Routledge Handbook of Human Rights in Asia

The *Routledge Handbook of Human Rights in Asia* provides a rich study of human rights challenges facing some of the most vulnerable people in Asia. While formal accession to core international human rights instruments is commonplace across the region, the realisation of human rights for many remains elusive as development pressure, violent conflict, limited political will and discrimination maintain human rights volatility.

This Handbook explores the underlying causes of human rights abuse in a range of contexts, considers lessons learnt from global, regional and domestic initiatives and provides recommendations and justifications for reform. Comprising 23 chapters, it examines the strengths and weaknesses of human rights institutions in Asia and covers issues such as:

- Participation, marginalisation, detention and exclusion
- Private sector responsibility and security
- Conflict and post-conflict rehabilitation
- Trafficking, displacement and citizenship
- Ageing populations, identity and sexuality.

Drawing together a remarkable collection of leading and emerging scholars, advisers and practitioners, this Handbook is essential reading for students, scholars, policy makers and advocates of human rights in Asia and the world.

Fernand de Varennes is United Nations Special Rapporteur on Minority Issues and Extraordinary Professor at the University of Pretoria, South Africa. He is the author of over 200 publications in more than 30 languages on human rights in Asia and other parts of the world.

Christie M. Gardiner is Lecturer of Law at the College of Law, Australian National University. Her research focuses on ageing, end of life law, human rights, life extension and technology.

Routledge Handbook of Human Rights in Asia

Edited by Fernand de Varennes and Christie M. Gardiner

Routledge
Taylor & Francis Group
LONDON AND NEW YORK

First published 2019
by Routledge

2 Park Square, Milton Park, Abingdon, Oxfordshire OX14 4RN
52 Vanderbilt Avenue, New York, NY 10017

Routledge is an imprint of the Taylor & Francis Group, an informa business

First issued in paperback 2020

British Library Cataloguing-in-Publication Data
A catalogue record for this book is available from the British Library

Library of Congress Cataloging-in-Publication Data
Names: Varennes, Fernand de, editor. | Gardiner, Christie M., editor.
Title: Routledge handbook of human rights in Asia / edited by Fernand de Varennes and Christie M. Gardiner.
Description: Abingdon, Oxon ; New York, NY : Routledge, 2019. | Includes bibliographical references and index.
Identifiers: LCCN 2018031942| ISBN 9781138855700 (hardback) | ISBN 9781315720180 (ebook) | ISBN 9781317518198 (epub) | ISBN 9781317518204 (Adobe Reader) | ISBN 9781317518181 (mobipocket encrypted)
Subjects: LCSH: Human rights—Asia.
Classification: LCC JC599.A78 R68 2019 | DDC 323.095—dc23
LC record available at https://lccn.loc.gov/2018031942

ISBN: 978-1-138-85570-0 (hbk)
ISBN: 978-0-367-65969-1 (pbk)

Typeset in Bembo
by Swales & Willis Ltd, Exeter, Devon, UK

Contents

Illustrations

Figures

Tables

Contributors

Raees Begum Baig is an assistant professor at the Chinese University of Hong Kong. Her research interests encompass issues relating to minority rights, gender and religion. Publications include *Hong Kong Muslims Self-representation in Cantonese: An Oriental Orientalism?* And *From Colony to Special Administrative Region: Ethnic Minorities' Participation in the Making of Legislation against Racial Discrimination in Hong Kong*.

Sharon Bessell is Associate Professor at the Crawford School of Public Policy, the Australian National University, Canberra. Her research interests focus on two broad areas: policy, social inclusion, social justice and the human rights of children; and the gendered and generational dimensions of poverty.

Emma Bowers is a lawyer at the leading Australian law firm Allens Linklaters. She combines her work as a commercial litigator with an active pro bono practice in the human rights space. Emma holds bachelor's degrees in Arts and Law (Hons) from the University of New South Wales, and was the recipient of the University Medal in Law.

Kathleen A. Cavanaugh is a socio-legal scholar and currently a lecturer in the Faculty of Law, Irish Centre for Human Rights (ICHR), National University of Ireland, Galway. She holds a PhD in Comparative Politics from the London School of Economics and Political Science (1997) and an LLM (Distinction) from Queen's University, Belfast (1998). Her areas of expertise include: nationalism, ethnic conflict, political violence, states of emergency, narratives on Islamic law and rights, freedom of religion and militant democracy. Selected recent publications include: 'Turkey's Hidden Wars', *Harvard Human Rights Journal* (Spring 2018), 'Rethinking What Is Necessary in a Democratic Society: Militant Democracy and the Turkish State', *Human Rights Quarterly* (August 2016), 'Unspoken Truths: Accessing Rights for Victims of Extraordinary Rendition', *Columbia Human Rights Law Review* (Winter 2015) and *Minority Rights in the Middle East* (2013) (with Joshua Castellino). Recent grant awards include a two-year Leverhulme/British Academy of Sciences project grant on Militant Democracy in Turkey.

Nick Cheesman is a fellow in the Department of Political and Social Change, the Australian National University, Canberra. Previously he was a desk officer with the Asian Legal Resource Centre, Hong Kong. He is the author of *Opposing the Rule of Law: How Myanmar's Courts Make Law and Order* (2015) and host of the New Books in Southeast Asian Studies podcast. Currently he holds an Australian Research Council grant to study torture in Southeast Asia.

Kenneth Christie PhD is a political scientist, author, editor and international academic who has taught and conducted research at universities in the USA, Singapore, South Africa, Norway, Dubai and Canada. Working all over the world has given him a unique perspective on peace, development and human security. His work has focused on issues of human rights, security and democratisation. He is widely published as an author and editor with ten books to his credit. His most recent book, *Freedom from Fear, Freedom from Want: An Introduction to Human Security* is co-authored with Dr Robert Hanlon. Today, he is working on issues of religion, ethnic and state formation/failure and human rights in the Middle East, North Africa and South Asia. He is head of the Human Security and Peacebuilding programme at Royal Roads University in Victoria, British Columbia.

Amal de Chickera is a co-director of the Institute on Statelessness and Inclusion. He leads the Institute's human rights engagement work and plays an important part in the Institute's work on childhood statelessness, gender discrimination, the Sustainable Development Agenda, engagement with civil society and the arts. Amal has researched, advocated, written, spoken, delivered training and served as an expert on statelessness and related issues for the UN, NGOs and academia, since 2008. He previously provided the lead on the Equal Rights Trust's statelessness work and was also a co-founder of the European Network on Statelessness.

Niki Esse de Lang holds two LLM degrees from the University of Amsterdam. He previously published an article in the *Asia-Pacific Journal on Human Rights and the Law* on the Myanmar National Human Rights Commission. He is currently serving as a legal consultant for UNODC, and previously worked for the Karen Human Rights Group as Capacity Building Manager – Research and Advocacy.

Fernand de Varennes is the United Nations Special Rapporteur on minority issues. He is also Extraordinary Professor at the University of Pretoria's Centre for Human Rights, and holds the Cheng Yu Tung Visiting Professorship at the Faculty of Law of the University of Hong Kong. He is renowned as one of the world's leading experts on the international human rights of minorities, has played a prominent role in promoting young Asian scholars in human rights as editor-in-chief of the *Asia-Pacific Journal on Human Rights and the Law*, and has worked and written extensively in areas such as the prevention of ethnic conflicts, the rights of migrants, the relationship between ethnicity, human rights and democracies, as well as the use of federalism and other forms of autonomy arrangements.

Debra L. DeLaet is Professor of Political Science at Drake University in Des Moines, Iowa. She serves as the David E. Maxwell Distinguished Professor of International Affairs. She has published numerous books, articles, and book chapters on human rights, global health and global gender issues, including *The Global Struggle for Human Rights* (2015) and (co-authored with David E. DeLaet) *Global Health in the 21st Century* (2012).

Basil Fernando is Director of Policy and Programmes at the Asian Human Rights Commission and Asian Legal Resource Centre, Hong Kong, where he was executive director for 16 years. Previously he served as a senior Human Rights Officer for the UN in Cambodia, and also practised law in Sri Lanka. Author of numerous books and articles in English and Sinhalese on human rights, law and democracy, in 2014 he received the Right Livelihood Award.

Christie M. Gardiner is a lecturer at the College of Law, Australian National University, Canberra and a solicitor of the Supreme Court of the Australian Capital Territory. She is an affiliate of the Centre for Excellence on Population Ageing Research (CEPAR) and a member of the Australian Network of Researchers for Law and Ageing, Council of the Ageing (COTA) (ACT) Policy Committee and the ACT Law Society Elder Law and Succession Law Committee. Her research focuses on the property, tort law and human rights aspects of ageing, end of life, life extension and technology. She teaches undergraduate and postgraduate law, including subjects in legal ethics, succession, tort law and property.

Alison Graham is an independent consultant, with her PhD examining states' obligations to implement the right to social security during financial crises. She has worked for a number of human rights organisations, including OHCHR, the International Service for Human Rights and the Office of the Independent Expert (now Special Rapporteur) on human rights and extreme poverty, for over 15 years in both field and headquarter locations. She has particularly extensive experience researching and drafting reports for publication, identifying and mapping trends, conducting rights-based analysis and formulating policy responses, particularly regarding economic and social rights. This includes identifying how violations of these rights can be read as early warning signs of conflict, unrest and other crises.

Raadhika Gupta is engaged as a consultant at the World Bank, having completed her BA, LLB (Hons) from NALSAR University of Law, Hyderabad and LLM from Harvard Law School. She earlier taught at the O.P. Jindal Global University and has published nationally and internationally in various areas, including constitutional law, jurisprudence and gender.

Robert J. Hanlon is a political scientist and consultant whose research explores the links between corporate social responsibility and human security in emerging Asian economies. He is an assistant professor at Thompson Rivers University (TRU), Kamloops, British Columbia and is an associate faculty member in the School of Humanitarian Studies at Royal Roads University, Victoria, British Columbia. Prior to joining TRU, Dr Hanlon served as a postdoctoral research fellow at the Institute of Asian Research, University of British Columbia. He has taught at the University of British Columbia, Kwantlen Polytechnic University, Simon Fraser University and the Royal Military College of Canada. Outside academia, Dr Hanlon has worked for the Asian Human Rights Commission, the Canadian Chamber of Commerce in Hong Kong, as well as the High Commission of Canada in Australia. He holds a PhD in international relations and Asian politics from City University of Hong Kong, a master's degree in peace and conflict resolution from the University of Queensland, as well as a BA in political science and philosophy from the University of Victoria. He has been a visiting scholar at the Centre for Socio-Legal Studies (Oxford), the Liu Institute for Global Issues (UBC), the Sasin Graduate Institute of Business Administration (Chulalongkorn) and the Balsillie School of International Affairs in Waterloo, Canada.

Naing Ko Ko is a PhD scholar at the School of Regulation and Global Governance (RegNet) at the Australian National University, Canberra. He joined the pro-democracy protests in Burma in 1988, serving six years in prison in solitary confinement. He has worked with UN agencies and activists on the Thai–Burma border and in Australia with former federal MP and lawyer Janelle Saffin. New Zealand accepted Naing Ko as a UN-sponsored refugee in 2007. He received a Human Rights Defender Award from Amnesty International New Zealand in 2010. He holds a BA (Hons) and an MA in political studies from the University of Auckland and an MA in international relations from the University of Queensland, under a Rotary Peace Centre Fellowship.

Anthony J. Langlois is an associate professor in international relations at Flinders University, Adelaide. He was educated at the University of Tasmania and the Australian National University, Canberra. His areas of academic endeavour include international relations, human rights, international political theory, global sexuality politics and global ethics.

Huong Le Thu is a visiting fellow at the Strategic and Defence Studies Centre (SDSC), Coral Bell School of Asia Pacific Affairs, Australian National University, Canberra, associate fellow at the Institute of Southeast Asian Studies (Singapore) and non-resident fellow at the Institute of International Relations (Taiwan). She is interested in the effect of external interventions on the politics of state formation, identity, nationalism as well as power projection and power perception. She has also done work as a consultant for intergovernmental organisations such as the United Nations and the ASEAN Intergovernmental Commission on Human Rights.

Upasana Mahanta is an associate professor and executive director, Centre for Women, Law and Social Change, Jindal Global Law School, O.P. Jindal Global University, Sonipat, Haryana. Prior to joining Jindal Global University, she was working as an assistant professor in the Centre for Women's Studies, Tata Institute of Social Sciences, Mumbai. Dr Mahanta completed her PhD at the Centre for Canadian, US and Latin American Studies, School of International Studies, Jawaharlal Nehru University, New Delhi. She was also a Shastri doctoral fellow in the Centre for Women's and Gender Studies, University of British Columbia, Vancouver. Dr Mahanta's research interests include the role of women in emergent political institutions; gendered understanding of conflict; women organising and resisting in insecure contexts; and examining development through a gendered lens.

Julia Mayerhofer is currently the Interim Executive Director of the Asia Pacific Refugee Rights Network (APRRN). She has been part of the APRRN Secretariat since 2011 and previously worked with refugee communities on the Thai–Myanmar border but also in Hong Kong. Her research interests are broadly focused on refugee rights protection in the Asia Pacific.

Elaine Pearson is the Australia Director at Human Rights Watch. She is an expert on migration and human trafficking issues and sits on the board of the Global Alliance Against Traffic in Women. She is an adjunct lecturer in law at the University of New South Wales.

Robin Ramcharan is Professor of International Relations at Webster University Geneva. He is a co-founder of the Asia Centre in Bangkok. His research interests centre on Southeast Asian security, traditional and non-traditional, human rights and intellectual property rights. Recent publications include a co-edited, special issue of *The Journal of Current Southeast Asian Affairs* (GIGA, Hamburg, Germany) on 'Democracy and Human Rights in Southeast Asia' and 'Democratic Transitions and Internal Political Conflict in Southeast Asia', *Strategic Security Analysis*, 12 (2015). He is currently conducting research for a forthcoming book on the protection of human rights in Southeast Asia.

Raja Devasish Roy is the hereditary *Chakma Raja*, an advocate (Barrister-at-Law) in Bangladesh, and a member of the UN Permanent Forum on Indigenous Issues. He held ministerial office in 2008–2009. His publications on indigenous peoples' rights, including customary law, have been published by Routledge, CUP, MRG, ILO and IWGIA.

Ambika Satkunanathan is a researcher and activist based in Sri Lanka. She was appointed as a member of the Human Rights Commission of Sri Lanka in October 2015. From 2007 to 2015 she functioned as National Legal Consultant to the Office of the UN High Commissioner for Human Rights in Sri Lanka. Her publications include, 'Collaboration, Suspicion and Traitors: An Exploratory Study of Intra-community Relations in Post-war Northern Sri Lanka' in *Contemporary South Asia* (2016), and 'Sri Lanka: The Impact of Militarization on Women' in the *Oxford Handbook of Gender and Conflict* (forthcoming). She has a Master of Laws (Human Rights) degree from the University of Nottingham, where she was Chevening Scholar, and earned bachelor's degrees (LLB/BA) at Monash University, Melbourne.

Alim Seytoff is the president of the Uyghur American Association (UAA) based in Washington, DC. He is also the director of the Uyghur Human Rights Project (UHRP). Mr Seytoff is one of the most prominent advocates worldwide for human rights in East Turkestan. He has been campaigning for the human rights and religious freedom of the Uyghur people since he came to the United States in 1996. He has written many articles on the political situation in East Turkestan. He has published in a number of journals including *The Wall Street Journal, Asia Times, Huffington Post, Index on Censorship* and *China Rights Forum*. He is frequently interviewed and/or quoted by CNN, BBC World Service, Al-Jazeera, Fox News, C-SPAN, PBS, WNYC, Voice of America, Radio Free Asia, *The New York Times, The Christian Science Monitor, The Weekly Standard,* the *Toronto Sun, The Australian, Al-Ahram Weekly* and the newswires. He testified many times before the US Congress and briefed US State Department officials on the situation in East Turkestan. Mr Seytoff holds a BA in Chinese studies from Xinjiang University and another BA in broadcast journalism from Southern Adventist University, Tennessee. He has an MA in public policy from the Robertson School of Government at Regent University, Virginia Beach, VA. Mr Seytoff received his JD degree from Regent University in 2006.

Rhona Smith is the United Nations Special Rapporteur on the situation of human rights in Cambodia and a professor of international human rights at Newcastle University Law School, Newcastle upon Tyne. She has taught and written on a range of human rights issues over 20 years. With a background in Scots' law, her specialism is in the UN human rights system, as well as in human rights at regional and national levels. She has a long-standing involvement in human rights education and capacity building.

Henryk Szadziewski is Senior Researcher at the Uyghur Human Rights Project. Mr Szadziewski has a BA (Hons) in modern Chinese studies from the University of Leeds and an MSc (Econ.) in development management from the University of Wales, Cardiff, where he was awarded a distinction for his work on Uyghur economic, social and cultural rights. Mr Szadziewski has authored numerous research and opinion articles on Uyghurs, Central Asia and development economics for a wide variety of publications. He lived in China for five years, three of those in Kashgar.

Laura van Waas is a co-director of the Institute on Statelessness and Inclusion, as well as a part-time assistant professor at the Department of European and International Law at Tilburg Law School. She leads the Institute's capacity building and academic engagement work, as well as playing an important part in the Institute's work on childhood statelessness and on the nexus between statelessness and forced displacement. Laura has worked on the issue of statelessness since 2004 and holds a PhD in international law from Tilburg University (manuscript 'Nationality Matters', 2008).

Foreword

Rita Izsák-Ndiaye[1]

Undoubtedly, the international community made significant progress during the past decades in establishing a normative framework for the protection of human rights for all, including for the most vulnerable communities. However, some current trends such as increasing hate speech, xenophobic rhetoric and incitement to hatred against minorities, coupled with the rise of extremists and far-right political parties and groups, threaten the progress achieved in the field of minority rights protection. Where democracy, rule of law and governance deficits are coupled with unequal competition over territory, resources and power, where bias politics and favouritism along ethnic or religious lines appear, and where minority rights are denied, violated or neglected, tensions between communities can evolve, threatening peace and stability and sometimes resulting in violence. We need strengthened legislative and institutional frameworks as well as an unequivocal political will to foster conditions for a cohesive society where there is unity in diversity.

The present *Routledge Handbook of Human Rights in Asia* is important reading for everyone who cares about the current state of the most vulnerable populations in Asia and the region's preparedness, capability and existing challenges to uphold their human rights. Women, migrants, children, older peoples, indigenous peoples, minorities, refugees, LGBTI and stateless persons, people with disabilities and other marginalised groups whose particular situation is highlighted in this publication are exposed to heightened risks of negligence, indifference, rights violations, and even violence, threats and attacks precisely because of who they are and the disadvantaged position they hold in the society. Moreover, discrimination and diminished economic and social rights make people more vulnerable to trafficking, especially affecting minority women and girls in poverty or in conflict and post-conflict settings who are exposed to a heightened danger of becoming victims of sexual exploitation, forced labour or services, slavery, servitude and other forms of exploitation. Such marginalised communities often do not hold any political, economic, social or media power, hence their ability to get their voices heard and to influence decisions can be hindered. When governments, businesses, the military and others in power fail to protect and promote the human rights of all, it is up to civil society, human rights activists and all concerned individuals to support those persons and remind the powerholders that it is not only a moral imperative to uphold the rights and dignity of every individual but indeed a human rights obligation. This right for holding actors accountable is the legal power which is indeed at the disposal of each of us and we must use that well and wisely, whether it is through advocacy, strategic litigation, peaceful protests or any other means.

Some writers claim in this Handbook that human rights are being increasingly labelled as a western concept, hence the applicability of international human rights standards and protection mechanisms are being challenged by several Asian states. The Association of Southeast Asian Nations (ASEAN) and the ASEAN Declaration of Human Rights therefore carry a huge importance in bringing legitimacy and relevance of human rights to the region and enable as well as inspire enforceability and action. This Handbook also offers a useful review of the existing mechanisms on the international, regional and national levels, and describes what UN entities, ASEAN, national human rights institutions, governments and others are doing or should be doing to uphold human rights in the region.

Many of the concrete situations that are discussed here have been a concern during my term as the UN Special Rapporteur on minority issues and the subject of my letters to governments or of my public press releases. Many of them have also been addressed by other UN entities as well, such as the situation of Rohingya in Myanmar, which is discussed in several chapters in this publication, highlighting its ongoing significance. On 11 September 2017, the UN High Commissioner for Human Rights Zeid Ra'ad al-Hussein, denounced the situation in Myanmar as 'a textbook example of ethnic cleansing'. When the UN Secretary-General, António Guterres was confronted with the question a few days later as to whether he believes that there is ethnic cleansing against the Rohingya, he responded: 'I would answer your question with another question. When one third of the Rohingya population had to flee the country, can you find a better word to describe it?' Right afterwards, on 13 September, the Security Council, while acknowledging the initial attacks on Myanmar security forces in its statement, condemned the subsequent violence, and called for immediate steps to end the violence in Rakhine state, to de-escalate the situation, re-establish law and order, and to ensure the protection of civilians.

While these are all welcome steps, one wonders why it still takes so much time and tragically so many lives to have such situations considered by the Security Council and the high powers of the international community. Indeed, until today, consultations about the protection of minorities, pluralistic societies, or the importance not only to protect but also to promote different identities tend to take place from a strictly human rights angle where the peace, security and development dimensions of these issues are often ignored. History has shown us how exclusionary ideologies, deficits of democracy and rule of law, unbalanced power, hate speech, past and unresolved grievances, a history of ethnic and religious tensions between groups without reconciliation, agitation of ethnic or religious components by political leaders, and impunity when perpetrators of human rights violations are permitted to act without consequences can all lead to irreversible conflict situations. Therefore, we must remain vigilant and take action as soon as we see the first signs of threats on our peaceful coexistence. In that context, some urge here the creation of a human rights early warning and risk assessment procedure by the ASEAN Regional Forum.

Comprehensive implementation of minority rights, non-discrimination and equality standards constitute an important foundation for the prevention of violence against minority communities and help establish conditions for stability and harmonious relations amongst various population groups. Mechanisms to ensure dialogue, consultation and participation, the fundamental principles of minority rights, should be established to assist states in understanding the situations of minorities, their issues and concerns. Where violence has previously taken place, such mechanisms are of particular relevance, including in post-conflict and post-violence reconciliation and peacebuilding processes. Establishing institutions for the protection of minority rights and ensuring attention to minority rights within existing national and human rights institutions are essential violence prevention measures.

What struck me during my tenure as Special Rapporteur was the limited, or often complete lack of a minority presence in political and public offices, including in municipal and government structures, law enforcement bodies, the judiciary, legislative bodies, criminal justice systems and other relevant bodies and mechanisms, especially when their decisions affect minorities. Without their participation, such bodies are less able to take vital decisions for the benefit of the entire society and may be less trusted by minorities, who may be reluctant to access them, or discouraged from doing so. Moreover, good and inclusive governance, which includes minorities and measures to ensure equality, are key conflict-prevention prerequisites.

It is my sincere hope that after reading this important Handbook, all readers will feel well-informed, empowered and further inspired to continue working towards achieving human rights for all. Let us not lose sight of the most fundamental principle, enshrined in Article 1 of the Universal Declaration of Human Rights, that we are born free and equal in dignity and rights and we are endowed with reason and conscience and should act towards one another in a spirit of brotherhood.

Note

1 Former UN Special Rapporteur on minority issues, elected member of the UN Committee on the Elimination of Racial Discrimination (2018–2021).

Acknowledgements

Despite significant progress in the recognition, promotion and protection of human rights toward the end of the 20th century, the rights of all peoples continue to remain vulnerable into the 21st century and are challenged in new, compounding and complex ways. Thankfully, the champions of human rights are many and they share a far more empowered and coherent voice than ever before. Beyond the often chaotic political rhetoric that engulfs human rights discourse and stymies progress, the contributors to this Handbook are among those champions. Their work critically examines and continues to make visible important issues of substance and, for many, seeks to identify and explore solutions to some of the most complex issues of our time. We are truly indebted to all of the contributors for agreeing to be a part of this important publication and for staying committed to this lengthy task, which can unnerve even the most resolute academics.

The editors extend a special gratitude to Rita Izsák-Ndiaye for writing the Foreword to this Handbook. Ms Izsák-Ndiaye's dedication and contribution to the field of human rights, specifically in relation to minority issues, has spanned the duration of her professional career. Serving two terms as United Nations Special Rapporteur on minority issues and as a member of the United Nations Committee on the Elimination of Racial Discrimination, she has repeatedly stressed the importance of the United Nations in advocating stronger human rights protection at national, regional and international levels, as well as within the mechanisms of the United Nations system.

For those who have supported each of us in different ways, enabling us to contribute our perspectives without oppression, unlike many of our colleagues around the world, we thank you.

Abbreviations

ACRS	Advisory Commission on Rakhine State
ACWC	ASEAN Commission for the Promotion and Protection of Women and Children
AHRC	Asian Human Rights Commission
AHRD	ASEAN Human Rights Declaration
AICHR	ASEAN Intergovernmental Commission on Human Rights
ALRC	Asian Legal Resource Centre
APF	ASEAN People's Forum
ARF	ASEAN Regional Forum
ASEAN	Association of Southeast Asian Nations
CAT	Convention against Torture or Other Cruel, Inhuman or Degrading Treatment or Punishment 1984
CED	Committee on Enforced Disappearances
CEDAW	Committee on the Elimination of All Forms of Discrimination Against Women
CERD	Committed on the Elimination of Racial Discrimination
CIA	Central Intelligence Agency
CMW	Committee on Migrant Workers
COMMIT	Coordinated Mekong Ministerial Initiative against Trafficking
CRC	Convention on the Rights of the Child
CRPD	Committee on the Rights of Persons with Disabilities
CSOs	Civil Society Organisations
CSR	Corporate Social Responsibility
DIS	Danish Immigration Service
EMRIP	Expert Mechanism on the Rights of Indigenous Peoples
EU	European Union
EW/RA	Early Warning/Risk Assessment
FCNM	Framework Convention for the Protection of National Minorities
HKSAR	Hong Kong Special Administrative Region
HRC	Human Rights Council
HRW	Human Rights Watch
ICCPR	International Covenant on Civil and Political Rights
ICERD	International Convention on the Elimination of All Forms of Racial Discrimination
ICESCR	International Covenant on Economic, Social and Cultural Rights
ICG	International Crisis Group
ICHR	Irish Centre for Human Rights

ICRC	International Committee of the Red Cross
IDP	Internally Displaced Person
IHL	International Humanitarian Law
ILO	International Labour Organization
INGO	International Non-governmental Organisation
IOM	International Organization for Migration
LGBTI	Lesbian, gay, bisexual, transgender and intersex
LGBTIQ	Lesbian, gay, bisexual, transgender, intersex and questioning
LTTE	Liberation Tigers of Tamil Eelam
MDG	Millennium Development Goals
MENA	Middle East and North Africa
MNHRC	Myanmar National Human Rights Commission
NGO	Non-governmental Organisation
NHRI	National Human Rights Institutions
NLD	National League for Democracy (Myanmar)
OECD	Organisation for Economic Cooperation and Development
OEWGA	Open-ended Working Group on Ageing
OHCHR	Office of the High Commissioner for Human Rights
OSCE	Organization for Security and Cooperation in Europe
RDO	Race Discrimination Ordinance (HKSAR)
RNDP	Rakhine Nationalities Development Party
RSCIC	Rakhine State Conflicts Investigation Commission
RSD	Regional Status Determination
SDG	Sustainable Development Goals
SEA	Southeast Asia
SGBV	Sexual and gender based violence
SOGI	Sexual orientation and gender identity
TOR	Terms of Reference
UDHR	Universal Declaration of Human Rights
UN	United Nations
UNACT	United Nations Action for Cooperation against Trafficking in Person
UNDESA	United Nations Department of Economic and Social Affairs
UNDMR	United Nations Declaration on Minority Rights
UNDP	United Nations Development Programme
UNDRIP	United Nations Declaration on the Rights of Indigenous Peoples
UNESCO	United Nations Educational, Scientific and Cultural Organization
UNGA	United Nations General Assembly
UNGC	United Nations Global Compact
UNGP	United Nations Guiding Principles on Business and Human Rights
UNHCR	United Nations High Commissioner for Refugees
UNIAP	United Nations Inter-agency Project on Human Trafficking
UNICEF	United Nations Children's Fund
UNOCHA	United Nations Office for the Coordination of Humanitarian Affairs
UNODC	United Nations Office for Drug Control and Crime Prevention
UNPFII	United Nations Permanent Forum on Indigenous Issues
UNRWA	United Nations Relief and Works Agency for Palestine Refugees in the Near East

UPR	Universal Periodic Review
USA	United States of America
USCIRF	United States Commission on International Religious Freedoms
USDP	Union State and Development Party
WHO	World Health Organization

Part I

Strengthening Asian human rights institutions

1

The rights of the marginalised in Asia

Increasing protection or vulnerability?

Fernand de Varennes

Introduction

I am neither of the East nor of the West, no boundaries exist within my breast.
– *Jalāl ad-Dīn Muhammad Balkhī (Rumi)*

As other contributors in this Handbook have pointed out, Asia remains the only part of the world without a regional human rights protections system, despite some more localised attempts and other sectoral efforts in this regard, such as the ASEAN Intergovernmental Commission on Human Rights (AICHR),[1] the ASEAN Commission on the Promotion and the Protection of the Rights of Women and Children (ACWC),[2] the ASEAN Committee to Implement the Declaration on the Protection and Promotion of the Rights of Migrant Workers,[3] and the Arab Human Rights Committee.[4]

Human rights are not necessarily less recognised in the region, nor are countries in Asia particularly unreceptive environments. After all, 'Asia' is a vast part of the world,[5] home to the world's largest populations and arguably most diverse societies in religious, cultural, linguistic, economic and social terms. As others have also pointed out, it was always going to be a greater challenge here to reach any kind of consensus than where there were more shared traditions in cultural terms, such as in the Americas or in Europe.

Indeed, if one were to limit oneself to an admittedly simple measurement as to whether there is less support for international human rights standards in Asia – by looking at the relative rate of support for the UN's main treaties dealing with some of the more vulnerable segments of society – Asian states cannot be said to deviate much in terms of ratification from the states in other parts of the globe. For example, all Asian states have ratified the *Convention on the Rights of the Child*,[6] only one Asian state (Iran) has not ratified or acceded to the *Convention on the Elimination of All Forms of Discrimination Against Women*,[7] and although only nine of the 51 states which had ratified the *International Convention on the Protection of the Rights of All Migrant Workers and Members of Their Families* are in Asia, it is still a proportion higher than that of Europe, since ratification has mainly been from Africa and Latin America.[8]

Unfortunately, even if by this simple measure Asian states cannot be said to greatly lag behind their counterparts in other parts of the world, ratification of human rights instruments does not automatically equate with compliance with the standards which they contain. This may be particularly true in relation to some of the world's most vulnerable or marginalised segments of society.

Asia and the world's most vulnerable

> You can only have lasting peace based on justice.
>
> – *Mahatma Gandhi (Wrench 1942)*

Asia as a region does not display any intrinsic rejection of general human rights treaties, nor of those that deal specifically with some of the world's most marginalised or vulnerable segments of society, such as migrant workers, refugees, children, women or minorities. However, in practice and in recent years this part of the world has been convulsed – some might say increasingly so – by deeply disturbing developments, from the ravages of conflicts and atrocities committed against minorities during times of conflicts (Yazidis and other religious minorities in Iraq; Hazara in Afghanistan) to the denial of basic human rights such as that of citizenship targeting specific ethnic groups (such as the Rohingya in Myanmar). Many of these in turn contribute to massive refugee and IDP (Internally Displaced People) movements – the largest the world has experienced since the end of the Second World War,[9] and with Asian regions figuring very prominently. Nor can it be said that the situation of women and children has markedly improved, except in countries where economic stability and prospects have had positive consequences in relation to access to education, health and public services. Even here, apparent statistical improvement can be misleading when it does not equally benefit all segments of a country's population. There are undoubtedly positive developments in some areas that should not be discounted, whether in relation to some initial positive steps for women in Saudi Arabia, such as a decree taking effect in June 2018 allowing women to drive, or right to vote and to run for office in municipal elections in 2015, or the increased access to education for most children in recent decades in the People's Republic of China.

It is of course impossible to provide a comprehensive picture covering both progress or failures in relation to all human rights matters in all of Asia. A much more modest approach is to focus on particularly vulnerable segments in those countries where there appear more clearly serious challenges that remain to be addressed. Unfortunately, this focus on 'negativity' may give the lopsided impression that Asian governments, as a whole, are not responding properly to their human rights obligations. This is not necessarily the case since the constraints of this chapter do not permit a comprehensive examination of all relevant aspects – the positive and the negative – of any given issue. This is the reason one should keep in mind that the focus in the next sections will be on the more notable areas of challenges and failures dealing with the human rights of some of the most marginalised in the region.

Refugees, IDPs and statelessness

> Imagine being told you don't belong because of the language you speak, the faith you follow, the customs you practice or the colour of your skin. This is the stark reality for many of the world's stateless. Discrimination, which can be the root cause of their lack of nationality, also pervades their everyday lives – often with crippling effects. If we want to end statelessness, we must address this discrimination. We must insist on equal nationality rights for all.
>
> – *Filippo Grandi, United Nations High Commissioner for Refugees (2017c)*

Recent figures from the United Nations High Commissioner for Refugees (UNHCR) identify Asia as home to more stateless people[10] and a source of more refugees and IDPs than any other part of the world. At the end of 2016, almost half the world's refugees come from only three Asian countries when one includes the 5.3 million Palestinian refugees registered by the United Nations Relief and Works Agency for Palestine Refugees in the Near East (UNRWA) (UNHCR 2017b: 2). While it should be kept in mind that as of 2017, about 59.63% of the global population was living in Asia, it should still be acknowledged that when considered in its entirety, it seems undeniable that Asia as a whole is disproportionately a source of and the home to many more refugees, IDPs and stateless people than any other continent. It is also noteworthy that the UNHCR launch in November 2014 of the #IBelong Campaign to End Statelessness with the goal of ending statelessness in ten years has helped raise awareness of statelessness and focus political attention to address it. This has led to regional initiatives such as the *Abidjan Declaration of Ministers of ECOWAS Member States on Eradication of Statelessness*[11] and the *Brazil Declaration and Plan of Action*.[12] Unfortunately no such momentum exists yet in this regard in Asia, though ASEAN mechanisms have not been completely silent on at least the connection between statelessness and human trafficking.[13] There have also been a number of global and regional NGO initiatives to address the particular vulnerability of children in situations of statelessness, though none of these specifically aimed at or emanating from the Asian region (Institute on Statelessness and Inclusion 2017: 14). Though not identical to situations of statelessness, it is thought that as many as '135 million children under five years old across Asia and the Pacific have not had their births registered', with consequences not entirely dissimilar to statelessness since 'registration is often a prerequisite in establishing a child's legal identity' (Institute on Statelessness and Inclusion 2017: 61). Thus, tens of millions of people in Asian countries lack proof of legal identity, including birth certificates, though not all of them are stateless. As in other parts of the world, the vast majority of stateless children in Asia are from minority groups such as the Rohingya who face discrimination in nationality laws.

Asian states have perhaps also been more timid from an international legal point of view, with few accessions or ratifications of the two UN treaties on statelessness: the 1954 *Convention Relating to the Status of Stateless Persons*[14] and the 1961 *Convention on the Reduction of Statelessness*.[15]

Further aggravating this unfortunate state of affairs, and demonstrating the interlocking human rights dimensions affecting sections of society who can be doubly marginalised, women in more Asian countries than anywhere else in the world can be denied the right to transmit their citizenship to their children because of their gender, including in some cases in combination with their ethnicity. Some 25 countries maintain nationality laws that discriminate against women in this manner, with the vast majority of them in Asia.[16] The consequences of this not only involve gender discrimination: these situations also revolve around contexts which compound the extreme vulnerability of their children as well since, because of their statelessness, they will likely encounter numerous and burdensome disadvantages or even complete denial in accessing medical care, education and formal employment, thus becoming highly vulnerable to exploitation, drugs, hopelessness and ultimately disenfranchisement from participation in society.[17]

Multilayered marginalisation in cases of statelessness in Asia are not limited to women and children – it in particular impacts on minorities disproportionally, as can be seen in dramatic and tragic fashion by the plight of Myanmar's Rohingya, that of Palestinians, of Bidoons in the Arabian Peninsula, Tibetans in India, Kurds of Syria, and Nepali from Bhutan, amongst others. According to the UNHCR, '[d]iscrimination, exclusion and persecution most commonly describe the existence of stateless minorities. More than 75% of the world's known stateless populations belong to minority groups' (UNHCR 2017c: 1). As with the children of women who cannot transmit their citizenship because of gender discrimination, stateless minority children find themselves particularly vulnerable 'to poverty and difficulties in accessing education, health care, and other state services' (UNHCR 2017c: 3), as well as to trafficking and sexual or economic exploitation.[18]

Many other cases of statelessness can be associated to situations of conflict where individuals fleeing instability and warfare may find themselves unable to prove their nationality or otherwise obtain citizenship of the country where they resided. They themselves are multiply vulnerable: as refugees or IDPs, as stateless individuals, as minorities, or even further as marginalised women or children. Indeed, this is one of the reasons the 1951 *Convention Relating to the Status of Refugees* recognises a link, in its definition of a refugee, of the particular vulnerability of minorities as 'persons who flee persecution . . . because of their race, religion, nationality, or membership in a particular social group'. The point must be emphasised because it is at times misunderstood or not sufficiently acknowledged: the very definition of those who can claim refugee status are recognised to be individuals vulnerable because of 'their race, religion, nationality'; in other words, they are likely to be minorities in the countries they must flee. Put another way, the relationship between persecution of minorities, and the human rights abuses they suffer, and refugee flows has been too frequently demonstrated.

In addition, forced displacement experienced by refugees and IDPs in Asia creates unstable circumstances that increase the risk of statelessness. Refugees may for example 'lose their identity documents and be unable to prove the bond with their home country. Being undocumented does not equate to being stateless, but it makes it challenging to prove nationality and increases the risk of statelessness' (Norwegian Refugee Council and Institute on Statelessness and Inclusion 2016), particularly over time and as new generations grow up in exile. Children are particularly at risk in these situations: they can become stateless if their parents cannot fulfil the citizenship conditions of their home country and the laws of the host country do not envisage stateless children born on their territory automatically acquiring citizenship.

There is also the issue of conflicts worldwide as drivers of refugee and IDP movements and the frequently misunderstood minority dimension. As explained in the next section, most conflicts since the end of the Second World War are internal conflicts, usually involving inter-ethnic or inter-religious dimensions. Almost unavoidably, ethnic, linguistic and religious minorities, as well as women and children,[19] are particularly vulnerable in these conflicts, as expressed in the preamble of the following resolution of the UN Commission on Human Rights (2002):

> Concerned at the growing frequency and severity of disputes and conflicts regarding minorities in many countries and their often tragic consequences, and that persons belonging to minorities are particularly vulnerable to displacement through, inter alia, population transfers, refugee flows and forced relocation . . .[20]

The most recent and striking example in Asia of such a close relationship between the vulnerability of minorities in conflicts and subsequent population transfers and refugee flows is that of the Rohingya of Myanmar, who by 11 January 2018 were more than 1 million needing assistance in that country alone (Inter Sector Coordination Group 2018).

Thus, the main drivers of the refugee and IDP crisis and of statelessness in Asia – conflicts, persecution and discriminatory laws and practices that particularly affect women, children and minorities – overlap and create huge burdens on millions of individuals across Asia – with disastrous consequences in human and social terms and increasingly heavy burdens for the international community and Asian states. At the same time, the generosity of some governments and populations in Asia cannot be overstated: many countries in a band from Turkey to the Philippines have shouldered disproportionally within their borders millions of IDPs, refugees or stateless individuals, and thus taken up the challenge of sheltering and protecting many of those who are among the most vulnerable in the world.[21]

Human rights, conflicts in Asia and their most vulnerable victims

> [It] is not difficult to establish that violations of the rights of free exercise and non-discrimination intensify conflict in divided multiethnic societies, nor to project with reasonable confidence that the observance and implementation of those norms will serve to reduce conflict.
>
> *(Little 1996)*

Some of the world's most serious patterns of human rights violations are related to conflict and violent crisis situations, blighting the lives of millions. In addition to the brutality and suffering often encountered by civilians in such contexts – including death, torture, rape and other forms of gender-based violence, hunger and a whole range of humanitarian consequences – there are often more indirect effects, ranging from loss of property and livelihoods, little or no access to education or health care because of a breakdown of basic services, and so on. Some of these violations may even constitute genocide, war crimes or crimes against humanity.

Two aspects of these patterns are not always appreciated. First, the changing nature of violent conflicts in Asia (and elsewhere) since the end of the Second World War have made vulnerable groups in many countries the specific targets of attack. Violent conflicts today are mainly intrastate rather than interstate,[22] and civilians have increasingly borne the heavy toll of warfare, much more than was previously the case before the second half of the 20th century, as recognised in a study sponsored by the International Red Cross:

> The research reveals, in essence, that modern wars have become conflicts without limits. Civilians have – both intentionally and by accident – been moved to center stage in the theater of war, which was once fought primarily on battlefields. This fundamental shift in the character of war is illustrated by a stark statistic: in World War I, nine soldiers were killed for every civilian life lost. In today's wars, it is estimated that ten civilians die for every soldier or fighter killed in battle.
>
> *(Greenberg & Boorstin 2001: 18–19)*[23]

Second, since the overwhelming majority of armed conflicts are now fought within states, and most have an ethnic dimension (Fearon & Laitin 2009: 199–211), women, children and ethnic minorities increasingly becoming the victims – intentionally or not – of these new conflict patterns. It is also no coincidence that all of the case studies of conflicts (Aceh, Mindanao and Southern Thailand) highlighted in a recent Asia Foundation report involved minorities:

> Subnational conflict is the most widespread, enduring, and deadly form of conflict in Asia. Over the past 20 years (1992–2012), there have been 26 subnational conflicts in South and Southeast Asia, affecting half of the countries in this region. These conflicts are among the world's longest running armed struggles, often lasting for multiple generations, and 45.2 years on average.
>
> *(Parks, Colletta & Oppenheim 2012: 1)*

This is a fact particularly noticeable in Asia, more so than in other parts of the world. In addition,

> Asia has by far the highest number of conflicts, and the longest running conflicts . . . the number of active subnational conflicts in four major regions (Asia, Africa, Europe, and Middle East) since 1946. Over this 65 year period, Asia had more subnational conflicts than the rest of the world combined in 55 of the 65 years, and has had the highest number of subnational conflicts since 1949.
>
> *(Parks, Colletta & Oppenheim 2012: 17)*

While some conflicts gradually took on more evident ethnic or religious dimensions (such as in Yemen, Syria, Southern Thailand, the Philippines and Iraq), most of the ongoing conflicts in Asia derive from deeply rooted claims of exclusion or discrimination by state authorities and other struggles by linguistic, religious or ethnic groups over minority rights. It should be added, however, that while most of these conflicts in Asia may have involved in the main a struggle between an aggrieved minority and a central government, there are often other contributing factors such as internal divisions within a minority group itself as between clans, some of which may be supportive of central authorities (Torres 2007).

The consequences of these evolving conflict patterns obviously also hold true for Asia. Particularly vulnerable and marginalised segments of society in Asia – minorities, children, women – are disproportionally at the receiving end in these internal, ethnic conflicts. Examples abound in this regard: the lives of millions of children are disrupted in Asia, with little or no access to education or health care. Tens of thousands of children every year are used as child soldiers, killed or abducted and victims of sexual violence; women can become targeted victims of violence, especially of sexual violence, in the context of these conflicts and even after, as they can be attacked by armed forces, militia or security personnel when arrested, at border crossings, in refugee camps, at homes or in detention centres.[24] As indicated in the 1996 report on children and conflict:

> the struggles that claim more civilians than soldiers have been marked by horrific levels of violence and brutality. Any and all tactics are employed, from systematic rape, to scorched-earth tactics that destroy crops and poison wells, to ethnic cleansing and genocide. With all standards abandoned, human rights violations against children and women occur in unprecedented numbers. Increasingly, children have become the targets and even the perpetrators of violence and atrocities.
>
> *(United Nations 1996)*

The stories can be horrific, the human costs tremendous, and the longer-term consequences disastrous. To focus on just one recent conflict situation, out of some 1.2 million Rohingya at the end of November 2017 in refugee camps in Bangladesh, most of who are denied citizenship in Myanmar, some 60% of them are children under the age of 18:

> Moreover, children, adolescents and women in both the Rohingya and host communities are exposed to high levels of violence, abuse and exploitation including sexual harassment, child labour and child marriage and are at high risk of being trafficked. Finally, an estimated 450,000 total Rohingya children aged 4–18 years old are in need of education services.
>
> *(UNICEF 2017)*

From a human rights point of view, the above are not isolated occurrences, but rather part of a vast interlocked pattern of violations and vulnerability: when minorities suffer long-term violations of basic rights, including discriminatory practices in terms of citizenship, education, employment or access to public services, this can lead to escalating grievances and instability that are conducive to further instability and violence, and eventually conflict, which in turn fuel ever increasing cycles of violations of other human rights (Parks, Colletta & Oppenheim 2012: 26).[25] Minorities, women and children are never winners in such cases. The result in Myanmar and Bangladesh and other parts of Southeast Asia in this particular case is hundreds of thousands of individuals experiencing extreme suffering and violations of the most basic human rights, including the right to life.

Unfortunately, the ordeal of so many in Bangladesh and Myanmar is far from unique. As pointed out earlier, Asia as a region has more internal conflicts than the rest of the world combined. Out of 26 interstate conflicts in South and Southeast Asia during a 20-year period between 1992 and 2012, all were ethnic conflicts. They all therefore involved aggrieved minorities and affected a vast population of 131 million people, including Myanmar, even when only taking into account the regions directly affected in each country (Parks, Colletta & Oppenheim 2012: 17).[26] Though the Myanmar situation may be relatively atypical in terms of recent scale, the significant elements to retain are the particular vulnerability and marginalisation of millions of minorities, children and women, and the massive and appalling violations of human rights Asia, more than other regions of the world, is currently experiencing.

The vulnerability of migrants in Asia

> This is what I order you to do, my son: Take care of your foreigners, esteem and support them. They should favour your country to others. Keep in mind, everybody has been born as a free human being.
>
> – *Stephen the Great, King of Hungary*[27]

Migration[28] is part and parcel of the globalisation phenomenon, with a record 257.7 million migrant workers spread out in all regions of the world in 2017, 79.6 million of which are in Asia – once again the largest proportion of any region (United Nations 2017). These historically massive population movements are particularly significant in specific countries or parts of the continent, with migrants for example representing some 88% of the United Arab Emirates' total population. Other Asian countries with very high proportions of migrant workers are Qatar, Jordan, Singapore and Saudi Arabia, while the region's major sending countries are the Philippines, Indonesia, Sri Lanka, Nepal and Bangladesh.

Migrant workers in Asia are another group particularly vulnerable to violations of human rights in Asia and elsewhere. Living in host states where they may not master the official language(s), are unfamiliar with the workings of the legal system and administration, detached from traditional support and family networks, exposed to a society with ways of life or cultures which they may find at times alien, they face obstacles that can leave them disoriented, unable to assert themselves or defend their rights. Their vulnerability means that migrant workers can experience

> assaults and killings by government security forces and private individuals, extensive use of torture and ill-treatment in detention, sexual abuse, widespread labor rights abuses, and pervasive extortion. Many employers still confiscate migrant workers' passports and work permits. Meanwhile, those filing grievances have often faced retaliation from police, officials, and employers.
>
> *(Human Rights Watch 2017)*

It is also those who are again most marginalised – minorities, women, and children – who can find themselves more susceptible to rights violations and even targeted by abuses.

The numbers of those vulnerable to human rights violations can also be staggering. There were estimated to be 20.2 million migrant workers originating from Southeast Asia alone in 2015 (United Nations 2015). In Thailand, migrant workers from Myanmar, Cambodia and Laos may make up between 1.8 to 3 million workers, or 5 to 10% of the country's workforce. Some of them have been trafficked, others are in situations of forced labour or even held in slave-like conditions. As in many other parts of the world, there are overlapping and intersecting issues faced by migrants and minorities, with minority women and children in particular falling victims of sexual abuse or employed in the sex industry. Though perhaps less often noted in the West, minority women and girls, such as Nepali in India or Burmese in Thailand, among other examples, increasingly appear to become caught up in situations of human trafficking and prostitution:

> From the 1990s to the present, an increasing number of the women and girls in prostitution in Thailand are from Burma. NGOs that work directly on rescuing victims have also reported that the majority of people in forced prostitution are from Burma. Some Thai NGOs estimate that 20,000 Burmese women and girls have been trafficked into Thailand and that the number of Burmese women in the Thailand sex industry totals 40,000. Thus, while the risk of prostitution and trafficking for sexual exploitation is decreasing for Thai and tribal women in Thailand, because the demand for prostitution remains the same the supply has shifted to people from Burma, in particular from the Shan State.
>
> *(Foster Crawford 2009)*

The extent of discrimination, exclusion and denial of basic rights of migrants, and particularly minority migrants, can impinge on almost every aspect of life:

> Beyond threats of ill-treatment, extended detention, and deportation, migrants constantly fear extortion by the police. Nearly all migrants held in police custody that we interviewed said that police had demanded money or valuables from them or their relatives in exchange for their release. Migrants reported paying substantial bribes depending on the area, the circumstances of the arrest, and the attitudes of the police officers involved. . . . Migrant workers are prohibited from forming associations and trade unions, taking part in peaceful assemblies, and face restricted freedom of movement. Often they cannot leave the area where their work is located without written permission from employers and district officials. The government prohibits migrants from obtaining driver's licenses.
>
> *(Human Rights Watch 2010)*

Even when legislation is supposed to protect migrants and nationals equally, in practice migrant workers may experience unequal and discriminatory treatment, with the problem 'compounded by ineffective mechanisms for resolving migrant worker complaints in most South-East Asian countries, which do not provide an accessible means for reporting and denouncing abuses when they occur' (Harkins & Åhlberg 2017: 1). This is even more so in relation to women migrants in the region:

> Males migrate into male-dominated sectors of employment which are often recognized in labour laws and codes, better paid and with better working conditions. Women migrate into more traditionally 'feminized' sectors of employment like domestic work and care work, which reinforce gender stereotypes. These sectors which are seen as a realm of the

> private household are still not part of labour laws nor recognized as work. Hence women do not earn adequate wages or have decent working conditions and the informality of the sector renders women prone to violence and exploitation of various kinds. Women migrating to low or unskilled work often do not have adequate education or understanding of basic human rights or means of access to justice in the case of violation of rights.
>
> *(UN Women 2013: 6)*

In other words, migrant women can experience compounded disadvantages due to forms of discrimination or other abuses due to the intersection of gender with other factors such as ethnicity, refugee or migrant status.

The above descriptions in relation to the unique challenges faced by migrants, though focused primarily on Southeast Asia, largely holds true in other parts of Asia, whether they involve Filipino or Nepali workers in the Middle East, Hong Kong, overstaying or hospitality workers in Japan, and many others. During their recruitment and employment, migrants often face barriers in accessing assistance, rendering them particularly vulnerable to labour rights violations, severe exploitation and other abuses. Most migrants at the same time also belong to ethnic minorities in their host countries, with often linguistic, cultural or religious factors compounding their vulnerability to human rights violations. The same difficulties remain true of minority women and girls who additionally can find themselves caught up by human trafficking or sexual exploitation, with once again Asia being the world's main source of people trafficked around the world according to one conservative estimate: some 400,000 persons from Southeast and South Asia alone, compared to 100,000 from the former Soviet Union, 100,000 from Latin America, 75,000 from Eastern Europe and 50,000 from Africa (Agbu 2003: 1–13).

This is not to say that no progress is being made in Asian countries or at the regional level in relation to protecting the human rights of migrants. On the contrary, there are regional and national efforts which have been ongoing in more recent years. For example, in 2002 the Regional Ministerial Conference on People Smuggling, Trafficking in Persons and Related Transnational Crime in Bali initiated what has become known as the Bali Process which has been ongoing since then, with about 50 Asian countries involved. The Bali Process has led to, amongst others, a Regional Support Office 'to support and strengthen practical cooperation on refugee protection and international migration, including human trafficking and smuggling, and other components of migration management in the region'.[29] It must be said that the Bali Process is mainly concerned with irregular migration as a challenge to be addressed, and does not focus particularly on the rights of those who are affected and often victimised.

In 2003, the Colombo Process was established as a regional state-driven consultative process on the management of migrant workers originating in Asia. Among its key objectives is 'protecting migrant workers from abusive practices in recruitment and employment and providing appropriate services to them in terms of pre-departure information, orientation and welfare provisions.[30]

As for ASEAN, it adopted the *Declaration on the Protection and Promotion of the Rights of Migrant Workers* (the *Cebu Declaration*) in 2007,[31] and some of the Declaration's obligations require host countries to facilitate access to justice for migrant workers, though not addressing explicitly irregular migrant workers.[32] Since 2008, the ILO has supported an annual ASEAN Forum on Migrant Labour. Additionally, Asian countries have not fared worse than other parts of the world in ratifying the main International Labour Organization's instruments dealing with the rights of migrant workers.[33] Finally, one of the more recent initiatives is a network of government, trade union and NGO service providers involved in a 2015–2025 programme known as the Tripartite Action to Enhance the Contribution of Labour Migration to Growth and Development in ASEAN (TRIANGLE in ASEAN programme).[34]

Through these and other initiatives too numerous to mention,[35] legislation in a number of countries in the Asia region has been gradually more responsive to the protection of vulnerable migrants and their human rights, though as this and other contributions in this Handbook point out, the scale, diversity and complexity of contexts make these issues extremely difficult to address – and one of the greatest challenges for many of the region's governments.

Conclusion

> 不怕慢，就怕站 – bù pà màn, jiù pà zhàn [It does not matter how slowly you go, as long as you do not stop].
>
> – *quote attributed to Confucius (28 September 551 BC–479 BC)*

There were always going to be tremendous human rights challenges facing a continent vastly more populated and heterogeneous than any other part of the world. Perhaps this means that a single human rights system is never going to be feasible or desirable, and that other sub-regional approaches could grow organically and should be encouraged. This would seem to be what has been occurring on the ground in recent years in relation to ASEAN and in areas of more regional concern such as migrant workers.

Be that as it may, there is no denying the disproportionate scale of the vulnerability of segments of society in many parts of Asia. While the marginalisation of migrants, minorities, children and women is not unique to the region, the general review in this chapter of the practices and circumstances in place around Asia highlights the need to be particularly aware of the need for the recognition and protection of human rights. While universal human rights are applicable to everyone, these are the individuals who find themselves particularly susceptible to harm or abuse, and therefore most in need of protection against the denial of their human individuality and dignity that one finds in the prohibition of discrimination and other fundamental standards.

Despite some positive developments in some sectors and Asian states, the extent of statelessness in the region, the massive numbers of refugees and internally displaced persons – often linked to ethnic and religious conflicts which are themselves often fuelled by discriminatory practices against minorities – and the all too common denial of some of the most basic rights of women and children in parts of Asia all suggest huge challenges remain to be acknowledged, and addressed.

Notes

1 The ASEAN Intergovernmental Commission on Human Rights is a consultative body of the Association of Southeast Asian Nations (ASEAN) which began operation in 2009. For general information on the Commission, see https://humanrightsinasean.info/asean-intergovernmental-comission-human-rights/about.html.

2 The ASEAN Commission on the Promotion and the Protection of the Rights of Women and Children was established in 2010. See in general https://humanrightsinasean.info/asean-commission-rights-women-and-children/about.html.

3 Established by the ASEAN Foreign Ministers in July 2007, the ASEAN Committee to Implement the Declaration on the Protection and Promotion of the Rights of Migrant Workers is responsible for overseeing the implementation of the 2007 ASEAN Declaration. See https://humanrightsinasean.info/asean-committee-migrant-workers/about.html.

4 The Arab Human Rights Committee was established in 2009 to oversee the application of the *Arab Charter on Human Rights* which entered into force in March 2008. The Council of the League of Arab States approved in September 2014 the statute for the establishment of a future Arab Court for Human Rights to be based in Bahrain. It was not yet in operation at the time of writing in

2018. For a non-official English translation of the statute, see www.acihl.org/texts.htm?article_id=44&lang=ar-SA.

5 Asia, for the purposes of this chapter, refers to the geographic sense of the term, referring therefore to the continent stretching from Turkey to Japan.

6 Only the United States of America has not ratified this treaty.

7 Once again, the United States of America has not ratified this treaty, nor have Somalia, Sudan, Tonga, Niue and Palau.

8 For the state of ratification as of 20 July 2017, see http://indicators.ohchr.org/.

9 In its 2016 Global Trends report, the UNHCR identified 65.6 million people around the world who had been forced from home, possibly the highest number in human history and exceeding even the massive population movements as a consequence of the Second World War. This figure includes nearly 22.5 million refugees, 40.3 million internally displaced people, and some 10 million stateless people without citizenship – an increase of 300,000 from 2015, itself a 'record' year. Most of these occurred as a result of persecution, conflict, violence or human rights violations. See United Nations High Commissioner for Refugees (2017b).

10 See Institute on Statelessness and Inclusion (2014: 56). There is no precise number of stateless people worldwide, though the most commonly invoked numbers are between 10 and 12 million.

11 Adopted by Member States of the Economic Community of West African States (ECOWAS), Abidjan, Nigeria, 25 February 2015, www.unhcr.org/ecowas2015/ENG-Declaration.pdf.

12 Governments of Latin America and the Caribbean met in Brasilia to mark the thirtieth anniversary of the *Cartagena Declaration on Refugees* of 1984. At the end of the Ministerial Meeting, 28 countries and three territories in Latin America and the Caribbean adopted by acclamation on 3 December 2014 the *Brazil Declaration*, also known as the *Framework for Cooperation and Regional Solidarity to Strengthen the International Protection of Refugees, Displaced and Stateless Persons in Latin America and the Caribbean*, www.refworld.org/docid/5487065b4.html.

13 The *Bali Process on People Smuggling, Trafficking in Persons and Related Transnational Crime* is an ASEAN forum where more recently in 2016 there was an acknowledgement of a relationship between irregular migration and statelessness during the Sixth Bali Process Ministerial Conference. The *Bali Process Declaration on People Smuggling, Trafficking in Persons and Related Transnational Crime* adopted in Bali on 23 March 2016 refers to the objective of adopting 'measures to prevent and reduce statelessness, consistent with relevant international instruments'. The declaration is available at www.baliprocess.net/UserFiles/baliprocess/File/Bali%20Declaration%20on%20People%20Smuggling%20Trafficking%20in%20Persons%20and%20Related%20Transnational%20Crime%202016%20%281%29.pdf.

14 www.unhcr.org/protection/statelessness/3bbb25729/convention-relating-status-stateless-persons.html.

15 www.unhcr.org/protection/statelessness/3bbb286d8/convention-reduction-statelessness.html.

16 For a general description of the marginalisation of women through gender-based denial of citizenship, see United Nations High Commissioner for Refugees (2017a).

17 For a description of the consequences of the double marginalisation of minority women and their children, see United Nations High Commissioner for Refugees (2012).

18 Minority Rights Group International (2017). See in particular the report's section on Asia at http://stories.minorityrights.org/statelessness/chapter/asia/.

19 One major UN report indicates that women and children may make up an estimated 80% of displaced populations. See United Nations (1996).

20 UN Commission on Human Rights, Resolution 2002/57 on the rights of persons belonging to national or ethnic, religious and linguistic minorities, UN Doc. E/CN.4/2002/57, 25 April 2002.

21 The world's top four refugee-hosting countries are all from Asia: Turkey (2.9 million), Pakistan (1.4 million), Lebanon (1 million) and Iran (979,400). Bangladesh could soon be added to this list if most Rohingya were to be considered refugees. UNHCR Global Appeal 2018–2019, http://reporting.unhcr.org/sites/default/files/ga2018/pdf/Global_Appeal_2018_full_lowres.pdf.

22 See Human Security Report Project (2010).

23 For a thorough analysis of the changing patterns in warfare, see also Epps (2013).

24 CEDAW Committee General Recommendation No 30 on women in conflict prevention, conflict and post-conflict situations, UN Doc No CEDAW/C/GC/30 (2013).

25 Economic development in and of itself does not alleviate internal conflicts involving minorities. On the contrary, economic development accompanied by continuing or increasing economic equality for a significant minority population can increase 'the widespread perception of injustice, unequal opportunities and marginalization that fuels resistance movements' (Parks, Colletta & Oppenheim 2012: 26).

26 The countries are Afghanistan, Pakistan, India, Nepal, Sri Lanka, Maldives, Bangladesh, Bhutan, Myanmar, Thailand, Lao People's Democratic Republic, Vietnam, Cambodia, Philippines, Indonesia, Malaysia, Singapore, Brunei, Timor-Leste and Papua New Guinea.
27 From *Scriptores rerum Hungaricum Tempore ducum regumque stirpis Arpadianae gestarum, Emericus Szentpétery*, Budapest, 1938 (quoted in de Varennes 2003: 5).
28 While the term migrant itself may be subject to different understandings, for the purposes of this section it is used in the sense of voluntary migration for educational, economic or similar purposes, and excludes refugees, forcibly displaced populations and asylum seekers.
29 See generally Bali Process, *About the Bali Process Official Website*, www.baliprocess.net/.
30 The twelve Asian member states are Afghanistan, Bangladesh, Cambodia, China, India, Indonesia, Nepal, Pakistan, Philippines, Sri Lanka, Thailand and Vietnam. See generally Colombo Process. *About the Colombo Process Official Website*, www.colomboprocess.org/about-the-colombo-process.
31 Cebu, 13 January 2007, www.ilo.org/dyn/migpractice/docs/117/Declaration.pdf.
32 It is thought about one-third of migrants in Asia are irregular, meaning their entry was not through the formal immigration process or they lack a valid work permit. International Labour Organization (2011: 4).
33 These are the *Migration for Employment Convention (Revised), 1949 (No. 97)* and *Recommendation (Revised), 1949 (No. 86)*, the *Protection of Migrant Workers (Underdeveloped Countries) Recommendation, 1955 (No. 100)*, the *Migrant Workers (Supplementary Provisions) Convention, 1975 (No. 143)*, and the *Migrant Workers Recommendation, 1975 (No. 151)*.
34 This is described as 'part of the International Labour Organization's (ILO) global efforts to promote fair migration ... through delivery of technical assistance and support to governments, social partners, civil society and regional bodies'. See *TRIANGLE in ASEAN*, ILO Programmes and Projects, at www.ilo.org/asia/projects/WCMS_428584/lang--en/index.htm.
35 Including amongst others the ASEAN Intergovernmental Commission on Human Rights, the ASEAN Commission on the Promotion and the Protection of the Rights of Women and Children, the ASEAN Committee to Implement the Declaration on the Protection and Promotion of the Rights of Migrant Workers, and the Arab Human Rights Committee.

References

Agbu, O (2003), Corruption and Human Trafficking: The Nigerian Case. *West Africa Review*, vol. 4, no. 1, pp. 1–13.

Bali Process, About the Bali Process Official Website, www.baliprocess.net/.

Colombo Process, *About the Colombo Process Official Website*, www.colomboprocess.org/about-the-colombo-process.

de Varennes, F (2003), *Strangers in Foreign Lands: Diversity, Vulnerability and the Rights of Migrants*, Paris: UNESCO, http://unesdoc.unesco.org/images/0014/001466/146681e.pdf.

Epps, V (2013), Civilian Casualties in Modern Warfare: The Death of the Collateral Damage Rule. *Georgia Journal of International and Comparative Law*, vol. 41, pp. 307–355.

Fearon, J & Laitin, D (2009), Sons of the Soil, Migrants, and Civil War. *World Development*, vol. 39, no. 2, pp. 199–211.

Foster Crawford, C (2009), Cultural, Economic and Legal Factors underlying Trafficking in Thailand and Their Impact on Women and Girls from Burma. *Thailand Law Journal*, vol. 12, no. 1, www.thailawforum.com/articles/Trafficking-in-Thailand-4%20.html.

Greenberg, SB & Boorstin, RO (2001), People on War: Civilians in the Line of Fire. *Public Perspective*, vol. Nov/Dec, pp. 18–22.

Harkins, B & Åhlberg, M (2017), *Access to Justice for Migrant Workers in South-East Asia*, Bangkok: International Labour Organization, www.ilo.org/wcmsp5/groups/public/---asia/---ro-bangkok/documents/publication/wcms_565877.pdf.

Human Rights Watch (2010), *From the Tiger to the Crocodile: Abuse of Migrant Workers in Thailand*, New York: Human Rights Watch, www.hrw.org/report/2010/02/23/tiger-crocodile/abuse-migrant-workers-thailand.

Human Rights Watch (2017), *Thailand: Migrant Worker Law Triggers Regional Exodus: Revise New Decree to End Disproportionate Penalties, Protect Rights*, New York: Human Rights Watch, www.hrw.org/news/2017/07/07/thailand-migrant-worker-law-triggers-regional-exodus.

Human Security Report Project (2010), *Human Security Report 2009/2010*, www.colorado.edu/geography/class_homepages/geog_4712_s12/geog4712_S12/materials_files/20092010HumanSecurityReport-Part1-CausesOfPeace.pdf.

Institute on Statelessness and Inclusion (2014), *The World's Stateless*, Oisterwijk: Wolf Legal Publishers, www.institutesi.org/worldsstateless.pdf.
Institute on Statelessness and Inclusion (2017), *The World's Stateless: Children*, Oisterwijk: Wolf Legal Publishers, www.institutesi.org/worldsstateless17.pdf.
Inter Sector Coordination Group (2018), *Situation Update: Rohingya Crisis, Cox's Bazar*, www.humanitarianresponse.info/en/operations/bangladesh/document/situation-update-rohingya-crisis-coxs-bazar-14-january-2018.
International Labour Organization (2011), *Asian Decent Work Decade Resource Kit: Protecting Migrant Workers*, Bangkok: ILO Regional Office for Asia and the Pacific.
Little, D (1996), *Belief, Ethnicity and Human Rights*, Washington, DC: United States Institute of Peace Press.
Minority Rights Group International (2017), *Statelessness and Minorities Globally*, London: MRG International, http://stories.minorityrights.org/statelessness/chapter/statelessness-and-minorities-around-the-world/.
Norwegian Refugee Council and Institute on Statelessness and Inclusion (2016), *Toolkit: Understanding Statelessness in the Syria Refugee Context*, www.syrianationality.org/index.php?id=8.
Parks, T, Colletta, N & Oppenheim, B (2012), *The Contested Corners of Asia: Subnational Conflict and International Development Assistance*, San Francisco, CA: Asia Foundation, https://asiafoundation.org/resources/pdfs/ContestedCornersOfAsia.pdf.
Torres, WM (ed) (2007), *Clan Feuding and Conflict Management in Mindanao*, San Francisco, CA: Asia Foundation, http://pdf.usaid.gov/pdf_docs/pnaea170.pdf.
UN Women (2013), *Laws, Policies and Regulations Governing Labour Migration in Asian and Arab States: A Gender and Rights Based Perspective*, Bangkok: UN Women Asia Pacific Regional Office, www2.unwomen.org/-/media/field%20office%20eseasia/docs/publications/2013/review%20of%20laws%20policies%20and%20regulations%20governing%20labour%20migration%20in%20asian%20and%20arab%20states.pdf?la=en.
UNICEF (2017), *Bangladesh: Humanitarian Situation Report No. 9 (Rohingya Influx) 27 October–2 November 2017*, https://reliefweb.int/report/bangladesh/bangladesh-humanitarian-situation-report-no9-rohingya-influx-27-october-2-november.
United Nations (1996), Impact of Armed Conflict on Children, Report of the expert of the Secretary-General, Graça Machel, submitted pursuant to General Assembly Resolution 48/157, New York: United Nations, www.unicef.org/graca/a51-306_en.pdf.
United Nations (2015), *Trends in International Migrant Stock: The 2015 Revision*, New York: United Nations Department of Economic and Social Affairs, Population Division, www.un.org/en/development/desa/population/migration/data/estimates2/data/UN_MigrantStockTotal_2015.xlsx.
United Nations (2017), *International Migrant Stock: The 2017 Revision*, New York: United Nations Department of Economic and Social Affairs, Population Division, www.un.org/en/development/desa/population/migration/data/estimates2/estimates17.shtml.
United Nations High Commissioner for Refugees (2012), *Gender Equality, Nationality Laws, and Statelessness: Testimonials of the Impact on Women and Their Families*, Geneva: United Nations, www.unhcr.org/protection/statelessness/4f587d779/gender-equality-nationality-laws-statelessness-testimonials-impact-women.html.
United Nations High Commissioner for Refugees (2017a), *Background Note on Gender Equality, Nationality Laws and Statelessness 2017*, Geneva: United Nations, www.refworld.org/docid/58aff4d94.html.
United Nations High Commissioner for Refugees (2017b), *Global Trends: Forced Displacement in 2016*, Geneva: United Nations, www.unhcr.org/statistics/unhcrstats/5943e8a34/global-trends-forced-displacement-2016.html.
United Nations High Commissioner for Refugees (2017c), *This Is Our Home: Stateless Minorities and Their Search for Citizenship*, Geneva: United Nations, www.unhcr.org/ibelong/wp-content/uploads/UNHCR_EN2_2017IBELONG_Report_ePub.pdf.
Wrench, E (1942), Mahatma Gandhi's Interview to Evelyn Wrench, *The Spectator*, http://gandhiking.ning.com/profiles/blogs/mahatma-gandhi-s-interview-to-evelyn-wrench-1.

2

Why Asian legal institutions fail to protect the human rights of the vulnerable

Nick Cheesman and Basil Fernando

Introduction

We begin with some illustrations of the problem with which we are here concerned.

A roadside vendor accuses a rickshaw driver of stealing bottles of petrol from his stall. Police detain the driver. For three days, they do not take him to court or file a charge, as required by law. Then they take him to hospital, where his relatives find him covered in bruises and scars, incurred while in custody. The vendor gives the family the equivalent of a few dollars for treatment costs, and a few more to the police, to close the case. The driver dies of his injuries, but the examining doctor records cause of death as alcohol poisoning. The family cannot get a copy of the medical report, and tries unsuccessfully to open a post mortem inquest (AHRC 2014a).

Human rights defenders find a group of children working as bonded labourers at a brick kiln. They notify a judge, who issues an order for a government officer to act. The rights defenders take the order to the officer. He asks them to come back after a week. They refuse. He tells them to come back the next day, and forms a team of police and other officials. They go to the kiln and find 20 children, whom they put in a vehicle. The officials have a conversation with the kiln owner, and then order the children to get out of the vehicle and go back to the kiln. The human rights defenders protest. The kiln management and some local thugs assault them. The police and government officers do not intervene. The kiln owner lodges criminal complaints against the rights defenders for interfering in his business (AHRC 2014c).

Six known criminals abduct and rape a teenage girl nearby a police station. Nobody comes in response to her cries. After finding her, villagers rally outside the station. Senior police warn the station chief not to lay charges because the rapists are politically connected. He opens cases anyway. A hospital confirms the girl was raped. She identifies the perpetrators. The criminals threaten her and her father. They approach the police through a political party to do a deal that only one of the six will be prosecuted. The station chief is suspended. An inquiry clears him of wrongdoing but he is not reinstated to his position. Instead he is transferred to another district (AHRC 2014f).

Prison guards beat and electrocute a detainee, who complains of the abuse. Legal aid lawyers bring a criminal case against the guards. A court finds the guards guilty of maltreating the detainee.

The judges emphasise that the guards had tortured the detainee because he had repeatedly violated prison rules. They appreciate that the guards had confessed and were contrite. They release the guards on a two-year suspended sentence (AHRC 2014d).

These stories illustrate events played out daily in Asia, different in details but common in their general features. From the hills of Pakistan to the islands of Indonesia, legal institutions fail to protect the human rights of the vulnerable in multitudinous but routine ways. State officers collude to defeat complaints of human rights abuse before they have even been heard. Where under pressure to act they may do something to demonstrate that they have complied with the orders of a judge, but the ties that bind them to influential business people or political parties may be stronger than the binding authority of the courts. In some places state officers are afraid of organised criminals with political connections, and a policeman who works according to law may be reprimanded rather than praised. And even where cases reach courts, judges may act as apologists for human rights violators, excusing rather than punishing them for wrongdoing.

The problem

Why do Asian legal institutions fail to protect the human rights of the vulnerable? The problem thus stated has two parts: *that* they fail to do so, and the reasons they fail to do so. We explore both parts together, along six routes to failure. But before going down those routes, we examine the elements of the problem further.

By 'legal institutions' we refer to state agencies responsible for providing, determining and enforcing effective judicial remedies for violations of human rights 'notwithstanding that the violation has been committed by persons acting in an official capacity'.[1] They include courts, prosecutors and police. They do not include national human rights institutions or analogous bodies charged with advising governments on human rights issues, and promoting international standards in domestic jurisdictions, because their general mandate does not refer primarily to judicial processes.[2] For the same reason, we exclude fact-finding commissions, inquiry committees and other institutions concerned with making recommendations rather than providing redress to people whose human rights have been violated.[3]

We understand 'vulnerability' to mean, drawing on Goodin (1985: 779), a situation in which the actions and choices of one person or group of persons can have a great impact on the interests of another person or group of persons. It is a condition of domination, such that someone can arbitrarily do some damage to somebody else (Pettit 1997). Vulnerability in this sense is relational. It emerges from asymmetrical power relations. One person or group of persons has disproportionate power to decide to do things, or refrain from doing things, that greatly affect another's interests.

Framed in terms of our problem, a vulnerable person is someone who in ordinary life is exposed to the possibility of an arbitrary, destructive attack on his or her human rights by someone else occupying a position of relative power, and is unable to do anything about it after an attack occurs. This understanding of vulnerability departs from the literature classing people as vulnerable according to whether or not they are of a particular religious, ethnic, cultural, linguistic, sexual or age group (see de Varennes and Gardiner in this volume). Although we acknowledge that people are always vulnerable in some way or another by virtue of how they are classed, and that particular classes of people are more or less vulnerable than others, in this chapter we concentrate on relations of vulnerability because our concern is expansive: troubled less by how Asian legal institutions fail to protect the human rights of particular vulnerable groups—a theme amply addressed by other contributors to this volume—than by how they fail to do so generally.

Our argument is that legal institutions fail to protect the human rights of the vulnerable not for want of resources or education, or not only for that reason, but for want of an institutionalised notion of 'task responsibility' to protect the vulnerable (Goodin 1985: 780). Asian legal institutions fail to protect the human rights of the vulnerable because it is not taken to be their job to protect them.

We are not being so crude as to suggest that legal institutions in Asia are absent of the notion of human rights altogether. Anyone can easily point to framework documents for the protection of human rights, such as bills of fundamental rights in constitutions, some laws to protect rights in accordance with international standards, and so on. And in some Asian countries, judges, prosecutors, police and administrators get training and receive handbooks on human rights via domestic programmes and international initiatives.[4] We also encounter officials of goodwill with a genuine concern to protect human rights. But the institutionalisation of task responsibility to do so is not just about institutional formalities or well-meaning individuals. It is evidenced through routine arrangements and practices to provide, determine and enforce effective judicial remedies where the human rights of the vulnerable are violated.

We restrict our discussion of the problem to physical integrity rights: rights not to be killed, not to be taken or detained arbitrarily, not to be sexually assaulted or tortured. These rights transcend debate about cultural particularities and go to the fundamental linkage between the dignity of the human and the necessity of legal institutions to protect rights, consistent with the contents of criminal codes and other domestic laws.

With Peerenboom, Petersen and Chen (2006) we adopt a case-based approach, drawing on accounts of destructive attacks on human rights in South and Southeast Asia over the last decade so as to counter abstract debate about universal human rights.[5] And like Haugen and Boutros (2014) we concentrate on unexceptional cases and times: on the everyday abuses heaped on people who while being most in need of protection are characteristically least able to make trouble for society when denied it (Goodin 1988: 166); on the 'everyday impunity' enjoyed by those responsible for attacks (see Cheesman, D'Costa & Haberkorn 2016). We also omit from the discussion circumstances where legal institutions may barely exist or not exist at all, such as in civil-war-prone areas of Myanmar; where emergency military regulations make the protection of human rights unusually difficult, like Manipur in the northeast of India (ALRC 2006a; see chapter by Mahanta in this volume), or times of 'manufactured chaos' (Thomson-Senanayake 2014), such as in the last days of Nepalese monarchy in the early 2000s (ALRC 2004), or during the anti-Muslim carnage in Gujarat under the government of Narendra Modi. The cases discussed in this chapter are indicative of the general problem with which we are concerned precisely because they are mundane.

Six routes to failure

Where a vulnerable person or persons suffer a destructive attack on their human rights, if legal institutions are to protect them, they should provide the vulnerable with effective judicial remedies, and offer certainty of competent investigation, fair hearing, and enforced determination. However, Asian legal institutions fail to protect the human rights of the vulnerable, because the person:

1. Does not make a complaint, because of fear or low expectation of redress.
2. Tries to make a complaint but cannot, because no legal institution exists to receive it, or because it exists but is inaccessible, or because it declines to receive the complaint.
3. Makes a complaint, but legal institutions have no authority, either in law or in fact to do anything about it.

4 Makes a complaint, but legal institutions do nothing, because they do not interpret their role as being to protect human rights, or because of threats or influence from other quarters, or because of lack of resources or inefficiency, or because they are paid not to act, or for more than one of these reasons.
5 Makes a complaint and legal institutions act, but in a way that is unreliable or arbitrary, that falls short of—or runs contrary to—human rights standards and expectations of the complainant.
6 Makes a complaint and one or more legal institutions act, but other institutions ignore or fail to enforce their directions.

To be sure, these six routes to failure are not the only ones. We are not implying that they are comprehensive. Nevertheless, from our observation of cases documented in the last ten years by the Asian Human Rights Commission (AHRC) on which the contents and findings of this chapter are based, although varying in their properties and frequency from one country to the next, in Asia these routes are primary.[6]

No complaint

A vulnerable person who suffers a destructive attack on his or her human rights may not complain to a legal institution. Two reasons for non-complaint are fear of what will happen in the event of complaint, and low expectation that anything will come from a complaint. Fear of complaining is both particular and general. A person tortured to confess to a crime when brought by police to a judge or doctor is unlikely to complain because of fear that they will be tortured further if they do, or if they otherwise fail to do as instructed. A person who has been released from custody after torture may be threatened that if they tell anyone about what has happened to them then they will suffer consequences, as in the case of an Indonesian man whom police accused of theft and hit around the head with a wooden block until he suffered contusions. On taking him for treatment at hospital, the police warned him to tell the doctor only that he had sustained the injuries in a fall or fight; notwithstanding, his mother filed a complaint (AHRC 2013b: 64–65). Sri Lankan torture survivors tell similar stories of being threatened to lie to doctors or run the risk of not being released from custody (Fernando 2009b). Released survivors of abuse may also receive visits from people representing their torturers, like one survivor of genital electrocution by police in Thailand, whom officers visited while in hospital (ALRC 2006b: 32–33). Having received money to cover his medical expenses, the torture survivor quietly, and sensibly, left the district.

Even where vulnerable people are not directly threatened, they may fear to complain because of what happens to people who do. A gunman shot Gerald Perera dead as he travelled on a public bus in Colombo, Sri Lanka shortly before he was due to give evidence in court against police who had tortured him (Fernando & Puvimanasinghe 2005: 60–65). Absent the key witness, the torture case has remained in court for over 12 years—although in 2015 the murder trial ended with the conviction of two policemen (AHRC 2015b), after intense and protracted efforts by the victim's family, human rights defenders, journalists and others to obtain justice. The successful conviction in this case notwithstanding, as a general rule the killing of a complainant in Sri Lanka has efficacy at two levels: it defeats the specific case, and it delivers a general message to the public, that it is foolish to think of going to court against the police and not to expect consequences, in response to which legal institutions will be either unable or unwilling to respond.

Whether or not a witness protection law that the parliament of Sri Lanka passed in 2015 proves to be effective remains to be seen, but the evidence from other Asian countries suggests that measures to protect complainants and witnesses under such laws are not particularly efficacious. In the Philippines and Thailand, complainants report feeling less secure as a result of being given official protection. In both, protection is provided haphazardly, and typically only for the life of a case in court. Complainants and witnesses are put into situations in which they are exposed to threats or inducements (ALRC 2006b), as in the case of Myrna Reblando (2012), the wife of one of 58 journalists and colleagues massacred on a hilltop in Mindanao, southern Philippines during 2009. Reblando learned that a man appointed to guard her as the case against the accused went to court had connections with the family that organised the massacre. To her surprise and dismay, he was even willing to act as a go-between to negotiate a price for her to withdraw from court proceedings against the accused. She subsequently fled the country to seek asylum abroad.

Complainants are also inhibited from coming forward by threats to their liberty. In Myanmar, government officials accused of wrongdoing lodge counter-criminal complaints in the courts, either to have complainants withdraw cases, or with a view to jailing anyone who has dared challenge their authority (Cheesman 2015: 237–247). In Bangladesh, the police and perpetrators also lodge fabricated criminal cases against the survivors of destructive attacks on their human rights to discourage potential complainants. In the case of F.M. Abdur Razzak and family, not only have they been brutally assaulted over a property dispute by an army officer's relatives and gang; they also have had no less than 15 cases registered against them with the connivance of the police (AHRC 2014h: 71–73), for their refusal to submit to the officer's presumption that he and his family are entitled to interfere arbitrarily in the affairs of other people.

In Thailand, human rights violators have access to a powerful 'defamation regime' (Streckfuss 2011) that is effective at intimidating actual or potential complainants, and inimical to the protection of human rights. Thai police torturers are able to attack their victims twice over, first by the act of torture and second, by having them imprisoned for criminal defamation when they dare complain (Khongkachonkiet 2013). Under such circumstances, it is hardly surprising that the survivors of destructive attacks on their human rights do not speak up, and instead accept money, where offered, to remain quiet.

Thwarted complaint

Complainants' attempts to obtain redress for destructive attacks on their human rights in Asia fail for a host of reasons. Most obviously, where countries lack laws consistent with international standards and institutions to enforce them, complainants lack avenues for effective redress. Whereas it is a crime everywhere in South and Southeast Asia to steal and destroy property, only in the Philippines is it a crime to abduct and kill somebody and dispose of their body parts in a manner that they are not traceable,[7] and only Sri Lanka and Cambodia have ratified the convention to prevent enforced disappearances.[8] Although a majority of countries in South and Southeast Asia are party to the anti-torture convention, only Sri Lanka and the Philippines have introduced laws to criminalise torture (AHRC & Redress 2013). That complaints of torture in these two countries are also for the most part unsuccessful (Fernando 2013; Reyes 2013) is indicative of how legal institutions in each still lack a notion of task responsibility to protect human rights, despite being assigned it on paper.[9] That practically nowhere in Asia do survivors of torture have avenues to complain and obtain restitution is also symptomatic of the generalised lack of effective remedies of the sort envisaged in treaties like the International Covenant on Civil and Political Rights.

When vulnerable people seek redress, the simplest expedient to thwart complaint is to refuse to listen to them, or not to record what they are saying. Police officers in the Philippines, for instance, have declined to take down complaints on spurious grounds such as that the following day is a public holiday or that an incident occurred outside their station's jurisdiction—even though they could still document and refer it to the relevant station (AHRC 2012a). Where pressured to record a complaint, they may write it down in the station diary and do nothing more. Research in Pakistan has found the majority of complainants have difficulty lodging a report to initiate a case because they need to pay bribes that they cannot afford (Saleem 2004). And two women in Bangladesh who tried unsuccessfully to register a case against the police who allegedly tortured them not only had their attempt rebuffed but were again detained and forced to recant their complaints in front of a judge (AHRC 2014b). The police thereafter reportedly fabricated a murder charge against the women with which to prevent them from pursuing the matter further.

While refusing to record a complaint, police officers may act against the wishes of the aggrieved and try to negotiate an informal settlement with the person who has committed an offence. Police in Sri Lanka told the mother of a disabled woman to accept money from her daughter's rapist and drop the matter on the spurious grounds that as the young woman was mentally incapacitated no complaint could be made (Fernando & Singh 2012: 136–139). Their counterparts in Nepal refused to register a complaint against a man responsible for abducting, raping and selling a teenage girl, saying that they would first seek a settlement with the accused and only if he refused to negotiate would they investigate (AHRC 2014e). In this instance, even attempts by the family of the girl to pay for the complaint to be lodged were not successful. And where complainants approach courts directly they may find that staff refuse to accept their plaints. Court clerks in Myanmar have handed documents back to lawyers rather than register cases against senior government officials or army officers. Magistrates in Pakistan are chary to accept cases lodged against military personnel, since these cases are unlikely to do their careers any good, and may put them or their families in danger.

Structural arrangements can also obstruct complainants trying to access legal institutions that on paper purport to protect their rights. One of the most widely known remedies for arbitrary arrest and detention is the writ of habeas corpus. Although Myanmar reintroduced habeas corpus via its 2008 Constitution, aspiring petitioners need to have money, time and knowhow to approach the Supreme Court in the country's hinterland capital to submit an application. Even then, that habeas corpus petitions have proven to be 'futile exercises that led to the exertion of significant time and expense without any tangible success' (Crouch 2014: 155) encourages potential petitioners to look for relief with the help of executive officers in their localities, who can intervene promptly on their behalf, rather than legal institutions that have neither the inclination nor capacity to assist.

No authority

The Supreme Court in Myanmar is an example of an institution that even if it did have the inclination to protect the human rights of the vulnerable lacks the authority to do so, because the army, not the judiciary or legislature, is the supreme organ of the state. The army for its part brooks no interference in matters it considers its internal affairs, even if these matters involve destructive attacks on the human rights of civilians that in no way relate to military operations or duties. Consequently, when low-ranked soldiers absconded from their base to rob a young couple in 2013, murdering one of the two and attempting to murder the other, a superior officer came and plucked them from police custody (AHRC 2013a). Although police had enough evidence to prosecute, the army conducted an internal inquiry that was closed off from the families, which reportedly punished the murderers with short periods of in-camp detention, not for murder but for violating the army code of conduct.

In other Asian countries with politically active militaries we find parallel ideas and practices. In Thailand, even where courts have imputed that army officers have been responsible for gross human rights abuses, such as the murder of 32 militants at a mosque (AHRC 2006), and the death in custody of an imam, their findings have not resulted in criminal prosecutions. In the former case, and in the 2004 killing of 78 men—most in army custody—the attorney general issued orders not to prosecute the commanding officers. In the case of the imam, the court averred that 'civilians cannot bring charges against soldiers for actions carried out while on duty' (Haberkorn 2015: 56). Similarly, in Pakistan, police refuse to investigate cases involving military intelligence, claiming that they are unable to file a case or institute any investigation against intelligence agents (AHRC 2014g).

In the event that aggrieved persons succeed in making complaints, they may also find that they require special dispensation to prosecute state officers—either because procedures require it, or because the concerned agencies are too powerful to act against their personnel without explicit permission, or both. Indonesian police can block the investigation and prosecution of their own personnel (Kerrigan & Dalton 2006). Only by doing deals with them do prosecutors have any hope of advancing a case. Police in Myanmar require that the home affairs ministry approve criminal inquiries against one of their own. In the event that the ministry—which is headed by an army officer—for whatever reason declines, legal institutions take no further action.

Where laws and institutions do not exist to protect human rights but nevertheless complaints are received and recorded, officials may push them on to agencies with neither the mandate nor knowledge to do anything about them. Complaints can spend years gathering dust in the filing cabinets of agencies that are not actually expected to provide redress. In Thailand, for instance, absent an agency to investigate torture, complaints of torture have in the past been transferred to the National Counter Corruption Commission (ALRC 2005) (now the National Anti-Corruption Commission), where they lingered for years without any information being made available to the complainants, or evidence of action. And why should anyone expect otherwise? The commission, after all, was established to investigate corruption, not torture. Meanwhile, people who have suffered torture and unlawful or incommunicado detention since the resurgence of military dictatorship in Thailand have had no judicial recourse at all (Thai Lawyers for Human Rights 2014; Cross Cultural Foundation 2016).

No action

In developmental discourse on human rights and law reform, legal institutions are said to fail in protecting human rights because they are under-resourced, slow and inefficient, or corrupt. The problems of legal institutions are identified with reference to a suite of conventional proposed solutions: more funding, more training, more restructuring (see for example World Bank 2003; Asia Foundation 2014; International Bar Association's Human Rights Institute 2015).

Like most facile accounts of obstacles to the achievement of human rights in the world today, including in Asia, these discourses are partly true. Even simple cases can take years for courts to conclude. In a study of Delhi criminal proceedings, for instance, Salar Khan (2008) found that around 88% of criminal cases had been awaiting prosecution evidence for over a year; 18%, for over five years. Around half the criminal cases in the city's courts were pending for one to five years, and some 29%, over five years. Delays had been caused by non-appearance of prosecution witnesses, pending paperwork, and by incompetence or cunning—evidence not lost was reported lost, or could not be made available in court, for reasons such as because the briefcase containing it was locked and the key to open it could not be found. While cases drag on for years, complainants, defendants and witnesses die or move away, making successful completion of trial impossible.

Delays afford perpetrators opportunities to despoil a case, and threaten complainants and witnesses. An army officer in Nepal against whom a case of alleged torture has been pending since 2011 has threatened the survivor and family repeatedly that he will kill them 'with the support of goons' (AHRC 2015a). And where a senior policeman, government administrator or powerful clan leader or businessman is the accused, the opportunities to destroy a case are multiplied, thanks to longer than usual delays. In West Bengal, India it took ten years for a court just to begin to prosecute a high-ranking policeman for abduction and murder (AHRC & Masum 2004). The young man's father died shortly before a court granted leave to proceed. The leading alleged perpetrator was never convicted, and has since been promoted to a top position in the state police force.

Payments also encourage inaction. The marketplace for justice across the region is sophisticated and vast. The manner in which criminal complaints are treated as commodities that accrue value for officials involved as they pass along the justice supply chain varies tremendously, whether in Indonesia (Butt & Lindsey 2011), Bangladesh (Islam 2010) or Myanmar (Cheesman 2015: 161–191). Nevertheless, the overriding imperative is that violators of human rights with money and resources easily outbid the vulnerable to forestall, foreclose or wreck a case brought against them. Inaction can also occur because illicit payments have not been received, precisely because officials are waiting expectantly to be paid before they act.

Although developmental discourse is partly correct about the routes by which legal institutions in Asia fail to protect the human rights of the vulnerable, it resists critical or probing analysis of reasons for failure for which it lacks ready-made solutions. Yet it is at exactly this point that we have the opportunity for insights that 'move the debate from one of state "incapacity" and "inability" to one of structured intent' (Baker & Milne 2015: 153). In Sri Lanka, dysfunction is not simply a developmental failure. It is a consequence of wilful neglect and political sabotage (Fernando 2009a). In Bangladesh, it is not just that the courts are overloaded. It is also that the prosecution service has been purposefully politicised (Ashrafuzzaman 2008). In the Philippines, it is not only that agencies lack funds or training. It is a consequence of embedded familial influence, such that in some cases involving rich and connected parties 'the judge is relegated to the background, as if he is no longer a judge' (Lagare 2013: 79).

Even if conditions in Sri Lanka, Bangladesh or the Philippines might be ameliorated through new legislation, retraining and restructuring, the failure of legal institutions in each of these countries to protect the human rights of the vulnerable is at bottom a failure to take task responsibility, and one that is indicative not merely of the absence of the rule of law in many parts of Asia, but of the hostility of existing institutions to the rule-of-law idea. Consequently, in Myanmar, despite political change since 2012, courts have shown little inclination to protect the human rights of the vulnerable, because the politics that animate them are still the politics of old: the politics of law and order, not human rights (Cheesman 2015). Law and order's goal is not to make people less vulnerable but to make the state more secure, and to do so via administrative rather than legal means.

A similar arrangement exists in Thailand, where top officials in the courts, police force and administrative departments 'almost see themselves as modern-day courtiers presiding over a giant court society, dispensing the royal benevolence to the king's loyal subjects' (Jory 2014: 4). This self-perception cultivates an attitude of contempt for the political ideal of equality on which human rights are founded, an attitude that is manifest through legal and extralegal projects for the subordinating of anyone failing to show appropriate respect for officials' benevolent dispensations, whether alleged drug dealers (ALRC 2003), or demonstrators protesting the repeated removal of elected governments by means of military coup.

Despite the semblance of a relatively high level of respect for human rights, legal institutions in the Philippines convey a similar albeit more subtle message when they decline to prevent destructive attacks on the rights of political activists or others whom they characterise as troublemakers—in some cases even saying as much (AHRC 2012b). Hence, a judge in the case of a man whom Filipino soldiers set on fire, alleging he was a member of a rebel group, remanded him in custody even though his burned face and neck were clearly visible in court (AHRC 2012b: 50–52). And the medico-legal officer in another case made only a cursory examination of an abused detainee, failing to record the physical evidence of torture on the medical report and declaring him fit to remain in custody (AHRC 2011: 14–15). When an institutionalised attitude that legal institutions have no task responsibility to protect the human rights of the vulnerable is combined with conditions that permit general incompetence and disregard for the basics of the job, as in this case, the chances for the complainant to succeed in obtaining redress are remote at best.

Limited action

Where legal institutions in Asia do respond to complaints, their responses may fall far short of whatever is needed to protect the human rights of the vulnerable. Government officials may announce that they have taken disciplinary action against violators of human rights rather than prosecuting them, or have charged them with relatively minor offences. In Myanmar, for example, police are demoted, transferred or sacked in response to deaths in custody, torture and malfeasance—responses that police spokesmen characterise as evidence of their responsiveness to complaints, and their concern to prevent such practices (Cheesman 2015: 153–154). Similarly, in Indonesia, survivors of torture may be told that 'administrative sanctions' have been imposed against police officers for violating their code of conduct (Arifin 2013), rather than criminal sanctions that survivors seek.

In parts of Asia, such managerial techniques for dealing with destructive attacks on human rights are described as 'eyewash'. Yet, they do more than simply give a good public impression. Far from protecting the human rights of the vulnerable, they help to reinforce existing arrangements, because they afford superiors opportunities to decide under what circumstances they will absolve subordinates of wrongdoing, and thereby obtain their gratitude and loyalty, while also enabling them to take action against those officers they consider 'in need of being brought into line' (Fuller 1969: 213). In other words, they perform an important internal policing function—just not one that has the effect of protecting the human rights of the vulnerable, since it does not signal that destructive attacks on human rights are unacceptable, but only that certain practices are unacceptable at certain times, if performed by certain personnel and if they have the effect of damaging the institutional reputation. The message delivered is in every respect conditional.

Courts may issue rulings in favour of vulnerable people long after destructive attacks on human rights have occurred. Some habeas corpus petitioners in Sri Lanka, for instance, have waited for over a decade before the courts have finally concluded in their favour (Pinto-Jayawardena & Guneratne 2011). After such a wait, the answers to the questions for which the petitions had been submitted have become academic, the failure of abducted and disappeared loved ones to return home in the interim speaking far more loudly to the abject failure of Sri Lankan legal institutions to protect rights than any pronouncements that the courts themselves can make.

Legal institutions also issue orders to pay survivors of destructive attacks on human rights, rather than punish perpetrators. In Thailand, relatively large amounts of compensation have been paid out to survivors of torture, people wrongly imprisoned, the families of persons forcibly disappeared and some of the relatives of people extrajudicially killed by police or men working with them. Very few perpetrators of these crimes and others have ever been investigated, let alone tried in court. In these cases, compensation serves not as a complement but as a substitute for substantive redress.

No enforcement

Where legal institutions occupy low rungs on the ladders of state authority, they struggle to give their orders effect. Even where judges issue instructions advantageous to the vulnerable, police, soldiers or administrators may simply ignore the orders, or respond inadequately, knowing full well that the court either does not care what happens after the order is made, or will not in any case be able to do anything about it.

The disregard of legal institutions' orders is not always malicious. It may also be due to laziness or symptomatic of a general lack of respect for courts, such as where a judge in Nepal ordered that a detainee get a medical examination, and police took him to hospital, but brought him back without being examined because he could not pay for the doctor's services himself (Fernando & Singh 2012: 268–270). In other cases, it is wilful, such as when a woman in West Bengal whose husband was found dead on railway tracks was forced to go to a judge to have a case opened after police refused to investigate. The judge ordered the police open a case, but they refused, saying the officer responsible was absent. The officer subsequently told a local human rights group that although the police had received the judge's order they had no intention of acting on it because the case was a suicide and the matter, closed. A second order from the judge was shunted over to the railway police on the basis that as the deceased was found on railway tracks, the 'place of occurrence' was under their jurisdiction (Human Rights Correspondence School 2006: 116).

The High Court in Bangladesh in 2012 issued an order to the home affairs ministry that it submit an investigation report concerning the alleged abduction and disappearance of a young man at the hands of a joint police–military unit, which had allegedly demanded ransom from his family (AHRC 2014b). Over two years since, no such report is known to have been submitted, and nor have the court's questions about the man's whereabouts been answered. In the interim the family has been threatened and monitored to prevent them from pursuing their complaints. And in the case from Myanmar with which we began the chapter, after the police refused to open a post mortem inquest, the family with the help of some political party members got a court order for one. The police ignored the order, and threatened the family and people helping them. The wife of the deceased was forced to move to another town.

Conclusion

In this chapter we have discussed, through a small selection of cases drawn from the thousands documented by the Asian Human Rights Commission over the last decade, how legal institutions in Asia fail to protect the human rights of the vulnerable—people who in ordinary life are exposed to the possibility of an arbitrary, destructive attack on their human rights by someone else occupying a position of relative power. Concentrating on South and Southeast Asia, we have argued that the underlying reason that legal institutions fail to protect the human rights of the vulnerable is an absence of task responsibility. We have examined the empirical features of that failure along six routes: non-complaint, failed attempt at complaint, absence of authority, inaction, inadequate or unreliable action, and non-enforcement.

None of these routes to failure are difficult to discern for anyone who chooses to look. Yet up to the present, we encounter resistance to admit to the failure, and a firm insistence—based on uncritical readings of institutional arrangements on paper or quantitative data of questionable validity—that Asian legal institutions can and do protect the vulnerable. Sometimes groups and individuals working to promote and protect human rights prefer to cooperate with legal institutions and governments in the region, and they do not want to jeopardise close relationships by speaking plainly about reasons for failure. At other times, human rights advocacy driven by international groups with limited knowledge of local conditions takes for granted the existence of legal institutions that can already protect the human rights of the vulnerable, but that just need new tools and training with which to do so.

Although we acknowledge that protection of human rights requires a variety of approaches and involvement of people with divergent skills and interests across a range of sectors, we also think insufficient attention has been paid to where established approaches have been going wrong. Technical solutions come up short of their goals because they are neither intended nor able to inculcate task responsibility to protect human rights. Advocacy for the human rights of particular vulnerable groups is vital, but has little merit if it neglects or insufficiently recognises chronic vulnerability across other classes and communities. And projects for human rights work based on templates from countries where legal institutions are already relatively good at providing, determining and enforcing effective judicial remedies for violations of human rights do not recommend themselves to places where they are not.

So, the problem in certain respects comes back to rest with the human rights movement itself. Although the routes to failure are manifest, existing responses to destructive attacks on human rights in Asia pay insufficient heed to the reasons the vulnerable are forced down them again and again, because the methodology of mainstream human rights work on legal institutions is today concentrated on implementation of specific provisions and measures consistent with international standards. It equips its practitioners to identify when, where and how states fail to comply with the particulars of international law, and gives them narrow and well-defined entry points for ritualised dialogue with like-minded practitioners and government officials versed in their language. What it does not do is push its practitioners to recognise and assess chronic failures to protect the human rights of the vulnerable against destructive attacks of the sort we have described in this chapter. It does not equip them with solutions to the kinds of deep institutional and political barriers to the protection of human rights that we have touched on. It does not encourage them to engage more critically with problems of institutional design and intentionality, to ask questions about when, where, how and why Asian legal institutions might fail to protect the human rights of the vulnerable as a matter of strategy rather than as a consequence of incapacity.

Recognition of the causes for failure to protect the human rights of the vulnerable in Asia obligates a different approach to human rights work from what is commonly done today. This different approach still recognises the need for technical improvement, but does not fixate on it. It still necessitates the monitoring and reporting on individual instances of abuse, but does not stop there. While working for technical change, it exposes the political reasons that improved training and better equipment do not necessarily deliver the results they promise. Through monitoring and reporting, it also builds a persuasive account of the larger structural causes of failure. It not only documents but also explains the characteristics of legal institutions' failure to protect the human rights of the vulnerable. And it treats the failure of Asian legal institutions to protect human rights as a problem not only of their practices, but also of their animating ideas, because—formal expressions of support for human rights and well-intended individuals notwithstanding—absent an institutionalised notion that they have a task responsibility to protect the human rights of the vulnerable, Asian legal institutions can but continue down their routes to failure.

Notes

1 International Covenant on Civil and Political Rights, Article 2. The Asian Legal Resource Centre (ALRC), which is the sister organisation of the Asian Human Rights Commission (AHRC), named its periodical *article 2* to emphasise that insufficient attention has been paid to how effective remedies are delivered to vulnerable people who have suffered destructive attacks on their human rights. All issues of *article 2*, which is cited throughout the chapter, are available online at www.article2.org.
2 Principles relating to the Status of National Institutions (the Paris Principles).
3 Arguably, the trend towards establishment of national human rights institutions and associated bodies in Asia has had less to do with the protection of human rights than with the appeasement of international criticism and ensuring of continued state control over nominal human rights agendas in the region (see chapter 8 in Cardenas 2014). Unsurprisingly, most official human rights institutions in Asia are hampered by a lack of institutional independence, and enjoy relatively few resources, making them institutionally and functionally peripheral to the questions at the centre of this chapter (see AHRC & Redress 2013).
4 Such as the World Programme for Human Rights Education, which in phase two targeted law enforcers and bureaucrats (UN 2012).
5 We draw on cases from South and Southeast Asia for reasons of practicability and because both authors have worked in these subregions extensively: Fernando in particular in Sri Lanka and Cambodia; and Cheesman, on Burma, or Myanmar, and Thailand.
6 In this chapter we draw on work done by the AHRC in ten countries—Bangladesh, Cambodia, India, Indonesia, Myanmar, Nepal, Pakistan, the Philippines, Sri Lanka and Thailand—in close consultation with desk staff. Since 2005, the AHRC has documented and reported in detail on approximately 2,100 cases of human rights violation from South Asia, and 900 cases from Southeast Asia. Details of cases can be found on the AHRC website, http://humanrights.asia.
7 Act Defining and Penalizing Enforced or Involuntary Disappearance, Republic Act No. 10353.
8 Convention for the Protection of All Persons from Enforced Disappearance.
9 In April 2016, a court in the Philippines for the first time convicted a police officer under the country's Anti-Torture Act, Republic Act No. 9745 (Mateo 2016), which was passed in 2009.

References

AHRC 2006, 'THAILAND: Three army officers identified as responsible for killings', viewed 29 March 2015, www.humanrights.asia/news/urgent-appeals/UA-398-2006.
AHRC 2011, 'The limitations of the Philippines' Anti-Torture Act', *Article 2*, vol. 10, no. 1, pp. 8–18.
AHRC 2012a, 'The tribulations and trials of complainants in the Philippines', *Article 2*, vol. 11, no. 2–3, pp. 8–18.
AHRC 2012b, 'Unsolved killings, disappearances, torture and arbitrary arrests [in the Philippines]', *Article 2*, vol. 11, no. 2–3, pp. 42–150.
AHRC 2013a, 'BURMA/MYANMAR: After five months no action against three soldiers who murdered a civilian', viewed 29 March 2015, www.humanrights.asia/news/urgent-appeals/AHRC-UAC-122-2013.
AHRC 2013b, 'Unsolved cases of torture, custodial deaths and extrajudicial killings [in Indonesia]', *Article 2*, vol. 12, no. 2, pp. 56–96.
AHRC 2014a, 'BURMA/MYANMAR: Police illegally arrest, detain and torture rickshaw driver to death', viewed 29 March 2015, www.humanrights.asia/news/urgent-appeals/AHRC-UAC-110-2014.
AHRC 2014b, 'Forty-seven cases of unresolved killing, torture and disappearance in five years', *Article 2*, vol. 13, no. 2–3, pp. 74–126.
AHRC 2014c, 'INDIA: Human rights defenders assaulted by traffickers and the AHTU look on', viewed 29 March 2015, www.humanrights.asia/news/urgent-appeals/AHRC-UAC-100-2014.
AHRC 2014d, 'INDONESIA: Judges grant probation to prison guards involved in torture', viewed 29 March 2015, www.humanrights.asia/news/urgent-appeals/AHRC-UAU-012-2014.
AHRC 2014e, 'NEPAL: Police refuse to investigate abduction and rape of teenager', viewed 29 March 2015, www.humanrights.asia/news/urgent-appeals/AHRC-UAC-123-2014.
AHRC 2014f, 'PAKISTAN: Threats to the lives of a minor who was gang raped and her father', viewed 29 March 2015, www.humanrights.asia/news/urgent-appeals/AHRC-UAC-098-2014.
AHRC 2014g, 'PAKISTAN: Three missing after arrest and police reject the filing of the First Information Report', viewed 29 March 2015, www.humanrights.asia/news/urgent-appeals/AHRC-UAC-099-2014.

AHRC 2014h, 'Wild West in the east: Four stories of state persecution', *Article 2*, vol. 13, no. 2–3, pp. 68–73.
AHRC 2015a, 'NEPAL: Torture victim threatened by army officer', viewed 29 March 2015, www.humanrights.asia/news/urgent-appeals/AHRC-UAC-008-2015.
AHRC 2015b, 'SRI LANKA: Sub-Inspector and his assistant convicted, sentenced to death for murder', viewed 29 June 2015, www.humanrights.asia/news/ahrc-news/AHRC-STM-090-2015.
AHRC & Masum 2004, 'Bhikari Paswan: Ten years of waiting for justice in West Bengal end with a funeral', *Article 2*, vol. 3, no. 4, pp. 29–36.
AHRC & Redress 2013, 'Torture in Asia: The law and practice', *Article 2*, vol. 12, no. 3, p. 184.
ALRC 2003, 'Extrajudicial killings of alleged drug dealers in Thailand', *Article 2*, vol. 2, no. 3, p. 44.
ALRC 2004, 'The mathematics of barbarity and zero rule of law in Nepal', *Article 2*, vol. 3, no. 6, p. 124.
ALRC 2005, 'Rule of law versus rule of lords in Thailand: Stronger institutions needed', *Article 2*, vol. 4, no. 3, pp. 10–34.
ALRC 2006a, 'Militarisation and impunity in Manipur', *Article 2*, vol. 5, no. 6, p. 56.
ALRC 2006b, 'Protecting witnesses or perverting justice in Thailand?', *Article 2*, vol. 5, no. 3, p. 80.
Arifin, S 2013, 'A torture victim's story of his quest for justice', *Article 2*, vol. 12, no. 2, pp. 40–44.
Ashrafuzzaman, M 2008, 'The disposable prosecutors of Bangladesh', *Article 2*, vol. 7, no. 1, pp. 59–65.
Asia Foundation 2014, '60 years addressing the critical issues facing Asia', Asia Foundation, San Francisco, CA.
Baker, J & Milne, S 2015, 'Dirty money states: Illicit economies and the state in Southeast Asia', *Critical Asian Studies*, vol. 47, no. 2, pp. 151–176.
Butt, S & Lindsey, T 2011, 'Judicial mafia: The courts and state illegality in Indonesia', in Edward Aspinall and Gerry Van Klinken (eds), *The state and illegality in Indonesia*, KITLV Press, Leiden, pp. 189–213.
Cardenas, S 2014, *Chains of justice: The global rise of state institutions for human rights*, University of Pennsylvania Press, Philadelphia, PA.
Cheesman, N 2015, *Opposing the rule of law: How Myanmar's courts make law and order*, Cambridge University Press, Cambridge.
Cheesman, N, D'Costa, B & Haberkorn, T 2016, 'Anticipating the struggle against everyday impunity in Myanmar through accounts from Bangladesh and Thailand', *Asia & the Pacific Policy Studies*, vol. 3, no. 1, pp. 45–58.
Cross Cultural Foundation 2016, '54 cases of torture and ill treatment in the deep south documented in 2014–2015', Cross Cultural Foundation, Duayjai & Patani Human Rights Organization, Bangkok.
Crouch, M 2014, 'The common law and constitutional writs: Prospects for accountability in Myanmar', in M Crouch and T Lindsey (eds) *Law, society and transition in Myanmar*, Hart Publishing, London, pp. 141–157.
Fernando, B 2009a, 'An essay on abysmal lawlessness and the zero status of Sri Lankans', *Article 2*, vol. 8, no. 4, p. 44.
Fernando, B (ed.) 2009b, *Recovering the authority of public institutions: A resource book on law and human rights in Sri Lanka*, Asian Human Rights Commission, Hong Kong.
Fernando, B (ed.) 2013, *Narrative of justice in Sri Lanka: Told through stories of torture victims*, Asian Legal Resource Centre, Hong Kong.
Fernando, B & Puvimanasinghe, S (eds) 2005, *An X-ray of the Sri Lankan policing system and torture of the poor*, Asian Human Rights Commission, Hong Kong.
Fernando, J & Singh, SK (eds) 2012, *The practice of torture: A threat to the rule of law and democratisation*, Asian Human Rights Commission and DIGNITY, Hong Kong & Copenhagen.
Fuller, LL 1969, *The morality of law*, Yale University Press, New Haven, CT & London.
Goodin, RE 1985, 'Vulnerabilities and responsibilities: An ethical defense of the welfare state', *American Political Science Review*, vol. 79, no. 3, pp. 775–787.
Goodin, RE 1988, *Reasons for welfare: The political theory of the welfare state*, Princeton University Press, Princeton, NJ.
Haberkorn, T 2015, 'When torture is a duty: The murder of Imam Yapa Kaseng and the challenge of accountability in Thailand', *Asian Studies Review*, vol. 39, no. 1, pp. 53–68.
Haugen, GA & Boutros, V 2014, *The locust effect: Why the end of poverty requires the end of violence*, Oxford University Press, Oxford & New York.
Human Rights Correspondence School 2006, *Rule of law and human rights in Asia*, Asian Human Rights Commission, Hong Kong.
International Bar Association's Human Rights Institute 2015, 'Annual Report 2014', International Bar Association's Human Rights Initiative, London.

Islam, MS 2010, *Politics-corruption nexus in Bangladesh: An empirical study of the impacts on judicial governance*, Asian Legal Resource Centre, Hong Kong.

Jory, P 2014, 'Thailand's "twilight of the gods": Understanding Thai politics in the interregnum', Public lecture, Griffith University.

Kerrigan, F & Dalton, P 2006, 'The Human Rights Courts and other mechanisms to combat impunity in Indonesia', *Article 2*, vol. 5, no. 2, pp. 13–24.

Khan, SM 2008, 'Judicial delays to criminal trials in Delhi', *Article 2*, vol. 7, no. 2, p. 80.

Khongkachonkiet, P 2013, 'Victims are not sons of rich men, they are poor', *Article 2*, vol. 12, no. 4, pp. 82–90.

Lagare, D 2013, 'Police, prosecutors and judges do not perform according to the law', *Article 2*, vol. 12, no. 4, pp. 79–81.

Mateo, J 2016, 'Pampanga cop gets 2 years for torture', *Philippine Star*, viewed 15 June 2016, www.philstar.com/nation/2016/04/03/1568750/pampanga-cop-gets-2-years-torture.

Peerenboom, R, Petersen, CJ & Chen, AHY (eds) 2006, *Human rights in Asia: A comparative legal study of twelve Asian jurisdictions, France and the USA*, Routledge, Oxford & New York.

Pettit, P 1997, *Republicanism: A theory of freedom and government*, Oxford University Press, Oxford & New York.

Pinto-Jayawardena, K and Guneratne, J 2011, *Habeas corpus in Sri Lanka: Theory and practice of the great writ in extraordinary times*, Law and Society Trust, Colombo.

Reblando, M 2012, 'Testimony of Myrna Reblando and her daughter', *Article 2*, vol. 11, no. 2–3, pp. 31–37.

Reyes, D 2013, *Torture in Indonesia and the Philippines: A jus cogens right with or without remedy?* Faculty of Law, University of Hong Kong, Hong Kong.

Saleem, A 2004, 'Inaccessible justice in Pakistan', *Article 2*, vol. 3, no. 5, pp. 11–14.

Streckfuss, D 2011, *Truth on trial in Thailand: Defamation, treason, and lèse-majesté*, Routledge, London & New York.

Thai Lawyers for Human Rights 2014, 'The human rights situation 100 days after the coup d'etat', Thai Lawyers for Human Rights, Bangkok.

Thomson-Senanayake, J 2014, *A sociological exploration of disappearances in Sri Lanka*, Asian Human Rights Commission, Hong Kong.

UN 2012, 'World Programme for Human Rights Education, second phase: Plan of action', United Nations, Geneva.

World Bank 2003, 'Legal and judicial reform: Strategic directions', World Bank, Washington DC.

3

An emerging Asian human rights regime as a tool for protecting the vulnerable in Asia?

Lessons from the UN human rights system and other regional human rights regimes

Debra L. DeLaet

Introduction

In advance of the 1993 World Conference on Human Rights in Vienna, a group of governmental representatives from Asian states met in Thailand to formalise their support for the Final Declaration of the Regional Meeting for Asia of the World Conference on Human Rights.[1] This document, which has come to be known as the 'Bangkok Declaration', represented the position of these Asian governments at the 1993 World Conference and Human Rights.

The Bangkok Declaration includes a number of provisions that articulate support for universal human rights, including reaffirmation of commitment to the Universal Declaration on Human Rights (para. 1) and to the 'interdependence and indivisibility' of economic, social, and cultural rights and of civil and political rights (para. 10). Although the document recognises interdependence and indivisibility among rights, it includes numerous provisions emphasising the importance of economic rights as foundational, including highlighting the right to development (para. 17) and identifying global inequities and poverty as fundamental obstacles to the attainment of human rights (para. 18 and para. 19). The Bangkok Declaration notably stresses the importance of guaranteeing fundamental human rights for vulnerable groups, including ethnic, national, racial, religious, and linguistic minorities, migrant workers, disabled persons, indigenous populations, and refugees and displaced persons (para. 11).

The Bangkok Declaration qualifies its support for universal human rights in a number of significant ways. It discourages the use of human rights conditionality in the provision of development assistance (para. 4) and stresses the ongoing importance of respect for the principles of national sovereignty, territorial integrity, and non-interference in the internal affairs of states (para. 5). Relatedly, it reaffirms the importance of self-determination, encompassing rights to freely determine both political systems and economic, social, and cultural development (para. 6 and para. 12). The Bangkok Declaration emphasises that universal human rights must be considered in the context of 'national and regional peculiarities and various historical, cultural, and religious backgrounds' (para. 8) and claims for states the primary responsibility for promoting and protecting universal human rights (para. 9).

In its expression of both commitments and qualifications to universal human rights, the Bangkok Declaration balances an aspirational rhetoric, inspired by a universalistic normative framework, and a more pragmatic discourse deferring to state interests and cultural values. This delicate balancing act is evident in the potential institutional responses that the Declaration identifies for advancing human rights in Asia. The declaration calls for a 'balanced and non-confrontational approach' in pursuit of human rights (para. 3). To this end, it acknowledges the need to explore the possibilities for establishing regional approaches to human rights protection and promotion (para. 26) but does not provide significant detail regarding the necessary elements for an effective regional human rights regime.

The Bangkok Declaration highlights an ongoing debate over the compatibility of 'Asian values' and universal human rights (Ciorciari 2012: 700–703). Lee Kuan Yew, the former prime minister of Singapore, famously argued in favour of an 'Asian values' perspective that would justify authoritarian governance. In a high-profile piece in *The New Republic*, Amartya Sen strongly contested the notion that 'Asian values' are inconsistent with human rights. Characterising the tendency to depict Asia as a single, homogenous entity as a Eurocentric view, Sen countered, 'there are no quintessential values that separate the Asians as a group from people in the rest of the world and which fit all parts of this immensely large and heterogeneous population' (Sen 1997: 34).

The fact that Asia, unlike other world regions, does not have a well-developed human rights regime has been used to support the argument that a cohesive set of 'Asian values' are inconsistent with human rights. Conversely, others have argued that it is precisely the lack of cultural, economic, or political cohesion in Asia that helps to explain the lack of established regional human rights procedures and mechanisms (Donnelly 2013: 179). Regardless of the reason, the lack of strong regional human rights norms and institutions distinguishes Asia from most other regions in the world; only the Arab world has been similarly slow to institutionalise human rights at a regional level (Donnelly 2013: 178).

Despite limited progress to date, a nascent human rights regime is emerging in Asia, or at least in sub-regions across Asia. In 2009, the Association of Southeast Asian Nations (ASEAN) created the Intergovernmental Commission on Human Rights (AICHR). Following this development, ASEAN created the ASEAN Commission on the Promotion and Protection of the Rights of Women and Children (ACWC) in 2010. The Asia Pacific Forum of National Human Rights Institutions (APF), a body that coordinates the activities of national-level human rights commissions in the area, also represents progress on the goal of institutionalising human rights in Asia. Because this body involves institutions *within* states, it arguably does not constitute the beginnings of a truly regional regime. Similarly, the ASEAN bodies are limited to a sub-region within Asia and, as such, cannot be described as a regime for the entire region. At the same time, these institutional developments indicate the emergence of bodies that represent a potentially unique path to institutionalising universal norms within a regional context.

In examining these institutional developments, this chapter compares and contrasts the emerging human rights regime in Asia with the global human rights regime and with other regional regimes. In doing so, the chapter challenges the notion that the institutionalisation of human rights at the regional level in Asia reflects a distinctly Asian approach to human rights, rooted in divergent 'Asian values'. Undoubtedly the development of formal human rights mechanisms in Asia has proceeded slowly, and the institutionalisation of human rights in Asia lags far behind that of most other regions. At the same time, the obstacles to human rights institutionalisation in Asia are similar to barriers to the effective promotion and protection of human rights via formal law and institutions at the global level and in regional regimes elsewhere. Further, the limitations of the emerging Asian human rights regime, a system characterised by a limited number of institutions governed by ambivalent norms with weak enforcement mechanisms, are shared, to varying degrees, with international human rights law as institutionalised in the UN system and with other regional regimes.

The UN human rights system

The United Nations (UN) system is the primary site of governance for the international human rights regime. The impressive body of international human rights treaties developed in the aftermath of the Second World War provides the legal foundation for this regime. Although these treaties codify human rights as universal rights, international human rights law ultimately remains a state-centric body of law. Likewise, UN human rights institutions reflect the statist dynamics of the international system, which limits its capacity to generate substantial and meaningful change.

The progressive codification and institutionalisation of international human rights law has been one of the most impressive and hopeful political developments in the twentieth century and beyond. Before the Second World War, distinct international human rights laws and institutions did not exist, apart from humanitarian laws governing state conduct during war and the 1926 Slavery Convention. In the aftermath of the Second World War, the development of international human rights laws was rapid and prolific, beginning with the adoption of the non-binding Universal Declaration of Human Rights by the General Assembly in 1948.

The International Covenant on Civil and Political Rights (ICCPR) and the International Covenant on Economic, Social and Cultural Rights (ICESCR), both signed in 1966 and entering into force in 1976, are binding treaties that codify an expansive list of universal human rights. They constitute the core of the international human rights regime. In addition to these core legal documents, the international human rights regime consists of numerous specialised human rights treaties that codify human rights norms in specific issue areas, including genocide, refugees, slavery, racial discrimination, torture, enforced disappearance, the protection of migrant workers, women's rights, and children's rights (DeLaet 2015: 31–35).

The codification of international human rights norms represents an important development in the emergence of a system of global governance, operating primarily within the framework of the United Nations. Governments and non-governmental actors leverage international human rights norms in domestic policy-making and legislative processes, an indication that international norms may contribute to the advancement of human rights in specific countries. Moreover, national courts have drawn on international human rights laws in domestic legal decisions. Yet, states and non-state actors continue to commit systematic and gross violations of human rights across the globe without consequence, and meaningful progress in improving the status of global human rights via international law and institutions has, to date, been limited.

The institutionalisation of international human rights laws within the UN illustrates the state-centric nature of the UN human rights system and helps to explain why international human rights law has not been more effective in promoting global human rights. The core of the UN human rights system includes nine treaty-monitoring bodies, one for each of the major treaties that constitute the international human rights regime: (1) the Human Rights Committee (ICCPR); (2) the Economic, Social and Cultural Rights Committee (ICESCR); (3) the Committee Against Torture (UNTC); (4) the Committee on the Elimination of Racial Discrimination (CERD); (5) the Committee on the Elimination of Discrimination Against Women (CEDAW); (6) the Committee on the Rights of the Child (CRC); (7) the Committee on the Rights of Persons with Disabilities (CRPD); (8) the Committee on Enforced Disappearances (CED); and (9) the Committee on Migrant Workers (CMW). In each case, the pertinent treaty establishes a committee with only weak monitoring powers, largely based in the voluntary submission of regular reports to the associated treaty-monitoring body followed by committee review and constructive dialogue with state parties (Office of the High Commissioner for Human Rights, 'United Nations Human Rights Programme'). Because treaty-monitoring bodies may only make non-binding recommendations in this process, states commonly do not follow these recommendations (DeLaet 2015: 139–141). Each treaty-monitoring body also issues general comments that offer interpretations of treaty obligations intended to influence state implementation efforts and that may be used by human rights groups in their advocacy efforts (Donnelly 2013: 167–168).

International complaint procedures also allow individuals to bring claims to the pertinent treaty-monitoring bodies, with the exception of the CRPD and the CMW for which complaint mechanisms have not yet entered into force. These complaint procedures allow individuals to lodge claims with treaty-monitoring committees against states if the state in question has both ratified the relevant treaty *and* recognises the competence of the committee to hear such claims. If a treaty-monitoring committee decides against a state in regards to an individual complaint, it will invite the state party to supply information within a specified time period regarding steps it has taken in response to the committee's findings. Although the decisions of human-rights-monitoring committees are considered authoritative interpretations of the treaties over which they have jurisdiction, their recommendations and rulings are not legally binding on states (Office of the High Commissioner for Human Rights, 'Human Rights Treaty Bodies: Individual Communications').

In addition to the treaty-monitoring bodies, the UN human rights system includes subsidiary bodies and specialised agencies with particular responsibilities for the promotion of human rights. The Human Rights Council (HRC), a body comprising 47 members elected by a majority of the General Assembly, has responsibility for promoting universal respect for the protection of all human rights and for making recommendations regarding human rights violations. This responsibility is carried out primarily through a 'universal periodic review' of the human rights records of all member states. The universal periodic review is based on state submission of reports detailing their records for fulfilling treaty-based human rights obligations, and the HRC does not have any mechanism to sanction states for non-compliance. The HRC also can receive and investigate specific complaints from states, non-governmental organisations, and individuals regarding patterns of systemic violations of human rights. However, the HRC may not publicise the nature of specific complaints or its discussion and, upon reaching decisions, can do little more than condemn rights violations (DeLaet 2015: 137–139). Notably, even absent strong enforcement mechanisms, these complaint procedures may be perceived as too adversarial to generate cooperative behaviour from states against which complaints have been brought (Donnelly 2013: 164). Nonetheless, Donnelly contends that the reporting process itself can be valuable in encouraging states to reflect on their human rights processes, procedures, and institutions, especially in countries with an active civil society, and that such reflection may lead to incremental change (Donnelly 2013: 166).

The UN Office of the High Commissioner for Human Rights (OHCHR) serves as a coordinating agency for human rights activities in the UN system. In this capacity, it plays an advisory role to other human rights institutions, supports and conducts research, and writes reports. Other specialised agencies with responsibilities for promoting specific human rights include the UN International Children's Emergency Fund, the UN High Commissioner for Refugees, and the UN Development Programme. In all cases, these agencies have responsibilities limited largely to norm creation, information gathering and dissemination, and the coordination of aid. The UN human rights system also includes offices of special rapporteurs or working groups in specific issue areas, including torture, arbitrary detention, freedom of religion, and the right to food that have had success in improving the human rights situations of particular individuals (Donnelly 2013: 163).

Collectively, the institutions in the UN human rights system emphasise norm creation, information gathering, monitoring, and, sometimes, public condemnation as tools for promoting international human rights. The international human rights regime includes only fledgling judicial mechanisms for rendering authoritative interpretations and applications of international human rights law that have not developed into effective mechanisms for consistently and comprehensively prosecuting violations of human rights. The limitations of the UN human rights system reflect the lack of political will on the part of states to engage in serious efforts to implement human rights norms rather than an inherent flaw in the UN system. As Nigel White (2002: 232) concludes, 'the problem is not the lack of human rights standards and mechanisms but the willingness of states to comply with obligations. The law is binding on states; the lack of enforcement is a combination of institutional deficiency and state unwillingness'.

Regional human rights regimes

Regional human rights systems offer an alternative path for promoting and protecting universal human rights in specific regions of the globe. Regional regimes have been institutionalised to varying degrees in Europe, the Americas, and in Africa. To a lesser extent, Arab countries have begun to institutionalise a regional framework for implementing human rights in the Arab world. Similarly, governments in Asian countries have begun to develop mechanisms for coordinating the promotion of human rights in parts of Asia.

The regional human rights regimes vary significantly in terms of the degree of institutionalisation, the scope of their activities, and the extent to which they create meaningful mechanisms for enforcement. Despite significant differences, regional regimes mirror the UN human rights system in replicating a predominantly state-centric and non-adversarial approach to the advancement of human rights. This section provides a brief overview of the human rights institutions in different regions to illustrate the similarities and differences among them as well as between regional regimes and the UN system.

The European human rights system

The European human rights system is the strongest and most fully developed among the regional human rights regimes. In fact, the human rights regime in Europe goes beyond the UN human rights system in creating concrete obligations for states. The foundational treaties for the European human rights regime include the European Convention for the Protection of Human Rights and Fundamental Freedoms, which codifies civil and political rights, and the European Social Charter, which delineates economic, social, and cultural rights.

Currently, the European Court of Human Rights provides the institutional core of the European human rights system. This Court has the strongest of any regional human rights regime and, indeed, surpasses the enforcement authority of existing institutional mechanisms in the UN human rights system. Under Protocol 11 to the European Convention for the Protection of Human Rights and Fundamental Freedoms, adopted in 1997 and entered into force in 1998, individuals as well as states have direct standing and can bring complaints before the Court. Prior to this time, a now-defunct European Commission on Human Rights, a political body with elected members from states parties to the Convention, had automatic jurisdiction in the case of state complaints and optional jurisdiction in the case of complaints from individuals or NGOs. The Commission could engage in fact finding, help to negotiate settlements, and issue non-binding recommendations regarding its review of complaints received in either manner. The Court has the authority to issue binding decisions, and the Committee of Ministers of the Council of Europe has responsibility for overseeing the 'execution of judgments' by states.

The enforcement authority of the Court has function as well as form—member states have altered human rights policies in numerous cases involving a range of issues, including the treatment of immigrants, prisoner detention policies, and matters related to privacy and freedom of the press (Donnelly 1998: 69–70). Beyond the fact that its rulings have directly led to policy changes, the Court's decisions also have shaped domestic court decisions in member states. Despite having meaningful enforcement powers, the European Court of Human Rights does not entirely displace the statist politics that characterise the international human rights regime. The Court's membership, elected by the Consultative Assembly of the Council of Europe, comprises a member from each state party to the European Convention.

Enforcement mechanisms for economic, social, and cultural rights are not as strong as the framework for protecting civil and political rights. Under the European Social Charter, member states are supposed to submit biennial progress reports that are reviewed by a Committee of Experts, appointed by the Committee of Ministers of the Council of Europe. The Committee of Experts issues its findings to the Committee of Ministers that may make non-binding recommendations (Weston, Lukes & Hnatt 1992: 247). In addition to this obligatory review process, the European Committee of Social Rights, the body responsible for overseeing the implementation of the European Social Charter, may receive and review complaints from individuals against states who have accepted an optional protocol to the Charter (Forsythe 2000: 119).

The European human rights regime also includes the Office of the European Commissioner for Human Rights, created by the Council of Europe in 1999. Elected by the Parliamentary Assembly of the Council of Europe for a six-year term, the European Commissioner has the responsibility and authority to raise awareness and promote human rights education in member states, to monitor member states' human rights records in order to identify shortcomings in their compliance with human rights obligations, and to promote and advance human rights norms among member states. The Commissioner is not authorised to receive or evaluate individual complaints of human rights abuses and pursues a largely non-adversarial engagement with governments.

One of the reasons that the European human rights regime has been relatively successful is that, generally speaking, European countries have relatively strong human rights records and share a basic commitment to the idea of universal human rights. As Jack Donnelly has noted,

> A cynic might argue that the breadth and strength of the European human rights regime simply illustrate the paradox of international action on behalf of human rights: strong procedures exist where they are least needed. Because they require the permission of states, they are likely only where states have a high interest and good records.
>
> *(Donnelly 1998: 71)*

In sum, the European human rights regime has been effective largely because of the political commitment among European states to fundamental human rights norms and not because the regime has superseded the statist nature of politics in the region.

The inter-American human rights system

The Inter-American Commission on Human Rights (CHR), created by the Organization of American States (OAS) in 1959, is the core institution in the inter-American human rights system.

The Commission comprises 11 members, elected by the OAS General Assembly, and has limited authority for promoting human rights. The CHR may engage in activities to raise awareness about human rights and can request information about human rights issues from member states. The CHR also has the authority to engage in efforts to negotiate friendly settlements to disputes. In these cases, the Commission reports its involvement to the OAS secretary-general and, in the event that a settlement is reached, the secretary-general issues a public report. If efforts to resolve disputes fail, the secretary-general can issue a confidential report or can make non-binding recommendations to the parties involved. The Inter-American Commission also receives, reviews, and issues non-binding recommendations on annual human rights reports from member states. Although the Inter-American Commission may receive and review individual complaints, it has rarely exercised this authority. When it has reviewed individual complaints, its decisions in these cases have generally been disregarded by member states (Donnelly 1998: 72).

The Commission also may file cases with the Inter-American Court of Human Rights, at which individuals do not have standing and may not bring cases directly to the Court. The Court, with 11 members elected by member states, issues binding decisions that the OAS General Assembly may seek to enforce by imposing sanctions on states. However, the OAS has not widely used its enforcement authority in the limited number of cases decided by the Court (Baehr 2001: 79).

The African human rights system

The 1981 African Charter on Human and Peoples' Rights provides the legal framework for the African human rights system. The African Commission on Human and Peoples' Rights is the institutional core of the African human rights system. With a membership comprising 11 members elected by the heads of state of the African Union, the Commission fundamentally reflects the statist nature of the regional system in Africa, even though members are supposed to serve in an independent capacity and do not represent their home governments. The African Commission has adopted a non-adversarial approach to human rights promotion, primarily centred on educational initiatives, information exchange, and the capacity to negotiate friendly settlements to disputes. Like other monitoring bodies in the UN and other regional systems, the Commission reviews biannual reports that states parties are required to submit under the African Charter. However, the Commission may only issue non-binding recommendations in response to these reports.

The Commission also has the power to receive communications from individuals and non-governmental organisations as well as states regarding state violations of human rights. Upon receiving a complaint and deciding it is admissible, the Commission first seeks to mediate a friendly settlement among parties. If efforts at friendly dispute settlement fail, the Commission rules on whether or not a violation has taken place and, in cases of violations, may make non-binding recommendations. The Commission's recommendations are only made public if accepted by the state that is the subject of the complaint (African Commission on Human and Peoples' Rights). In general, the Commission emphasises cooperative mechanisms rather than adversarial processes.

The African Court on Human and Peoples' Rights (ACHPR), which came into existence in 2004, is charged with interpreting and protecting the rights enumerated in the African Charter. To date, the Court has not been terribly active and has only issued rulings in a few cases. In a manifestation of the ways in which regional regimes might actually undermine the promotion of universal human rights, the African Union actively discourages the prosecution of international crimes in the ICC and asserts a preference for prosecuting human rights violations in the

ACHPR, despite its limited activity to date (*The Economist* 2012). In 2008, African Union states adopted a new protocol to the African Charter that calls for the African Court on Human and Peoples' Rights to merge with the Court of Justice of the African Union (created in 2003) to form a single court to be called the African Court of Justice and Human Rights. To date, no such merged court has been brought into existence, and judicial action in the African human rights system remains limited.

The human rights system in the Arab world

The human rights system in the Arab world remains underdeveloped. Since 1968, the Permanent Arab Commission on Human Rights, created by the League of Arab States, has operated with a focus on the occupation of the West Bank and Gaza (Donnelly 2013: 172). In 2004, the League of Arab States adopted the Arab Charter of Human Rights that entered into force in 2008. This Charter calls for the creation of a Committee of Experts on Human Rights that will receive reports and monitor progress toward human rights in member countries. To date, progress on the institutional development of this Charter has been limited. Like other regional commissions, the powers of this Committee are restricted to the review of state reports and the subsequent issuing of non-binding recommendations.

A new human rights regime for Asia?

Unlike most other regions of the world (with the exception of the Arab world), Asia has been slow to institutionalise international human rights. Asian states have generally low rates of ratifying international human rights treaties (Mayer 2013: 315; Rathgeber 2014: 158–160). Even when Asian states have ratified international human rights treaties, they have frequently attached reservations to their ratifications (Ciorciari 2012: 707). The Human Rights Council's universal periodic review processes have revealed significant gaps between treaty-based commitments to universal rights and actual respect for human rights in Asian countries (Rathgeber 2014: 158–160). Asian countries have also been resistant to monitoring by Special Rapporteurs (Rathgeber 2014: 158).

Further, the politics of human rights in Asia are characterised by a notable deficit in the development of regional norms and mechanisms for advancing rights. To the extent that Asian countries, collectively, have sought to institutionalise human rights, they have done so only to a limited extent. Unlike other regions, Asian states have not adopted a human rights treaty that covers the region in its entirety. Accordingly, there is no human rights commission or court that sets human rights standards or processes for the region as a whole. The region does not have a common complaint mechanism that might provide redress for individuals or groups whose rights have been violated.

One challenge to the creation of a broad regional human rights regime in Asia is the lack of a clear-cut demarcation of the geographical and cultural boundaries of Asia. The region as a whole includes a multitude of potential sub-regional divisions, including Central Asia, Eastern Asia, Southeastern Asia, Southern Asia, and Western Asia.[2] Asia is the world's most populous region and contains a multitude of languages, ethnicities, religions, and cultures. In this context, it is reasonable to ask whether Asia—broadly defined—can be expected to have a collective identity and a common approach to human rights (Mayer 2013: 315–316).

Despite the lack of a comprehensive set of human rights institutions across Asia, sub-regional institutional developments, especially in Southeast Asia, suggest the potential emergence of a nascent human rights regime in Asia. It is important to acknowledge and examine the sub-regional progress that has been made in recent years in order to accurately assess the ways in which the Asian approach to human rights differs from other regions.

The institutionalisation of human rights in the Association of Southeast Asian Nations

Formed in 1967, the Association of Southeast Asian Nations (ASEAN) did not adopt a formal charter until 2007. This Charter, which entered into force in 2008, represented a significant first step towards the creation of a sub-regional human rights system. Article 14 of the ASEAN Charter asserts that the organisation shall establish a human rights body with responsibilities for promoting and protecting human rights and fundamental freedoms in the region. The Charter includes other provisions that articulate support for universal human rights. At the same time, the Charter reaffirms the importance of the principle of non-interference in the internal affairs of member states. Ultimately, the Charter upholds the fundamental importance of state sovereignty as a norm that ultimately trumps universal human rights (Ciorciari 2012: 711).

Despite the statist underpinnings of the Charter, ASEAN followed through on its commitment to establish a human rights body soon after the Charter entered into force with the creation of the ASEAN Intergovernmental Commission on Human Rights (AICHR) in 2009. Soon thereafter, in 2010, ASEAN created the ASEAN Commission on the Promotion and Protection of the Rights of Women and Children (ACWC). The AICHR has already advanced the development of sub-regional human rights norms via its adoption of the ASEAN Human Rights Declaration in 2012 (Rathgeber 2014: 161). Although the creation of these two human rights bodies and the Declaration are noteworthy, it is important to acknowledge that these developments represent minimal steps towards the creation of a weak sub-regional human rights system.

The ASEAN Declaration is a non-binding set of norms. Although it articulates an ambitious set of human rights norms, it undercuts these aspirations with qualifications that defer to state sovereignty and the principle of non-interference. Its state-centric nature is underscored by the fact that state representatives were exclusively involved in its negotiation; civil society actors were excluded from the process (Davies 2014: 111–114).

The AICHR is primarily a consultative body and does not have investigative or enforcement powers. Instead, its responsibilities largely involve consultation and constructive dialogue with states parties. The commission does not have the authority to receive complaints from individuals or non-governmental organisations. Moreover, the body has sought to limit the capacity of non-governmental organisations to shape human rights policies by limiting its engagement to civil society organisations that have received governmental approval (Gomez & Ramcharan 2012: 27–28). AICHR decisions are to be made on the basis of consensus, which results in each member state having a de facto veto over Commission recommendations (Ciorciari 2012: 715). AICHR has the authority to gather information about human rights issues, to develop non-binding strategies for advancing human rights, and to issue reports about human rights conditions in the region. Underscoring the state-centric nature of this nascent human rights framework, the Commission reports to the foreign ministers of ASEAN (Rathgeber 2014: 161).

Not only have ASEAN human rights norms and institutions failed to create strong enforcement mechanisms, but they may also make it more difficult for non-state actors to pressure ASEAN governments on human rights issues (Ginbar 2010: 517–518). According to Ciorciari, the AICHR and the ACWC

> 'institutionalize' human rights in the sense of confining them to a controlled bureaucratic environment, enabling ASEAN members to address (or deflect) criticism by discussing human rights in a safe political space in which incumbent government officials control the pace and content of the discourse.
>
> *(Ciorciari 2012: 697)*

In short, the ASEAN human rights bodies provide legitimacy gains for member states without creating concrete obligations for these states to make progress on specific human rights commitments.

ASEAN states have also cooperated in developing norms in specialised issue areas. The ASEAN Declaration Against Trafficking in Persons, Particularly Women and Children, adopted in 2004, calls for further development of a regional regime to combat human trafficking. Similarly, in 2007, ASEAN states adopted the Declaration on the Protection and Promotion of the Rights of Migrant Workers, which includes non-binding recommendations for ASEAN governments to take steps to protect migrant workers and, to this end, to develop a formalised legal instrument codifying and institutionalising such protections. ASEAN progress in articulating new norms legitimates the international human rights project and may serve as a model for human rights standard-setting in the region (Davies 2014: 123; Rathgeber 2014: 161–163). However, non-binding declarations do not create concrete, enforceable commitments for states. In this way, they remain very deferential to state interests and preferences even as they articulate aspirational human rights norms.

Not surprisingly, human rights indicators from Freedom House, the US State Department, and Amnesty International demonstrate that most states in Southeast Asia have not made progress subsequent to the development of ASEAN human rights institutions (Ciorciari 2012: 708). Worse, the Commission may actually undermine the capacity of non-governmental organisations to advocate on behalf of human rights in Southeast Asia. Again, according to Ciorciari,

> if the Commission does just enough to placate some constituencies and outside observers, it may actually provide a thin layer of added political cover for continued abuses. This is the sense in which 'institutionalizing' human rights can mean something more akin to imprisonment than reification.
>
> *(Ciorciari 2012: 720)*

The Asia Pacific Forum of National Human Rights Institutions

The Asia Pacific Forum of National Human Rights Institutions (APF-NRI), a body that coordinates the activities of national-level human rights commissions in the region, represents another development in the formation of a nascent human rights regime in Asia. The Asia Pacific is the broadest geographical categorisation of the Asian region and encompasses a broad set of states, including Pakistan, India, China, Japan, Southeast Asia and other sub-regions, Australia, New Zealand, and other Pacific islands (Croyden 2014: 289–290). National human rights bodies of Australia, India, Indonesia, and New Zealand joined together to create the APF-NRI in 1996 as a means of coordinating their institutional activities. The APF-NRI shares expertise, fosters institutional partnerships, and leverages institutional networks in striving to advance human rights objectives among its membership.

As its name suggests, the APF-NRI consists of national-level human rights commissions from countries in the Asia Pacific region. Although these commissions have been formally established by national legislation in their respective countries, they operate with a degree of independence from the state. APF-NRI members must be accredited by the International Coordinating Committee of National Human Rights Institutions. To this end, national human rights institutions must demonstrate compliance with the Paris Principles, a set of international standards related to the independence of domestic human rights bodies, in order to be accredited. The Paris Principles, generated under UN auspices in 1991, identify six criteria for effective national human rights institutions, including a clearly defined and broad-based mandate based on universal human rights standards, autonomy from the government, independence explicitly protected by legislative measures or the constitution, pluralistic and representative membership, adequate resources, and adequate powers of investigation. Notably, APF members are subject to re-accreditation every five years, so their compliance with the Paris Principles must be ongoing (Croyden 2014: 292).

The APF-NRI currently has 15 full members that have been accredited as complying fully with the Paris Principles. These members include the national human rights institutions from Afghanistan, Australia, India, Indonesia, Jordan, Malaysia, Mongolia, Nepal, New Zealand, Palestine, the Philippines, Qatar, Republic of Korea, Thailand, and Timor-Leste. The APF-NRI also has seven associate members that have not been accredited as complying fully with the Paris Principles. National human rights institutions from Bangladesh, Kazakhstan, the Maldives, Myanmar, Oman, Samoa, and Sri Lanka are associate members.[3] In addition to fostering cooperation among their members, the APF-NRI seeks to improve human rights conditions in the region by expanding its membership. To this end, the APF-NRI has advocated on behalf of the creation of national human rights institutions in Japan, Taiwan, and China. APF-NRI efforts have generated some progress in Japan and Taiwan, where national human rights institutions are being formally considered (Croyden 2014: 296–302).

The APF represents a distinctive approach to balancing aspirational norms with statist politics in the effort to develop a regional human rights framework. On the one hand, the APF-NRI appears to preserve even more power for states than other regional regimes by locating the site of human rights institutions *within* states. In this regard, it arguably does not constitute the beginnings of a truly regional regime. On the other hand, the APF-NRI creates conditions for membership that transcend the authority of the state. Further, the independence of the national human rights commissions that are members of the APF-NRI may reflect a greater deal of autonomy than regional (or sub-regional) institutions whose authority fundamentally defers to state interests.

The fact that human rights are institutionalised *within* the state in the APF-NRI model does not necessarily mean that this approach is more state-centric than one built on regional institutions that transcend the state. Indeed, when human rights institutions are located beyond the state, state elites may be more likely to shape policy and implementation measures without pressures from civil society actors who do not have the same access to these institutions. In contrast, because national human rights institutions are located within particular states, they may be more likely to remain accessible to domestic human rights advocacy groups and to create political spaces in which civil society actors have opportunities to influence human rights policies. In this regard, the APF model may be more likely to generate bottom-up implementation efforts to advance human rights that fundamentally differ from the more top-down model of creating formal law and institutions above the state.

Conclusion

As this chapter has shown, Asia does not have a well-developed human rights regime. The development of regional human rights institutions has largely been limited to the sub-region of Southeast Asia, as represented by ASEAN human rights initiatives, and to the development of national human rights bodies coordinated by the APF. The low degree of human rights institutionalisation in Asia has been cited in support of the argument that a cohesive set of 'Asian values' are inconsistent with human rights and that the institutionalisation of human rights (or lack thereof) represents a distinct Asian approach to universal human rights. According to Acharya, an Asian approach to human rights implementation 'involves a high degree of discreteness, informality, pragmatism, expediency, consensus-building, and non-confrontational bargaining styles' (Acharya 1997: 329, quoted in Rathgeber 2014: 160).

If the institutionalisation of human rights in Asia is looked at in isolation, the argument that there is a unique Asian approach to human rights might be compelling. However, a close examination of other regional human rights systems suggests that the Asian approach is not as distinctive as it might appear at first glance. To be sure, the institutionalisation of human rights frameworks in other regions far surpasses what has happened in Asia to date. Yet, even the most well-established regional regimes face the same barriers to the effective promotion and protection of human rights that have constrained the development of a more comprehensive human rights system in Asia.

Regional human rights systems typically remain deferential to state sovereignty in their efforts to promote human rights. They tend to be governed by legal documents that contain ambivalent norms, loopholes, and ill-defined state obligations. Regional human rights institutions have minimal monitoring powers and weak enforcement mechanisms. The European human rights system, which challenges sovereignty more than any other regional system, provides a limited exception to these tendencies.

In comparison to Asia, most other regions may have more formal laws on the books and a larger number of institutions that are active in the sphere of human rights. However, these institutions are primarily engaged in monitoring, norm creation, and non-adversarial mediation roles. These activities may contribute to human rights improvements at the margins and may provide relief in a limited number of cases to individual victims of human rights violations. Yet, it is not evident that regional mechanisms have been effective at a macro-level in producing systemic improvements in human rights conditions.

Jack Donnelly (2013: 178) has observed that 'the character of regional mechanisms is a consequence, rather than a cause, of the regional pattern of human rights performance'. Human rights scholars and advocates are well-served to heed this insight. When it comes to the promotion of universal human rights and the protection of the vulnerable anywhere, the problems run far deeper than the absence of effective regional human rights mechanisms. Although the differences in the institutionalisation of human rights across regions matter at the margins, the similarities in state behaviour are more striking and meaningful.

The systemic causes of human rights violations lie within states and the state system. International human rights law—as a body of law created by states—is inherently state-centric and, as such, cannot provide the solution to systemic human rights violations. At the end of the day, regional human rights regimes do not escape the statist dynamics that characterise international human rights law and institutions. Ultimately, the state-centric nature of the international human rights system has had limited effects on actual state behaviour and policy (Hafner-Burton 2013: 44–66). The same can generally be said of regional human rights systems, regardless of how well they are institutionalised.

This reality is a difficult one to accept for proponents of human rights for whom formal law and institutions often seem an obvious response to persistent and pervasive human rights abuses across the globe. However, the limited effectiveness of regional human rights systems—and the international human rights regime in general—suggests that change must originate with politics and not the law. Public international law is rooted in a top-down conception of change. Instead, bottom-up pressures arising within states are more likely to leverage change than abstract and distant formal law and institutions (Ciorciari 2012: 724). To be sure, non-governmental organisations and civil society actors may leverage the law in their efforts to mobilise change (Davies 2014: 123). However, formal law and institutions are not sufficient. Further, in some cases, they may actually serve as an obstacle to change if states use their participation in formal human rights frameworks to gain legitimacy without taking concrete steps to improve human rights and if these frameworks create exclusionary political spaces that limit the extent to which non-governmental organisations and civil society actors participate in human rights discussions. In this regard, the APF may present a more promising model for regional implementation than formal regional human rights institutions.

At the end of the day, the nascent human rights regime in Asia does not represent a distinctly Asian approach to human rights. Rather, it represents the prevailing statist approach to international human rights that characterises the generally weak international legal order. The state-centric nature of the international system is deeply entrenched, and achieving advances in human rights in this context will never be easy. However, initiatives that focus on particular local contexts within states as potential sites of change may have more promise than efforts centred on international or regional legal frameworks given state dominance of these formal legal institutions.

Notes

1 Final Declaration of the Regional Meeting for Asia of the World Conference on Human Rights, available online at: http://daccess-dds-ny.un.org/doc/UNDOC/GEN/G93/125/95/PDF/G9312595.pdf?OpenElement.
2 These sub-regional divisions are categorised by the United Nations Statistics Division.
3 See Membership of the Asia Pacific Forum, www.asiapacificforum.net/members.

References

Acharya, A 1997, 'Ideas, Identity, and Institution-Building: From the ASEAN Way to the Asia-Pacific Way?', *Pacific Review*, vol. 10, no. 1, pp. 319–346.

African Commission on Human and Peoples' Rights, *Communications Procedure*, www.achpr.org/communications/procedure/.

Baehr, PR 2001, *Human Rights: Universality in Practice*, Houndmills, UK: Palgrave.

Ciorciari, JD 2012, 'Institutionalizing Human Rights in Southeast Asia', *Human Rights Quarterly*, vol. 34, no. 3, pp. 695–725.

Croyden, SA 2014, 'Towards a Regional Human Rights Mechanism in the Asia Pacific? Exploring the Potential of the Asia Pacific Forum', *Pacific Review*, vol. 20, no. 2, pp. 289–306.

Davies, M 2014, 'An Agreement to Disagree: The ASEAN Human Rights Declaration and the Absence of Regional Identity in Southeast Asia', *Journal of Current Southeast Asian Affairs*, vol. 33, no. 3, pp. 107–129.

DeLaet, DL 2015, *The Global Struggle for Human Rights* (2nd ed), Stamford, CT: Cengage.

Donnelly, J 1998, *International Human Rights* (2nd ed), Boulder, CO: Westview Press.

Donnelly, J 2013, *Universal Human Rights in Theory and Practice* (3rd ed), Ithaca, NY: Cornell University Press.

The Economist 2012, 'Justice for Dictators: History Rules', www.economist.com/node/21553010.

Forsythe, DP 2000, *Human Rights in International Relations*, Cambridge: Cambridge University Press.

Ginbar, Y 2010, 'Human Rights in ASEAN: Setting Sail or Treading Water?', *Human Rights Law Review*, vol. 10, no. 3, pp. 504–518.

Gomez J & Ramcharan R 2012, 'The Protection of Human Rights in Southeast Asia: Improving the Effectiveness of Civil Society', *Asia-Pacific Journal on Human Rights and the Law*, vol. 13, no. 2, pp. 27–43.

Hafner-Burton, EM 2013, *Making Human Rights a Reality*, Princeton, NJ: Princeton University Press.

Mayer, B 2013, 'Review of *Emerging Regional Human Rights Systems in Asia* by Tae-Ung Baik', *Journal of East Asia and International Law*, vol. 6, no. 1, pp. 315–317.
Rathgeber, T 2014, 'Human Rights and the Institutionalisation of ASEAN: An Ambiguous Relationship', *Journal of Current Southeast Asian Affairs*, vol. 33, no. 3, pp. 131–165.
Sen, A 1997, 'Human Rights and Asian Values: What Lee Kuan Yew and Li Peng Don't Understand about Asia', *The New Republic*, 14 July, pp. 33–40.
United Nations Office of the High Commissioner for Human Rights undated, 'Human Rights Treaty Bodies: Individual Communications', www.ohchr.org/EN/HRBodies/TBPetitions/Pages/Individual Communications.aspx#overviewprocedure.
United Nations Office of the High Commissioner for Human Rights undated, 'United Nations Human Rights Programme', www.unhchr.ch/html/abo-intr.htm.
Weston, BH, Lukes RA & Hnatt KM 1992, 'Regional Human Rights Regimes: A Comparison and Appraisal', in Richard Pierre Claude & Burns H. Weston (eds), *Human Rights in the World Community: Issues and Action* (2nd ed), Philadelphia, PA: University of Pennsylvania Press, pp. 244–255.
White, ND 2002, *The United Nations System: Toward International Justice*, Boulder, CO: Lynne Rienner.

4

Protecting the most vulnerable

Opportunities for employing the UN mechanisms in East Asia

Rhona Smith[1]

Introduction

International human rights benefit everyone, but in particular the international human rights system should provide a framework for the most vulnerable and oppressed in society to have their voices heard and their suffering ameliorated. This chapter will focus on the United Nations (UN) and examine the extent to which its mechanisms offer a voice to those whose rights are most neglected and abused. The geographical focus of the chapter is East Asia. This is taken to be Brunei, Cambodia, the People's Republic of China, Indonesia, Japan, the Democratic People's Republic of Korea, the Republic of Korea, Lao People's Democratic Republic, Malaysia, Myanmar, Philippines, Singapore, Taiwan, Thailand, Timor-Leste and Vietnam. All except Taiwan are UN member states.[2] Within this region, three countries have been identified by the United Nations as being of particular concern: the Democratic People's Republic of Korea, Cambodia and Myanmar.[3]

The UN framework

The UN was established in 1945, primarily with a mandate to secure and maintain international peace and security (UN 1945: Art. 1). Nevertheless, the importance of protecting vulnerable individuals from abusive actions by states was a concern, not least given the ongoing findings of the Nuremberg and Tokyo tribunals. The 1948 Universal Declaration of Human Rights (General Assembly Resolution 217A(III), 1948) is a 'milestone document' of human development and human rights (OHCHR undated) and the foundation for modern international and indeed regional human rights systems. The international human rights system is predicated on equality: 'All human beings are born free and equal in dignity and rights' (UDHR: Art. 1). However, minorities were singled out by the UN General Assembly as requiring particular attention (General Assembly resolution 217C(III), 1948), though minority rights have had a somewhat chequered history at the United Nations thereafter (Thornberry 1991; Henrard and Dunbar 2009). Rights and freedoms recognised in the Universal Declaration of Human Rights were subsequently tabulated in a series of treaties which are legally binding on states party to them (see Table 4.1). Of particular relevance for vulnerable people are the UN Convention on the Elimination of all Forms of Racial Discrimination (CERD), the UN Convention on the Elimination of all Forms of Discrimination Against Women (CEDAW), the UN Convention on the Rights of the Child (CROC), and the UN Convention on the Rights of Persons with Disabilities (CRPD) (see respectively, Thornberry 2015; Freeman, Chinkin and Rudolf 2012; Alen et al. various; Quinn and O'Mahoney forthcoming).

Having a framework of international treaties does not guarantee that the rhetoric is translated into reality for those requiring protection. As former High Commissioner, Mary Robinson (2003; 2008), regularly commented, action is needed to transform the rhetoric of human rights treaties and political statements into a reality for those who should benefit. States are obliged to protect, promote and respect those rights contained in treaties to which they are party to fulfil

Table 4.1 Ratification of core UN treaties[a]

	ICCPR	*ICESCR*	*ICERD*	*CEDAW*	*CAT*	*CRC*	*CMW*	*CED*	*CRPD*	*CTOC T*	*CTOC M*
Brunei Darussalam				R		R					
Cambodia	R	R	R	#R*	#R	R		#R	R	R	R
PR China		R	R	R	R	R			R	R	
Indonesia	R	R	R	R	#R	R	R		R	R	R
Japan	R	R	R	R	#R	R		#R	R		
DPR Korea	R	R		R		R					
Rep of Korea	R	R	R*	#R*	#R*	R			R		
Lao PDR	R	R	R	R	R	R			R	R	R
Malaysia			R			R			R	R	
Myanmar				R		R			R	R	
Philippines	R*	R	R	#R*	#R	R	R		R	R	R
Singapore				R		R			R		
Taiwan	A	A				A					
Thailand	R	R	R	#R*	#R	#R*			R	R	
Timor-Leste	R	R	R	#R*	R	R	R			R	R
VietNam	R	R	R	R		R			R	R	

Key
ICCPR = International Covenant on Civil and Political Rights
ICESCR = International Covenant on Economic, Social and Cultural Rights
ICERD = Convention on the Elimination of all forms of Racial Discrimination
CEDAW = Convention on the Elimination of all forms of Discrimination Against Women
CAT = Convention against Torture
CRC = UN Convention on the Rights of the Child
CMW = Convention on the Rights of Migrant Workers
CED = Convention on Enforced Disappearances
CRPD = Convention on the Rights of Persons with Disabilities
CTOC T = Protocol to Prevent, Suppress and Punish Trafficking in Persons, Especially Women and Children, supplementing the United Nations Convention against Transnational Organized Crime
CTOC M = Protocol against the Smuggling of Migrants by Land, Sea and Air, supplementing the United Nations Convention against Transnational Organized Crime
R = state has ratified or otherwise acceded to the treaty
* = state has agreed to accept the possibility of individual communications
# = state has agreed to accept the inquiry process
A = Taiwan has indicated acceptance of the provisions and standards but is not permitted to submit instruments of ratification to the UN.

Note
a Information compiled from treaty bodies database, www.ohchr.org, and www.unodc.org, 15 January 2015.

their obligations (see also the Vienna Convention on the Law of Treaties, Art. 18). Thus, they should neither act contrary to, nor condone infringements of, rights and freedoms. Treaties make clear the obligation incumbent on states party to take all measures to guarantee the listed rights (e.g. see Preamble CERD; Art. 3 CEDAW; Art. 4 CRC; Art. 4 CRPD). This means states must protect in law and policy those rights and freedoms they have accepted. Finally, states must promote or raise awareness of those rights and freedoms so individuals understand the obligations accepted by them. This strengthens the accountability of states internally – with chapters within this volume providing further details of such mechanisms, specific issues, options for redress and case studies. However, when internal challenges are thwarted, recourse may be had to regional systems or to the UN system's range of mechanisms offering oversight and monitoring. This chapter will focus on the opportunities for employing UN mechanisms in East Asian states. Three UN mechanisms will be considered: the universal periodic review (UPR) process of the Human Rights Council; the special procedures of the Human Rights Council; and the treaty-monitoring bodies responsible for ensuring compliance of states with their treaty obligations.

It should be noted that during the period covered in this chapter, the UN Human Rights Council mandated a Commission of Inquiry on Human Rights in the Democratic People's Republic of Korea (DPRK).[4] The DPRK Special Rapporteur was a member of the Commission, which reported in February 2014 (as was the first Cambodian mandate holder, who chaired it).[5] The Commission considered that 'systematic, widespread and gross human rights violations have been and are being committed by the Democratic People's Republic of Korea', going as far as to find crimes against humanity perpetrated (at para. 24). However, the state refused to cooperate with the Commission (see paras. 9–11) and has refuted all requests in relation to it from the Human Rights Council.

All UN member states now undergo universal periodic review of 'the fulfilment by each state of its human rights obligations and commitments' (General Assembly resolution 60/251 2006, 5(e)). Performance is 'peer reviewed' by other states which have the opportunity to ask questions, make recommendations and other comments on each state. The working reports, containing the questions, recommendations and comments offered to each East Asian UN member state will be considered. Turning to the next mechanism, most states in the region have acquiesced to requests from UN special procedure mandate holders for country visits. These are independent experts who focus on specific thematic human rights issues (there are several on vulnerable groups – women, migrants, indigenous peoples) or, exceptionally, on countries (including Cambodia, Democratic Peoples' Republic of Korea and Myanmar). Regular reports on the theme or the country are submitted to the Human Rights Council and sometimes the General Assembly.

Finally, treaty-monitoring bodies will be considered. All East Asian states accept at least two of the nine core international human rights treaties (see Table 4.1), and those UN member states thus must regularly report to specific UN committees on progress made fulfilling treaty obligations. These committees of experts hold dialogues with reporting states in an attempt to further advance its fulfilment of human rights obligations.

UN reports on universal periodic review, the special procedures and the treaty-monitoring bodies are publicly available (including on the website of the OHCHR). Accordingly, each recent report has been analysed to determine the extent to which voices of the most vulnerable in East Asian societies are being heard through the UN mechanisms. The most vulnerable people are identified following the categories specified for this Handbook project (for select overviews, see also Castellino and Dominguez-Redondo 2006). Timewise, this chapter uses the inception of the Human Rights Council as a starting point; thus the period covered is from 2006 through to January 2015.

It should further be noted that there is no regional human rights system in Asia, although the Southeast Asian states in ASEAN have intergovernmental cooperation on certain human rights (see www.aichr.org). There has also been considerable discussion over the years on whether human rights mean something different in Asia. Arguments posited note that in Asia harmony and order within the community, economic success and respect for family are emphasised and can be prioritised over individual freedoms. This 'Asian values' debate stimulated by Singapore, Malaysia and Indonesia, consolidated around the 1993 Vienna World Conference on Human Rights though interest appears to have waned (Langlois 2001; though note Asplund 2009). A growing discourse on human rights with Chinese characteristics raises similar issues (Chan 2013; Peerenboom 1993; see also PRC 2009; 2012). For the purpose of this chapter, international human rights will be taken as universal as derived from the core UN treaties.

Universal periodic review

Universal periodic review is the only mechanism which reviews the realisation of all human rights and all humanitarian law in all UN member states. This is a highly regulated peer review system, operating to a strict timetable, both of countries being reviewed and of the actual physical meetings during the review process. The first cycle ran from 2008 to 2011, the second, from 2012 through to 2016, and the third cycle will run thereafter so every country is reviewed every four and a half years (Human Rights Council 2011, annex. I.B.3). Each review is based on three documents: a state report; a report compiled by the Office of the High Commissioner for Human Rights summarising existing UN, treaty-monitoring body and special procedure reports on the country; and a report prepared by the Office of the High Commissioner of Human Rights summarising comments made by other stakeholders, including NGO and civil society organisations (Human Rights Council 2007, res. 5/1 annex, para. 15). The principal part of the process is a working group session held in the Human Rights Council at which any UN member state can raise questions or make comments on the state under review. This data is collated in the working group report.

Table 4.2 notes the subject matter of comments and recommendations made to each country concerning those identified in this volume as vulnerable peoples. To gather this data, the working group report of each state (Human Rights Council 2008–2011) during the first (completed) cycle of review was analysed.[6] It should be remembered that the peer review process is not consistently comprehensive and interventions made by states can be driven by political and other external factors, not simply an objective review of compliance with human rights and humanitarian law standards. As is apparent, many of the vulnerable groups and vulnerable characteristics identified as a focus of this volume have been highlighted during the universal periodic review process. Migrants, trafficked persons, minorities,[7] women and children were particularly frequent subjects. This is neither unique to East Asia nor especially surprising.

Malaysia, the Philippines, Singapore and Thailand (Human Rights Council 2009b; 2008d; 2011c; 2011b) had a notable number of comments on migrant workers.[8] Many migrants in the region are unauthorised (see Battistella 2002) though attempts are being made to regularise the position, inter alia, by the Cambodian government vis-à-vis the status of many migrant workers in Thailand.[9] Within China, many migrants are internal, moving from poorer rural areas, for example, the western provinces, to cities or larger industrialised areas (see, e.g. Zhang, Ding and Gao 2011). In the region, only the Philippines has ratified the Convention on Migrant Workers and the protocol on smuggling migrants (though Thailand has signed the latter) although other states were urged to consider ratifying this treaty during periodic review. There is also an ASEAN Declaration on the Protection and Promotion of the Rights of Migrant Workers 2007

Table 4.2 Subject of recommendations made in UPR working group reports mentioning selected vulnerable peoples[a]

	Women	*Children*	*Disabled persons*	*Indigenous peoples*	*Rural population*	*Migrants*	*Human rights defenders*	*Minorities*	*Trafficked persons*	*Elderly*
Brunei Darussalam	×	×	×	×	×					×
Cambodia	×	×		×	×		×			×
PR China	×	×	×		×	×	×	×		×
Indonesia	×	×				×	×	×	×	
Japan	×	×		×		×		×	×	
DPR Korea	×	×	×						×	×
Rep of Korea	×	×				×			×	
Lao PDR	×	×	×	×	×			×	×	
Malaysia	×	×	×	×	×	×				
Myanmar	×	×		×		×	×	×	×	
Philippines	×	×		×		×	×		×	
Singapore	×	×	×			×		×	×	×
Thailand	×	×			×	×		×	×	
Timor-Leste	×	×	×		×			×	×	
VietNam	×	×	×		×			×	×	

Note

a All Working Group reports are cited under Human Rights Council in the bibliography.

which seeks to regulate the matter. Migration inevitably links to human trafficking on which Indonesia, the Philippines and Thailand received many interventions (Human Rights Council, 2008a 2008d; 2011b) though all three of those have ratified the protocol to suppress human trafficking (see Table 4.1).

Ratification of all core UN human rights treaties is a relatively standard recommendation and, as Table 4.1 indicates, there are gaps although the conventions on women, children and persons with disabilities are widely ratified. Nevertheless, all states in the region had comments during review on women and children and over half had comments on disabled persons. Given the diversity of ethnicities and indigenous groups in the region, it is also concerning that violations of rights of minorities and indigenous peoples were frequently raised.

It is clear that respect for human rights across a range of vulnerabilities gives rise to concern in the reviews. The question is thus whether this mechanism protects vulnerable peoples. Undoubtedly, universal periodic review offers one key benefit when considered as a mechanism for holding states accountable – it is a public forum and, being a form of inter-state commentary, comparatively high profile. However, individual violations cannot really be raised or remedied through such a mechanism. Rather, it is effective at shining a spotlight on states and forcing each to justify or respond publicly to comments raised.

Special procedures

The Human Rights Council also operates a network of special procedures (see generally Gutter 2006; 2007; Lempinen 2001; Ramcharan 2009; Wheatley et al. special edition 2011). Special procedures are independent and impartial experts who serve in their private capacity and do not represent or take instruction from any state or organisation (Human Rights Council res. 5/2(2007), Annex Code of Conduct, Art. 3; see also Alston 2011; Smith 2011). There are two types of mandates: thematic, in which a particular human rights issue is examined in detail; and country, in which the focus is on potentially the full range of human rights but the geographical focus is a single country/area. All mandate holders should undertake factfinding visits to states, meeting with a range of stakeholders. Special procedures can receive complaints from individuals and groups. In this respect, they discharge a quasi-judicial function.

Only two countries in eastern Asia, Japan and Thailand, have extended standing invitations to all special procedures for country visits.[10] This is considerably below other regional averages: Asia-Pacific for example, has a 41% invitation rate, thanks in part to the high level of invitations issued by Pacific Island states, while globally 109 out of 193 states have extended standing invitations. For other states, mandate holders must seek and obtain specific invitations to undertake visits.

Table 4.3 notes the visits of special procedures to the region from 2006 through to January 2015. There have been a number of visits from thematic rapporteurs to East Asian UN member states. Many of these rapporteurs have mandates extending to vulnerable groups including discrimination against women in law and practice, migrants, trafficked persons, health, extreme poverty, internally displaced persons, freedom of religion and such like. However, as Table 4.3 also notes, there are many mandate holders who have sought invitations to visit the region, to no avail or with no confirmed dates. Outstanding requests include many from mandate holders considering vulnerable groups including those with responsibility for the rights of minorities, indigenous peoples, migrants, internally displaced persons and the sale of children. Without doubt the failure of states to extend invitations can limit the opportunities for vulnerable groups to have their voices heard.

Table 4.3 Visits of Special Procedure mandate holders 2006–January 2015[a]

	2006	2007	2008	2009	2010	2011	2012	2013	2014	2015	Outstanding requests
Brunei Darussalam											
Cambodia	C[b]	C[c]			C2[d]	C3[e]	C2[f]	C[g]	C2[h]	C	Independent judges and lawyers; sale of children; water and sanitation; peaceful assembly and association; human rights defenders; truth, justice and reparations
PR China					T[i]			T[j]			Freedom of religion (invitation extended, no dates); peaceful assembly and association; hazardous substances and waste; health; extrajudicial and summary executions; human rights defenders; housing; minorities; water; foreign debt, independence of judges and lawyers; WG on enforced disappearances
Indonesia	T[k] C[l]	T2[m]			C[n]			T[o]			Freedom of expression (accepted but postponed); health (accepted); extrajudicial and summary executions; freedom of religion; human rights defenders; foreign debt; water; minorities; assembly and association; cultural rights; indigenous peoples; truth, justice and reparation; hazardous substances and waste; WG enforced disappearances; WG discrimination against women
Japan	C[p]		C[q]	C[r] T[s]	T2[t]	C[u]	C[v] T[w]	T[x]		C[y]	WG arbitrary detention (accepted); racism; sale of children
DPR Korea[z]											Food
Rep of Korea	T[aa] C[ab]		C2[ac]		T[ad] C2[ae]	C[af]		T[ag]	T[ah] C[ai]		Migrants (accepted); Peaceful assembly and association
Lao PDR				T[aj]							Cultural rights (accepted); summary executions; housing; peaceful assembly and association
Malaysia	C[ak]	T[al]			WG[am]			T[an]	T[ao]		Indigenous people (accepted); human rights defenders; freedom of religion; migrants; counter-terrorism; minorities; racism; independence of judges and lawyers; peaceful assembly and association

Myanmar		C[ap]	C[aq]	C[ar]	C[as]	C[at]	C2[au]	C2[av]	C2[aw]	C	Summary executions; freedom of religion; arbitrary detention; independence of judges and lawyers; assembly and associations internally displaced persons; food; education
Philippines		T[ax]					T[ay]				Adequate housing, IDPs; food (all accepted); migrants; counter-terrorism; extreme poverty; human rights defenders' independence judges and lawyers; health; minorities; cultural rights; assembly and association; foreign debts; WG discrimination women; WG arbitrary detention
Singapore					T[az]						Extrajudicial and summary executions; cultural rights; peaceful assembly and association
Thailand	C[ba]		C[bb]		C[bc]	T[bd] C[be]	C[bf]	T[bg]	C[bh]		Sale of children (accepted); torture (accepted); extrajudicial and summary executions; minority rights; housing; counter-terrorism; human rights defenders; migrants; food; peaceful assembly and association; racism; IDPs, extreme poverty; WG disappearances; WG arbitrary detention
Timor-Leste			T[bi]			T2[bj]					Torture; minority issues
VietNam					T2[bk]	T2[bl]		T[bm]	T[bn]		Summary executions; food; torture; human rights defenders; migrants; sale of children; contemporary forms of slavery; peaceful assembly and association

Key

C = Visit by country mandate holder (number denotes number of visits that year)

T = Visit by thematic mandate holder (number denotes number of visits that year)

WG = Visit by working group

Notes

a Including agreed. Taken from www.ohchr.org/EN/HRBodies/SP/Pages/countryvisitsa-e.aspx (accessed 5 February 2015), with accuracy checked to the cited UN documentation where there are contradictions.

b SR on the situation of human rights in Cambodia, 19–28 March 2006, UN Doc. A/HRC/4/36.

c SR on the situation of human rights in Cambodia, 1–10 December 2007, UN Doc. A/HRC/7/42.

d SR on the situation of human rights in Cambodia, visits of 17–30 January 2010 and 8–18 June 2010, UN Doc. A/HRC/15/46.

e SR on the situation of human rights in Cambodia, visits of 15–24 February 2011 and 30 May–3 June 2011, UN Doc A/HRC/18/46; visit of 5–11 December 2011, UN Doc. A/HRC/21/63.

f SR on the situation of human rights in Cambodia, visit of 4–11 May 2012, UN Doc. A/HRC/21/63; visit of 8–15 December 2012, UN Doc. A/HRC/24/36.

g SR on the situation of human rights in Cambodia, visit of 19–25 May 2013, UN Doc. A/HRC/24/36.

h SR on the situation of human rights in Cambodia, visit of 12–17 January 2014 and 15–25 June 2014, UN Doc. A/HRC/27/70.

i SR on the right to food, visit of 15–23 December 2010, UN Doc. A/HRC/19/59/Add.1.

j Working Group on discrimination against women in law and in practice, visit of 12–19 December 2013, UN Doc. A/HRC/26/39/Add.2.

k SR on migrants, visit of 12–21 December 2006, UN Doc. A/HRC/4/24/Add.3.

l SR on Myanmar to India, Indonesia, Malaysia and Thailand, visit of 11–26 February 2006, UN Doc. A/HRC/4/14.

m SR on the situation of human rights defenders, visit of 5–13 June 2007, UN Doc. A/HRC/7/28/Add.2; SR on torture, visit November 2007, UN Doc. A/HRC/7/3/Add.7.

n SR on human rights in Myanmar, visit of 3–11 August 2010, UN Doc. A/65/368.

o SR on adequate housing, visit 31 May–11 June 2013, UN Doc. A/HRC/25/54/Add.1.

p SR on the situation of human rights in the DPRK, visit 10–14 December 2006, UN Doc. A/HRC/4/15.

q SR on the situation of human rights in the DPRK, visit 15–19 January 2008, UN Doc. A/HRC/7/20.

r SR on the human rights situation in the DPRK, visit 23–28 January 2009, UN Doc. A/HRC/10/18.

s SR on trafficking, visit 12–17 July 2009, UN Doc. A/HRC/14/32/Add.4.

t SR on migrants, visit 23 March–1 April 2010, UN Doc. A/HRC/17/33/Add.3; IE on the issue of human rights obligations related to access to safe drinking water and sanitation, visit 20–28 July 2010, UN Doc. A/HRC/18/33/Add.3.

u SR on human rights in DPRK, visit to Japan, 25–28 January 2011, UN Doc. A/HRC/16/58.

v SR on human rights in DPRK, visit 16–20 January 2012, UN Doc. A/HRC/19/65.

w SR on health, visit 15–26 November 2012, UN Doc. A/HRC/23/41/Add.3.

x IE on foreign debt, visit, 16–19 July 2013, UN Doc. A/HRC/25/50/Add.2.

y SR on the situation of human rights in DPRK, follow-up fact-finding visit, January 2015, not yet reported.

z During the period in question, the country mandate has not been invited to visit; visits were made to surrounding states instead.

aa SR on migrants, visit 5–12 December 2006, UN Doc. A/HRC/4/24/Add.2.

ab SR on the situation of human rights in DPRK, visit 14–18 December 2006, UN Doc. A/HRC/4/15.

ac SR on the situation of human rights in DPRK, visit 19–24 January 2008, UN Doc. A/HRC/7/20; SR on the situation of human rights in DPRK, visit 27–31 October 2008, UN Doc. A/HRC/10/18.

ad SR on the right to freedom of expression and opinion, visit 5–15 May 2010, UN Doc. A/HRC/17/27/Add.2.

ae SR on the situation of human rights in DPRK, visit 10–16 January 2010, UN Doc. A/HRC/13/47; SR on the situation of human rights in DPRK, visit 22–26 November 2010, UN Doc. A/HRC/16/58.

af SR on the situation of human rights in DPRK, visit 21–25 November 2011, UN Doc. A/HRC/19/65.

ag SR on human rights defenders, visit 29 May–7 June 2013, UN Doc. A/HRC/55/Add.1.

ah SR on contemporary forms of racism, racial discrimination, xenophobia and related intolerance, visit 29 September–6 October 2014, report not yet published.

ai SR on the situation of human rights in DPRK, visit 10–14 November 2014, UN Doc. A/HRC/55/Add.1.

aj SR on freedom of religion, visit 23–30 November 2009, UN Doc. A/HRC/13/40/Add.4.

ak SR on Myanmar to India, Indonesia, Malaysia and Thailand, visit 11–26 February 2006, UN Doc. A/HRC/4/14.
al SR on the right to education, visit 5–14 February 2007, UN Doc. A/HRC/8/10/Add.3.
am WG on arbitrary detention, visit 7–18 June 2010, UN Doc. A/HRC/16/47/Add.2.
an SR on food, visit 9–18 Dec. 2013, UN Doc. A/HRC/25/57/Add.2.
ao SR on the right to health, visit 19 November–2 December 2014, not yet reported.
ap SR on the situation of human rights in Myanmar, visit 11–15 November 2007, UN Doc. A/HRC/7/24.
aq SR on the situation of human rights in Myanmar, visit 3–7 August 2008, UN Doc. A/63/341.
ar SR on the situation of human rights in Myanmar, visit 14–19 February 2009, UN Doc. A/HRC/10/19.
as IE on the situation of human rights in Myanmar, visit 15–19 February 2010, UN Doc. A/HRC/13/48.
at SR on the situation of human rights in Myanmar, visit 21–25 August 2011, UN Doc. A/66/365.
au SR on the situation of human rights in Myanmar, visit 31 January–5 February 2012, UN Doc. A/HRC/19/67; SR on the situation of human rights in Myanmar, visit 30 July–4 August 2012, UN Doc. A/67/383.
av SR on the situation of human rights in Myanmar, visit 11–16 February 2013, UN Doc. A/HRC/22/58; SR on the situation of human rights in Myanmar, visit 11–21 August 2013, UN Doc. A/68/397.
aw SR on the situation of human rights in Myanmar, visit 14–19 February 2014, UN Doc. A/HRC/25/64; SR on the situation of human rights in Myanmar, visit 17–26 July 2014, UN Doc. A/69/398.
ax SR on extrajudicial, summary or arbitrary executions, visit 12–21 February 2007, UN Doc. A/HRC/8/3/Add.2.
ay SR on trafficking in persons, visit 5–9 November 2012, UN Doc. A/HRC/23/48/Add.3.
az SR on racism, visit 21–28 April 2010, UN Doc. A/HRC/17/40/Add.2.
ba SR on Myanmar to India, Indonesia, Malaysia and Thailand, visit 11–26 February 2006, UN Doc. A/HRC/4/14.
bb SR on the situation of human rights in Myanmar, working visit 6–13 August 2008, UN Doc. A/63/341.
bc SR on human rights in Myanmar, visit 3–11 August 2010, UN Doc. A/65/368.
bd SR on trafficking, visit 8–19 August 2011, UN Doc. A/HRC/20/18/Add.2.
be SR on the situation of human rights in Myanmar, visit 16–23 May 2011, UN Doc. A/66/365.
bf SR on the situation of human rights in the DPRK, visit 25–29 June 2012, UN Doc. A/67/370.
bg SR on safe drinking water and sanitation, visit 31 January–8 February 2013, UN Doc. A/HRC/24/44/Add.3.
bh SR on Myanmar, visit 10–13 February 2014, UN Doc. A/HRC/25/64.
bi RSG on internally displaced persons, working visit 7–12 December 2008, A/HRC/10/13.
bj WG on enforced disappearances, visit 7–14 February 2011, UN Doc. A/HRC/19/58/Add.1; SR on human rights and extreme poverty, visit 13–18 November 2011, UN Doc. A/HRC/20/25/Add.1.
bk IE on human rights and extreme poverty, visit 23–31 August 2010, UN Doc. A/HRC/17/34/Add.1; IE on minority issues, visit 5–15 July 2010, UN Doc. A/HRC/16/45/Add.2.
bl IE on foreign debt, visit 21–29 March 2011, UN Doc. A/HRC/20/23/Add.1; SR on health, visit 25 November–5 December 2011, UN Doc. A/HRC/20/15/Add.2.
bm SR on cultural rights, visit 18–29 November 2013, UN Doc. A/HRC/28/57/Add.1.
bn SR on freedom of religion (21–31 July 2014), UN Doc. A/HRC/28/66/Add.4.

Matching these requests to the UPR issues raised, it is clear that in many instances the special procedures offer an avenue for addressing issues of potential concern within states. Minorities, indigenous peoples, women, children and human rights defenders are obvious examples. However, Alston (2011) highlights the potential impact on independence and integrity of the procedures given the attempts by the Council to curtail their activities through certain provisions of the then new Code of Conduct. Piccone (2011) highlights the lack of consistency of special procedures, with mandates being discharged in markedly different ways (caused in part by the independence and autonomy of mandate holders), though notes the positive impact many have had on national laws and policies.

Turning to the three states in the region with a country mandate, Myanmar has the longest-standing country mandate (from 1992), followed by Cambodia (since 1993) and the DPR Korea (2004). In accordance with normal practice, each mandate has been renewed annually ever since (first by the Commission, later by the Human Rights Council).[11] Past mandate holders have offered insight into their experiences. Kirby (2010) and Subedi (2011a; 2011b) have written on their experiences in Cambodia; whilst Smyth (2014: 186) criticises the slow progress of government action on recommendations of the Cambodian mandate holders, in spite of many recommendations being backed up by General Assembly resolutions. Goedde (2010) argues that the particular political system in North Korea renders impotent, or at least reduced, the impact of bringing international human rights (and indeed international law) to bear on the country. Myanmar and Cambodia currently cooperate to facilitate country visits, the DPRK does not.

Special procedures can receive and consider communications from individuals or groups whose rights are violated, responding by raising the matter direct with the government concerned. They can also raise urgent appeals on alleged imminent violations or on pending legislation which would compromise human rights. Figure 4.1 lists those states in the region which have been the subject of six or more such communications to rapporteurs. Note, however, that the subject matter is confidential (unless parties decide otherwise).

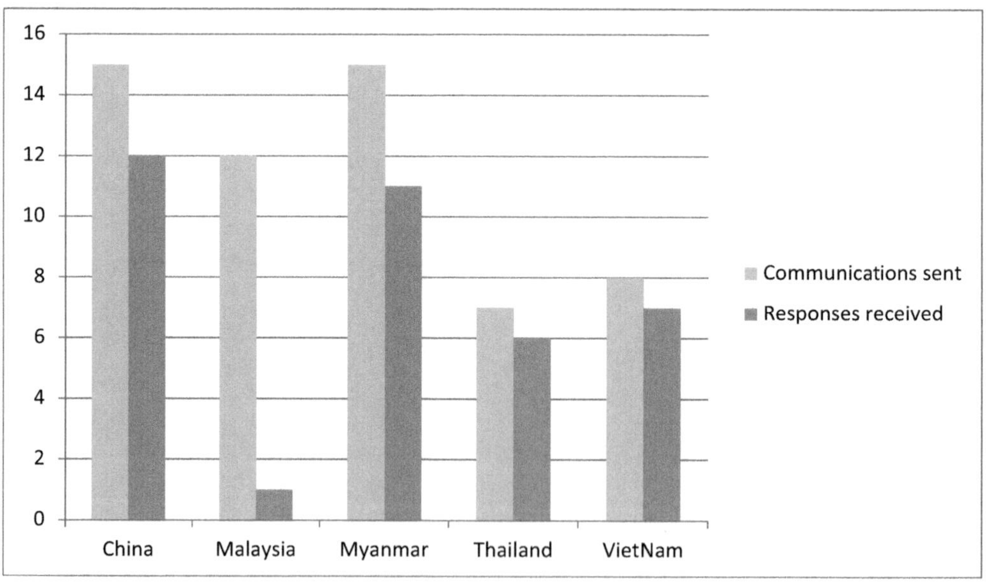

Figure 4.1 Communications from special procedures

Special rapporteurs offer a viable mechanism for highlighting lack of protection of vulnerable people. They also have a range of tools at their disposal (country visits, meetings, communications, reports). The main limitation is that their opinions can be ignored and they can be subjected to personal criticisms. Support from the Council and other states is essential for following through recommendations and suggestions.

Treaty-monitoring bodies

All nine of the core UN human rights treaties (see Table 4.1) contain reporting obligations. States party to each treaty are required to submit regular reports to a committee of independent experts. This committee and the state should engage in a continual cycle of state report, discussions between the committee and the state, concluding observations by the committee on the progress of the state, implementation then repeat state report etc. The periodicity of the reports varies from committee to committee though there is a general problem with delayed reports and backlogs of reports awaiting consideration by the committee (OHCHR 2012: pt. 2.3.2; Egan 2011). Nevertheless, all East Asian UN member states have submitted reports and received comments from committees. Emerging practice includes 'shadow' reports being submitted by non-state stake-holders (usually non-governmental organisations) in respect of each state. These reports often present information on individuals or groups and this allows voices to be 'heard' in a documentary process. However, such reports are not necessarily comprehensive or systematic.

The most recent concluding observations of each committee for each state were analysed to determine whether vulnerable people were mentioned. Obviously, vulnerable groups in terms of the scope of the present volume are the principal subject of discussion before several of the committees: women, disabled persons, migrant workers, racial groups and children. All East Asian UN member states have entered dialogues with the UN Committee on the Rights of the Child and the Committee on the Elimination of All Forms of Discrimination Against Women. Consideration is also given to vulnerability in the process of considering compliance with other treaties as all core treaties contain non-discrimination clauses.

With respect to individual voices, these may also be heard through individual complaints to the treaty bodies. As Table 4.1 shows, five states have accepted individual communications under CEDAW (Republic of Korea, Cambodia, Philippines, Thailand and Timor-Leste). There have been three communications considered on the Philippines, with violations found in respect of two complaints concerning rape laws, investigations and trials (CEDAW 2010; 2014). A series of communications concerning the Philippines have also been brought before the Human Rights Committee: most concern fair trial rights and investigations into deaths implicating the state.[12] The Republic of Korea has also been the subject of many communications before the Human Rights Committee. Although there have been communications on deportation and refoulement (Human Rights Committee 2014), most communications have concerned freedom of belief and conscription to military service.[13] Interestingly one complaint to CAT claimed a risk of torture for an individual whom the Republic of Korea sought to return to Myanmar (CAT 2014).

While arguably the individual complaint process has been invoked more in East Asia than elsewhere, as is often the case, complaints are bunched around certain topics (here, military service in Korea and fair trial and death investigation in the Philippines). The numbers of communications thus do not necessarily indicate extensive violations of rights, rather it is often multiple violations.

Voices heard or suppressed?

The UN should offer succour to vulnerable groups within East Asia, after all its human rights system was created to contribute to peace and security by ensuring that the rights and freedoms of all people are respected, promoted and protected by all states. Three mechanisms are particularly relevant: universal periodic review, which allows for all UN member states to be reviewed; special procedures, including the country mandates for the three states which are deemed to present particular human rights challenges; and the treaty bodies, which review state compliance with those core UN human rights treaties which have been accepted. In addition, there has been a commission of inquiry for the Democratic People's Republic of Korea.

Unfortunately, the UN system is far from ideal. As the foregoing analysis and tables make clear, a wide variety of issues concerning vulnerable people are regularly considered or otherwise tabled before these UN mechanisms. However, as many chapters in this volume demonstrate, and as a plethora of governmental, non-governmental organisation, inter-governmental organisation, civil society and academic literature proves, human rights of vulnerable people are breached almost daily. This suggests that the system does not function as a protection mechanism, but that was never the intention. The UN system provides the framework for protection, though states grant the UN mechanisms limited enforcement options. Rather, the primary obligees under the core UN treaties are the states themselves and they must ensure those rights and freedoms they voluntarily accept are given full effect in national law. Procedures for remedying infringements must also be provided. They choose to accept those human rights and fundamental treaties contained in the treaties they ratify (see Table 4.1) and by virtue of being members of the United Nations, they agree to undergo universal periodic review (see Table 4.2). What is apparent from the national reports to the working group for UPR and from the state reports to the treaty-monitoring bodies, is that the states themselves are often aware of the challenges they are facing and acknowledge some (but not all) of the areas in which rights are breached and compromised. In addition, NGOs and civil society organisations rarely miss opportunities to remind states of their failings. However, some states are reluctant to engage with the international mechanisms.

What remains to be done is for states in the region to systematically address the required areas of legal reform and policy and practice change. National road maps or action plans are one option, much favoured in some sectors of the UN. These offer the benefit of states publicly declaring the measurable steps they will take to ensure protection of human rights. Strengthening or establishing some form of national human rights institutions, whether formal in terms of the Paris Principles or not, could ensure more focus on human rights and give impetus to the need to conform to the treaties accepted. Such an entity could serve to steer the state towards better implementation of human rights and highlight perceived deficiencies in law and practice. Moreover, such an entity and the existing legal system in the state should ensure a robust national mechanism is available to receive and consider complaints from vulnerable individuals that rights are violated. Following such consideration, effective remedies must be available and the means to ensure future violations are prevented.

For individuals without such national mechanisms, the special procedures perhaps offer the best option for vulnerable groups in the region, given so few countries in the region accept individual communications to the treaty bodies. It is clear that special procedures have raised complaints with governments across the region. However, it is somewhat difficult to evaluate success, given the confidentiality of the process. Based on the information publicly available, Figure 4.1 extracts the information on numbers of communications sent and government responses received. China, Myanmar, Thailand and Vietnam all respond reasonably promptly to communications; Malaysia notably less so. Moreover, it is possible that at least some requests for visits, including outstanding requests, were raised pursuant to receipt of multiple complaints and/or specific concerns of the mandate holder.

Conclusion

The UN human rights system offers a lifeline for vulnerable groups but, although Ban Ki Moon (2007) stated that 'All victims of human rights abuses should be able to look to the Human Rights Council as a forum and a springboard for action', the UN is not a panacea for all violations. States themselves must actively accept the UN mechanisms and work with them to remedy violations. Moreover, national mechanisms should be created and/or strengthened to monitor the national position and offer a more effective and accessible remedy for vulnerable individuals and groups.

Notes

1 Details contained in this chapter are current to March 2015.
2 Taiwan, or the Republic of China, is regarded in the UN as part of the Peoples' Republic of China, see Winkler (2012).
3 Cambodian country mandate established by Commission on Human Rights resolution 1993/6; extended regularly; last extension HRC resolution 24/29 (2013) for two years. Democratic People's Republic of Korea mandate established by Commission on Human Rights resolution 2004/13; extended annually; last extension HRC resolution 25/25 (2014) for one year. Myanmar mandate established by Commission on Human Rights resolution 1992/58; extended regularly; last extension HRC resolution 25/26 (2014) for one year.
4 Human Rights Council resolution 22/13 (2013), UN Doc. A/HRC/RES/22/13 (2013). See generally, www.ohchr.org/EN/HRBodies/HRC/CoIDPRK/Pages/CommissionInquiryonHRinDPRK.aspx (accessed 15 February 2015).
5 See Report of the commission of inquiry on human rights in the Democratic People's Republic of Korea, UN Doc. A/HRC/25/63 and detailed supporting documentation in UN Doc. A/HRC/25/CRP.1 (2014).
6 Although the presentation of the working group reports changed during the first cycle, as far as possible, the data represented in the table is equivalent across all states. Note also that no account is taken of the recommendations made to the ratifying of treaties – all states which have not ratified all core UN treaties had recommendations to that effect. Accordingly, this information was excluded – it should be read as implicit. Table 4.1 lists the ratifications of the core UN treaties.
7 Note that minorities and indigenous peoples are sometimes treated as the same in reports. The terminology used in each report was used to determine the category in Table 4.2.
8 China (Human Rights Council 2009a) also had many comments though the migrant workers referenced were generally internal.
9 In June 2014, following a Royal Government of Cambodia's decree, migrant workers have been able to obtain a passport for a USD4 photo fee, rather than the normal USD124 passport fee. This measure was designed to regulate the status of undocumented migrant workers in Thailand and followed a mass exodus of Cambodian workers back to Cambodia following the assumption of power by the military in Thailand. For details of the joint government press release on measures taken to regularise and protect Cambodian migrant workers, see http://thainews.prd.go.th/centerweb/newsen/NewsDetail?NT01_NewsID=WNPOL5708180010011 (accessed 5 February 2015).
10 As of 1 January 2015, from www.ohchr.org/EN/HRBodies/SP/Pages/Invitations.aspx.
11 Note that exceptionally the Cambodian mandate was extended for two years with agreement of the government, most recently Human Rights Council resolution 24/29(2013).
12 See, for example, opinions on communications recorded in UN Docs CCPR/C/99/D/1559/2007; CCPR/C/98/D/1619/2007; CCPR/C/94/D/1560/2007; CCPR/C/92/D/1466/2006.
13 See, recently, UN Docs CCPR/C/106/D/1786/2008; C/98/D/1593-1603/2007; CCPR/C/88/D/11321–1322/2004.

References

Alen, A, Lanote, V, Verhellen, E, Ang, F, Berghmans, E, Verheyde, M and Abramson, B (eds) (various) *A Commentary on the United Nations Convention on the Rights of the Child*, Leiden, Brill.

Alston, P 2011, 'Hobbling the Monitors: Should U.N. Human Rights Monitors Be Accountable?', *Harvard International Law Journal*, vol. 55, no. 2, pp. 561–649.

Asplund, K 2009, 'Resistance to Human Rights in Indonesia: Asian Values and Beyond', *Asia Pacific Journal on Human Rights and the Law*, vol. 10, no. 1, pp. 27–47.

Ban, K 2007, Secretary-General's video message for the opening of the Fourth Session of the Human Rights Council, 12 March, Geneva, Switzerland, www.un.org/sg/STATEMENTS/index.asp?nid=2475.

Battistella, G 2002, 'Unauthorized Migrants as Global Workers in the ASEAN Region', *Southeast Asian Studies*, vol. 40, pp. 350–371.

Castellino, J and Dominguez-Redondo, E (eds) 2006, *Minority Rights in Asia: A Comparative Legal Analysis*, Oxford, Oxford University Press, chapters on China, Malaysia and Singapore.

CAT 2014, *TM v. Republic of Korea*, UN Doc. CAT/C/53/D/519/2012.

CEDAW 2010, *Karen Tayag Vertido v. Philippines*, UN Doc. CEDAW/C/46/D/18/2008.

CEDAW 2014, *RPB v. Philippines*, UN Doc. CEDAW/C/57/D/34/2011.

Chan, P 2013, 'Human Rights and Democracy with Chinese Characteristics?', *Human Rights Law Review*, vol. 13, no. 4, pp. 645–689.

Egan, S 2011, *The UN Human Rights Treaty System: Law and Procedure*, Dublin, Bloomsbury.

Freeman, M, Chinkin, C and Rudolf, B (eds) 2012, *The UN Convention on the Elimination of All Forms of Discrimination Against Women*, Oxford, Oxford University Press.

Goedde, P 2010, 'Legal Mobilization for Human Rights Protection in North Korea: Furthering Discourse or Discord?', *Human Rights Quarterly*, vol. 32, no. 3, pp. 530–574.

Gutter, J 2006, *Thematic Procedures of the United Nations Commission on Human Rights and International Law: In Search of a Sense of Community*, Antwerp, Intersentia.

Gutter, J 2007, 'Special Procedures and the Human Rights Council: Achievement and Challenges', *Human Rights Law Review*, vol. 7, no. 1, pp. 93–107.

Henrard, K and Dunbar, R (eds) 2009, *Synergies in Minority Protection: European and International Law Perspectives*, Cambridge, Cambridge University Press.

Human Rights Committee 2014, *X v. Republic of Korea*, UN Doc. CCPR/C/110/D/1908/2009.

Human Rights Council 2007, *Resolution 5/1 Institution-building of the United Nations Human Rights Council*, UN Doc. A/HRC/RES/5/1.

Human Rights Council 2008a, *Report of the Working Group on the Universal Periodic Review Indonesia*, UN Doc. A/HRC/8/23.

Human Rights Council 2008b, *Report of the Working Group on the Universal Periodic Review Japan*, UN Doc. A/HRC/8/44.

Human Rights Council 2008c, *Report of the Working Group on the Universal Periodic Review Republic of Korea*, UN Doc. A/HRC/8/40.

Human Rights Council 2008d, *Report of the Working Group on the Universal Periodic Review*, The Philippines, UN Doc. A/HRC/8/28.

Human Rights Council 2009a, *Report of the Working Group on the Universal Periodic Review China*, UN Doc. A/HRC/14/25.

Human Rights Council 2009b, *Report of the Working Group on the Universal Periodic Review Malaysia*, UN Doc. A/HRC/11/30.

Human Rights Council 2009c, *Report of the Working Group on the Universal Periodic Review Viet Nam*, UN Doc. A/HRC/12/11.

Human Rights Council 2010a, *Report of the Working Group on the Universal Periodic Review Brunei Darussalam*, UN Doc. A/HRC/13/14.

Human Rights Council 2010b, *Report of the Working Group on the Universal Periodic Review Cambodia*, UN Doc. A/HRC/13/4.

Human Rights Council 2010c, *Report of the Working Group on the Universal Periodic Review Democratic People's Republic of Korea*, UN Doc. A/HRC/13/13.

Human Rights Council 2010d, *Report of the Working Group on the Universal Periodic Review Lao People's Democratic Republic*, UN Doc. A/HRC/15/5.

Human Rights Council 2011, *Resolution 16/21 (2011), Outcome of the review of the work and functioning of the United Nations Human Rights Council*, UN Doc. A/HRC/RES/16/21.

Human Rights Council 2011a, *Report of the Working Group on the Universal Periodic Review Myanmar*, UN Doc. A/HRC/17/9.
Human Rights Council 2011b, *Report of the Working Group on the Universal Periodic Review Thailand*, UN Doc. A/HRC/19/8.
Human Rights Council 2011c, *Report of the Working Group on the Universal Periodic Review Singapore*, UN Doc. A/HRC/18/11.
Human Rights Council 2012, *Report of the Working Group on the Universal Periodic Review Timor-Leste*, UN Doc. A/HRC/19/17.
Kirby, M 2010, 'UN Special Procedures: Reflections on the Office of UN Special Representative for Human Rights in Cambodia', *Melbourne Journal of International Law*, vol. 11, pp. 1–24.
Langlois, A 2001, *The Politics of Justice and Human Rights: Southeast Asia and Universalist Theory*, Cambridge, Cambridge University Press.
Lempinen, M 2001, *Challenges Facing the System of Special Procedures of the United Nations Commission on Human Rights*, Turku, Abo Akademi Institute for Human Rights.
OHCHR (undated), Website on the Universal Declaration of Human Rights, www.ohchr.org/EN/UDHR/Pages/Introduction.aspx.
OHCHR 2012, *Report on Strengthening the UN Treaty Body System*, UN Doc. A/66/860.
Peerenboom, R 1993, 'What's Wrong with Chinese Rights?: Toward a Theory of Rights with Chinese Characteristics', *Harvard Human Rights Journal*, vol. 6, p. 29–57.
Piccone, T 2011, 'The Contribution of the UN's Special Procedures to National Level Implementation of Human Rights Norms' *International Journal of Human Rights*, vol. 15, no. 2, pp. 206–231.
PRC 2009, *National Human Rights Action Plan 2009–2010*, available in English, http://news.xinhuanet.com/english/2009-04/13/content_11177126.htm.
PRC 2012, *National Human Rights Act Plan 2012–2015*, available in English, http://news.xinhuanet.com/english/china/2012-06/11/c_131645029.htm.
Quinn, G and O'Mahoney, C (eds) (forthcoming), *The United Nations Convention on the Rights of Persons with Disabilities: Comparative, Regional and Thematic Perspectives*, Antwerp, Intersentia.
Ramcharan, B 2009, *The Protection Roles of UN Human Rights Special Procedures*, Leiden, Brill.
Robinson, M 2003, 'From Rhetoric to Reality: Making Human Rights Work', *European Human Rights Law Review*, vol. 1.
Robinson, M 2008, 'From Rhetoric to Reality: An Interview with Mary Robinson', *Bulletin of the World Health Organisation*, vol. 86, no. 8, pp. 587–588, viewed 13 February 2015, www.who.int/bulletin/volumes/86/8/08-040808/en/.
Smith, R 2011, 'The Possibilities of an Independent Special Rapporteur System', *International Journal of Human Rights*, vol. 15, no. 2, pp. 172–186.
Smyth, L 2014, 'Country Specific Mandate Holders: The Role of the Special Rapporteur on the Situation of Human Rights in Cambodia', *Melbourne Journal of International Law*, vol. 15, no. 1, p. 155–189.
Subedi, S 2011a, 'The UN Human Rights Mandate in Cambodia: The Challenge of a Country in Transition and the Experience of the Special Rapporteur for the Country', *The International Journal of Human Rights*, vol. 15, no. 2, pp. 249–264.
Subedi, S 2011b, 'Protection of Human Rights through the Mechanism of UN Special Rapporteurs', *Human Rights Quarterly*, vol. 33, pp. 201–228.
Thornberry, P 1991, *International Law and the Rights of Minorities*, Oxford, Clarendon Press.
Thornberry, P 2015, *The International Convention on the Elimination of All Forms of Racial Discrimination: A Commentary*, Oxford, Oxford University Press.
United Nations (1945), *Charter of the United Nations Organisation*.
Wheatley, S, Mukherjee, A, Subedi, S and Ngane, S 2011, 'The Role of the Special Rapporteurs of the United Nations Human Rights Council in the Development and Promotion of International Human Rights Norms', *The International Journal of Human Rights*, vol. 15, no. 2, Special Edition, pp. 155–161.
Winkler, S 2012, 'Taiwan's UN Dilemma: To Be or Not To Be', *Taiwan–US Quarterly Analysis*, Brookings Institution, www.brookings.edu/research/opinions/2012/06/20-taiwan-un-winkler.
Zhang, W, Ding, P and Gao, W 2011, 'Rights of Migrant Workers in Contemporary China: International Standards and Domestic Implementation', in J Plantilla and S Ahmad (eds), *Law, Jurisprudence and Human Rights in Asia*, Malaysia, HURIGHTS OSAKA and SIRD.

Part II
Participation and exclusion

5

Civil and political participation and minority rights protection in East Asia

Raees Begum Baig

Introduction

In 1992 the United Nations unanimously adopted the Declaration on the Rights of Persons Belonging to National or Ethnic, Religious and Linguistic Minorities; yet, the recognition and application of minority rights by states has remained controversial. The Declaration recognises the specific situations faced by minorities and to protect minority rights. However, without legally binding provisions, the extent to which minority rights are protected rests heavily on the state's discretion towards the recognition of minority rights.

With the criteria specified by the international mechanisms to define a 'minority', the state holds the ultimate power to determine who minorities are. Further, recognising and regulating access to specific minority rights also remains a state-driven exercise. Such conditions have created an opportunity for states to exempt themselves from protecting minorities, as states have absolute power to define what 'minority' officially means. When minorities fail to be recognised by the state, protection of their basic rights are at stake. Further, the exclusion—through non-recognition—of minorities from civil and political participation is contrary to perceptions of democracy and universality.

States and governments in East Asia, including Hong Kong, Japan and South Korea, which are democratic and semi-democratic in nature, have kept pace in terms of their national recognition of human rights; having ratified similar international human rights treaties since the 1960s. Yet, the growing denial of human rights by states has threatened the protection of minority rights. Though the governments have not denied the concepts of minority rights, minority rights have yet to be fully implemented in Asia under the tepid debate on human rights and 'Asian values' (Castellino & Redondo 2006). As homogenous and monocultural states, this chapter examines the scope of minority rights protection in Hong Kong, Japan and South Korea by analysing human rights protection mechanisms and the recognition and treatment of minorities by these states.

Limited provisions for minority rights protection

International human rights frameworks impose obligations on states and provide guidelines for the attainment of adequate human rights protections in each country. However, the international community is yet to endorse an appropriate mechanism for the protection of the rights of minorities (Rehman 2000), and without a specific international treaty concerning minority rights, it has been difficult for minorities to seek adequate enforcement of their rights.

In order to address specific concerns and needs of minorities, the United Nations General Assembly passed Resolution 47/135 in 1992 adopting the Declaration on the Rights of Persons Belonging to National or Ethnic, Religious and Linguistic Minorities (UN Declaration on Minority Rights or UNDMR). The UNDMR has established essential standards for the protection of minority groups and provides guidelines for the states' progressive realisation of the protection and promotion of the rights of minorities. However, unlike other international human rights treaties, such as the International Covenant on Civil and Political Rights (ICCPR), the UNDMR, unless ratified, does not compel states to implement consistent human rights standards, and thus confines them to do so out of a moral and political impetus.

Stringent protection of the rights of minorities instead falls on international treaties which have binding effect on states. Article 27 of the ICCPR contains a specific provision for the protection of minorities which states:

> In those States in which ethnic, religious or linguistic minorities exist, persons belonging to such minorities shall not be denied the right, in community with the other members of their group, to enjoy their own culture, to profess and practise their own religion, or to use their own language.

Out of the Asian states that have ratified the ICCPR, none held reservations concerning Article 27, suggesting a certain level of recognition of the existence and rights of minorities (Castellino & Redondo 2006). In addition to the ICCPR, Article 30 of the Convention on the Rights of the Child (CRC) contains similar provisions on minority recognition as follows:

> In those States in which ethnic, religious or linguistic minorities or persons of indigenous origin exist, a child belonging to such a minority or who is indigenous shall not be denied the right, in community with other members of his or her group, to enjoy his or her own culture, to profess and practise his or her own religion, or to use his or her own language.

Indeed, among all the international treaties, the International Convention on the Elimination of All Forms of Racial Discrimination (ICERD) may be the lynchpin for minority rights. The primary objective of ICERD is to combat discrimination on the basis of race, and includes provisions relating to ethnicity and gender. With ICERD recognising ethnicity as a specific group identity, ethnic minorities receive some acknowledgement under the protection provisions of ICERD.

The above three international treaties provide some scope for the protection of minority rights; and states which have ratified any of these treaties are obliged to render protection for minorities who are vulnerable of being marginalised by racially discriminatory practices. Despite this, it has been observed that international protection of the rights of minorities has remained passive. While major treaties for vulnerable groups in society (including for women, children, refugees, migrant workers, and persons with disabilities) have specific committees overseeing their implementation, as well as conduct periodic examinations of the situations in ratified states, the implementation of the UNDMR is not governed by an oversight committee. Further, unlike having a regional mechanism on human rights protection, such as the Council of Europe and the successive establishment of the Framework Convention for the Protection of National Minorities (FCNM), states in East Asia have been criticised for their insufficient protection of human rights, specifically minority rights.

The governments of Japan and South Korea assert that the protection provisions of international treaties are enshrined in their Constitutions, yet the Committee on the Elimination of Racial Discrimination has repeatedly condemned both countries for their lack of enacting specific legislation against discrimination.[1] Various treaty bodies have further condemned the Japanese government for not establishing a fully independent national human rights institution for the protection and promotion of human rights,[2] and have condemned the South Korean government for allocating insufficient resources for the promotion of human rights and education.[3]

Yet, to a certain extent, the ratification of various international human rights treaties has brought about positive changes for some minorities, such as the Zainichi Koreans in Japan. Zainichi Koreans are Koreans who came to Japan during colonial rule or are descendants of those persons. Rather than being granted Japanese nationality, Zainichi Koreans are stateless people who in the early days were offered a special passport by the Japanese government (Shipper 2010). To comply with the international standards of equality in the area of social rights, the Japanese government revised its social welfare policy in the mid-1980s, allowing Zainichi Koreans to access the welfare system (Kim 2011). Yet, when it comes to other rights protection, dominant culture has always been used to define those who do not belong to the Japanese society. The Japanese government removed various barriers, allowing Zainichi Koreans to access equality in education, employment and political participation. Most Korean schools in Japan are not recognised as 'regular schools' under the stringent education curriculum. The curriculum taught in Korean schools may not be accredited—as they promote Korean culture, which has been seen as alienating of Japanese dominant culture. Consequently, as 'vocational schools', Korean schools receive less support from the Japanese government, even when compared with private schools in Japan. Resources are further limited—as private donations to Korean schools are not popular, given there is no preferential treatment for the tax reduction of donors. Korean children studying in these schools are consequently prejudiced in further education and employment opportunities (Minority Rights Group 2005; Kim 2011). The lack of Japanese nationality also bars Zainichi Koreans from participating in elections, public-sector employment, and they are even denied freedom of re-entry into Japan.

Hong Kong passed legislation against racial discrimination in 2008, which entered into force in 2009 (Baig 2012). However, the Hong Kong Special Administrative Region (HKSAR) government has also taken the minimalist approach in its legislation by not imposing positive obligations on the government to promote minority rights or racial equality. Article 4 of ICERD stresses the importance of the states parties adopting positive measures designed to eradicate all forms of racial discrimination. During consultations for the proposed Race Discrimination Ordinance (RDO), civil society had repeatedly suggested that the RDO should impose on public authorities a positive duty to promote racial equality. However, the government did not include such provisions into the RDO which was finally enacted in 2008 without reason. Furthermore, treaty body committees have criticised the HKSAR government for not establishing an independent national human rights institution in accordance with the Paris Principles.[4]

Arbitrary recognition of identity

The introduction of the RDO in Hong Kong was a by-product of the government's initiative to recognise the existence and the rights of minorities in Hong Kong. With the growing number of non-Chinese residents in Hong Kong, predominantly Chinese,[5] the government began to formally recognise the challenges faced by non-Chinese in terms of social integration. The number of non-Chinese in Hong Kong began to increase sharply right before decolonisation in

1997, particularly due to migration from South Asia[6] with 100,906 in 1981 to 343,950 in 2001, a percentage of total population increase from 2.02% to 5.1%.

The large influx of migrants was a result of postcolonial migration. During decolonisation, certain people from the colonies were often granted certain forms of formal status within colonial countries, enabling them to settle in other colonial countries. Having their relatives working for the British colonial government, South Asians holding a right of abode status rushed to Hong Kong shortly before the handover of Hong Kong's sovereignty to China, fearing that their right of abode status would lapse following British handover to the Chinese (Baig 2012). Holding the right of abode in Hong Kong denotes a person has the right of ingress to Hong Kong, to be free from any condition attaching to their stay, and not to be deported and removed from Hong Kong. In order to secure a right of abode in Hong Kong, the influx of South Asians made the South Asian population in Hong Kong the largest group among all non-Chinese populations.

The new migrants mainly comprised South Asians with lower education levels and those working in elementary occupations (HKSAR Government 2000). Due to such characteristics, many new migrants have reported experiencing difficulties in employment, education, accommodation and seeking medical and social services (HKSAR Legislative Council 2003). Human rights advocates have found mounting cases of severe racial discrimination against South Asian migrants, including access to employment, education, and opening bank accounts; they have even experienced racial profiling by the police (South China Morning Post 1999). Publicising the situations facing migrants has caused the government to be unable to ignore ethnic integration and race relations. As a sign of recognising the existence of minority populations in Hong Kong—and the challenges faced by them—as of 2000 the government has proactively used the term 'ethnic minority' to refer to non-Chinese people.

Although the government showed positive signs of recognising the status of minorities, the process of recognition was indeed completely state-driven. Minorities seldom have the opportunity to participate in the process of minority status building and such a lack of participation contrasts with the idea of self-identification and self-determination enshrined by UNDMR.

Defining minority

Article 1 of the UN Declaration on Minority Rights adopted in 1992 defines minorities based on national or ethnic, cultural, religious and linguistic identity, and that states should protect their existence. A 'minority group' may be understood as a collective of persons with a shared cultural identity, based on language, religion, or other beliefs and customs, lineage, history and a way of life which differ from the dominant practices in the society (Henders 2004). Under the United Nations human rights system, the term 'minority' usually refers to national or ethnic, religious and linguistic minorities. However, determining the existence of a minority group depends on both objective factors, such as a shared ethnicity, language and religion among a group of people, and also the subjective identification of an individual viewing themselves as a member of a minority group (UN OHCHR 2010). Besides, 'minority' is not solely defined in terms of the population size, but also according to the power differences within the population. Even certain population groups with a large population size, but who hold less social and political power as compared to other population groups could also be regarded as minority groups.

Under such frameworks of defining minority, scholars have been critical of how minorities' rights entitlements are highly dependent on state interests, rather than on the genuine needs of minorities (Mihr 2006; Manchanda 2009). Caught in a paradox of protecting minority rights and building a cohesive nation-state, minority rights have often been sacrificed by democratic states in East Asia which claim to abide by international human rights standards.

Apart from the British whom came to Hong Kong during the early colonial days as administrators, other non-Chinese communities have been settling in Hong Kong, mainly working for the British colonial administration or for economic reasons (White 1994; Bickley 2005; Plüss 2005). Though British outnumbered other non-Chinese populations during the colonial days, a change in population demography shows an increasing number of South Asians. The rights of minorities have never appeared on the agenda of colonial governments, not only because non-Chinese, particularly British persons, were holding dominant power, but because colonialism traditionally embodied strong principles of racism, with colonial governments disregarding the status and interests of minorities. Hesse and Sayyid (2006) argue that European colonialism prioritised 'whiteness' as a precursor to colonial governance—it was the idea of the 'white man' to generate colonial relationships and form a specific authoritarian colonial cultural style. The fundamental ideas of 'whiteness' and racism were clearly expressed in different forms of colonial administration. The British limited the involvement of the Chinese in politics and policymaking by all means, as they thought the Chinese would alter their administrative style. Before the 1970s, all laws were written in English and only a few Hong Kong Chinese were capable of understanding them, as the vast majority of Hong Kong Chinese were unable to read English. Legislative Council members were not allowed to speak in Chinese and generally no interpretation was available in court. Different forms of racially discriminatory practices were observed and such practices only began being abolished when residential segregation ended in the 1960s (Sautman & Kneehans 2002).

As Vasconcellos (2007) put it, the idea of race is socially constructed by those in power in order to justify and legitimise their hegemony over colonial subjects, and it eventually became fundamental to maintaining colonial power. In order to maintain superiority and to continue the exploitation of resources, acts of oppression by the coloniser must be constantly maintained (Zahar 1974). Hong Kong is a typical example for the legacy of colonialism. The British suppressed the involvement of the Chinese and other ethnic groups in politics and policymaking participation (Baig 2012). However, a mass social movement by local Chinese called for the adoption of Chinese as an official language of Hong Kong during the 1970s in preparation for decolonisation. Local Chinese subsequently gained civil and political power from the British administration, yet this did not occur for other ethnic populations (Baig 2012). Being small in population size and having less political power, South Asians have been experiencing discrimination and unequal treatment from both the British administration and the majority Chinese population. Such unequal treatment has been experienced by minorities in other East Asian countries.

State failure to protect the rights of minorities could also be observed in Japan. As the largest non-Japanese population in Japan, the Zainichi Koreans have been denied state recognition as being minorities of the Japanese society, and are merely viewed as foreign residents (Minority Rights Group 2005). This lack of recognition has been attributed to the strong nationalism of the Japanese government. Korean migrants came to Japan, primarily to work as cheap labourers, after Japan colonised Korea in 1910. It has been estimated that 1.5 million Koreans were brought to Japan during colonisation (Strausz 2006: 646). Migrating Koreans were forced to take up Japanese citizenships and were stripped of their Korean nationality.

Following Japan's surrender after the Second World War, the remaining Koreans were asked to decide whether they would keep their Japanese citizenship. However, the adoption of the San Francisco Peace Treaty in 1952 caused Japan to abandon their claim over the Korean peninsula and Japanese nationality for Koreans immediately lapsed. Koreans who wished to regain Japanese nationality needed to be naturalised and to give up their Korean nationality (Strausz 2006). However, not many Koreans were prepared to do so, especially those who had strong ties with Korea (Strausz 2006). It was not until the fingerprinting refusal movement initiated by the Zainichi Koreans, and a better diplomatic relationship was formed between South Korea and

Japan, that the Japanese government started to grant 'Special Permanent Residents' status to the Zainichi Koreans. Without Special Permanent Residents, the Zainichi were still recognised as foreign nationals even though many have remained in Japan for generations. The non-recognition of Zainichi Koreans as a minority group within the Japanese community has been attributed to the Japanese government's attitude toward maintaining a monocultural and monolinguistic society in Japan. Accordingly, although the Zainichi Korean population in Japan satisfies the international concept of a 'minority' under the UN system, a lack of recognition by the Japanese government subjects this group to continuous discriminatory acts, including the granting of citizenship and other forms of rights protections, such as access to education and employment.

Minority exclusion

As state authorities determine the status and the degree of rights conferred upon minorities according to state interests; every so often, minorities are recognised to advance certain social needs, but not to advance their political rights—a consequence of their restricted nationality status.

The government of Hong Kong has not adopted international standards for the recognition of minorities, instead using the term 'minority' narrowly to only refer to ethnic minorities in Hong Kong. In a predominantly Chinese society, ethnic minorities generally refer to people who define themselves as ethnically non-Chinese (Hong Kong Census and Statistics Department 2011: 4). Census data from 2011 shows that there were more than 450,000 persons in Hong Kong identifying as being an ethnic minority, constituting 6.4% of the whole population. Among them there are 137,765 permanent residents who are entitled to the same civil and political rights as other ethnic Chinese permanent residents in Hong Kong. Furthermore, ethnic minorities consist of people with diverse ethnic backgrounds, including 'Asians (other than Chinese) (81.0%), Whites (12.2%), Mixed (6.4%) and Others (0.3%)' (Hong Kong Census and Statistics Department 2011). Among non-Chinese Asians, the majority of permanent residents have Indian, Pakistani and Nepalese ethnic backgrounds, with religious and linguistic diversities.

Moreover, on a policy level, the government of Hong Kong has taken an even narrower definition of 'ethnic minority', by referring to minorities with Indian, Pakistani and Nepalese ethnic backgrounds in Hong Kong as these groups face the greatest challenges in terms of economic and social integration in Hong Kong (HKSAR Legislative Council 2006; Baig 2012). With this narrow definition used by the Hong Kong government, it would be difficult for other ethnic groups to claim their rights, as they are not recognised as being ethnic minorities. Yet most minority ethnic persons suffer unique obstacles, particularly in terms of a lack of Chinese language proficiency, making access to information more difficult, further hindering their social and political participation.

As stated by the government of Hong Kong, the recognition of minority status is merely to assist with social and economic integration into the majority population, but not to facilitate the person's civil and political participation or rights, as these are highly correlated to the status of nationality (HKSAR Legislative Council 2003). With the rising importance of 'Chineseness' appearing during and after decolonisation, as stated in the Basic Law,[7] the social status of the ethnic minorities has become inferior to the ethnic Chinese. Subsequent to the handover to People's Republic of China in 1997, Chinese language and Chinese nationality has drastically increased in importance in Hong Kong. The Basic Law, the Constitution which governs the HKSAR, emphasises the importance of Chinese language and Chinese nationality in the government system (Xiao 2001: 123, 193). With the change in language and nationality requirements for civil servants (i.e. localisation policy), ethnic minorities who were able to engage with public sector employment have since decreased significantly.[8] A survey conducted in 2011 by the administration on racial profiles of civil servants found that 0.8% were of non-Chinese ethnicity (HKSAR Legislative Council 2013). Take the police force as an example: the number of non-local officers has fallen 70%, from 877 in 1997 to 282 in 2009 (South China Morning Post 2009). This decrease has been attributed to combined causes of localisation policies, where civil servants are expected to be primarily local Chinese nationals, and the language proficiency in mastering both Chinese and English languages as the major languages in the government structure as stated under the Basic Law (HKSAR Legislative Council 2010). Such dramatic and disproportionate exclusion of ethnic minorities is arguably a form of racial discrimination.

The naturalisation of ethnic minorities seeking to gain Chinese nationality has never been a clear process, as there are no guidelines to determine successful applications and there is a lack transparency in application and appeal systems (Xu & Shih 2013). According to the Basic Law, only permanent residents of Chinese nationality are eligible to run for the Chief Executive candidature in elections, or hold senior posts of government including members of the Executive Council. The Legislative Council should also comprise permanent residents of Chinese nationality with no right of abode in a foreign country (Xiao 2001). Permanent residents who are not of Chinese nationality may also be elected members, provided the proportion of such members does not exceed 20% of the total membership of the Council (Xiao 2001). Without the granting of Chinese nationality, minorities are thus barred from accessing their political and civil rights.

Minorities, human rights and political participation

The United Nations has drawn a strong nexus between democracy and human rights, for instance it states

> [t]he values of freedom, respect for human rights and the principle of holding periodic and genuine elections by universal suffrage are essential elements of democracy. In turn, democracy provides the natural environment for the protection and effective realization of human rights.[9]

With the protection of the rights of minorities, and particularly non-discrimination within the human rights framework, a true democratic society should be inclusive of minorities with regards to their specific national or ethnic, cultural, religious and linguistic identity. Scholars have tried to define democracy in respect of minority rights. Henders (2004: 9) argues that 'the process of democratization included, but it is much more than simply establishing free and fair competitive elections resulting in a government with binding authority. It also involves the constitution and reproduction of collective, including ethnic identities'.

Through ratification of ICCPR, states are obliged to incorporate the principles of the ICCPR into their domestic legislation or implement them directly in their constitutions. In Hong Kong, the principle of universality of civil and political rights, regardless of a person's race and ethnicity as stated in ICCPR is indeed enshrined in the Basic Law of Hong Kong. Not only has the Basic Law assured ICCPR and other international conventions ratified previously by the British government and extended the application to Hong Kong before the handover; and those ratified by the Chinese government with its application extended to Hong Kong 'shall remain in force and shall be implemented through the laws of the Hong Kong Special Administrative Region' (Art. 39). Article 26 of the Basic Law further states clearly that 'permanent residents of Hong Kong Special Administrative Region shall have the right to vote and the right to stand for election in accordance with law'. International conventions ratified by the state party have the same weight as domestic legislation, and similar legal provisions could be found in Japan and South Korea.[10] Under the Constitution of Japan, paragraph 1 of Article 14 states that 'all of the people are equal under the law and there shall be no discrimination in political, economic or social relations because of race, creed, sex, social status or family origin'. Similar provisions can be found in the Constitution of South Korea, pursuant to paragraph 1 of Article 11, which provides that 'all citizens shall be equal before the law, and there shall be no discrimination in political, economic, social, or cultural life on account of sex, religion, or social status'.

Yet the degree of civil and political rights afforded to persons often depends on the form of their legal status, as rights stipulated in domestic laws are granted to those with state-recognised status in society. It is found that Hong Kong, Japan and South Korea have all failed to adequately ensure that minorities are being fully included in society in non-discriminatory ways, particularly in the civil and political arenas.

Although Japan and South Korea are democratic countries in East Asia, both countries have been scrutinised for neglecting the rights of minorities, particularly in relation to discriminatory policies and practices, and for not upholding democratic values. In order to be granted social and political rights, unrecognised minorities need to abandon their ethnic identity by no longer identifying themselves with their ethnic background (Lie 2001). This would include such actions as adopting a name from the dominant culture rather than their ethnic name, in order to be included as a national in the state (Lie 2001). The need to hide one's ethnic background is contrary to the right of minorities to self-identify pursuant to Article 1 of the UNDMR.[11] Not only are the cultural needs of minorities not being recognised by the state, minorities are also prevented from fully integrating with the majority population because of their cultural heritage. In that sense, minorities are also excluded from nation participation and recognition.

The transformation of the colonial administration from authoritative governance to public political participation through the establishment of electoral systems of the Legislative Council and District Council suggests that Hong Kong is a semi-democratic society (Baig 2012). Even concerns raised by the minorities have been put on the government policy agenda; the Hong Kong government has addressed the issue of minorities merely as a social consideration, but not yet in terms of civil and political rights. Instead of facilitating minority political participation under the electoral systems, only selected minorities are incorporated into the administrative functions of the state through appointment to advisory and consultative positions.

Ethnic minorities have been appointed to the District Council—an administrative structure overseeing public facilities and services within the district—to serve as members of various committees in areas with higher minority concentrations, such as Khalid Kiani in the Kwai Tsing District Fight Crime Committee and Khan Nasab in Kwai Chung North East Area Committee (HKSAR Home Affairs Department 2016; HKSAR Kwai Tsing District Council 2016). Growing numbers of ethnic minorities have been appointed to statutory and advisory committees of the HKSAR government, especially those committees dedicated to race relations affairs, such as the Committee on the Promotion of Racial Harmony.[12] Appointees are mainly religious leaders of the Muslim community, and also ethnic group leaders of Indian, Pakistani and Nepalese origin.

The lack of genuine political participation is most commonly seen among minority groups. It is important to recognise that formal possession of political rights does not guarantee genuine political participation. Minority exclusion can be exacerbated by socioeconomic status, for instance by limiting access to language training and culturally inclusive activities. Political participation requires access to substantive resources in order to exercise informed political judgement. However, it has been well established that such resources and channels required to obtain adequate information are less likely to be available to minorities (Castles & Davidson 2000: 109; Baig 2012: 177). Access to information is a key precondition to exercising political rights and participating in political activities. To ensure equal rights are able to be exercised, equal access to information by all rights holders is essential so those persons may make well informed political decisions. With the majority of ethnic minorities being non-Chinese-language users, language has been the most significant barrier to ethnic minority participation in political debates. Further, various other platforms disseminating political information predominantly do so in Chinese language, including major media outlets such as news broadcasters and online political commentaries. Accessing information not only requires the relevant language ability, but also adequate skills and resources to access the internet, which could further hinder those with poor socioeconomic status (Conway 2000; Verba, Schlozman & Brady 1995; Woshinsky 1995).

Although inclusive minority representation could better reflect the needs of the minority community, such representative governance has often been criticised for being over-focused on collective ethnic identity, leading to favouring the government's political positions and disregarding the importance of democratic participation of minorities as individuals (Trebbi, Aghion & Alesina 2008: 350).

Co-opting ethnic minority elites into political structures may negatively impact individual minority political participation, as mere selective inclusion sets a limited parameter around the ideal model of minority inclusion, as perceived by the state (Brown 2004; Nagata 2004). Minorities who do not match this ideal model may find themselves alienated by the state and society (Brown 2004; Nagata 2004). In this regard, minority identity is constantly shaped by the state, which expects a level of conformity to the prescribed minority image. Accordingly, the resultant form of minority political participation becomes a mechanism to facilitate state interests and to build a nation according to the state's vision, even if this neglects the promotion and protection of the rights, interests and diversity of minorities.

Conclusion

Since the Second World War, the emergence of democracy in Easy Asia has unfortunately not developed in conjunction with the contemporary approach of placing human rights constructs at the core of this process. Rather, through the manipulation of legal systems and the limited recognition of minorities, as well as the degree of respect for their rights and related entitlements, democracy has been used as a tool to maintain state power and uphold perceptions of an ideal 'nation'.

Indeed, the discussion regarding the protection of minority rights is the most appropriate example to examine the degree of social and political inclusion and human rights protection in a democratic state. Effective democracy requires substantively equal access to official resources, which is ensured when the human rights of individuals within a community are upheld (Gould 2004). Exercising equal positive freedom and rights also requires the recognition of differences. A people-driven democratic system should be able to promote and protect the differences of individuals, acknowledging their identity and taking their interests and needs into consideration. Such recognition is essential to maintaining equal opportunity in democratic participation, as individuals may then participate in all contexts of the community, including social, economic and political life. It is only through such recognition that individuals and groups may effectively articulate their concerns with the confidence that the state will be responsive to these. Through such a structure, communities may truly develop according to people's rights and needs.

Yet, such levels of participation are only guaranteed when individual diversity is valued by the nation state. Whether a group or an individual has been considered as part of a nation often depends on the perceptions of identity, often revolving around the 'sameness' of nationals. Collective bonding may be established through 'common ethnic ancestry and similar ethnocultural attributes, and sometimes mainly on the claim that they occupy a particular territory and have a common pride in the public institutions and public way of life associated with that territory' (Brown 2004: 49). Nation building under nationalism is a way to strengthen such sameness through building one cohesive community. Such cohesion most often leads to the exclusion of minorities, as they may alter the social and cultural proximity of the nation. When the state endorses strong nationalism, minorities are excluded as part of the nation to the extent that a unified society takes priority, even under a democratic political system.

With states in East Asia holding strong nationalistic positions and maintaining monocultural societies, minorities are not being effectively recognised and do not have equal opportunities in social and political participation. A lack of recognition of the rights of minorities coupled with their exclusion through discriminatory practices in Japan, South Korea and Hong Kong has caused minority needs to be unarticulated. Rather than abiding by a 'people-driven democratic system' where people can fully participate in state affairs, democracy in East Asia most often barely refers to the transparency of the electoral system. Such democratic structures are entirely state-driven with limited capacity for public engagement in state affairs and are often used as a tool to sustain the state's authoritative rule rather than to build an inclusive society incorporating diverse ethnic, religious and linguistic groups.

The situation of minority rights protection in Hong Kong, Japan and South Korea clearly demonstrates the importance of state recognition on the status of minorities in order to fully protect the rights of minorities. Although international treaties have been signed and ratified by these governments, poor implementation within national human rights frameworks has deprived minorities of their rights and needs, while also limiting the efficacy of protection measures. The consequences of these shortcomings compound to marginalise and exclude minorities from effective participation in society.

Notes

1 In the concluding observations of the Committee on the Elimination of Racial Discrimination on its consideration of reports submitted by Japan at its seventy-sixth session (15 February–12 March 2010), the Committee urged the state party to consider adopting specific legislation to outlaw direct and indirect racial discrimination, in accordance with Article 1 of ICERD. And in the concluding observations on the fifteenth and sixteenth periodic reports of the Republic of Korea, adopted by the Committee on the Elimination of Racial Discrimination at its eighty-first session (6–13 August 2012), the Committee urged the state party to take immediate action on the finalisation and adoption of the Discrimination Prohibition Act or other comprehensive legislation to prohibit racial discrimination.

2 In the concluding observations of the Committee on the Elimination of Racial Discrimination on its consideration of reports submitted by Japan at its seventy-sixth session (15 February–12 March 2010), the Committee urged the state party to establish a well-financed and adequately staffed independent human rights institution, in compliance with the Paris Principles, with a broad human rights mandate and a specific mandate to address contemporary forms of discrimination.

3 In the concluding observations on the fifteenth and sixteenth periodic reports of the Republic of Korea, adopted by the Committee on the Elimination of Racial Discrimination at its eighty-first session (6–13 August 2012), the Committee urged the state party to provide the National Human Rights Commission of Korea with adequate financial resources and experienced human rights experts so as to enable it to carry out its mandate effectively, including promoting and monitoring the rights under the Convention.

4 In the concluding observations on the combined third and fourth periodic reports of China, adopted by the Committee on the Rights of the Child at its sixty-fourth session (16 September–4 October 2013), the Committee recommended that the state party promptly establish independent national human rights institutions in accordance with the Paris Principles to monitor the implementation of the Convention and to deal with complaints from children in a child-sensitive and expeditious manner. A similar recommendation could be found in the concluding observations on the third periodic report of Hong Kong, China, adopted by the Human Rights Committee at its 107th session (11–28 March 2013).

5 Residents of Hong Kong should have the right of abode and obtain a Hong Kong Identity Card. They shall enjoy civil and political rights granted in accordance with Chapter 3 of the Basic Law.
6 The total number of Indians, Pakistanis and Nepalese has increased from 27,313 in 1991 to 42,124 in 2001.
7 According to the Basic Law, Chinese language is the dominant language. Article 9 of the Basic Law states: '[i]n addition to the Chinese language, English may also be used as an official language by the executive authorities, legislature and judiciary of the Hong Kong Special Administrative Region'.
8 In 2003, the language requirement for the appointment to the civil service has been standardised, with at least Grade E in English language (Syllabus B) and Chinese in HKCEE for the non-graduate grades; and a pass in both language papers (Use of Chinese and Use of English) in the Common Recruitment Examination (CRE) for the degree/professional grades. According to the Basic Law, the chief executive and other top government officials, including the members of the Executive Council and chief justice of the Court of Final Appeal and the chief judge of the High Court of the Hong Kong Special Administrative Region, should be Chinese citizens and have no right of abode in other countries.
9 Definition on democracy and human rights is retrieved from the United Nations' website: www.un.org/en/globalissues/democracy/human_rights.shtml.
10 In the summary record of the 1,988th meeting of the Committee on the Elimination of Racial Discrimination on 20 October 2010, paragraph 20 stated that 'The international conventions ratified by the State party had the same weight as domestic legislation'.
11 Article 1 of UNDMR states that 'States shall protect the existence and the national or ethnic, cultural, religious and linguistic identity of minorities within their respective territories and shall encourage conditions for the promotion of that identity'.
12 The HKSAR government website states:

> The Government makes appointments to advisory and statutory bodies on the basis of the merit of individuals concerned, taking into account a candidate's ability, expertise, experience, integrity and commitment to public service and with due regard to the statutory provisions of statutory bodies, functions and nature of business of the bodies concerned.
>
> (www.hab.gov.hk/en/policy_responsibilities/District_Community_and_Public_Relations/t_advisory.htm)

References

Baig, R 2012, 'From colony to Special Administrative Region: Ethnic minorities' participation in the making of legislation against racial discrimination in Hong Kong', *Social Transformations in Chinese Societies*, vol. 8, no. 2, pp. 173–200.

Bickley, G 2005, 'Early beginnings of British community (1841–1898)', in CYY Chu (ed.), *Foreign communities in Hong Kong, 1840s–1950*, New York, Palgrave Macmillan, pp. 17–38.

Brown, D 2004, 'The democratization of national identity', in S Henders (ed.), *Democratization and identity: Regimes and ethnicity in East and Southeast Asia*, Lanham, MD, Lexington Books, pp. 43–66.

Castellino, J & Redondo, ED 2006, 'Asian states, international human rights law, and minority rights', in J. Castellino & ED Redondo (eds), *Minority rights in Asia: A comparative legal analysis*, Oxford, Oxford University Press.

Castles, S & Davidson, A 2000, *Citizenship and migration: Globalization and the politics of belonging*, Basingstoke, Macmillan.

Conway, M 2000, *Political participation in the United States*, Washing DC, CQ Press.

Gould, CC 2004, *Globalizing democracy and human rights*, New York, Cambridge University Press.

Henders, S 2004, 'Political regimes and ethnic identities in East and Southeast Asia: Beyond the "Asian values" debate', in S Henders (ed.), *Democratization and identity: Regimes and ethnicity in East and Southeast Asia*, Lanham, MD, Lexington Books, pp. 1–21.

Hesse, B & Sayyid, S 2006, 'Narrating the postcolonial political and the immigrants imaginary', in N Ali, VS Kalra & S Sayyid (eds), *A postcolonial people*, London, C. Hurst & Co.

HKSAR Government 2000, *Sample survey of the characteristics of the ethnic minorities in Hong Kong: Main findings*, Paper No. CB(2)590/00-01(01).

HKSAR Home Affairs Department 2016, *District Fight Crime Committee (Kwai Tsing District)*, viewed 23 October 2016, www.had.gov.hk/en/18_districts/t_my_map_11_dfcc.htm.

HKSAR Kwai Tsing District Council 2016, *Kwai Chung North East Area Committee*, viewed 23 October 2016, www.dckwaitsing.org.hk/ktdc-web/c/homeAffairsCommittee45_c.faces.

HKSAR Legislative Council 2003, *Panel on home affairs: Minutes of meeting held on 12.12.2003*, LC Paper No. CB(2)913/03-04.
HKSAR Legislative Council 2006, *Panel on education: Education for children of ethnic minorities*, LC Paper No. CB(2)2642/05-06(4).
HKSAR Legislative Council 2010, *LCQ1: Chinese language proficiency requirements for appointment to the civil service*, HKSAR government press release, 20 January 2010, www.info.gov.hk/gia/general/201001/20/P201001200143.htm.
HKSAR Legislative Council 2013, *Panel on public services: Employment of ethnic minorities in civil service*, LC Paper No. CB(4)545/12-13(05).
Hong Kong Census and Statistics Department 2011, *2011 population census thematic report: Ethnic minorities*, www.census2011.gov.hk/pdf/EM.pdf.
Kim, B 2011, '"Blatant discrimination disappears, but . . .": The politics of everyday exclusion in contemporary Japan', *Asian Perspective*, vol. 35, pp. 287–308.
Lie, J 2001, *Multiethnic Japan*, Cambridge, MA, Harvard University Press.
Manchanda, R 2009, *The no nonsense guide to minority rights in South Asia*, New Delhi, Sage.
Mihr, A 2006, 'Minority participation: A challenge for human rights', *Journal of Social Science Education*, vol. 5, no. 1, pp. 44–59.
Minority Rights Group 2005, *World directory of minorities and indigenous peoples*, viewed 24 March 2015, www.minorityrights.org/5369/japan/koreans.html.
Nagata, J 2004, 'Elusive democracy: appropriation of "rights" ideologies in Malaysian ethnic and religious political discourse', in S Henders (ed.), *Democratization and identity: Regimes and ethnicity in East and Southeast Asia*, Lanham, MD, Lexington Books, pp. 225–249.
Plüss, C 2005, 'Migrants from India and their relations with British and Chinese residents', in CYY Chu (ed.), *Foreign communities in Hong Kong, 1840s–1950*, New York, Palgrave Macmillan, pp. 155–170.
Rehman, J 2000, *The weaknesses in the international protection of minority rights*, London, Kluwer Law International.
Sautman, B & Kneehans, E 2002, *The politics of racial discrimination in Hong Kong*, Maryland Series in Contemporary Asian Studies, vol. 162, no. 2.
Shipper, AW 2010, 'Nationalisms of and against Zainichi Koreans in Japan', *Asian Politics & Policy*, vol. 2, no. 1, pp. 55–75.
South China Morning Post 1999, 'Minority groups racially targeted', 13 January.
South China Morning Post 2009, 'HK police force nears "localisation" goal with exit of expat officer', 12 October.
Strausz, M 2006, 'Minorities and protest in Japan: The politics of the fingerprinting refusal movement', *Pacific Affairs*, vol. 79, no. 4, pp. 641–656.
Trebbi, F, Aghion, P & Alesina, A 2008, 'Electoral rules and minority representation in U.S. cities', *The Quarterly Journal of Economics*, vol. 123, no. 1, pp. 325–357.
United Nations Office of the High Commissioner for Human Rights 2010, *Minority rights: International standards and guidance for implementation*, www.ohchr.org/Documents/Publications/MinorityRights_en.pdf.
Vasconcellos, CA 2007, 'Racism', in ME Page and PM Sonnenburg (eds), *Colonialism: An international, social, cultural and political encyclopaedia*, Santa Barbara, CA, ABC-CLIO.
Verba, S, Schlozman, K & Brady, H 1995, *Voice and equity: Civic voluntarism in American politics*, Cambridge, MA, Harvard University Press.
White, BS 1994, *Turbans and traders: Hong Kong's Indian communities*, Hong Kong, Oxford University Press.
Woshinsky, OH 1995, *Culture and politics: An introduction to mass and elite political behavior*, Englewood Cliffs, NJ, Prentice-Hall.
Xiao, W 2001, *One country, two systems: An account of the drafting of the Hong Kong Basic Law*, Beijing, Peking University Press.
Xu, J & Shih, C 2013, 'Getting a Hong Kong passport, becoming a Chinese national', *Varsity*, 10 January, viewed 25 March 2015, http://varsity.com.cuhk.edu.hk/index.php/2013/01/ethnic-minorities-chinese-passports/.
Zahar, R 1974, *Frantz Fanon: Colonialism and alienation*, London, Monthly Review Press.

6

China's most oppressed

Uyghur exclusion and discrimination

Alim Seytoff and Henryk Szadziewski

Introduction

The Uyghur people are one of the most ancient Turkic peoples who have lived in central and northern Asia for thousands of years, having established their own powerful states and empires on a par with China's Tang dynasty. Present-day Uyghurs are the indigenous Turkic-speaking Muslim ethnic group who live in what is now the Xinjiang Uyghur Autonomous Region (XUAR), also known as East Turkestan, of the People's Republic of China (PRC). The more than ten million Uyghur people have a culture, religion, language, and belief system that are distinct from the majority Han Chinese, who make up over 90% of the country's population. Until the Manchu Qing Empire conquered East Turkestan in the late nineteenth century (Millward 2007), Uyghurs did not have a shared history with the Han Chinese.

The modern history of the Uyghur people starts with the Manchu occupation of East Turkestan in 1884 and the changing of the name of the Uyghur homeland into Xinjiang, which literally means 'New Territory' in the Chinese language, Mandarin (*putonghua*). Since the Manchu occupation, Manchu and Chinese warlords ruled the Uyghur people for several decades until the overthrow of Manchu rule by Chinese nationalists in 1911 and subsequent communist Chinese occupation of East Turkestan in 1949. Prior to communist administration, the Uyghur people enjoyed brief periods of independence in the twentieth century establishing two independent states: the Islamic Republic of East Turkestan on 12 November 1933 and the East Turkestan Republic on 12 November 1944 (Millward 2007). However, both Uyghur republics were short-lived because of Soviet military support for the initial occupying Chinese nationalist forces and the later invading People's Liberation Army.

Xinjiang and the establishment of purported Uyghur autonomy

In the modern history of East Turkestan, Uyghurs view the Manchu conquest and the subsequent Republican and Communist Chinese administrations as forms of foreign occupation. This conceptualisation of the Uyghurs as a captured nation is solidified by the current Chinese government's hard-line position that Xinjiang is an inseparable part of China since ancient times (news.xinhuanet.com 2003). As a result, the relationship between the indigenous Uyghur people and the occupying Chinese authorities and the accompanying Chinese settlers has been one of distrust and hostility since the establishment of the PRC in October 1949.

After the formation of PRC, the Chinese Communist Party (CCP) established the XUAR in 1955 in an attempt to co-opt the Uyghur political and military leaders and assuage the opposition of Uyghur people toward communist Chinese rule. The XUAR was established against the backdrop of strong Uyghur political independence and a military presence of 40,000 standing troops from the Republican era, as well as Uyghurs numbering 87% of the total population in East Turkestan. With the establishment of the XUAR, the CCP declared the enactment of the Regional Ethnic Autonomy Law (REAL), in addition to the PRC Constitution, which guaranteed limited self-rule for East Turkestan and the special status of the Uyghur people in China. The REAL stipulated that only Uyghurs can be appointed as the head of all governmental offices and administration, including the position of XUAR chairman. The REAL also specified the Uyghur language has equal status to Mandarin, China's official language, in the XUAR administration, media and education. Furthermore, the REAL has specific clauses guaranteeing the religious freedom of the Uyghur people (cecc.gov 2013).

While the XUAR was declared and REAL was theoretically enacted in 1955, the Uyghur people did not enjoy the rights enshrined in the REAL. First, although Xinjiang was declared as a Uyghur autonomous region, it was divided into 13 prefectures with some of them given to ethnic minority groups in East Turkestan as autonomous administrations even though the Uyghur population was the majority there, such as the Ili Kazakh Autonomous Prefecture, Kizilsu Kyrgyz Autonomous Prefecture, Bortala Mongol Autonomous Prefecture and Bayingolin Mongol Autonomous Prefecture (Bovingdon 2010). Second, even though the XUAR chairman is an appointed Uyghur, usually a pro-CCP Uyghur handpicked by Beijing, the position holder is only a figurehead without real powers because political, economic, security and military-related decisions are made by a Han Chinese Communist Party secretary directly appointed by the central government. The Uyghur chairman cannot exercise any power independent of the Han Chinese party secretary or veto any decisions made by the incumbent or the central government. The chairman's job is to faithfully endorse all the decisions made by the Han Chinese party secretary and to follow all directives of the central government. The same situation exists for all Uyghur leaders in positions of power in the XUAR (Li 2008).

Marginalisation and exclusion of Uyghurs, despite their autonomy in Xinjiang

In 1954, the CCP established the Xinjiang Production and Construction Corps (XPCC or Bingtuan), a semi-military colonial administration in East Turkestan consisting of mostly decommissioned occupying Chinese soldiers and settlers, a year prior to the establishment of the XUAR. The XPCC was established under the direct order of PRC founder Mao Zedong to 'develop frontier regions, promote economic development, ensure social stability and ethnic harmony, and consolidate border defense' (news.xinhuanet.com 2003). The XPCC functions as a military organisation in times of Uyghur unrest and as a business corporation in times of peace in East Turkestan. It consists of 14 military-style divisions with a total population of nearly three million (Xinjiang Review 2011) strategically located near areas surrounding major Uyghur cities and towns and has a 120,000 strong militia force (The Economist 2013). The XPCC has administrative authority over several cities and towns, major agricultural farmlands, settlements and important water resources. It is heavily involved in regional and national business activities, as well as import–export businesses with neighbouring Central Asian countries. It has a separate governing body, courts, armed police forces, militia, media, schools and hospitals (Cliff 2009).

The administration, the decision-making bodies and most of its employees of the XPCC are Han Chinese and Uyghurs are almost completely excluded. Consequently, the XPCC is a Han Chinese run colonial entity in which Uyghurs have no influence or decision-making power (The Economist 2013). The Uyghur people have a deep suspicion and resentment of the XPCC due to the fact it was used many times in the past in support of Chinese military suppression of Uyghur protests against Chinese rule in East Turkestan, notably during the Barin Uprising in 1990 (Volodzko 2014).

The XPCC, as an instrument of the central government, has been the main driver of steady Han Chinese immigration into East Turkestan with the objective to dominate XUAR, colonise the resource-rich territory and marginalise the once dominant Uyghur population into an absolute minority in their own homeland. After the Chinese occupation of East Turkestan, the XPCC facilitated the transfer of millions of Han Chinese immigrants into the XUAR and resettled them in the XPCC-established cities and towns, including Shihezi, Kuitun and Shuanghe.

The Uyghur population in East Turkestan, which was nearly 90% in 1949 (Chung Chienpeng 2002), is now only 45% (BBC News 2014), while the Chinese immigrant population grew due to state-sponsored mass settlement from around 6% in 1953 (Toops 2004) to the current 40% (excluding the Chinese military, seasonal workers and floating population) (BBC News 2014). Furthermore, 86% of XPCC personnel are Han Chinese (The Economist 2013). Many Uyghurs believe Han Chinese settlers are already a majority, since Beijing continues to encourage their settlement.

This XPCC colonial project, which enjoys the full support of the current Xi Jinping administration, has produced severe consequences in the XUAR demography by systematically reducing the dominant position of the once majority Uyghur population, followed by social and employment discrimination against them in favour of Han Chinese immigrants. The XPCC is also one of the main employers in the XUAR and Uyghurs are vastly underrepresented in almost all facets of this entity that controls almost all levers of life in the Uyghur autonomy (cecc.gov 2009a).

Notwithstanding the fact that REAL stipulates that every head of the administration and government departments in the XUAR should be a Uyghur, the REAL does not apply to the XPCC and there is no Uyghur chairing any important position in the corps. In fact, the XPCC prioritises providing housing, employment and funding, including low interest bank loans, and other opportunities to the incoming Han Chinese settlers. At the same time, it denies similar opportunities to the indigenous Uyghurs. As a result of such direct racial discrimination, Uyghurs account for little in the XPCC administration and work force (Bhattacharji 2012).

Human rights violations of Uyghurs in the name of the 'war on terror'

The Chinese government often exploits the Uyghurs' faith in Islam in order to justify repressive 'anti-terror' measures in East Turkestan, in order to consolidate political and economic supremacy in the region through militarisation (Narramore 2012). The human rights violations of the Uyghur people by the Chinese authorities dramatically increased after 9/11. Since the Uyghurs believe in Islam, Chinese leaders saw the terrorist attacks on the United States and the subsequent 'Global War on Terror' as an historic opportunity to complete Chinese empire building by repackaging its repression of the Uyghur people as a 'fight against terrorism' and forcibly assimilating the Uyghur people into Chinese culture.

In the immediate aftermath of 9/11, the CCP went on a global public relations campaign claiming: 'China is a victim of Uyghur terrorism' (Ramzy 2014). The CCP launched a campaign against what it termed a 'fight against the three evil forces of terrorism, separatism and religious extremism' in East Turkestan, targeting all expressions of Uyghur dissent (Muldoon 2004). Over the past 15 years, using 'terrorism' as a justification, Beijing has undertaken a renewed, systematic and sustained crackdown on all forms of Uyghur dissent. Chinese security forces often target Uyghurs who express any type of dissent, as they 'strike hard' against the 'three evil forces'. In May 2014, President Xi Jinping initiated an 'anti-terror campaign' in the XUAR, which extended until the end of 2015.

In an attempt to further restrict legitimate Uyghur political and human rights demands, China adopted a new Counter-Terrorism Law on 27 December 2015, effective as of 1 January 2016. The broad and vague definitions of 'terrorism' and 'religious extremism' contained in the legislation potentially criminalise peaceful expressions of religious belief and legitimise heavy-handed repression in the region. The law measure was heavily criticised by the US government and human rights organisations in the west (state.gov 2015; Uyghur Human Rights Project 2016).

The 5 July 2009 Urumchi unrest and its ramifications

On 5 July 2009, the XUAR capital Urumchi erupted into unprecedented unrest that resulted in the deaths of an unknown number of Uyghur people at the hands of Chinese security forces. The unrest began with a peaceful demonstration by Uyghurs. The XUAR government deployed fully armed security forces to suppress the demonstration and, according to eyewitnesses, deadly live fire was used against Uyghurs (Uyghur Human Rights Project 2010: 3).

For the next ten months, Chinese authorities initiated the world's longest-running information blockade by cutting off the Internet and telephone communications throughout the XUAR, effectively preventing information regarding the atrocities of Chinese security forces from being leaked to the outside world. In particular, the Chinese authorities have actively sought to silence the voice of the Uyghur people since 5 July 2009. Many Uyghur journalists, bloggers and website staff have been detained, arrested or sentenced since 5 July 2009. Arbitrary detentions and enforced disappearances of Uyghur men throughout Urumchi after 5 July 2009 left entire Uyghur neighbourhoods with only women and children (Uyghur Human Rights Project 2013a: 4; Human Rights Watch 2009).

Chinese officials and state media widely reported the violence that was allegedly committed by Uyghurs against Han Chinese, but ignored Han Chinese attacks committed against Uyghurs in July 2009. Government accounts of the unrest in Urumchi in July 2009 have consistently demonised Uyghurs as violent criminals and terrorists, and Urumchi residents said government propaganda fanned public hatred against Uyghurs and deepened ethnic discord not only in Urumchi, but also in the entire XUAR (Uyghur Human Rights Project 2010).

Recent increasing repression and human rights violations

Chinese authorities have not only exploited the international security environment and Islamophobia in the aftermath of 9/11, but also most recently the rise of Islamic State of Iraq and Levant (ISIS) to silence peaceful Uyghur dissent to state policies. The Chinese state's conflation of terrorism with peaceful dissent has effectively limited Uyghurs from speaking out against state policies that disregard their economic, social and cultural interests during a time of systematic human rights violations in the XUAR.

In the XUAR, repression of Uyghur individuals has manifested most notably in the arrest of moderate Uyghurs critical of the Chinese government. The 2014 arrest, conviction and life sentencing of Ilham Tohti, a professor at Beijing's Minzu University, marked the seriousness of the Chinese government's determination to root out any opposition to its policy approach in the region. Professor Tohti often questioned the efficacy of Chinese government policies targeting Uyghurs, citing worsening economic, social and cultural conditions. In addition to severely cracking down on Uyghur political and human rights activists, China also imposes zero tolerance on dissenting Uyghur views regarding issues of social or cultural relevance.

On 7 January 2014, Xi Jinping announced a 'major strategy shift' in the XUAR, which reprioritised regional policies toward state security from an emphasis on development to create conditions of regional stability (Uyghur Human Rights Project 2010). Ten days later, Chinese state media detailed how regional officials planned to double the budget for the Xinjiang Public Security Bureau (english.peopledaily.com.cn 2014). The role of Chinese policies under Xi Jinping in fostering an atmosphere of tension and fear in the XUAR should not be underestimated. Invariably, the Chinese government's response to dissent is further repression of Uyghur political and cultural rights. China's willingness to lock the regional tensions in the XUAR into a cycle of additional repression following incidents sparked by repressive policies is an approach from which state officials will find it increasingly hard to retreat. In a society that is ever more militarised and surveilled, in which Uyghurs expressing peaceful dissenting ideas are punished and silenced, and where Uyghurs are socially stigmatised, the likelihood of further violence is an unavoidable conclusion.

China's discriminatory language policy in the XUAR

In the past decade, and with increasing intensity since 2002, the PRC has pursued a monolingual language policy aimed at removing Uyghur as a language of instruction in the XUAR. Employing the term 'bilingual' education, the PRC has, in reality, moved in stages towards making Mandarin Chinese the only language of instruction in the XUAR, undermining the linguistic basis of Uyghur culture. The exclusion of the Uyghur language from public institutions, and its absence as a working language and language of employment for civil servants are discriminatory practices—and also result in the marginalisation of the Uyghurs in public life and their poor performances in areas such as higher education.

Children reach their education potential better if instructed in their mother tongue. According to Kishore Singh, United Nations (UN) Special Rapporteur on the Right to Education: 'A child learns best in its mother tongue, especially at the early stage in education, and among linguistic minority groups' (UNESCO 2012). Their right to receive education in their mother tongue is recognised by the UN Declaration of Human Rights, Convention on the Rights of the Child and the Declaration on the Rights of Persons Belonging to National or Ethnic, Religious and Linguistic Minorities. Under these international instruments, China is required to take appropriate measures to guarantee that Uyghur children have adequate opportunities to learn their mother tongue or to receive instruction in their mother tongue. Furthermore, China's Constitution and the REAL guarantee the rights of minorities and the use of minority languages in government, education, media and on a daily basis.

However, in violation of both domestic and international laws, the Chinese government has implemented the compulsory monolingual Mandarin language education in the XUAR since the mid-1980s. The new 'bilingual' education imperative is designed to transition Uyghur students from education in their Uyghur mother tongue to education in Mandarin, resulting eventually in the complete loss of the Uyghur mother tongue.

The exclusive use of Mandarin in the XUAR is completely unreasonable where the Uyghur population accounts for nearly half of the Uyghur autonomous region's 22 million population. The XPCC, as one of the region's main employers, in effect neither uses nor employs Uyghur-speaking individuals since only Putonghua is used for official purposes (cecc.gov. 2009a). The exclusive use of Mandarin has the negative effects of marginalising Uyghur language in the educational sphere with the goal of eliminating it as a language of instruction in the XUAR, forcing Uyghur students at levels ranging from preschool to university to study in a second language, removing Uyghur children from their cultural environment and placing them into Chinese language 'Xinjiang classes' located in inland China, using Chinese language requirements and school mergers to force veteran Uyghur teachers out of the classroom, and taking decisions on language of instruction for Uyghur children out of the hands of parents (Uyghur Human Rights Project 2007). In the end, this policy increases the already high tensions between Uyghurs and the Chinese state because the Uyghur people perceive China's 'bilingual' education as an affront to their unique identity and culture and is aimed at forcibly assimilating them into the Chinese culture.

Human rights and religion

Many Uyghurs perceive their belief in Islam not only as a personal expression of faith, but also as a statement of their cultural distinctiveness. For many Uyghurs, the incursion of the state into this private aspect of their lives and the role it plays in establishing a broader identity is viewed as part of a considered assimilative process.

In the XUAR, the twofold implementation of strict national and regional regulations concerning religious belief and practice mean the Uyghur people are subjected to the harshest conditions governing religious life in the PRC. This occurs even though China's domestic laws, such as the Constitution and the REAL, guarantee religious freedom. Discriminatory restrictions that target Uyghur Muslims and not other Muslims in China places the Chinese government in violation of Article 2 of the Declaration on the Rights of Persons Belonging to National or Ethnic, Religious and Linguistic Minorities. For example, age limits are only placed on Uyghurs when applying for a space on state-sponsored Hajj pilgrimages (Ananth 2011).

Rather than simply forbid religious practice, Chinese authorities have implemented regulations that progressively narrow the definition of lawful activity. As a result, many Uyghurs often discover that traditional religious customs are increasingly not permitted (Uyghur Human Rights Project 2014). However, Chinese officials justify many of the restrictions through claims that outlawed practices have been imported from overseas and that it faces an organised threat to public security in the form of the 'three evil forces of terrorism, separatism and religious extremism' (Dynon 2014).

China's highly politicised criminal-legal system, as well as the state apparatus governing and monitoring religion, have ensured the government is the ultimate arbiter in the interpretation of religious affairs. In effect, the bodies established by the Chinese state to oversee administration in China do little to protect religious believers, but assist the government's repression of religious freedom by helping to formulate and promote restrictive regulations.

Religious leaders, such as imams, are required to attend political education classes to ensure compliance with CCP regulations and policies; only state-approved versions of the Qur'an and sermons are permitted, with all unapproved religious texts treated as 'illegal' publications liable to confiscation and criminal charges against whoever was found in possession of them; any outward expression of faith in government workplaces, hospitals and some private businesses, such as men wearing beards or women wearing headscarves, is forbidden; state employees and persons under the age of 18 are prohibited from entering a mosque, a measure not in force in the rest of China; organised private religious education is proscribed and facilitators of private classes in Islam are frequently charged with conducting 'illegal' religious activities; and students, teachers and government workers are prohibited from fasting during Ramadan. In addition,

Uyghurs are not permitted to undertake Hajj, unless it is with an expensive official tour, in which state officials carefully vet applicants (Uyghur Human Rights Project 2013b).

Uyghurs found to have contravened religious regulations are punished severely. In a disturbing number of cases, Uyghurs have been given long prison sentences for 'illegal' religious activities for actions considered normal by international human rights standards (Radio Free Asia 2014). An area of considerable concern is the open discrimination against Uyghurs, especially women, who choose to lead religious lives publicly (cecc.gov 2009b). The ban on Islamic veiling in Urumchi in 2015 and reports of withholding state assistance unless pledges are signed guaranteeing non-participation in 'illegal' religious activities indicate the extent of the problem (Grose & Leibold 2015; Congressional-Executive Commission on China 2012).

Racial and ethnic discrimination in employment and the economy

Primarily through a series of centrally led campaigns, the state has been the key driver of development priorities among the Uyghur. Although it is not unprecedented for a central government to define regional development policy, in China, the manner of its negotiation invariably places ethnic minorities outside its formation, as interventions emphasise material development from a top-down and state-centric perspective.

The Western Development (2000) and First Xinjiang Work Forum (2010) initiatives were designed to address inter- and intraregional economic disparities. However, economic measures indicate that while Xinjiang's economy has experienced high rates of growth, inequities between Uyghurs and Han Chinese have exacerbated since the implementation of these initiatives. These disparities represent forms of discrimination with highly visible consequences, such as hiring discrimination and higher levels of poverty.

Employment discrimination based on ethnicity has occurred despite domestic laws preventing such practices. Article 4 of the Chinese Constitution, Articles 9 and 22 of the Regional Ethnic Autonomy Law, Articles 12 and 14 of the Labour Law and Articles 3 and 28 of the Employment Promotion Law all state that ethnic minorities should receive equal opportunity in the job market (cecc.gov 2009c). Despite a dearth of state-produced evidence on the ethnic composition of regional unemployment and poverty rates, non-Chinese state accounts describe the ethnic discrimination faced by Uyghurs in securing employment across professions and localised poverty concentrated in Uyghur areas.

Against a backdrop of imbalanced economic growth between its eastern and western regions, the Chinese government initiated Western Development as part of its Tenth Five Year Plan (2001–2005) (Howell & Fan 2011). In the XUAR, Western Development was characterised by investment in large-scale natural resources projects and infrastructure development (Bellér-Hann 2012). In a tacit admission of Western Development shortcomings in the wake of ethnic unrest in Urumchi in 2009, the central leadership convened a Work Forum in Beijing in May 2010 to assess and adjust economic policies in the region toward greater spatial distribution of state investment.

Research conducted by the Congressional-Executive Commission on China (CECC) spanning six years of Western Development illustrates discrimination against Uyghur candidates for jobs with the XPCC, the civil service and in the regional education sector (cecc.gov 2005; cecc.gov 2006; cecc.gov 2009a; Congressional-Executive Commission on China 2011). Differences in distribution between ethnicities employed in the natural resources industry span the Western Development period. In 2000, *The Washington Post* stated that the '[oil] industry is now almost completely run by Han. The China National Petroleum Co. has brought most of its workers here from other parts of China' (Pomfret 2000). More than 15 years later, CECC had seen no improvement among natural resource industry employers. The Commission documented 50 jobs advertised by the Xinjiang PetroChina Pipe Engineering Co. had been exclusively reserved for Han Chinese (cecc.gov 2010a).

As reported in a 2009 article, scholars Ben Hopper and Michael Webber asked Uyghur and Han Chinese correspondents their opinions on employment opportunities. In the survey, 76% of Uyghurs stated the employment situation was worse than that of ten years ago, as opposed to 49% of Han Chinese.

According to a Hong Kong-based scholar, discriminatory practices in Xinjiang have aggravated economic disparities between Uyghurs and Han Chinese (Yang 2010). In 2004, scholar Calla Wiemer documented a pattern of lower incomes and higher poverty rates among ethnic minorities in Xinjiang. She described: 'a strong pattern of disparity related to ethnicity. Han Chinese tend to be concentrated in more economically developed areas, whereas Turkic peoples predominate in poorer regions' (Wiemer 2004). Six years later and ten years into Western Development, Huhao Cao's study of spatial and ethnic income disparity found: '80% of the total poverty designated counties in the province consist of minority communities where, in most cases, minority populations represent over 90% of the total population' (Cao 2010).

Data available in the 2013 Xinjiang Statistical Yearbook, demonstrates how increased state investment under the terms of the First Xinjiang Work Forum in the Uyghur majority south of Xinjiang did not have a direct impact on Uyghur communities. Kashgar, Hotan and Aksu Prefectures fell into the bottom third of the 15 region-wide administrative areas surveyed in terms of GDP per capita (Xinjiang Uygur Autonomous Region Statistical Bureau 2013). A 2015 Phoenix Weekly report showed that the per capita GDP in Kashgar, Hotan, Kizilsu and Aksu is less than 45% of the regional average. In addition, 85% of the rural poor and 63% of the unemployed were found in these four Uyghur majority prefectures (Phoenix Weekly 2015).

Economic development is a recurrent feature of ethnic minority policy in the PRC. Progress in standards of living is one gauge of successful ethnic minority management according to the official rhetoric (news.xinhuanet.com 2000). As a member of the UN General Assembly and a signatory to the UN Charter, the PRC is obliged to respect the articles of the UN Universal Declaration of Human Rights (UDHR). In Articles 19 and 21, the UDHR contains provisions that protect the right of individuals to freely participate in public decision-making processes.

The Declaration on the Right to Development, adopted by the UN General Assembly in 1986, is also relevant to the protection of popular participation. Article 2 of the Declaration establishes 'active, free and meaningful participation in development' and its associated benefits as a necessary foundation of state development policies. Article 9 of the Declaration specifies: 'States should encourage popular participation in all spheres as an important factor in development and in the full realisation of all human rights' (United Nations 2001).

However, discriminatory practices and a denial of the Uyghurs' right to participation in the development process have resulted in imbalanced policies favouring Han Chinese with greater economic, social and cultural capital to exploit opportunity in the region. The lack of monitoring procedures inherent in state economic initiatives in Xinjiang ensures that Uyghur input on policy performance is absent and any consequent reassessment and realignment of policy in their interests appears unlikely.

The full implications of the Second Xinjiang Work Forum (2014) remain to be understood; however, the initiative appears aimed at encouraging more Han Chinese to migrate to the south of the region as the state has placed a focus on 'ethnic mingling' in the policy (Liebold 2014). Reports of cash rewards for couples entering mixed marriages in Cherchen and the announcement of a new mixed ethnicity settlement near Hotan were illustrative of the approach (Phillips 2014). The relaxing of *hukou* requirements in southern Xinjiang has been another means the state has attempted to stimulate migration (Haas 2015). Should the state succeed in motivating Han Chinese to settle in the south it may localise economic exclusion of the Uyghurs, especially among those Uyghurs excluded from the incentives prompted by 'ethnic mingling'.

Culture and the rights of the Uyghurs: the demolition of Kashgar old city

Many cultures are under pressure to survive due to the homogenising effects of globalisation; however, the Uyghur people face an additional threat to their identity from state imposed measures. Uyghur cultural loss is traceable through a history of policies targeting tangible and intangible heritage. Chinese government officials and Chinese official media often portray the cornerstones of Uyghur culture as backward. For example, in 2002, former XUAR party secretary Wang Lequan commented: 'The languages of the minority nationalities have very small capacities and do not contain many of the expressions in modern science and technology, which makes education in these concepts impossible. This is out of step with the 21st Century' (Bequelin 2004: 45).

The demolition of Uyghur neighbourhoods in East Turkestan is another example of the state's modernisation narrative regarding minority cultures. According to Harrell (1996), the approach to modernisation in Communist ideology is not defined by the conversion of peripheral peoples into those of the centre, but rather to raise them to a standard of modernity that is universal. Harrell (1996) adds that in China, including the period of CCP government, Han Chinese culture instead is promoted as a measure of centrality and modernity.

In February 2009, Chinese authorities announced a 'residents' resettlement' project that aimed to demolish 5 square kilometres of Kashgar's 8 square kilometres of old city, and resettle 45,000 households by 2014. At its conclusion, the demolition will affect approximately 65,000 households. This is an estimated 220,000 people representing about 42% of Kashgar's total population (Uyghur Human Rights Project 2012). The Chinese authorities stated motivation for the demolition is public safety. Authorities considered the 65,000 houses in Kashgar's old city were suffering from poor drainage and were vulnerable to collapse from earthquakes. Residents of the old city would therefore be moved to newly constructed buildings up to 8 kilometres away from the old city area, spurring social isolation and impacting livelihoods (cecc.gov 2009d; cecc.gov 2010b).

The Chinese government's reasoning for the demolition has been criticised, most notably from within China. Wu Dianting, a professor at Beijing Normal University, as well as Wu Lili, of the Beijing Cultural Heritage Protection Center, have stated that the resettlement of old-city Uyghurs is not only 'cruel' because of the destruction to the Uyghur lifestyle, but also unnecessary. Professor Wu believes that reinforcing and repairing existing housing could better serve the large amount of money used to destroy Uyghur homes (Fan 2009; Wines 2009).

The demolition of Kashgar's old city is a great loss to world heritage and a serious threat to the survival of what is most distinctive about Uyghur material culture, architecture and human community. The Chinese government argues that the demolition is necessary to the modernisation of the Uyghur people. Modernisation is important in the development of all cultures, but the Chinese government neglects two vital points: whether there was an alternative to outright destruction of homes that have so long withstood climatic and political changes and whether Uyghurs were genuinely consulted on the terms of the demolitions.

International legal instruments stipulate the need to protect the property rights and housing rights of Uyghurs and others living in China. These legal instruments regulate the evictions of residents from their homes and property, the relocation and resettlement of individuals and communities, consultation with affected communities, compensation for the loss of homes and property, and preservation of cultural heritage and the environment. Land and housing rights in international law are thus inextricably intertwined with a number of human rights issues. They are also intertwined with development issues, as an expansion in urban development in China has created significant conflicts between residents and developers, and many international conventions are designed to protect indigenous communities' rights to develop according to their own principles.

The International Covenant on Economic, Social and Cultural Rights (ICESCR), which has been signed and ratified by China, is an important document in evaluating the property and housing rights affected in the destruction of Uyghur communities. The protection of property rights is enshrined in the ICESCR, as is protection against forced eviction. General Comment 7 of the ICESCR calls for a degree of security that 'guarantees legal protection against forced eviction, harassment and other threats', and concludes by saying that 'forced evictions are prima facie incompatible with the requirements of the Covenant'. It further states that indigenous people and ethnic minorities, together with women, children, youth and the elderly, all suffer disproportionately from the practice of forced eviction (ohchr.org 2011).

Conclusion

In her 2005 monograph, *The Xinjiang Conflict: Uyghur Identity, Language Policy, and Political Discourse*, scholar Arienne Dwyer writes:

> Youths will only become radicalized if they sense that their language and religion is under threat. If Beijing would support peaceful local forms of religious expression and the maintenance of major minority languages as it did in the 1980s, then the PRC will win back the support of many Uyghurs.
>
> *(Dwyer 2005)*

In this regard, George Washington University professor Sean Roberts has said: 'The ongoing development and further marginalization of the Uighurs, and particularly the suppression of Uighur dissent and constantly associating it with terrorism by the state, is likely to eventually lead to a self-fulfilling prophecy' (Tang 2014). This conclusion was taken a step further by Chinese writer Wang Lixiong. Speaking about the harassment of Ilham Tohti, he told journalist Ian Johnson:

> [T]he only conclusion is dark: it's that they don't want moderate Uighurs. Because if you have moderate Uighurs, then why aren't you talking to them? So they wanted to get rid of him and then you can say to the West that there are no moderates and we're fighting terrorists.
>
> *(Johnson 2014)*

China's strict management over information means Chinese officials are in almost absolute control of how the world interprets conditions in East Turkestan. The Chinese government has not portrayed the situation with the complexity that undeniably exists over prevailing conditions. Incidents reported by the state are habitually characterised as 'terror' related without the means for the outside world to check such claims. To simply explain the recent violence as having been orchestrated from overseas validates failing domestic policies in critical need of reform. As scholar James Millward wrote in a 2014 article for *The New York Times*:

> It is unclear if China's leaders entirely believe their own propaganda—that all Uighur troubles derive from external sources and are unrelated to government policies—but local and regional authorities certainly benefit from it: Whereas common people elsewhere in China enjoy some de facto freedom to protest official and business malfeasance, Uighurs enjoy no such latitude.
>
> *(Millward 2014)*

However, further violence should not be viewed as inevitable, especially among Chinese officials seeking to cast East Turkestan's problems into the 'Global War on Terror'. Loosening curbs on freedom of speech, participatory development planning, sensitive policing, religious tolerance and depoliticised migration policies are all also within the control of the Chinese government and their implementation will ease tensions between Uyghurs, Han Chinese and the state. These are not policies of preference for one ethnicity over another, but policies of inclusion into a state from which Uyghurs feel increasingly estranged.

References

Ananth, K 2011, 'China's Uighur Muslims yearn for liberal Hajj regime', *The Hindu*, viewed 6 July 2016, www.thehindu.com/news/international/article2580392.ece.

BBC News 2014, 'Xinjiang territory profile: Overview—BBC News', viewed 9 March 2016, www.bbc.com/news/world-asia-pacific-16860974.

Bellér-Hann, I 2012, 'Violence in Xinjiang: Indicative of deeper problems?', *East Asia Forum*, viewed 9 March 2016, www.eastasiaforum.org/2012/03/30/violence-in-xinjiang-indicative-of-deeper-problems/.

Bequelin, N 2004, 'Criminalizing ethnicity: Political repression in Xinjiang', *China Rights Forum*, (1), pp. 39–46, viewed 10 March 2016, www.hrichina.org/sites/default/files/PDFs/CRF.1.2004/b1_Criminalizing1.2004.pdf.

Bhattacharji, P 2012, 'Uighurs and China's Xinjiang region', *Council on Foreign Relations*, viewed 9 March 2016, www.cfr.org/china/uighurs-chinas-xinjiang-region/p16870.

Bovingdon, G 2010, *The Uyghurs*, New York: Columbia University Press.

Cao, H 2010, 'Urban–rural income disparity and urbanization: What is the role of spatial distribution of ethnic groups? A case study of Xinjiang Uyghur Autonomous Region in western China', *Regional Studies*, vol. 44, no. 8, pp. 965–982.

Cecc.gov 2005, 'Xinjiang government says ethnic Han Chinese will get 500 of 700 new civil service appointments', Congressional-Executive Commission on China, viewed 9 March 2016, www.cecc.gov/pages/virtualAcad/index.phpd?showsingle=10319.

Cecc.gov 2006, 'Civil servant recruitment in Xinjiang favors Han Chinese', Congressional-Executive Commission on China, viewed 9 March 2016, www.cecc.gov/pages/virtualAcad/index.phpd?showsingle=61191.

Cecc.gov 2009a, 'Recruitment for state jobs in Xinjiang discriminates against ethnic minorities', Congressional-Executive Commission on China, viewed 9 March 2016, www.cecc.gov/publications/commission-analysis/recruitment-for-state-jobs-in-xinjiang-discriminates-against-ethnic.

Cecc.gov 2009b, 'Xinjiang authorities train, seek to regulate Muslim women religious figures', Congressional-Executive Commission on China, viewed 9 March 2016, www.cecc.gov/pages/virtualAcad/index.phpd?showsingle=125102.

Cecc.gov 2009c, 'Governments in Xinjiang continue to sponsor, sanction job recruitment that discriminates against ethnic minorities', Congressional-Executive Commission on China, viewed 9 March 2016, www.cecc.gov/publications/commission-analysis/governments-in-xinjiang-continue-to-sponsor-sanction-job.

Cecc.gov 2009d, 'Demolition of Kashgar's old city draws concerns over cultural heritage protection, population resettlement', Congressional-Executive Commission on China, viewed 9 March 2016, www.cecc.gov/publications/commission-analysis/demolition-of-kashgars-old-city-draws-concerns-over-cultural.

Cecc.gov 2010a, 'Discriminatory job hiring practices continue in Xinjiang', Congressional-Executive Commission on China, viewed 10 March 2016, www.cecc.gov/publications/commission-analysis/discriminatory-job-hiring-practices-continue-in-xinjiang.

Cecc.gov 2010b, 'Chinese media reports on continued demolition in Kashgar, resettlement numbers vary', Congressional-Executive Commission on China, viewed 9 March 2016, www.cecc.gov/publications/commission-analysis/chinese-media-reports-on-continued-demolition-in-kashgar.

Cecc.gov 2013, 'Regional Ethnic Autonomy Law of the People's Republic of China (Chinese and English text)', Congressional-Executive Commission on China, viewed 9 March 2016, www.cecc.gov/resources/legal-provisions/regional-ethnic-autonomy-law-of-the-peoples-republic-of-china-amended.

Chung, C 2002, 'China's "War on Terror": September 11 and Uighur separatism', Council on Foreign Relations, viewed 9 March 2016, www.cfr.org/china/chinas-war-terror-september-11-uighur-separatism/p4765.

Cliff, T 2009, 'Neo oasis: The Xinjiang Bingtuan in the twenty-first century', *Asian Studies Review*, vol. 33, no. 1, pp. 83–106.

Congressional-Executive Commission on China 2011, *Annual Report 2011*, Washington, DC: US Government Printing Office, viewed 9 March 2016, www.cecc.gov/publications/annual-reports/2011-annual-report.

Congressional-Executive Commission on China 2012, *Annual Report 2012*, Washington, DC: US Government Printing Office, viewed 9 March 2016, www.gpo.gov/fdsys/pkg/CHRG-112shrg76190/pdf/CHRG-112shrg76190.pdf.

Dwyer, A 2005, *The Xinjiang Conflict: Uyghur Identity, Language Policy, and Political Discourse*, 1st ed [e-book], Washington, DC: East-West Center, viewed 10 March 2016, www.eastwestcenter.org/fileadmin/stored/pdfs/PS015.pdf.

Dynon, N 2014, 'The language of terrorism in China: Balancing foreign and domestic policy imperatives', *The Jamestown Foundation*, viewed 9 March 2016, www.jamestown.org/single/?tx_ttnews%5Btt_news%5D=41799&no_cache=1#.VEE5yYvF-i4.

English.peopledaily.com.cn 2014, *Xinjiang Doubles Terror Fight Budget—People's Daily Online*, viewed 9 March 2016, http://english.peopledaily.com.cn/90785/8515157.html.

Fan, M 2009, 'An ancient culture, bulldozed away', *Washingtonpost.com*, viewed 9 March 2016, www.washingtonpost.com/wp-dyn/content/article/2009/03/23/AR2009032302935.html.

Grose, T & Leibold, J 2015, 'Why China is banning Islamic Veils', *ChinaFile*, viewed 9 March 2016, www.chinafile.com/reporting-opinion/viewpoint/why-china-banning-islamic-veils.

Haas, B 2015, 'China seeks new wave of migrants for restive Xinjiang', *Yahoo News*, viewed 9 March 2016, http://news.yahoo.com/china-seeks-wave-migrants-restive-xinjiang-022820733.html.

Harrell, S 1996, 'Introduction', in S Harrell (ed.), *Cultural Encounters on China's Ethnic Frontiers*, 1st ed., Seattle, WA: University of Washington Press.

Howell, A & Fan, C 2011, 'Migration and inequality in Xinjiang: A survey of Han and Uyghur migrants in Urumqi', *Eurasian Geography and Economics*, vol. 52, no. 1, pp. 119–139.

Human Rights Watch 2009, *China: Detainees 'Disappeared' after Xinjiang Protests*, viewed 9 March 2016, www.hrw.org/news/2009/10/21/china-detainees-disappeared-after-xinjiang-protests.

Johnson, I 2014, 'They don't want moderate Uighurs', *The New York Review of Books*, viewed 10 March 2016, www.nybooks.com/blogs/nyrblog/2014/sep/22/trial-ilham-tohti-they-dontwant-moderate-uighurs/.

Li, C 2008, 'Ethnic minority elites in China's party-state leadership: An empirical assessment', *China Leadership Monitor*, vol. 25, pp. 1–13.

Liebold, J 2014, 'Xinjiang work forum marks new policy of "ethnic mingling"', *The Jamestown Foundation*, viewed 9 March 2016, www.jamestown.org/regions/chinaasiapacific/single/?tx_ttnews%5Btt_news%5D=42518&tx_ttnews%5BbackPid%5D=52&cHash=e382c60e99ad9bfe6cd7453376dc25a0#.VEE-y4vF-i4.

Millward, J 2007, *Eurasian Crossroads*, New York, Columbia University Press.

Millward, J 2014, 'China's fruitless repression of the Uighurs', *The New York Times*, viewed 10 March 2016, www.nytimes.com/2014/09/29/opinion/chinas-fruitless-repression-of-theuighurs.html?_r=0.

Muldoon, JP 2004, 'The impact of 9/11 on Chinese regional security cooperation', *The Jamestown Foundation*, viewed 10 March 2016, www.jamestown.org/single/?tx_ttnews%5Btt_news%5D=26645&no_cache=1#.VuG8JpMrIo8.

Narramore, T 2012, 'Exercising sovereignty: China's "core interests" and unfinished national unification', the 2012 APSA Annual Conference, Australian Political Studies Association, pp. 855–883, viewed 9 March 2016, www.auspsa.org.au/publications/apsa-conference-2012.

News.xinhuanet.com 2000, *National Minorities Policy and Its Practice in China*, viewed 9 March 2016, http://news.xinhuanet.com/zhengfu/2002-11/18/content_633175.htm.

News.xinhuanet.com 2003, *History and Development of Xinjiang*, viewed 10 March 2016, http://news.xinhuanet.com/zhengfu/2003-06/12/content_916306.htm.

Ohchr.org 2011, *Forced evictions: Adequate housing*, viewed 9 March 2016, www.ohchr.org/EN/Issues/Housing/Pages/ForcedEvictions.aspx.

Phillips, T 2014, 'China plans to fight terror with "dozens" of new cities', *Telegraph.co.uk*, viewed 9 March 2016, www.telegraph.co.uk/news/worldnews/asia/china/11042528/China-plans-to-fight-terror-with-dozens-of-new-cities.html.

Phoenix Weekly 2015, 'Shū fù xiànwěi shūjì: Kàn shénme wèntí dōu cóng mínzú jiǎodù chūfā, shì xīnjiāng zuìdà yǐnhuàn [Shufu county secretary: The biggest danger in Xinjiang is to view every problem that arises from the perspective of ethnicity], viewed 9 March 2016, www.guancha.cn/local/2015_02_01_308223.shtml.

Pomfret, J 2000, 'Go west young Han', *The Washington Post*, viewed 9 March 2016, www.hartford-hwp.com/archives/55/470.html.

Radio Free Asia 2014, 'Uyghur religious leader on hunger strike after fifth jail term', viewed 9 March 2016, www.rfa.org/english/news/uyghur/hunger-04252014152239.html.

Ramzy, A 2014, 'China criticizes U.S. terrorism report', *Sinosphere Blog*, viewed 9 March 2016, http://sinosphere.blogs.nytimes.com/2014/05/02/china-criticizes-u-s-terrorism-report/?_r=0.

State.gov 2015, 'Country reports on human rights practices for 2014', viewed 9 March 2016, www.state.gov/j/drl/rls/hrrpt/humanrightsreport/index.htm#wrapper.

Tang, D 2014, 'Experts skeptical of Kunming link to global terror', *Associated Press*, viewed 10 March 2016, http://bigstory.ap.org/article/experts-skeptical-kunming-link-global-terror.

The Economist 2013, 'Circling the wagons', viewed 9 March 2016, www.economist.com/news/china/21578433-region-plagued-ethnic-strife-growth-immigrant-dominated-settlements-adding.

Toops, S 2004, *Demographics and Development in Xinjiang after 1949*, 1st ed. [ebook], Washington, DC, East-West Center, viewed 9 March 2016, www.eastwestcenter.org/fileadmin/stored/pdfs/EWCWwp001.pdf.

UNESCO 2012, *Articles IMLD 2012 | Education | United Nations Educational, Scientific and Cultural Organization*, viewed 9 March 2016, www.unesco.org/new/en/education/themes/strengthening-education-systems/languages-in-education/international-mother-language-day/articles-imld-2012/.

United Nations 2001, 'Declaration on the right to development', A/RES/41/128, viewed 9 March 2016, www.un.org/documents/ga/res/41/a41r128.htm.

Uyghur Human Rights Project 2007, *Uyghur Language under Attack: The Myth of 'Bilingual' Education in the People's Republic of China*, Washington, DC: Uyghur Human Rights Project, p. 1, viewed 9 March 2016, http://docs.uyghuramerican.org/UyghurLanguageUnderAttack.pdf.

Uyghur Human Rights Project 2010, *Can Anyone Hear Us? Voices from the 2009 Unrest in Urumchi*, Washington, DC: Uyghur Human Rights Project, p. 3, viewed 9 March 2016, http://docs.uyghuramerican.org/Can-Anyone-Hear-Us.pdf.

Uyghur Human Rights Project 2012, *Living on the Margins: The Chinese State's Demolition of Uyghur Communities*, Washington, DC, Uyghur Human Rights Project, viewed 9 March 2016, http://docs.uyghuramerican.org/3-30-Living-on-the-Margins.pdf.

Uyghur Human Rights Project 2013a, *To Strike the Strongest Blow: Questions Remain over Crackdown on 2009 Unrest in Urumchi*, Washington, DC, Uyghur Human Rights Project, p. 4, viewed 9 March 2016, http://docs.uyghuramerican.org/to-strike-the-strongest-blow.pdf.

Uyghur Human Rights Project 2013b, *Sacred Right Defiled: China's Iron-Fisted Repression of Uyghur Religious Freedom*, Washington, DC, Uyghur Human Rights Project, viewed 9 March 2016, http://docs.uyghuramerican.org/Sacred-Right-Defiled-Chinas-Iron-Fisted-Repression-of-Uyghur-Religious-Freedom.pdf.

Uyghur Human Rights Project 2014, *China Attempts to Criminalize Every Aspect of Uyghur Religious Belief and Practice*, Washington, DC, Uyghur Human Rights Project, viewed 9 March 2016, http://docs.uyghuramerican.org/5-8-14_Briefing-Religious_Restrictions.pdf.

Uyghur Human Rights Project 2016, *China's New Counter-Terrorism Law and Its Human Rights Implications for the Uyghur People*, Washington, DC, Uyghur Human Rights Project, viewed 6 July 2016, http://uhrp.org/press-release/briefing-chinas-new-counter-terrorism-law-and-its-human-rights-implications-uyghur.

Volodzko, D 2014, 'The economics of the Kunming massacre', *East by Southeast*, viewed 9 March 2016, www.eastbysoutheast.com/tag/bingtuan/.

Wiemer, C 2004, 'The economy of Xinjiang', in S Starr (ed.), *Xinjiang: China's Muslim Borderland*, 1st ed., New York, M.E. Sharpe.

Wines, M 2009, 'To protect an ancient city, China moves to raze it', *Nytimes.com*, viewed 9 March 2016, www.nytimes.com/2009/05/28/world/asia/28kashgar.html?pagewanted=all&_r=0.
Xinjiang Review 2011, 'The Xinjiang production and construction corps: China's East Turkistan company, viewed 9 March 2016, https://xinjiangreview.wordpress.com/2011/02/28/xinjiang-production-and-construction-corps-china's-east-turkistan-company/.
Xinjiang Uygur Autonomous Region Statistical Bureau 2013, *Statistical Yearbook of Xinjiang 2013*, Urumqi: China Statistical Publishing House.
Yang, I 2010, 'Violence, ethnicity and economics: Can the government spend its way towards ethnic peace in Xinjiang? Evidence from official data', Unpublished paper, Hong Kong University of Science and Technology.

7

The politics of human rights in Myanmar

Naing Ko Ko[1]

Introduction

Myanmar's[2] historical legacy is one of the world's worst human rights records. Systemic human rights violations, including arbitrary arrests, forced labour,[3] recruitment and enlistment of child soldiers, imprisonment of political opponents, extrajudicial killings, torture, rape, war crimes, land confiscation, ethnic cleansing and discrimination against minorities were widespread up until the political transition that began under President Thein Sein in 2011, and many of these problems persist to the present.

Myanmar's path to the current democratically elected government, that took office in 2016, was initiated by the student-led people's demonstrations that occurred between the 1970s and 1980s. In the most famous of these uprisings, millions of Burmese protested on 8 August 1988, demanding an end to the military-dominated political and economic system and the re-establishment of democracy, human rights and social justice in the country: this became known as the '8888' movement. During the months of August and September in 1988, a power vacuum was created within state mechanisms because the government of the day, the Burmese Social Program Party (BSPP), was unable to govern effectively due to the nationwide demonstrations. Those demonstrations in support of democracy included participation by the state's public servants, including the police force, the air force, the navy and a few army officials who were involved in the movement. However, the movement faltered due to lack of internal leadership and the military adopted a 'shoot first' policy, resulting in the second generation of military generals[4] taking power in a coup d'état on 18 September 1988.

After the failure of the 8888 movement, Myanmar was ruled by military elites for 25 years. There were many political opportunities during that period that should have led to the establishment of human rights norms and a society that enjoyed rule of law, including the 8888-democracy uprising, the 1990 multiparty elections,[5] the short-lived Committee Representative People Parliament (CRPP)[6] and the military-designed Seven-Points-Road-Map[7] to a disciplined democracy. However, none of these initiatives bore fruit; as a consequence, the adoption of universal human rights norms, and democratic values and practices in Myanmar remains incomplete.

This chapter investigates the politics of human rights in Myanmar, with an emphasis on the years between 1988 and 2011, and a coda for the period 2016 to 2017. I look at human rights in Myanmar through the theoretical framework developed by Gramsci (1971) and elaborated by Cox (1981), in order to identify 'hegemonic' and 'counter-hegemonic' agents within Myanmar that have framed political culture and discourse. In the Burmese context, the military and their business cronies are the hegemonic actors and human rights and democracy activists of Myanmar are counter-hegemonic forces and social entrepreneurs. I also note the involvement of transnational non-state actors in Western democracies that have contributed to shaping Myanmar's political development.

This chapter first seeks to apply the Gramscian approach to Myanmar. Second, it describes how Burmese human rights and democracy activists tried to shape the political landscape of Myanmar during the military regime years to 2011. Third, it examines the policy impact of their actions. Finally, the chapter concludes with the current norms and practices of human rights in Myanmar and a coda about how these are faring under the new National League for Democracy (NLD)-led government.

Human rights in Myanmar through a Gramscian lens

> Structures and superstructures form an 'historic bloc'. That is to say the complex contradictory and discordant ensemble of the superstructure is the reflection of the ensemble of the social relations of production.
>
> *(Gramsci 1971: 366)*

Since the fall of the Berlin Wall in 1989, the Gramscian concept of non-state actors, such as global civil society, transnational advocacy networks, transnational social movements and international non-governmental organisations, has become widely accepted. Within Anglo-American international relations scholarship, the promises and idealisation of the Gramscian non-state actor are contested. However, as an empirical matter, Burmese non-state actors have framed various aspects of human rights policy and processes in Myanmar in recent years and continue to challenge the military's sovereignty there.

Cox (1981: 138) would explain this process as occurring on three levels (shown below in Figure 7.1):

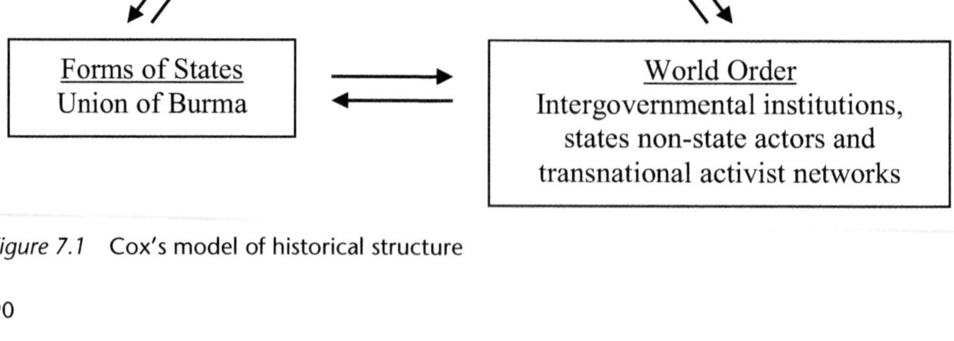

Figure 7.1 Cox's model of historical structure

1 the organisation of production, more particularly with regard to the *social forces* engendered by the production process;
2 *forms of state* as derived from a study of state/society complexes; and
3 *world orders*, i.e. the uses of armed force, which define the problematic war or peace for the ensemble of states.

In the Myanmar context, we can think of human rights activists of Myanmar as the first level, *social forces*. After the 8888 uprising,[8] approximately 3,000 people died and an estimated 30,000 people escaped to the borders that ethnic armed forces controlled. In 1989, in the border areas, some students who wanted to carry out an armed struggle against the military, set up the All Burma Student Democratic Front (ABSDF). Inside the country, organisations such as the All Burma Federation of Student Unions (ABFSU) and the National League for Democracy (NLD) followed Daw Aung San Suu Kyi's non-violent approach for challenging gross human rights violations and promoting democracy. These human rights and democracy activists united against the military's hegemony from both within and outside the country.

Many of these Burmese activists were exiled and many of them resettled as political refugees in high-wage countries. Some of them turned themselves into non-state actors and joined with transnational advocacy networks to continue the struggle against the military's hegemony over their birthplace. After that, as *social entrepreneurs*, these actors testified in relation to their treatment in the prisons, their experiences of atrocities by the authorities, and crimes against humanity at the parliaments, congresses and senates of liberal democracies and in the forums of multilateral institutions. These expatriates and stateless activists became the pressure forces against the Burmese military and their cronies, in particular at international labour and trade conferences. By using a naming-and-shaming strategy, Burmese democracy activists particularly targeted economic sanctions, trade and arms embargos against the military elites of Myanmar.

At the *forms of state* level in Cox's model (see Figure 7.1), global investors and business elites such as multinationals Unocal and Total, invested jointly in military-owned and controlled production in Myanmar. Financial revenue and expenditure of the military derived from resource extraction with the help of multinational companies and foreign direct investment, while donations from global civil society underpinned human rights activists. The United States National Endowment for Democracy (NED) and its affiliates funded border-based human rights organisations.

Nonetheless, the military succeeded in securing its state hegemony because there were no demarcation lines between state, society and market forces. Law and regulations were made by the generals, not by elected civilians and not via a democratic process. The military monopolised the economy, while cronies exploited the country's resources. During the dark-ages of militarism in Myanmar (1988–2011), there were limited options for those seeking economic advancement: (a) work in business with the generals; or (b) be marginalised by the generals; or (c) escape to refugee camps or neighbouring countries. Thus, students and workers-turned-human rights activists who chose the third path emerged as counter-hegemonic social entrepreneurs for democracy, rule of law and human rights.

The third level of Cox's model (see Figure 7.1), the *world order*, has changed significantly in South East Asia in the twenty-first century. While ASEAN countries were debating 'constructive vs. flexible' engagement with Myanmar, the northern hemisphere countries adopted diplomatic and economic sanctions against the Burmese generals and their cronies. Although gross human rights violations by Myanmar's neighbouring countries, such as Vietnam and Cambodia, share some historic similarities to the Myanmar case, Myanmar was the only country in ASEAN where the West imposed economic sanctions against its leadership. Hundreds of military generals and their cronies were listed as Specially Designated Nationals[9] (SDN) by the law enforcement agencies of the United States of America, which had the practical effect of restricting their ability to do business with the United States or with American corporations or individuals. One consequence of the West's economic sanctions against the military elites was that Myanmar's economy remained fairly closed—seen in the lack of market competition, and the underdeveloped production mechanisms that characterise Myanmar today. Business elites in Asian countries that did not impose sanctions, such as Singapore, Thailand, China and Korea, have enjoyed much greater access to the Myanmar economy, with no pressure to apply or uphold human rights norms, corporate social responsibility, business ethics, corporate governance standards and integrity and anticorruption measures in their businesses.

The lack of job creation in Myanmar, historically and at present, means that millions of undocumented Burmese workers have migrated to (and continue to migrate to) neighbouring economies for economic survival reasons. Despite winning the 2015 general election, the National League for Democracy government has a fragile grip on political power and has been unable, legally and structurally, to significantly move the military and business cronies out of control of the state and economy.

In the pre-transition period, at the level of international institutions, the most practical, robust global pressures came from the International Labour Organization (ILO), the United States,[10] particularly through the Burmese Freedom and Democracy Act (2003) and the Tom Lantos' Junta's Anti-Democratic Efforts Act (2008) and the European Union Common Position on Burma/Myanmar that was adopted in 1996, which also imposed an arms embargo, a widespread visa ban and suspension of humanitarian assistance. Without those convincing international policy actions and tough pressure, the military would not have embarked on its 2011 dialogue with Daw Aung San Suu Kyi as the leader of the National League for Democracy, and with leaders of the ethnic armed forces.

How did activists seek to shape the Burmese political landscape?

After brief periods of Westminster-style democracy in Myanmar during 1948–1958 and 1960–1962, the country reverted to military dictatorship for half a century. From 1962 to 2011, there was no independent civil society, no political liberty, no rule of law, and no independent social, legal, political and economic institutions and entities operating freely within the country. Gramsci conceptualises state and civil society as separate: the state as a legal, political, administrative entity and the civil society as family, friends and individual spheres (Hoare & Nowell Smith 1999: 445–450). True (2003: 131) adds that 'it is the space lying between the public realm of the state and the private realm of the family'. In Myanmar, until very recently, we have had very little separation between the state and society—the military *was* the state, with decision and policy-making power coming from the generals, not from the elected individuals and civilians. That situation remains entrenched in the 2008 Constitution (Art. 436, sect. a), where the military reserves for itself the final decision-making power.

The challenge for human rights activists in Myanmar has been how to occupy and then expand the space that would usually belong to civil society. Figure 7.2 shows how these activists framed the politics of human rights in Myanmar up until 2011. This happened through three major policy-making processes or strategies. First, Burmese activists/social entrepreneurs provided training for their members in human rights, trade union rights, child rights, women's rights, media engagement and environmental issues at the border towns of Thailand, China and India. These trained activists then went back to the country to collect raw data about human rights violations, such as cases of forced labour, land grabbing, torture and civil rights violations by the authorities. They also documented lists of political prisoners and their condition in the

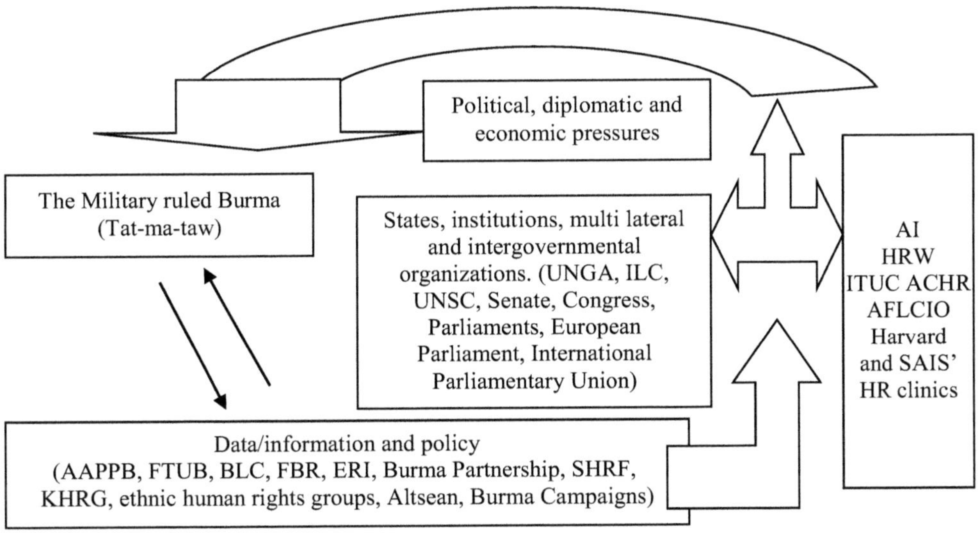

Figure 7.2 Framing and mobilising for human rights in Myanmar

prisons and collected facts and figures about multinational corporations that had invested in business with the military and its cronies.

Second, the raw data collected in different ethnic languages was translated into English and edited by transnational human rights researchers in order to get robust evidence on the violations of international human rights treaties and norms. When human rights reports and position papers were finalised, human rights activists in Myanmar dispatched them on an 'under embargo' or 'strictly confidential' basis to transnational human rights networks and the human rights researchers for consultation, before launching their campaigns.

Finally, after those consultations, a specific time and targeted cities were defined for launching the human rights reports. Campaigns were initiated in partnership with Myanmar issues-oriented organisations, such as Burma Partnership, Equality Myanmar, Burma Campaign United Kingdom, the United States Campaigns for Burma, Earth Rights International, Burma Campaign New Zealand, Burma Campaign Australia, Christian Solidarity Worldwide and Altsean (see Figure 7.2).

Human rights organisations linked to Myanmar also pursued pressure on democratic governments such as the United Kingdom, the United States, Australia and New Zealand, and members of the EU and ASEAN, as well as the UN Security Council and the ILO. None of the activists in exile sought personal revenge: the highest policy demand of these Myanmar civil society actors was national reconciliation and political dialogue, not regime change.

The domestic human rights activists in Myanmar shown in Figure 7.2 provided humanitarian services, such as assisting families of political prisoners to visit their loved ones, supporting political prisoners by providing necessities such as food and medicine, and monitoring conditions in prisons. Internationally, former political prisoners from Myanmar and transnational non-state actors testified about their interrogation, torture experiences and solitary confinement by the military personnel and prison wardens. Numerous 'Burma campaign' groups and issues-oriented organisations combined with transnational advocacy networks to carry out their respective grass-roots actions, lobby tours, parliamentary testimony and hearings, and a global action day for Burma (Myanmar).

Finally, as part of these campaigns, key human rights documents were invoked: Table 7.1 shows some of the international human rights treaties and conventions that have been utilised by activists of Myanmar over the past 25 years. These nascent civil society groups established

Table 7.1 Human rights treaties and conventions used by Myanmar civil society advocates

No.	*Name of organisation*	*Names of human rights treaties and conventions*	*SLORC/SPDC*
1	Assistant Association of Political Prisoners	Freedom of Association and Protection of the Right to Organise Convention Convention Against Torture and other cruel, inhuman and degrading treatment or punishment (1984)	Ratified 1955 UNTC has not been ratified yet.
2	Burma Partnership	The UN Charter Convention on the Prevention and Punishment of the Crime of Genocide Rome Statute of the International Criminal Court International Covenant on Civil and Political Rights	Ratified 1956
3	Earth Rights International	The Alien Tort Claims Act (1789) Corporate Social Responsibility	Even though ATC (1978) is not an HR convention, it was utilised by the Burmese Human Rights movements, in particular, ERI and FTU-B.
4	Free Burma Coalition	Corporate Social Responsibility	
5	Federation of Trade Unions-Burma	Forced Labour Convention, 1930 (No. 29) Freedom of Association and Protection of the Right to Organise Convention, 1948 (No. 87)	Ratified 1955
6	Women's League of Burma	Convention on the Elimination of All forms of Discrimination against Woman (1979) Convention on the Prevention and Punishment of the Crime of Genocide Rome Statute of the International Criminal Court	Accessed 1997
7	Karen Human Rights Group	Convention on the Prohibition of the Use, Stockpiling, Production and Transfer of Anti-Personnel Mines and on Their Destruction (Mine Ban Convention, 1997)	Ratified 1956
8	Shan, Chin, Rakhine, Kachin, Karanni, Mon, Human Rights Groups	International Covenant on Civil and Political Rights Convention on the Prevention and Punishment of the Crime of Genocide Rome Statute of the International Criminal Court	
9	Equality Myanmar	International Covenant on Civil and Political Rights Convention on the Rights of the Child	ICCPR has not been ratified. Ratified 1997

issues-based organisations in the border areas and advocated for international labour and human rights and norms such as those within the Forced Labour Convention 1930 (No. 29) and Freedom of Association and Protection of the Right to Organise Convention 1948 (No. 87). These were particularly championed by the Federation of Trade Unions Burma (FTUB), with gender mainstreaming and women's rights emphasised by the Women's League of Burma (WLB), which is an umbrella organisation comprising 12 pre-existing women's organisations representing different ethnic nationalities.

The Burma Lawyers' Council (BLC) provided legal services and advocacy. Earth Rights International (ERI) focused on policy issues of environmental and corporate social responsibility. The All Burma Federation of Student Unions (Foreign Affairs Committee) and the Assistance Association for Political Prisoners (AAPP) advocated for the implementation of the Freedom of Association and Protection of the Right to Organise Convention, and Convention Against Torture and other cruel, inhuman and degrading treatment or punishment. The Democratic Voices of Burma (DVB), Mizzima News and the Irrawaddy formed a media organisation, standing for freedom of speech and of the press. All of these social groups within, and connected to, Myanmar targeted the UN mechanisms, and in particular, the UN Chapter VII of the Convention on the Prevention and Punishment of the Crime of Genocide and the Rome Statute of the International Criminal Court.

A labour rights case study

Myanmar's emerging civil society actors and advocates benefitted greatly from their links with transnational actors. Forced labour issues show how this was accomplished. The practice of forced labour had been a routine element in business undertaking by the military and its cronies for many decades. Since the 1990s, the Federation of Trade Unions - Burma (FTUB) reported the violation of forced labour by the military and its commercial businesses at the International Labour Conference (ILC), via the International Confederation of Trade Unions (ICFTU). After analysing the complaints and reports of the ICFTU for many years at the ILC, the governing body of the ILO established a Committee of Inquiry in 1996 and a very High Level Team (vHLT) in 2004 for investigating the use of forced labour in Burma. The intent was to pressure the Myanmar government to scrap the legal authority it used for the use of forced labour, to order all government authorities to cease using it, and to prosecute those responsible, especially military personnel.

In 1998, the ILO Committee of Inquiry found:

> a saga of untold misery and suffering, oppression and exploitation of large sections of the population inhabiting Myanmar by the Government, military, and other public officers. It is a story of gross denial of human rights to which the people of Myanmar have been subjected particularly since 1988 and from which they find no escape except fleeing the country.
>
> *(ILO 1998)*

So, we see here a significant point of intersection between forms of the state and the world order. The ILO approved a special resolution adopted by the Conference in June 2000, under Article (33) of the ILO Constitution. It was the first time in the ILO's 96-year history that the Conference had recourse to measures under Article (33), a procedure that was designed to be invoked only in the event of a country failing to carry out the recommendations of an ILO Committee of Inquiry, which is itself a procedure reserved for grave and persistent violations of international labour standards.

Civil society actors in Myanmar had shifted the advocacy to the international institutional forum due to the lack of an independent judiciary in Myanmar and the lack of rule of law.

In 2003, the National Council of the Union of Burma (NCUB)[11] advocated for the intervention of the United Nations Security Council (UNSC), and released a report, 'Time for UN intervention in Burma/Myanmar' by referring the UNSC Article (VII) to the International Criminal Court (ICC).

In 2008, Amnesty International (AI) documented: 'official impunity for serious human rights violations, including war crimes and crimes against humanity during the 2006–2008 military offensive in Karen State and asserted that the Myanmar army violated the Geneva Conventions of 1949' (AI 2008).

In 2008, the International Crisis Group (ICG) recommended to like-minded countries in the Western democracies (including Japan) that the mechanism of human rights be deployed to push for change in Myanmar:

While allowing the UN and regional governments to take the diplomatic lead, work was underway to establish an international environment conducive to their success, including by:

a maintaining focus on key human rights issues in all relevant forums, including the Security Council, and by supporting active engagement and access to Myanmar by the Special Rapporteur and other representatives of the relevant thematic human rights mechanisms;
b preparing and structuring a series of escalating targeted sanctions, focusing on:
   i restrictions on access by military, state and crony enterprises to international banking services;
   ii limiting access of selected generals and their immediate families to personal business opportunities, health care, shopping, and foreign education for their children; as well as
   iii a universal arms embargo; and
c offering incentives for reform in order to balance the threat and/or imposition of sanctions and give the military leadership positive motivation for change (ICG 2008).

In 2010, the United Nations' Special Rapporteur on the situation of human rights in Myanmar, Tomas Ojea Quintana, reported:

> there is a pattern of gross and systematic violations of human rights which has been in place for many years and still continues. Given the extent and persistence of the problem, and the lack of accountability, there is an indication that those human rights violations are the result of a State policy, originating from decisions by authorities in the executive, military and judiciary at all levels.

The Special Rapporteur called on the United Nations to consider the possibility of establishing a Commission of Inquiry into crimes in violation of international law committed in Myanmar. In 2011, Human Rights Watch called on:

> relevant UN bodies to establish a Commission of Inquiry to investigate reports of violations of international human rights and humanitarian law in Burma by all parties, and to identify the perpetrators of such violations with a view to ensuring that those responsible are held accountable.
>
> *(HRW 2011)*

In 2012, Amnesty International also found 'most political prisoners in Myanmar have been sentenced under laws that place the country well outside of international norms and standards on the freedoms of expression, peaceful assembly and association' (AI 2012).

In 2014, the International Human Rights Clinic of Harvard Law School that focuses on 'indiscriminate attacks and wilful killings of civilians in Myanmar' discovered that:

> based on evidence gathered during its investigation, the Clinic has concluded that Myanmar Army personnel from Southern Command and Light Infantry Division 66 committed crimes against humanity and war crimes, as defined by Articles 7 and 8, respectively, of the Rome Statute of the International Criminal Court.
>
> *(IHRC 2014)*

When intergovernmental institutions and global civil society actually imposed diplomatic and economic pressure, and showed themselves ready to take action for crimes against humanity, the military was faced with limited options. On some readings of these events, the military had to open the door to international engagement and at least pay lip service to human rights. The generals did this largely by maintaining the status quo, so that, rather than sharing power and resources with civilian citizens, they swapped their uniforms for civilian clothes and adjusted democracy and human rights norms in ways that would not threaten their grip on political and economic power. We see this in the 2008 Constitution and the sham election of 2010, which was boycotted by the opposition National League for Democracy.

At the same time, the generals ratified several international agreements including the Convention on the Elimination of All Forms of Discrimination Against Women in 1997, Convention on the Rights of the Child in 1997 and the ILO's recommendations on 'an ILO liaison officer' for monitoring labour rights in the country. Due to global civil society pressures, the Thein Sein administration—a nominally civilian government—also implemented a second wave of economic liberalisation and macroeconomic reforms from 2011.[12]

The culmination of the internal and external pressure for political transition ultimately led to the 2015 general election, which was contested and resoundingly won by the National League of Democracy and which saw Daw Aung San Suu Kyi become de facto political leader of the country.

Human rights norms in Myanmar today

With the transition to the civilian National League for Democracy government that took office in 2016, hopes were raised within and outside Myanmar that the country will quickly embrace human rights and start to transform its dark record as a repressive state.

Those hopes have diminished in the face of slow progress, particularly on justice and security sector reforms. Daw Aung San Suu Kyi has also been criticised domestically and internationally for her failure to take leadership on the pressing issue of the treatment of the Rohingya minority and to address state complicity in human rights abuses in Rakhine State.

To date Myanmar has not ratified some human rights treaties and conventions such as the Convention against Torture and Other Cruel, Inhuman or Degrading Treatment or Punishment (CAT), the International Covenant on Civil and Political Rights (ICCPR) and the International Covenant on Economic, Social and Cultural Rights (ICESCR). But clearly the form and shape of U Thein Sein's 2011 reforms and the political changes that followed were influenced by the liberal world order.

We can identify at least three barriers to swift adoption of universal rights norms in Myanmar, even under a new government. The first of these is normative path dependence among justice and security elites. Cheesman's (2015) path-breaking study of authoritarian attitudes to law in Myanmar shows that 'rule by law' has been the norm in modern Myanmar and that 'law and order' is a much higher value for most agents of the government than rule of law values such as equality before the law or access to justice. The military and the police have been accustomed to acting with impunity. Coupled with risk aversion among bureaucrats who were historically punished for taking the initiative, new concepts such as human rights must compete with these powerful default attitudes.

Structurally the new government is hampered by the division of real political power enshrined in the 2008 Constitution which reserves places for the military in the government. The civilian government does not have jurisdiction over home affairs (including policing), security, border affairs or defence. In practical terms, this means that it controls neither the police nor the military. This then flows into the administrative machinery. The Thein Sein administration, for example, set up the Myanmar National Human Rights Commission (NHRC) in 2011, with technical assistance from some international human rights groups. But, the commission has not addressed ongoing human rights violations in the country, in particular, discrimination against minority ethnic groups. Nor is it likely to tackle what has been a coordinated campaign of violence against Rohingya people, particularly in Rakhine State, complicated by the fact that local retaliation has targeted the military and the police.

A third issue is a complex mix of ethnic and religious intolerance of the kind that flourishes in conditions of instability. It is implicated in—but not limited to—the 'Rohingya issue' and it has deep historical roots. The Rohingya are Muslims who live predominantly but not exclusively in the poorest state in Myanmar, Rakhine (formerly known as Arakan). There are conflicting origin stories. According to the Rohingyas and some scholars, they are indigenous to Rakhine State; while other historians claim that the group represents a mixture of precolonial and colonial immigrations. The official stance of the Myanmar government, past and present, has been that the Rohingyas are illegal immigrants who arrived following Burmese independence in 1948 or after the Bangladesh liberation war in 1971. Those who subscribe to this view deny the existence of 'Rohingya' and call them 'Bengali'. A real consequence is that Rohingya are, for the most part, denied citizenship and the rights that flow from this. Regardless of which view of their origins you take, the human rights abuses against this group are irrefutable.

State repression of this group began with the first-generation generals led by General Ne Win, who carried out a number of military operations in (then) Arakan State in the 1970s. An early violation was documented by Amnesty International in 1992 when 250,000 Rohingya refugees escaped to Bangladesh. The 'Rohingya crisis' escalated under U Thein Sein's administration, and the opening up of Myanmar meant that this issue became much more visible to the international community. A leading Burmese scholar, Maung Zarni, has argued that 'since 1978, the Rohingya, a Muslim minority of Western Burma, have been subject to a state-sponsored process of destruction' (Zarni & Cowley 2014). A Human Rights Watch (2013) report argues that 'The criminal acts committed against the Rohingya and Kaman Muslim communities in Arakan State beginning in June 2012 amount to crimes against humanity carried out as part of a campaign of ethnic cleansing'. A number of legal scholars have asked 'Is genocide occurring in Myanmar's Rakhine State?' (Lowenstein et al. 2015). The real situation on the ground is undoubtedly more complex than these claims suggest. But determining that is difficult because Rakhine State remains closed to most international visitors and the Myanmar government has declined to cooperate with UN efforts to investigate human rights abuses in Rakhine, most recently through the UN Human Rights Council's appointment of three independent legal experts and rights advocates to carry out a fact-finding mission. Instead, the government has opted for a domestic inquiry, chaired by the vice-president and former general, U Myint Swe. From her position as state counsellor, Daw Aung San Suu Kyi has little formal authority to countermand this move.

Notwithstanding the acute problem of the Rohingya, the gradual embrace of international rights law has been a significant shift in Myanmar, after more than five decades in which political and social development was deadlocked. Freedom of expression and freedom of assembly have been reinstated, although memories of the 2012 crackdown on the media arrests of journalists are still fresh memories. U Thein Sein's suspension of a dam construction project in 2011 due to public concern was also considered a significant change, as this was the first time in Myanmar's modern history that the president or the head of state had listened to the people's concerns.

The problem for the former activist supporters of the new government, however, is that the human rights advances in Myanmar threaten to be completely overshadowed by government determination to treat the Rohingya issue as 'a domestic matter'—which will ensure that it remains an international concern. The plight of the Rohingya are discussed in further detail throughout this volume.

Conclusion

Myanmar in 2017 is a distillation of 'transition'. The path towards full democracy and the full implementation of human rights in Myanmar is neither straight nor short. No military dictators have ever respected or willingly established universal human rights, rule of law or democratic principles, and certainly not in Myanmar. And yet U Thein Sein did consent to elections in which the opposition won government in 2015, albeit with a structurally constrained jurisdiction. Unlike the transition to civilian rule in Indonesia following the fall of Soeharto in 1998, the Burmese generals have not relinquished control over the economy, domestic affairs and security. This makes them major gatekeepers to the substantive implementation of human rights norms in Myanmar.

The challenge for political elites in Myanmar is how to civilise its armed forces and politically, how to install civilian oversight of Myanmar's military. What we can see from the 2000s onwards, however, is that advocacy by civil society within and outside Myanmar has been effective in drawing the generals into dialogue, internally with Daw Aung San Suu Kyi and other ethnic armed forces and externally with transnational actors who are promoters and influencers of normative change.

Notes

1 PhD scholar at Regulatory Institutions Networks, College of Asia and the Pacific, Australian National University (ANU): naing.ko@anu.edu.au. My thanks to Professor Veronica Taylor (ANU) for advice on the content and editing of this chapter; all errors are my own.

2 I prefer the formulation Burma to describe my country, but in this chapter I use Myanmar, which was adopted widely after the ruling military junta changed the country's name from Burma to Myanmar in 1989, a year after the 1988 popular uprising. Rangoon also became Yangon at the same time.

3 The Forced Labour Convention, 1930 (No. 29) was adopted by the International Labour Organization (ILO) on 1 May 1932 and Burma is a party to the convention and ratified it in 1955.

4 The first generation of military generals led by General Ne Win overthrew the elected U Nu government on 2 March 1962.

5 The 1990 multi-party general election was held on 27 May 1990 and the National League for Democracy won 392 out 492 seats; however, the result was not honoured by the second-generation military-led regime.

6 The Committee Representative People Parliament (CRPP) was formed on 16 September 1998 and was dissolved by the military.

7 A former Prime Minister, Lt. Gen. Khin Nyunt announced this on 30 August 2003 in the state media.

8 After killing 3,000 civilians in the democracy uprising, the military generals claimed themselves as State Law and Order Restoration Council (SLORC) on 18 September 1988, and changed into the State Peace and Development Council (SPDC) in November 1997.
9 See more on the Burmese SDN list at www.treasury.gov/resource-center/sanctions/SDN-List/Pages/default.aspx.
10 The US has also adopted an additional five executive orders against the generals of Burma, including EO 13047, EO 13310, EO 13448, EO 13464 and EO 13651.
11 NCUB was established on 22 September 1992, and comprises 22 democracy and human rights organisations.
12 The first liberalisation reforms were implemented in 1989, but the results were limited.

References

Amnesty International 1992, *Union of Myanmar (Burma): Human Rights Violations against Muslims in the Rakhine (Arakan) State*, ASA16/06/92.

Amnesty International 1997, *Myanmar/Bangladesh, Rohingyas: The Search for Safety*, ASA 13/07/97, www.amnesty.org/en/documents/asa13/007/1997/en/.

Amnesty International 2008, *Crimes against Humanity in Eastern Burma*, London, ASA 16/011/2008, www.amnesty.org/en/documents/ASA16/011/2008/en/.

Amnesty International USA 2012, 'Ensuring U.S. Businesses Respect Human Rights in Myanmar (Burma)', www.amnestyusa.org/pdfs/EnsuringUSBusinessesRespectHumanRightsInMyanmar.pdf.

Cheesman, N 2015, *Opposing the Rule of Law: How Myanmar's Courts Make Law and Order*, Cambridge: Cambridge University Press.

Cox, RW 1981, 'Social Forces, States and World Orders: Beyond International Relations Theory', *Millennium: Journal of International Studies*, vol. 10, no. 2, pp. 126–155.

Gramsci, A 1971, *Selections from the Prison Notebooks*, translated and edited by Quintin Hoare and Geoffrey Nowell Smith, New York: International Publishers.

Hoare, Q & Nowell Smith, G 1999, *Selections from the Prison Notebooks of Antonio Gramsci*, London: Elecbook.

Human Rights Watch 2011, *Burma: Q & A on an International Commission of Inquiry*, New York.

Human Rights Watch 2013, *'All You Can Do Is Pray': Crimes against Humanity and Ethnic Cleansing of Rohingya Muslims in Burma's Arakan State*, New York.

International Crisis Group 2008, 'Burma/Myanmar: After the Crackdown', *Asia Report*, no. 144, www.crisisgroup.org/asia/south-east-asia/myanmar/burmamyanmar-after-crackdown.

International Human Rights Clinic (IHRC) 2014, *Legal Memorandum: War Crimes and Crimes against Humanity in Eastern Myanmar*, November, Cambridge, MA: Harvard Law School.

International Labour Organization 1998, *Forced Labour in Myanmar (Burma)*, Report of the Commission of Inquiry appointed under Article 26 of the Constitution of International Labour Organization to examine the observance by Myanmar of the Forced Labour Convention, 1930 (No. 29), Geneva.

Lowenstein, AK, International Human Rights Clinic & Yale Law School 2015, *Persecution of the Rohingya Muslims: Is Genocide Occurring in Myanmar's Rakhine State? A Legal Analysis*, Fortify Rights, www.fortifyrights.org/downloads/Yale_Persecution_of_the_Rohingya_October_2015.pdf.

True, J 2003, *Gender Globalization and Postsocialism: The Czech Republic after Communism, Importing Civil Society*, New York: Columbia University Press.

Zarni, M & Cowley, A 2014, 'The Slow-Burning Genocide of Myanmar's Rohingya', *Pacific Rim Law & Policy Journal Association*, vol. 23, no. 3, pp. 683–754.

8

An architecture of exclusion

Palestinian Arab citizens of Israel

Kathleen A. Cavanaugh

Introduction

Palestinian citizens of Israel experience an architecture of exclusion that is deeply embedded within the socio-legal framework in Israel. Although separated from Palestinians living in the West Bank and Gaza, Palestinian citizens of Israel remain inextricably connected to the conflicts (Israeli–Arab as well as Israeli–Palestinian) that characterise this region. At the same time, this physical separation creates a double minority status for Israeli Arabs—they are a minority within Israel but also, politically and socially, a minority within the larger Palestinian community. This has created a 'lived' experience for Israeli Arabs that is both tied to *and* distinct from the larger political struggle.

Events such as the first and second *intifada* (uprising), the failure of the Oslo Peace Accords (and other endeavours) to deliver a sustainable road map to peace, as well as the uninterrupted expansion of Jewish settlements in the West Bank and East Jerusalem have underpinned the political mobilisation of the Palestinian community in Israel and created a security narrative which maps relations between Israeli Arabs and Jews onto the wider Palestinian struggle. Yet the experience of Palestinians living within Israel is also distinct in a number of important ways. For one, a resolve of the wider Palestinian question of statehood does not address the situation of Palestinians living within Israel. Second, and more immediately, the marginalisation (and indeed exclusion) from civil and political life in Israel is constructed through a complex series of legal measures that are quite specific to Israeli Arabs. Against this backdrop, this chapter will examine the status of Palestinian citizens of Israel by looking at the legal measures which regulate their engagement in the civil and political sphere. Although Israel has argued a security basis for restrictions placed on its Arab population, I suggest a more complex underpinning; one in which race continues to define the concept of citizen in Israel—who is included and excluded from socio-economic and political decision-making institutions.

A meta-conflict

The Israeli–Palestine conflict is a 'meta-conflict'; it is both a protracted conflict between two peoples and a conflict about the nature of the conflict itself. Whilst the political and legal situation that has unfolded in Israel and the Occupied Territories is complex and extends beyond the remit of this chapter, some mapping of the political and legal geography is useful. As part of the 1949 armistice agreements, which marked the end of the 1948 Arab–Israeli war, Israel and neighbouring Egypt, Lebanon, Jordan, and Syria, established armistice demarcation lines (often referred to as the 'Green line'), that divided the new Jewish state of Israel from other parts of Mandate Palestine. The West Bank and the Gaza Strip became distinct political units. From 1948 to 1967, Palestinians living in the West Bank, including East Jerusalem were governed by Jordan, and were extended citizenship. During this same period, Palestinians living in the Gaza Strip fell under Egyptian military administration.

Since the 1967 war, when Israel captured and occupied West Bank and Gaza and annexed East Jerusalem, Palestinians have been subject to Israeli rule that has been jurisdictionally divided into three areas, each of which has a distinct legal status. The first is the sovereign territory of Israel, located within the 1949 armistice or 'Green line'. The second consists of those units/parts of the Occupied Territories, which have been *de facto* annexed (e.g. East Jerusalem, confiscated lands, Jewish settlements and military installations). Finally, there is the Israeli military administration that was established to govern Palestinians in the West Bank and Gaza. In 2005, Israel 'withdrew' from the Gaza strip and, since August 2005, the military legal administration (which includes the military courts) *only* applies to citizens of the West Bank.

Although Palestinians who remained within the 'Green line' (hereafter referred to as Palestinian Arab citizens of Israel)[1] were physically separated from Palestinians living in the West Bank and Gaza, Israeli–Palestinian and Israeli–Arab conflicts that would come to characterise this region had a profound effect on relations between Palestinian Arab citizens of Israel and Jews. The 1967 war, the first *intifada* (uprising) from 1987 to 1991, the failure of the Oslo Peace Accords to deliver a sustainable road map to peace, the murder of Israeli prime minister, Yitzhak Rabin, in 1995, and the beginning of a new chapter of Palestinian resistance in 2000 as well as the uninterrupted expansion of Jewish settlements in the West Bank, Gaza Strip and East Jerusalem ensured that those writing on the 'intractability' of the conflict would not be proved wrong. The decision by Israel to construct a separation barrier in 2002, incorporating parts of the West Bank, effectively separated Palestinian Arab citizens of Israel from family members who found themselves on the other side of the wall. For Israeli Arabs, these events also served to politically mobilise the community to demand equal treatment within Israel.

Conflict, identity and exclusion

Endeavours to provide a historical backdrop to the origins of the conflict inevitably give rise to counter-narratives. Contestations over the authenticity of Palestinian identity are part of a broader hegemonic contestation over how the histories of this contested space are read and exported. Endeavours to challenge the rootedness of the Palestinian national identity have become part of the 'official history' of the state (Shlaim 2004).[2] The intent is clear; de-link the peoples from the territory (and, therefore, their self-determination claims) by suggesting an imagination of community.

Questions over just how national identities are constructed have produced long and rich literatures extending beyond the Palestinian case. The crafting of a memory of state that attempts to exert hegemonic control over a 'national' narrative as part of a larger political project is not unique to Israeli or Palestinian discourses. What makes the Palestinian case 'unique' is 'the intertwining of, and the tension between, the Palestinian and Israeli national narratives [that] may have reached a level of intensity in Palestine itself, and in American and European public discourse' (Khalidi 1997: 147). In the 'grafting of modern political Zionism on to Jewish history' (Khalidi 1997: 147), the Zionist political project has been particularly successful in narrating and exporting its particular memory of state. By contrast, Palestinians have never 'enjoyed such success [and] since the beginning [Palestinian identity] struggled for acceptance and legitimacy in the outside world, and even for recognition of its very existence as a category of being' (Khalidi 1997: 147). This struggle for hegemonic control of the discourse on Palestine is not merely some esoteric debate; it goes to the heart of Palestinian self-determination claims.

Within Palestinian scholarship, analysis of the emergence of Palestinian identity tends to focus either on the emergence of a Zionist movement in the early 1900s or on the post-1948 period. Yet in rooting discussions of Palestinian national identity in these points of departure, the issue is trapped in a paradigm in which the 'Palestinians exist not as an independent entity with an independent narrative but only in relation to another entity and another narrative [e.g., that of Israel and the Jewish people]' (Khalidi 1997: 146). That the question of Palestinian identity is inextricably linked to the Israeli–Palestinian meta-conflict has complicated what is, otherwise, a fairly straightforward story:

> In the case of national identities of peoples of other Arab countries which came in to being in their modern form in the wake of World War 1, similar processes of the construction of new identities building on elements of old ones as part of a novel synthesis (for this is what we are talking about in the Palestine case and most other cases of the development of new national identities in the modern era) have occasioned relatively little attention, and limited controversy, within these countries or elsewhere.
>
> *(Khalidi 1997: 147)*

The idea that identity can be shaped and formed over time is not new. This does not suggest, however, that Palestinian identity is not real, nor does it suggest that it can only be recognised in opposition to the other (in this case, Israeli or Jewish identity). If such a definition of what comprises a 'peoples' were accepted, then most national identities would fail to pass such a test. De-linked from the political project, a clinical reading of the history of the formation of a Palestinian identity suggests that it existed in some form and had been evolving since the mid-nineteenth century. That 'Palestine was a geographical location and a site of identity' (Banko 2011) is evident in the writings at the times. Research undertaken by Khalidi, Gerber and others (Khalidi 1997; Lybarger 2007; Gerber 2008) show that under Ottoman rule, those living in this contested space, 'understood themselves as living in a territory called Palestine (not Greater Syria). In 1911, the newspaper *Filastin* (Palestine) began publication in Jaffa and it is evident that even at this time, 'Palestine was a geographical location and a site of identity' (Banko 2011). As Banko has argued, a reading of 'Palestinian history from the perspective of nationality, rather than nationalism, shows that "the Palestinian people" were anything but a hasty invention' (2011).

'Citizens' of Israel? Inequality and marginalisation

Palestinian Arab citizens of Israel have been referred to as a 'trapped minority', a term first introduced by Israeli sociologist Dan when examining the effects of 're-territorialization' on the identity and consciousness of Palestinian citizens living within Israel (Rabinowitz 2001: 73–74). Rabinowitz defines trapped minorities as marginalised, and in the case of Palestinian-Israelis, doubly marginalised (Rabinowitz 2001:76–77). In reality, Palestinians living in Israel became threefold marginalised (or 'triple minorities')—marginalised within Israel, the Arab world and the broader Palestinian community. Within Israel, a legal architecture of exclusion was constructed. Although ostensibly these rules and regulations were applicable to everyone within the state, in practice, these restrictions fell, disproportionately, on the Palestinian community.

Within the wider Palestinian community, Palestinian Arab citizens of Israel were separated from the political struggles that would evolve within the Occupied Palestinian Territories of the West Bank and Gaza. This was coupled with a physical separation that impacted social and kinship networks—separating Palestinians from both the territory as well as each other. Within the Arab world, they were often regarded by other Arabs as traitors for remaining in Israel.

Up until 1966, Palestinian Arab citizens of Israel were governed under a military regime. Although they were granted citizenship and voting rights, a number of restrictions were imposed during this period on their rights to work, speech, association and movement. For example, travel restrictions severely restricted Palestinians from travelling outside their villages (unless with permits) and, as many Palestinians were farmers, this significantly impacted their economic independence. This period also marked the beginning of a systematic confiscation of land by the state which would irrevocably alter its territorial complexion. The exclusion of Palestinian Arab citizens of Israel from participating fully in the socio-economic and decision-making institutions of the new Israeli state would continue well after the military government ended in 1966. The systemic nature of the marginalisation is mapped out in a number of ways across the civil and political, and socio-economic landscape in Israel and was detailed in a 2003 report of the Orr Commission set up in the wake of the second *intifada* (Dalal 2003). Although the government argues a security basis for restrictions placed on its Arab population, which comprise approximately 20% of Israel's population (numbering 1.42 million persons) and include both Christians and Muslims,[3] an audit of these measures suggests a more complex underpinning, one in which race continues to define the concept of citizen in Israel—just who is included and excluded from socio-economic and political decision-making institutions. For Israel's Palestinian citizens, the 'lived' experience of inequality within Israel's landscape is found in two main areas,

> substantial discrimination in terms of the distribution of economic resources, particularly as regards housing and land allocation; education; budgets for local authorities; the maintenance of holy places; and employment as a result of preferences given to those who serve in the army. Secondly, they seek better opportunity to express their national identity in the cultural, educational, linguistic and other realms.
>
> *(IGC 2012)*

The remaining sections of this chapter will detail the legal architecture that has been built around the Palestinian-Israeli community in five particular areas: citizenship, the economy, education, political participation and land.

Citizenship

Endeavours to define the notion of citizenship can be traced to The Law of Return 5710 (1950)[4] which states that, '[e]very Jew has the right to come to this country as an *oleh* [a Jew immigrating to Israel]'. This law provides that every Jewish person has a right to immigrate to Israel and was amended in 1970 so as to extend this right to the children and grandchildren of Jews, as well as their spouses and the spouses of their children and grandchildren. The Nationality Law, 5712, passed by the Knesset 1 April 1952 and its Amendments (3.3.58) (8.7.68) (5.17.71)[5] provides '[e]very "oleh" under the Law of Return, 5710–1950(1)' with citizenship.[6] However under Article 3, Israeli nationality is limited to Palestinians who were in Israel 'from the day of the establishment of the State to the day of the coming into force of this Law or entered Israel legally during that period'. This provision effectively prohibits from obtaining citizenship Palestinians who were residents of Palestine prior to 1948 but left during the 'War of Independence' or the 'al-Nakbah'. A 2008 amendment to Article 11 of this law provides the state with the ability to revoke citizenship if it deems that the person 'has committed an act of disloyalty towards the State of Israel'. Such acts have been broadly defined and include obtaining naturalisation or permanent residency in one of nine Arab and Muslim states (Afghanistan, Iran, Pakistan, Iraq, Lebanon, Libya, Sudan, Syria and Yemen) or the Gaza Strip. Citizenship can be revoked without requiring a criminal conviction.

In March 2011, the Citizenship Law (Amendment No. 10) 5771[7] was passed by the Knesset and extended the authority of the state, if requested by the Ministry of the Interior as part of a criminal sentence, to revoke the citizenship of any person who has been found guilty of 'an act of terror' as defined under the Prohibition on Terrorist Financing Law (2005) or of treason, espionage, assisting the enemy in time of war, violating state sovereignty, serving in enemy forces (as defined in the Israeli penal law).

The 2003 Citizenship and Entry into Israel Law (Temporary Order)[8] introduced legislation preventing Palestinian Arab citizens of Israel from acquiring citizenship for spouses in the occupied territories. There were some amendments to this in 2005,[9] but the discriminatory nature of the law remained. In 2007, this was expanded to include citizens and residents from a number of 'enemy states' defined and listed in the law as Lebanon, Syria, Iran and Iraq.[10] In 2008, a cabinet decision extended the Order to citizens of Gaza. Although the law was meant to be temporary, it remains in place. The government has argued, and a 2006 Israeli High Court ruling concurred,[11] that the continued use of the Order was a necessary part of its 'war on terror' and efforts to curb violent attacks within Israel. A 2011 Report by the CEDAW noted:

> its concern that this Law, which suspends the possibility, subject to limited and subjective exceptions, of family reunification, especially in cases of marriages between an Israeli citizen and a person residing in the Occupied Palestinian Territories, has recently been extended for another six months and thus continues to adversely affect the marriages and right to family life of Israeli Arab women citizens and Palestinian women from the Occupied Territories.[12]

The Committee's concerns echoed remarks made on a number of occasions by the Committee on the Elimination of Racial Discrimination (CERD). In their 2012 Concluding Observations, CERD raised 'concern at the maintenance of discriminatory laws especially targeting Palestinian citizens of Israel such as the Citizenship and Entry into Israel Law (Temporary Provision)' and called on Israel 'to revoke the Citizenship and Entry into Israel Law (Temporary Provision) and to facilitate family reunification of all citizens irrespective of their ethnicity or national or other origin'.[13] In January 2012, a constitutional legal challenge to the law was rejected. In a six to five decision, the Israeli High Court upheld the law's constitutionality arguing that given the exigencies of the situation, such restrictions were necessary in order to protect the lives of Israeli citizens and that, 'human rights are not a prescription for national suicide'.[14] As Jabareen and Zaher have noted,

> The two Supreme Court decisions on family unification from 2006 and 2012 have generated an intense legal debate in Israel over whether demographic considerations—the desire to preserve a Jewish majority within the Green Line—were the real impetus for the law. The security arguments presented by the state before the Supreme Court are unconvincing given official data indicating that the family unification process does not, in fact, pose a security threat to Israel. In our opinion, the true debate between the justices is that surrounding the identity of Israel as a 'Jewish and democratic' state. One side of this debate

> argues that the Jewish state should preserve the Jewish majority and views the ban on family unification between Palestinians within Israel as a means of safeguarding these values. The other side, which concurs that Israel should maintain a Jewish majority, nonetheless regards this sweeping ban as a threat to the democratic character of the state, since no democratic state in the world prohibits family unification based solely on a person's ethnicity or national belonging . . . This debate in and of itself calls the equality of Palestinian citizens of Israel into question.
>
> *(Jabareen and Zaher 2012)*

The economy

The economic disparity between Palestinian Arab citizens of Israel and Jews in Israel is evident in a number of areas. Despite a significant improvement in the Israeli economy in more recent years, the country's poverty rate is among the highest in the OECD. A 2017 IMF paper on Israel's socio-economic development reports high levels of unemployment, particularly amongst Haredi (ultra-Orthodox Jewish) men and Palestinian women (IMF 2017: 23). An earlier report which focused on labour productivity within Israel noted that amongst the Palestinian citizens of Israel, the poverty levels were much higher than among the rest of the population (IMF 2015: 19). In 2003, the rate of poverty amongst Palestinians was 50.9% (compared to 19.3% for all Israelis); by 2011 that rate had increased to 58%, 'more than double the overall poverty rate' (IMF 2015: 20).[15]

Whilst the IMF report notes an overall decline in unemployment in 2016 to 4.8% from 6.3% in 2013, employment amongst Arab-Israeli men and women is still lower than the rest of the population (IMF 2015: 20). The IMF study notes that there remains an approximate ten-percentage point difference between the employment rate between all Israeli men and Israeli Palestinian men but this gap is much more significant for women. As of 2015, employment amongst Palestinian women was at 34.6%, compared to 87.4% for the non-Haredi, non-Arab population (IMF 2017: 5).

There are a number of factors that contribute to Palestinian unemployment in Israel. Military service as a prerequisite for employment in high-tech companies and for working in Israeli Airports (by the Israeli Airports Authority) as a baggage handler is one significant factor. Military service is also a requirement for senior level government positions. This affects employment opportunities for Palestinian citizens who, for historical and political reasons are exempt from serving in the Israeli Defence Forces (or IDF). Whilst the Minister of Economy and Labour had previously eliminated the military service requirement for Orthodox Jews (who, for religious reasons, are also exempt from service), this remains an obstacle for Palestinians.[16] Palestinian employment is also impacted by the political climate in Israel. For example, during the July 2014 conflict in Gaza, Adalah[17] received a number of complaints from Palestinians who were dismissed from their employment for having anti-war views. Employers would gather information about an employee's political view through Facebook and other social media which led to 'an increasing wave of dismissals by Israeli Jewish employers of Arab workers from their place of employment due to their anti-war political opinions' (Adalah 2014).

Education

There are two separate education systems operating within Israel—one for Israeli Jews and another for Palestinian citizens of Israel. For Palestinian children within the Israeli education system, disparities in both access and quality have been mapped out in a number of ways.

Historically, the Israeli government has allocated 'less money per head for Palestinian Arab children than it does for Jewish children' (Coursen-Neff 2004: 102), and has offered 'far fewer facilities and educational opportunities than those offered to other Israeli children' (Coursen-Neff 2004: 102).[18] These disadvantages are most acutely felt amongst children in preschool where the rates of attendance in preschool amongst Jewish children was between 10 and 15% higher than Arab children of the same age group (Adalah 2015b: 2).

Differences also exist in the curriculum available to Palestinian children. State curriculum provides readings of history and culture that emphasises Jewish, Zionist and Israeli identity but excludes Palestinian experiences and representations. The State Education Law (1953),[19] amended in 2000, defined the aims and objectives of education strictly in Jewish terms. Although, under Article 2(11), the cultural and linguistic needs of Palestinian Arab citizens of Israel are recognised:

> this rather weakly worded article is not being implemented, and this objective has not been realized. In reality, students in Arab state-run schools receive very little instruction in Palestinian or Arab history, literature and culture, and spend more time learning the Torah than the Qur'an or the New Testament.[20]

Whilst Israeli Arab students are taught in Arabic, the curriculum is the same as that of Jewish schools. A 2007 government-approved history textbook, used only in Arab Israeli schools, did allow for a Palestinian historical narrative to be used but following the 2009 election of one of the most right-wing coalitions in the history of the state a new curriculum was introduced.

In 2009, the government issued a report, entitled 'The Government of Israel Believes in Education', which outlined a new education curriculum approved by the then Education Minister Gideon Sa'ar. The stated objectives of the programme included 'building, strengthening and implementing programs to deepen Jewish, Zionist and Israeli identity'; and fostering 'awareness and identification with Jerusalem, the capital of Israel and the Jewish people'; and 'encouraging recruitment to the IDF and to national civic service'. Under the Sa'ar programme's implementation plan a new syllabus, called Israel's Culture and Tradition was created in which pupils would learn about 'nation and homeland—symbols and customs; Zionism and the yearning for Zion; Judaism and Zionism—leaders and role models; the Jewish life cycle; Bar and Bat Mitzvah; Judaism and Zionism—social and ethical values; the test of fulfilling Judaism and Zionism'. The programme also assigns more teaching hours on the Israeli national anthem, *Hatikva*, and by encouraging enlistment in the Israeli military and national-civic service. Indeed, the rate of enlistment among the former pupils of a school into the military would be one of the criteria for assessing the school's performance for the purpose of determining its future funding, which instructs that references to the word 'Nakba' be removed from these new Arabic textbooks (Zaher 2010).

At the same time as this report was issued, an amendment to The State Budget Law (1985), referred to as the 'Nakba Law', proposed to ban all bodies that receive state funding from spending money on any activity that, *inter alia*, 'commemorates Independence Day or the day of the establishment of the state as a day of mourning'.[21] The Bill was passed in 2011, as one of many laws or bills enacted under a newly configured—and right leaning—Knesset. Since 2009,

> a flood of discriminatory legislation . . . continue[s] to surface on a near weekly basis, seek[s], inter alia, to dispossess and exclude Arab citizens from the land; turn their citizenship from a right into a conditional privilege; undermine the ability of Arab citizens of Israel and their parliamentary representatives to participate in the political life of the

> country; criminalize political expression or acts that question the Jewish or Zionist nature of the state; and privilege Jewish citizens in the allocation of state resources. It is particularly disturbing that some of the legislation appears to be specifically designed to pre-empt, circumvent or overturn Supreme Court decisions providing protection for these rights.
>
> *(Adalah 2011: 1)*

Political participation

The marginalisation of Palestinian Arab citizens of Israel is particularly acute in the political sphere. Since 1948, no Arab party has been included in a ruling government coalition. To date, Arab Israelis are represented by 18 members (16 men, two women) in the 120-member parliament (Knesset), or just over 15% of the seats.[22] This figure reflects a rise in the number of seats gained by Arab MKs from the previous Knesset where ten Arab MKs sat with Arab parties and Hadash, and two Arab MKs sat with Jewish parties Yisrael Beiteinu and Meretz. The decision by the three Arab parties and the Jewish–Arab Hadash to unify in a joint electoral list was made following the enactment of the Governance Law (2014), which raised the electoral threshold from 2% to 3.25% of total valid votes; an electoral threshold all four parties would have had difficulty reaching. The Governance Law is but one of a number of laws that have been adopted by the Knesset that, although ostensibly neutral, effectively limit the political participation of Palestinian Arab citizens of Israel.

Under Section 7(A) of a 1985 amendment to the 1958 Basic Law:

> A list of candidates shall not participate in the elections for the Knesset if its aims or actions, expressly or by implication, point to one of the following: (1) denial of the existence of the State of Israel as the state of the Jewish people: (2) denial of the democratic nature of the state; and (3) incitement to racism.

In 2002, Section 7(A)(1) of this Amendment was changed to read as, 'denial of the existence of the State of Israel as a Jewish and democratic state' and Section 7(A)(3) was added which states, 'support for armed struggle by a hostile state or a terrorist organization against the State of Israel'. Any of these provisions can be used to disqualify candidates and candidates' lists, and whilst these provisions ostensibly apply to all members of the Knesset, in reality they are directed at Arab parliamentarians. The government argued that this was to prevent meetings between Arab Knesset members and militant groups or states that were enemies of Israel, but Arab parliamentarians argued that such a measure amounted to racial discrimination.[23]

Land

Land confiscations and restrictions placed on land and planning rights—an architecture of exclusion—has continued despite growth in the Israeli Arab population. The legal framework includes: The Israel Land Administration (ILA) Law (2009);[24] Amendment (2010) to The Land (Acquisition for Public Purposes) Ordinance (1943);[25] The 2010 Amendment to the Negev Development Authority Law (1991): Individual settlements;[26]Law to Amend the Cooperative Societies Ordinance (No 8) 5771–2011[27] and The Israel Lands Law (Amendment No. 3) (2011).[28]

Under the Israel Land Administration (ILA) Law, enacted by the Knesset in August 2009, land previously confiscated from Palestinians or land held by the state as 'absentees' property' could be legally sold to private individuals or investors and would not be subject to future restitution claims. This measure effectively dispossessed Palestinian refugees, or those internally displaced, from their land. This decision applies to an estimated 800,000 dunams of land and includes refugees' properties located in cities with mixed Israeli–Palestinian communities.[29] The Land Authority Council, which replaced Israel Land Administration, manages 93% of the land. It comprises 13 members, six of which are members of the Jewish National Fund (JNF).[30]

Under the Land (Acquisition for Public Purposes) Ordinance (1943), the finance minister was allowed to confiscate land for 'public purposes'. The Ordinance was widely used to confiscate Palestinian-owned land, often applied in conjunction with other laws[31] related to property. Under a 2010 Amendment to the Ordinance, land that was confiscated under the original Ordinance was confirmed even if the land was not used for the original confiscation purposes. The ordinance, in addition:

> allows the state not to use the confiscated land for the original confiscation purpose for 17 years and prevents landowners from demanding the return of confiscated land not used for the original confiscation purpose if it has been transferred to a third party, or if more than 25 years have elapsed since the confiscation. The amendment expands the Finance Minister's authority to confiscate land for 'public purposes', which under the law includes the establishment and development of towns and allows the Minister to declare new purposes. The new law was designed to prevent Arab citizens of Israel from submitting lawsuits to reclaim confiscated land: over 25 years have passed since the confiscation of the vast majority of Palestinian land, and large tracts have been transferred to third parties, including Zionist institutions like the JNF.
>
> *(Adalah 2011: 2)*

The 2011 Admissions Committees Law makes lawful 'administration committees' that oversee development on state land in the Naqab and Galilee area. The law gives full discretion to these committees to select (or reject) applicants who apply to live in housing units or to purchase land. The criteria used to determine the suitability of applicants is subjective[32] and suggests that the law may have been enacted to circumvent the 2009 Israeli High Court's *Ka'adan* decision,[33] which deemed that the exclusion of Arabs from state land was discriminatory.

The 2010 Amendment[34] to the Negev Development Authority Law (1991) recognises individual settlements in the Negev. There are approximately 60 settlements in this area, many established without planning permits. This amendment provides a tool kit for individual settlements to gain recognition and, therefore, to be entitled to basic services. The law vests the Negev Development Authority with the power to recommend allocation of lands for individual settlements to the Israel Land Administration. The Amendment did not address or provide recognition to approximately 100,000 inhabitants of Arab Bedouin villages in the Negev which remain without the most basic services.

Finally, the 2011 Israel Lands Law (Amendment No. 3) prohibits the owner from selling land or renting property to individuals or a party (public or private) for a period of over five years or from bequeathing or transferring private ownership rights in Israel to 'a foreigner, whether in exchange or not in exchange'.[35] The term 'foreigner' is applied to anyone who is not 'an Israeli citizen or Israeli resident; or a person who is entitled to immigrate to Israel under the Law of Return, 5710–19502'.[36] This law negates the previous approach to the question of 'absentee' owners (e.g. Palestinian refugees), whereby Israel undertook a 'custodian' role, holding the land until a final solution to the conflict was reached. Under this law, Palestinians are 'foreigners' and, despite being original owners, are unable to reclaim their land or property.

Conclusion

A database compiled by the Legal Centre for Arab Minority Rights in Israel (Adalah) details more than 50 Israeli laws, that 'directly or indirectly discriminate against Palestinian citizens of Israel in all areas of life, including their rights to political participation, access to land, education, state budget resources, and criminal procedures'.[37] What emerges from a review of these laws, some of which have been discussed in this chapter, is an intricate framework of inequality that has been embedded in Israel's legal landscape.

In 2011, a proposal to constitutionally determine the identity of the State of Israel as the 'nation-state' of the Jewish people was introduced. In 2014, a government-sponsored bill[38] subsuming two other 'nation-state' proposals were to be introduced. The attempt to redefine the state and legally anchor an asymmetry between the state's 'Jewish and democratic' components[39] has ignited debate within civil society in Israel. Proponents argue that this merely reflects the 'widespread consensus amongst the Israeli public about the definition of the State of Israel as a Jewish state', whilst those opposed suggest that if such a law were adopted it, 'negates every national right and every community symbol of Israel's Arab citizens, that annuls the status of Arabic as the state's second official language, and above all, erases "equality". This is the law that changes us while we sleep' (Sarid 2014).[40] The government fell before the bill was formally presented to the Knesset, but the 2015 elections shifted Israel's political landscape further to the right and gave renewed impetus for the initiative to be resurrected. Right-wing parties as well as the Israeli prime minister, Benjamin Netanyahu support such a bill; those from within Israeli centrist parties remain, for the moment, opposed.

Yet the fault line between the two opposing political camps should not be read as a contestation between those opposed to and those supporting equality for Israel's Palestinian-Arab citizens. Rather, as Jabareen has argued, opposition to codifying laws which are ethnically based or 'clearly written in discriminatory language' challenges 'the longstanding "Ben-Gurionist" tradition regarding the rule of law'—a desire for Israel to be seen 'as democratic in the international arena' (Jabareen 2015).For Palestinian Arab citizens of Israel, it is a debate 'not about whether discrimination should or should not be stopped, but rather about how to continue it' (Jabareen 2015).

Notes

1 This community is also referred to as Israeli Arabs, Palestinian citizens of Israel or Palestinian-Israelis.

2 There have been attempts, most notably by Benny Morris, to challenge aspects of the official state history. Dubbed 'New Historians', this group of historians emerged in the 1980s and, using material that had been declassified 30 years after the founding of the state, they began to push back against official state narratives on seminal historical events. They did find some traction with public opinion in the 1990s, but their work came under strong critique, in large part because their critics allege they did not use Arab sources sufficiently. Morris would, in 2002, distance himself from some of his stated earlier political positions but he did not withdraw any of his writings.

3 According to the Central Bureau of Statistics, the population of Israel was 8,463,400 at the end of 2015: 6,705,600 (79.2%) were Jews or other non-Arabs and 1,757,800 (20.8%) were Arabs. However, this figure includes 335,000 Palestinian residents of East Jerusalem, who do not hold Israeli citizenship. The in-text figure excludes residents of East Jerusalem from the total. See www.cbs.gov.il/www/publications/isr_in_n16e.pdf, last accessed 28 February 2018.

4 Passed by the Knesset on the 20th Tammuz 5710 (5 July 1950) and published in Sefer Ha-Chukkim No. 51 of the 21st Tammuz 5710 (5 July 1950), p. 159; the Bill and an Explanatory Note were published in Hatza'ot Chok No. 48 of the 12th Tammuz 5710 (27 June 1950), p. 189.

5 *Laws of the State of Israel: Authorized Translation from the Hebrew*, Volume 6. Government Printer, Jerusalem (1948–1987), pp. 50–53.

6 Under Article 2(a).
7 Enacted by the Knesset on 22 Adar Bet 5771 (28 March 2011); the legislative proposal and explanations were published in Knesset Bills—366, on 27 Shvat 5771 (1 February 2011), p. 73. This amends the Nationality Law, 5712–1952.
8 The Nationality and Entry into Israel Law, 31 July 2003.
9 The Nationality and Entry into Israel Law (Amendment), 27 July 2005.
10 The Nationality and Entry into Israel Law (Amendment), 21 March 2007.
11 See HCJ cases 7052/03, 7102/03, *Adalah and others v. The Minister of the Interior*, 14 May 2006.
12 UN Committee on the Elimination of Discrimination Against Women (CEDAW), *Concluding Observations: Israel* (16 December 2011) CEDAW/C/ISR/CO/5 paras. 24–25.
13 UN Committee on the Elimination of Racial Discrimination (CERD), Consideration of reports submitted by States parties under Article 9 of the Convention: concluding observations of the Committee on the Elimination of Racial Discrimination: Israel, 3 April 2012, CERD/C/ISR/CO/14-16 at para. 18.
14 HCJ case 466/07, *MK Zahava Galonv v. The Attorney General, et al.*
15 The report also noted that the rate of poverty for Haredi Jews was also at 58%.
16 In June 2013, the Ministerial Committee on Legislation approved the proposed 'Contributors to the State Bill' which, as written, afforded those who had military service records preferences in hiring for civil service jobs, in job salaries and in services such as student housing, higher education and land allocation. In wake of this approval and fearing that the Bill would violate the Basic Law on Human Dignity and Freedom, a revised and 'softer' version of the Bill was drafted. For more information on this see, *Haaretz* Op-Ed (28 October 2013). Available at: www.haaretz.com/opinion/1.554919, last accessed 28 February 2018.
17 Adalah (meaning Justice in Arabic) is a local based human rights NGO located in Haifa, Israel which deals primarily with issues related to Palestinian Arab citizens of Israel.
18 Although Coursen-Neff (2004) is a dated article, the disparity in funding and the allocation of resources remains disproportionate. In a 2015 report by Adalah, using information provided by the State Comptroller's office, the organisation reported that, 'Jewish pupils receive at least 16% more money per child from the Education Ministry than Arab children: Jewish children receive NIS 807, while Arab children get only NIS 693' (Adalah 2015a).
19 7 Laws of the State of Israel (LSI) 113 (5713–1952/53).
20 Adalah, 'Submission to the UN Committee on the Elimination of Racial Discrimination to assist it in its consideration of Israel's 14th to 16th periodic reports to the Committee (October 2010/ January 2011), and in its upcoming review of Israel in February 2012', 8 December 2011, p. 28.
21 Book of Laws 5745, 15; 5771, 195.
22 This figure is current as of March 2018 and includes 12 members from the Joint (Arab) List, which comprises three Arab parties and the Jewish-Arab Hadash party. This brings the total number of Arab MKs to 18—12 in the Joint (Arab) list (one Hadash MK on the list is Jewish) and four in Jewish parties—Likud, Yisrael Beiteinu, Meretz, and Zionist Union. A breakdown of all MPs and their biographies can be found at: www.knesset.gov.il/mk/eng/mkindex_current_eng.asp?view=1.
23 Both the Legal Centre for Arab Minority Rights in Israel (Adalah) and the Association for Civil Rights in Israel (ACRI) have undertaken significant litigation in these areas. For details on their work see: www.acri.org.il/en/category/arab-citizens-of-israel/arab-minority-rights/ and www.adalah.org, last accessed 28 February 2018.
24 The Israel Land Administration Law, Amendment No. 7 (5769–2009), the Official Gazette: the Book of Laws 2209, 10 August 2009.
25 Law to Amend the Land (Acquisition for Public Purposes) Ordinance, No. 3 (5770–2010), the Official Gazette: the Book of Laws 2228, 15 February 2010.
26 The Negev Development Authority Law, Amendment No. 4 (5770–2010), the Official Gazette: the Book of Laws 2250, 22 July 2010, 591–593.
27 Cooperative Associations Ordinance (Amendment No. 8), 5771–2011, SH No. 2286, p. 683.
28 Israel Lands Law, Amendment No. 3 (5771–2011), the Official Gazette: the Book of Laws 2291, 5 April 2011, 754–756.
29 E.g. Haifa, Lod (Led), Ma'alot-Tarshiha, Nazareth Ilit, Akka (Acre), Ramle and Tel Aviv–Jaffa.
30 The Jewish National Fund (Hebrew: Keren Kayemeth Leyisrael, KKL) is a non-governmental organisation that was founded more than a century ago by the fifth Zionist Congress at Basle in 1901 for the purpose of land purchase and development in Palestine. See www.jnf.org/about-jnf/.

31 Land Acquisition Law (1953) and the Absentees' Property Law (1950).
32 Amongst these are whether or not the applicant is deemed suitable to live in the community and whether s/he would contribute to the social and cultural life. As well, the committees allow individual towns to apply specific criteria based on the 'unique characteristics' of a particular town. See Law to Amend the Cooperative Societies Ordinance, No. 8 (5771–2011), the Official Gazette: the Book of Law 2286, 30 March 2011, 683–686, Section 2, 6(c).
33 HCJ case 6698/95, *Ka'adan v. the Israel Land Administration*, PD 54(1) 258 (2000).
34 This follows a 2010 Israeli High Court ruling that allowed for recognition of these settlements. A petition lodged by Adalah, Bimkom and the Negev Coexistence Forum in 2006 against what was referred to as the Wine Path Plan failed. The Court failed to address two points in the petitioners submission; the question of unequal land distribution and discrimination of the Arab villages (which were not recognised in the plan). See HCJ case 2817/06, *Adalah, et al. v. The National Council for Planning and Building, et al.* (decision delivered 15 June 2010).
35 Israel Lands Law (n 31).
36 Ibid.
37 www.adalah.org/en/content/view/7771.
38 For the text of the proposed Bill, in English, see: www.acri.org.il/en/2014/06/19/kru16jun14/, last accessed 29 May 2015.
39 This language is common to each of the bills that have been proposed but explicitly noted in the version of the Bill (1550/19/P) proposed by Yariv Levin (Likud), Ayelet Shaked (Jewish Home) and Robert Ilatov (Yisrael Beytenu) in the attached Explanatory Notes, which states, in part,

> [d]espite widespread consensus amongst the Israeli public about the definition of the State of Israel as a Jewish state, the character of the State of Israel as the nation-state of the Jewish people has never been enshrined in the State's basic laws . . . Enshrining the Jewish character of the State of Israel in a basic law will enable a widespread acceptance of a complete and comprehensive constitution in the future.

40 These comments were made in relation to the 2014 bills, which remained the most recent versions of the Bill to be submitted at the time this chapter was written (February 2018). For full text of bills, see Gild-Hayo (2017). For commentary on the bills see Sarid (2014).

References

Adalah 2011, 'New Discriminatory Laws and Bills in Israel', June Haifa: Adalah.

Adalah 2014, 'Adalah Demands That Israeli Academic Institutions and Employers Retract Punitive Measures Taken against Arab Students and Workers for their Anti-War Opinions on Gaza', 6 August, www.adalah.org/en/content/view/8315, last accessed 28 February 2018.

Adalah 2015a, 'On the International Day for the Protection of the Child: Blatant Discrimination in Early Childhood Education for Arab Children in Israel', June, www.adalah.org/en/content/view/8563, accessed 28 February 2018.

Adalah 2015b, 'Inequality of Opportunity in Early Childhood Education: The Case of 3- and 4-Year-Old Palestinian Arab Children in Israel', May, www.adalah.org/uploads/Position-Paper-Early-Childhood-Education-Eng-May-2015.pdf, accessed 28 February 2018.

Banko, L 2011, 'The Invention of Palestine', *Jadaliyya*, 27 December, www.jadaliyya.com/pages/index/3783/the-invention-of-the-palestinian, accessed 8 March 2018.

Coursen-Neff, Z 2004, 'Discrimination against Palestinian Arab Children in the Israeli Education System', *International Law and Politics*, vol. 36, no. 749, pp. 101–162.

Dalal, M (ed.) 2003, *October 2000: Law and Politics before the Or Commission*, Haifa: Adalah.

Gerber, H 2008, *Remembering and Imagining Palestine: Identity and Nationalism from the Crusades to the Present*, Houndmills: Palgrave Macmillan.

Gild-Hayo, D 2017, *Overview of Anti-Democratic Legislation Advanced by the 20th Knesset*, Association for Civil Rights in Israel (ACRI), 10, December 2017, www.acri.org.il/en/wp-content/uploads/2018/02/December-Overview-of-Anti-Democratic-Legislation-2017.pdf.

IMF 2015, Country [Israel] Report No. 15/262, September.

IMF 2017, Country [Israel] Report No. 17/75, March.

International Crisis Group (ICG) 2012, 'Back to Basics: Israel's Arab Minority and the Israeli–Palestinian Conflict', 14 March, Middle East Report No. 119, www.crisisgroup.org/en/regions/middle-east-north-africa/israel-palestine/119-back-to-basics-israels-arab-minority-and-the-israeli-palestinian-conflict.aspx, accessed 8 March 2018.

Jabareen, H 2015, 'The Real Debate Over Israel's "Jewish Nation-State" Bill', *The Nation Magazine*, 29 January, www.thenation.com/article/196577/real-debate-over-israels-jewish-nation-state-bill#, accessed 28 February 2018.

Jabareen, H and Zaher, S 2012, 'The Israeli Supreme Court's Decision in the Citizenship Law Case HCJ 466/07, MK Zahava Galon v. The Attorney General, et al.', 31 January, www.jadaliyya.com/pages/index/4205/the-israeli-supreme-courts-decision-in-the-citizen, accessed 8 March 2018.

Khalidi, R 1997, *Palestinian Identity: The Construction of Modern National Consciousness*, New York: Columbia University Press.

Lybarger, LD 2007, *Identity and Religion in Palestine: The Struggle between Islamism and Secularism in the Occupied Territories*, Princeton, NJ: Princeton University Press.

Rabinowitz, D 2001, 'The Palestinian Citizens of Israel: The Concept of Trapped Minority and the Discourse of Transnationalism in Anthropology', *Ethnic and Racial Studies*, vol. 24, no. 1, pp. 64–85.

Sa'ar, G 2009, 'The Government of Israel Believes in Education', August (Hebrew), http://meyda.education.gov.il/files/owl/hebrew/alsederhayom/education_presentation_final_opt.pdf, accessed 8 March 2018.

Sarid, Y 2014, 'Jewish Nation-State Bill: Time to Remove the Fig Leaf', *Haaretz*, 23 November, www.haaretz.com/news/israel/.premium-1.628105, accessed 1 March 2018.

Shlaim, A 2004, 'The War of Israeli Historians', *Annales*, vol. 59, no. 1 (January–February), pp. 161–167.

Zaher, S 2010, 'The Prohibition on Teaching the Nakba in the Arab Educational System in Israel', Adalah Newsletter, September, www.adalah.org/uploads/oldfiles/newsletter/eng/sep10/docs/Sawsan%20Nakba%20English%20final.pdf, accessed 1 March 2018.

Part III
The private sector

9

Human rights and corporate social responsibility in Southeast Asia

Kenneth Christie and Robert J. Hanlon

Introduction

Business actors in Southeast Asia are a prominent authority in a region that experiences endemic human rights abuse. And yet, the private sector often sees human rights as an issue that falls outside its sphere of influence and responsibility. Arguably, this is changing with the concept of corporate social responsibility (CSR) bringing an ideational shift on how companies think about their human rights impact. However, the issue of business and human rights in Southeast Asia (SEA) is largely industry driven; and multilateral initiatives developed by United Nations (UN) agencies have had little success in bringing real change to the region. Despite nearly two decades of high-level UN talks on how to develop international business norms around the concept of rights, little has changed in the protection of vulnerable populations. In SEA, the past few years has seen a human rights rollback, with governments showing less interest in holding the private sector to account for committing violations.

In this chapter, we give three reasons why human rights are a marginalised business issue in Southeast Asia. First, there is weak political will to monitor business actors given a general rollback in state interest to protect human rights. Governments are dependent on the private sector to maintain growth targets and are willing to ignore rights violations in order to enhance economic performance while the so-called 'war on terror' has reprioritised political interests. Second, international efforts to promote human rights and business through global rights discourse has fallen short. Initiatives such as the UN Global Compact (UNGC) and the UN Guiding Principles on Business and Human Rights (UNGP) are perceived as being unrealistic initiatives falling outside the scope of many organisations. Finally, the Association of Southeast Asian Nations (ASEAN) has struggled to establish itself as a legitimate advocate and protector of human rights. ASEAN's inability to protect human rights defenders at the expense of powerful stakeholders from government and industry minimises the issue of rights and sidelines civil society groups. This chapter concludes with a premise that, until governments start consistently promoting human rights as a business issue, there is little incentive for companies to take rights, let alone UN voluntary initiatives, seriously. In this light, civil society must take on more of a role in publicising and acting to protect vulnerable groups. Indeed, government and private sector actors in the region have yet to emerge as meaningful advocates for a comprehensive approach to the issue of business and human rights.

We start with an overview of the problem of, and views on, human rights in the region, even though there are major differences in the ways that human rights are perceived by regions and states within Southeast Asia. Second, we draw on corporate social responsibility literature and assess how business actors in SEA have responded to international calls for industry to develop a human rights strategy. Lastly, a summary of the prospects and challenges for business and human rights in SEA will be offered. Overall, there is no single, uniform version of human rights shared in the region, nor is there an agreed upon political approach to improving rights. Divergent rights policy and weak political will have thus disincentivised the regional business case for human rights. Attempts to superimpose the UNGC and the UNGPs have therefore proved to be difficult, if not impossible.

To begin, we provide an overview of human rights in Southeast Asia while arguing that the region is experiencing a human rights rollback. Efforts to curb terrorism and stimulate economic growth have sidelined many of the early human rights gains that had been achieved since the end of the Cold War. Given the variety of regimes and states, ranging from dictatorships to democracies and beyond, the forces of globalisation coupled with the post-9/11 political environment has led to a securitisation of rights in this vast, diverse and complex region. Such an atmosphere has led to significant barriers for achieving a meaningful business case for human rights in Southeast Asia.

Southeast Asia's human rights rollback

One of the most dramatic changes affecting global human rights took place in the aftermath of the attacks on the USA on 11 September 2001, perpetrated by the Islamist fundamentalist organisation, al-Qa'ida. The reaction of the US government against terrorism (the so-called 'war on terror') generated a crisis for human rights prospects in many parts of the Asia-Pacific region, as neo-conservative, authoritarian regimes were reinvigorated in the pursuit of long-standing agendas against domestic oppositions. The stance claiming that 'you're either for us or against us', heavily promoted by US President George W. Bush following the attacks, enabled states in Asia that were previously seen to be improving their human rights records to suppress dissent by 'securitising' the argument. That is, in view of acts of terrorism, the issue of national security acquired a new political significance. This resulted in the restriction and the abolition of many civil liberties, a policy adopted by many governments in the region. These governments further increased repressive internal security measures, many of which had been inherited from former colonial masters.

From 2005 this 'securitisation' intensified; the dominant theme remained the US 'war on terror', which had negative connotations for human rights in the Southeast Asian region. There seemed to be no end in sight to this 'war' during President Bush's second term of office (which ended in early 2009), and the situation appeared to change little with regard to the protection of rights across the region. This was particularly so in the People's Republic of China, Indonesia, Singapore, Malaysia and Thailand. These 'hard' and 'soft' authoritarian governments seized much of the context of the attacks of 11 September 2001 as a means of increasing suppression of internal dissent against their particular rule, and as a way of bolstering their own legitimacy. This followed the disappearance of the debate on Asian values, which was made redundant in the aftermath of the regional financial crisis of 1997/98. These trends reflect a far more anxiety-driven notion that human rights can be completely discarded on account of 'internal' and 'external' threats.

The revival of the nation-state in terms of the assertion of sovereignty has grown, as cosmopolitan claims to rights confront state security needs. The election of Barack Obama as US president in late 2008 appeared to mark a change in the USA's policy towards human rights. In early 2009 Obama ordered the closure of the Guantánamo Bay detention centre in Cuba and also of secret prisons operated by the Central Intelligence Agency (CIA), the existence of which had significantly tarnished the human rights policy of the previous administration. In the meantime, human rights abuses remained fairly constant across the region. Overall, areas of Southeast and Northeast Asia seem beset by issues of poor, weak, or simply bad, governance. Thailand's political system was seriously jeopardised in 2009/10, with the eruption of political violence and mass demonstrations eventually leading to the government being overthrown in a 2014 coup. The Philippines continues to be adversely affected by corruption and weakness, as does Indonesia. The Democratic People's Republic of Korea (North Korea) is simply a rogue state, which adheres to no international conventions and does not heed the opinions of the wider world. It would also appear that regional mechanisms such as ASEAN have been unable and essentially unwilling to exercise much influence in terms of procuring change in human rights; however, there has been some incremental change at this level. Reports also suggest that human rights defenders and advocates have been targeted by regimes with poor human rights records, in clear efforts to deflect criticism (FORUM-ASIA 2016). This is a worrying trend for the reporting of human rights abuses, not just in the region but on a global scale. Indeed, the region's authoritarian tendencies impact all areas of civil society including the private sector, which will be discussed later in this chapter.

Some observations form a context for the discussion of human rights in the Asia-Pacific region. As Parekh (2004) has noted, East Asian political elites have argued that there is no history of 'human rights' in the region as understood in Western, liberal terms. The West's advocacy of rights in their initial form not only applied to all groups of people in all societies, regardless of status, but are also seen as basic entitlements, which eclipse other considerations that may arise from an individual's relationship to social networks or to the state. However, in Asia there is no tradition or political history of such entitlements according to the states and regimes present. Citizens are believed to have 'basic duties', not 'basic rights', because such societies did not adhere to the same liberal trajectory of Western modernisation whereby rights were won from the state in political struggle. 'Asian' duties in this sense arise from a person's status or group affiliation (Parekh 2004).

For many Southeast Asian governments, the priority of second-generation (economic and social) rights has always featured heavily in political agendas, much more so than first-generation (civil and political) rights. In some ways, the relationship is the opposite of that found in the West, where individuals are highly prioritised. Asian governments have been seen to value the group more than the individual; if the group means the nation-state, then individual rights can justifiably be abrogated in defence of the larger national community. Although the size and diversity of the region induce caution in making generalisations, authoritarianism in Asia is on the rise and is consistently undermining human rights (Case 2010).

The promotion of a security agenda in the aftermath of the attacks of September 2001, and the response to those attacks, could not have come at a worse time for defenders of human rights in the East Asian region, who believe that human rights are vital for a country's well-being (AHRC 2015). Although Western governments and Asian activists long ago rejected the Asian values argument, after the events of 11 September some Western governments expressed sympathy for, and even encouraged, the prioritising of security over human rights. For many who struggled against excessive national security laws and anti-crime campaigns aimed at quelling political dissent, this was a major set-back. This region is a crucial battleground in the 'war on terror', owing to the activities of a minority of the significant number of Muslims. Nearly 240 million Muslims live in Southeast Asia, residing in overwhelming numbers in Malaysia, Brunei and Indonesia and other areas of the Malay Archipelago, as well as Thailand and the Philippines. Levels of terrorist activity have remained very high in the region, and senior US officials have been concerned that Southeast Asia has become susceptible to terrorism and instability. As repeatedly documented by the International Crisis Group (2016), most countries in the region have experienced a relatively high degree of political violence and terrorism in recent years.

Overall, human rights in the region have undergone change in terms of the agendas pursued. From the neo-conservative emphasis on Asian values and their political implications in the early 1990s to the hegemonic imposition of the 'war on terror' in the new millennium, it seems certain that these issues will remain contentious for some time to come. It appears that there has been a general degradation of human rights in favour of regime security. Moreover, fiscal growth continues to take precedence over human rights with governments consistently prioritising the interests of the economy. This preference has impacted vulnerable populations who are unable to hold political and corporate power to account. The following section outlines the impact of the private sector on human rights in Asia.

Business and human rights in Southeast Asia

Southeast Asia is one of the world's most dynamic regions and home to over 600 million people. It is also a region that has seen waves of financial uncertainty, from stunning economic growth rates in the early 1990s to near economic ruin by the end of the decade. Today the region has recovered from the Asian Financial Crisis and has positioned itself as a leading investment hub, representing some of the world's leading emerging markets. Markets such as Cambodia, Myanmar and Laos are expected to be some of the fastest-growing markets, while the Asian Development Bank has suggested that SEA could offset China's slow economic deceleration (ADB 2015).

Business actors play a major role in the region's economic growth and are deeply connected with government. Studwell (2007: xviii) referred to Southeast Asia's business elite as 'godfathers' and rightly noted that they work 'hand in glove' with the state. The close relationship between industry and government has raised questions of accountability and transparency. Race-to-the-bottom economics, coupled with endemic corruption, has led to serious human rights abuses in the region and the intimidation of activists.

For example, in Laos, civil society groups concerned with land rights violations have come under pressure from government to stay away from the ASEAN People's Forum (APF) and have reported being in 'fear for their safety'. The Office of the High Commissioner for Human Rights has noted:

> One trend that stands out in the communications received is related to human rights defenders. Communications have addressed alleged murders of, attacks on and acts of intimidation against human rights defenders who campaign against the adverse impacts of extractive company operations and allegations regarding the impact of mining and hydroelectric projects on indigenous peoples. The Working Group is gravely concerned about a disturbing increase in attacks and acts of intimidation by State and non-State actors against those who protest against the actual and potential adverse impacts of business operations and major development projects.
>
> *(OHCHR 2014: 17)*

Indeed, activists have long complained that the government was more interested in providing industry with land concession rights rather than address public concerns. One activist noted that the Laotian government was going to great lengths to manipulate the rights dialogue at the

ASEAN Peoples Forum (RFA 2015). Meanwhile, in Thailand, Natural Fruit has recently sued human rights activist Andy Hall while filing a criminal defamation complaint against him for publishing a report that highlighted abuse committed by the company (Sherwell 2016).

Cases of companies committing human rights violations are common. According to FORUM-ASIA (2015: para. 4), in Thailand there has been 'systematic killings and attacks on human rights defenders'. Citing the murder of a land rights activist in Surat Thani Province, there has been 'a series of killings designed to intimidate communities who are seeking to protect their land and livelihood against encroachments of destructive agricultural industries in the province' (FORUM-ASIA 2015: para. 2). Indeed, Southeast Asia's agri-business industry has seen its share of controversy. Land acquisitions can be contentious and involve violent seizures of property carried out by state security forces against powerless communities.

According to the Forest Peoples Programme (2013), the scale of land rights violations carried out in the region varies from country to country, although corruption, legal irregularities and a lack of compensation for those impacted are all common themes associated with forced land seizures. The agribusiness industry also sees the convergence between political and private sector interests seeking to enhance economic performance through infrastructure development projects and the accumulation of resources destined for export markets. For example, in Cambodia, the Forest Peoples Programme (FPP) notes:

> [A] lack of law enforcement and irregularities in the implementation of existing legislation has led to the proliferation of human rights abuses in recent years in the country's agribusiness sector. Many development projects underway have been implemented without disclosure of information or public consultation with affected local communities. Food insecurity has increased in rural areas and families have become impoverished as a result of the loss of their farmland and grazing land to large-scale agribusiness investors.
>
> *(FPP 2013: 7)*

The extractive industry is another frequently targeted sector by human rights activists over alleged abuses. In 2011, Canadian mining firm Barrick Gold was subject to a 94-page Human Rights Watch (HRW) report (HRW 2011) that accused the company of complicity in human rights violations carried out by its security guards involving rape at its Porgera gold mine in Papua New Guinea. In the report, HRW noted 'Five alleged incidents of gang rape by mine security personnel in 2009 and 2010, and a sixth in 2008. We believe these incidents represent a broader pattern of abuse by some PJV [Porgera Joint Venture] security personnel' (HRW 2011: 9). As a result, Barrick cooperated with HRW and conducted an internal investigation leading to the firing of six employees, some of whom would be later arrested by police.

The idea that the business community in SEA can serve as a human rights defender is a missing narrative. Industry often perceives rights as falling outside their sphere of influence and responsibility, arguing instead that they fall inside the realm of the state. Yet a human rights approach to business can provide industry with a framework 'to prevent, mitigate and remedy abuses or workers and local communities by corporate activities' (Business and Human Rights Resource Centre 2015: 4). Still, businesses in Asia often avoid the issue of rights while preferring to commit to less controversial community programmes such as education and the environment. A central reason why industry avoids human rights can be attributed to the gap in knowledge of how rights impact business.

The United Nations Secretary-General's Special Representative on business and human rights, John Ruggie, has found that outside basic labour rights, there is little incentive for industry to develop human rights policy. Ruggie notes:

> Beyond workplace issues companies similarly lack shared understandings of any hierarchy of duties they may have and to whom they may have them. Many of the policies they have adopted are phrased in language that makes it difficult for the company itself, let alone the public, to measure performance against commitments. As a result, companies committed to human rights themselves often are the losers. They may be unable adequately to monitor their performance, defeating a primary purpose of their policy; and they may get little external credit for admirable things they do.
>
> *(OHCHR 2007: 59)*

Ruggie proceeded to undertake a six-year consultation with industry to develop what would become human rights norms for the private sector. The result was the production of the UN Guiding Principles on Business and Human Rights (UNGP).

As Kaufmann (2013) notes, the UNGP operates around a three-pillar framework. First, the 'Protect, Respect and Remedy' framework seeks to reaffirm the state responsibility to protect human rights. The responsibility to investigate and prevent rights violations by companies must be considered within a state-centric legal model. Second, business should develop corporate social responsibility programmes that incorporate human rights into their model. Companies should perform due diligence within their operations to ensure rights are not being violated while operations fall within legal compliance of national and international laws. The final pillar calls for human rights victims to have access to remedies, which should be seen as a joint responsibility between the state and private sector (Kaufmann 2013: 5). As Ruggie has stressed, governments must play a stronger role in communicating human rights risks to industry with expectations being made clear and enforced.

Still, the prospects for business and human rights in Asia are unclear. As Richard Welford at CSR Asia correctly notes, many companies fail to accept that rights violations such as human trafficking and child labour could be occurring in their supply chains (Welford 2015; CSR Asia 2014). Welford stresses that firms will avoid the issue out of fear they will be perceived as a company with a rights problem, or they see human rights outside their sphere of influence; while NGOs are perceived as adversarial organisations looking to undermine business interests (Welford 2015; CSR Asia 2014). Yet as Welford writes, many NGOs are seeking to work with industry to help minimise human rights problems that may be occurring within the organisation (CSR Asia 2014).

The next section tackles the future challenge of business and human rights within the ASEAN context. Asia remains the only region in the world without a formal human rights body that is empowered to assess the domestic rights policy and progress of each country within the region. While ASEAN has started to take human rights more seriously, the organisation's ability to hold its members to account is limited. Thus, ASEANs capacity to enforce business and human rights norms is also weak.

ASEAN prospects for business and human rights

Founded in 1967 as a security regime, ASEAN has seen its mandate evolve from one that advocated a strong policy of political non-interference towards a more collaborative multilateralism. ASEAN has rapidly emerged as a progressive regional organisation developing policy around everything from economic integration to climate change. Developing a formal human rights framework has been one of ASEANs recent policy goals. As highlighted in the ASEAN Charter, 'ADHERING to the principles of democracy, the rule of law and good governance, respect for and protection of human rights and fundamental freedoms' (ASEAN Secretariat 2015: 2). In 2009, the ASEAN Intergovernmental Commission on Human Rights

(AICHR) was established to find ways of integrating and operationalising human rights policy within the ASEAN framework. Three years later, the group formally introduced the ASEAN Human Rights Declaration (AHRD).

While the AHRD has been welcomed by many as ground-breaking and having the potential to become binding obligations, human rights defenders were quick to point out that the declaration is inconsistent with international law considering that certain rights language was not included in the document. As *The Diplomat* (2012) reported, over 50 regional human rights NGOs called the declaration 'anti-human rights'. Indeed, the AHRD included a special provision that gives governments the ability to deny basic rights based on a broad range of subjective criteria as set by the state. The AHRD states 'rights must be considered in the regional and national context bearing in mind different political, economic, legal, social, cultural, historical and religious backgrounds' (ASEAN 2013: 4–5). As Mohan (2011) notes, ASEANs refusal to deal with internal issues has hindered its ability to promote human rights.

The American Bar Association (2014) has also stressed that the AHRD should be considered both progressive and problematic. First, while the AHRD is a path-breaking initiative launched by ASEAN, it is still legally non-binding, allowing governments the latitude to avoid implementation at the national level. Second, although civil society in the region has welcomed greater political interest in rights, the AHRD has been categorically rejected by NGOs who see the initiative as falling short, given the various loopholes that could be used by governments to suppress rights. Finally, while the AHRD is seen as a notable first attempt at human rights norm setting, if it is not carefully amended to reflect international standards it could very well undermine human rights protection in Southeast Asia (ABA 2014). Yet as Jones (2014) notes, the organisation's rights approach is consistent with ASEAN's typical policy processes dating back to the early 1990s. Jones (2014) sees the AHRD as a hybrid between international human rights standards and culturally relativist discourses that seek to consolidate authoritarian governance models.

Although ASEANs commitment to human rights is controversial, the organisation has moved forward with several initiatives concerned with the social and environmental impact of business investment. Most ASEAN governments began drafting CSR policy prior to 2010 (Shaba & Meuter 2013). According to the AICHR, Western practices of CSR are being brought to the region by multinational corporations. Concepts such as the 'triple-bottom line' that promote social, economic and environmental sustainability are gaining in popularity and being adapted within a regional context. Yet philanthropy continues to be the dominant and preferred form of CSR, given the desire for Asia-based family-run firms to build legacies and contribute to religious and cultural specific initiatives such as Buddhist temples in Thailand or Christian churches in the Philippines. The AICHR notes that one of its objectives is to expand CSR competence beyond philanthropy while ensuring that such charity continues (AICHR 2014: 19).

Established in 2011, the ASEAN CSR Network has argued human rights must be considered a priority issue for business in the region. The network, which evolved from a 2008 initiative led by the ASEAN Foundation and the Asian Institute of Management (AIM), is registered as a limited company in Singapore. Driven by business, the organisation's purpose is to 'ensure that Corporate Social Responsibility (CSR) is incorporated in the corporate agenda and to contribute towards sustainable socio-economic development in ASEAN Member States' (ASEAN CSR Network 2015). The network shares an office with UN Global Compact Singapore and is frequently involved in high-level discussions throughout the region on themes such as human rights, corruption and food security. The association has also been active in promoting the UNGP, contributing to the ASEAN Business Coalition on HIV-AIDS, as well as running seminars on business and human rights with diverse stakeholders. Indeed, human rights due diligence is on the rise in some circles, recently leading to the first Asia Regional Forum on Business and Human Rights in 2016 (OHCHR 2016). Still, companies developing human rights strategies tend to be those operating in high-risk industries such as extractives, agribusiness and garment manufacturing. There is also a stronger CSR push from multinational companies as opposed to regional firms.

Still, there are examples of Southeast Asian firms incorporating international human rights norms into their business model. For example, Indonesia-based Asia Pulp and Paper was accused of human rights violations when its security guards beat a farmer to death who campaigned against land grabbing. International condemnation resulted in Greenpeace ending its relationship with the company that had seen the NGO support its zero-tolerance policy of deforestation (*The Jakarta Post* 2015). As a result, Asia Pulp and Paper replaced the security company, met with the victim's family and helped investigate the crime with the Indonesia National Human Rights Commission. Another example stems from 2014, which saw brands Puma, the Gap and H&M threaten to pull out of Cambodia if the government did not improve conditions for the country's 600,000 garment workers. The companies had been responding to violent labour unrest that led to at least four deaths and dozens of arrests.

The prospects for establishing a human rights culture within business circles have appeared a little clearer in the region in recent years. For example, there are real prospects for improving the overall rights situation in Myanmar following the release of Aung San Suu Kyi. Following the 2015 election, some observers note that Myanmar may be on the brink of real transformation although the country faces a long and protracted struggle in achieving legitimate change (Bünte 2016). The private sector has the opportunity to play a meaningful role in assisting Myanmar reach its development and human rights goals. For example, the launch of the UNGC in the country has the potential to raise the profile of social and environmental problems caused by industry (Kell 2013).

In Myanmar, business is the driving force even behind UNGC. According to one original UNGC signatory in Myanmar, 'For a signatory, we have committed ourselves to be [a] more socially responsible business entity. As for the country, other biz [sic] will follow this noble attitude that will be leading to a better world' (Personal Interview 2012a). The CEO went on to say that UNGC raises the level of CSR in the country and can bring increased expectations to future partners and agencies (Personal Interview 2012a). The UNGC is an opportunity to learn more about the UN's work, while signing the agreement is an important personal promise; a self-commitment to sustainability and corporate social responsibility (Personal Interview 2012a). A second UNGC signatory noted that public statements of support for the UNGC not only show a commitment to CSR, but also signal to potential clients the corporate values they are expected to hold should they enter into future partnerships (Personal Interview 2012b).

As of May 2016, some 326 participants have signed up to the UNGC in Myanmar, thereby establishing a Global Compact Network Myanmar (GCNM) which helps each company liaise with New York and develop expert knowledge. According to one UN official who works on the Myanmar portfolio, the UNGC provides business with new opportunities to learn pragmatic implementation skills involving corporate sustainability (Personal Interview 2012c). He went on to note that the UNGC can develop:

- an association with the UN, the universality of the UNGC principles;
- opportunities to network on a national, regional and global level with like-minded businesses;
- the vast learning platform on sustainability challenges and solutions;
- an opportunity to engage in collective action;

- an opportunity to enter into partnership projects with the UN and its agencies;
- access to practical resources and cutting-edge guidance on relevant sustainability issues (Personal Interview 2012c).

Recent initiatives of the GCNM have included stakeholder engagements, trainings, as well as outreach programmes. For example, in 2014, the network hosted the event 'Advancing the UN Global Compact in Myanmar: Delivering Prosperity and Opportunity Widely'. The half-day conference brought together over 100 participants and introduced them to the UN's recently launched initiative 'Business for Peace', a programme which acknowledges companies that use their influence to advance themes of peace and security. The local network also works in conjunction with UNGC officials in New York on various stakeholder engagement programmes. For example, in 2013 the UNGC facilitated a webinar in conjunction with the Atlantic Council and LexisNexis entitled 'Business Action in Support of the Rule of Law: An Example in Myanmar'. The event brought together UN officials, the private sector and activists highlighting the connection between rule of law, human rights, socio-economic stability, education and investment (UNGC 2013).

But there are more examples of firms in Myanmar working to include UNGC principles in their business operations, including ones driven by multinational firms. The Coco-Cola Company for instance requires its truck drivers in Myanmar to carry cards stating that any bribe that they are asked to pay will be reported to management. According to Coca-Cola, the cards have proven successful in minimising requests for bribes from traffic police (UNGC 2015). Total S.A., a global energy firm which has also signed up to the UNGC principles, has been active in promoting human rights, as well as community outreach and economic development programmes. The French firm manages a socio-economic programme that operates in 33 villages in Total's Yadana pipeline area that provides support for local schooling and infrastructure development. The company organises frequent stakeholder dialogues and has launched nationwide initiatives that support orphanages, health programmes and hospitals. Yet Total's human rights presence in Myanmar has come under scrutiny by the US-based Collaborative for Development Action (CDA). While the group acknowledges the company's positive steps, CDA stresses the firm can do more to improve its reputation, reduce corporate risk and maintain strong human rights standards (CDA 2014). The CDA argues Total needs to consider a more rigorous and long-term strategy for ensuring the sustainability of its socio-economic programmes in the country (CDA 2014).

Overall, the future prospects for business and human rights in SEA have potential, yet much of this will depend on the political will of sovereign governments in positioning the rights discourse as an important element for protecting the vulnerable and marginalised in Southeast Asia's emerging economies. Multilateral efforts to mainstream human rights within the region's business community are dependent on support from a range of actors including political elites, multinational corporations, intergovernmental agencies, activists and communities. Volatile socio-economic climates and political instability, especially in Myanmar and Thailand, have raised questions on whether governments have the capacity to hold business accountable for rights violations. Although the UNGC and the UNGPs have been criticised by those who see voluntary CSR platforms as weak given their lack of enforcement, the idea and purpose of each initiative continues to be integrated within the regional CSR lexicon.

Conclusion

In many parts of Asia, human rights abuses associated with the private sector are prevalent. The problem of child labour, much sought after in the neo-liberal development model as cheap labour, continues to be an enduring issue, along with persistent encroachments in terms of women's rights. It is also hard to hold up the 'dictum' of economic rights anymore either. According to the Asia Monitor Resource Centre, the workplace is killing millions of Asians every year through various illnesses, poisons and unhealthy workplaces throughout East Asia (*The Guardian* 2012). Moreover, women in Southeast Asia and East Asia have been vulnerable to trafficking. Land grabbing is another area of concern for human rights defenders and an issue that seems unlikely to end anytime soon. Land concessions benefit powerful elites who face slim repercussions for violating rights of the vulnerable under the appearance of economic development.

It is difficult to discuss the development of human rights in the Asia-Pacific region without reference to globalisation, which not only played its part in the region's dramatic economic growth but was a factor in its rapid downfall, with the onset of the Asian economic crisis in mid-1997. The financial crisis and the attendant currency turmoil of the late 1990s simply brought these issues into sharp focus. There are serious questions of illegal (and legal) migration, labour standards, prostitution, child labour, child prostitution and discrimination against ethnic minorities, to name just a few. However, globalisation has also had positive effects in that at least these debates have started to take place, and a consciousness of rights is developing. Indigenous groups have now become more assertive in their claims to political and economic rights. The tension between economic development, rapid growth and the state of governance is an important one.

After September 2001 the global 'war on terror' produced a more difficult and complex world than ever before. More often than not, such efforts were at the expense of individual human rights. The USA has continued to support countries like the Philippines and Indonesia in their anti-terrorist measures and often this has led to abuses. The accession of Barack Obama as US president might have raised hopes for a gentler policy, reversing these trends; unfortunately, this does not seem to have been the case. The 'war on terror' has continued and, most importantly for human rights, this 'war' has allowed states to reinvigorate their internal security mechanisms and justify repression. They can be assured that they will suffer little criticism or adverse measures from the USA as a result. The 'war on terror' has given these countries a new opportunity to exploit the security nexus of the state in violating human rights. This trend appears likely to continue.

Overall, human rights in Southeast Asia remains a marginalised business issue. The UN Global Compact and UN Guiding Principles on Business and Human Rights have yet to materialise into any type of meaningful rights implementation strategy. The regional debate on CSR and human rights is largely being driven by a host of foreign multinational corporations that see human rights due diligence as a mechanism to minimise non-financial risk. Asia-based firms have little interest in human rights as they perceive it as outside their sphere of influence; while these groups tend to view CSR as a public relations strategy. Local civil society groups are generally weak stakeholders and depend on international NGOs to help raise awareness surrounding human rights violations committed at the local level. The launch of the UNGC in Myanmar should be considered as symbolic rather than a serious type of mechanism to help improve the social and environmental record of corporations in the country, while serving as a marketing tool for domestic actors looking to diversify their foreign investment portfolios.

References

American Bar Association 2014, *The ASEAN Human Rights Declaration: A Legal Analysis*, viewed 24 April 2015, www.americanbar.org/content/dam/aba/directories/roli/asean/asean-human-rights-declaration-legal-analysis-2014.authcheckdam.pdf.

ASEAN CSR Network 2015, *Mission and Objective*, viewed 17 August 2015, www.asean-csr-network.org/c/about-us/our-mission-a-objectives.

ASEAN Intergovernmental Commission on Human Rights 2014, *AICHR's Thematic Study on CSR and Human Rights in ASEAN*, viewed 24 April 2015, http://aichr.org/documents/.

ASEAN Secretariat 2015, 'The ASEAN Charter', 18th reprint, viewed 26 May 2016, www.asean.org/wp-content/uploads/2012/05/11.-October-2015-The-ASEAN-Charter-18th-Reprint-Amended-updated-on-05_-April-2016-IJP.pdf.

Asian Development Bank 2015, *Asian Development Outlook 2015: Financing Asia's Future Growth*, viewed 24 April 2015, www.adb.org/publications/asian-development-outlook-2015-financing-asias-future-growth.

Asian Human Rights Commission 2015, *Human Rights Day Report 2015*, viewed 26 May 2016, www.humanrights.asia/resources/hrreport/2015.

Association of Southeast Asian Nations 2013, *ASEAN Human Rights Declaration*, viewed 26 May 2016, www.asean.org/storage/images/ASEAN_RTK_2014/6_AHRD_Booklet.pdf.

Bünte, M 2016, 'Myanmar's Protracted Transition', *Asian Survey*, vol. 56, no. 2, pp. 369–391.

Business and Human Rights Resource Centre 2015, 'Briefing: Development for All, or a Privileged Few? Business and Human Rights in Southeast Asia', viewed 24 April 2015, http://business-humanrights.org/en/development-for-all-or-a-privileged-few-business-human-rights-in-southeast-asia.

Case, W 2010, *Contemporary Authoritarianism in Southeast Asia: Structures, Institution and Agency*. New York: Routledge.

Collaborative for Development Action 2014, *Corporate Engagement Program: Field Visit Report – Total E&P Myanmar*, viewed 18 August 2015, www.cdacollaborative.org/publications/corporate-engagement/cep-case-studies/total-ep-myanmar-seventh-site-visit/.

CSR Asia 2014, *Why Businesses Fail to Engage with Human Rights*, viewed 23 April 2015, http://csr-asia.com/csr-asia-weekly-news-detail.php?id=12401.

The Diplomat 2012, 'Human Rights Declaration Falls Short', viewed 24 April 2015, http://thediplomat.com/2012/11/human-rights-declaration-falls-short/.

Forest Peoples Programme 2013, *Agribusiness Large-scale Land Acquisitions and Human Rights in Southeast Asia*, viewed 24 April 2015, www.forestpeoples.org/sites/fpp/files/publication/2013/08/lsla-briefings.pdf.

FORUM-ASIA 2015, 'Thailand: Regional Human Rights Group Condemns Murder of Land Rights Defender', viewed 24 April 2015, www.forum-asia.org/?p=18323.

FORUM-ASIA 2016, 'Open Letter to the Cambodian Prime Minister: End Legal Harassment of Cambodian Human Rights Defenders Including ADHOC Staff Members', viewed 24 May 2016, www.forum-asia.org/?p=20669.

The Guardian 2012, 'Workplace Poisoning Killing Millions of Asians Each Year, Says New Report', viewed 26 May 2016, www.theguardian.com/world/2012/apr/26/workplace-poisoning-killing-millions-of-asians.

Human Rights Watch 2011, 'Gold's Costly Divide', viewed 24 April 2015, www.hrw.org/node/95767/section/2.

International Crisis Group 2016, Southeast Asia: Recent Reports, viewed 24 May 2016, www.crisisgroup.org/en/regions/asia/south-east-asia.aspx.

The Jakarta Post 2015, 'Greenpeace Halts APP Deal after Brutal Murder', viewed 24 April 2015, www.thejakartapost.com/news/2015/03/03/greenpeace-halts-app-deal-after-brutal-murder.html.

Jones, W 2014, 'Universalizing Human Rights The ASEAN Way', *International Journal of Social Sciences*, vol. 3, no. 3, pp. 72–89.

Kaufmann, C 2013, 'Introduction: Situating the Debate', in Human Rights Resource Centre, *Business and Human Rights in ASEAN: A Baseline Study*, viewed 24 April 2015, http://hrrca.org/system/files/u6/Business%20and%20Human%20Rights%20in%20ASEAN%20Baseline%20Study%20ebook.pdf.

Kell, G 2013, Executive Director of the United Nations Global Compact. Interview conducted via phone, 19 August 2013.

Mohan, M 2011, 'Regulating Business Impacts on Human Rights in Southeast Asia: Lessons from the EU', *Asia Europe Journal*, vol. 9, no. 1, pp. 57–65.

Office of the High Commissioner for Human Rights 2016, 2016 UN Asia Regional Forum on Business and Human Rights, viewed 26 May 2016, www.ohchr.org/EN/Issues/Business/Pages/2016AsiaRegionalForum.aspx.

Office of the United Nations High Commissioner for Human Rights 2007, *Report of the Special Representative of the Secretary-General on the Issue of Human Rights and Transnational Corporations and Other Business Enterprises*, viewed 26 May 2016, www2.ohchr.org/english/bodies/hrcouncil/docs/4session/A.HRC.4.35.Add.4.pdf.

Office of the United Nations High Commissioner for Human Rights 2014, *Report of the Working Group on the Issue of Human Rights and Transnational Corporations and Other Business Enterprises*, viewed 22 April 2015, www.ohchr.org/EN/HRBodies/HRC/.../A_HRC_26_25_ENG.doc.

Parekh, B 2004, 'Non-ethnocentric Universalism', in T Dunne & NJ Wheeler (eds), *Human Rights in Global Politics*, New York: Cambridge University Press.
Personal Interview 2012a, CEO of Burmese Corporation, personal communication between Robert Hanlon and Original Signatory of UNGC Myanmar, interview conducted via Skype, 6 June 2012.
Personal Interview 2012b, CEO of Burmese Corporation, personal communication between Robert Hanlon and Original Signatory of UNGC Myanmar, interview conducted via phone, 4 June 2012.
Personal Interview 2012c, UNGC Official, personal communication between Robert Hanlon and Project Manager of UNGC Myanmar Portfolio, interview questions sent via email, 3 June 2012.
Radio Free Asia 2015, 'Lao Civil Society Pressured to Drop Rights Issues from ASEAN Forum', viewed 21 April 2015, www.rfa.org/english/news/laos/forum-04222015150409.html.
Shaba, L & Meuter, J 2013, *RBC Initiatives in Southeast Asia: An Overview Insights for RBC Policy Making*, viewed 24 April 2015, www.oecd.org/daf/inv/mne/RBC-Initiatives-in-Southeast-Asia-an-Overview.pdf.
Sherwell, P 2016, 'British Activist Faces Jail Threat in Thailand as Trial Starts over Worker Abuse Research', *The Telegraph*, 19 May, viewed 26 May 2016, www.telegraph.co.uk/news/2016/05/19/british-activist-faces-jail-threat-in-thailand-as-trial-starts-o/.
Studwell, J 2007, *Asian Godfathers: Money and Power in Hong Kong and Southeast Asia*, New York: Grove Press.
United Nations Global Compact 2013, 'Business Action in Support of the Rule of Law: An Example in Myanmar', viewed 17 August 2015, www.unglobalcompact.org/library/731.
United Nations Global Compact 2015, 'Coca-Cola's Fight against Corruption in Myanmar', viewed 17 August 2015, www.unglobalcompact.org/take-action/action/case-example/113.
Welford, R 2015, personal communication between Robert Hanlon and Richard Welford, Chairman of CSR Asia, via Skype, 22 April 2015.

10

Human rights defenders, foreign investment and land in Myanmar

A question of power and marginalisation

Alison Graham

Introduction

The free functioning of human rights defenders is critical for the protection of all human rights. Yet, while Myanmar is being praised for opening up and supposedly working towards ensuring democratic freedoms, human rights defenders have remained under threat. Particularly at risk are those protesting against urban development, land acquisition and the expropriation of natural resources by national and international companies threatening the human rights of many small-hold farmers, especially the right to an adequate standard of living. Many of these human rights defenders have been detained, threatened and in some cases killed. As well as violating key civil and political rights, this is undermining protection for economic and social rights, and is increasing inequality, particularly for ethnic minorities, many of whom depend on land to provide for themselves and who have limited access to justice or political power. This further exacerbates the vulnerability and marginalisation of these ethnic minorities. It could also contribute to increasing tensions in their resource-rich homelands that are only just beginning to recover from the conflict that has characterised these regions from independence in 1948 (*The Economist* 2013). Although the political reforms of 2011 and the initiation of a peace process have been followed by several ceasefires, tensions remain (*The Economist* 2013).

Background

Myanmar was ruled by a military dictatorship from 1962 to 2010 with severe restrictions on the freedom of expression, assembly and association amongst other rights (Quintana 2011). Ethnic and religious minority groups have also faced systematic and endemic discrimination (Quintana 2011). In 2011, Myanmar transitioned to a quasi-civilian government, which started a process of political and economic reform. This new government under President Thein Sein released political prisoners (including Aung San Suu Kyi from house arrest), loosened media restrictions, initiated dialogue with armed groups, established the Myanmar National Human Rights Commission, and promised to allow for international monitoring of human rights (Karen Human Rights Group 2015: 18). Despite this, however, many people advocating for the implementation of human rights have continued to be arrested and imprisoned under Thein

Sein's government (Amnesty USA 2015). Protestors against land acquisitions that are resulting in the forced eviction of farmers and entire communities for infrastructure and commercial projects, usually without compensation, are particularly at risk (Human Rights Watch 2016). While in 2016 the democratically elected National League for Democracy (NLD) became the new government with Htin Kyaw as the president, to make substantial progress in guaranteeing human rights it must break away from much of the still remaining deeply repressive legislation (Amnesty USA 2016).

Human rights defenders are 'people who, individually or with others, act to promote or protect human rights' (Office of the High Commissioner for Human Rights 1996). This term can thus include those people directly affected by human rights violations providing they are advocating for the implementation of their rights. The importance of human rights defenders in exposing human rights violations and promoting accountability for governments, and increasingly for corporations, has been recognised by the United Nations (UN) and the European Union (EU) (Ministry of Foreign Affairs, the Netherlands 2009). Academics have similarly noted that social movements, often made up of human rights defenders, including labour unions and welfare rights groups, have played a critical role in shaping domestic policy and law that protects economic and social rights and in ensuring equality (Young 2012: 224). Their repression is therefore clearly not just an issue in itself but one that threatens the very fabric of the national human rights protection systems.

The importance of human rights defenders and a robust human rights protection system remains particularly crucial in a post-conflict society such as Myanmar to ensure that the voices of the most marginalised and vulnerable are heard, and their human rights respected and protected. Their free functioning is essential in guaranteeing an inclusive society that ensures and promotes peace. The importance of human rights defenders to securing peace includes those working on economic and social rights such as land rights activists. Violations of economic and social rights are being increasingly recognised as a critical factor in igniting, perpetuating or promoting a return to conflict (Office of the High Commissioner for Human Rights 2016: 1–3). In fact, in Myanmar, access to and control over land was one of the principal economic grievances that fuelled the conflict in the ethnic states[1] (Transnational Institute 2013: 1). Ethnic groups living in these resource-rich regions accused the central government of exploiting natural resources without reinvesting profits back into the local population (Transnational Institute 2013: 1).

OHCHR has also identified a number of other risk factors for conflict and/or serious human rights violations that include a lack of access to effective grievance mechanisms and shrinking democratic space for civil society. (Office of the High Commissioner for Human Rights 2016: 16–19). Certainly, it seems logical that with limited ability to change their situation and to secure their rights, tensions amongst the affected communities will rise and conflict could ignite.

Human rights obligations

Myanmar is yet to ratify core human rights treaties such as the International Covenant on Civil and Political Rights and the Convention on the Elimination of Racial Discrimination. It has, however, signed the International Covenant on Economic, Social and Cultural Rights, and ratified both the Convention on the Rights of the Child (CRC) and the Convention on the Elimination of Discrimination Against Women (CEDAW). Both these conventions recognise the right to an adequate standard of living. Article 14 of the CRC obligates states parties to ensure 'the right of every child to a standard of living adequate for the child's physical, mental, spiritual, moral and social development'. This clearly then obligates states to respect and protect families' and women's access to livelihoods.

States parties are also obligated to ensure that these rights are enjoyed without discrimination (CEDAW: Art. 2; CRC: Art. 2). This requires both protecting people against both direct and indirect discrimination and ensuring the equal enjoyment of people's rights in reality (Committee on the Elimination of Discrimination Against Women 2004). This may often require positive measures to overcome the real impediments preventing certain groups from accessing and enjoying their human rights such as providing free interpreters for linguistic minorities to help them access social services (*Eldridge v British Columbia (Attorney General)* 1997). In some cases, it might also require affirmative action, i.e. temporary special measures that allow justifiable preferential treatment for certain population groups to correct past and present forms and effects of discrimination (Committee on the Elimination of Discrimination Against Women 2004).

Myanmar is morally and to a certain extent legally bound by the Universal Declaration of Human Rights (UDHR). Many scholars argue that the UDHR remains the primary source of global human rights standards, and is recognised by states worldwide as a source of rights and law (Hannum 1998: 146). Other academics acknowledge that only certain articles of the UDHR have the status of customary international law, such as the prohibition of racial discrimination (Lawyers Rights Watch Canada [undated]). Nonetheless the UDHR remains the articulation of the UN Charter's human rights provisions, and is 'the primary source of the global consensus on human rights' (Hannum 1998: 144). The UDHR includes all rights be they civil, cultural, economic, political and social.

The Declaration on the Right and Responsibility of Individuals, Groups and Organs of Society to Promote and Protect Universally Recognised Human Rights and Fundamental Freedoms (the Declaration on Human Rights Defenders) elucidates states' human rights obligations regarding human rights defenders. While again, the Declaration is not, in itself, a legally binding instrument, the principles and rights contained therein have been enshrined in other international instruments. It therefore does not create new rights but instead articulates existing rights to make them more applicable to the practical role and situation of human rights defenders.

Notably Article 1 of the Declaration reaffirms the rights of everyone 'to promote and to strive for the protection and realization of human rights and fundamental freedoms at the national and international levels'. The Declaration further stipulates the right to be protected 'against any violence, threats, retaliation, de facto or de jure adverse discrimination, pressure or any other arbitrary action as a consequence of his or her legitimate exercise of the rights referred to in the present Declaration' (Art. 12); and the rights to freedom of expression, assembly, and of association (Arts 5 and 6). It also articulates the rights of human rights defenders: to develop and discuss new human rights ideas and to advocate for their acceptance; to criticise government bodies and agencies and make proposals to improve their functioning; to provide legal assistance or other advice and assistance in defence of human rights; to gain unhindered access to and communication with non-governmental and intergovernmental organisations, and international bodies; and to access resources for the purpose of protecting human rights, including the receipt of funds from abroad (Office of the High Commissioner for Human Rights 2011).

Foreign investment and land reform in Myanmar

Land has been and remains a crucial issue in Myanmar. Seventy five per cent of Myanmar's population consists of subsistence farmers who are reliant on access to land and forests in order to provide for themselves and their families (Buchanan, Kramer & Woods 2013: 3). This is particularly true in the ethnic states 'that occupy 57% of the total land area (and) are home to poor and often persecuted ethnic minority groups' (Transnational Institute 2013: 1). For the most part these ethic communities practice small-scale farming with few alternative means of livelihood open to them due to systematic and entrenched discrimination over decades. Furthermore, over half of the subsistence farmers in Myanmar lack formally recognised land titles and instead rely on a traditional land use system that was created and functions at the community level, but is not recognised by the government (Aguirre 2015).

These farmers are vulnerable to land acquisition, or 'land grabbing' by corporations that is currently being aided and abetted by the government (Asian Legal Resource Centre 2012). In his 2011 inauguration speech President Thein Sein made it clear he was opening Myanmar for foreign investment in order to drive economic growth (Transnational Institute 2013), and soon after started to liberalise the economy, implementing reforms to attract foreign investment (Buchanan, Kramer & Woods 2013: 12). Thein Sein's government wanted to secure development through stimulating industrial agricultural production – especially for rubber, palm oil and paddy rice – through massive foreign investment (Transnational Institute 2013: 2). Particularly of interest to many companies are the resource rich-ethnic states where land is more readily available due to the ceasefires and peace process (Buchanan, Kramer & Woods 2013: 3). In Karen State for instance human rights groups have noted that villagers southeast continue to face widespread land confiscation, mostly due to 'the rapid expansion of domestic and international commercial interest and investment in southeast Myanmar since the January 2012 preliminary ceasefire between the Karen National Union and the Myanmar Government' (Karen Human Rights Group 2015: 1).

While it is often claimed that FDI promotes economic growth and development, increased FDI has not always translated into benefits for local communities, particularly those most marginalised such as the ethnic minorities and indigenous communities. International investment law is based on a web of bilateral investment treaties (BITs), usually agreed between a developed and a developing country. They are designed to facilitate investment in the developing country by providing legal guarantees and stability for investors through clauses that protect investors from any future changes in the law including those that might improve the protection of human rights, public health and/or the environment to the detriment of investors. BITs are therefore often regarded as asymmetric, with foreign investors being 'accorded substantive rights' without incurring any obligations (Dumberry & Dumas Aubin 2013). With developing countries competing against each other for foreign direct investment, the requirements and regulations imposed on foreign investors including to respect and protect human rights are consistently minimal. In 2003 the High Commissioner for Human Rights had observed that 'this race to attract investment might lead to a race to the bottom to the severe detriment of human rights' (Office of the High Commissioner for Human Rights 2003).

Any disputes between foreign investors and host governments are settled outside the national court system through investment arbitration dispute settlement mechanisms on a case-by-case basis according to procedural rules[2] with the aim of providing 'a fair and neutral dispute settlement system . . . to protect their corporations' investments from perceived bias and corruption within national courts' (Eberhardt & Olivet 2012). Civil society organisations have therefore frequently observed that such mechanisms are far from neutral (Eberhardt & Olivert 2012). While their procedural rules differ, over the past decades such mechanisms have proved effective at holding governments to account for the way they treat investors, granting investors substantial compensation for host breaches of contracts or treaties (International Institute for Environment and Development 2009).

In Myanmar civil society organisations have noted with concern that there is little legislation in place to protect the human rights of Myanmar's most vulnerable populations and that it is in fact instead primarily orientated towards attracting investors (Burma Project 2014; International

Federation for Human Rights 2013). In particular the Farmland Act and the Vacant, Fallow and Virgin Land Act have been criticised for opening up the land market to foreign investment and benefitting large corporate interests without protecting the rights of those who need access to land/or forests for their livelihoods (Chung Ho 2013). The 2012 Farmland Act repeals the 1953 Land Nationalization Act, which directed that all land in Myanmar is property of the government. While the 2008 Constitution of Myanmar stipulates that all land is to remain the property of the state, the Farmland Law, establishes a system of land registration for farmers that provides land use certificates (LUCs) that, once secured, create rights to sell, exchange, access credit against, inherit and lease the land over which they hold rights (Displacement Solutions 2015: 9). While in theory this is designed to expand rights to those in rural areas, to secure LUCs, farmers must have some sort of deed of title or legal registration document (Displacement Solutions 2015: 9). Without this, they have effectively no rights to the land concerned under statutory law (Displacement Solutions 2015: 9–10). This is particularly concerning since it is estimated that only 15%, or less, have such land registration documents (Denmark 2013). There are also significant questions about whether subsistence farmers are aware of their rights and the administrative processes involved in obtaining such LUCs (Henley 2014: 10). Moreover, even if a farmer has an LUC his or her tenure rights are not secure since the government can revoke the LUCs for failing to comply with the strict conditions of use (Displacement Solutions 2015: 9).

The Vacant, Fallow and Virgin Land Law, passed as an amendment to the Farmland Act, stipulates that any unused land can be claimed and utilised by willing individuals (foreign or local investors included) for 30 years (Oberndorf 2012: 22). However, it is unclear what constitutes 'vacant, fallow and virgin land' and there is a risk of those who, for generations, have engaged in sustainable rotation crop practices, having their land passed to domestic and foreign investors (Transnational Institute 2013).

Displacement Solutions director Scott Leckie criticises the legislation for ignoring customary land titles and for making it easier for well-connected business persons and military cronies to seize land from small-scale farmers (Chung Ho 2013). It was further observed that 'The new laws willingly give *carte blanche* to the government and their closest allies the power to essentially do whatever they want in areas that they would like to exploit', and believes that they represent a 'clear obstacle to a sustainable peace throughout the country' (Chung Ho 2013). NGOs have further accused the Thein Sein government of not taking into account the land rights of ethnic minorities and their particular situation when drafting and adopting the two Acts.

The effects of land grabbing by corporations can be catastrophic for those affected. The land is usually taken away without consultation, and the occupiers often do not receive compensation even if the land is currently under cultivation (Karen Human Rights Group 2013). Without land, the former subsistence farmers are usually unable to secure an adequate standard of living with limited means of alternative livelihood (Karen Human Rights Group 2015). Several organisations have noted that many women and girls affected by land grabbing turn to prostitution in order to provide for themselves and their families (Partners Relief & Development 2012). Typically, those from the minority ethnic populations are particularly affected since they inhabit the 'most isolated and impoverished areas' (Buchanan, Kramer, & Woods 2013: 2). Such 'land grabbing' therefore often increases poverty, marginalisation and inequality.

To help address some of the concerns over land use and tenure, the Thein Sein government drafted a National Land Use Policy (NLUP) that was released in the final days of the outgoing parliament in late January 2016. The NLUP is essentially a framework to guide the development of a National Land Use Law and the harmonisation of the many existing land-related laws in Myanmar. Daniel Aguirre of the International Commission of Jurists has praised the policy for using 'rights-based language in its basic principles' and referring 'directly to human rights standards in chapters related to land acquisition, the land use rights of ethnic minorities' and being 'framed with explicit reference to the equality of men and women' (Aguirre 2016). However, the NLD government now needs to build on this and enshrine its principles into law (Aguirre 2016). At the moment it lacks the teeth necessary to protect the most marginalised against land grabs and forced evictions.

The situation of human rights defenders

In Myanmar, in addition to unequal access to and control over natural resources that is exacerbating inequality, marginalisation, particularly in the ethnic states, there is shrinking civil society space. This is particularly vital and worrying given the power imbalance between corporations and subsistence farmers, and the fact that the 'least-advantaged citizens are still getting steamrolled across the country, losing their land to powerful elites and their international partners' (Motlagh 2013).

This need for a robust civil society is increased by the very few avenues available to victims of 'land grabbing' to seek redress. Myanmar's judiciary is not independent from political and executive branches of government, and lacks the resources or the capacity to deal with complex land cases (Aguirre 2015). Moreover, the implementing bodies related to various land laws, such as the Farmland Management Body (the main institution for resolving farmland disputes under the Farmland Law) are often considered final, and therefore, the judiciary does not fulfil its role in overseeing executive decisions (Aguirre 2015). According to Henley 'appeals can be made up to the state-level FMB, but there is no provision for appeal to the judiciary' (Henley 2014: 10).

Additionally, although the Land Acquisition Inquiry Commission, created in 2012, is mandated to investigate past cases of land acquisition and whether confiscation has been carried out in compliance with the law, it has 'no power to resolve disputes or provide compensation. Its role is limited to informing parliamentary initiatives' (Henley 2014: 10). Similarly, while a parliamentary commission (Land Investigation Commission) was established on 26 July 2012 to investigate land confiscation cases, civil society groups claim that the Commission 'has been unable to deal effectively with these cases or move forward on reforms to prevent further occurrence' (International Federation for Human Rights 2013). Furthermore, when villagers have tried to follow the available avenues to protest and secure compensation, they have been reportedly threatened by government authorities (Karen Human Rights Group 2013).

The robustness of civil society is being undermined by legislation that falls short of international standards by failing to protect freedom of association, assembly and expression, which is crucial if human rights defenders are to be able to work freely and effectively (Sekaggya 2013: para. 66). In 2015 one international human rights organisation expressed deep concern 'at reports of an increase in the arrest, prosecution and imprisonment of people exercising their fundamental rights to freedom of expression, association and assembly, particularly those protesting against land grabs and major development projects' (International Service for Human Rights 2015). This is discussed more fully in the paragraphs below.

While recognising the right of peaceful assembly, the 2011 Right to Peaceful Assembly and Peaceful Procession Law has been heavily criticised for falling short of international human rights standards. It prohibits unauthorised outdoor assemblies of more than five persons, and specifies that such authorisation must be sought at least five days in advance. In addition to basic information such as the date, time and place of the planned assembly, the application process requires information on the assembly's purpose and schedule, the names and addresses of organisers and speakers, and details of any proposed chants or slogans (Lee 2015: para. 13). Even when authorised, those taking part must not 'talk or behave in a way to cause any disturbance or obstruction, annoyance, danger or a concern that these might take place' and/or 'that could negatively affect the country or the Union, race, or religion, human dignity and moral principles' (Human Rights Watch 2015). They also 'must not spread rumors or incorrect information' (Human Rights Watch 2015). A violation of any of these restrictions may result in a term of imprisonment (Human Rights Watch 2015). While the Law was amended in June 2014 to supposedly address some of these shortcomings, many remain. It clarified that the request for authorisation shall be rejected only if the authorities provide 'valid reasons' (International Service for Human Rights 2015). However, without further elaboration on what constitutes 'valid reasons', this can be arbitrarily interpreted (Article 19 2014: 3). Moreover, to comply with international standards, people should not have to ask permission in order to exercise their right to peaceful assembly (Human Rights Watch 2015). The amendments also retained imprisonment as a penalty for violating the Act, only halving the maximum prison sentence for causing unrest to one year and for failing to seek permission for protesting to six months (International Center for Not-For-Profit Law 2016).

Many organisations, including Amnesty International, have continued to document the frequent arrest and detention of land rights activists protesting against land acquisition for allegedly violating the Peaceful Assembly and Peaceful Procession Law (Amnesty International 2014). This includes the arrest and sentencing of human rights defenders for attending a farmers' demonstration against land confiscation on 10 June 2013 in Nattalin (AHRC 2013). Also in 2013, ten individuals were sentenced to three months in prison for demonstrating against the Shwe Gas Project in Arakan State. They were arrested for violating Article 18 of the Peaceful Assembly and Peaceful Procession Law, which requires a permit from the authorities for any public assembly.[3] The demonstrators had previously been denied a permit twice on the purported grounds that a state of emergency had been declared under Article 144 of the Penal Code following ethno-religious clashes in other parts of Arakan State. This was despite the fact that there had been no incidence of violence in Maday Island (Forum Asia 2013).

Human rights defenders have also been arrested and charged under the Unlawful Associations Act (1908) that prohibits aiding and abetting members of an unlawful association. Since the president has the power to declare an association unlawful (Unlawful Associations Act, Art. 16, part II), local NGOs have expressed concern that they might unwittingly come under the scope of the Act. Nilar Myaing of the Local Resource Centre, for instance, has noted that, although the original law does not mention civil society organisations, the wording 'associations stated in the act' could include non-government organisations (*Myanmar Times* 2013). In August 2015, several prominent land rights campaigners in Karen State were arrested under this Act (*Karen News* 2015).

There is potential for abuse against human rights defenders under the Penal Code due to ambiguity. For example, Article 505(b) prohibits the 'inducement of crimes against the state or against public order by means of any statement, rumor or report'. As Burma Partnership and Forum Asia note, it has often been 'used in conjunction' with section 18 of the 2011 Right to Peaceful Assembly and Peaceful Procession Law (amended in 2014) to 'target peaceful protestors who are legitimately exercising their fundamental rights to freedom of assembly and expression' (Burma Partnership & Forum Asia 2014). Other concerns include Article 447 of the Penal Code that stipulates that 'criminal trespass shall be punished' with imprisonment or a fine. Protestors have often been accused of and imprisoned for 'trespassing' on what they regard as their own land (Aljazeera America 2014). On 23 July 2015, for instance, police arrested human rights defender Su Su Nway, who had been assisting local farmers in Bago to claim back their land. She was arrested on charges of trespassing under Article 447 of Myanmar's Penal Code (Frontline Defenders 2015) and was sentenced to 15 days in prison with hard labour (AWID 2015).

In addition to arrests and detention, security forces have also used excessive force against land rights activists. One of the most notable cases concerned the Chinese backed Letpadaung Copper Mine, in Monywa, Sagaing Region. First initiated in the 1970s, from 2010/11 the site has been developed and operated by Wanbao Mining Ltd in collaboration with the Thein Sein government (Amnesty International 2015b). Many people have been forcibly evicted from the land they depend on, and expressing their dissatisfaction with the resettlement process, compensation schemes, environmental and health effects, the local community has organised numerous protests and demonstrations in 2012 and 2014 (Amnesty International 2015b). On 29 November 2012 local authorities used excessive force against the protesters (Lee 2015). Authorities reportedly used white phosphorus[4] grenades and over 100 people were injured, with some suffering horrific burns and lifelong disability (Amnesty International 2015a). So far there has been no investigation into the event (Amnesty International 2015a). On 22 December 2014 security forces used live ammunition against the protesters, injuring many people and killing one human rights defender (Amnesty International 2015b). In a statement, Myanmar's National Human Rights Commission (MNHRC) found that the police and security forces did not take adequate steps to de-escalate or disperse the protest before resorting to force (MNHRC 2014).

The cases mentioned above are just a snapshot of the problems facing human rights defenders working on land-related issues in Myanmar. In 2015 Phil Robertson, Human Rights Watch's deputy Asia director, highlighted:

> The Burmese authorities' repeated use of oppressive laws against land rights activists is a heavy-handed attempt to silence them. These activists are forced to run a gauntlet of government intimidation, arrests – and now, trumped-up charges – just to try and help villagers stay on their land.
>
> (Karen News *2015)*

Conclusion

As the UN Special Rapporteur on Myanmar has noted 'While the growing economy has benefited some in the country, there remain large sections of the population who have been left out' (Lee 2015: para. 62). This is being exacerbated by the land grabbing that is perpetuating the cycle of poverty and marginalisation, particularly amongst the ethnic minorities who by living in the resource-rich ethnic states are the most at risk of having their means of livelihood taken from them.

With a systemic imbalance of power in favour of the corporations acquiring the land over land users, and a lack of access to justice and remedies, the attacks on human rights defenders and civil society, in particular land-rights activists, is also especially worrying.

Land issues are a well-known source of conflict (Office of the High Commissioner for Human Rights 2016). However, when also accompanied by decreasing space for human rights activists and no opportunities for justice, a potent cocktail is created (Office of the High Commissioner for Human Rights 2016). While these issues are grave human rights concerns in themselves, they must also be viewed by all actors in Myanmar as together significantly undermining the peace process, jeopardising the creation of a fair, inclusive society and risking a return to conflict. The NLD government has inherited an increasingly volatile situation and it is imperative that it takes the necessary action to secure people's human rights to avoid a return to conflict.

Notes

1 These states are named after the seven main ethnic groups living there and are Kachin, Kayah, Kayin, Chin, Mon, Rakhine and Shan States.
2 The most common arbitration options include the International Centre for Settlement of Investment Disputes (ICSID) (World Bank), United Nations Commission on International Trade Law (UNCITRAL), Stockholm Chamber of Commerce and the International Chamber of Commerce (Peterson 2009).
3 The pipeline project passes through 20 townships across Myanmar and has thus far resulted in a long list of human rights abuses, including forced labour, forced eviction and land confiscation, and arbitrary taxation.
4 White phosphorus can cause injuries and death in three ways: by burning deep into tissue, from being inhaled as a smoke, and from being ingested.

References

Aguirre, D 2015, *Outdated Laws and an Inadequate Judiciary: A Recipe for Land Related Human Rights Violations and Conflict*, 21 October, viewed 6 June 2016, https://businesshumanrightsburma.wordpress.com/2015/10/21/outdated-laws-and-an-inadequate-judiciary-a-recipe-for-land-related-human-rights-violations-and-conflict/.

Aguirre, D 2016, *Myanmar: A Sound Basis for Land Reform*, 19th February, viewed 6 June 2016, https://landportal.info/news/2016/02/myanmar-sound-basis-land-reform.

Aljazeera America 2014, *Plow Protesters Lose Land and Liberty in Myanmar*, 12 November, viewed 8 June 2016, http://america.aljazeera.com/articles/2014/11/12/myanmar-arrests-pointtodangerousfuture.html.

Amnesty International 2014, *Myanmar: Stop Using Repressive Law against Peaceful Protesters*, viewed 10 June 2016, www.amnesty.org/download/Documents/4000/asa160252014en.pdf.

Amnesty International 2015a, *Myanmar: Letpadaung Mine Protesters Still Denied Justice*, 27 November, viewed 20 June 2016, www.amnesty.org/en/latest/news/2015/11/myanmar-letpadaung-mine-protesters-still-denied-justice/.

Amnesty International 2015b, *Open for Business? Corporate Crime and Abuses at Myanmar Copper Mine*, viewed 20 June 2016, www.amnesty.nl/sites/default/files/public/amnesty_letpadaung_-_final_report.pdf.

Amnesty USA 2015, *Going Back to the Old Way*, viewed 23 June 2016, www.amnestyusa.org/sites/default/files/amnesty_myanmar_pocs_briefing.pdf.

Amnesty USA 2016, *New Expression Meets Old Repression: Ending the Cycle of Political Arrests and Imprisonment in Myanmar*, 24 March, viewed 24 June 2016, www.amnestyusa.org/research/reports/new-expression-meets-old-repression-ending-the-cycle-of-political-arrests-and-imprisonment-in-myanma.

Article 19 2014, *Myanmar: Amended Right to Peaceful Assembly and Peaceful Procession Law*, August, viewed 10 June 2016, www.article19.org/data/files/medialibrary/37666/14-08-01-LA-myanmar-assembly.pdf.

Asian Human Rights Commission (AHRC) 2013, *Burma/Myanmar: Three People Detained and Charged for Fighting for Farmers' Land Rights*, 26 July, viewed 20 June 2016, www.humanrights.asia/news/urgent-appeals/AHRC-UAC-101-2013.

Asian Legal Resource Centre (ALRC) 2012, *Myanmar at Risk of Land-grabbing Epidemic*, Statement to the Human Rights Council on 6 June.

AWID 2015, *Burma/Myanmar: Release of Ms. Su Su Nway Leader of the Myanmar Farmers Union*, 26 August, viewed 10 June 2016, www.awid.org/get-involved/burmamyanmar-release-ms-su-su-nway-leader-myanmar-farmers-union.

Buchanan, J, Kramer, T & Woods, K 2013, *Developing Disparity: Regional Investment in Burma's Borderlands*, Amsterdam: Transnational Institute and Burma Centre.

Burma Partnership & Forum Asia 2014, *Briefing Paper on the Situation of Human Rights in Burma/Myanmar 25th Regular Session of the UN Human Rights Council*, Myanmar/Geneva: Burma Partnership and Forum Asia, viewed 1 April 2015, www.burmapartnership.org/2014/03/briefing-paper-on-the-situation-of-human-rights-in-burmamyanmar-25th-regular-session-of-the-un-human-rights-council.

Burma Project 2014, CSO Statement on Myanmar investment treaties, 25 June, viewed 6 June 2016, www.tni.org/declaration/cso-statement-myanmar-investment-treaties.

Chung Ho, E 2013, 'The Peace Process and Land Rights', *DVB News*, 18 June, viewed 5 April 2015, www.dvb.no/analysis/the-peace-process-and-land-rights/28846.

Committee on the Elimination of Discrimination Against Women 2004, *General Recommendation No. 25, on Article 4, Paragraph 1, of the Convention on the Elimination of All Forms of Discrimination Against Women, on Temporary Special Measures*, viewed 5 July 2016, www.un.org/womenwatch/daw/cedaw/recommendations/General%20recommendation%2025%20(English).pdf.

Denmark, M 2013, 'Land Rights Key to Peace Process', *Myanmar Times*, 10 June, viewed 6 April 2015, http://displacementsolutions.org/myanmar-times-on-ds-report-land-rights-key-to-peace-process/.

Displacement Solutions 2015, *Land Acquisition Law and Practice in Myanmar: Overview, Gap Analysis with IFC PS1 & PS5 and Scope of Due Diligence Recommendations, May*, viewed 6 June 2016, http://displacementsolutions.org/wp-content/uploads/2015/05/LAND-ACQUISITION-LAW-AND-PRACTICE-IN-MYANMAR.pdf.

Dumberry, P & Dumas-Aubin, G 2013, *How to Incorporate Human Rights Obligations in Bilateral Investment Treaties?* Canada: International Institute for Sustainable Development.

Eberhardt, P & Olivet, C 2012, *How Law Firms, Arbitrators and Financiers Are Fuelling an Investment Arbitration Boom?* Amsterdam: Transnational Institute, viewed 6 April 2015, www.tni.org/briefing/profiting-injustice.

The Economist 2013, 'Myanmar Ethnic Conflicts: Waiting for the Dividend', 5 October, viewed 3 June 2014, www.economist.com/news/asia/21587272-despite-hopes-nationwide-ceasefire-agreement-trust-needed-lasting-peace-remains-long.

Eldridge vs. British Columbia (Attorney General) (1997) Canada Supreme Court, 2 S.C.R. 624.

Forum Asia 2013, *Burma: Imprisonment of Arakan Human Rights Defenders Exposes Government's Continued Complicity in Corporate Human Rights Abuses. Bangkok, Forum Asia, 30 September*, viewed 7 April 2015, www.forum-asia.org/?p=16416, http://www.hrw.org/news/2015/01/26/burma-peaceful-assembly-law-fails-end-repression.

Frontline Defenders 2015, *Myanmar (Burma): Human rights defender Su Su Nway Arrested*, 24 July, viewed 6 August 2015, http://frontlinedefenders.org/node/29194.

Hannum, H 1998, 'The Status of the Universal Declaration of Human Rights in National and International Law', *Health & Human Rights*, vol. 3, pp. 144–158.

Henley, G 2014, *Case Study on Land in Burma*, London: Overseas Development Institute.

Human Rights Watch 2015, *Burma: 'Peaceful Assembly Law' Fails to End Repression*, New York: Human Rights Watch, 26 January, viewed 4 April 2015, www.hrw.org/news/2015/01/26/burma-peaceful-assembly-law-fails-end-repression.

Human Rights Watch 2016, *Burma: Growing Political Prisoner Population Students, Land Rights Activists, and Journalists Face Bogus Charges*, 17 January, viewed 6 June 2016, www.hrw.org/news/2016/01/17/burma-growing-political-prisoner-population.

International Center for Not-For-Profit Law 2016, *NGO Law Monitor: Myanmar (Burma)*, 23 January, viewed 6 June 2016, www.icnl.org/research/monitor/Myanmar.html.

International Federation for Human Rights 2013, *Burma/Myanmar Not Ready for Rights-compliant Investment*, 28 February, Paris: FID, viewed 4 April 2015, www.fidh.org/en/asia/burma/Burma-not-ready-for-rights-12969.

International Institute for Environment and Development 2009, *'Land Grabs' in Africa: Can the Deals Work for Development?* IIED briefing note, London: IIED, viewed 4 April 2015, www.iied.org/pubs/pdfs/17069IIED.pdf.

International Service for Human Rights 2015, *Myanmar: End Restrictions, Reprisals and Use of Force against Protesters and Human Rights Defenders*, 20 January, Geneva: ISHR, viewed 4 April 2015, www.ishr.ch/news/myanmar-end-restrictions-reprisals-and-use-force-against-protesters-and-human-rights-defenders.

Karen Human Rights Group (KHRG) 2013, *Losing Ground: Land Conflicts and Collective Action in Eastern Myanmar*, 5 March, Myanmar: KHRG, viewed 4 April 2015, http://khrg.org/2013/03/losing-ground-land-conflicts-and-collective-action-eastern-myanmar.

Karen Human Rights Group 2015, *With Only Our Voices What Can We Do?*, June, viewed 6 June 2016, http://khrg.org/sites/default/files/full_with_only_our_voices._-_english.pdf.

Karen News 2015, 'Jailed Land Rights Activists Are "Political Prisoners", says Human Rights Watch', 16 August, viewed 6 June 2016, http://karennews.org/2015/08/jailed-land-rights-activists-are-political-prisoners-says-human-rights-watch.html/.

Lawyers Rights Watch Canada (undated), *International Human Rights Law: Non-Treaty Standards*, viewed 6 June 2015, www.lrwc.org/education/international-law/non-treaty-standards/.

Lee, Y 2015, *Report of the Special Rapporteur on the Situation of Human Rights in Myanmar to the Human Rights Council*, A/HRC/28/72, Geneva: Human Rights Council.

Ministry of Foreign Affairs, the Netherlands 2009, *Manual for Embassies of EU Member States: Strengthening the National Human Rights Protection System*, viewed 10 June 2016, www.globalequality.org/storage/documents/pdf/manual%20nhrps-web.pdf.

Motlagh, J 2013, 'Land-grabbing Endures in New Burma', *The Washington Post*, 31 January, viewed 10 June 2016, www.washingtonpost.com/world/asia_pacific/land-grabbing-endures-in-new-burma/2013/01/31/429ace6e-6a3d-11e2-95b3-272d604a10a3_story.html.

Myanmar National Human Rights Commission (MNHRC) 2014, *Press Statement on the Inquiry of Riots of 22nd December 2014 at Latpadaungtaung Copper Mine Project in Salingyi Township Statement No.(1/2015)*, Yangon: MNHRC, viewed 10 June 2016, www.mnhrc.org.mm/en/2015/01/myanmar-national-human-rights-commission-press-statement-on-the-inquiry-of-riots-of-22nd-december-2014-at-lat-padaungtaung-copper-mine-project-in-salingyi-township/.

Myanmar Times 2013, 'Amendments to Unlawful Associations Act Proposed', 25 March, viewed 10 June 2016, www.mmtimes.com/index.php/national-news/5695-amendments-to-unlawful-associations-act-proposed.html.

Oberndorf, RB 2012, *Legal Review of Recently Enacted Farmland Law and Vacant, Fallow and Virgin Lands Management Law*, November, viewed 10 June 2016, www.forest-trends.org/documents/files/doc_3274.pdf.

Office of the High Commissioner for Human Rights 1996, *Who Is a defender?*, Geneva: OHCHR, viewed 10 June 2016, www.ohchr.org/EN/Issues/SRHRDefenders/Pages/Defender.aspx.

Office of the High Commissioner for Human Rights 2003, *Report of the High Commissioner for Human Rights on Human Rights, Trade and Investment to the 55th Session of the Sub-Commission on the Promotion and Protection of Human Rights*, E/CN.4/Sub.2/2003/9, Geneva: Sub-Commission on the Promotion and Protection of Human Rights.

Office of the High Commissioner for Human Rights 2011, *Commentary to the Declaration on the Right and Responsibility of Individuals, Groups and Organs of Society to Promote and Protect Universally Recognized Human Rights and Fundamental Freedoms*, viewed 10 June 2016, www.ohchr.org/Documents/Issues/Defenders/CommentarytoDeclarationondefendersJuly2011.pdf.

Office of the High Commissioner for Human Rights 2016, *Early Warning and Economic, Social and Cultural Rights*, Geneva: OHCHR, viewed 8 June 2016, http://ohchr.org/Documents/Issues/ESCR/EarlyWarning_ESCR_2016_en.pdf.

Partners Relief & Development 2012, *Land Grabbing in Burma Forcing Young Girls into Prostitution*, Oslo: Partners Relief & Development, viewed 5 June 2016, www.partnersworld.org/news/land-grabbing-burma-forcing-young-girls-prostitution.

Peterson, LE 2009, *Human Rights and Bilateral Investment Treaties: Mapping the Role of Human Rights Law within Investor–State Arbitration*, Montreal: Rights and Democracy, viewed 5 June 2016, www.dd-rd.ca/site/_PDF/publications/globalization/HIRA-volume3-ENG.pdf.

Quintana, T 2011, *Report of the Special Rapporteur on the Situation of Human Rights in Myanmar*, A/66/365, New York: General Assembly.

Sekaggya, M 2013, *Report of the Special Representative on the Situation of Human Rights Defenders to the Human Rights Council*, A/HRC/25/55, Geneva: Human Rights Council.

Transnational Institute 2013, *Access Denied: Land Rights and Ethnic Conflict in Burma*, Burma Policy Briefing Paper No. 11, Amsterdam: Transnational Institute, viewed 6 June 2016, www.tni.org/briefing/access-denied.

Young, K 2012, *Constitution Economic and Social Rights*, Oxford: Oxford University Press.

Part IV
Security and conflict

11

Human rights and conflict prevention in Southeast Asia

The protection gap

Robin Ramcharan

Introduction

Given the serious and ongoing internal nation-building challenges within the ASEAN states, the protection of human rights is an integral part of conflict prevention strategies and the forging of lasting peace.[1] This chapter argues, however, that a major pitfall in the Southeast Asian region's nascent human rights regime is the absence of a real 'protection' architecture and consequently a capacity for conflict prevention. The latter is a vital part of good governance and the legitimacy of states. The positive linkages between the protection of human rights and the absence of violent conflict are evident in European Union and North American experience since the Second World War, both of which have highly developed human rights mechanisms, including courts that have the capacity to secure redress and remedies.

Dispute settlement in society through the protection of human rights by the emerging ASEAN human rights architecture should be a central element in the prevention of conflicts within Southeast Asia in the global context of 'wars of the third kind'. These are internal conflicts, resulting from internal problems of legitimacy of states, that are transformed into international conflicts. Such wars have comprised the majority of conflicts since the Second World War (Bercovitch & Jackson 2009: 4). They have generated unprecedented interest among states in what happens in other states and have led some to adopt a 'human security' foreign policy.

Southeast Asia's human rights architecture, as defined here, encompasses the ASEAN Inter-Governmental Commission on Human Rights (AICHR), National Human Rights Institutions (NHRIs), Civil Society Organisations (CSOs) and the ASEAN Regional Forum (ARF). The last of these, though not a human rights forum per se, cannot fail to address the obvious human rights dimensions at the heart of many conflicts in the region, Myanmar being a case in point. In the context of weak and ineffective protection mechanisms at the regional and national levels in Southeast Asia, wider Asia-Pacific-centred avenues for the protection of human rights must complement ongoing efforts to foster effective protection. The ARF can and must forge a role in advancing human rights protection so as to prevent 'wars of the third kind' through human rights-based early warning and risk assessment. This surely is within its mandate.

After a brief review of dilemmas of nation-building that constitute the contemporary complex security challenges facing Southeast Asian states, this chapter outlines the difficulties confronting national and regional mechanisms comprising the nascent human rights architecture. It then examines the potential role of the ARF in early warning and risk assessment (EW/RA) aimed at advancing the protection of human rights.

Internal security challenges, nation-building and 'wars of the third kind'

ASEAN's main security challenges from its inception lay between and within the member states. While the prospect of war between the members has faded as a security community emerges, conflict within states and their spill-over effects remain a serious concern. Recent religious violence (Buddhist vs. Muslim in Myanmar), violence due to historical and socio-economic grievances (Southern Thailand), continuing tensions in Mindanao in the Philippines, ethnic conflict in Myanmar and border tensions between Malaysia and the Philippines are pointed reminders of the same. Globally, the number of inter-state conflicts has decreased from less than five per year in 1946, to almost zero by 2010 (Backer & Huth 2014: 19). The number of intra-state conflicts,[2] however, has increased from about seven per year in 1946, to over 35 per year in 1990 and then to 25 per year in 2010 (Backer & Huth 2014: 19). One feature of such conflicts is their recurrence over the past 25 years, as opposed to termination. The prospect of internal political unrest and conflict remains significant in Southeast Asia.

Problems of nation-building, civil unrest and the potential for 'wars of the third kind'

Southeast Asia has historically faced communist insurgencies, ethnic conflicts and secessionist movements. The first of these has disappeared, but the latter two persist. A cursory reading of the Uppsala conflict database for Southeast Asia quickly reveals as much. In the context of democratic transitions, especially uncertain in situations of irregular leadership transfers, the prospect of political instability and conflict is heightened (Frantz 2014: 29).

A leading conflict ledger has assessed the risk of potential conflict in 164 countries using internationally recognised methodologies.[3] The likelihood of conflict in the Southeast Asian region transitioning to democratic governance was highest in Timor-Leste, whose risk ratio was approximately 10.1 or ten times higher than that of the OECD.[4] Timor-Leste featured at number 25, in the top 25, with Afghanistan at number one, followed by Guinea-Bissau (2), Djibouti (3), Guinea (4) and so on. Countries with the largest increases in risk of instability included Thailand and Myanmar. The former's risk ratio increased from 0.9 (2007–2009) to 2.8 (2012–2014). Myanmar's risk ratio increased from 4.8 to 5.8 in the same periods. Thailand, on a path to democracy since the landmark democratic constitutional reforms of 1997, has seen many setbacks to democratic governance since the overthrow of Thaksin in 2006. This has been accentuated by the return of military rule. Myanmar's military regime has set in motion a transition to democratic governance, all the while aspiring to preserve the influence of the military establishment as per the Indonesian model.

The greatest increases in risk of instability have taken place in countries that were classified as partial democracies, which 'are at greater risk for instability than autocracies or full democracies' (Backer, Wilkenfeld & Huth 2014: 5). 'Repressive tactics adopted by autocratic governments often smother the potential for significant political instability' (Backer, Wilkenfeld & Huth 2014: 10). Coherent and mature democracies, which constituted some 58% of the world's states by 2011, compared with 12% autocracies and 30% anocracies (democratic and autocratic features) (Frantz 2014: 26), 'possess the capacity to address group grievances and manage the competition between groups that vie for political power and other resources'

(Backer, Wilkenfeld & Huth 2014: 19). Mature democratic states, replete with the rule of law and corresponding rights, that provide access to justice and do secure redress and remedies for victims of violations, retain authority and legitimacy.

Causal linkages between human rights violations and the onset of conflict have been posited by many scholars and policymakers. Empirically, a 'direct' causal linkage may yet emerge as scholars test this proposition. 'Proximate' causes (or 'triggers') that mobilise groups to use violence are important in generating violent conflict. They include political factors such as regime change, instability and uncertainty, external intervention, elections, democratic transitions or military coups, protests or insurgent violence, which provoke brutal government crackdowns; and discriminatory policies. Proximate causes are frequently linked to abuses of civil and political rights, and for Thomas and Ron (2007), this basket of rights is more directly linked to the outbreak of violent conflict. Underlying reasons for conflict and wars of the third kind include socio-economic factors, that implicate economic, social and cultural rights (Thomas and Ron 2007). For example, empirical testing by the Minorities at Risk Project (Gurr 1993) of the correlation between the inequalities experienced by minority ethnic groups and incidences of 'ethnic violence' have led researchers to conclude that 'members of politically, economically and culturally disadvantaged groups are more likely to stage protest and rebellion against incumbent governments than those who enjoy a more secure position in society' (Cederman, Girardin & Wucherpfennig 2014: 74). Research on the linkages between inequality, grievances and civil war have concluded that grievances do cause civil war. Using quantitative tools, Cederman, Gleditsch and Buhaug (2013: 205), have found that economic horizontal inequality 'contributes powerfully to the risk of civil war outbreak'. Among the policy tools the authors prescribe is power-sharing that involves minority groups in exercising authority (Cederman, Gleditsch & Buhaug 2013). Refinements in research methodologies have led to the propositions related to correlation between conflict and the 'alien' quality of dominant political groups, the political exclusion of minority groups and the relative wealth of ethnic groups. Cederman, Girardin and Wucherpfennig (2014: 84) note that grievances can emanate 'from resentment linked to backwardness and governmental neglect, or, in case of relatively affluent groups, frustration with having to support less effective parts of the state'. Analysis has also shown that civil wars last longer when rebel organisations are linked to excluded groups that are active in the fighting (Cederman, Girardin & Wucherpfennig 2014: 86). Economic deprivation has also been identified as a major reason for conflict escalation (Bercovitch & Jackson 2009: 92; Collier et al. 2003). Such analyses complement other areas of research such as basic needs theory of John Burton and the structural violence approach of Johan Galtung. The former posited a relationship between violent conflict and the frustration of basic human needs. The latter posited structural violence as a situation in which members of an ethnic or other minority 'out-group' 'are denied access to political, social and economic and other resources typically enjoyed and presided over by a mainstream in-group' (Sandole 2013: 31). Del Rosso (2013) has usefully reminded us that sub-state and irredentist nationalisms are still features of the modern 'nation-state' system.

Multiple and complex problems in the Southeast Asian region bear the potential for violent internal conflict and 'wars of the third kind': poverty, social dislocations from rapid development, misappropriation of land, inevitable inequities from rapid regional integration, the preservation of identities in a multi-ethnic Southeast Asia with some 100 million indigenous peoples, the demands for self-determination and inclusive growth by indigenous peoples and other minorities, corruption and varying degrees of imperfect governance. These are compounded by remaining border and maritime disputes (Bercovitch & Jackson 2009: 3). Dispute settlement in society through the protection of human rights by the emerging ASEAN human rights regime must be a central element of a conflict prevention mechanism in the global context of wars of the third kind.

Non-violent nation-building: human rights protection as a *sine qua non*

A credible and effective human rights protection regime is a *sine qua non* for an inclusive and peaceful nation-building process. As such it constitutes a core element in any conflict prevention strategy. Ultimately, a society will be peaceful if all parts of that society share in the national vision and feel that they have a stake in the future of the country, a country that is equitable towards them. In framing a national vision for each country, the basic rights of the human being as they have been developed since 1945 in international instruments and that have been brought home in varying ways in regions such as Southeast Asia must be kept in view. Each society must have laws, policies and institutions for giving effect to the human rights of everyone, for monitoring the implementation of these rights, for detecting and preventing to the extent possible human rights grievances that can descend into violent conflict. Every ASEAN member should be able to show, at minimum, that it has in place an adequate and effective national protection system that has six main elements: legislative measures, administrative arrangements for implementing rights, protection of rights by the judiciary, specialised institutions such as national human rights institutions, arrangements to detect and head off human rights grievances, and ongoing efforts to teach and disseminate human rights. The national protection system has as its rationale the development of a culture of human rights within the society. It is through such an approach that one can hopefully head off situations that might deteriorate into violent conflicts (Ramcharan, BG 2010).

In the Southeast Asian region, the following elements need to be borne in mind in considering human rights approaches to conflict prevention: countries of varying stages of development with a great deal of poverty and inequality; many minority and indigenous groups in very vulnerable situations; some national protection systems with varying degrees of or no effectiveness at providing redress and remedies; an ASEAN Charter of human rights that has been the subject of many (adverse) comments and an AICHR that is just beginning to function and that has also attracted much scepticism because of its inter-governmental character and its limited peer-review mandate.

Southeast Asia's weak human rights protection architecture

The nascent but weak human rights architecture created by ASEAN is the outcome of a regional human rights movement that began after the World Conference on Human Rights in Vienna, Austria, in 1993 that proclaimed the universality of human rights. The concerns of East Asian states over the universality of human rights have been well documented. Two decades later, Southeast Asia's timid human rights 'protection' regime finally took shape. In 2007, the ASEAN Charter paved the way for a regional human rights body. By 2009, the Terms of Reference were adopted. In 2010 the AICHR began operating, though in great secrecy and amidst resounding international and regional CSO criticism over the new body's 'lack of teeth'.

Access to justice by rights holders is a fundamental aspect of any human rights regime. In comparison with other regional mechanisms and the international architecture, Southeast Asia's does not provide direct access to individuals and civil society organisations (Ramcharan, R 2010). The AHRD provides maximum leeway to governments nervous about their human rights records and external scrutiny of the same. Moreover, the AHRD registered continuing regional disaffection with universal human rights standards, as it provided for human rights to be considered in the context of local cultures and traditions. The AICHR and AHRD are firmly anchored in the 'ASEAN Way', that is of non-interference in the affairs of member states.

While doctrinal debates continue in academic circles over the philosophical foundations of fundamental human rights, citizens and states the world over have nevertheless acknowledged the indivisibility and universality of conventional human rights. Many states and their citizens have come to accept and expect that they would collectively benefit from the rights guaranteed under international human rights law. It is well established that the latter is part of the national responsibility of states. Where domestic jurisdictions fail to protect their citizens' rights, regional and universal human rights protection mechanisms increasingly become involved in providing some protection. A strong system of 'protection' is yet to emerge in Southeast Asia.

Problems of protection

The intergovernmental human rights system at present seems more of a device to protect governments' international reputations rather than as a dispute resolution system that can provide redress and remedies to victims of violations of fundamental rights. Frustrated attempts at securing justice are at the heart of wars of the third kind.

The AICHR's weak foundations

In the drafting phase of the Terms of Reference (TORs) of the AICHR, concluded in July 2009, the general requirements of an ASEAN regional human rights body were highlighted by the National Human Rights Institutions of Indonesia, Malaysia, Philippines and Thailand. They had posted a position paper of 2008 on the draft terms of reference of the eventual ASEAN human rights body, available through the National Human Rights Commission of Indonesia website (National Human Rights Institutions 2008). It had noted that the TORs should provide for an 'independent deliberative body' that provides 'an effective level of promotion, protection and monitoring of human rights throughout the ASEAN region'. Formation of the human rights body had to be undertaken in a transparent and participatory manner, along with an inclusive process of consultation with all stakeholders, including the NHRIs and the civil society. The human rights body required both promotion and protection functions. The human rights body also had to have, at the initial phase, a role to monitor the implementation of international human rights obligations and the respective treaty bodies' recommendations at the national level for ASEAN member states. The protection function of the human rights body should have included human rights situation analysis of the ASEAN sub-region, which could have been undertaken through country visits and the assessment of the impacts of the blueprints for the ASEAN communities, i.e. political and security, economic and socio-cultural. The human rights body needed to be adequately funded and supported by staff members and facilities.

The 'protection' regime under AICHR is devoid of a crucial aspect of any protection regime worthy of that name: an individual petitions/complaints system to which ASEAN citizens have direct access. Other credible regional human rights mechanisms have designed such systems. Moreover, there is no institutionalised access for CSOs that might compensate for this lack of a petitions system. The AICHR operates secretively. Governmental representatives, appointed by states and thus lacking independence, generally view their role as that of 'defending' their respective governments.

The formal sessions of the AICHR have been conducted in secrecy, unaffected by public scrutiny. Their public engagements have largely been of a promotional nature. One innovation, introduced by an increasingly confident Indonesia, was the submission for consideration by AICHR of its report to the Universal Periodic Review of the Human Rights Council.

An inability to secure redress and remedies

National Human Rights Institutions (NHRIs) have been widely acclaimed by academics and practitioners as the most promising way of enhancing the protection of human rights at the domestic level (Gomez & Ramcharan 2016). Despite the positive ratings of regional NHRIs, their effectiveness as protection entities is in doubt. Gomez and Ramcharan (2016) highlight NHRIs' incapacity at mobilising executive, parliamentary or judicial action in pursuit of remedies and redress.

It has been argued cogently that 'the judicial protection of human rights should be our goal in every country' (Ramcharan 2006). While all NHRIs have documented receipt of complaints and have undertaken investigations and issued recommendations, effective protection requires stronger action of a quasi-judicial nature. Judging from reports to date, few, if any, undertake the latter, which requires actions akin to those normally undertaken by a court of law or a judge. Generally, from the primary sources there is little evidence of the exercise of such capacity by the NHRIs to provide remedies. Across the region NHRIs' responses to violations are generally of a soft nature, varying from public awareness, to mediation, to investigation, to visiting detainees, to involvement in court cases, and to reports to national assemblies for follow up.

Ineffectiveness of CSOs

In an assessment of the contribution of CSOs to advancing human rights in the region, Dinah PoKempner argued in 1997:

> NGOs are likely to play a key role in coming years, not only in monitoring and exposing abuses, but in standard-setting as well. This is due to Asia's unique position as the only region of the world without a regional intergovernmental mechanism for the protection of human rights.
>
> *(PoKempner 1997)*

Until the establishment of the AICHR, Southeast Asia lacked a wider human rights institution. During this time, Track III diplomacy emerged in the region as involving transnational non-governmental advocacy groups in Southeast Asia, alongside formal governmental (Track I) and informal governmental interaction with think tanks (Track II) (Kraft 2002).

CSOs have indeed usefully and powerfully criticised the process and outcomes of various stages of the establishment of the human rights architecture. As Termsak Chalermpalanupap, then ASEAN's Director of Political and Security Directorate has noted, the new ASEAN human rights body was 'not supposed to have teeth' but was to generate consensus (Salaveria 2009). 'To moan on the human rights body's "lack of teeth" is to bark up the wrong tree' (Chalermpalanupap c.2012). Commentators have offered useful suggestions on the enhancement of the protection of human rights in the region (Ramcharan, R 2010).

CSOs, however, were largely excluded from all stages of the establishment of the regional inter-state architecture and continue to be excluded. Trenchant criticisms have plagued the closed-door approach to drafting an ADHR. This was epitomised in July 2012 by calls from the UN High Commissioner for Human Rights, Navi Pillai, for a meaningful consultation on the draft with the widest spectrum of people in the region. The Indonesia-based Human Rights Working Group (HRWG) deplored the 'blocked access to information relating to the draft, which is so important and which will affect millions of people in Southeast Asia' (Ririhena 2012; Wahyuningrum 2012).

Historically, CSOs have played a vital role in advancing the protection of human rights in many parts of the world, though by themselves they do not have capacity to guarantee the protection of human rights. The media (traditional and new) must continue and intensify their push for more transparency in the ASEAN human rights regime, for the respect of international commitments already binding upon ASEAN states, for the respect for universal standards under the UN Charter and the Universal Declaration of Human Rights and for real protection of fundamental rights. Given the extremely limited interaction between CSOs and the AICHR, one cannot say that CSOs in Southeast Asia are effective in providing protection within the current human rights regime.

The ineffectiveness of CSOs in advancing the protection of human rights in Southeast Asia leaves room for doubt about the emergence of a strong protection regime in the near future (International Justice Resource Centre 2012). Should the ARF play a role in human rights protection? If yes, how can it do so?

ARF, human rights and the prevention of 'wars of the third kind'

In the context of wars of the third kind and the ASEAN Regional Forum,[5] a wider regional ASEAN-centred conflict management and prevention exercise cannot fail to address internal causes of conflicts and the linkages between human rights violations and such conflicts. It has been noted by a former UN High Commissioner for Human Rights that 'a country's human rights record is a crucial factor in assessing the level of risk – whether for the prevention of conflict, assessment of stability or decisions on business opportunities' (Ramcharan 2004).

States in the region individually have the responsibility to protect their populations from human rights violations. For example, Myanmar has the responsibility to address grievances leading to ethnic conflicts and Rohingya fleeing from persecution in Myanmar. The Philippines has the responsibility to address grievances of the Moros in Mindanao. Thailand has the responsibility of addressing grievances inciting conflict in Southern Thailand where Muslim minorities, once part of Malaya, militate for some autonomy over their lives. As noted above, human rights protection is not currently a major focus of the ARF. Given the propensity of ASEAN to deal with conflicts regionally and in accordance with the 'ASEAN Way', which can complicate the resolution of conflicts, it is incumbent upon the ARF to place under scrutiny the human rights dimensions of regional conflicts.

Human rights early warning assessments

The ARF already has a conflict prevention mandate and could undertake human rights early warning and risk assessments to analyse the likelihood of outbreak of violent conflicts that have a 'spill-over' capacity through its Track II processes. These processes engage with think tanks and academic institutions that inform its Track I (inter-governmental) processes. At a minimum and for a start, neutral and widely respected Track II think tanks could engage in conceptualisation of the modalities of such a capacity and then submit their findings to the ARF members for consideration in inter-governmental sessions. Learning can be derived from the OSCE's Office for Democratic Institutions and Human Rights whose practice of preventive diplomacy encompasses action to forestall policies that create political and social tension. These include policies affecting or potentially violating human rights (Tivayanond 2004: 2). The OSCE High Commissioner on National Minorities has also played an important role in heading off conflicts within the OSCE space. In many ways, the High Commissioner's functions act as a 'conflict prevention mechanism', specifically addressing situations involving human rights violations of vulnerable minorities at the centre of many contemporary ethnic conflicts.

Early warning in the field of human rights can build on work related to human rights indicators done by the Office of the High Commissioner for Human Rights (OHCHR 2012). An indicator is

> specific information on the state or condition of an object, event, activity or outcome that can be related to human rights norms and standards; that addresses and reflects human rights principles and concerns; and that can be used to assess and monitor the promotion and implementation of human rights.
>
> *(OHCHR 2012: 16)*

Whether quantitative (statistical) or qualitative (narrative or categorical form), these complementary approaches serve to monitor the progress in realisation of universally recognised human rights. Indicators may also be fact-based (objective, verifiable, based on events) and judgement-based (subjective, based on perceptions, opinions, assessments or judgements). In selecting indicators, capturing not only national averages but also a micro-level assessment of the enjoyment of rights on an individual and personal level are important. OHCHR (2012: 23) notes that indicators 'can be meaningful and are more likely to be used when they are contextually relevant'. For example, collecting malaria rates in the European Union is futile. The OHCHR (2012) notes that attempts to develop indicators thus far have led to an 'artificial dichotomy' that is undesirable. The dichotomy is between a 'violation' approach (based on civil and political rights) and a 'progressive realisation' approach (based on economic, social and cultural rights). This dichotomy is undesirable given the indivisibility of all human rights. The overall aim is to measure the 'enjoyment of rights by rights holders' and not to identify a fully comprehensive list of all indicators for all human rights standards or all treaty provisions. Capturing a few outcomes may be sufficient to provide an accurate overview of the state of realisation of human rights, notably those that lead to exclusion and discrimination against vulnerable minorities and indigenous peoples (OHCHR 2012: 28).

In the area of EW/RA, to collect sufficiently broad data needed to produce a conflict analysis, information must be obtained from a range of relevant sources, including from academics, NGOs, national governments, regional organisations and the UN. Early warning findings could then be presented to formal ARF meetings each year. In relation to minorities and indigenous peoples in Southeast Asia, this list might be better adapted by the inclusion of issues such as economic exclusion, discriminatory practices in relation to land rights, lack of employment opportunities, and language of education.

There is increasing evidence that violations of ESCRs are causes, consequences and often predictors of social or civil unrest, violence and even violent conflict (OHCHR 2015: 3). For example, the discussion paper on 'Economic, Social and Cultural Rights, Social Unrest, Conflict and Early Warning' highlighted analysis on the causes of the conflict between the Philippine state and the Moros, a Muslim minority, which was

> related to the failure of the government to provide public goods; its control over rich resources; a dysfunctional legal system in the Moro community; the fact that the Moro people suffer from the highest levels of poverty in the Philippines; and discrimination by the Christian majority towards Muslims. Inequality seems to be a key determinant of the Moro conflict.
>
> *(OHCHR 2015: 6)*

It noted further, that 'economic and financial issues, unemployment and inequalities inside society have increased social tensions' (OHCHR 2015: 6). While guarding against a one-size-fits-all model to predict with certainty where and when unrest and conflict will erupt, and in the absence of preventive measures, the paper argued that there may be core elements, particularly regarding economic, social and cultural rights, that could be identified as part of an early warning system. The discussion paper noted that in many circumstances, demonstrations, riots and other manifestations of social discontent are rooted in violations and denial of ESCRs. They are often accompanied by lack of access to justice, accountability and political participation. Specific issues or indicators for an early warning model include: the right to water and affordability, the availability of public expenditures and state expenditures prioritisation, the right to food and freedom from hunger, unemployment and adequate standards of living, austerity, marginalisation and other inequalities. Research has also pointed to gender inequality as a risk factor, with the OHCHR (2015: 9) noting 'evidence that States characterised by gender inequality that is rooted in discrimination and structural violence are more tolerant of violence as a means of resolving grievances, and thus significantly more likely to experience internal conflict'.

Quantitative work on the determinants of abuses of human rights has emerged over the past two decades, but little work on early warning and risk assessment. This body of work has generated correlations between abuses and the level of democracy, economic development, population size, past repression and involvement in international and civil war (Poe, Rost & Carey 2006: 486). Democracy was associated with the least amounts of repression. Economic scarcity on the other hand was associated with increased tensions and likely repression. Early warning models were developed for inter-state conflicts, refugee movements, genocide and politicide, to predict ethnic conflict in terms of which groups were most at risk (Poe, Rost & Carey 2006: 487–488). Some early warning templates for human rights included pattern recognition[6] and structural risk assessment.[7] Poe, Rost and Carey (2006) offer a glimpse into the efforts of testing the predictive accuracy of methodologies of the structural approach developed earlier by Poe and Tate (1994). The latter's structural risk factors aimed at generating a list of countries deserving of greater attention. In addition to these, work by Bhavnani et al. (2014) has examined grievances and violent conflicts in urban settings, which is highly appropriate in today's world in which over half of the population lives in urban areas.

A more judgement-based and policy-oriented human rights risk assessment can also be undertaken. In assessing country situations, the ARF may usefully deploy the following checklist in its efforts to head off conflicts (Ramcharan 2004: 1): What is the ethnic composition of the country? Is there a minority, indigenous or migrant population? Is there a unifying vision for the country? What is the state of governance and is there a functioning democracy? What is the state of the rule of law and the courts? Is there an effective national protection system? Are there major grievances? Is there an internal system for early warning to head off grievances? Are there gross violations of human rights? What is the state of women's rights? Is there a human trafficking problem? What is the state of respect for the rights of the child? Is there freedom of expression, religion and belief? What are the UN human rights treaty bodies and investigations reporting about the country? What are the leading international human rights organisations reporting? Are there reputable human rights non-governmental organisations and what are they saying? Are perpetrators of gross violations of human rights brought to justice?

Crafting an ARF human rights-based early warning capacity

In light of the emerging evidence linking human rights violations to conflict, crafting an ARF-based human rights EW mechanism that will serve to enhance the protection of human rights is in order. In doing so relevant experiences within institutions designed to address human rights grievances and to head off conflicts may be kept in mind. The experiences in conflict prevention of the Organization for Security and Cooperation in Europe (OSCE) High Commissioner on National Minorities may hold vital lessons (OSCE 2015a). The Conflict Prevention Centre of the OSCE was established in 1990 out of recognition that in Europe there are many minority populations with frustrated aspirations and grievances that include human rights violations. Indeed, historically, Europe has had its share of violence related to minority grievances. A century ago, the repression of minority group aspirations in the despotic Austro-Hungarian Empire contributed to generating not only internal strife but also conditions that produced the First World War and the demise of that empire. In the late 1980s, Bulgaria and Turkey confronted each other as Bulgaria imposed discriminatory laws on Bulgarians of Turkish origin, such as forced name changes. Early warning action by the United Nations Secretary-General defused the situation. The problem of genocide resurfaced in the former Yugoslavia at the end of the Cold War, occasioning UN mediation efforts. The then newly independent Baltic countries also faced internal civil conflict as Russian-speaking groups, suddenly thrust into a minority situation after the collapse of the Soviet Union, faced discriminatory laws and practices, once again leading to UN conflict prevention efforts. Canada, an OSCE member and one of the most peaceful countries, experienced a small but nevertheless armed conflict for 78 days between the state and indigenous Mohawk people over land rights in Oka, Quebec, in 1990. The potential for violent conflict due to denial of rights to minority and indigenous groups is thus real.

The OSCE has acknowledged that heading off violence required constant efforts to promote the acceptance of human rights standards and standards for the protection of minorities, and that one must engage in ongoing dialogue with groups and governments with a view to fostering solutions grounded in human rights norms (OSCE 2015b). The OSCE Conflict Prevention Centre 'acts as an OSCE-wide early warning focal point, facilitates negotiation, mediation, and other conflict prevention and resolution efforts, and supports regional co-operation initiatives' (OSCE 2015b). In general, the OSCE monitors the rights of minorities and 'identifies and seeks early resolution of ethnic tensions that might endanger peace or stability. It promotes the rights of national minorities' (OSCE 2015b).

In this vein, it is noteworthy that within Southeast Asia, in relation to internal conflict, individual ASEAN states have not been averse to involvement in resolving conflict through preventive diplomacy techniques. Indonesia, for example, was involved in the Philippines's Moro dispute in Mindanao (Tivayanond 2004). Malaysia has been involved in finding a resolution to the Southern Thai conflict, that has seen violent conflict between minority Muslim Thais and the Thai government, by acting as a facilitator in 2005, 2013 and 2015 (Funston 2010; Chanintira 2015).

Given the central position of ASEAN in the ARF process and its members' adherence to the principle of non-interference, can external pressure push ASEAN to consider placing the protection of human rights on the ARF's conflict prevention agenda? Such pressure may come from the European Union (EU) and the USA. They have demonstrated their will and capacity to effect positive changes in the region through their policies aimed at isolating Myanmar and obstructing the latter's enjoyment of its full membership within ASEAN. The promotion of human rights worldwide is a pillar of EU foreign policy and may impact on the promotion and protection of human rights in Southeast Asia. The EU constitutes itself internally on a rule of law basis and in its external relations. It emphasises the primacy of rules, both in terms of the social contract at the level of the nation-state and in its inter-state relations. As such, EU's foreign policy towards Asia is likely to contain a strong human rights component (see, for example, de Búrca 2013). In the case of the USA, its 2010 National Security Strategy noted that 'we see it as fundamental to our own interests to support a just peace around the world – one in which individuals, and not just nations, are granted the fundamental rights that they deserve' (United States Government 2010). It noted that it will 'actively support the leadership of emerging democracies as they assume a more active role in advancing basic human rights and democratic values in their regions and on the global stage' (United States Government 2010). Indeed, there has been a 'globalisation of freedom', which refers to the expansion of democracy from some 25 democracies around 60 years ago to over 120 today. The 'protection' of human rights in Southeast Asia is potentially served by President Obama's pivot, or re-balancing, to the Asia-Pacific, which was intended to be an all-encompassing enterprise, concerning not just military strategists. President Obama argued in Australia in 2011, that human rights were being applied through the pivot in three specific ways: by strengthening civil society; advancing the rights of all people, including minorities; and encouraging open government (Obama 2011).

However, thus far, analysis has pointed to the fact that while external pressure on ASEAN members does have an effect on regional responses to conflict situations, it does not necessarily bring about greater attention to human rights (Stensland 2012: 3). In July 2013, US Secretary of State Kerry called on North Korea to cooperate with external human rights institutions to evaluate the situation there (US State Department 2013). Despite this positive omen, the human rights impact of President Obama's pivot to Asia has been criticised for encouraging authoritarian regimes on mainland Southeast Asia at the expense of more democratic partners, such as Indonesia and the Philippines (Kurlantzik 2015).

It seems, therefore, that the grafting of an EW/RA human rights assessment capacity onto the ARF agenda would necessarily have to be championed by non-western powers, such as Indonesia, which are more confident in asserting their domestic human rights credentials. In a multi-polar world marked by the diffusion of power horizontally (geographically away from the North Atlantic) and vertically (great powers, middle powers, emerging powers) the 'human rights diplomacy' of western liberal states, notably the US and the EU, is meeting with greater resistance, in particular by an emerging superpower, China.

The importance of a regional champion is underscored by resistance to the western human rights diplomacy that has emanated from regional states, as well as academics and even former UN rights officials who have criticised insensitive human rights diplomacy by big powers. Southeast Asian states have long resisted western 'interventionist' human rights diplomacy and have demonstrated a 'will to differ' in relation to the content of rights (Tay 1996). China's inevitable rise to global superpower status is the greatest challenge to western human rights diplomacy. It recalls a 'century of humiliation' at the hands of western powers and resents efforts to intervene in its internal affairs. This is seen as an attempt to foster US global hegemony. More fundamentally, even if China has very recently engaged with international human rights discourse and law, its historical experience is rather different. Qi has argued that, beyond the differing political systems of the US and China, there is no tradition of rights in the western sense. In the Confucian tradition, the state exists to take care of the ruled and there are no 'equal rights' between ruled and rulers. Political order is given pride of place and emphasis is placed on the duty of each person to preserve a stable political order. Academics such as Hopgood (2013) have levelled powerful critiques against the international human rights movement, which he deems as having been usurped by elites away from grass-roots movements and by the US in service of its foreign policy. The 'liberal agenda' of western powers in UN peacebuilding, inclusive of universal human rights standards, for example, has come under attack as being ineffective in consolidating and building peace in post-conflict situations (Geneva Peacebuilding Platform 20154). Former High Commissioner for Human Rights, Louise Arbour of Canada, while not doubting the universality of human rights, has stated that 'One doesn't have a sense that there's a general direction that is encouraging'. In particular,

> I now find it incredible how the West seems to be absolutely incapable of hearing what it sounds like to the rest of the world – a total disconnect, in the promotion of what it rightly believes are universal values, while being completely oblivious to the fact that others don't take this at face value as being a good-faith pursuit of universal goods. It just doesn't work.

She suggested that a way out of the impasse was to stop imposing everything at once and opt for a humbler, 'micro' approach, a 'quiet, mediating role in fixing individual wrongs'. A 'kind of political empathy' would provide strategic advantage (Arbour quoted in Saunders 2015).

Conclusion

A regional champion for an ARF human rights EW capacity can usefully build on academic research pointing to convincing linkages between human rights violations and conflict. The potential for internal violence from minority grievances and its international spill-over is nowhere more evident than in the Buddhist-majority state of Myanmar, where the denial of very basic, universally recognised rights such as food, health, shelter and work to the Rohingya people, a Muslim minority group, has led to violence and displacement across borders in recent years. The denial by the state of civil and political and economic, social and cultural rights to multiple ethnic groups in Myanmar has resulted in decades-long violent conflict between the state and most of that country's other ethnic groups. It has resulted in refugee flows to neighbouring countries and to cross-border tensions. Ongoing conflicts in the Philippines and Thailand involving minorities and indigenous populations are also cases in point.

These situations obviate the need for placing a human rights EW capacity on the ARF agenda in the context of weak human rights protection mechanisms in the region. The ARF is a conflict prevention exercise, which may usefully deploy a human rights EW assessment as a 'stress test' in order to head off conflicts. In doing so, it could enhance the protection by inciting established national and regional mechanisms to improve their protection capacities.

Notes

1 'Peace' in this chapter is taken to mean the absence of violent conflict within and between societies (Lund 1996).

2 The Uppsala Conflict Data Program (UCDP) and the Peace Research Institute Oslo (PRIO) Armed Conflict Dataset have defined conflict as 'a contested incompatibility that concerns government and/or territory where the use of armed force between two parties, of which at least one is the government of a state, results in at least 25 battle-related fatalities'. Backer and Huth focus on conflicts that have produced at least 25 battle-related fatalities in any given year and has accumulated 1,000 fatalities over the entire course of the conflict (Backer & Huth 2014: 18).

3 The Peace and Conflict Instability Ledger represents a synthesis of leading research on conceptualising, explaining and forecasting political instability. The definition of the latter is that used by the Political Instability Task Force (PITF) at the University of Maryland Center for International Development and Conflict Management. This definition encompasses a wide variety of types of state failure events, including revolutionary wars, ethnic wars, adverse regime changes and genocides or politicides. The heterogeneous events share a fundamental characteristic in that their appearance signals the onset of disruption in government capacity to deliver core services and to exercise meaningful authority, thereby threatening overall stability (Backer, Wilkenfeld & Huth 2014: 1). Key factors influencing the risk of inability include:

> Institutional consistency (extent to which the institutions comprising a country's political system are uniformly and consistently autocratic or democratic). Political institutions with a mix of democratic and autocratic features are inconsistent, a common feature of polities in the midst of democratic transition.

Economic openness (extent to which a country's economy is integrated into the global economy).

Infant mortality rate (an indicator that serves as a proxy for overall economic development), level of social welfare policy and its capacity to deliver core services to the population. It taps into both economic and social domains.

Militarisation (indicator of availability of infrastructure, skill and human resources that increase the likelihood for civil conflict).

Neighbourhood security (instability is increased when a neighbouring state is currently experiencing armed conflict) (Backer, Wilkenfeld & Huth 2014: 5).

The Ledger presents each country's likelihood of future instability as a risk ratio, which is the relative risk of instability in a country compared to the average estimated likelihood of instability for the 28 members of the Organisation for Economic Cooperation and Development (OECD), who are widely held to be the most stable countries. The estimated probability of the average OECD country experiencing instability in the period 2012–2014 is 0.007 (Backer, Wilkenfeld & Huth 2014: 6).

4 The Ledger presents each country's likelihood of future instability as a risk ratio, which is the relative risk of instability in a country compared to the average estimated likelihood of instability for the 28 members of the Organisation for Economic Cooperation and Development (OECD), who are widely held to be the most stable countries. The estimated probability of the average OECD country experiencing instability in the period 2012–2014 is 0.007 (Backer, Wilkenfeld & Huth 2014: 6).

5 The ASEAN Regional Forum (ARF), which was established in 1994, deals with regional security issues and is held in conjunction with the ASEAN Post Ministerial Conference. It aims to enhance peace and security through regional confidence-building measures. It has emphasised dialogue between foreign ministers and other senior officials. Its members are the ASEAN member states plus Australia, Bangladesh, Canada, China, the European Union, India, Japan, North Korea, South Korea, Mongolia, New Zealand, Pakistan, Papua New Guinea, Russia, Sri Lanka, Timor-Leste and the United States.

6 Pattern recognition uses a recognition algorithm to forecast political instability over a period of time.

7 Structural risk assessment uses ordinary least squares (OLS) regression or logit analysis to test theory-based models that generate expectations of future events. It identifies long-term structural factors that would lead one to expect a country to have a greater than normal risk of ethnic conflict (Poe, Rost & Carey 2006: 289).

References

Backer, D, & Huth, P 2014, 'Global Trends in Armed Conflict, 1946–2012', in DA Backer, J Wilkenfeld & PK Huth (eds), *Peace and Conflict 2014*, Boulder, CO, Paradigm, pp. 18–22.

Backer, D, Wilkenfeld, J & Huth, P 2014, 'The Peace and Conflict Instability Ledger: Ranking States on Future Risks', in DA Backer, J Wilkenfeld & PK Huth (eds), *Peace and Conflict 2014*, Boulder, CO, Paradigm, pp. 4–17.

Bercovitch, J & Jackson, R 2009, *Conflict Resolution in the Twenty-First Century: Principles, Methods and Approaches*, Ann Arbor, MI: University of Michigan Press.

Bhavnani, R, Donnay, K, Miodownik, D, Mor M & Helbing, D 2014, 'Group Segregation and Urban Violence', *American Journal of Political Science*, vol. 58, no. 1, pp. 226–245.

Búrca, G de 2013, 'EU External Relations: The Governance Mode of Foreign Policy', in B Van Vooren, S Blockmans & J Wouters (eds), *The EU's Role in Global Governance: The Legal Dimension*, Oxford, Oxford University Press, pp. 39–58.

Cederman, L, Girardin, L & Wucherpfennig, J 2014, 'Exploring Inequality and Ethnic Conflict: EPR-ETH and Grow', in DA Backer, J Wilkenfeld & PK Huth (eds), *Peace and Conflict 2014*, Boulder, CO, Paradigm, pp. 74–87.

Cederman, L, Gleditsch, K & Buhaug, H 2013, *Inequality, Grievances and Civil War*, Cambridge, Cambridge University Press.

Chalermpalanupap, T c. 2012, 'Facts About ASEAN's Human Rights Cooperation', ASEAN Secretariat, www.aseansec.org/HLP-OtherDoc-1.pdf.

Chanintira Na Thalang 2015, e-mail exchange on conflicts in Thailand and Southeast Asia, 28 August.

Collier, P, Elliot V, Hegre, H, Hoeffler, A, Reynal-Queyrol, M & Sambanis, N 2003, *Breaking the Conflict Trap*, Washington, DC, Oxford University Press.

Del Rosso, S 2013, 'Hiding in Plain Sight: The Neglected Dilemma of Nationalism for Statebuilding', in D Chandler & TD Sisk (eds), *The Routledge Handbook of International Statebuilding*, Abingdon and New York, Routledge, pp. 64–82.

Frantz, E 2014, 'Global Trends in Democratization: Leadership Transitions and Systemic Change', in DA Backer, J Wilkenfeld & PK Huth (eds), *Peace and Conflict 2014*, Boulder, CO, Paradigm. pp. 23–28.

Funston, J 2010, 'Malaysia and Thailand's Southern Conflict: Reconciling Security and Ethnicity', *Contemporary Southeast Asia*, vol. 32, no. 2, pp. 234–257.

Geneva Peacebuilding Platform 2015, *White Paper on Peacebuilding*, viewed 30 March 2015, www.gpplatform.ch/white-papers/whitepapers.

Gomez, J & Ramcharan, R 2016, 'The "Protection" Capacity of National Human Rights Institutions in Southeast Asia', Working Paper Series, No. 172, February, www.cityu.edu.hk/searc/Resources/Paper/16021610_172%20-%20WP%20-%20Dr%20Gomez.pdf.

Gurr, T 1993, *Minorities at Risk: A Global View of Ethnopolitical Conflicts*, Washington, DC, United States Institute of Peace.

Hopgood, S 2013, *The Endtimes of Human Rights*, Ithaca, NY, Cornell University Press.

International Justice Resource Centre 2012, 'Civil Society Organizations Worry ASEAN Human Rights Declaration Falls Short of International Standards', 24 September, http://ihrlaw.org/2012/09/24/civil-society-organizations-worry-asean-human-rights-declaration-falls-short-of-human-rights-standards/.

Kraft, H 2002, 'Track Three Diplomacy and Human Rights in Southeast Asia: The Asia Pacific Coalition for East Timor', *Global Networks*, vol. 2, no. 1, pp. 49–63.

Kurlantzik, J 2015, 'U.S. *Administration Fails in Southeast Asia, Scholar Says'*, www.cfr.org/asia-and-pacific/us-administration-fails-southeast-asia-scholar-says/p35999.

Lund, M 1996, *Preventive Violent Conflict: A Strategy for Preventive Diplomacy*, Washington, DC, United States Institute of Peace.

National Human Rights Institutions 2008, 'Position Paper of the National Human Rights Institutions of Indonesia, Malaysia, Philippines, and Thailand on Terms of Reference of The ASEAN Human Rights Body', submitted at the meeting with the HLP on 10 September, www.komnasham.go.id/portal/en.

Obama, B 2011, 'Remarks by President Obama to the Australian Parliament', 17 November.

Office of the High Commissioner for Human Rights (OHCHR) 2012, *Human Rights Indicators: A Guide to Measurement and Implementation*, Geneva, OHCHR. HR/PUB/12/5.

Office of the High Commissioner for Human Rights 2015, 'Economic, Social and Cultural Rights, Social Unrest, Conflict and Early Warning', Discussion Paper, prepared for the Expert Group Meeting on Economic, Social and Cultural Rights in Social Unrest, Conflict and Early Warning, Palais des Nations, Geneva, 10–13 July.

Organization for Security and Cooperation in Europe (OSCE) 2015a, 'Conflict Prevention and Resolution', www.osce.org/secretariat/conflict-prevention.

Organization for Security and Cooperation in Europe 2015b, *Minority Rights*, www.osce.org/what/minority-rights.

Poe, SC, Rost, N & Carey, SC 2006, 'Assessing Risk and Opportunity in Conflict Studies: A Human Rights Analysis', *Journal of Conflict Resolution*, vol. 50, no. 4, pp. 484–507.

Poe, SC & Tate, CN 1994, 'Repression of Human Rights to Personal Integrity in the 1980s: A Global Analysis', *American Political Science Review*, vol. 88, no. 4 (December), pp. 853–872.

PoKempner, D 1997, 'Asia's Activists and the Future of Human Rights', *Fordham Law Review*, vol. 66, no. 2, pp. 677–686.

Ramcharan, BG 2004, 'Rights and Risk', *The World Today*, June, www.theworldtoday.org.

Ramcharan, BG 2006, 'Contemporary Challenges of Human Rights Protection: A Call for Preventive Strategies', *Rutgers Law Journal*, vol. 37, pp. 495–516.

Ramcharan, BG 2010, *Preventive Human Rights Strategies*, Abingdon, Routledge.

Ramcharan, R 2010, 'ASEAN'S Human Rights Commission: Policy Considerations for Enhancing Its Capacity to Protect Human Rights', *UCL Human Rights Review*, vol. 3, pp. 199–233.

Ririhena, Y 2012, 'Maintaining Transparency Key to ASEAN Human Rights Declaration', *The Jakarta Post*, 28 June.

Salaveria, L 2009, 'Toothless Rights Body Would Hurt ASEAN Group', *Philippine Daily Inquirer*, 30 June, http://newsinfo.inquirer.net.

Sandole, D 2013, 'Extending the Reach of Basic Human Needs: A Comprehensive Theory for the Twenty-first Century', in K Avruch & C Mitchell (eds), *Conflict Resolution and Human Needs: Linking Theory and Practice*, London and New York, Routledge, pp. 21–39.

Saunders, D 2015, 'Why Louise Arbour Is Thinking Twice', *Globe and Mail*, 28 March, viewed 30 March 2015, www.globeandmail.ca.

Stensland, A, Lotze, W & Ng, J 2012, 'Linking Regional Security and Human Rights in ASEAN', Norwegian Institute of International Affairs, Policy Brief no. 7.

Tay, S 1996, 'Human Rights, Culture and the Singapore Example', *McGill Law Journal*, vol. 41, pp. 743–780.

Thomas, O & Ron, J 2007, 'Do Human Rights Violations Cause Internal Conflict?', *Human Rights Quarterly*, vol. 29, no. 3 (August), pp. 674–705, https://jamesron.com/documents/scholarly-2007-rights-violations.pdf.

Tivayanond, MJ 2004, 'Pre-evaluating Preventive Diplomacy in Southeast Asia', Working Papers in Contemporary Asian Studies, Centre for East and Southeast Asian Studies.

United States Government 2010, National Security Strategy, The White House, www.whitehouse.gov/sites/default/files/rss_viewer/national_security_strategy.pdf.

United States, State Department 2013, Secretary Kerry's Participation in the ASEAN Regional Forum Ministerial Meeting, Office of the Spokesperson, 2 July, www.state.gov/r/pa/prs/ps/2013/07/211503.htm.

Wahyuningrum, Y 2012, 'ASEAN Human Rights Declaration', a letter to civil society, 12 September, www.dtp.unsw.edu.au/documents/ASEANHUMANRIGHTSDECLARATION.pdf.

12

The Rohingya and other Muslim minorities in Myanmar

Human rights and the marginalisation of the most vulnerable

Niki Esse de Lang

Introduction

This chapter considers the scale and seriousness of human rights violations against the Rohingya and other Muslim minorities in Myanmar. The first section of this chapter provides a background on these minorities and the recent upsurge and spread of violence against them since 2012. The second section addresses the government's failure to intervene and its own involvement in severe human rights violations. The third section discusses the root causes for the Rohingya's marginalisation and vulnerability, such as the denial of citizenship and the government's inaction or even involvement in violence targeting the Rohingya and other Muslim minorities. The fourth and fifth sections describe how human rights breaches, such as discrimination, denial of citizenship, hate speech, and incitement to violence against the Rohingya, create an extreme climate of systematic exclusion and vulnerability and how these are important contributing factors to the increased and continuing violence in the country. According to the Special Rapporteur Tomás Ojea Quintana in May 2013, the Rohingya are 'the most vulnerable and marginalised group in Myanmar' (OHCHR 2013).

Background

Rohingya and other Muslims in Myanmar

To understand why the Rohingya are particularly marginalised and denied basic human rights in Myanmar, it is necessary to understand how they are perceived – and treated – as distinct from other ethnic groups in society.

Out of a total national population of about 51.4 million (Department of Population 2014: 4), between 4% (CIA 2014) and 13% are Muslim (Matthews 2001: 5). Between 800,000 and one million of these are Rohingya, the majority living in Northern Rakhine (Arakan) State (Euro-Burma Office 2009: 1; Department of Population 2014: 4). The rest of Myanmar's Muslims are Indian Muslims, Pakistani Muslims, Kaman/Kamein (hereafter Kaman) Muslims, Malay Muslims, Chinese Muslims (Panthays), Burmese converts, and Muslims from mixed marriages

(Yegar 1972: 58; Yegar 2002: 24; Matthews 2001: 5; Priestley 2006). The Kaman are the only Muslim minority in Myanmar which are part of the 135 officially recognised national ethnic groups with full citizenship rights (Than Tun Win [undated]).

The Myanmar government under former president Thein Sein and the Buddhist majority in Rakhine State refer to the Rohingya as 'Bengalis', claiming that the name Rohingya is actually a Bengali word for Arakan, the former name for Rakhine State, and that the Bengali falsely took this name for themselves (Human Rights Watch 1996: 9; Zarni & Cowley 2014: 683). Even the Myanmar National Human Rights Commission (MNHRC) referred to the Rohingya as 'Bengalis' when it released a statement in 11 February 2014 on the alleged killing of 48 Rohingya in Ducheeratan village tract, Rakhine State, in which it stated:

> The news of the killing of 8 Bengalis and 40 Bengalis did not emerge in the Ducheeratan village tract and it is therefore concluded that the said news is unverifiable and unconfirmed.
>
> *(MNHRC 2014)*

According to Zarni and Cowley (2014: 682–683) the Rohingya 'are a borderland people' whose identity was recognised after independence in 1948 but denied after the 1962 military take-over. The name Rohingya itself seems to date back to 1799 and is derived from the words *Rohang* or *Roshang*, earlier names for Arakan in their language (Shafer 2013: 7; Alam 2011: 3; Charney 2005). For their part, the Rohingya assert being indigenous to Arakan (Rakhine State) and descendants of Muslims who settled there hundreds of years ago (Human Rights Watch 1996: 9). The Rohingya are said to be an 'ethnic mix of Bengali, Persian, Moghul, Turk and Pathan' (Shafer 2013: 7) and have a 'culture and language which is absolutely unique to the region' (Alam 2011: 1 as cited in Shafer 2013: 7). The consensus outside Myanmar is that the Rohingya have long been present in Arakan, perhaps even pre-dating Arakan's incorporation into Burmese territory in the eighteenth century (Staples 2012: 139; Shafer 2013: 7).

Whatever the period of their physical presence in Myanmar, the similarities of the Rohingya with Bangladeshi citizens just across the border (Chittagonians) are indisputable, as noted by the Danish Immigration Service (DIS):

> this group of Myanmarese nationals [Rohingya] look like Bangladeshi people from that area [Chittagong], they speak the same dialect and understand the language although there are some differences. Furthermore they have the same culture and the same religion. According to the [Bangladesh] Director of [the] MFA [Ministry of Foreign Affairs], even people from Bangladesh are confused and cannot distinguish the two groups.
>
> . . .
>
> A well informed diplomatic source . . . said that there is no difference in ethnicity and language between Rohingya and the local Bangladeshi population in the border area. . . . However, in the villages everybody will know who is a Rohingya which make them vulnerable as they are not citizens.
>
> *(DIS 2011: 9)*

The newly elected government which is led by Aung San Suu Kyi's National League for Democracy (NLD) party has refrained from using the derogatory term 'Bengalis' but they also refuse to use the term 'Rohingya' and in doing so deny the Rohingya their right to self-identify as a minority. In May 2016, a Foreign Ministry official in the new government, Mr Kyaw Zay Ya, stated:

> We won't use the term Rohingya because Rohingya are not recognized as among the 135 official ethnic groups. . . . Our position is that using the controversial term does not support the national reconciliation process and solving problems.
>
> *(Paddock 2016)*

Aung San Suu Kyi herself stated in a press briefing on 22 May 2016:

> The Rakhine Buddhists object to the term 'Rohingya' just as much as Muslims object to the term 'Bengali' because they have all kinds of political and emotional implications, which are unacceptable to the opposite party.
>
> *(Lun Min Mang 2016)*

Responses to the upsurge and spread of anti-Muslim violence

The history of the Rohingya is replete with tales of persecution and mistreatment after the collapse of British India, and there is a wealth of credible reports on massive human rights violations, including crimes against humanity at various periods (e.g. *inter alia* HRW 1996; HRW 2000; EBO 2009; ICHR 2010). Yet in recent years, and particularly since 2012, their plight has reached a crescendo of violence and exclusion.

The catalyst for the 2012 upsurge in violence against the Rohingya was the rape and murder of a Buddhist woman in Rakhine State by three Muslim men on 28 May of that year which resulted in riots in which ten Muslims were killed (Aung Hla Tun 2012). Despite the establishment of an investigation group, the Rakhine State Conflicts Investigation Commission (RSCI Commission), by the Myanmar government, violence continued to escalate, with further people being killed and property destroyed, leading to the declaration of a state of emergency on 10 June in Rakhine State (ICG 2012). The RSCI Commission reported in April 2013 that as a result of the 2012 sectarian conflicts there were 192 deaths, 265 injured, 8,614 houses destroyed and 100,000 people displaced (RSCIC 2013). Other organisations have estimated that the actual death toll was much higher. The Burmese Rohingya Organisation for its part claimed that 'within June alone, at least 650 Rohingya had been killed in the unrest' (Mizzima News 2012). The US Commission on International Religious Freedoms (USCIRF 2013: 21) estimated that over 1,000 Rohingya had been killed as a result of the violence.

In September 2013, the Special Rapporteur on the situation of human rights in Myanmar, Tomás Ojea Quintana, expressed to the UN General Assembly his belief that Rakhine State was in a continuous profound crisis and that the government was doing little to tackle the underlying causes of the targeted violence (Quintana 2013a: 12). He further criticised the RSCI Commission because their 'report fails to address the issue of impunity and the allegations of widespread and systematic human rights violations against the Rohingya community in Rakhine State' and he reiterated 'that the State has not fulfilled its obligation to properly investigate allegations, dating from June 2012, of extrajudicial killings, rape and sexual violence; arbitrary detention and torture and ill-treatment in detention; deaths in detention; and denial of due process and fair trial rights' and '[i]t also has not held those responsible to account' (Quintana 2013a: 12–13).

Initially localised to Northern Rakhine State, the violence spread to other parts of the country against other Muslim minorities. Special Rapporteur Quintana (2013a: 15–16) reported that on 20 March 2013 there were incidents of incitement to hatred against Muslim minorities in Meiktila and Mandalay regions. These contributed to an outbreak of violence between 20 and 23 March 2013 leading to 43 more deaths, including students at an Islamic boarding school and a Buddhist monk and the displacement of some 13,000. The Special Rapporteur (Quintana 2013a: 15–16) expressed his concerns on the involvement of the 969 Movement (a Buddhist nationalist movement) in the spread of anti-Muslim sentiment adding fuel to the violence. He further highlighted the worrying allegations of police failing to intervene to stop the violent mobs and protect local Muslim populations throughout the country – and even acting in ways which could be deemed supportive of the activities by the 969 Movement. He for example reported in April 2014 that he

> has continued to receive allegations of serious human rights violations being committed during [a] police operation [on 13 and 14 January 2014 in Maungdaw Township, Rakhine State] which also involved Rakhine mobs, including allegations of the brutal killing of [Muslim] men, women and children, sexual violence against women and the looting and burning of properties.
>
> *(Quintana 2014: 12)*

The USCIRF (2014: 44) additionally reported that 'though police reportedly participated in anti-Muslim violence during the past year, no member of the police or other security units were held responsible' and that '[i]ndividuals who incited violence against Muslims, including Buddhist monks and leaders of the "969" anti-Muslim movement, also were not held accountable'.

In October 2016 a new wave of violence engulfed Rakhine State. Reportedly, nine Myanmar police officers were killed by insurgents of the Rohingya Solidarity Organisation (RSO) in the night of 9 to 10 October 2016 which sparked a military operation in retribution to the attacks. The military operation which included the use of ground troops and helicopter gunships has led to serious human rights violations according to the Special Rapporteur on the situation of human rights in Myanmar, Yanghee Lee (Special Rapporteur Lee) such as torture, summary executions, sexual violence and the destruction of homes and mosques (OHCHR 2016). In response, Special Rapporteur Lee expressed her concern that 'tens of thousands of people have fled their homes' and '[h]umanitarian programmes providing health, food, education and nutrition assistance have been suspended' and she called for investigation of allegations of human rights abuses, including alleged rape and sexual assault (OHCHR 2016). Shockingly, Human Rights Watch (HRW 2016b) reported that after analysing high resolution satellite images recorded between 10 and 18 November 2016 around 1,250 buildings were destroyed by arson.

Since August 2016, former Secretary-General Kofi Annan, upon request by State Counsellor Aung San Suu Kyi, has been leading a commission composed of six local[1] and three international experts[2] to study the conditions in Rakhine State. According to the commission's website 'the Advisory Commission on Rakhine State has been founded as a neutral and impartial body which aims to propose concrete measures for improving the welfare of all people in Rakhine state' (ACRS 2016a). The mandate of the Advisory Commission flows from a Memorandum of Understanding between the Ministry of the Office of the State-Counsellor and the Kofi Annan Foundation (MOSC 2016). The Advisory Commission published its Interim Report in March 2017 in which it stated:

> The Commission is not mandated to investigate specific alleged human rights violations [and] [i]n line with the request of the State Counsellor, the Commission uses neither the term 'Bengali' nor 'Rohingya', who are referred to as 'Muslims' or 'the Muslim community in Rakhine'.
>
> *(ACRS 2017: 4–5)*

The report makes several 'interim recommendations' on topics such as humanitarian access, media access, justice and rule of law, border issues, socioeconomic development, training of security forces, citizenship, freedom of movement, birth certificates, closure of IDP camps, cultural issues, inter-communal dialogue, representation and participation in public life and regional relations. The Advisory Commission's final report is expected somewhere in the second half of 2017 but human rights experts and academia have already criticised the mandate of Annan's commission as flawed for several reasons, such as having to operate in accordance with the widely criticised Citizenship Law 1982 and focusing on development issues instead of investigating human rights abuses (Ives 2016; Ying-Kit Chan 2017: 10). Also, none of the commissioners are Rohingya, although one of them is Muslim, U Aye Lwin.

On 24 March 2017 the UN Human Rights Council adopted resolution 34/22 in which it decided to dispatch an independent international fact-finding mission,

> to establish the facts and circumstances of the alleged recent human rights violations by military and security forces, and abuses, in Myanmar, in particular in Rakhine State, including but not limited to arbitrary detention, torture and inhuman treatment, rape and other forms of sexual violence, extrajudicial, summary or arbitrary killings, enforced disappearances, forced displacement and unlawful destruction of property, with a view to ensuring full accountability for perpetrators and justice for victims.

The members of the fact-finding mission were appointed on 31 May 2017 and include Ms Indira Jaising (advocate of the Supreme Court of India and former member of the Committee on the Elimination of Discrimination Against Women), Ms Radhika Coomaraswamy (member of the Sri Lankan Constitutional Council and former Chairperson of the Sri Lanka Human Rights Commission) and Mr Christopher Dominic Sidoti (former director of the International Service for Human Rights and former Australian Human Rights Commissioner) (OHCHR 2017).

The NLD-government led by Aung San Suu Kyi has publicly stated that it will not support the fact-finding mission and not provide visas for the fact-finding mission members. An official in Suu Kyi's Ministry of Foreign Affairs stated to the press: 'If they are going to send someone with regards to the fact-finding mission, then there's no reason for us to let them come. . . . Our missions worldwide are advised accordingly' (Lewis 2017). Aung San Suu Kyi herself stated earlier in May 2017 to the press: 'We are disassociating ourselves from the resolution because we don't think the resolution is in keeping with what is actually happening on the ground' (Ives 2017).

Massive internal and regional displacement

The widespread and unprecedented level of disenfranchisement and denial of the most basic of human rights has led the Rohingya to flee the country in massive numbers. Their desperation at the scale of violations has left them with little choice but to seek refuge elsewhere. Since June 2012 at least 200,000 Rohingya have fled their homes and more than 138,000 Rohingya and Kaman Muslims were internally displaced in Rakhine State as of November 2013 and are living in camps, not able to return home (Fortify Rights 2014: 18). As of December 2015, there were still 145,062 IDPs that remain internally displaced in Rakhine State according to the UN Office for the Coordination of Humanitarian Affairs (UNOCHA 2015).

The above figures only concern Rohingya which were 'internally displaced' since 2012. The plight of the Rohingya is one that spans a long period of time and has created a steady flow of refugees across international borders and waters for decades. In their 2014 Annual Report the USCIRF (2014: 44) estimated that 'About 300,000 Muslims Rohingya live, often in squalid conditions, in refugee camps in Bangladesh, Thailand, and other Southeast Asian countries, and face discrimination, trafficking, and other hardships'. The number of Rohingya fleeing the persecution has increased since 2012 and is creating an unprecedented humanitarian crisis in the region. The UNHCR (2014) reported that it:

> estimates more than 86,000 people have left on boats since June 2012. This includes more than 16,000 people in the second half of 2012, some 55,000 in 2013 and nearly 15,000 from January to April this year [2014] . . . The majority are Rohingya.

In the first quarter of 2015 the UNHCR (2015: 1–2) reported:

> 25,000 people are estimated to have departed in irregular maritime movements from the Bay of Bengal. . . . Based on interviews with those who have reached Thailand and Malaysia, 300 people are estimated to have died at sea while attempting maritime journeys from the Bay of Bengal in the first quarter of 2015 – and as many as 620 since October 2014 – primarily as a result of starvation, dehydration, and beatings by boat crews. . . . Between 40 to 60 per cent of the estimated 25,000 people who departed from the Bay of Bengal in the first quarter of 2015 are thought to originate from Rakhine State, Myanmar, though many embarked on their maritime journeys from Bangladesh.

According to a more recent report by UNHCR published in April 2017, a total number of 168,500 Rohingya refugees have fled Myanmar since 2012, including 44,000 in 2016 (UNHCR 2017: 2).

These provide the background explaining Special Rapporteur Quintana's description of the Rohingya as the 'most vulnerable and marginalised group in Myanmar' (OHCHR 2013). As a result of these disturbing developments, the UN General Assembly (UNGA) adopted UNGA resolution 69/248 (2015, paras. [8]–[9]) on 29 December 2014 urging:

> the Government of Myanmar to accelerate its efforts to address discrimination, human rights violations, violence, hate speech, displacement and economic deprivation affecting various ethnic and religious minorities and attacks against Muslims and other religious minorities and reiterating its serious concern about the situation of the Rohingya minority in Rakhine State, including further instances of violence and other abuses in the past year.

The government's failure to intervene and involvement in severe violations of human rights

Right to life and use of force

Human Rights Watch (HRW) reported on several instances where police and security forces were allegedly involved in the upsurge of violence from 10 June 2012 onwards, such as:

> Residents in Sittwe and northern Arakan State . . . witnessed groups of [Buddhist] Arakan villagers armed with sticks, swords, spears, metal rods, and knives traveling together with police and appearing to work in concert.
>
> . . .
>
> Rohingya witnesses said that police and paramilitary Lon Thein – units specially trained to handle riots, and physically distinguished by red scarfs – opened fire on Rohingya as they attempted to extinguish fires that had been set by Arakan groups.

> . . .
>
> In northern Arakan State, Rohingya witnesses described how the security forces conducted violent sweeps, opening fire on fleeing villagers, killing what they said were dozens of Rohingya and wounding dozens more.
>
> *(HRW 2012: 24, 26–27)*

In the previous section it was also described how the Special Rapporteur has received reports on a police operation in January 2014, also involving Rakhine mobs, during which Muslim men, women and children were brutally killed. No members of the police or security units were held responsible. The level of impunity on behalf of officials was confirmed by Fortify Rights (2014: 18) which reported: 'there have been no prosecutions of members of Myanmar's state security forces for abuses committed in Rakhine State'.

The government's failure to prevent civilians being killed in the violence, or its participation in extrajudicial killings or executions of civilians is a violation of the right to life protected in treaties such as the International Covenant on Civil and Political Rights 1966 (ICCPR: Art. 6) – not yet ratified by Myanmar – and with regard to children in the Convention on the Rights of the Child 1989 (CRC: Art. 6) which is ratified by Myanmar and therefore binding. Moreover, the right to life has the status of customary international law and possibly *jus cogens* and can therefore be considered binding on Myanmar (Ramcharan 1985: 121, 161; Forrest Martin et al. 2006: 34–35).

The UN has developed the Basic Principles on the Use of Force and Firearms by Law Enforcement Officials 1990 which can be used as a tool by the Myanmar government to ensure its military and (border) police refrain from using force and firearms unless it is absolutely unavoidable, and even then they should exercise restraint, minimise damage and injury and respect and preserve human life (Basic Principles 1990: ss. 4–5). Arbitrary or abusive use of force should be punished as a criminal offence (Basic Principles 1990: s. 7).

Arbitrary arrest, detention and right to a fair trial of Rohingya

In the last few years the Rohingya have been increasingly targeted and persecuted by state authorities in Myanmar. HRW (2012: 27–28) reported large-scale security operations targeting Rohingya 'in which police, Lon Thein [paramilitary "riot" police], Nasaka [border police], and Burmese Army [also: Tatmadaw] soldiers systematically went village to village around Maungdaw Township rounding up residents and taking them to unknown locations'. HRW (2012: 28–29) also received reports of mass arrests of Rohingya in June 2012 and that some of those arrested were sentenced to one-year jail sentences for violating immigration laws. These arrests are arbitrary because these Rohingya are not citizens from another country who immigrated to Myanmar (they do not have Bangladeshi citizenship). They are from Myanmar and are stateless as a result of the government's discriminatory Citizenship Law 1982 which will be discussed in more depth in the third section of this chapter.

Special Rapporteur Quintana (2013b: 13) noted that 'more than 1,100 persons have been detained in relation to the violence in June and October, the vast majority of whom he understands are Rohingya men and boys'. He raises concerns over the violation of their 'due process rights, including access to legal counsel, judicial control over arrest, guarantees of habeas corpus, pre-trial detention as the exception rather than the norm, and the right to be tried without undue delay'. Quintana (2013a: 14) added to this list in his September 2013 report:

> Defendants have subsequently been denied legal representation, tried in closed trials with no access to the public, including family members, not received adequate interpretation of court proceedings, not received clear information on the charges against them (and requested to submit witness lists even so), have been tried in mass trials of more than 70 persons and have been chained together during trial proceedings.

As a result, in a period of just three days between 21 and 23 August 2013, the court in Buthidaung sentenced a total of 78 Rohingya to prison with sentences ranging from seven years to life (Quintana 2013a: 14).

HRW (2013: 39) also reported that Rohingya working for the UN and international NGOs were arrested and sentenced for crimes such as promoting hatred between Buddhists and Muslims and participating in arson attacks. While it was reported by Special Rapporteur Quintana (2013b: 13) that 'all United Nations staff detained in relation to the violence in Rakhine State have been released', he 'remains concerned that the four INGO workers . . . remain in detention'. The Special Rapporteur Lee (2014: 14) also expressed her concern 'about the status of the three [one was released] international NGO staff' and 'believes they were arrested under spurious charges and have been denied fair trial and due process rights'.

These arrests and convictions of Rohingya, including those working for the UN and NGOs, while denying their due process rights – is arbitrary and are against their right to liberty and security of person (ICCPR 1966: Art. 9) and their right to a fair trial (ICCPR 1966: Art. 14). The arbitrary nature of the imprisonment is further underlined by the reported fact that some of the UN staff members were sentenced to two and six years' imprisonment by the Maungdaw court and then four days later received a presidential pardon by President Thein Sein (HRW 2013: 39).

Torture and cruel, inhuman or degrading treatment

The vulnerability and marginalisation of the Rohingya leads to ill-treatment, including even torture, at the hands of state officials, who seem to have little concern for their basic human rights. HRW (2013: 37) reported on numerous such abuses, including this one:

> A well-educated Rohingya man was apprehended by Burmese intelligence services in June [2012] and interrogated for 19 consecutive days, deprived of sleep, hooded for extended periods, and threatened with physical harm. Authorities accused him of violating the Electronics Transactions Act by communicating abroad about the violence in June. He has since been released and the charges against him have been dropped.

HRW (2013: 37) also reported on one of their interviews with a UN official who claimed first-hand knowledge of conditions in detention in Arakan State:

> There is torture, humiliating torture. They are kept without food, water, clothes, in very bad conditions. They could be forced to work, to do things against their will. That is the reason why people are so afraid of being detained. Even in the process of detention, beatings can start immediately, even in the street . . . people die from beatings.

Special Rapporteur Quintana (2013a: 4) reported on allegations of systematic torture and ill-treatment of Muslim men and boys by prison guards in Buthidaung prison following the violence in June 2012. He also reported that 'up to 20 prison inmates . . . appear to have been brought into the prison for the specific purpose of administering beatings to Muslim prisoners'. Quintana (2013a: 4) reported further 'that the practice of systematic torture and ill-treatment of detainees in Buthidaung prison has now ceased, although inmates continue to experience arbitrary acts of ill-treatment, including beatings'.

The prohibition of torture and cruel, inhuman or degrading treatment is a generalised principle of international law protected by Article 7 of the ICCPR and the Convention against Torture or Other Cruel, Inhuman or Degrading Treatment or Punishment 1984 (CAT). The prohibition of torture has attained *jus cogens* status (Dratel 2005: 598). According to Special Rapporteur Lee (2014: 18) 'The Constitution is noticeably silent on the prohibition of torture, inhuman or degrading treatment or punishment, as well as the presumption of innocence until proved guilty'.

Rape and sexual violence against the Muslim minority

Special Rapporteur Quintana (2014: 13) has stated that rape and other forms of sexual violence have taken place on a large scale and been directed against the Rohingya population in Rakhine State. In international human rights law there is no specific definition on rape or sexual violence, but according to the Special Rapporteur on torture and other cruel, inhuman or degrading treatment or punishment, Manfred Nowak (2008: 34), 'rape constitutes torture when it is carried out by or at the instigation of or with the consent or acquiescence of public officials'. An Al-Jazeera documentary contained for example one shocking account by a Rohingya victim of rape by such officials during the civil unrest in Rakhine State. The woman, named Jannat Ara, recounted her ordeal at the hands of paramilitary police:

> After Friday prayers, when the violence erupted everyone panicked. People were running, trying to hide. I remained at home and closed all the doors. Paramilitary police [Lon Thein] surrounded our house and pushed open the doors. They found me upstairs. It happened on the bed. I was grabbed. They held me down and kicked me. After that I knew nothing. When I regained consciousness in [the] hospital I realised what had happened to me.
>
> [The woman's account stops here and the Al-Jazeera narrator continues:]
>
> According to medical records Janette was raped by more than 20 men. As a result of her rape she contracted kidney disease and aborted a pregnancy. On November 2nd 2012 Jannat Ara died from her injuries.
>
> *(Al-Jazeera 2013)*

After the renewed outbreak of violence in Rakhine State in October 2016 '[d]ozens of rapes' were reported by different rights groups, such as the Arakan Project and Burma Human Rights Network (MacGregor 2016). When *Myanmar Times* journalist, Fiona MacGregor, brought this to light in a news article she was dismissed due to alleged pressure on the newspaper by the Myanmar government (Holmes 2016).

The above cases against Rohingya and other Muslim women and girls involve 'conflict-related sexual violence'. This is defined as 'rape, sexual slavery, forced prostitution, forced pregnancy, enforced sterilization and other forms of sexual violence of comparable gravity perpetrated against women, men, girls or boys that is linked, directly or indirectly (temporally, geographically or causally) to a conflict' (UN S-G 2015, para. [2]). The UN Secretary-General (2015, para. [41]) outlined Myanmar in general and Rakhine State in particular as locations where conflict-related sexual violence is taking place. With regard to Rakhine State, he reported that 'Intercommunal fighting in Rakhine State has placed Muslim women in particular in a precarious position owing to restrictions on movement and lack of services'.

Citizenship and statelessness

Marginalisation, the Rohingya and the Citizenship Law 1982

Most Rohingya are today denied citizenship because of how their ethnicity is dealt with under the Citizenship Law 1982. Fortify Rights (2014: 16) reported an estimate of 40,000 Rohingya having citizenship, which means that only around 5% of the estimated 800,000 Rohingya living in Myanmar have a nationality. The Citizenship Law 1982 defines three classes of citizens, mainly based on ethnic criteria: full, associate and naturalised.

Full citizenship is reserved for those whose ancestors settled in Myanmar before 1823 (Citizenship Law 1982: s. 3) and who are members of one of Myanmar's 135 officially recognised national ethnic groups (not including the Rohingya) (Citizenship Law 1982: ss. 3–4; Than Tun Win [undated]). The Kaman Muslims, also a marginalised and vulnerable minority in Myanmar, are listed as a national ethnic group and therefore have full citizenship rights.

Associate citizenship is for those who are both eligible and have applied for citizenship under the previous Union Citizenship Act 1948 (Citizenship Law 1982: s. 78). The deadline for applying for associate citizenship passed on 15 October 1982 and according to the Burma Rohingya Organisation UK (BROUK 2015: 2): 'Few Rohingya are believed to have applied because most were unaware of the 1948 Act or of its significance'.

Finally, naturalised citizenship is available only for those who have entered and resided in the state before 4 January 1948, and their offspring born within the state, provided 'conclusive evidence' can be furnished (Citizenship Law 1982: s. 42) of their 'lineage or history of residence' (HRW 2000: 10). HRW (2000: 10) reported: 'Even for those Rohingya whose families settled in the region before 1823, moreover, the onerous burden of proof has made it nearly impossible for all but a handful to secure citizenship'.

The Burma Rohingya Organisation UK reported: 'The only documentation available to most Rohingya is a "family list" which indicates the names and dates of birth of each member of a household [but this] is insufficient because it does not record place of birth' (BROUK 2015: 2–3). Rohingya are also excluded or seriously disadvantaged in obtaining citizenship through other requirements. Section 44 of the Citizenship Law 1982 requires that applicants must be older than 'eighteen years' old, 'be able to speak well one of the national languages', a major hurdle for most Rohingya (HRW 2000: 10; ICHR 2010: 96), and be of 'good character' and 'sound mind'.

There are additionally worrying reports that Rohingya who already had 'conclusive evidence' on which they could establish citizenship, such as the lucky few who gained citizenship under the Union Citizenship Act 1948 and who received National Registration Cards (NRCs) under the Residents of Burma Registration Act 1949 and Residents of Burma Registration Rules 1951, were ordered to hand in these NRCs and reapply under the Citizenship Law 1982. According to a Rohingya journalist Aman Ullah from Kaladan Press Network (based in Bangladesh):

> [An] NRC is a bona fide document that allowed one to carry on all his national activities, without let or hindrance: to possess moveable and immovable or landed properties, pursue education, including higher studies and professional courses in the country's seats of learning, right to work and public services, including armed forces, and to obtain Burmese passport for travelling abroad, including pilgrimage to Holy Makkah.
>
> *(Ullah 2014)*

The policy of seizing NRCs started in 1974 and only applied to the Rohingya (Ullah 2014). As a result, their position changed retroactively from having citizenship and 'conclusive' proof for citizenship to becoming stateless and being issued Foreign Registration Cards (FRCs) or Temporary Registration Cards (TRCs, also White Cards) (HRW 1996: 27; ICHR 2010: 97; BROUK 2015: 3). In 1989 all residents in Burma that wanted to be recognised as citizens under the Citizenship Law 1982 had to apply for Citizenship Scrutiny Cards, pink for full citizens, blue for associate citizens and green for naturalised citizens (Ullah 2014). Most Rohingya were denied these cards or did not apply for them because they could not provide 'conclusive evidence' as required under the Citizenship Law 1982, since their NRCs were seized and they had no other documentation to proof their citizenship.

Most of the Rohingya up until this point had TRCs, which did allow them to take part in the 2008 referendum on the Myanmar Constitution 2008 and the 2010 elections (Zawacki 2012–2013: 20; BROUK 2015: 3). However, on 11 February 2015, President Thein Sein announced that all TRCs would expire on 31 March 2015 (BROUK 2015: 3). According to the Burma Rohingya Organisation UK 'this move has disenfranchised around a million people, mostly ethnic Rohingya from the upcoming general election due in Burma in November 2015' (BROUK 2015: 1). Special Rapporteur Lee (2015) confirmed this in a statement at the UN General Assembly on 28 October 2015, less than two weeks before the elections took place:

> I am also concerned by the disenfranchisement of hundreds of thousands of individuals from across Myanmar society. This includes Rohingya and individuals of Chinese and Indian descent who previously held temporary registration cards and had the right to vote in past elections. Given its disproportionate impact on minority communities, in particular the Rohingya, this decision is discriminatory. Also, the cancellation of voting rights without due process runs counter to international human rights standards and good practice.

According to Special Rapporteur Lee (2017: 4),

> about 470,000 TRCs were surrendered (of about 760,000 originally disbursed). While the highest number surrendered came from Rakhine (almost 400,000), the rest mostly came from Shan, Kayin and Mon States as well as Tanintharyi, Bago and Ayeyarwaddy Divisions.

The replacement for the TRC is the identity card for national verification (ICNV), which is, according to Special Rapporteur Lee (2017: 4), 'a document that is a prerequisite for applying for citizenship if the applicant no longer holds an identity card'. She adds that ICNV holders cannot freely move within Rakhine State and the rest of Myanmar but are free to cross to Bangladesh legally with border passes (Special Rapporteur Lee 2017: 4)

These citizenship requirements raise serious issues of state discrimination on racial, ethnic or linguistic grounds against the Rohingya.

The international response to the statelessness of the Rohingya

The consequences for the Rohingya of not being recognised as citizens because of discriminatory racial, ethnic and linguistic criteria are extreme, and without a doubt one of the main causes for their marginalisation in Myanmar. One of the main effects of the denial of citizenship is that most Rohingya have effectively been rendered stateless. Citizenship is after all 'the right to have rights' (a famous quote from philosopher Hannah Arendt) (Zawacki 2012–2013: 20; Kesby 2012), and means that the discriminatory exclusion of the Rohingya due to their ethnicity results in them more easily falling victims of other violations of human rights. Since the

Rohingya have been living in Myanmar for generations, it also means that they are rendered stateless – and extremely vulnerable to massive human rights abuses.

Rita Izsák, former UN Special Rapporteur on minority issues, stated that not recognising the Rohingya as citizens has 'implications for the enjoyment of all their human rights' (Izsák 2014: 19). Among the human rights affected, which will be described in more detail in the fourth section of this chapter are the rights to access employment, education, and health, rights to property and adequate housing, freedom of movement, freedom from arbitrary detention, reproductive rights, and even the rights to marry and to family life.

Special Rapporteur Quintana (2014: 13) for his part recommended that the Citizenship Law 1982 be reformed and brought 'into line with international standards' by removing 'race and ethnicity' as 'determining factors in the granting of citizenship', and that it should 'provide for objective criteria that comply with the principle of non-discrimination, such as birth in the territory and descent'. Special Rapporteur Lee (2014: 15) reiterated the same in her report, stating: 'The Citizenship Law of 1982 is in contravention of international law . . . thus it should not be exempt from reform'.

The racial, ethnic or even linguistic criteria for citizenship in the case of the Rohingya is a violation of the principle of non-discrimination, including the rights to equality before the law and equal protection of the law. This principle of non-discrimination is codified in Article 2(1) ICCPR and the rights to equality before the law and enjoying equal protection of the law in Article 26 ICCPR. Even though Myanmar has not ratified the ICCPR, the Myanmar Constitution 2008, section 347 reads: 'The Union shall guarantee any person to enjoy equal rights before the law and shall equally provide legal protection'. Moreover, the principle of non-discrimination is widely considered as customary international law (Eriksson 2000: 138–139) and can therefore be considered binding on Myanmar.

The Human Rights Committee held in its General Comment 18 on non-discrimination (1989: para. [13]) that only 'if the criteria for such differentiation are reasonable and objective and if the aim is to achieve a purpose which is legitimate under the Covenant' it might not be unlawful. This is clearly not the case as the criteria for full citizenship in Myanmar exclude the Rohingya only because they are not a recognised ethnic/racial group. The unreasonable and non-objective nature of the differentiation is further illustrated by the arbitrary revocation of some Rohingyas' NRCs (depriving them of *de facto* citizenship) and the vague 'conclusive evidence' criteria for naturalised citizenship – including language requirements – which are applied arbitrarily specifically with regard to the Rohingya. Together with the large-scale denial of services, benefits, right to property, health and education, which will be discussed in more depth below, these criteria cannot be considered reasonable, objective and with a legitimate aim.

Systematic discrimination and exclusion of Rohingya and other Muslims in Myanmar

A climate of systematic discrimination

Special Rapporteur Lee (2014: 13) stated that 'By virtue of its lack of legal status, the Rohingya community continues to face systematic discrimination'. This systematic discrimination 'includes restrictions on the freedom of movement, on access to land, food, water, education and health care, and on marriages and birth registration' (Lee 2014: 13).

Not only the lack of legal status, but also the discriminatory criteria used by the government of Myanmar in determining who is entitled to citizenship – itself a violation of international human rights law – often opens the door for state authorities to deny them other human rights when combined with the intolerance and hatred being directed at them as minorities, the unwillingness of the authorities to protect the Rohingya and other Muslims, and even their active involvement in disregarding these rights.

HRW's Asia director Brad Adams pointed out in this regard that 'Burma's discriminatory citizenship law not only deprives Rohingya of citizenship, but for decades has encouraged systematic rights violations' (HRW 2015).

As was stressed in the section of this chapter exploring background matters, as of December 2015 more than 140,000 Rohingya and Kaman Muslims remain internally displaced and are living in government-designated IDP camps, not being able to return to their homes (Fortify Rights 2014: 18; UNOCHA 2015). Also 168,500 Rohingya refugees have fled Myanmar since 2012, including 44,000 in 2016 (UNHCR 2017: 2).

Numerous reports demonstrate that the Rohingya more than any other group in Myanmar are being subjected because of their ethnicity to laws, policies and practices which illustrate a climate of systematic discrimination by state authorities. These laws, policies and practices lead to land confiscations, forced evictions, destruction of houses, forced labour, extortion, arbitrary taxation and restrictions on the freedom of movement. The Rohingya are also subjected to various discriminatory restrictions in relation to marriage, employment, access to land, food, water, education and health care (Lee 2014: 13; Zawacki 2012–2013: 19).

While many of these appear to be widespread in recent years, they are known to have occurred as early as 2001, when the United States reported in its International Religious Freedom Report on Burma that the Rohingya 'continued to experience severe legal, economic, and social discrimination' (US Department of State 2001). It was indicated that the Rohingya faced severe government restrictions on their ability to travel and engage in economic activity: if they wanted to leave their village area they had to obtain permission from the authorities.

Other examples include secondary education which legislation in Myanmar reserves for citizens and thus most Rohingya students did not have access to state-run schools beyond primary education (US Department of State 2001). This also applies to other Muslim minorities, not Rohingya, in other parts of Myanmar, which an interview in the section on right to education below illustrates.

These forms of denial of basic human rights have continued by state authorities and been exacerbated by the climate of violence and intolerance. Special Rapporteur Quintana (2014: 11) visited a Muslim neighbourhood, Aung Mingalar, in Sittwe, which he described as a 'ghetto'. Residents are prevented from leaving the neighbourhood by 'armed guards and wire fencing' and that there is 'Only one medical assistant . . . provided, by an international NGO, for all 4,375 residents of the ward'. He further reported that 'university students have been unable to access education since May 2012' and a lot of 'residents, many of whom are traders, remain unable to access their livelihoods' since they cannot leave the area (Quintana 2014: 12). The Special Rapporteur describes a similar situation in the Khoung Dote Khar Rohingya internally displaced persons (IDP) camp, near Sittwe and also that '[o]f the six public hospitals in Rakhine State, only two are currently accepting Muslim patients'. All of these show an inability or unwillingness of state authorities to ensure the protection and respect for the human rights of the Rohingya minority, whereas members of the Buddhist majority are mostly free to continue their daily activities with no similar restrictions.

The Myanmar government established in July 2014 the Rakhine State Action Plan. This plan contains a section on 'Citizenship Assessment of Bengalis' (2014: 8–10), which provides for steps to assess whether Rohingya are entitled to citizenship, using as a guideline the Citizenship Law 1982. According to HRW (2013), the use of the 'pejorative label' of Bengali already indicates a negative predisposition – and how detached this plan is to any concern for the human rights of the Rohingya:

> For any Rohingya failing to meet the criteria for citizenship, the authorities will 'construct temporary camps in required numbers for those who refuse to be registered and those without adequate documents' and sequester them in closed camps in what amounts to arbitrary, indefinite detention with the possibility of deportation.

Even the Government of Myanmar's solutions in the 'Permanent Resettlement' section of the Rakhine State Action Plan (2014: 6–7) proposed steps for eventually relocating some 133,000 Rohingya from Internally Displaced Persons (IDP) camps to other sites are problematic from a human rights point of view. HRW (2014) has voiced its concerns that the Action Plan does not discuss the possibility of these Rohingya returning to their original homes, and that the proposed resettlement zones might 'deepen the isolation and marginalization of the Rohingya' which is 'in violation of their freedom of movement and other rights'.

Forced evictions: the right to adequate housing and the prohibition of arbitrary or unlawful interference with a person's home

After the violence in 2012 a lot of Rohingya were forced off their land, their houses destroyed and their land confiscated. HRW (2013: 59–60) gave a few examples of how Muslims in Rakhine State lost the roofs over their heads, including the following:

> A Kaman man, 31, from Kyauk Pyu said:
>
> On October 23 many Arakanese came into the village and said, 'This is not your place, this is our property because this country is ours'. The military and police entered the village and said the same things to us. They said we should go. . . . The police and military came and told people to come out of their house, and they said if we didn't we'd all be killed. They said they couldn't provide us with security. At that time, the Arakanese people had started setting fires. They set the mosque on fire first and then the houses. . . . And in the presence of the military and police, they entered our homes and took what they wanted. Most of the people in Kyauk Pyu possess property. They took our belongings and then set fires [to our houses]. They [the authorities] didn't take any action against them.
>
> *(HRW 2013: 59)*

As was mentioned above, HRW (2016b) obtained satellite imagery showing proof of arson of around 1,250 buildings in November 2016. Allegedly the military denied burning down these buildings and blamed the Rohingya for setting their own houses on fire (AFP 2016).

Land confiscations, forced evictions and the destruction of houses by authorities which particularly target Muslims are violations of human rights recognised in international human rights treaties such as, among other things, the right to adequate housing in Article 11 of the International Covenant on Economic, Social and Cultural Rights 1966 (ICESCR), recently signed by Myanmar but not yet ratified, and Article 17 ICCPR on the prohibition of arbitrary or unlawful interference with a person's home.

Freedom of movement and access to livelihood

The Irish Centre for Human Rights (ICHR 2010: 12) reported that Rohingya are being detained for travelling beyond their villages and neighbourhoods without permits as specified in the Foreigners Act 1864, ss. 10 and 12, and for travelling without authorisation under the

Emergency Provision Act 1950, s. 5(j). These restrictions are once again linked in part to their status and vulnerability as non-citizens and the result of discrimination on the ground of ethnicity. These are clearly violations of their right to freedom of movement protected in treaties such as Article 12 of the ICCPR. It is also a violation of the prohibitions against arbitrary arrest and detention, which were already discussed.

HRW gave an example of the situation in Myebon, Rakhine State in December 2012 that shows the Buddhist Rakhines (also: Arakanese) are not as affected by the restrictions as the Rohingya Muslims:

> In Myebon, for example, a relatively small number of displaced Arakanese were provided adequate shelter in tents – and elsewhere in local schools and monasteries – sanitation, food, and medical supplies. At the same time, 4,000 displaced Rohingya just kilometres away were living in squalor, without adequate shelter, sanitation, or other basic necessities weeks after their displacement. They were also guarded by soldiers and prevented from leaving.
>
> *(HRW 2013: 80)*

Rapporteur Lee (2014: 12) reported that the 'Restrictions on the freedom of movement severely affected basic rights, [among other things] access to livelihoods, food, water and sanitation' protected by Article 11 of the ICESCR.

Right to health and reproductive rights

Having been located against their will by state authorities in various camps, Rohingya now find themselves with very limited or even no medical facilities available to them. Special Rapporteur Lee (2014: 12) reported that she 'received disturbing reports of deaths in camps owing to the lack of access to emergency medical assistance and owing to preventable, chronic or pregnancy-related conditions' (Lee 2014: 12). She stressed that the situation is 'deplorable' for both communities that have been displaced (including Buddhist Rakhines) but she 'observed that the conditions in the Rohingya camp were undeniably worse' (Lee 2014: 12).

Also outside the camps official government policies such as 'Regional Order 1/2005' imposes only for the Rohingya a strict two-child policy and also does not allow them to have children out of wedlock (Fortify Rights 2014: 24). Fortify Rights (2014: 28–29) reported that this policy has led to illegal and unsafe abortions and in some cases to serious health issues and even death. Allegedly, the policy has also led to degrading methods for the government to confirm women are truly the birth mothers by forcing Rohingya women to breastfeed infants in the presence of soldiers (Fortify Rights 2014: 24).

To make matters worse, in December 2014, Myanmar's former President Thein Sein submitted four draft laws, the Religious Conversion Law, the Buddhist Women's Special Marriage Law, the Population Control Healthcare Law and the Monogamy Law, known collectively as the 'Race and Religion Protection Laws' to the Myanmar parliament. Even though these laws were widely criticised by national and international civil society organisations, including Aung San Suu Kyi's National League for Democracy, they were adopted by the Myanmar parliament before the elections took place in November 2015 (HRW 2016a: 139–140; Yale IHRC & Fortify Rights 2015: 33–34; AI & ICJ 2015; GIWPS 2015). The Committee on the Elimination of Discrimination Against Women (CEDAW Committee 2016: 15) in its Concluding Observations on Myanmar's state report held that the four laws 'discriminate against women and girls based on, inter alia, their ethnicity and religion'.

According to a report by Yale Law School's International Human Rights Clinic for Fortify Rights (Yale IHRC & Fortify Rights 2015: 34):

> One of the laws [the Population Control Healthcare Law] authorizes local authorities to force women to have a gap of 36 months between births. The law does not explicitly mention the Rohingya but states that local authorities can enforce the law selectively, taking into account a high number of migrants in the area, a high population growth rate and a high birth rate.

These practices, policies and recently enacted Population Control Healthcare Law are in violation of the Rohingya's right to health in Article 12 of the ICESCR and Article 12 of the Convention on the Elimination of All Forms of Discrimination Against Women 1979 (CEDAW) and their reproductive rights which are defined in the Programme of Action of the International Conference on Population and Development International Conference (1994, para. [7.3]).

Right to education

Rohingya children and students have been severely restricted in terms of access to education since 2012. A Rohingya man from Sittwe stated to HRW in an interview: 'We haven't had access to any education since the violence. At the same time, the Arakanese living downtown . . . their children can attend school. They [the Arakanese] can attend primary class but for us, it's not available here' (HRW 2013: 89). A Rohingya student of university-age stated to HRW: 'In Maungdaw and Buthidaung the [Muslim] students can't attend university, and even the students living near the university here [in Sittwe] can't attend the university. The government said they could not provide security for us' (HRW 2013: 89). Muslims in other areas of Myanmar also face restrictions, mostly resulting from a lack of ID cards, as the following interview by the Karen Human Rights Group (KHRG) in early 2016 with a Muslim villager from Thaton Township, Mon State, illustrates:

> [T]he Myanmar government came to make ID card[s] for the students at the school but our Muslim children were rejected because they [the government] said we have to go and ask for ID cards at the Township level if we want to make one. It is not easy to make an ID card if we go to the Township office. Also, we have to pay a lot of money. Some Muslim people reported the case many times but in the end, they just lost their money. So I withdrew my daughters from the school that year. . . . We sent our children to the school for 9 or 10 years but finally we lost everything before they could get to college, because of the ID card issue. Most of the Muslim children left the school.
>
> *(KHRG 2016: 3)*

The above accounts are clear violations of the right to education, protected by treaties such as Article 13(2)(b) and (c) of the ICESCR 1966 and Article 28(1) of the CRC.

Right to marry and have a family life

There are indications of particularly intrusive and discriminatory state practices towards the Rohingya in relation to private matters such as marriage and family life. Fortify Rights (2014: 30) identified a number of restrictions on marriage being imposed on Rohingya. Examples of these include the requirement of appearing before the official cleanly shaven (most Rohingya men have a beard due to religious customs) or for women not being allowed to wear a headscarf (Fortify Rights 2014: 30). The greatest hurdle for most Rohingya, however, is that authorities may demand 'unofficial' payments as high as US$100 and an extensive waiting period for approval of often up to two years (Fortify Rights 2014: 30–31) – and plainly for the Rohingya and not others. The newly adopted Buddhist Women's Special Marriage Law places restrictions on interfaith marriages between Buddhist women and non-Buddhist men. According to Yale IHRC and Fortify Rights (2015: 34): 'The law permits township officials to publicly display an interfaith couple's application for marriage for two weeks and permits objections to the marriage to be taken to local court'. These practices, policies and newly enacted law are in violation of Article 16 of the Universal Declaration of Human Rights 1948 (UDHR) and Article 16(1) of the CEDAW.

Freedom of religion

The right to freedom of religion of the Rohingya Muslims and other Muslims in Myanmar is also being violated. HRW (2012: 30–31) reported that after the upsurge of violence in Rakhine State in 2012 the authorities have 'prevented Muslims from burying their dead as required by Islam, and some were allegedly cremated', which was 'highly distressing to the Muslim community'. In their 2014 annual report, the USCIRF (2014: 44) wrote that 'The government recently ordered the destruction of mosques, religious centers, and schools'. The USCIRF (2013: 25) reported earlier that in the whole of Myanmar the 'Police often restricted the number of Muslims who could gather in one place, effectively banning public worship, religious ceremonies and education'. It was also reported that 'It is almost impossible for Muslims to obtain building permits for either mosques or schools and unlicensed venues are regularly closed or destroyed' (USCIRF 2013: 25).

A further example of the infringement of the freedom of religion and religious discrimination is the newly adopted Religious Conversion Law which in practice, according to the Georgetown Institute for Women, Peace and Security (GIWPS 2015: 8), is 'aimed at preventing Buddhists from converting to another religion, especially Islam, and to stop non-Muslim women from marrying Muslim men by putting obstacles in their paths to conversion'.

This is not in line with international human rights standards which require that 'Everyone has the right to freedom of thought, conscience and religion' (ICCPR: Art. 18).

Hate speech and incitement to discrimination, hostility or violence

Background

The climate in Myanmar has become violently intolerant towards the Muslims and the Rohingya in particular, but this is not something which has occurred spontaneously. It has directly been fuelled by hate speech activities and incitements to discrimination, hostility or violence which have remained unchallenged and unpunished by state authorities, and even in some cases facilitated and supported by them. According to Van Klinken and Su Mon Thazin Aung (2017: 1):

> Recent anti-Muslim violence in Myanmar cannot be understood primarily as a spontaneous outburst of religious feeling among the general population. Rather it was a shocking repertoire deployed by a semi-organised social movement with clear political goals, which overlapped with those of Myanmar's military elite.

The most influential groups in organising anti-Rohingya activities are the local order of Buddhist monks in Rakhine State, the Arakan National Party and the 969 Movement (also: Ma Ba Tha).[3]

The hatred and incitement to violence expressed by local Rakhine Buddhist monks can at first glance seem startling, as is shown by the content of pamphlets distributed on 29 June 2012 by the Association of Young Monks (HRW 2013: 25) which included statements such as:

> [Arakanese] [m]ust not do business with Bengalis.
>
> [Arakanese] [m]ust not associate with Bengalis.
>
> Bengalis who dwell on Arakanese land, drink Arakanese water, and rest under Arakanese shadows are now working for the extinction of the Arakanese.
>
> *(HRW 2013: 25)*

Another Buddhist organisation in Myanmar, the Alliance to Protect Buddhism Group (Thar Tha Nar) issued on 10 September 2012 a leaflet with four rules:

1 Traditionally Buddhist owned houses, compounds and farms are not to be sold, rented or pawned to Muslims.
2 Buddhist women are not to marry Muslim men.
3 Buddhists are to buy goods only from Buddhists' shops.
4 Buddhists are not to use their Burmese names to buy property, build or rent property for Muslims (Burma Campaign UK 2013: 1).

While these are views expressed by private parties, it is unfortunately the case that state officials have tended to support such hate speech, rather than condemn and prohibit it as can be seen from this letter from Myanmar's Consul-General in Hong Kong:

> In reality, Rohingya are neither 'Myanmar People' nor Myanmar's ethnic group. You will see in the photos that their complexion is 'dark brown'. The complexion of Myanmar people is fair and soft, good looking as well. . . . It is quite different from what you have seen and read in the papers. (They are as ugly as ogres).
>
> *(Ye Myint Aung 2009: 1; ICHR 2010: 114)*

Other Muslims, such as the Kaman, have also been targeted by similar hate speech. The head monk at the Than Phyu Monastery is reported to have said:

> Kaman are also Kular [dark-skinned] and They are a kind of Kular race. They are the same blood. When incidents happen they unite with Kular, they don't stay on the Rakhine side.
>
> *(Schearf 2012)*

Special Rapporteur Quintana (2013a: 15–16) in particular expressed his concerns about the role of the 969 Movement in incidents of incitement to discrimination, hostility or violence throughout Myanmar. The 969 Movement is led by a Buddhist monk named Wirathu who was initially sentenced to 25 years in prison in 2003 for inciting religious conflicts, but subsequently released in January 2012.

Muslims throughout Myanmar are affected by the hate speech of the 969 Movement as the below interview by KHRG with a Muslim villager from Thaton Township in Mon State in early 2016 shows:

> [T]he people (969) from here said they would destroy or burn our religious school and our Muslim temple [mosque]. So I discussed about it with the Township leader. Then, he told me that he would come to call a meeting for us after two days but we, *Ka la* [*Kular*], were not invited to come to the meeting . . . Even though we did not go to the meeting, people still criticised the Township leader [accused him of supporting Muslims] when the Buddhist monk came to preach here. In my life, I have never seen those who have bad attitudes [hate] towards other people. Now it happens like that. . . . It became a noise [rumour] that people should not buy things from *Ka la* shops. Most *Ka la* are poor people. Maybe you may see many *Ka la Malay* who are street sellers in the street. During that whole year [after the 2013 riots], it became a serious concern because they [street sellers] were afraid to sell outside. If we go out for fishing, we worry that we will be beaten by other non-*Ka la* people because we are a minority ethnic group.
>
> *(KHRG 2016: 6)*

What remains less said is how state authorities in Myanmar in recent years have appeared to support those responsible for the wave of violence and abuse against the Rohingya and Muslims in general. When the leader of the 969 Movement, Wirathu was featured on the front page of the July 2013 issue of *TIME Europe* and *TIME Asia* magazine with the cover title 'The Face of Buddhist Terror: How Militant Monks are Fuelling Anti-Muslim Violence in Asia' (*TIME* 2013), both were banned in Myanmar (Williams 2013), as well as Sri Lanka (AP 2013). President Thein Sein even went so far as to publicly defend Wirathu and accuse *TIME* magazine of 'slandering the Buddhist religion and harming the national reconciliation process by accusing the outspoken cleric'. The Myanmar president then went on to describe Wirathu as a 'son of Buddha' and a 'noble person committed to peace', while a spokesperson for the president stated that Wirathu had the right to 'express [his] opinion' (Hindstrom 2013).

However, statements attributed to Wirathu by independent international media make it difficult to perceive how a 'noble person committed to peace' could espouse what would reasonably appear to others as incompatible with peace:

> 'Now is not the time for calm. . . . Now is the time to rise up, to make your blood boil'; '[Muslims] are breeding so fast, and they are stealing our women, raping them'; 'Taking care of our own religion and race is more important than democracy' *TIME magazine*.
>
> *(Beech 2013)*

> 'Myanmar is currently facing a most dangerous and fearful poison that is severe enough to eradicate all civilization'; 'If we are weak, our land will become Muslim' *New York Times*.
>
> *(Fuller 2013)*

> 'In every town, there is a crude and savage Muslim majority'; 'Once we [have] won this battle, we will move on to other Muslim targets' *The Guardian*.
>
> *(Hodal 2013)*

Incitement to discrimination, hostility or violence

As pointed out by Special Rapporteur Quintana (2014: 6–7), the Myanmar 'Government is not fulfilling its international human rights obligation to tackle incitement to violence based on national, racial or religious hatred', and 'Community-based, political and religious groups have been conducting, with impunity, well-organized and coordinated campaigns of incitement to discrimination, hostility and violence against Rohingya and other Muslims minorities'. His successor, Special Rapporteur Lee (2014: 15) reported in September 2014 that 'She is concerned at the spread of hate speech and incitement to violence, discrimination and hostility in the media and on the Internet, which have fuelled and triggered further violence'. She advised:

> A comprehensive series of measures is needed as a priority, encompassing the review of existing legislation to prohibit and combat hate speech, and, if necessary, the adoption of additional measures – but these must comply with international human rights standards, and be carefully construed and applied by the judiciary so as not to excessively limit the freedom of expression.
>
> *(Lee 2014: 15)*

There is, under Article 20(2) of the ICCPR, a clear positive obligation to legally prohibit any advocacy of national, racial or religious hatred that constitutes incitement to discrimination, hostility or violence, and this prohibition reflects customary international law (General Comment 24 1994: para. [8]).

Therefore, Myanmar authorities have a duty to investigate and prosecute those responsible for such incitements which have fuelled and continue to encourage attacks on Rohingya. While there is in place national criminal legislation against hate speech, its restrictions apply only to 'persons' resident in the Union (Myanmar Penal Code 1860: s. 153A) and thus it may still leave the Rohingya without protection. In addition, Special Rapporteur Lee (2014: 15) advised:

> New legislation or stricter enforcement of existing measures is never a panacea in quelling hate speech, however. There should be an accompanying set of policy measures to address the root causes and underlying grievances, foster dialogue and bring about a change in mindset and discourse. This should include awareness-raising measures, as well as support for intercommunal and interfaith cooperation initiatives.

The Special Rapporteur stressed that 'political leaders and public officials have a special responsibility, and in that respect, President Thein Sein's clear and public call against hate speech and incitement in early July is welcomed' (Lee 2014: 16). In March 2017 the Special Rapporteur (Lee 2017: 3) acknowledged 'the Government's decision to draft a hate speech law that should address incitement to discrimination and violence, while protecting freedom of speech'. However, it was added that 'she is concerned that the draft has not yet been open for public consultation, and that several proposed provisions are not in accordance with international standards' (Lee 2017: 3). She further encouraged the government to hold meaningful consultations and revise the text in accordance with the Rabat Plan of Action on the prohibition of advocacy of national, racial or religious hatred that constitutes incitement to discrimination, hostility or violence (Lee 2017: 3; OHCHR 2012).

Attacks against and the disenfranchisement of the Rohingya remain the order of the day in Myanmar: there continues to be no steps taken against Buddhist leaders and others who continue to incite in complete impunity discrimination, hostility or violence against the Rohingya and other Muslims.

Conclusion

Severe human rights violations continue to be committed since the 2012 upsurge of violence in Rakhine State and the subsequent spread of violence against Muslims throughout Myanmar, leading among others to an unprecedented refugee and humanitarian crisis in neighbouring Southeast Asian countries. State authorities continue to fail to protect Muslims in the country from abuse and violence. What is worse, there are credible reports that they have been involved in the abuse and violence and through discriminatory practices, policies and laws created and maintained a climate that is supportive of it.

One of this chapter's main points of focus has been how the Rohingya have been victims of discrimination due to their ethnicity and thus denied citizenship, and how this discrimination and denial of citizenship are root causes for their marginalisation and vulnerability as 'foreigners' and how it has led the Rohingya being seen as a threat by state and non-state actors alike. Other human rights violations by state authorities such as forced evictions, restrictions on the freedom of movement, religion, marriage, employment, education and health care illustrate the deeply rooted systematic nature of the discrimination committed against the Rohingya.

Hate speech and incitement to discrimination, hostility or violence has, since 2012, fuelled the intolerance and violence against Rohingya and other Muslims in Myanmar. Politicians in Rakhine State and Buddhist monks in the 969 Movement have contributed greatly to an environment which has led to numerous incidents of hate speech and incitement to discrimination, hostility or violence which have in the end poisoned whole segments of society. These groups seem to have been allowed to operate with relative impunity and even to have the implicit support of state authorities, including even that of the former President U Thein Sein. Myanmar's international obligations clearly require that the government investigate and punish these incidents of hate speech and incitement in order to protect those who are the most vulnerable and marginalised in Myanmar: the Rohingya.

As events since 2012 have been showing, the systematic failure to recognise, respect and protect effectively the rights of the Rohingya and other Muslim minorities has not only caused horrific human suffering and a humanitarian crisis, it has also resulted in a refugee crisis which carries real risks of destabilising and causing tensions in neighbouring Southeast Asian countries.

With a new government in place under leadership of Nobel Peace Prize Laureate Aung San Suu Kyi – albeit not as president but as State Counsellor, Minister of the President's office and Foreign Minister – expectations were high for an improvement in the situation of the Rohingya and other Muslims in Myanmar. Unfortunately, over the last year that the NLD-led government has been in place these expectations have not been met. Aung San Suu Kyi herself and her government have been criticised widely for not speaking out on the subject and trying to avoid making statements that might affect her relationship with the military. This might have to do with the fact that the elected government is not in control of the 'key' ministries of Defence, Home Affairs and Border Affairs, which are appointed and *de facto* controlled by the military. However, what Aung San Suu Kyi and the NLD government could have done was speak out on the subject and ensure the UN Fact Finding Mission would be allowed to conduct independent and transparent investigations on alleged violations of human rights. As she is Minister of Foreign Affairs she should have tried to use that power to ensure the Fact Finding Mission members are allowed to visit Myanmar, but her ministry has publicly stated it will not issue visas.

Notes

1 The local commissioners are: U Win Mra (MNHRC Chairman), Dr Tha Hla Shwe (former president of the Myanmar Red Cross), U Aye Lwin (chief convener of the Islamic Centre of Myanmar and founding member of Religions for Peace, Myanmar), Dr Mya Thida (president of Obstetrical and Gynecological Society of the Myanmar Medical Association), U Khin Muang Lay (MNHRC member), Daw Saw Khin Tint (Chairperson of the Rakhine Literature and Cultural Association, Chairperson for Saving

Arakan Committee, Vice Chair of Rakhine Women's Association, and Vice Chair of the Arakan Farmers Development Committee) (ACRS 2016b).

2 The international commissioners are: Kofi Annan (former Secretary-General of the UN), Ghassan Salamé (former Minister of Culture in Lebanon and former Senior Advisor to UN Secretary-General), Laetitia van den Assum (former Netherlands Ambassador to Thailand, South Africa, Kenya, Mexico and the UK) (ACRS 2016b).

3 Ma Ba Tha is most commonly translated as Organization for the Protection of Race and Religion.

References

Advisory Commission on Rakhine State (ACRS) 2016a, *About the Commission*, viewed 18 July 2017, www.rakhinecommission.org/.

Advisory Commission on Rakhine State (ACRS) 2016b, *Staff*, viewed 18 July 2017, www.rakhinecommission.org/staff.

Advisory Commission on Rakhine State (ACRS) 2017, *Interim Report and Recommendations*, March, www.rakhinecommission.org/app/uploads/2017/03/Advisory-Commission-Interim-Report.pdf.

Agence France Presse (AFP) 2016, 'Myanmar Pursuing "Ethnic Cleansing" of Rohingya: UN Official', *Bangkok Post*, 25 November, viewed 30 November 2016, www.bangkokpost.com/news/asean/1144205/myanmar-pursuing-ethnic-cleansing-of-rohingya-un-official.

Al-Jazeera 2013, *The Hidden Genocide (Myanmar)*, 16 January, viewed 22 May 2015, www.aljazeera.com/programmes/aljazeerainvestigates/2012/12/2012125122215836351.html.

Alam, MA 2011, *Marginalization of the Rohingya in Arakan State of Western Burma*, 30 January, viewed 22 May 2015, www.scribd.com/doc/96809398/Marginalization-Rohingya.

Allard K. Lowenstein International Human Rights Clinic, Yale Law School & Fortify Rights (YALE IHRC & Fortify Rights) 2015, *Persecution of the Rohingya Muslims: Is Genocide Occurring in Myanmar's Rakhine State?*, viewed 22 May 2016, www.fortifyrights.org/downloads/Yale_Persecution_of_the_Rohingya_October_2015.pdf.

Amnesty International (AI) & International Commission of Jurists (ICJ) 2015, *Myanmar: Parliament Must Reject Discriminatory 'Race and Religion' Laws*, Joint statement, 3 March, viewed 22 May 2016, www.amnesty.org/download/Documents/ASA1611072015ENGLISH.pdf.

Associated Press (AP) 2013, 'Sri Lanka: Time Magazine Is Banned', *The New York Times*, 3 July, viewed 22 May 2015, www.nytimes.com/2013/07/04/world/asia/sri-lanka-time-magazine-is-banned.html?_r=0.

Aung Hla Tun 2012, 'Myanmar Assigns Top Cop, Minister to Probe Muslim Deaths', *Reuters*, 7 June, viewed 22 May 2015, www.reuters.com/article/2012/06/07/us-myanmar-violence-idUSBRE8560LH20120607.

Basic Principles on the Use of Force and Firearms by Law Enforcement Officials (Basic Principles 1990), adopted in Havana at Eighth United Nations Congress on the Prevention of Crime and the Treatment of Offenders, 27 August–7 September 1990, UN Doc A/CONF.144/28/Rev.*1 at* 112.

Beech, H 2013, 'The Face of Buddhist Terror', *Time Magazine*, 1 July, viewed 22 May 2015, http://content.time.com/time/magazine/article/0,9171,2146000,00.html.

Burma Campaign UK 2013, 'Examples of Anti-Muslim Propaganda', *Burma Briefing*, 21 March, viewed 22 May 2015, www.burmacampaign.org.uk/images/uploads/Examples_of_Anti-Muslim_Propaganda.pdf.

Burma Rohingya Organisation UK (BROUK) 2015, *Briefing Paper: The Rohingya, the Citizenship Law, Temporary Registration, and Implementation of the Rakhine State Action Plan*, Briefing Paper, 2 April, viewed 21 May 2015, http://brouk.org.uk/wp-content/uploads/2015/04/Briefing-Paper-on-White-Card.pdf.

Charney, MW 2005, 'Buddhism in Arakan: Theory and Historiography of the Religious Basis of the Ethinym', a paper submitted to the Forgotten Kingdom of Arakan Workshop, Bangkok, 23–24 November, viewed 22 May 2015, www.kaladanpress.org/index.php/scholar-column-mainmenu-36/58-seminar-and-event-sp-541/arakan-historical-seminar/718-buddhism-in-arakantheories-and-historiography-of-the-religious-basis-of-ethnonyms.html.

Charter of the United Nations (UN Charter), adopted 26 June 1945, entered into force 24 October 1945, 1 UNTS XVI.

Citizenship Law 1982, Pyithu Hluttaw Law No. 4, 15 October, viewed 22 May 2015, www.refworld.org/docid/3ae6b4f71b.html.

Committee on the Elimination of Discrimination Against Women (CEDAW Committee) 2016, 'Concluding Observations on the Combined Fourth and Fifth Periodic Reports of Myanmar', 25 July, UN Doc CEDAW/C/MMR/CO/4-5.

Convention Against Torture or Other Cruel, Inhuman or Degrading Treatment or Punishment (CAT), adopted 10 December 1984, entered into force 26 June 1987, 1465 UNTS 85.

Convention on the Elimination of All Forms of Discrimination Against Women (CEDAW), adopted 18 December 1979, entered into force 3 September 1981, 1249 UNTS 13.

Convention on the Rights of the Child (CRC), adopted 20 November 1989, entered into force 2 September 1990, 1577 UNTS 3.

Danish Immigration Service (DIS) 2011, *Rohingya Refugees in Bangladesh and Thailand: Fact Finding Mission to Bangladesh and Thailand 4 to 17 February 2011*, Copenhagen, May, viewed 22 May 2015, www.nyidanmark.dk/NR/rdonlyres/B08D8B44-5322-4C2F-9604-44F6C340167A/0/FactfindingrapportRohingya180411.pdf.

Dratel, JL 2005, *The Torture Papers: The Road to Abu Ghraib*, New York, Cambridge University Press.

Eriksson, MK 2000, *Reproductive Freedom: In the Context of International Human Rights and Humanitarian Law*, The Hague, Kluwer Law International.

Euro-Burma Office (EBO) 2009, *The Rohingyas: Bengali Muslim or Arakan Rohingyas?*, Briefing Paper 2, viewed 22 May 2015, www.burmalibrary.org/docs6/EBO_Briefing_Paper_No._2_-_The_Rohingyas.pdf.

Foreigners Act 1864 (India Act III), 12 February, viewed 22 Ma 2015, www.refworld.org/docid/3ae6b54c4.html.

Forrest Martin, F, Schnably, SJ, Wilson, R, Simon, J & Tushnet, M 2006, *International Human Rights and Humanitarian Law: Treaties, Cases, and Analysis*, Cambridge, Cambridge University Press.

Fortify Rights 2014, *Policies of Persecution*, 25 February, viewed 22 May 2015, www.fortifyrights.org/downloads/Policies_of_Persecution_Feb_25_Fortify_Rights.pdf.

Fuller, T 2013, 'Extremism Rises among Myanmar Buddhists', *The New York Times*, 20 June, viewed 22 May 2015, www.nytimes.com/2013/06/21/world/asia/extremism-rises-among-myanmar-buddhists-wary-of-muslim-minority.html.

Georgetown Institute for Women, Peace and Security (GIWPS) 2015, *Protection for Whom? Violations of International Law in Myanmar's New 'Race and Religion Protection' Laws*, December, viewed 22 May 2016, https://giwps.georgetown.edu/sites/giwps/files/violations_of_international_law_in_myanmar.pdf.

Hindstrom, H 2013, 'Burma President Backs Anti-Muslim "Hate Preacher" Wirathu', *Democratic Voice of Burma*, 24 June, viewed 22 May 2015, www.dvb.no/news/politics-news/burma-president-backs-anti-muslim-%E2%80%98hate-preacher%E2%80%99-wirathu/28955.

Hodal, K 2013, 'Buddhist Monk Uses Racism and Rumours to Spread Hatred in Burma', *The Guardian*, 18 April, viewed 22 May 2015, www.theguardian.com/world/2013/apr/18/buddhist-monk-spreads-hatred-burma.

Holmes, O 2016, 'Myanmar Journalist Says She Was Fired Over Story on Military Rape Allegations', *The Guardian*, 4 November, viewed 30 November 2016, www.theguardian.com/world/2016/nov/04/myanmar-times-journalist-fired-fiona-macgregor.

Human Rights Committee, *General Comment 18 on Non-discrimination* 1989, UN Doc HRI/GEN/1/Rev.1: 26 (1994).

Human Rights Committee, *General Comment 24 on Issues Relating to Reservations Made upon Ratification or Accession to the Covenant or the Optional Protocols thereto, or in Relation to Declarations under Article 41 of the Covenant*, 1994, 4 November, UN Doc CCPR/C/21/Rev.1/Add.6.

Human Rights Watch (HRW) 1996, *The Rohingya Muslims: Ending a Cycle of Exodus?*, vol. 8, no. 9, viewed 22 May 2015, www.hrw.org/reports/pdfs/b/burma/burma969.pdf.

Human Rights Watch (HRW) 2000, *Burma/Bangladesh, Burmese Refugees in Bangladesh: Still no Durable Solution*, vol. 12, no. 3, viewed 22 May 2015, www.hrw.org/sites/default/files/reports/burm005.PDF.

Human Rights Watch (HRW) 2012, *The Government Could Have Stopped This: Sectarian Violence and Ensuing Abuses in Burma's Arakan State*, August, viewed 22 May 2015, www.hrw.org/sites/default/files/reports/burma0812webwcover.pdf.

Human Rights Watch (HRW) 2013, *'All You Can Do Is Pray': Crimes against Humanity and Ethnic Cleansing of Rohingya Muslims in Burma's Arakan State*, April, viewed 22 May 2015, www.hrw.org/sites/default/files/reports/burma0413webwcover_0.pdf.

Human Rights Watch (HRW) 2014, *Burma: Government Plan Would Segregate Rohingya: Forced Resettlement, Discriminatory Citizenship Creates Dangers*, 3 October, 22 May 2015, www.hrw.org/news/2014/10/03/burma-government-plan-would-segregate-rohingya.

Human Rights Watch (HRW) 2015, *Burma: Amend Biased Citizenship Law*, 13 January, viewed 22 May 2015, www.hrw.org/news/2015/01/13/burma-amend-biased-citizenship-law.

Human Rights Watch (HRW) 2016a, *World Report 2016*, viewed 22 May 2016, www.hrw.org/sites/default/files/world_report_download/wr2016_web.pdf.

Human Rights Watch (HRW) 2016b, *Burma: New Wave of Destruction in Rohingya Villages*, viewed 30 November 2016, www.hrw.org/news/2016/11/21/burma-new-wave-destruction-rohingya-villages.

Independent Expert (IE) Izsák, R 2014, 'Report of the Independent Expert on minority issues', 6 January, UN Doc A/HRC/25/56.

International Conference on Population and Development (ICPD) 1994, *Programme of Action of the International Conference on Population and Development*, 5–13 September, UN Doc A/CONF.171/13/Rev.1.

International Covenant on Civil and Political Rights (ICCPR), adopted 16 December 1966, entered into force 23 March 1976, 999 UNTS 171.

International Covenant on Economic, Social and Cultural Rights (ICESCR), adopted 16 December 1966, entered into force 3 January 1976, 993 UNTS 3.

International Crisis Group (ICG) 2012, *Myanmar Conflict Alert: Preventing Communal Bloodshed and Building Better Relations*, 12 June, viewed 22 May 2015, www.refworld.org/docid/4fd85cdd2.html.

Irish Centre for Human Rights (ICHR) 2010, *Crimes against Humanity in Western Burma: The Situation of the Rohingyas*, Galway, viewed 22 May 2015, www.nuigalway.ie/media/intranet/Crimes-Against-Humanit-in-Western-Burma.pdf.

Ives, M 2016, 'Kofi Annan, in Myanmar, Voices Concern Over Reported Abuses of Rohingya', *The New York Times*, 6 December, viewed 7 December 2016, www.nytimes.com/2016/12/06/world/asia/kofi-annan-myanmar-rohingya.html?_r=0.

Ives, M 2017, 'Myanmar Vows to Block U.N. Investigators from Entering', *The New York Times*, 30 June, viewed 19 July 2017, www.nytimes.com/2017/06/30/world/asia/myanmar-united-nations-rohingya.html?mcubz=0.

Karen Human Rights Group (KHRG) 2016, *Thaton Interview: U A---* 2016, 7 December, viewed 7 December 2016, http://khrg.org/sites/default/files/16-40-a1-i1.pdf.

Kesby, A 2012, *The Right to Have Rights: Citizenship, Humanity, and International Law*, Oxford, Oxford University Press.

Lewis, S 2017, 'Myanmar Says It Will Refuse Entry to U.N. Investigators Probing Rohingya Abuses', *Reuters*, 30 June, viewed 19 July 2017, www.reuters.com/article/us-myanmar-rohingya-un-idUSKBN19L0CP.

Lun Min Mang 2016, 'State Counsellor Urges Avoidance of Words "Rohingya" and "Bengali"', *Myanmar Times*, 23 May, viewed 18 July 2017, www.mmtimes.com/index.php/national-news/yangon/20438-state-counsellor-urges-avoidance-of-words-rohingya-and-bengali.html.

Macgregor, F 2016, 'Dozens of Rapes Reported in Northern Rakhine State', *Myanmar Times*, 27 October, viewed 30 November 2016, www.mmtimes.com/index.php/national-news/23326-dozens-of-rapes-reported-in-northern-rakhine-state.html.

Matthews, B 2001, *Ethnic and Religious Diversity: Myanmar's Unfolding Nemesis*, Institute of South East Asian Studies, Visiting Researchers Series 3, viewed 22 May 2015, www.iseas.edu.sg/documents/publication/vr32001.pdf.

Ministry of the Office of the State Counsellor (MOSC) 2016, *Establishment of the Advisory Commission on Rakhine State*, 23 August, viewed 18 July 2017, www.president-office.gov.mm/en/?q=issues/rakhine-state-affairs/id-6535.

Mizzima News 2012, *British Lawmakers Hear Testimony on Rakhine State Unrest*, viewed 22 May 2015, http://archive-2.mizzima.com/news/world/7408-british-lawmakers-hear-testimony-on-rakhine-state-unrest.html.

Myanmar Constitution 2008, accessed 22 May 2015, www.burmalibrary.org/docs5/Myanmar_Constitution-2008-en.pdf.

Myanmar Department of Population 2014, *The Population and Housing Census of Myanmar 2014: Summary of the Provisional Results*, August, viewed 22 May 2015, http://countryoffice.unfpa.org/myanmar/drive/SummmaryoftheProvisionalResults.pdf.

Myanmar National Human Rights Commission (MNHRC) 2014, 'Statement of the MNHRC on the Findings of the Commission Team from Its Investigation of the Incident at the Ducheeratan village', Statement No. (2/2014), 17 February, viewed 18 July 2017, www.mnhrc.org.mm/en/2014/02/statement-of-the-mnhrc-regarding-the-findings-of-the-commission-team-from-its-investigation-of-the-incident-at-the-ducheeratan-village-tract-statement-no-22014/.

Myanmar Penal Code 1860, (INDIA ACT XLV (45)), as amended in 1948, viewed 22 May 2015, www.burmalibrary.org/docs17/1861-Penal_Code-ocr-en+bu.pdf and www.wipo.int/edocs/lexdocs/laws/en/mm/mm004en.pdf.

Myanmar Rakhine State Action Plan (Action Plan) 2014, 7 July, viewed 22 May 2015, www.burmamuslims.org/resources/Action%20Plan_Eng_07072014.pdf.

Office of the United Nations High Commissioner for Human Rights (OHCHR) 2012, *Rabat Plan of Action on the Prohibition of Advocacy of National, Racial or Religious Hatred That Constitutes Incitement to Discrimination, Hostility or Violence*, 5 October, Rabat, viewed 22 May 2015, www.ohchr.org/Documents/Issues/Opinion/SeminarRabat/Rabat_draft_outcome.pdf.

Office of the United Nations High Commissioner for Human Rights (OHCHR) 2013, *Myanmar: UN Expert Urges Government to Act on Local Regulations Targeting Rohingya Muslims in Rakhine State*, 31 May, viewed 22 May 2015, www.ohchr.org/EN/NewsEvents/Pages/DisplayNews.aspx?NewsID=13391&LangID=E.

Office of the United Nations High Commissioner for Human Rights (OHCHR) 2016, *Myanmar: UN Expert Warns of Worsening Rights Situation after 'Lockdown' in Rakhine State*, 18 November, viewed 30 November, www.ohchr.org/EN/NewsEvents/Pages/DisplayNews.aspx?NewsID=20895&LangID=E.

Office of the United Nations High Commissioner for Human Rights (OHCHR) 2017, *President of Human Rights Council Appoints Members of Fact-finding Mission on Myanmar*, 30 May, viewed 18 July 2017, www.ohchr.org/EN/NewsEvents/Pages/DisplayNews.aspx?NewsID=21671&LangID=E.

Paddock, RC 2016, 'Aung San Suu Kyi Asks U.S. Not to Refer to "Rohingya"', *The New York Times*, 6 May, viewed 21 May 2016, www.nytimes.com/2016/05/07/world/asia/myanmar-rohingya-aung-san-suu-kyi.html.

Priestley, H 2006, 'The Outsiders', *The Irrawaddy*, January, viewed 22 May 2015, www2.irrawaddy.org/article.php?art_id=5380.

Rakhine State Conflicts Investigation Commission (RSCIC) 2013, 'The Rakhine State Conflicts Investigation Commission Released Its Report: Executive Summary', *New Light of Myanmar*, 29 April, viewed 22 May 2015, www.burmalibrary.org/docs15/Rakhine_Conflicts_Commission_Report-Executive_Summary.pdf.

Ramcharan, BG (ed.) 1985, *The Right to Life in International Law*, Dordrecht, Martinus Nijhoff.

Residents of Burma Registration Act 1949, viewed 22 May 2015, www.burmalibrary.org/docs12/The_Residents_of_Burma_Registration_Act-1949.pdf.

Residents of Burma Registration Rules 1951, viewed 22 May 2015, www.burmalibrary.org/docs12/Residents_of_Burma_Registration_Rules-1951.pdf.

Schearf, D 2012, 'Kaman Muslims Raise Concerns of Wider Conflict', *Voice of America News*, 29 November, viewed 22 May 2015, www.voanews.com/content/burmas-kaman-muslims-cite-religious-ethnic-conflict-in-rakhine-state/1555524.html.

Shafer, N 2013, 'The Rohingya: Impediments to Inclusive Citizenship', Unpublished dissertation, University of London, http://cosmopolistoronto.com/wp-content/uploads/2013/12/The-Rohingya-Impediments-to-Inclusive-Citizenship-by-Colin-Boyd-Shafer.pdf.

Special Rapporteur (SR) Lee, Y 2014, 'Report of the Special Rapporteur on the Situation of Human Rights in Myanmar', 23 September, UN Doc A/69/398.

Special Rapporteur (SR) Lee, Y 2015, *Statement by Yanghee Lee, Special Rapporteur on the Situation of Human Rights in Myanmar at the 70th Session of the General Assembly*, 28 October, viewed 21 May 2016, www.ohchr.org/en/NewsEvents/Pages/DisplayNews.aspx?NewsID=16674&LangID=E.

Special Rapporteur (SR) Lee, Y, 2017, 'Report of the Special Rapporteur on the Situation of Human Rights in Myanmar', 14 March, UN Doc A/HRC/34/67.

Special Rapporteur (SR) Nowak, M 2008, 'Report of the Special Rapporteur on Torture and Other Cruel, Inhuman or Degrading Treatment or Punishment', 15 January, UN Doc A/HRC/7/3.

Special Rapporteur (SR) Quintana, TO 2013a, 'Report of the Special Rapporteur on the Situation of Human Rights in Myanmar', 23 September, UN Doc A/68/397.

Special Rapporteur (SR) Quintana, TO 2013b, 'Report of the Special Rapporteur on the Situation of Human Rights in Myanmar', 17 April, UN Doc A/HRC/22/58.

Special Rapporteur (SR) Quintana, TO 2014, 'Report of the Special Rapporteur on the Situation of Human Rights in Myanmar', 1 April, UN Doc A/HRC/25/64.

Staples, K 2012, *Retheorising Statelessness: A Background Theory of Membership in World Politics*, Edinburgh, Edinburgh University Press.

Than Tun Win (undated), *Composition of the Different Ethnic Groups under the 8 Major National Ethnic Races in Myanmar*, viewed 22 May 2015, www.embassyofmyanmar.be/ABOUT/ethnicgroups.htm.

TIME 2013, 'The Face of Buddhist Terror' (Cover only), 1 July, viewed 22 May 2015, http://content.time.com/time/covers/asia/0,16641,20130701,00.html.

Ullah, A 2014, 'Rohingyas and the Residents of Burma Registration Act', *Kaladan Press Network*, 11 October, viewed 22 May 2015, www.kaladanpress.org/index.php/feature-mainmenu-28/365-2014/4664-rohingyas-and-the-residents-of-burma-registration-act.html.

UN Office of the High Commissioner for Refugees (UNHCR) 2014, *As Thousands Continue to Flee Myanmar, UNHCR Concerned about Growing Reports of Abuse*, 10 June, viewed 22 May 2015, www.unhcr.org/5396ee3b9.html.

UN Office of the High Commissioner for Refugees (UNHCR) 2015, *South-East Asia, Irregular Maritime Movements, January–March 2015*, viewed 22 May 2015, www.unhcr.org/554c6a746.html.

UN Office of the High Commissioner for Refugees (UNHCR) 2017, *Mixed Movements in South-East Asia 2016*, April, viewed 18 July 2017, www.refworld.org/pdfid/590b18a14.pdf.

UN Secretary-General (UN S-G) 2015, *Conflict-related Sexual Violence*, 23 March, UN Doc S/2015/203.

Union Citizenship Act 1948 (Act No. LXVI of 1948 as amended 1 December 1960), viewed 22 May 2015, www.burmalibrary.org/docs/UNION_CITIZENSHIP_ACT-1948.htm.

United Nations General Assembly (UNGA) Resolution 69/248, adopted 29 December 2014, published 21 January 2015, *Situation of Human Rights in Myanmar*, UN Doc A/RES/69/248.

United Nations Human Rights Council (HRC) Resolution 34/22, adopted 24 March 2017, published 3 April 2017, *Situation of Human Rights in Myanmar*, UN Doc A/HRC/RES/34/22.

United Nations Office for the Coordination of Humanitarian Affairs (UNOCHA) 2015, *Myanmar: IDP Sites in Rakhine State*, December, viewed 21 May 2016, http://reliefweb.int/sites/reliefweb.int/files/resources/Affected_Map_IDP_Sites_Rakhine_OCHA_Dec2015_A0.pdf.

United States of America, Central Intelligence Agency (CIA) 2014, *World Factbook: Burma*, under 'Religions', viewed 22 May 2015, www.cia.gov/library/publications/the-world-factbook/geos/bm.html.

United States of America, Commission of International Religious Freedoms (USCIRF) 2013, *Annual Report*, April, viewed 22 May 2015, www.uscirf.gov/sites/default/files/resources/2013%20USCIRF%20Annual%20Report%20(2).pdf.

United States of America, Commission of International Religious Freedoms (USCIRF) 2014, *Annual Report*, viewed 22 May 2015, www.uscirf.gov/sites/default/files/USCIRF%202014%20Annual%20Report%20PDF.pdf.

United States of America, Department of State, Bureau of Democracy, Human Rights and Labor 2001, *Burma: International Religious Freedom Report*, viewed 22 May 2015, www.state.gov/j/drl/rls/irf/2001/5581.htm.

Universal Declaration of Human Rights (UDHR) 1948 Un Doc A/810/71.

Van Klinken, G & Su Mon Thazin Aung 2017, 'The Contentious Politics of Anti-Muslim Scapegoating in Myanmar', *Journal of Contemporary Asia*, vol. 47, no. 3, pp. 353–375.

Williams, A 2013, 'Myanmar Bans TIME Magazine over "Buddhist Terror" Cover Story', *Investvine News*, 28 June, viewed 22 May 2015, http://investvine.com/myanmar-bans-time-magazine-over-buddhist-terror-cover-story.

Ye Myint Aung 2009, *Letter by the Consul-General of the Consulate General of the Union of Myanmar to Hong Kong & Macau SAR*, 9 February, viewed22 May 2015, http://asiapacific.anu.edu.au/newmandala/wp-content/uploads/2009/02/the-consul-generals-letter.pdf and https://democracyforburma.wordpress.com/2009/02/14/burmese-consular-says-rohingya-do-not-belong-to-burma.

Yegar, M 1972, *The Muslims of Burma: A Study of a Minority Group*, Wiesbaden, O. Harrassowitz.

Yegar, M 2002, *Between Integration and Secession: The Muslim Communities of the Southern Philippines, Southern Thailand, and Western Burma/Myanmar*, Lanham, MD, Lexington Books.

Ying-Kit Chan 2017, 'The Advisory Commission on Rakhine State in Myanmar: An Introduction', unpublished paper presented to International Conference on National Human Rights Institutions in Southeast Asia: Challenges of Protection, Bangkok, 13–14 July 2017.

Zarni, M & Cowley, A 2014, 'Slow-Burning Genocide of Myanmar's Rohingya', *Pacific Rim Law & Policy Journal*, vol. 23, no. 3, pp. 681–752.

Zawacki, B 2012–2013, 'Defining Myanmar's "Rohingya Problem"', *Human Rights Brief*, vol. 20, pp. 18–25.

13

The treatment of former combatants in post-war Sri Lanka

A form of arbitrary detention or rehabilitation?

Ambika Satkunanathan

Introduction

During the three-decades-long armed conflict in Sri Lanka, Emergency Regulations issued under the Public Security Ordinance and the Prevention of Terrorism Act served as a comprehensive and draconian legislative framework to counter terrorism. These laws were used to target mainly Tamil men who were often arrested largely due to their ethnicity, and region of residence or origin, i.e. the north and east of the country, and arbitrarily detained for months, without charges being filed. The armed conflict between the government of Sri Lanka and the Liberation Tigers of Tamil Eelam (LTTE) came to an end in May 2009 with the military victory of the government. When hostilities ended in May 2009 and internally displaced persons (IDPs) began entering government-controlled areas, the government separated those suspected of being LTTE cadre or of having had links with the group from the IDPs. In the post-war period, national security laws, and the extra-legal practices that had come into being as a result, continued to be applied to deal with the alleged former LTTE combatants.

The aim of this chapter is to trace the violation of the rights of those who were identified by the state as LTTE combatants (termed 'surrendees' by the government) from the point of custody to their release from government-run rehabilitation centres and their post-release status. Although child combatants were subjected to the rehabilitation process this chapter will focus only on adults. This chapter, which is based primarily on interviews with alleged former combatants, aims to map the violations these persons experienced to contribute to addressing the paucity of research on the rehabilitation process in Sri Lanka. From December 2009 to December 2013 individual interviews were conducted in the Northern Province (Jaffna, Kilinochchi, Mullaitivu, Vavuniya and Mannar) with 26 women and 17 men who were sent to rehabilitation centres. Six focus groups of 15 participants, each of those whose family members were in detention, rehabilitation or prison, were held, with each discussion lasting between 90 to 120 minutes. Further, nine lawyers who represent those detained under national security laws were also interviewed. This chapter will use the legal term used by the government, 'surrendees', only when discussing the legal framework. In other instances, the term rehabilitees, i.e. those who were sent to rehabilitation centres, will be used in order to avoid categorising even those who did not surrender as surrendees.

This chapter will begin by setting out the national security framework, particularly the laws relating to former combatants, to identify the provisions and lack of protections that enabled the violation of rights of persons termed as surrendees by the law. The following section will focus on the rehabilitation process itself, and conclude with a description of the post-release context, including how this context itself led to further violation of the rights of the surrendees who have been released from rehabilitation centres.

The national security framework

Background

Sri Lanka, which has experienced insurgencies since the 1970s, both in the northern and southern parts of the country, was governed by a state of emergency during most of its post-independence life. These insurgencies led to the imposition of states of emergency and the promulgation of Emergency Regulations. Article 155 of the Constitution bestows upon the president the power to declare a state of emergency. The substantive powers brought into effect by the declaration of a state of emergency, which must be renewed each month in parliament, are found in the Public Security Ordinance No. 25 of 1947 as amended. Section II of the Public Security Ordinance, confers wide powers on many officials, including the president, ministers (through delegation by the president) and members of the armed forces and police, to arrest and detain suspects for extended periods without trial. When the Ceasefire Agreement was signed in 2002 the state of emergency was not renewed in parliament and the Prevention of Terrorism Act No. 48 of 1979 (the Act) was effectively suspended under Article 2.12 of the Agreement.

Following the tsunami in December 2004 the government declared a state of emergency on 4 January 2005 in 14 tsunami-affected districts. The state of emergency lapsed after 14 days but was renewed by parliament on 11 February 2005. In December 2006, following a suicide attack on Defence Secretary Gotabhaya Rajapaksa, the government announced the re-activation of the Act, also introducing tough new emergency regulations (Freedom House 2009).

On 25 August 2011, President Mahinda Rajapakse announced in parliament that the state of emergency would not be renewed when it came to an end on 30 August 2011 (Jayasinghe 2011). On 31 August 2011, the attorney general announced that new regulations would be issued under section 27 of the Act, which empowers the minister of defence (hereinafter the Minister) to make regulations under the Act for the purpose of carrying out or giving effect to the principles and provisions of the Act (Bandara 2011).

Law relating to former combatants

On 5 September 2011 four gazetted regulations, which were dated 29 August 2011, became publicly available. These included the Prevention of Terrorism (Surrendees Care and Rehabilitation) Regulation No. 5 of 2011, which is applicable to those categorised as former LTTE combatants.

According to principles of statutory interpretation, rules and other subordinate legislation can never override the specific provisions of the Act itself, since the purpose of the regulations 'is to provide for procedural matters or matters which are subsidiary to the provisions of the Act' (Bindra & Shanmukham 1997: 737). Regulations also cannot impose onerous restrictions not envisaged by the Act or which exceed the provisions of the Act (Bindra & Shanmukham 1997: 746), widen the purposes of the Act or 'add new and different means for carrying out or to depart from, and vary its terms' (Bindra & Shanmukham 1997: 756). The preamble to the Act states that it was promulgated

> for the prevention of acts of terrorism in Sri Lanka, the prevention of unlawful activities of any individual, group of individuals, association, organisation or body of persons within Sri Lanka or outside Sri Lanka and for matters connected therewith or incidental thereto.

The government could hence argue that the intention of the Act as set out in the preamble is broad enough to capture the said regulations. However, it is a well-established rule of statutory interpretation that regulations that restrict the liberty of citizens should be construed strictly. Further, principles of interpretation also state that 'when a statute interferes with the liberty of the subject it will not be taken to deprive him of that liberty to any greater extent than is expressly stated' (Bindra & Shanmukham 1997: 523) and 'care must be taken to see that no one is brought within it, who is not within the express language' (Bindra & Shanmukham 1997: 721). Sri Lankan courts have also articulated this principle (*Sebastian Fernando v. Katana Multi-purpose Co-operative Society Ltd, and Others* (1990) SLR, vol. 1: 342).

Hence, regulations can be issued under the Act only 'for the purpose of carrying out or giving effect to the principles and provisions of this Act'. The Minister therefore does not have the power to create new offences, which can only be done either through new legislation passed by parliament or by way of a proclamation of a state of emergency under the Public Security Ordinance, which would give the president the power to issue Emergency Regulations under Part II of the Public Security Ordinance. In contravention of these principles, the Prevention of Terrorism (Surrendees Care and Rehabilitation) Regulation No. 5 of 2011 issued under the Prevention of Terrorism Act on 29 August 2011 stipulates that a person can be held at a rehabilitation centre for a maximum period of 24 months, which exceeds the maximum period of detention stipulated by the Act, which is 18 months.

With the lapse of the state of emergency on 30 August 2011, the limited safeguards which offered protection to citizens when armed forces engaged in searches and arrests that existed in the Emergency (Miscellaneous Provisions and Powers) Regulation No. 1 of 2005, such as the requirement to issue arrest receipts to the family members of arrested persons confirming arrest as a precaution against enforced disappearances (reg. 20(9)), were removed.

The safeguards created by the Public Security Ordinance (s. 20) are also minimal in comparison to the lapsed Emergency Regulations, since these provisions only state that any person arrested by the armed forces, functioning under an order issued by the president pursuant to s. 12, shall be handed over to the police without unnecessary delay. No strict time lines are stipulated for such handover. The Human Rights Commission Act No. 21 of 1996 provides some protection via s. 28(1), which requires the armed forces to inform the Commission of those detained and/or arrested under the Prevention of Terrorism Act or the Emergency Regulations, but this provision was not observed, with the Commission often not informed of arrests.

Until 31 August 2011, surrendees were held under the Emergency Regulation No. 22 of 2005 as amended by Emergency Regulation 1462/8 of 2006. Thereafter, the Prevention of Terrorism (Surrendees Care and Rehabilitation) Regulation No. 5 of 2011 was applied. However, the 2011 regulations to the Prevention of Terrorism Act merely reproduced Emergency Regulation 22 and contained no substantive changes addressing concerns related to the violation of the rights of those held at rehabilitation centres. Moreover, the attorney general, in his letter dated 24 December 2009 to the International Organisation for Migration (IOM) (on file with the author), stipulated additional modalities to deal with surrendees that were not within the legal framework. For instance, the letter stated that 'an amnesty could be considered to those who were marginally involved having regard to their age, family status, educational background and skills and health', but the attorney general did not indicate how the amnesty would be effected legally. Further, the criteria the attorney general listed for determination of eligibility for amnesty, such as family status and skills, do not conform with established international practice. Usually, the eligibility for amnesty is determined based on factors such as the level of involvement in the armed group, seriousness of crimes committed by the individual etc. Despite these remarks legally, an amnesty was not granted.

Definitions and categorisation

Prevention of Terrorism Act Regulation No. 3(2) issued in 2011, like Regulation 22, does not provide a clear definition of 'surrendee', except to state that anyone who surrendered in relation to an offence under certain laws, such as the Prevention of Terrorism Act would be considered a surrendee. It further required the person to submit a written statement that s/he surrendered voluntarily. It should be noted that all persons who were held at rehabilitation centres were termed 'surrendees' by the government, although many were forcibly taken away by the armed forces from IDP camps, or were detained by the military when they crossed into government-controlled territory. According to Patrick Cammaert, Special Envoy of the Special Representative of the Secretary-General on Children and Armed Conflict, the government broadcast announcements in IDP camps instructed everyone who had spent 'even five minutes' with the LTTE to surrender, which led many people to surrender or hand over their family members to the military (Office of the Special Representative of the Secretary-General for Children and Armed Conflict 2010). However, most of these persons had been forcibly recruited by the LTTE, particularly during the last stages of the war, with many having spent perhaps only a few hours directly participating in hostilities. This therefore raises questions regarding the voluntariness of the statement that is required to be signed by those being sent to rehabilitation.

There is no publicly available information on the process the government utilised to determine eligibility for rehabilitation. The National Action Plan of the National Framework Proposal for Reintegration of Ex-combatants into Civilian Life in Sri Lanka, presented by the government in 2009, which was drafted through a multi-stakeholder process, contained a sliding scale that provided a guide to categorising those who required rehabilitation as opposed to those who should be prosecuted, based on various factors including the period spent with the armed group (Ministry of Disaster Management and Human Rights 2009). Yet, this Plan was never implemented and decisions regarding rehabilitation of those categorised as former LTTE combatants were taken in a non-transparent manner. If there was a plan or process with objective criteria regarding categorisation of persons as combatants to which the government adhered during the decision-making process, it was never made public.

It was known that the rehabilitation process was within the purview of the Ministry of Defence and Secretary of the Ministry, Gotabaya Rajapaksa, the brother of President Mahinda Rajapaksa. Gotabaya Rajapaksa was the primary authority where decision making was concerned, which is evidenced by wide reportage by the Ministry of Defence. For instance, the Ministry of Defence website stated that 'The Sri Lankan government under direction and supervision of Secretary Defence Mr. Gotabaya Rajapakse designed a comprehensive programme to rehabilitate those ex-combatants at the Rehabilitation Centres established in Jaffna and Vavuniya' (Ministry of Defence 2010). According to the Bureau of Commissioner-General of Rehabilitation (2013: 17) the 'Sri Lankan model of rehabilitation for ex-combatants was initiated, designed, developed and implemented by the Sri Lanka Army'. This points to the lack of transparent institutional processes, and confirms that decisions regarding the lives of thousands of persons were made without consultation, transparency or oversight.

In 2017 the rehabilitation process was within the purview of the Ministry of Resettlement but the Secretary, Ministry of Defence is the only entity empowered to determine the period of rehabilitation. The only remaining rehabilitation centre Poonthottam continues to be run by a military officer and all other staff too appear to be military officials. Decision making is done by multiple authorities, including the attorney general's department, resulting in lack of clarity regarding the authority responsible for the implementation of the process (Human Rights Commission 2016: 15).

As mentioned earlier in this chapter, a large portion of surrendees were not combatants but instead were employed by the LTTE through non-military structures such as the 'police force, political, propaganda and media divisions, and administrative cells, the banking, immigration, taxation, prisons sectors etc.' (Jeyaraj 2010). It should be noted that in the areas controlled by the LTTE, administrative structures, as well as several businesses, were run by the LTTE. Accordingly, most persons living in the area were employed by or engaged directly or indirectly with the LTTE. The International Committee of the Red Cross note on Interpretive Guidance on the Notion of Direct Participation in Hostilities under International Humanitarian Law (Melzer 2009) recognises that

> As with State parties to armed conflicts, non-State parties comprise both fighting forces and supportive segments of the civilian population, such as political and humanitarian wings. The term organized armed group, however, refers exclusively to the armed or military wing of a non-State party: its armed forces in a functional sense.
>
> *(Melzer 2009: 32)*

It goes on to state:

> [i]ndividuals who continuously accompany or support an organized armed group, but whose function does not involve direct participation in hostilities, are not members of that group within the meaning of IHL. Instead, they remain civilians assuming support functions, similar to private contractors and civilian employees accompanying State armed forces.
>
> *(Melzer 2009: 34)*

Within this framework, those who were part of non-combat divisions and did not directly participate in hostilities would not be considered combatants under international humanitarian law. Contrary to this, in Sri Lanka anyone who functioned even in a civilian capacity in one of the civilian organisations of the LTTE was treated as a combatant.

This form of categorisation was not in line with IHL, but appears to be in line with the policy of the government articulated in the earlier mentioned letter of the attorney general to the IOM in which he notes that 'it would be a mandatory requirement for those who surrender to be compulsorily rehabilitated under the law'. Therefore, a person taken in by the armed forces who was subjected to rehabilitation in lieu of prosecution has no recourse to refuse such rehabilitation. Further, in the same letter the attorney general noted that persons undergoing rehabilitation 'shall not be entitled to legal counsel whilst undergoing rehabilitation'.

Period of rehabilitation

According to Regulation 8 of the Prevention of Terrorism (Surrendees Care and Rehabilitation) Regulation No. 5 of 2011, a surrendee could be held for a period of twelve months. At the end of this period there were three potential options:

1 Following a review by the Secretary to the Ministry of Defence the person could be released; or
2 The period of rehabilitation could be extended for a period of three months at a time. In this case, the aggregated period of such extensions should not exceed a further 12 months; or
3 Within three months of the person being assigned to a rehabilitation centre the government could begin investigations to ascertain whether the person committed any offences, and the person could be charged with an offence.

Hence, being part of the rehabilitation programme did not preclude the person from being arrested for an offence at any point during or even after the rehabilitation process if, because of the investigation, the government decided to prosecute the person. There was no mention of the period within which the investigation should be concluded. Further, as the 'screening' process[1] continued throughout the duration of the rehabilitation process, the surrendee had no certainty regarding his or her legal position which was in a perpetual state of limbo. For instance, in 2016 a member of the LTTE's Political Division who had been through the rehabilitation process following the end of the war and was later employed as a university lecturer was indicted for forcible recruitment of a minor and, in July 2017, was sentenced to life imprisonment (*Thinakkural* 2017: 1). This case illustrates the impact of the lack of a coherent and transparent policy on rehabilitation, particularly the lack of a coherent process of categorisation of persons for rehabilitation that adheres to international human rights standards. While prosecutions, such as the aforementioned, are part of the accountability process with regard to gross violations of human rights and humanitarian law, they fail to provide legal certainty to those who have been made to believe they will not be prosecuted since they were part of the rehabilitation process.

In the letter to the IOM the attorney general stated that the extension of the period of rehabilitation rests with an Advisory Committee appointed by the president in accordance with regulation 19(4) of Emergency Regulation of August 2005. It should be noted that no such committee existed at any point during the period in question. To date, the decision-making authority regarding surrendees lies entirely with the secretary to the Ministry of Defence, and there are no oversight or review mechanisms in place. According to testimonies of those released from rehabilitation centres, none were informed of the laws under which they were being held, nor was this information produced in court during this period, leading to a reasonable conclusion that persons were arbitrarily detained.

As per Regulation 9(2), if the person was prosecuted and found guilty the court had the discretion to order an undefined extension of the period of rehabilitation as part of the sentence. The Commissioner-General for Rehabilitation at the time, Major General Chandana Rajaguru, stated 'there is another category of people who had been produced before courts and had received rehabilitation as the verdict. They are with us, and are around 1,000 in number. We intend to keep them only for one year' (Wijayapala 2011). If rehabilitation was imposed as part of a judicial order, then the 1,000 persons should have been prosecuted and convicted of an offence. However, instead, those persons were told that if they pleaded guilty for a less serious offence under the Prevention of Terrorism Act they would be sentenced to only one year of rehabilitation. Given that trials can take up to several years to conclude, even those against whom there would have been negligible evidence chose this plea option and as a result now have a recorded criminal conviction. It should be noted that at no point were these persons able to retain a legal representative, nor access the evidence against them. Hence, this process denied them the right to due process or fairness. In 2016 the Human Rights Commission of Sri Lanka in its report to the UN Committee Against Torture reported that those on remand under the PTA who have not been indicted were asked if they wish to go to rehabilitation, and upon signing consent letters 'surrendering' were sent to rehabilitation. If there is no evidence to indict the person it is unclear on which criteria these persons were deemed eligible to be sent to rehabilitation. In 2016 court records revealed that in a number of cases the court was informed by the Terrorism Investigation Department that the attorney general (AG) had ordered the person to rehabilitation. Yet, in many cases persons have refused in court to be sent to rehabilitation, leading to the conclusion the person's consent was not deemed relevant by the authorities to subject them to the process. It should be noted that in law the AG is not the decision-making authority in this regard (Human Rights Commission 2016: 15).

It should be noted that unlike emergency regulations, regulations issued under the Prevention of Terrorism Act cannot override any law or restrict fundamental rights since they are not extraordinary legislation. Hence, all persons being held at the rehabilitation centres following the lapse of the state of emergency in 2011 can lawfully challenge their rehabilitation. Despite this, in the interviews conducted with lawyers, it was found many held at rehabilitation centres refused to do so for fear it would lead to reprisals including the prolongation of their rehabilitation period.

Misuse of the law

In 2015 and 2016 instances of the law being used to send to rehabilitation persons who had not passed security checks required for certain state employment, such as Grama Niladari officers (village officers), for three months prior to their employment being confirmed were reported. According to the Human Rights Commission (2016: 15),

> in May 2015 and March 2016, sixteen and six GN officers respectively in the North were informed by the Ministry of Home Affairs, which according to the law has no authority to order persons to rehabilitation, they would have to undergo rehabilitation. In total eleven persons completed this programme and were released after three months—seven women and four men. Of the seven women, one woman had a baby three months ago prior to being sent to rehab and hence her baby along with her mother lived with her at Poonthottam.

In these instances the authority that directed the persons be sent to rehabilitation was the Ministry of Home Affairs, which had no authority to do so. Hence, the existence of such a law that established a system that is not subject to judicial oversight creates space for abuse and enables state authorities to act in a manner that is ultra vires.

The rehabilitation process

At the end of the armed conflict, soon after they were separated from the internally displaced population, the surrendees were held at public buildings such as schools, which were not equipped to house large numbers of persons. Due to this, rehabilitees experienced poor living conditions, such as lack of water and proper sanitation. They were thereafter transferred to sites that were better equipped to house larger numbers of persons.

Lack of verifiable statistics

Government statements on the total number of persons subjected to rehabilitation processes have been inconsistent. Until the ICRC was denied entry to the centres in July 2009, it registered just under 10,000 persons (US State Department Report 2009). This is also based on information stated by the ICRC at its meetings and is publicly known. In December 2009, Sri Lanka's Permanent Representative to the United Nations in New York stated 12,700 former combatants had been identified (*Asian Tribune* 2009). However, a 2013 official government publication contains two contradictory figures. In a section describing the situation at the end of the war and the process leading up to rehabilitation, it states that a total of 10,196 adults were sent to rehabilitation (Bureau of Commissioner-General of Rehabilitation 2013: 16) but later mentions that, as at 31 May 2013, a total of 12,167 were rehabilitated (Bureau of Commissioner-General of Rehabilitation 2013: 66). As at July 2017, the website of the Bureau of the Commissioner-General of Rehabilitation states that of the total number of 12,000 only 11,406 were adults while 594 were children. The initial number is likely to be the total population of those identified by the government as LTTE combatants at the end of the war, while the second statistic shows an increase because it most likely includes those arrested under national security laws, such as the Prevention of Terrorism Act, who were sent to rehabilitation centres after the end of the war and in cases where the state did not have adequate evidence to file charges.

Often, when a person detained under the Act files a fundamental rights petition in the Supreme Court seeking relief as per Article 126 of the Constitution—challenging his or her detention on the basis that it has violated his/her fundamental right—the state offers rehabilitation as an option to encourage the person to withdraw their Fundamental Rights petition. There have been instances of detainees filing Fundamental Rights cases only to be sent to rehabilitation for a maximum of two years, rather than spend many years in administrative and thereafter judicial custody.

As at October 2016, there were 18 men at a rehabilitation centre located at Poonthottam in the Northern Province. Since July 2009, when the ICRC's access to the rehabilitation centres was stopped, no independent agency had visited the centre to undertake protection monitoring until the ICRC was granted access in late 2013. Hence, there is no independent means of verifying the actual total number of persons who have been subjected to the rehabilitation process and released. The lack of monitoring by an independent entity also created space for possible violations such as torture and other forms of ill-treatment.

Transfers from rehabilitation centres to detention centres

Research conducted found instances in which rehabilitees have been transferred from a rehabilitation centre, where the maximum period of detention is 24 months, to a detention centre such as Boosa, where persons are held on detention orders issued by the minister of defence for a maximum period of 18 months under the Act. Transfers from rehabilitation to detention centres usually take place towards the end of the maximum period for which a rehabilitee can be held, i.e. 24 months. In some cases, persons have been transferred from the rehabilitation centre to a detention centre, and back to a rehabilitation centre. By transferring a person back and forth from a rehabilitation centre to a detention centre the government can essentially hold an individual in indefinite administrative detention. Even if a person is placed in fiscal custody, i.e. on remand, then provided the remand is renewed every 14 days the person can also be remanded indefinitely.

On 7 September 2010, then Deputy Economic Development Minister Lakshman Yapa Abeywardena, referring to surrendees, told the BBC that the 'detainees are providing us with information about others who are still at large. The authorities need to keep them for longer to extract more information about the rebel activities and people involved', acknowledging the real reason for the prolonged detention of these persons, i.e. interrogation not rehabilitation (Perera 2010). While the state has the right to interrogate persons suspected of committing terrorist offences, in the case of Sri Lanka it has been used as an excuse to disregard due process and detain a large number of persons for long, indeterminate periods without access to legal representation. Hence, at no point during the rehabilitation process did surrendees enjoy procedural safeguards. Instead, they were denied information on the timeframe of rehabilitation and their right to legal representation to contest the lawfulness of the rehabilitation process.

The rehabilitation process

Prevention of Terrorism Act Regulation 5(1) states that the surrendee should be assigned to a centre that provided the person with appropriate vocational, technical or other training. However, according to testimonies of persons released from the rehabilitation centres,[2] most (particularly those who were released prior to 2011) received no vocational training during the period of rehabilitation.

Although the government claimed it provided vocational training to all those held in rehabilitation centres, according to interviewees only a handful appear to have received any form of training at all. Many interviewees stated that of the thousands of persons in detention, only a limited number of around 20 to 30 were chosen for each training course at any given time. The courses were in carpentry, masonry, welding, electrical and bulldozer operation. As discrimination and disempowerment were the main causes of the ethnic conflict that led to the armed uprising, alleged former combatants who in many instances were already socially, economically and legally marginalised sought to be trained in vocations that would enable rather than restrict upward social mobility. Training such persons in blue collar industries with limited scope for upward social mobility keeps them bound to their relative 'place' in society. If this is the intended strategy, it will sow the seeds for future social conflict. Further, the training available to women was gender stereotyped and this has been illustrated by the Bureau of Commissioner-General of Rehabilitation's publication which states 'courses on bridal dressing, hair dressing and make-up were conducted exclusively for the female ex-combatants who were really excited to learn these new subjects just like any other girl in society' (2013: 33). Several female former combatants that had undertaken tasks such as driving heavy vehicles, were part of technical or mechanical units or were students, stated they were extremely dissatisfied with the training that was offered at the centres, as it would not help them earn a livelihood in their villages and was also not what they wished to be trained in. Many said that despite this, they enrolled for the few available places in courses because of the need to feel useful and engage in some sort of activity while at the centres.

Jeyaraj (2010) describes on-the-job training that women were being given at garment factories in the south, noting 'The girls are given free food and lodging and paid 12,000 to 15,000 rupees per month as allowance. This money is actually a saving for them'. It is not clear whether this training was part of their rehabilitation, and if so whether they were able to choose to work in the factories as opposed to undergoing other training programmes available at the centre. Moreover, if they were working in the factories as part of their rehabilitation, as they were not convicted of a crime, the work would constitute forced labour if it was against their will.

According to the Prevention of Terrorism Act Regulation 7 of 2011, the surrendee was entitled to meet his/her parents, relations or guardian every fortnight with the permission of the officer in charge of the centre; but uniform rules on procedures and conditions of visits were not applied at all centres. Until mid-2009 those held at the centres were only allowed restricted communication with their families and therefore in many instances families were unaware of the person's whereabouts. In the case of persons who were taken away from the centres for further investigation, often family members complained they were not even informed of the transfer from the rehabilitation centre to detention centre, and were not provided with arrest receipts.

Post-release monitoring and surveillance

Those released from rehabilitation centres were instructed by the local government agent, the Grama Sevaka, to register with the Civil Affairs Office which is run by the military. Thereafter rehabilitees were required to report to the Civil Affairs Office weekly, fortnightly or monthly, a decision dependent entirely on the area military commander. Some former rehabilitees reported that during these visits they were asked to sign documents that were in Sinhala, a language they don't understand. They were also reportedly interrogated, indicating they were asked the same questions that were posed to them in the rehabilitation centres, being which section/battalion/unit they were a member of; who their commander was; how long they were in the LTTE; whether they know where weapons were hidden etc. Some who were forcibly recruited by the LTTE lamented that these questions only reminded them of a period they wished to forget when they were trying to move forward with their lives. Others expressed anger about the constant harassment and suspicion with which they were viewed, and said this made them feel like second-class citizens. Post-release monitoring and surveillance was conducted outside existing legal frameworks in an ad hoc manner by multiple military/intelligence agencies who regularly visited homes of former rehabilitees and often interrogated them. The officers/visitors frequently failed to identify themselves. Former rehabilitees were given no information on the likely duration of surveillance and reporting, and some have also been subjected to travel restrictions.

The continued monitoring and harassment by the security services restrict the ability of this population to successfully re-integrate into the community—as they continued to be viewed with suspicion by the community due to their regular visits to the Civil Affairs Office and/or army camps and due to the visits by security agencies to their homes. These visits by the security forces resulted in creating a degree of suspicion within the community that these persons were providing information to the military. Women are particularly affected by this because they are also thought to be providing sexual favours to, or being abused or exploited by the military, and are thereby stigmatised by a society which in turn refuses to engage, or limits engagement, with them (Satkunanathan 2016). There were also those who complained that they were unable to engage in income-generating activities due to regular visits by the intelligence agencies or the army to their place of employment. This unsurprisingly caused problems at their workplaces, particularly in the case of those who are self-employed and provide services to homes, such as electricians, plumbers and masons.

The most pressing need of those released from rehabilitation centres continues to be the lack of livelihood opportunities. Although the IOM has provided a grant to those released from rehabilitation centres to enable them to kick-start income-generating activities, some released persons experienced long delays in accessing these grants. Others utilised the grant to engage in one-off economic activities that did not provide a sustainable income. In other instances, with no guidance or advice, some undertook income-generating projects which they were not qualified to run, and thereby incurred losses, most often resulting in the loss of capital as well. Also, the fixed grant provided by the IOM did not cover all costs related to certain income-generating activities, which prevented some from engaging in the activity productively.

Former combatants have also found it difficult to obtain loans, since banks or other institutions require guarantors, which former combatants are unable to secure. For instance, a former rehabilitee who wished to obtain a bank loan explained that when she approached an individual known to her to sign as the guarantor for the loan, he refused. He did so by expressing concerns that he would ultimately become responsible for the loan and be forced to pay it given she might later be abducted by state forces.

The Bureau of Commissioner-General of Rehabilitation established a follow-up mechanism known as the Socio Economic and Welfare Coordinating Office for Rehabilitated Beneficiaries, with the purpose of providing 'assistance to improve the livelihood of [the] reintegrated' (Bureau of Commissioner-General of Rehabilitation 2011). Ex-combatants can borrow up to 250,000 rupees (USD$2,000) with a below-market interest rate of 4% and a repayment period of ten years. A total of 1,568 loans amounting to 259,195,000 rupees (USD$2,073,560) have been disbursed. However, a study of 20 loan recipients from Jaffna and Kilinochchi in the north found that:

> [m]ost ex-combatants continue to live a very low quality of life and are not doing well through their businesses. Some regret that they took the loan in the first place. Overall, their loans have not provided the needed economic stimulus to uplift their living standards, and many continue to live at a subsistence level. Nine mentioned that because the loan was not sufficient to make ends meet they had to go out in search of another job, but many found it difficult to find other work. Most had undertaken their business venture because there was no other choice, and they had not received sufficient entrepreneurship or technical training before the loan was given.
>
> *(Miriyagalla 2014: 257)*

Conclusion

At the end of the armed conflict in Sri Lanka the government separated those suspected of being members of the LTTE and sent them to rehabilitation centres run by the military. Decision making regarding those sent for rehabilitation was entirely within the purview of the secretary for the Ministry of Defence, and was done with no transparency or judicial oversight. Those persons separated were denied the right to challenge their detention and even the right to legal representation. Due to a lack of objective criteria to determine eligibility for rehabilitation, even those who were forcibly recruited and were in the LTTE for only a few days or hours, and those who worked in a civilian capacity in LTTE institutions and did not take direct part in hostilities were also sent to rehabilitation. During the rehabilitation process, which was not monitored by any independent protection agency, the government repeatedly stated that it was providing vocational training to those at the centre. However, particularly during the first couple of years after the conclusion of the armed conflict, most rehabilitees did not receive any vocational training. Further, the available training was gender stereotyped and often not in line with market demands or likely opportunities. The Emergency Regulations and thereafter the Prevention of Terrorism Act enabled the government to keep people under indefinite administrative detention by transferring persons between rehabilitation centres and detention centres. Following release, most rehabilitees were subject to regular surveillance, interrogation and harassment by the military and intelligence services, which hampered their re-integration. This was further exacerbated by societal perceptions and a level of suspicion and fear that those persons were informants for the military. Further, the socio-economic needs of those released from rehabilitation centres were unmet, with state initiatives falling short of addressing the legitimate needs of those persons. Even throughout 2016 the effective socio-economic re-integration of rehabilitees remained low and the support services provided to the rehabilitees continued to be within the purview of the military. One rehabilitation centre, Poonthottam, remains open and receives persons who have been detained under the Prevention of Terrorism Act including long-term detainees pre-2009 and those arrested at different times after that—sent either because there isn't adequate evidence to file charges against them or because they have pleaded guilty to lesser offences under the Prevention of Terrorism Act. Facilities at the Poonthottam centre remain rather basic and rehabilitees are provided only three vocational training options: welding, masonry and carpentry. Hence, there has been little change to the structural and legal framework governing rehabilitation with the ongoing military treatment and social marginalisation experienced by former rehabilitees continuing to hamper their productive reintegration into civil society.

Notes

1 Interviewees stated they were subjected to numerous rounds of interrogation by different sections of the security apparatus. In addition, many of them were also required to complete questionnaires of close to a hundred questions, related to time they spent within the LTTE, their lives in the LTTE-controlled areas and opinions on politics and the LTTE, several times.
2 Based on interviews with 43 former combatants released from rehabilitation centres between 2010 and 2013.

References

Asian Tribune 2009, 'The "Elders" Statement on IDPs in Sri Lanka: Sadly Outdated and Inaccurate—Dr. Kohona', 5 December.

Attorney General of Sri Lanka 2009, 'Letter to the International Organisation for Migration (IOM)', 24 December.

Bandara, K 2011, 'New Regulations under PTA to Deal with LTTE', *Sri Lanka Brief*, vol. 31, August, viewed 16 March 2017, http://srilankabrief.org/2011/08/new-regulations-under-pta-to-deal-with-ltte/.

Bindra, NS & Shanmukham K 1997, *N.S. Bindra's Interpretation of Statutes*, Law Book Co., Allahabad.

Bureau of Commissioner-General of Rehabilitation 2011, *Socio Economic and Welfare Coordinating Offices for Rehabilitated Beneficiaries*, viewed 16 March 2017, www.bcgr.gov.lk/followup.php-.

Bureau of Commissioner-General of Rehabilitation and Department of Government Information 2013, *Rehabilitation of Ex-combatants*, viewed 15 June 2015, http://bcgr.gov.lk/flip_book.html#/0.

Constitution of the Democratic Socialist Republic of Sri Lanka.

Emergency (Miscellaneous Provisions and Powers) Regulation No. 1 of 2005.

Emergency Regulation No. 22 of 2005 as amended by ER 1462/8, 2006.

Freedom House 2009, *Sri Lanka: Freedom in the World 2009*, viewed 16 March 2017, https://freedomhouse.org/report/freedom-world/2009/sri-lanka.

Human Rights Commission of Sri Lanka Act, No. 21 of 1996.

Human Rights Commission of Sri Lanka 2016, 'Report of the Human Rights Commission to the UN Committee Against Torture', October, viewed 10 August 2017, http://hrcsl.lk/english/wp-content/uploads/2016/11/Report-to-CAT-Committee-.pdf.

Jayasinghe, A 2011, 'Sri Lanka Scraps Emergency Laws', *Sri Lanka Brief*, 25 August, viewed 16 March 2017, http://srilankabrief.org/2011/08/sri-lanka-scraps-emergency-laws/.

Jeyaraj, DBS 2010, 'What Is Happening to the Ex-LTTE Cadre Surrendees?', viewed 1 June 2015, http://dbsjeyaraj.com/dbsj/archives/1599.

Melzer, N 2009, *Interpretive Guidance on the Notion of Direct Participation in Hostilities under International Humanitarian Law*, ICRC, Switzerland, www.icrc.org/eng/assets/files/other/icrc-002-0990.pdf.

Ministry of Defence 2010, *Jobs for Ex-LTTE Cadres*, viewed 1 June 2016, www.defence.lk/new.asp?fname=20100907_02.

Ministry of Disaster Management and Human Rights 2009, *National Action Plan of the National Framework Proposal for Reintegration of Ex-combatants into Civilian Life in Sri Lanka*, www.ilo.org/wcmsp5/groups/public/---ed_emp/documents/genericdocument/wcms_504728.pdf.

Miriyagalla, D 2014, 'Socio-economic Reintegration of Former LTTE Combatants in Sri Lanka: Self-employment, Sustainable Incomes and Long-term Peace', *Global Change, Peace & Security 2014*, viewed 5 October 2014, http://dx.doi.org/10.1080/14781158.2014.953469.

Office of the Special Representative of the Secretary-General for Children and Armed Conflict 2010, Mission report: Visit of Major General (ret.) Patrick Cammaert, Special Envoy of the Special Representative for Children and Armed Conflict to Sri Lanka, 5–11 December 2009, viewed 16 March 2017, www.un.org/children/conflict/_documents/SriLankavisitReport09.pdf.
Perera, S 2010, *ICJ Report Accuses Sri Lankan Government of Violating Rights*, viewed 15 June 2015, www.wsws.org/articles/2010/oct2010/sril-o07.shtml-.
Prevention of Terrorism Act Regulation No. 3(2) of 2011.
Prevention of Terrorism (Surrendees Care and Rehabilitation) Regulation No. 5 of 2011.
Prevention of Terrorism (Temporary Provisions) Act No. 48 of 1979.
Public Security Ordinance No. 25 of 1947.
Satkunanathan, A 2016, 'Collaboration, Suspicion and Traitors: An Exploratory Study of Intra-community Relations in Post-war Northern Sri Lanka', *Contemporary South Asia*, vol. 24, no. 4, Special Issue: *Post-War Sri Lanka: State, Capital, Labour and the Politics of Reconciliation*, pp. 416–428.
Sebastian Fernando v. Katana Multi-purpose Co-operative Society Ltd, and Others [1990] 1 SLR 342.
Thinakkural 2017, 'Jaffna University Lecturer Sentenced to Life by Vavuniya High Court', 26 July.
US Department of State, Bureau of Democracy, Human Rights, and Labor 2010, *2009 Country Reports on Human Rights Practices*, Report, 11 March 2010, www.state.gov/j/drl/rls/hrrpt/2009/sca/136093.htm.
Wijayapala, R 2011, 'Rehabilitation, Resettlement of ex-LTTEers, a Success', *Sunday Observer*, 9 October, viewed 16 March 2017, www.sundayobserver.lk/2011/10/09/fea01.asp.

14

Recognising the rights of conflict widows

Insights from Manipur, India

Upasana Mahanta

Introduction

In situations of armed conflict, ensuring the legal protection of human rights becomes a significant challenge for many countries. This is a cause of immense concern, especially when the nature of armed conflict has changed considerably in the last few decades from conflicts between states to conflicts within them. Armed conflicts today are being fought due to 'quest[s] for self-determination, demands for fair access to resources, resistance to forces acculturation and discrimination, and – most often a combination of such factors' (Merths & Helsing 2006: 4). With the blurring of the so-called 'war front' and the 'home front' a vast burden of these conflicts are being borne by civilians. It is estimated that around 90% of casualties in armed conflicts today are civilian (Goodhand 2010: 13). Consequently, armed conflicts create new categories of vulnerability, with the impact of conflict falling disproportionately between men and women. This is not to imply that women are always the 'victims' of violence and men are the 'perpetrators' of violence. However, research suggests that women are engaged with armed conflicts 'as combatants, as grassroots peace advocates, as targets of physical and sexual violence, as the bearers of contested communal identities and as the group in society that is expected to sustain everyday life, even under catastrophic conditions' (Reilly 2007: 155). Armed conflicts thus lead to both individual and societal-level consequences. Most significantly, they often cause a shift in gender roles within the larger household and family (the most salient being the emergence of women-headed households), requiring systematic attention.

The Beijing Platform for Action adopted at the Fourth World Conference on Women (United Nations 1995) recognises women in armed conflict as a critical area of concern. It states:

> In addressing armed or other conflicts, an active and visible policy of mainstreaming a gender perspective into all policies and programmes should be promoted so that before decisions are taken an analysis is made of the effects on men and women.
>
> *(United Nations 1995: para. 141)*

The United Nations Security Council Resolution 1325 (2000) acknowledges the changing nature of warfare, with the chief burden falling on civilians, and calls for incorporating the 'special needs of women and girls during repatriation and resettlement and for rehabilitation, reintegration and post-conflict reconstruction' (United Nations 2000: para. 222). However, despite international commitments, gender concerns are yet to be integrated into many national and transnational justice delivery mechanisms.

In this context, this chapter seeks to address the critical phenomenon of conflict widowhood. Widowhood is one of many significant fallouts resulting from high levels of civilian casualties in armed conflict. It is estimated that in certain parts of the conflict-torn eastern Democratic Republic of Congo, almost 50% of women have been widowed (United Nations 2011: 2). There are an estimated three million widows in Iraq and over 70,000 in Kabul, Afghanistan (United Nations 2011: 2). In post-war Sri Lanka, 90,000 widows are struggling for survival (Al Jazeera 2015). Although estimates on actual numbers of widows are unclear, the three-decades-long Maoist conflict in Nepal has created thousands of young widows between the ages of 20 and 30 (International Centre for Transnational Justice 2010: 28).

These numbers have serious implications in terms of the protection and promotion of human rights in situations of armed conflict. Widows facing social stigma both in private and public spaces under the garb of tradition and culture is common practice in many societies. Widowhood across societies mostly implies 'a loss of social status and reduced economic circumstances' (United Nations 2001: 5). During armed conflict, widows face additional constraints as they often have to assume the role of heads of households[1] in an environment that imposes severe restrictions on their mobility and access to livelihood. Moreover, customary laws or cultural practices in many societies ostracise widows by restricting their right to inheritance and barring them from owning land and property. Widows of armed conflict thus face structural and systemic barriers in accessing justice delivery mechanisms.[2] At the same time, widowhood leads to a fundamental shift in traditional gender roles, with women assuming the roles of household heads. However, the realities and experiences of conflict widows are often not reflected in the assistance programmes designed for survivors of armed conflict.

This chapter seeks to further explore this issue by examining the situation of conflict widows in the state of Manipur, India. It is argued that conflict widows have special needs in terms of mechanisms that provide economic, social, and psychological support. However, assistance offered to survivors of armed conflict often discounts the experiences and realities of widows. The chapter, therefore, emphasises the need to recognise the rights of conflict widows within the larger framework of human rights. The vulnerability and marginalisation faced by conflict widows must be perceived as violations of basic human rights to live without fear and to live with dignity. Further, this chapter draws attention to the distinction between state-led and civil-society-led assistance programmes, making a case for an evidence-based approach to understanding the nature of marginalisation faced by conflict widows.

Armed conflict in Manipur

The history of political development in India since independence has been replete with several cases of intense internal armed conflicts. This has led to a large-scale impact on the civilian population, resulting in loss of life, severe injuries, and mass displacement. Further, it has resulted in disruptions to service delivery mechanisms by breaking down critical sectors such as health and education. It is estimated that between the years 1994 to 2015,[3] fatalities due to conflicts in India have reached around 64,282, of which 24,560 were civilian (South Asia Terrorism Portal 2015a).[4] Currently, India has major ongoing internal armed conflicts in three regions: in Jammu and Kashmir, in the northeastern region, and in Maoist dominated areas of central and eastern India.

The northeastern region of India consists of seven states (known as the 'seven sisters') – Assam, Manipur, Mizoram, Tripura, Arunachal Pradesh, Nagaland, and Meghalaya. The region is of great significance as it shares over 2,000 km of border with Bhutan, China, Myanmar, and Bangladesh. The region has been witnessing intense militarisation ever since India's independence. The states of Manipur, Assam, Nagaland, and Tripura have been experiencing conflicts of such scale, even being 'categorised as low intensity wars, defined as conflicts in which fatalities are over 100 but less than 1000 per annum' (Sahni 2001).

Manipur remained as a semi-autonomous 'princely' state under British colonial rule and was annexed as part of the Indian Union in October 1949. There was tremendous resentment in Manipur against this 'forced' merger. Although initially a part of the province of Assam, Manipur became a separate state after much agitation in 1972. However, armed violence and separatist movements demanding secession from India continued to fester. The divergent political aspirations of various ethnic groups within Manipur further add to the existing conflict dynamics of the state. In fact, the conflict situation in Manipur has, over the past three decades, evolved from a purely separatist struggle to a complex multi-layered low-intensity conflict involving three broad strands: confrontation between state and non-state armed groups, factional clashes among the non-state groups, and periodic clashes between the three major ethnic groups – Meitei, Kuki, and Naga. A major dimension to the contemporary conflict are claims made by ethnic groups (especially the Nagas and Kukis) residing in the Hill Districts regarding systematic discrimination by the provincial government (which is Meitei dominated, especially in terms of the distribution of development entitlements).[5]

It is estimated that Manipur currently has around 35 militant groups of which 12 are active, 18 are at ceasefire and 5 are inactive (Centre for Development and Peace Studies 2015). Between 1992 and 2015,[6] 6,014 deaths have been recorded in Manipur as a result of the ongoing conflict of which 2,248 are civilians (South Asia Terrorism Portal 2015b).

Responding to the conflict in Manipur, the Indian government in the late 1980s declared the state as a 'disturbed area' and imposed the Armed Forces Special Powers Act (AFSP Act) 1958 on the state. The AFSP Act, which has been severely critiqued as a draconian law, provides complete impunity to the armed forces in initiating actions against suspected insurgents. It allows an officer of the armed forces (commissioned and non-commissioned) to exercise a range of powers, for example:

> if he is of [the] opinion that it is necessary so to do for the maintenance of public order, after giving such due warning as he may consider necessary, fire upon or otherwise use force, even to the causing of death, against any person who is acting in contravention of any law or order for the time being in force in the disturbed area . . .
>
> *(AFSP Act 1958: sect. 4(a))*

> . . . arrest, without warrant, any person who has committed a cognizable offence or against whom a reasonable suspicion exists that he has committed or is about to commit a cognizable offence and may use such force as may be necessary to effect the arrest . . .
>
> *(AFSP Act 1958, sect. 4(c))*

> . . . [and] enter and search without warrant any premises to make any such arrest as aforesaid.
>
> *(AFSP Act 1958: sect. 4(d))*

The powers granted by the AFSP Act have been subjected to serious abuse in Manipur, leading to extrajudicial killings, rape, torture, and forced disappearances (Human Rights Law Network 2009). The state has witnessed mass agitations and civil society movements demanding the repeal of the AFSP Act. The agitations reached a peak on 11 July 2004 with the alleged rape and murder of Thangjam Manorama Devi (Pandey 2004). The incident outraged people across the state and led to one of the most defiant protests in the history of social movements, with Manipuri women discarding their clothes outside an Assam Rifles base and challenging the Indian army to rape them. Irom Sharmila Chanu, known as the Iron Lady of Manipur, went on a fast for 16 years from November 2000 to August 2016 (Singh 2016). Her fast occurred in the aftermath of the alleged killing by Assam Rifles personnel of ten civilians, who were waiting for a bus in Malom, a town in the Imphal valley of Manipur (Bhonsle 2016).

Despite the large-scale violence, the household-level impacts of the armed conflict in Manipur have drawn little attention. The conflict situation has led to the breakdown of the traditional social structures in the state and has severely impacted the social and economic stability of the region. It has impaired people's daily lives, mobility, livelihood, and access to service delivery institutions. There is a deep psychological impact of the conflict, with people living in perpetual fear and reeling under the trauma of large-scale violence. The conflict has created new sets of vulnerabilities, especially for women, children, and the elderly, which remain largely untold. Consequently, the strategies of response to the conflict have adopted homogenous policies that do not address the concerns emerging from these vulnerable groups.

Conflict widows of Manipur

Human rights groups have reported that the conflict in Manipur creates at least 500 widows every year, many of whom have become widows at a very young age (Jha 2011). However, there is very little systematic data available on the conflict widows of Manipur. Most statistics available come from non-governmental organisations that collect data for their own work. Insights into the lives of conflict widows, therefore, are principally drawn from the narratives of widows that have been documented by grassroots organisations or featured in the local media. These narratives bring to light the vulnerabilities faced by conflict widows in Manipur, where they have become easy targets of social exclusion, discrimination, and violence and are being forced to live impoverished lives.

For instance, in the case of Nitan Elangbam (aged 29), the death of her husband in an alleged staged encounter by Manipur Police Commandos also meant that she was denied the right to her marital home. Her in-laws were no longer willing to take the responsibility for her upkeep and she was forced to return to her natal home (Karmakar 2014). When she wanted to remarry, she faced massive opposition from both families. While Nitan overcame this opposition, many others have not been able to do so. 'We aren't just fighting the system for justice; we are fighting social battles too', claims Edina Yaikhom, General Secretary Extrajudicial Execution Victim Families' Association, Manipur (Karmakar 2014).

The life of Mumtaz, as documented in *We, Widows of the Gun* (van Lierde 2011: 21), is a story of fighting such battles:

> Mumtaz Singga Mayum Ongbi is 38 and has five growing children: a son and four daughters. After her husband's murder, three of them were placed under the guardianship of her husband's family, and that family is now keeping the children from their mother. Mumtaz is a Muslim, a member of the Meitei Pangal community, and lives in Phoudel Mamang Leikai, in the Thoubal district south of the capital city of Imphal. Her husband, Mohammed Azad Khan Shekhar, was murdered on 7 March 2009 by a combined team of Assam Rifles and the Manipur Police Commandos of Imphal East.

While unravelling her life and struggles, Mumtaz laments:

> I haven't been allowed to see my son and my two youngest daughters in months. I know that they do not go to school anymore. Apart from that, I know nothing. Sometimes at night the fear drives me mad. Sometimes I faint. Sometimes I call my sisters to see if anyone can come over in the night. But no one comes. No one wants to have anything more to do with me. I am the cause of Azad's death, I am the wife of a terrorist, I am dangerous. My in-laws don't want to see me at all, let alone take care of me or support me financially. What has become of Nyhaad, Niphaad and Injam-amul? They aren't going to school anymore. That is a disaster. Three months ago I went to Azad's sister. Like the rest, she could not or would not tell me where they were. Here in Manipur, so many children disappear. They get sold, young boys disappear into the hands of the rebels or paramilitaries, and young girls disappear into the sex trade, or they get addicted to drugs. Sometimes children are sold to rich families as house slaves. The very thought . . . .
>
> *(van Lierde 2011: 36)*

Mumtaz now lives at her father's place with two of her children:

> When we have no more food, my father says 'Eat what you have, and if not, starve' . . . And my mother goes on stirring things up. She says that my sister's husband wants to kill me because I gossip too much, because I want to know too much about my husband's death, that everyone in the village knows that I cannot be trusted, and that I have nowhere to go.
>
> *(van Lierde 2011: 36)*

Conflict widows of Manipur are struggling to meet the daily needs of their families. Becha Devi (aged 38), whose husband was killed by unknown assailants in February 2009, now lives with her old mother and her three minor daughters:

> I am now the lone bread earner of the five-member family. I stopped sending my two children to school, as I could not pay the monthly fees of Rupees 150 each. I managed the family with the money I earned from the national rural employment guarantee scheme. Now it's off-season. So I sold all my belongings to feed my mother and three children. I have no more belongings to sell. I often thought of committing suicide with my three children. But I could not. Now I am thinking of selling my piece of land.
>
> (The Telegraph *2010)*

Hardships of widows are further accentuated by the frequent economic blockades that Manipur has been facing.[7] It leads to artificial price rises of fuel and essential commodities. Phairembam Katnao Devi (aged 29), whose husband was killed by unknown assailants in 2006, is now the sole breadwinner for her two minor daughters and is earning her living by knitting clothes:

> The price of 1kg of rice is Rupees 26. Kerosene is not available. Prices of all the commodities have gone up after the blockade. I borrowed money to feed my children. Now shops are not willing to give us commodities on credit. I also used to borrow money. But no one is willing to lend us money any longer. Our future is really bleak.
>
> (The Telegraph *2010)*

Conflict widows also become soft targets of violence and sexual assault. For instance, as reported in *The Sangai Express* (e-Pao 2008), widow Laishram Ningol (aged 24), was killed and her body abandoned in a paddy field by unknown assailants. There were strangulation marks on her neck and also blood stains in her 'private parts' (e-Pao 2008). Her husband Laimujam Rojen was shot down two years earlier by unidentified gunmen allegedly for acting as an informant. After his death Laishram had returned to her maternal home with her two sons aged five and three years (e-Pao 2008).

In the case of Wahengbam Bilashini (aged 55), as reported by *The Sangai Express* on 30 March 2009 (cited in e-Pao 2009), two unknown youths entered her house at night and sought her help in carrying a small gun to a nearby place. Upon her refusal to do so, they asked her to keep the weapon in her house. When she refused this proposition and closed the door on them, the youths fired through her window severely injuring her (e-Pao 2009). In another case reported by Hueiyen News Service (see e-Pao 2010), a widow (aged 36) and her daughter (aged 17) were abducted and later found murdered in an open paddy field at Tampha Loukon of Phayeng Chingkhounou in Imphal West district. The report said,

> The way the dead bodies were found suggests possible gang rape of both mother and daughter as their clothing including inner wears was found displaced even though police is yet to confirm the same owing to the highly decomposed state of the bodies.
>
> *(e-Pao 2010)*

Widows are also fighting the social stigma of being viewed as a threat to society. In fact, many cases have been reported where widows were subjected to social persecution for allegedly practising black magic. For instance, as reported by Hueiyen News Service (see e-Pao 2011), a widow was paraded in a public place at Wangoi of Imphal West District of Manipur for allegedly causing the defeat of a candidate from a particular political party in the civic body polls through the practice of black arts. She was alone when nearly 50 men entered her house and dragged her to the market place (e-Pao 2011). It is also important to note that many such cases go unreported, thereby masking the magnitude of the prejudice faced by widows.

While the widows of conflict in Manipur are fighting to survive, the conflict has also led to the creation of 'half-widows'. Half-widows are women whose husbands have disappeared involuntarily – either they have been abducted by security forces or kidnapped by rebel groups. Although in many cases their husbands have been missing for years and are presumed dead, there is no official proof of their death (under sect. 108 of the Indian Evidence Act 1872, a person can be declared dead only if he or she has gone missing without trace for a period of seven years). As 'half-widows', these women live their lives with the agony of not knowing the fate of their husbands. The phenomenon of half-widows has gained prominence due to the work of the Association of Parents of Disappeared Persons (APDP) in Jammu and Kashmir that has estimated that the state has around 1,500 half-widows (APDP 2011: 6). However, there is no available data providing an estimate on the number of half-widows in Manipur, though many cases of alleged forced disappearances by security forces have been reported. In a writ petition submitted to the Supreme Court of India by the Extra Judicial Execution Victim Families Association Manipur, it has been stated that between May 1979 to May 2012, 1,528 extrajudicial killings were committed in Manipur (Human Rights Law Network 2015: 1). The discovery of eight human skulls and other skeletal remains at a construction site in the capital city of Imphal in December 2014 has further strengthened the allegations of enforced disappearances and extra-judicial killings. The site was an abandoned school complex occupied by the central paramilitary forces from 1980 to 1999 (*Deccan Herald* 2014).

The half-widows of Manipur are not only suffering from social and economic deprivations, but are also living each day with the agony of not knowing whether their husbands are alive or dead. Mina Kheratun was two months pregnant when her husband was abducted by unknown assailants on 25 July 1999 (*The Sangai Express* 2015a). Speaking to Families of the Involuntarily Disappeared Association, Manipur (FIDAM), Mina says that she heard reports of her husband being taken to the Kangla Fort which was then occupied by 17 Assam Rifles. Mina has not heard from her husband since. She says, 'For the past many years, I have been suffering silently. The question whether my husband is still alive or dead has been tormenting me every night' (*The Sangai Express* 2015a). With her husband's fate unknown, Mina is struggling every day to meet the daily needs of her family of three sons and three daughters.

State assistance to conflict widows

Widowhood as a consequence of armed conflict has largely remained unaddressed in India's attempt to offer assistance to survivors of armed conflict. Conflict widows remain invisible in the policies and programmes designed to counter the ill effects of armed conflict. In fact, most of the policies and programmes designed for widows are meant for peace time and do not take into account the vulnerabilities faced by conflict widows. Four key social welfare programmes through which conflict widows can seek state assistance will now be discussed briefly to evaluate their effectiveness.

Indira Gandhi National Widow Pension Scheme (IGNWPS)

This mechanism came into existence in February 2009 and is an important component of the National Social Assistance Programme (NSAP) that seeks to ensure a minimum national standard for social assistance. To be eligible for assistance under the programme, the age of the applicant should be between 40 and 64 years and the applicant must belong to a household below the poverty line, according to criteria prescribed by Government of India. The assistance provided by the centre under this scheme is 200 rupees per month per beneficiary. State governments are urged to contribute at least equally towards the pension amount.

Project Assist, National Foundation for Communal Harmony (NFCH)

Project Assist of NFCH (an autonomous organisation with the Ministry of Home Affairs, Government of India) aims to provide financial assistance to children who have been orphaned or have been reduced to destitution due to either communal, caste, ethnic or terrorism-related violence. Under the project, a child is deemed to be an orphan or a destitute in cases where either both parents or the surviving parent or main breadwinner is killed or permanently incapacitated due to communal, caste, ethnic or terrorism-related violence. To be eligible for receiving assistance, the annual income of the family must not exceed 100,000 rupees.

SWADHAR GREH: a scheme for women in difficult circumstances

This is a scheme by the Ministry of Women and Child Development, Government of India. It aims to respond to the needs of women in difficult circumstances such as: widows; destitute and deserted women; women ex-prisoners; victims of sexual abuse and crimes, including those trafficked and rescued from brothels; migrant or refugee women who have been rendered homeless due to natural calamities; mentally challenged women; and women victims of terrorist violence. The scheme is implemented through social welfare functions of the government, including the Ministry of Women and Child Development, as well as women's development corporations, urban local bodies, reputed public/private trusts or voluntary organisations who are willing to take up the responsibility of rehabilitating such women. The services made available through the SWADHAR scheme include provisions for shelter, clothing, health care, food, counselling and legal support, social and economic rehabilitation through education, and awareness generation.

Central Scheme for Assistance to Civilian Victims of Terrorist, Communal and Naxal Violence

Launched by the Ministry of Home Affairs, the scheme was initially called the 'Central Scheme for Assistance to Civilian Victims of Terrorist and Communal Violence' and became effective in April 2008. Later, in June 2009, the scheme was extended to include victims of Naxal violence. For purposes of this scheme, the term 'terrorism' is taken to include militancy and insurgency-related violence.[8] The chief objective of the scheme is to provide assistance for sustenance and rehabilitation to families of victims of violence, especially affected dependent spouses, children, and aged parents, on account of death or the permanent disability of one or more of the family members. Under the scheme, a financial assistance of 300,000 rupees is given for each death or permanent incapacitation (disability of 50% or above) of a family member. In addition to financial assistance, those permanently incapacitated and members of the families of the victims killed are entitled to a Health Card given by the District Health Society under the National Rural Health Mission.

A preliminary overview of these programmes leads to the identification of some critical problems with their implementation. For instance, to be eligible to apply for assistance under the Indira Gandhi National Widow Pension Scheme, a widow should be within the age bracket of 40 to 64 years. Many widows of conflict in Manipur are very young and are thus not eligible to apply for assistance under this scheme. Moreover, the scheme is applicable only if an applicant is belonging to a below-poverty-line (BPL) household.[9] In addition, there have been several lacunae identified in shortlisting BPL families for government assistance schemes such as corruption, difficulty in obtaining accurate data, and the exclusion of deserving families (Alkire & Seth 2013: 409–410). In situations of armed conflict where institutional machineries break down, accumulating correct data on BPL families or applying for a BPL card through proper channels become immensely difficult. Also, the assistance offered under the programme (200 rupees per month) is a meagre sum. With increasing prices of essential commodities, surviving on that small amount is almost impossible. Although state governments are encouraged to contribute towards this assistance, it is not mandatory for them to do so.

It is also difficult for conflict widows to seek assistance for their children under Project Assist, as the scheme only offers assistance to children whose fathers have been killed by rebel groups, not the security forces. Manipur has had a number of cases of alleged fake encounters by security forces under the protection offered by the AFSP Act. It has been reported that since 2006 there have been around 32 cases of alleged fake encounters in Manipur for which no enquiry has been instituted and no one has been put on trial (Bhattacharjee 2009). All of these families, however, fall outside the purview of assistance provided by Project Assist. It is estimated that in the years 2012 to 2013, 46 civilians and 103 suspected insurgents have lost their lives due to the conflict in Manipur (South Asia Terrorism Portal 2015b). However, in the same timeframe, reported cases of assistance under Project Assist for child victims is recorded as just five (National Foundation for Communal Harmony 2013: 14).

The situation is similar with the other two assistance programmes, as they do not offer assistance to the victims of the families of 'suspected terrorists'. In the years 2009 to 2013, a total of 80 persons in Manipur received assistance under the Central Scheme for Assistance to Civilian

Victims of Terrorist, Communal and Naxal Violence (Government of India 2013: annex. 1). However, within the same timeframe the South Asia Terrorism Portal records 730 insurgency-related killings, of which 174 are civilians and 556 are 'terrorists' (South Asia Terrorism Portal 2015b). This raises serious concerns, as widows of 'suspected terrorists' have nowhere to turn for assistance and support. Moreover, since the Scheme has only been effective since 2009, it excludes all victims prior to 2009. According to the South Asia Terrorism Portal, from 1994 to 2008, 21,588 civilians were killed in India as a result of armed violence[10] (South Asia Terrorism Portal 2015c).

Another critical lacuna is that none of these programmes cater to the concerns of half-widows. Since their husbands have disappeared and are not officially dead, half-widows are not in a position to submit documents that confirm their status as a 'widow', which is a primary requirement in order to avail themselves of assistance under any of these programmes.

Thus, it is evident that state assistance programmes during armed conflict tend to vastly exclude the experiences and concerns of conflict widows. Many widows in Manipur are currently struggling to survive, with their fundamental human right to live with dignity being violated daily:

> After the shock of losing their husbands the real fight of these widows only begins: the fight for their children's future, the fight against the stigma that comes with being the widow of a suspected terrorist. The fight against impunity, corruption, extortion, crippling inflation and strangling black markets. In short, they struggle to live life in dignity – as a woman, a mother, a widow and as a citizen.
>
> *(van Lierde 2011)*

Organising beyond the state

However, amidst the stories of despair and hopelessness, there are also stories of courage, of widows organising beyond the state and fighting for their rights. *The Sangai Express* (2015b) documents the story of Preeti Devi:

> Although justice and assistance from the Government is not at sight, Preeti Devi, who lost her husband at the hands of a militant group in 2008, is committed to raise her two little children by the sweats of her brows. Preeti, who hails from Ahallup Makha Leikai, rented a Sangam of agriculture land belonging to one of her aunts and started cultivating seasonal vegetables since June last year. Soon after, some widows of the locality joined her and they together formed Lanleima Self Help Group. Their creativity, sincerity and social skills combined are keeping them going in the face of hardships. Grit and strength sustain them as they courageously take care of their families. Buoyed by the success of their venture, the [Self Help Group] is now planning to cultivate mushrooms too on their rented land.

Preeti Devi's story is not an isolated incident. There are many such instances where widows have joined hands and overcome social and administrative barriers to survive with dignity. There are various voluntary, community-led initiatives that have been initiated in Manipur offering financial, psycho-social, and legal assistance to widows and half-widows. For instance, Manipur Women Gun Survivors Network, Extrajudicial Execution Victim Families' Association, Manipur, Conflict Widows Forum, and Gun Victims' Survivors Association are a few such significant initiatives. The membership base of these initiatives includes widows of civilians and also widows of 'terrorists' who fall outside the purview of state assistance schemes. Talking about Extrajudicial Execution Victim Families' Association, Manipur (EEVFAM), its secretary Neena Ningombam writes:

> EEVFAM is an organization of widows and mothers of those killed by police and security forces. We are discriminated as young widows and also as families of the 'terrorists'. We cannot access the basic schemes for widows namely widow pension given by the Social Welfare Dept. because they had not attain [sic] the age of 40 years. We cannot access the ex-gratia given by the State Government because our husbands are killed in 'encounters'. We also cannot access the children's education support under the National Foundation for Communal Harmony given by the District Commissioner because they were meant only for children killed by 'non-state actors'. Having nowhere to go we decided to help each other.
>
> *(Ningombam 2012)*

What sets these initiatives apart from the state-driven assistance schemes is that they approach the issue of conflict widowhood from the perspective of a survivor. Organisers are thus driven by the actual needs of widows, rather than being imposed upon through top-down socio-political measures. As a consequence, such organisations are more inclusive and holistic in their approach. To quote Binalaksmi Nepram (Women's Web 2012), founding member of the Manipur Women Gun Survivors Network:

> Whenever there is news of a killing, we go as soon as we can to meet the family. In some cases, there is a need for immediate intervention since the breadwinner has been killed and the women have almost nothing. We ensure that they have some funds to keep the house running at the moment. The next step is to open a bank account in the woman's name. In most cases, women have nothing of their own. Plus, it also helps their own safety to have an account in their name since widows may face trouble from other family members such as in-laws. . . . Then, we assess their skills and ask them what it is they can do or would like to learn. In most cases, the women have been housewives and never earned money before. We don't teach them, but we ask them to come up with what they would like to work on. We help them with small loans needed to start a business . . . Once they are assured of food and the children's education, then they start looking for their legal rights. . . . Recently, we have also started a support program where we ask doctors in the state to donate a small amount of time where we can bring in these women and get them treated for their health issues. As you would know, anaemia is rampant in Indian women and especially in Manipuri women. The trauma of losing a loved one, mental depression and abuse, physical abuse, the stigma attached to being a widow, poverty – all these worsen their health. A lot of doctors have responded beautifully and give us pro-bono consultation for these women, and even free medication.

Instead of only offering monetary assistance to widows or half-widows, grassroots initiatives in Manipur have been seeking to find long-term solutions to a widows' struggle for survival. Widows, for instance, can apply for interest-free loans to the Manipur branch of the Indian Red Cross Society under their livelihood project (Imphal Free Press 2015). The aim behind these loans is to enable widows to start small commercial businesses of their own (*The Sangai Express* 2015c). Further, the Integrated Rural Development Social Organization, with the support of the Foundation for Social Transformation, has initiated the 'Supporting Gun Widows Survivors for Sustainable Development Project' in Manipur, which perceives gun widows as significant stakeholders in the peacebuilding process rather than treating them merely as victims. The project seeks to empower gun widows through the creation of self-help groups and by enabling them to gain economic independence.

Offering legal support is also a significant aspect of the types of assistance being offered to widows from various initiatives and civil society organisations. Organisations such as the Extrajudicial Execution Victim Families' Association, Manipur (EEVFAM) offer assistance to widows by referring them to pro-bono lawyers or by organising their meetings with human rights activists; and also by enabling widows to understand their rights and entitlements. This is extremely crucial as widows often have no information or awareness regarding the existing government mechanisms in place for accessing assistance. Financial constraints also prevent widows from commencing legal proceedings concerning the extrajudicial killing of their husbands. It was because of the support provided by the Human Rights Law Network (HRLN) that Sagolshem Ongbi Latani Devi was able to fight the case of her husband's wrongful killing by the security forces (Human Rights Law Network 2010). As judgement in this case, the Guwahati High Court Imphal Bench ordered the Assam Rifles authorities to pay Sagolshem Ongbi Latani Devi 400,000 rupees as compensation (Human Rights Law Network 2010).

However, civil society initiatives often face several barriers often imposed by the provincial administration and also the society at large. The efforts of the EEVFAM to register itself with the Social Welfare Department were futile, as the Department required removal of the word 'Extrajudicial' from the association's name (Manipur Online 2011). Narrating her experience Renu Takhellambam, the chair of EEVFAM who lost her husband in an alleged extrajudicial killing by the Imphal-West Police Commandos in April 2007, states:

> the more you act out in the open, the more you demand your rights and the rights of your murdered husbands, the more you are known as a critical organization of troublesome widows, and the more you risk the government, the army or the police making your life difficult.
>
> *(van Lierde 2011: 88)*

However, such social prosecution does not deter women like Renu who pledge to go on 'resisting and conquering taboos and fears' (van Lierde 2011: 88). Through their relentless courage and work, widows in Manipur have been able to break several stereotypes and forge support networks within their communities. As Renu claims,

> In reality, with our work for widows we are also raising the men. The men who just a few years ago were belittling me because they found me too free and impertinent for a widow, today show me respect because they see and hear that I lead workshops and talk to journalists.
>
> *(van Lierde 2011: 89)*

Conclusion

The indirect impacts of armed conflict continue far beyond the de-escalation and cessation of direct violence. Widows of conflict in Manipur experience discrimination on a daily basis in the form of societal prejudice and exclusionary state assistance policies. State assistance offered to widows is mostly top-down and does not recognise a woman's agency in finding durable solutions to her circumstances. However, conflict widows of Manipur have not remained silent accomplices to their own suffering. They have come together, organised themselves and have created forums through which they can begin to fight for their rights. It must also be emphasised that the problem of conflict widowhood is not an isolated one involving select regions – it is a global concern. The Beijing Declaration and Platform for Action, 1995, states, 'Violations of the human rights of women in situations of armed conflict are violations of the fundamental principles of international human rights and humanitarian law' (para. 131). The UN has recognised that the 'abuse of widows and their children constitute one of the most serious violations of human rights' (United Nations 2011: 1).

It is therefore important to confront the treatment of widows of conflict in a direct and holistic manner. Instead of merely incorporating 'widows' as a vulnerable group within policy frameworks for the receipt of welfare assistance based exclusively on discriminatory criteria, it is essential that their lived experiences and perspectives are integrated into broader peacebuilding, re-integration and development-based policy frameworks. Assistance programmes designed for survivors of armed conflict need to specifically address the economic, social, and psychological needs of widows. The paucity of reliable data is one of the key obstacles in designing an appropriate policy framework. The continual discrimination and violence experienced by widows of conflict render meaningless any cash grant scheme. Rather, the approach should be to incorporate holistic programmes that combine livelihood support with long-term psychosocial care. Therefore, there is an urgent need to encourage evidence-based policy design both at a regional and a global level. A further causal problem experienced by widows is corruption and impunity, leaving unpunished those who contribute to extrajudicial killings – and further exacerbating the extreme vulnerability of conflict widows. It is, therefore, imperative that justice delivery mechanisms are strengthened and become more transparent and accountable. It is further important to integrate widows into post-conflict reconstruction and peacebuilding efforts, thereby recognising and facilitating their contribution to sustainable peace and security. To build a human rights system that recognises gender equality, one must also be conscious of the heterogeneity of gender experience and account for it. In addition, conventional human rights approaches that focus primarily or exclusively on the state must now go beyond the state and engage with non-state, civil society actors in a robust and consultative way. The vulnerabilities faced by conflict widows globally must be recognised and addressed with utmost urgency.

One must not forget that, for many, 'The deadly bullet that enters and exits the body of the husband in an extrajudicial killing or rebel encounter, freezes forever in his wife and children' (van Lierde 2011: 7).

Notes

1 It has been documented that female and widow -headed households account for around '20–25% of all households in post-conflict situations' (UN Habitat 2007: 66).

2 A study conducted by the University of Kashmir highlights three sets of problems that widows in the conflict-torn state face:

> The first difficulties surface soon after the death of their partners, in the forms of emotional stress, denial of inheritance rights, sexual harassment and general social undesirability. The second wave of difficulties arises gradually, as loss of control over the children, and a growing sense of inferiority. Finally, the widows are burdened by the long-term and growing demands of house care and the assignment of menial responsibilities. Altogether, the women find their position thoroughly compromised.
>
> *(Bukhari 2002: 39)*

3 Data current to 31 May 2015.
4 This data does not include fatalities due to left-wing extremism until the year 2004.
5 As stated by Sajjad Hassan (2006: 23):

> Aggravating the situation is the perception among tribal communities of poor investments in hill areas, poor implementation of development programmes and absence of basic infrastructure. The Hills make up some 9/10ths of the total area of the state. Tribal communities, who exclusively inhabit them, constitute 37 per cent of the state's total population. A survey of budget allocations for hill districts in fiscal 2004–05 throws up some interesting figures: only 26 per cent of the total budget of the Education Department was allocated for the five hill districts. It wasn't any better in other departments: 25 per cent of the Health Department's budget and 22 per cent of the budget of the Public Works Department (PWD), the agency responsible for roads and other works. In other key departments of social welfare and agriculture, the allocation was 14 per cent and 12 per cent respectively. A similar imbalance characterizes credit to the Hills as proportion of total credit to the state: 21.4 per cent in 2003 and only 7.8 per cent in 2002. The outcome of low levels of investment in the Hills has been along predictable lines. Four out of five hill districts figure at the bottom of the heap on the human development index. These districts also have a larger proportion of the poor than their valley counterparts.

6 Data current until 7 June 2015.
7 Economic blockades are a frequently employed tool by various ethnic and rebel groups to press for their demands.
8 See Revised Guidelines of Central Scheme for Assistance to Civilians Victims / Family of Victims of Terrorist, Communal and Naxal Violence, http://mha1.nic.in/pdfs/T-Guide141008.pdf.
9 BPL is an indicator used by the Government of India that provides the poverty threshold for identifying households in need of assistance. Identifying the BPL threshold has been a contentious issue in India. For more on this, please see Sangal (2015).
10 Data to 2004 does not include fatalities in left-wing extremism.

References

Al Jazeera 2015, *Sri Lanka: Widows of War*, viewed 22 May 2015, www.aljazeera.com/programmes/101east/2015/04/sri-lanka-widows-war-150421161203533.html.

Alkire, S & Seth, S 2013, 'Identifying BPL Households: A Comparison of Methods', *The Indian Journal of Human Development*, vol. 2, no. 2, pp. 407–424.

Armed Forces Special Powers Act 1958, viewed 24 January 2017, http://nagapol.gov.in/PDF/The%20Armed%20Forces%20Special%20Powers%20Act%201958.pdf.

Association of Parents of Disappeared Persons (APDP) 2011, *Half-Widow, Half-Wife? Responding to Gendered Violence in Kashmir*, APDP, Srinagar, viewed 22 December 2016, www.jkccs.net/wp-content/uploads/2015/02/Half-Widow-Half-Wife-APDP-report.pdf.

Bhattacharjee, K 2009, *Manipur's Widows of Conflict*, viewed 2 February 2015, www.ndtv.com/india-news/manipurs-widows-of-conflict-399643.

Bhonsle, A 2016, *Mother, Where Is My Country? Looking for the Light in the Darkness of Manipur*, Speaking Tiger Books, New Delhi.

Bukhari, F 2002, 'Dying Day by Day: Taking Stock of Mental and Social Health in Kashmir', *Himal South Asian*, vol. 15, no. 11, pp. 38–40.

Centre for Development and Peace Studies 2015, Militant Groups Active, Inactive and Under Ceasefire, viewed 22 September 2016, www.cdpsindia.org/manipur_outfits.asp.

Deccan Herald 2014, '8 Human Skulls Found in School Complex in Manipur', viewed 10 May 2015, www.deccanherald.com/content/450241/8-human-skulls-found-school.html.

e-Pao 2008, *Young Widow Found Dead, Abandoned at Kakching*, viewed 12 August 2016, http://e-pao.net/epRelatedNews.asp?heading=2&src=110408.

e-Pao 2009, *Lady LDC Shot*, viewed 14 October 2016, http://e-pao.net/epRelatedNews.asp?heading=7&src=310309.

e-Pao 2010, *Widow, Daughter Found Murdered, Gang Rape Suspected*, viewed 26 November 2016, http://e-pao.net/epRelatedNews.asp?heading=18&src=240110.

e-Pao 2011, *Widow Ostracized for Alleged Black Art to Ensure Candidate's Loss*, viewed 28 October 2016, http://e-pao.net/GP.asp?src=16..110111.jan11.

Goodhand, J 2010, 'From Wars to Complex Political Emergencies: Understanding Conflict and Peacebuilding in the New World Disorder', *Third World Quarterly*, vol. 20, no. 1, pp. 13–26.

Government of India 2010, Ministry of Home Affairs, *Revised Guidelines of Central Scheme for Assistance to Civilians Victims / Family of Victims of Terrorist, Communal and Naxal Violence*, viewed 30 September 2016, http://mha1.nic.in/pdfs/T-Guide141008.pdf.

Government of India 2012, Ministry of Rural Development (Office Memorandum No. J-11015/1/2012-NSAP), 2012, *Guidelines for Central Assistance under the Indira Gandhi National Widow Pension Scheme (IGNWPS)*, viewed 23 December 2016, http://nsap.nic.in/Guidelines/wps.pdf.

Government of India 2013, Ministry of Home Affairs, Lok Sabha, Unstarred Question No. 4824, annexure 1, viewed 14 November 2016, http://mha1.nic.in/par2013/par2013-pdfs/ls-230413/4824.pdf.

Government of India 2015, Ministry of Women and Child Development, *SWADHAR GREH (A Scheme for Women in Difficult Circumstances)*, viewed 30 December 2016, http://wcd.nic.in/schemes/swadhar-greh-scheme-women-difficult-circumstances.

Human Rights Law Network 2009, *Manipur in the Shadow of AFSPA: Independent People's Tribunal Report on Human Rights Violations in Manipur*, HRLN, Imphal.

Human Rights Law Network 2010, *Compensation Awarded through HRLN Manipur to Victim of Unjustified Killing by Assam Rifles*, viewed 14 March 2015, www.hrln.org/hrln/newsroom/press-release/591--compensation-awarded-through-hrln-manipur-to-victim-of-unjustified-killing-by-assam-rifles.html.

Human Rights Law Network 2015, *SC Appointed Commission Gave Report on Its Investigation of the Extra-judicial Killings in Manipur*, viewed 10 May 2015, www.hrln.org/hrln/criminal-justice/pils-a-cases/1509-sc-appointed-commission-gave-report-on-its-investigation-of-the-extra-judicial-killings-in-manipur.pdf.

Imphal Free Press 2015, *Red Cross Society Distributes Interest Free Loans to 50 Widows of Conflict*, viewed January 2017, http://ifp.co.in/page/items/25424/red-cross-society-distributes-interest-free-loans-to-50-widows-of-conflict.

International Centre for Transnational Justice 2010, *Across the Lines: The Impact of Nepal's Conflict on Women*, viewed 17 May 2015, www.ictj.org/sites/default/files/ICTJ-Nepal-Across-Lines-2010-English.pdf.

Jha, R 2011, *Young Widows of India's 50-Year-Old Conflict in Manipur*, viewed 20 March 2015, http://news.bbc.co.uk/2/hi/programmes/from_our_own_correspondent/9421267.stm.

Karmakar, R 2014, *Conflict Widows: Left to Fight Social Battles*, 7 November, viewed 18 December 2016, www.hindustantimes.com/india/conflict-widows-left-to-fight-social-battles/story-KwbOcptpTsUp6qtUFkBrDN.html.

Manipur Online 2011, *Young Widows Bear the Brunt of Conflict Situation*, 8 March, viewed 8 April 2015, http://manipuronline.com/headlines/young-widows-bear-brunt-conflict-situation/2011/03/08.

Merths, J & Helsing JW 2006, 'Introduction', in J Merths & JW Helsing (eds), *Human Rights and Conflict: Exploring the Links Between Rights, Law and Peacebuilding*, United States Institute of Peace Press, Washington, DC.

National Foundation for Communal Harmony 2013, *Annual Report 2012–13*, NFCH, New Delhi.

National Foundation for Communal Harmony, *Project Assist*, viewed 19 October 2016, http://nfch.nic.in/?q=project-assist.

Ningombam, N 2012, *Resisting Extrajudicial Execution in Manipur*, 30 September, viewed 2 March 2015, www.countercurrents.org/ningombam300912.htm.

Pandey, G 2004, 'Woman at the Centre of Manipur Storm', BBC News, 27 August, news.bbc.co.uk/2/hi/south_asia/3604986.stm.

Reilly, N 2007, 'Seeking Gender Justice in Post-conflict Transitions: Towards a Transformative Women's Human Rights Approach', *International Journal of Law in Context*, vol. 3, no. 2, pp. 155–172.

Sahni, A 2001, *Survey of Conflicts and Resolution in India's Northeast*, viewed 25 April 2015, www.satp.org/satporgtp/publication/faultlines/volume12/Article3.htm#@.

Sajjad Hassan, M 2006, *Explaining Manipur's Breakdown and Manipur's Peace: The State and Identities in Northeast India. Crisis States Programme*, Working Paper No. 79, viewed 11 October 2014, eprints.lse.ac.uk/28150/1/wp79.pdf.

Sangal, PP 2015, 'Defining Poverty Line for India', *The Financial Express*, viewed 18 November 2016, www.financialexpress.com/opinion/defining-a-poverty-line-for-india/74725/.

Singh, SS, 2016, 'Irom Sharmila Ends 16-Year Fast', *The Hindu*, 9 August, viewed 12 December 2016, www.thehindu.com/news/national/Irom-Sharmila-ends-16-year-fast/article14562315.ece.

South Asia Terrorism Portal 2015a, *India Fatalities: 1994–2015*, viewed 4 June 2015, www.satp.org/satporgtp/countries/india/database/indiafatalities.htm.

South Asia Terrorism Portal 2015b, *Insurgency Related Killings 1992–2015*, viewed 9 June 2015, www.satp.org/satporgtp/countries/india/states/manipur/data_sheets/insurgency_related_killings.htm.

South Asia Terrorism Portal 2015c, *India Fatalities: 1994–2015*, viewed 10 June 2015, www.satp.org/satporgtp/countries/india/database/indiafatalities.htm.

The Sangai Express 2015a, *'Half-widows' Wait for Lost Husbands*, 22 January, viewed 12 March 2015, www.thesangaiexpress.com/half-widows-wait-for-lost-husbands/.

The Sangai Express 2015b, *Although Justice and Assistance Not at Sight . . . Widow Commits to Raise Children by Sweat of Brows*, 12 March, viewed 8 February 2015, www.thesangaiexpress.com/page/items/49400/although-justice-and-assistance-not-at-sight-widow-commits-to-raise-children-by-sweat-of-brows.

The Sangai Express 2015c, 'Loan for Widows', 21 February, viewed 10 March 2015, www.thesangaiexpress.com/loan-for-widows/.

The Telegraph 2010, 'Manipur Conflict Widows Cry for Help', 12 June, viewed 12 February 2015, www.telegraphindia.com/1100612/jsp/northeast/story_12554627.jsp.

United Nations 1995, Beijing Declaration and Platform for Action, adopted at the Fourth World Conference on Women, viewed 2 April 2015, www.un.org/womenwatch/daw/beijing/pdf/BDPfA%20E.pdf.

United Nations 2000, Resolution 1325, adopted by the Security Council at its 4213th Meeting, on 31 October 2000, viewed 30 August 2016, www.securitycouncilreport.org/atf/cf/%7B65BFCF9B-6D27-4E9C-8CD3-CF6E4FF96FF9%7D/WPS%20SRES1325%20.pdf.

United Nations 2001, *Widowhood: Invisible Women, Secluded or Excluded*, viewed 28 April 2015, www.un.org/womenwatch/daw/public/wom_Dec%2001%20single%20pg.pdf.

United Nations 2011, *Backgrounder: International Widow's Day*, viewed 2 June 2015, www.un.org/en/events/widowsday/pdf/backgrounder.pdf.

United Nations (UN Habitat) 2007, *From Emergency to Reconstruction: A Post-conflict Administration and Peace-building Handbook*, United Nations Human Settlements Programme.

United Nations Security Council 2000, S/RES/1325 (2000), viewed 2 February 2015, www.un.org/en/ga/search/view_doc.asp?symbol=S/RES/1325(2000).

van Lierde, F 2011, *We, Widows of the Gun*, Cordaid, The Hague.

Women's Web 2012, *Interview with Binalakshmi Nepram: Women in the Shadow of the Gun*, 28 March, viewed 12 March 2015, www.womensweb.in/articles/binalakshmi-nepram-interview-manipur/.

Part V

Trafficking, displacement and citizenship

15

Statelessness in Asia

An entrenched but solvable problem

*Amal de Chickera and Laura van Waas**

Introduction

Each time the tragic stories of Rohingya boat refugees make international headlines, as they did again in mid-2015,[1] the global press reports on the enormous human suffering experienced by this group—both in their home country of Myanmar and in exile in Bangladesh, Malaysia, Thailand and elsewhere. The media explains how the Rohingya minority in Myanmar are ethnically, religiously and linguistically distinct from the majority of the country's population and how this makes them a target of discrimination at the hands of state and non-state entities alike. The press may also highlight how the Rohingya have been cast as outsiders, labelled as 'illegal immigrants' by their own country, further fuelling all manner of rights violations. Yet, relatively little consideration is given to the fact that they have been arbitrarily deprived of their nationality and are the largest known stateless population in Asia and the Pacific. Statelessness is a consequence and a marker of the extreme marginalisation, discrimination and persecution the Rohingya face, and it acts as a vector and catalyst for the subsequent human rights problems suffered. This is a reality that must be acknowledged if the root causes of the Rohingya's suffering and their displacement are to be successfully addressed.

That statelessness is a relatively neglected phenomenon is not only apparent in respect of the Rohingya. There are many more stateless populations in Asia, whose lack of nationality poses a severe challenge to their full enjoyment of human rights. Indeed, in absolute numbers, statelessness is documented as affecting far more people in Asia and the Pacific than in any other region of the world. Furthermore, in many Asian countries, statelessness is inadequately documented or even completely undocumented. Statelessness remains poorly understood and its interaction with other issues of international concern—including minority rights, women's rights, children's rights, migration, democratic governance and the rule of law—often fails to attract the attention it deserves.

This chapter places statelessness at its heart and explores different dimensions of this human rights issue. It offers a snapshot of statelessness in Asia, commenting on the scale and reach of the problem across the region. It then explores the interaction between statelessness and other human rights concerns in Asia, looking both at how different human rights violations have contributed to the denial and deprivation of nationality and how being stateless exposes those affected to subsequent, cumulative, human rights violations.[2]

Statelessness as a human rights concern

Statelessness is a problem of global proportions. It affects people all over the world and can have a harmful impact on them, their families and wider communities. Under international law, a stateless person is someone 'who is not considered as a national by any state under the operation of its law' (UN Convention on the Status of Stateless Persons 1954). Nationality, in this context, refers to a particular type of legal bond between an individual and a state.[3] It is a type of formal membership that results in rights and duties on both sides. The individual, for instance, holds the right to reside in the territory and the state a corresponding duty of admission; the individual holds a duty of allegiance (which may include a duty to perform military and/or national service) and the state the right to exercise diplomatic protection on behalf of its nationals abroad (Edwards 2014). Where a person lacks any nationality, he or she does not enjoy the attached rights or duties, resulting in a lack of protection.[4] A stateless person is seen and treated as a foreigner everywhere, as a national nowhere.

A person can be stateless in the country in which he or she was born, has always lived and has all family ties. Equally, a person can be stateless in a migratory context—for instance, losing nationality prior to, as a consequence of or at some point after crossing an international border. Statelessness rests on the fact of lacking any nationality, nothing more. Most stateless persons have not moved from their homes and live in what can be described as their own country. Yet, due to the added vulnerability of stateless persons to discrimination, human rights abuse and even persecution, statelessness can also prompt forced displacement.[5] Some stateless persons, then, become internally displaced persons (IDPs), asylum seekers and refugees,[6] as will also be apparent when looking more closely at the Asia regional context.

Wherever it occurs and whoever it affects, statelessness presents a human rights problem. All people have the right to a nationality, as set out in Article 15 of the Universal Declaration of Human Rights and reaffirmed in a host of other human rights instruments.[7] Statelessness is the worst possible result of the denial of this right. Moreover, statelessness often also results from the violation of other human rights. Each state sets the conditions for acquisition and loss of its nationality—an act which is an expression of self-determination and a legitimate exercise of sovereignty—within the limits set by international law. A person is left stateless either where he or she has failed to acquire any nationality to begin with (i.e. at birth), or where he or she has lost or been deprived a nationality that was once held, without acquiring another. Law, policy or practice which leaves people without nationality is commonly motivated by discrimination, for instance on the grounds of gender or race. Elsewhere, statelessness is a tool in the arsenal of those who would seek to manipulate the democratic process, with deprivation of nationality a means of silencing the opposition. Statelessness can also be a consequence of a failure to fulfil fundamental child rights such as the right to be registered at birth, or of a breakdown in the rule of law such that decisions on nationality are characterised by arbitrariness.

Having been denied the right to a nationality, stateless persons find themselves more vulnerable to other human rights problems. The universality of human rights rests on the premise that everyone enjoys a nationality (which is why this has also been affirmed as a human right). Indeed, the human rights system recognises that states may reserve some rights for their citizens—such as the right to participate in government[8]—placing these out of reach for stateless people. So, until statelessness is eradicated, the fundamental aspiration of universal human rights remains just that, an aspiration. Moreover, in practice, statelessness is a proven barrier to the ability to exercise a wide range of other rights, and discrimination between citizens and non-citizens in the enjoyment of rights is commonplace.[9]

The harsh reality for many stateless persons is a story of lack of opportunity, of lack of protection and of lack of participation. They face challenges in all areas of life, including: entering or completing schooling; accessing healthcare services for preventative medicine or to treat an injury or illness; finding gainful employment or signing a labour contract; buying or inheriting a house; registering a car or a business; obtaining a birth certificate, driving licence, marriage certificate or even death certificate; opening a bank account or getting a loan; falling back on social security; and enjoying a pension. Obtaining a passport or indeed being issued any form of identity documentation is extremely difficult if you are not the national of any country, such that many stateless persons have no proof that they exist and no means by which to identify themselves in their day-to-day interactions with the state or with private entities. International travel is almost inconceivable, unless by illicit—and dangerous—means. Free movement within the state of residence, even if it is where the person was born and has all his or her ties, can also be difficult due to the inability to provide proof of identity if stopped at a security checkpoint or in a random check by the police. Arbitrary arrest and detention, including in the person's home country, is not uncommon. In some cases, detention becomes prolonged or even indefinite, if the state is intent on expulsion, but no other country can be found which would allow the person to enter. Where a stateless person wants to assert their rights, or where they have become a victim of crime or exploitation, their statelessness can also stand in the way of getting help from the authorities or finding their way to a court. Their complaint may be readily dismissed or ignored, and they are powerless to take a stand against this due to their status of disenfranchisement.[10]

In response to the problem of statelessness, the United Nations (UN) developed two dedicated international treaties: the 1954 Convention Relating to the Status of Stateless Persons and the 1961 Convention on the Reduction of Statelessness.[11] As their names imply, the former—very similar in content and structure to the 1951 Convention relating to the Status of Refugees—sets out the protection framework for stateless persons, whereas the latter sets out the international standards related to the avoidance and reduction of statelessness. These two statelessness treaties complement and are informed by the many human rights treaties that contain standards relevant both to the protection of stateless persons and the avoidance/reduction of statelessness. For instance, the Convention on the Rights of the Child, which enjoys almost universal ratification, includes a safeguard against childhood statelessness,[12] and the Convention on the Elimination of all forms of Discrimination Against Women protects against gender discriminatory nationality laws—one of the causes of statelessness.[13] As such, statelessness is to be understood as a human rights concern for which international law provides a significant arsenal of norms and standards to counter both its occurrence and consequences.

A snapshot of statelessness in Asia

States hold the primary duty to identify stateless persons in order to implement their international obligations towards these populations under the two UN statelessness Conventions and in accordance with international human rights law. In the fulfilment of its statelessness mandate,[14] the United Nations High Commissioner for Refugees (UNHCR) has been tasked to undertake and share research on various aspects of statelessness, including on the scope of the problem. Other UN agencies, NGOs and academia also have a role to play in the identification and quantification of situations of statelessness through their respective mandates, missions and work.

At present, UNHCR is the only organisation which systematically collates statistics from a wide range of sources and regularly reports on the number of stateless persons in the world. UNHCR's statistical reporting currently covers a total tally of some 3.5 million stateless persons. Yet, gaps in the collection of data by governments, the UN and civil society, including as a result of methodological and other challenges inherent in identifying and counting stateless persons,[15] means that this number is not representative of the full scale of statelessness globally. UNHCR estimates that there are in fact 'over 10 million' stateless persons in the world and other research has verified that statelessness is indeed likely to be at least this number (Institute on Statelessness and Inclusion 2014).

In absolute numbers, statelessness is documented as affecting far more people in Asia and the Pacific than in any other region of the world, with UNHCR reporting a total of 1,422,850 persons under its statelessness mandate in Asia (Institute on Statelessness and Inclusion 2014). There are six countries in which the number of stateless persons is reported to be over 10,000 and a further nine which are currently marked by an asterisk in UNHCR's statistics (see Table 15.1), signifying that there is a large but undocumented stateless population. This means there are no less than 15 countries in which statelessness affects a significant number of people (out of 45 countries in total), more than in any other region.[16] It is furthermore evident that statelessness is severely underreported in Asia and the Pacific, with research suggesting that the true number of stateless persons in Asia and the Pacific is more than double what is currently accounted for in global statelessness statistics (Institute on Statelessness and Inclusion 2014). It may be far higher if, indeed, there are widespread problems of statelessness in India, Indonesia, Nepal and Pakistan, as some of the available information suggests there might be.

State succession, state-building and statelessness in Asia

The political map of the world is forever changing, with international borders shifting, emerging where previously there were none or disappearing as countries (re)unite. In Asia, the decolonisation process and, later, the dissolution of the USSR have been the cause of the most

Table 15.1 Stateless populations in Asia and Pacific

Countries in Asia and Pacific with over 10,000 stateless persons or marked with * (meaning there is a large population but no accurate data)	
Myanmar	810,000
Thailand	506,197
Malaysia	40,000
Brunei Darussalam	20,524
Kyrgyzstan	11,425
Viet Nam	11,000
Bhutan	*
Cambodia	*
India	*
Indonesia	*
Nepal	*
Pakistan	*
Papua New Guinea (PNG)	*
Sri Lanka	*
Uzbekistan	*

Source: UNHCR

significant such changes in recent history. Sri Lanka, Pakistan, Bangladesh, Cambodia, Laos, Brunei, Uzbekistan, Kyrgyzstan and Tajikistan: none of these—and more—existed as sovereign states in 1945. Wherever sovereignty over a particular territory is transferred, be it from one state to another or by way of the establishment of a newly independent state, the question emerges as to what happens to the nationality of the persons affected (Ziemele 2014). The establishment of new rules relating to nationality is therefore part-and-parcel of any case of state succession and indeed often this process plays an important role in the development or assertion of the new national identity of the state(s) concerned. For instance, when Bangladesh gained independence from Pakistan in 1971, Bangladeshi nationality had to be constituted for the first time and Pakistani nationality regulations had to be readjusted to factor in the new situation. In these circumstances, the potential for statelessness to arise is significant as the alignment of nationality rules to ensure that no-one is left behind is not necessarily given sufficient attention. Problems can be particularly acute where discrimination against minority groups or (historically) migrant communities also influences the content and application of nationality laws.[17]

Asia is no exception and many of the situations of statelessness that have arisen in the region stem from post-state-succession nationality policy. Some of these have now been largely resolved—including the Urdu-speaking or 'Bihari' community in Bangladesh who were finally confirmed as citizens by a High Court ruling in 2008.[18] Elsewhere, however, statelessness that was prompted by state succession has yet to be fully addressed. Across former Soviet states in Central Asia, in particular, statelessness continues to affect many tens of thousands of people—now almost a quarter of a century after dissolution. Moreover, although the numbers are diminishing as these states take efforts to further facilitate access to nationality for stateless persons on their territory, the problem is likely still to be larger than current statistical reporting would suggest.[19]

It is also important to acknowledge that state-building processes, including the (re)definition of nationality policy, enumeration of populations and solidification of borders, can occur independently of state succession or at a different moment in a state's history. In Thailand, for instance, the 1950s saw the first concerted efforts by the state to document its nationals. Indigenous communities living in the outer reaches of the kingdom and whose traditional tribal areas indeed straddled the rather porous—and previously largely meaningless—borders, such that their kin could also be found living in neighbouring states, were not fully included in these exercises. This had a lasting impact on their access to nationality: today, there are still over half a million stateless persons in Thailand, predominantly members of these communities collectively known as 'hill tribes' for whom the seeds of exclusion were sowed by these state-building processes many decades ago.[20]

Statelessness and minority rights in Asia

As alluded to above, there is a strong nexus between statelessness and discrimination. In many instances, discrimination is the root cause of statelessness and inevitably, statelessness results in further discrimination. While the harmful impact of gender discrimination will be discussed below, ethnic and religious discrimination can disenfranchise entire groups over multiple generations, leaving them with little hope of accessing nationality and integrating in society on equal terms. The politics of identity and belonging also make this type of statelessness among the most difficult to solve, for it is not just about changing laws, but about engaging minds and deconstructing socio-political prejudices and stereotypes that have endured decades, even centuries.

The 1982 Citizenship Act of Myanmar is a prime example of how racially discriminatory laws can create mass-scale statelessness for entire groups over multiple generations. According to this law and a subsequent Schedule, automatic acquisition of nationality is reserved for members of the 135 recognised 'ethnic nationalities' of Myanmar (Citizenship Law 1982). The Rohingya and several other ethnic groups have been excluded from this list. The impact has been harshest on the Rohingya, an ethnic, religious (Muslim), and linguistic minority who predominantly live in northern Rakhine state, who have suffered severe social and institutional marginalisation for decades.[21] Described as one of the most persecuted minority groups in the world, the treatment of the Rohingya has attracted the attention and indeed condemnation of the international human rights community.[22] Other communities stripped of nationality on the grounds of ethnicity include persons of Chinese, Indian and Nepali ancestries.[23] According to Minority Rights Group International, persons of Chinese descent account for some 3% of Myanmar's population and persons of Indian descent a further 2% (Minority Rights Group 2009). Many of them are likely to still be stateless.[24] There are no other reports on how many persons from these, or other minority groups in Myanmar, are stateless.

Malaysia is another country in the region that has a large stateless population as a result of ethnic discrimination. UNHCR reports an estimated 40,000 stateless persons in Peninsular Malaysia,[25] who are ethnic Indians (mainly Tamils), are not treated as Malaysian nationals.[26] They were brought to Malaysia from India several generations ago while the country was under British rule and are elsewhere described as 'stateless Indians'.[27] In all, ethnic Indians constitute a total of 7.8% of Malaysia's population, or 1.9 million people (DHRRA Malaysia 2014). The exact number of people affected by statelessness within Malaysia's Indian community remains highly contested (and heavily politicised), with some suggesting it is as low as 9,000 and others claiming that as many as 300,000 are stateless (Izwan 2012). In Brunei Darussalam, according to UNHCR statistics, there are 20,524 stateless persons of Indian and Chinese descent, which is equal to 5% of the population or one in every 20 people in the country.

Bhutan, while marked by an asterisk in UNHCR statistical data (see Table 15.1), has an estimated stateless population of over 80,000. People of Nepali origin have been migrating to Bhutan as workers since the nineteenth century, settling mostly in the south of the country, where they are also referred to as Lhotshampas. Descendants of these ethnic Nepali in Bhutan were granted Bhutanese nationality pursuant to the 1958 Citizenship Act. However, in the 1980s, they came to be seen as a security threat. Bhutan passed a new Citizenship Act in 1985 with strict nationality criteria that were applied retroactively, essentially recognising only those who could prove their residence in Bhutan prior to 1958 as nationals. As the new Citizenship Act was being enforced, Bhutan forcibly expelled over 100,000 ethnic Nepali to Nepal, where they became stateless refugees. Many ethnic Nepali remain in Bhutan where they are reportedly still affected by statelessness, explaining why UNHCR marks the country in its statistical table with an asterisk (see Table 15.1). The 2005 national census identified 81,976 people in Bhutan as 'non-national residents'—amounting to approximately 13% of the total population of the country. Bhutanese NGO groups claim that these are mainly ethnic Nepali and they are not recognised as nationals (Bhutanese Refugee Support Group & Association of Human Rights Activists 2007). Human Rights Watch (2007) also reported that those registered as 'non-national residents' in the 2005 census were not being issued citizenship identification cards. There are no more recent estimates of the size of the population and no information of the problem being addressed in Bhutan.[28]

Statelessness and women's and children's rights in Asia

A disregard for ethnic or religious minorities is not the only way in which discrimination manifests itself in nationality law and practice—there may also be discrimination on the basis of gender. In its most severe form, gender-biased nationality policy precludes women from passing their nationality to their children on the same terms as men, creating a risk of statelessness for children whose father, for instance, is stateless, absent, deceased, or unwilling or unable to transmit his own nationality. This is evidently problematic from both a women's and a children's rights perspective—violating the provisions of Article 9 of the Convention on the Elimination of All Forms of Discrimination Against Women and Articles 2, 3 and 7 of the Convention on the Rights of the Child. Globally, there are 27 countries where such discriminatory nationality laws are still in place, of which five are in Asia and the Pacific.[29] Yet there are also signs of change in the region, with Sri Lanka, Indonesia and Bangladesh all having reformed their laws on this point since 2000 (UNHCR 2015a).

One country in which gender discrimination in nationality law is a current and highly contentious issue is Nepal, where women cannot confer, acquire, change and retain citizenship fully, independently and on equal terms with men. While Article 8(2)(b) of the Interim Constitution of 2007 states that anyone 'whose father *or mother* is a citizen of Nepal at the birth of such person' is eligible for Nepali citizenship, other constitutional provisions, the Citizenship Act and Rules of Nepal, and the discriminatory manner in which the law is implemented by authorities, all contribute to a reality which is discriminatory of women, with significant negative impacts on their offspring.[30] For example, according to Article 8(7) of the Interim Constitution, the children of Nepali women and foreign men can only access citizenship through naturalisation, and not by right, through descent. There is no similar restriction on men. One of the consequences of Article 8(7) is that state authorities in practice refuse to accept citizenship applications submitted only by mothers, as they require proof of the father's identity to establish that he is not a foreigner. According to a study undertaken in 2013, 4.3 million Nepalese people aged 16 and above did not have citizenship certificates, representing nearly 24% of the total population of Nepal (Forum for Women, Law and Development (FWLD) 2013) with men more likely than women to be in possession of citizenship certificates (Forum for Women, Law and Development (FWLD) 2014). The US Department of State (2013) acknowledges the range of estimates for stateless persons to be 2.3 to 2.6 million in Nepal. It is important to be mindful that where a person lacks citizenship documentation, this does not necessarily mean in all cases that the person is not recognised as a national, yet these statistics provide some insight into the potential scope of the problem of statelessness and its discriminatory nature. Significantly, both boys and girls have been deprived of Nepali citizenship because their mothers have not been allowed to pass their nationality to them, thus the victims of gender discriminatory law are as likely to be men as they are women.

Discriminatory nationality laws are not the only threat to the realisation of the child's right to a nationality. Another significant challenge is posed by birth registration systems which are inaccessible to certain populations and leave them without proof of place and date of birth, or parentage. This can create a risk of statelessness if the claim to nationality by those affected is likely to be contested by the state concerned, such as where the nationality status of the parents is also unclear or the children are perceived as foreign by the authorities. In Malaysia, for instance, the Bajau Laut (also known as Sama Dilaut or 'sea-gypsies')[31] is one population widely reported to be affected by or at risk of statelessness, although the numbers are unclear. Ambiguity surrounds the nationality status of many within this community who are undocumented and whose ties with the state are contested. The number of Bajau Laut children without documents is expected to be high due to their nomadic lifestyle even if they are born in Malaysian waters, with one report suggesting that 60% of one Marine Park's 2,500 resident Bajau Laut population (or 1,500 people) were stateless (Wood, Suliansa & Brunt 2007). This is just a small proportion of the total Bajau Laut population estimated at being approximately 450,000 (Minority Rights Group 2016) and it is unclear whether the level of statelessness among this group is representative.

In China, where the problem of statelessness has not been mapped and the number of persons affected is unknown,[32] significant problems have been reported with regard to access to birth registration. Births are documented through the family booklet called the 'hukou', which also serves as the primary ID document and is key for access to education, state welfare, legal employment, and is necessary for daily life in China. According to the 2010 census around 13 million children in China lack birth registration (*People's Daily* 2011), although independent analysis revealed the number could be as high as 37 million children (Goodkind 2004). One group that is particularly affected is that of children denied birth registration as a result of family planning policies, better known as the 'one child policy'. Until the parents have paid a 'social compensation fee', their children are denied birth registration (Greenhalgh 2006).[33] Single mothers are usually also fined social compensation fees, and some mothers face great difficulty registering their child's birth even if they pay a fine, because they lack a marriage certificate (Wu 2013). Many children manage to secure birth registration later in their life, but some do not. At present, there is no indication that the denial of registration in the hukou system leads to non-recognition of Chinese nationality and therefore directly results in statelessness. Yet, those who continue to be refused registration in the system are denied legal identity, and may be at risk of statelessness, particularly if they leave the country, further complicating the establishment or recognition of their ties to China.

Statelessness, migration and forced displacement in Asia

Given the nexus between statelessness and discrimination, it is not surprising that some stateless groups are also victims of persecution and have had to flee their homes in search of security and stability elsewhere. Others migrate in search of better economic prospects. Thus, statelessness is sometimes a root cause of forced displacement and migration. It can also be a consequence of displacement or migration, particularly when the children of refugees are not documented or provided with adequate protection.

As previously discussed, during the 1990s, over 100,000 ethnic Nepali Bhutanese—often referred to as 'Lhotshampas'—were displaced across the border into Nepal after being arbitrarily deprived of their nationality. Those who were forcibly expelled have not since been allowed to return and despite repeated attempts to negotiate solutions with both the governments of Bhutan and Nepal, neither country is willing to offer them a way out of their plight. More than 83,000 have now been resettled to eight countries which have agreed to provide a durable solution (UNHCR 2016).[34] By the end of 2013, just over 30,000 remained in refugee camps in Nepal—all of whom are *stateless* refugees.

India has long been seen as a country where statelessness is a real problem, but reliable data remains unforthcoming. There are, in fact, various migrant groups in India which are reported to be affected by statelessness, which makes it a complex environment in which to map the issue. For example, the Chakmas and Hajongs migrated to India decades ago from the Chittagong Hill Tracts of what was then East Pakistan (now Bangladesh) and have settled in Arunachal Pradesh. Despite a Supreme Court judgment in favour of recognising the Chakmas as Indian citizens, this is reportedly still not the case in practice (Singh 2010). The number of Chakmas is estimated to be some 60,000–65,000 persons (Singh 2010).[35] Other populations in India which are reportedly affected by statelessness include: Hindus from Pakistan who came to India after the 1947 partition riots and are not considered as Indian citizens; inhabitants of the Chitmahals (Indian enclaves in Bangladesh); persons of Chinese origin in Kolkata; Nepali speakers in the north-eastern states; Bhutanese of Nepali origin living in eastern/north-eastern India; Bihari Muslims from Bangladesh (Calcutta Research Group 2011); and Rohingya refugees in India. Neither the total size of these populations nor the prevalence of statelessness among them is clear—additionally, in some reporting on these groups it is not evident that the term 'stateless' is being applied in the sense of the international legal definition.[36]

In Cambodia, the populations of ethnic Vietnamese, ethnic Chinese and children of other ethnic minorities have been variously identified as possibly being impacted by statelessness.[37] The extent to which this is the case remains largely unmapped and the overall size of these populations is also uncertain—perhaps unsurprisingly, against the historic backdrop of persecution and ethnic cleansing of minorities during the rule of the Khmer Rouge.

There is a sizeable stateless population of an estimated 9,378 West Papuan *refugees* in Papua New Guinea.[38] In the mid-1980s, several thousand West Papuans fled from the Indonesian part of New Guinea Island, across the border into Papua New Guinea, to escape political turmoil. Many remain there to this day. Their long-term absence from Indonesia led to the loss of Indonesian citizenship under the operation of the nationality law, though most have not been able to naturalise as Papuan citizens because they did not meet the criteria or could not pay the fee.

As previously discussed, the overwhelming majority of Rohingya in Myanmar are stateless and this has acted as a catalyst or even a conduit for severe human rights violations and prompted displacement on a massive scale. Stateless Rohingya refugees can be found in large groups in several nearby states and further afield, while smaller numbers have sought asylum in many more countries. In Bangladesh, forcibly displaced stateless Rohingya account for almost all of the 231,145 persons reported in UNHCR's statistical data as refugees or in refugee-like situations.[39] According to other sources, the number of Rohingya in Bangladesh is in excess of 300,000 and perhaps as high as 500,000.[40] Since a new wave of increased and sustained violence against the Rohingya began in 2012, an estimated 100,000 have fled Myanmar, but their situation is very fluid and difficult to map, hence it is difficult to establish where they are presently located.[41] According to UNHCR, Malaysia currently hosts 45,910 Rohingya refugees registered with the agency (UNHCR Malaysia 2015). UNHCR has also registered 12,320 'Myanmar Muslims', a category that is likely to include within it Rohingya who are stateless (UNHCR Malaysia 2015). There are likely to be many Rohingya who have also not registered with UNHCR (Equal Rights Trust 2014). There are also Rohingya populations of varying sizes in Thailand and Indonesia; India and Pakistan; and further afield in the Arab Gulf, in particular Saudi Arabia (Institute on Statelessness and Inclusion 2014).

Malaysia is also home to a large population of Indonesian and Filipino migrant descent or Filipino refugees. According to the 2010 census, almost 900,000 of Sabah's 3.2 million population consists of non-Malaysian citizens (Department of Statistics Malaysia 2010). Even though it remains unclear if this figure accounts for all the undocumented populations, an estimate of 200,000 to 500,000 undocumented migrants live in Sabah.[42] Within this undocumented population, an unknown number of Indonesian migrants or migrant workers may be affected by statelessness because they lost their nationality on the basis of their more than five years' residence abroad without consular registration under the pre-2006 Indonesian nationality law, and have not reacquired it.[43] In the case of irregular Filipino migrants, the absence of a permanent consular presence for the Philippines due to the unresolved dispute between the governments of Malaysia and the Philippines over the sovereignty of Sabah combined with low levels of birth registration can result in irregular Filipino migrants and their children lacking documentation to prove their link to the Philippines, risking difficulties in proving citizenship.

Conclusion

This chapter has provided a brief overview of the complex and little-documented story of statelessness in Asia, and the resultant human rights challenges. It has shown that there are multiple factors which cause statelessness, including state succession, the legacy of colonialism, arbitrary deprivation of nationality, administrative barriers and lack of documentation and the inheritance of statelessness. Also evident is that there is almost always an element of discrimination and/or arbitrariness at play when individuals or entire groups become stateless. Discrimination and arbitrariness can manifest in an overt, aggressive or even persecutory manner, such as when large communities are deprived of their nationality based on ethnicity or religion; or it may be subtler and more latent, such as the failure of states to prioritise legal reform that would plug gaps in the law which could cause statelessness. Thus, it is worth recalling that while states do have significant freedom to set out their own membership criteria, they also have a responsibility to protect against discrimination and arbitrariness, and to uphold international standards. Statelessness most often occurs when states fail to do so—and this is the story of statelessness in Asia. Before concluding with a few positive examples of what has and what can be done to solve statelessness in Asia, it is important to reflect on some of the barriers to addressing this complex human rights issue.

The relatively poor treaty ratification record and lack of strong regional human rights mechanisms in Asia

Only a handful of Asian countries (including Fiji, Kiribati, Turkmenistan and the Philippines) are party to the 1954 Convention Relating to the Status of Stateless Persons, and even fewer are party to the 1961 Convention on the Reduction of Statelessness. While ratification of the core human rights treaties (including the CRC, CEDAW, ICCPR and ICESCR) is much stronger in the region, this is not complemented by strong regional human rights frameworks. The ASEAN Inter-governmental Commission on Human Rights (AICHR) has very few powers and is in its infancy, other sub-regional groupings like the South Asian Association for Regional Cooperation (SAARC) have no human rights bodies whatsoever. Thus, human rights actors in Asia are at a disadvantage when compared with those in Europe, the Americas and Africa, and it is difficult to envisage strong regional pressure or solutions for Asia's statelessness (or indeed any other human rights) challenge. The failure to galvanise strong regional action on the Rohingya issue is an example of how significant a handicap the lack of a strong regional framework can be.

The politics of belonging, exclusion and discrimination

Possibly the biggest barrier to ending the injustice of statelessness and ensuring the inclusion of formerly stateless persons is that discrimination, prejudice, notions of who belongs and who does not, and socio-political stereotypes are at the heart of statelessness. There is no easy fix to such historically rooted problems, which can only be addressed through engaging and challenging societal prejudices and attitudes. While legal reform helps, reform alone is never adequate. Furthermore, reform is often not possible until dominant attitudes have softened.

The challenge of intergenerational statelessness

The single biggest cause of statelessness in Asia (and globally) is the inheritance of statelessness. Many contemporary situations of statelessness have their roots at a particular moment in history, such as state succession, the first registration of citizens or the adoption of a discriminatory nationality decree denationalising an entire group, as outlined earlier in this chapter. Yet these situations endure and even grow over time because the states concerned have not put any measures in place to stop statelessness being passed from parent to child—or do not implement existing measures to that effect. Furthermore, these situations migrate to new countries along with the (often forced) migration of stateless persons abroad, as in migratory contexts too, statelessness is allowed to continue into the next generations. This means that most new cases of statelessness affect children, from birth, such that they may never know the protection of nationality. It also means that stateless groups suffer from intergenerational marginalisation and exclusion, which snowballs with each generation, affecting the social fabric of entire communities.

The multi-faceted nature of statelessness

Statelessness cannot be seen or addressed in isolation. It impacts on—and is impacted by—other issues and disciplines such as international development, humanitarian affairs, human rights, children's rights, economics, healthcare, democracy, peace and security and forced migration. Statelessness will only be successfully addressed if such disciplines recognise its relevance and respond to it in an integrated way.

There are various other challenges and barriers to addressing statelessness in Asia. But these four broadly encapsulate why statelessness can be such an entrenched problem. However, it is important to hold onto the fact that statelessness is nonetheless solvable. The following are some examples of good practices in this regard.

Vietnam has taken steps to facilitate the naturalisation of part of its resident stateless population in recent years, as well as to improve safeguards against statelessness in the country's nationality laws.[44] However, today, some 11,000 stateless persons in the country still await a solution, including many women who previously renounced Vietnamese nationality following marriage to a foreign national and were left stateless. In Sri Lanka, statelessness has largely been addressed by successive legislative initiatives and in particular by a 2003 law recognising the so-called 'hill Tamils' (Tamils of south Indian origin whose ancestors were brought to Ceylon as it was then known by the British colonisers to work on hill country plantations) as nationals and a subsequent citizenship campaign that distributed identity documents as proof of citizenship to those concerned.[45] In Indonesia, statelessness had in the past affected large numbers of persons of Chinese origin—as many as 300,000 in 1992, according to one report (Minority Rights Group [undated]). This appears to have since been largely resolved due to both facilitated acquisition of Chinese citizenship by much of this population and later the reform of Indonesia's nationality law in 2006 which made it easier for ethnic Chinese to acquire Indonesian nationality (Suryadinata 2008). Sri Lanka, Indonesia and Bangladesh have also amended gender discriminatory nationality laws to ensure that women can now pass on their nationality on equal terms with men.

These success stories are examples to hold up and provide lessons that can be learned, when attempting to solve some of the most entrenched and complex statelessness problems in the world. They demonstrate how often strong national-level commitment (many a time initiated and sustained by civil society movements) is an essential ingredient for such change. Nevertheless, particularly when there does not appear to be strong will at the national level to address statelessness, there are also global frameworks which can be drawn on. In November 2014, the UNHCR launched an ambitious campaign to end statelessness by 2024. The impetus that this campaign has provided is placing statelessness on the international agenda, and it brings with it greater visibility and potential for global collaboration to support national efforts.[46] Given the central interplay between statelessness and human rights, the Universal Periodic Review and UN Treaty Body processes provide critical opportunities to raise questions pertaining to statelessness for states to answer, and also for the international community to recommend action. Through strategic, collaborative and concerted action, it is possible to address statelessness holistically and to protect and include the stateless and formerly stateless.

Notes

*Co-Directors of the Institute on Statelessness and Inclusion. See www.InstituteSI.org for more information. The authors would like to thank María José Recalde Vela for her editorial assistance.

1 For an overview of the 2015 boat crisis, please see the Institute on Statelessness and Inclusion (2015a), which has a special spotlight section on it.
2 Please note that this chapter summarises and updates relevant sections of the following report by the same authors: Institute on Statelessness and Inclusion, 2014, *The World's Stateless*, http://institutesi.org/worldsstateless.pdf.
3 Citizenship is commonly used as a synonym for nationality, also referring to this specific type of legal bond between a person and a state. In some disciplines and various domestic or regional contexts, nationality and citizenship can also have distinct meanings, but within writing on statelessness—and in this report—the two terms are used interchangeably.
4 It is important to note, however, that all persons—including those who are stateless—are protected by international human rights law. Thus, while the stateless may not necessarily benefit from rights attached to citizenship (such as the right to vote), they are entitled to the general protection of international human rights law.
5 See, for the interaction between statelessness and displacement, Norwegian Refugee Council and Tilburg University (2015).
6 Where a person who 'is not considered as a national by any state under the operation of its law' also falls within the scope of the 1951 UN Convention relating to the Status of Refugees, he or she is a *stateless refugee*.
7 See, for a compilation of extracts relating to nationality and statelessness from selected universal and regional human rights instruments, UNHCR (2009).
8 See, for instance, Article 25 of the International Covenant on Civil and Political Rights, 1966, UNTS, vol. 999.
9 See, for instance, Office of the High Commissioner for Human Rights (OHCHR) (2006); see also, UN Human Rights Council (2011).
10 See, for more on the human impact of statelessness, UNHCR (2014a).
11 United Nations Convention on the Reduction of Statelessness, 1961, UNTS vol. 989.
12 See Articles 7 and 8, read in conjunction with Article 3, Convention on the Rights of the Child, 1989, GA Res. A/RES/44/25.
13 See Article 9, Convention on the Elimination of All Forms of Discrimination Against Women, 1979, GA Res. A/RES/34/180.
14 On UNHCR's mandate to assist states to deal with statelessness, see, for instance, Manly (2014).
15 See Institute on Statelessness and Inclusion (2015b).
16 Please note that UNHCR has updated its statistics in its Global Trends report for 2014, which is available at: http://unhcr.org/556725e69.html. Page 44 onwards has various tables annexed to the report, providing the statistical breakdown of populations of concern to UNHCR, including the stateless. Accordingly, UNHCR now estimates the stateless population in Uzbekistan at 86,703, and the total counted stateless population for Asia is 1,509,696.
17 See also the below section on statelessness and minority rights.
18 See further on the cause and eventual resolution of these situations of statelessness, UNHCR (2015b).
19 For instance, with the UNHCR reported figure of 6,942 falling under the 10,000 benchmark for 'significant' stateless populations used throughout this report, Kazakhstan is not included in the table above showing the largest situations of statelessness in Asia and the Pacific. Nevertheless, alternative sources of data suggest that the number of stateless persons may be substantially higher—possibly into the tens of thousands. See further Institute on Statelessness and Inclusion (2014: 82–83).
20 There are many reports discussing the situation of this group. For a summary, see the series of blog posts by L. van Waas entitled 'Reflections on Thailand', the first of which is available here: http://statelessprog.blogspot.nl/2013/02/reflections-on-thailand-1-protracted.html.

21 It is important to note that according to the letter of the law, most Rohingya should still be eligible for naturalised citizenship (a 'lesser' form of citizenship with fewer rights attached, the acquisition of which is not automatic and which can, once acquired, be deprived on multiple grounds). However, due to discriminatory implementation of the law and (related) lack or loss of documentation, very few have been able to acquire citizenship by naturalisation.
22 See, for instance, Human Rights Council Resolutions A/HRC/19/L.30 of 20 March 2012; A/HRC/22/L.20 of 15 March 2013; A/HRC/25/L.21 of 24 March 2014; and A/HRC/29/L.30 of 3 July 2015.
23 See, for instance, IRIN News (2014); see also High-Level Committee on the Indian Diaspora (2001: 60).
24 See the country section on Myanmar in chapter 20 of the Report of the High-Level Committee on the Indian Diaspora (2001: 60), which suggested that despite the government of Myanmar continuing to grant citizenship to ethnic Indians in 'small batches', between 200,000 and 400,000 are still stateless.
25 According to a footnote in UNHCR's statelessness statistical table for Malaysia, the estimate is 'based on NGO and media reports, some citing official sources'.
26 See, more recently, UNHCR (2014b).
27 See, for instance, Human Rights Watch (2011).
28 For a more recent discussion of the problem of statelessness in the country, including the 2008 constitutional changes which 'formalise the high bar to citizenship established by the 1985 Citizenship Act', see Ferraro (2012).
29 These are Brunei Darussalam, Iran, Kiribati, Malaysia and Nepal. See further UNHCR (2015c).
30 For a more detailed analysis see, Nepal Civil Society Network of Citizenship Rights, the Global Campaign for Equal Nationality Rights and the Institute on Statelessness and Inclusion (2015). See also, Forum for Women, Law and Development (FWLD) and National Women Commission (2014).
31 See, for instance, Clifton et al. (2014).
32 This section is based on research and analysis conducted by Stephanie Gordon, consultant and PhD candidate specialising in the study of civil registration laws and practices in China—see further Institute on Statelessness and Inclusion (2014: 81–82).
33 For case studies see Wu (2013) or Baklinski (2014).
34 For an impression of life as a Bhutanese stateless refugee, see Das (2014).
35 See also, Calcutta Research Group (undated).
36 See, for instance, media reports relating to the enclaves between Bangladesh and India; Behar (2011).
37 See, for instance, Asia Pacific Refugee Rights Network webpage on Cambodia, available at: http://aprrn.info/wiki/tiki-index.php?page=Cambodia; Duoos (2012); Miller (2012); Jesuit Refugee Service (JRS) (2013); Radio Free Asia (2014). Relevant literature also identifies the Khmer Krom as a group affected by statelessness in Cambodia but in fact this group is likely to possess Vietnamese nationality on the basis of previous historic residence in Vietnam and the fact that access to Cambodian nationality is experienced as problematic is erroneously conflated with statelessness.
38 However, we believe that it is necessary and correct for these and all other stateless refugees to also be included in statelessness statistics.
39 Country of origin data for refugees in Bangladesh indicates that all but 20 of this number are from Myanmar. Some 31,000 of these Rohingya refugees are officially registered and reside in two refugee camps. The remaining displaced Rohingya population living in Bangladesh is not registered with either UNHCR or the authorities but is estimated by UNHCR as 200,000 persons.
40 In media, estimates for the number of Rohingya in the country varies between 200,000 and 500,000 persons. See, for instance, IRIN News (2013); and Kaladan National Press Network (2014).
41 The Arakan Project estimates that approximately 94,500 Rohingya made the boat journey between June 2012 and July 2014. The majority of the boats found their way to Malaysia, either directly or after being 'helped on' by Thai authorities, a few proceeded to Indonesia or Australia while some only made it to Sri Lanka. As many as 2,000 are believed to have gone missing at sea—presumably drowned (making this one of the most dangerous irregular migration routes in the world).
42 Compare the figures cited in the Malaysian press, here: *Free Malaysia Today* (2011); and here: *The Borneo Post* (2012).
43 According to IOM statistics, Malaysia hosts well over a million labour migrants from Indonesia. See IOM (2010).
44 See, for instance, McKinsey and Tan (2011); US Department of State (2013).

45 See, for instance, Wijetunga and Tan (2004).
46 For more information on the global campaign, visit the #ibelong campaign's website, http://ibelong.unhcr.org/en/home.do.

References

Baklinski, T 2014, 'Chinese father of four commits suicide over one-child policy fines so his children can go to school', *Life Site News*, 26 May, www.lifesitenews.com/news/chinese-father-of-four-commits-suicide-over-one-child-policy-fines-so-his-c.

Behar, C 2011, 'The land that maps forgot', *The Economist*, 15 February, www.economist.com/blogs/banyan/2011/02/enclaves_between_india_and_bangladesh.

Bhutanese Refugee Support Group & Association of Human Rights Activists 2007, *NGO Response to the Second Periodic Report of the Kingdom of Bhutan under the Convention on the Rights of the Child.*

The Borneo Post 2012, 'Najib announces setting up of RCI to probe issue of illegal immigrants in Sabah', 2 June, www.theborneopost.com/2012/06/02/najib-announces-setting-up-of-rci-to-probe-issue-of-illegal-immigrants-in-sabah-new/.

Calcutta Research Group (undated), *Executive Summary of the Report on 'The State of Being Stateless: A Case Study of the Chakmas of Arunachal Pradesh'.*

Calcutta Research Group 2011, *Mapping the Stateless in India—phase 2*, www.mcrg.ac.in/Statelessness/Statelessness_Report_2011.pdf.

Clifton, J, Acciaioli, G, Brunt, H, Dressler, WH, Fabinyi, M & Singh, S 2014, 'Statelessness and conservation: exploring the implications of an international governance agenda', *Tilburg Law Review*, vol. 19, no. 1–2, pp. 81–89.

Das, B 2014, 'In pictures: Nepal's Bhutanese refugees', *Aljazeera*, 28 January, www.aljazeera.com/indepth/inpictures/2014/01/pictures-nepal-bhutanese-refug-2014127134634213108.html.

Department of Statistics Malaysia 2010, *Population Distribution and Basic Demographic Characteristics 2010*, Kuala Lumpur, www.statistics.gov.my/portal/download_Population/files/census2010/Taburan_Penduduk_dan_Ciri-ciri_Asas_Demografi.pdf.

DHRRA Malaysia 2014, 'Factsheet on mapping and registration', 14 September, http://dhrramalaysia.org.my/fact-sheet-on-mapping-registration/.

Duoos, T 2012, *To Be Determined: Stories of People Facing Statelessness*, JRS Asia Pacific.

Edwards, A 2014, 'The meaning of nationality in international law in an era of human rights: procedural and substantive aspects', in A Edwards & L van Waas (eds), *Nationality and Statelessness under International Law*, Cambridge University Press.

Equal Rights Trust 2014, *Equal Only in Name: The Human Rights of Stateless Rohingya in Malaysia*, www.equalrightstrust.org/content/equal-only-name-malaysia-full-report.

Ferraro, M 2012, 'Stateless in Shangri-La: minority rights, citizenship and belonging in Bhutan', *Stanford Journal of International Law*, vol. 48, pp. 305–435.

Forum for Women, Law and Development (FWLD) 2013, *Acquisition of Citizenship Certificate in Nepal: Estimating Prevalence.*

Forum for Women, Law and Development (FWLD) 2014, *Acquisition of Citizenship Certificate in Nepal: Understanding Trends, Barriers and Impacts.*

Forum for Women, Law and Development (FWLD) & National Women Commission 2014, *Analysis of Nepalese Citizenship Laws from a Gender Perspective.*

Free Malaysia Today 2011, 'Illegal immigrants in Sabah: a numbers game', 28 August, www.freemalaysiatoday.com/category/nation/2011/08/28/illegal-immigrants-in-sabah-a-numbers-game/.

Goodkind, D 2004, 'China's missing children: the 2000 census underreporting surprise', *Population Studies*, vol. 58 no. 3, pp. 281–295.

Greenhalgh, S 2006, 'Planned births, unplanned persons', *American Ethnologist*, vol. 30, no. 2, pp. 196–215.

High-Level Committee on the Indian Diaspora 2001, *Report of the High-Level Committee on the Indian Diaspora*, www.indiandiaspora.nic.in/diasporapdf/chapter20.pdf.

Human Rights Watch 2007, *Last Hope: The Need for Durable Solutions for Bhutanese Refugees in Nepal*, New York, www.hrw.org/reports/2007/bhutan0507/.

Human Rights Watch 2011, 'Stateless: Undocumented Indians, South East Asia'.

Institute on Statelessness and Inclusion 2014, *The World's Stateless*, www.institutesi.org/worldsstateless.pdf.

Institute on Statelessness and Inclusion 2015a, *Statelessness Monthly Bulletin*, May 2015, www.institutesi.org/stateless_bulletin_2015-05.pdf.
Institute on Statelessness and Inclusion 2015b, 'Counting the world's stateless: reflections on statistical reporting on statelessness', in *UNHCR Statistical Yearbook 2013*, UNHCR, Geneva, www.unhcr.org/54cf9bd69.html.
IOM 2010, *Labour Migration from Indonesia*, Geneva, www.iom.int/jahia/webdav/shared/shared/mainsite/published_docs/Final-LM-Report-English.pdf.
IRIN News 2013, 'Bangladesh's "Rohingya strategy" stokes concern', 26 November, www.irinnews.org/feature/2013/11/26/bangladesh%E2%80%99s-%E2%80%9Crohingya-strategy%E2%80%9D-stokes-concern.
IRIN News 2014, 'The forgotten Ghurkhas of Burma', 20 May.
Izwan 2012, 'Najib debunks 300,000 stateless Indian claim, says only 9000', *The Malaysian Insider*, www.themalaysianinsider.com/malaysia/article/najib-debunks-300000-statelessindian- claim-says-only-9000.
Jesuit Refugee Service (JRS) 2013, *Brief on the Khmer Krom*, www.jrscambodia.org/publication/Brief/KhmerKrom_JRSCambodia_June13.pdf.
Kaladan National Press Network 2014, 'Bangladesh bars on marriage with Rohingya refugees', www.kaladanpress.org/index.php/news/371-news2014/july-2014/4588-bangladesh-bars-on-marriage-with-rohingya-refugees.html.
McKinsey, K & Tan, V 2011, 'Statelessness: former refugees win citizenship, and now dream of home ownership', UNHCR, Geneva, www.unhcr.org/news/latest/2011/9/4e7204db6/statelessness-former-refugees-win-citizenship-dream-home-ownership.html.
Manly, M 2014, 'UNHCR's mandate and activities to address statelessness', in A. Edwards and L. van Waas (eds), *Nationality and Statelessness under International Law*, Cambridge University Press.
Miller, M 2012, *Ethnic and Racial Minorities in Asia: Inclusion or Exclusion?*, Routledge.
Minority Rights Group (undated), *World Directory of Minorities and Indigenous Peoples: Indonesia—Chinese*, http://minorityrights.org/minorities/chinese-3/.
Minority Rights Group 2009, *World Directory of Minorities and Indigenous Peoples: Myanmar/Burma*, http://minorityrights.org/country/myanmarburma/.
Minority Rights Group 2016, '*World Directory of Minorities and Indigenous Peoples: Malaysia—Indigenous Peoples and Ethnic Minorities in Sabah*', http://minorityrights.org/minorities/indigenous-peoples-and-ethnic-minorities-in-sabah/.
Nepal Civil Society Network of Citizenship Rights, the Global Campaign for Equal Nationality Rights & the Institute on Statelessness and Inclusion 2015, *Joint Submission to the Human Rights Council at the 23rd Session of the Universal Periodic Review: Nepal*, www.institutesi.org/NepalUPR2015.pdf.
Norwegian Refugee Council & Tilburg University 2015, 'Statelessness and Displacement: Scoping Paper', www.nrc.no/arch/_img/9197390.pdf.
Office of the High Commissioner for Human Rights (OHCHR) 2006, *The Rights of Non-citizens*, Geneva, www.ohchr.org/Documents/Publications/noncitizensen.pdf.
People's Daily 2011, '统计局:中国1300万人没户口 绝大多数为超生' (The general bureau of statistics says, most of the people who have no legal citizenship registration are the ones who were not born under the one-child policy), 10 May, http://politics.people.com.cn/GB/1026/14523741.html.
Radio Free Asia 2014, 'Ethnic Vietnamese left in limbo without citizenship', 19 March, www.rfa.org/english/news/cambodia/vietnamese-03192014205359.html.
Singh, D 2010, *Stateless in South Asia: The Chakmas between Bangladesh and India*, Sage.
Suryadinata, L 2008, *Ethnic Chinese in Contemporary Indonesia*, ISEAS.
UNHCR 2009 'Extracts relating to nationality and statelessness from selected universal and regional human rights instruments', Geneva, www.refworld.org/docid/4c29aec02.html.
UNHCR 2014a, *Ending Statelessness within 10 Years: A Special Report*, Geneva, www.unhcr.org/546217229.html.
UNHCR 2014b, *2014–2015 Global Appeal: Malaysia*, Geneva, www.unhcr.org/528a0a320.html.
UNHCR 2015a, 'Figures at a glance', www.unhcr.org.my/About_Us-@-Figures_At_A_Glance.aspx.
UNHCR 2015b, 'Good practices paper—Action 1: resolving major existing situations of statelessness', 23 February, Geneva, www.refworld.org/docid/54e75a244.html.
UNHCR 2015c, 'Background note on gender equality, nationality laws and statelessness', www.refworld.org/docid/54f8369b4.html.
UNHCR 2016, 'Country page on Nepal', www.unhcr.org/pages/49e487856.html.
UNHCR Malaysia 2015, 'Figures at a glance in Malaysia', July 2015, www.unhcr.org/figures-at-a-glance-in-malaysia.html.

UN Human Rights Council 2011, *Human Rights and Arbitrary Deprivation of Nationality: Report of the Secretary General*, A/HRC/19/43, Geneva, www.refworld.org/docid/4f181ef92.html.
United Nations Convention on the Reduction of Statelessness, 1961, UNTS vol. 989.
United Nations Convention on the Status of Stateless Persons, 1954, UNTS vol. 360.
US Department of State 2013, *Country Reports on Human Rights Practices 2013: Nepal*, Washington DC, www.state.gov/j/drl/rls/hrrpt/2013/sca/220400.htm.
US Department of State 2013, *Government Responses to Statelessness*, remarks by Senior Policy Officer for the Bureau of Population, Refugees and Migration, Washington DC, www.state.gov/j/prm/releases/remarks/2013/207642.htm.
Wijetunga, CP & Tan, V 2004, 'Sri Lanka makes citizens out of stateless tea pickers', UNHCR, Geneva, www.unhcr.org/news/latest/2004/10/416564cd4/feature-sri-lanka-makes-citizens-stateless-tea-pickers.html.
Wood, E, Suliansa, MS & Brunt, H 2007, *Results of the 2006 Community Census*, Semporna Islands Darwin Project.
Wu, N 2013, 'Single mothers in China face higher legal hurdles from "outdated" policies', *South China Morning Post*, 17 July, www.scmp.com/news/china/article/1284550/single-mothers-%20china-face-higher-legal-hurdles-outdated-policies.
Ziemele, I 2014, 'State succession and issues of nationality and statelessness', in A Edwards & L van Waas (eds), *Nationality and Statelessness under International Law*, Cambridge University Press.

16

Protecting the rights of refugees in South and Southeast Asia

Julia Mayerhofer[1]

Introduction

Refugee flows continue to increase unabated. In 2014 the number of forcibly displaced persons worldwide exceeded 50 million people for the first time since the Second World War (UNHCR 2015a). Ongoing and emerging violent conflicts, as well as discrimination and persecution of minorities in Asia and outside the region, are the primary drivers of displacement. South[2] and Southeast Asia[3] host a large number of the world's refugees and are also the site of some of the world's most acute and protracted refugee situations.[4] Despite the fact that South and Southeast Asian states are hosting such a high number of refugees, the majority of them do not provide adequate protection or access to the most basic rights.

Refugees from Afghanistan residing in Pakistan and Iran represent one of the most protracted refugee situations in the world. Of the 2.6 million Afghan refugees worldwide, 2.5 million can be found in Iran and Pakistan alone (UNHCR 2014a). The continuing political instability in Afghanistan suggests that the situation for refugees is unlikely to improve anytime soon. Bangladesh hosts one of the largest stateless populations in the world with over 200,000 Rohingya refugees[5] living largely in the southeastern district of Cox's Bazar. A further estimated 300,000 to 500,000 unregistered and undocumented live in Bangladesh (UNHCR 2015b). Most are living in a state of limbo, unable to seek legal employment, heavily reliant on humanitarian assistance and with no durable solutions in sight.[6] India is home to a rising number of urban refugees from various countries, with the majority living around New Delhi, though sizable populations can also be found in other cities. India also hosts Sri Lankan Tamils in camps in the south of the country, and Tibetan refugees in different parts of India. In 2013, 272,000 refugees lived in the country, including 150,000 Tibetans and more than 68,000 Sri Lankans in 112 refugee camps, with 32,000 located outside the camps (US Bureau of Democracy, Human Rights and Labor 2014). While Nepal has a small urban refugee population, there are 24,000 Bhutanese refugees remaining in two camps (92,000 have been resettled since 2007) as well as 15,000 Tibetans who are spread throughout the country (UNHCR 2014b).

In Southeast Asia, refugees from Myanmar continue to be the largest refugee group; also constituting a protracted situation—as many have been displaced for over two decades. In Malaysia, refugees from Myanmar live largely in the urban areas surrounding Kuala Lumpur, whereas in Thailand, the majority of refugees from Myanmar are living in nine 'temporary' camps along the Thailand–Myanmar border. Since 2012, there have been some signs of political change inside Myanmar with on-going talks between the government and various ethnic groups. However, many refugees are reluctant to return to Myanmar due to the ongoing conflict and rights abuses, as well as the absence of key safeguards that need to be in place before refugees can return. Additionally, there are over 400,000 Internally Displaced Persons (IDPs) inside Myanmar, the majority of whom are in Kachin and Rakhine states (UNHCR 2015c). In Thailand, Malaysia and Indonesia, the number of urban refugees from countries such as Pakistan, Afghanistan, Sri Lanka, Syria, Iran, Iraq, Somalia and Vietnam continues to grow. Among the ASEAN member states, the Philippines and Cambodia are the only two countries that have signed the 1951 Convention relating to the Status of Refugees and its 1967 Protocol (UNHCR 2015f), and both host a comparatively small number of refugees.

The South and Southeast Asian sub-regions are characterised by three trends. First, as with other populations moving to urban areas, refugees too are increasingly moving towards urban centres. It is estimated that more than half of the world's refugees now reside in cities rather than in refugee camps (UNHCR 2015d). In comparison to closed camps, cities present obvious opportunities for people seeking asylum to remain inconspicuous, make money and build a better future. However, they also present dangers and new challenges. Refugees often do not hold legally recognised or respected documentation, are vulnerable to exploitation, arrest and detention, and are exposed to discrimination and xenophobia. In addition, the anonymity afforded by urban situations provides considerable challenges for service provision, particularly in reaching out and accessing different communities.

The second trend in the region is that of mixed migration. In addition to refugees, other vulnerable groups, such as asylum seekers,[7] internally displaced persons (IDPs), stateless persons, victims of trafficking and those displaced by natural disasters and climate change, are often also in need of international protection. In reality, the boundaries between forced and economic migration in this region are difficult to define and overlap. Patterns of migration are usually mixed with refugees and migrants using the same routes of migration which are mostly irregular. Providing protection to such diverse migratory populations provides obvious challenges.

Third, the Southeast Asia region, in the context of mixed migration, is characterised by complex maritime movements. According to the UNHCR (2014c), 54,000 people undertook irregular journeys by boat in 2014. In the absence or inadequacy of safe migration channels, people smugglers and traffickers are provided with a fertile ground to exploit people desperate to flee persecution. The ongoing plight of Rohingya refugees who originate from Myanmar and are trying to reach Malaysia or Indonesia in small, unseaworthy vessels floundering in the Andaman Sea was highlighted in May 2015. While the Rohingya have fled from persecution and gross human rights violations in Myanmar for many years, numbers skyrocketed throughout 2015. In the first quarter of 2015, the United Nations High Commissioner for Refugees (UNHCR 2015e) estimated that 25,000 people had departed by sea from Bangladesh and Myanmar trying to reach Southeast Asian nations. Many have lost their lives at sea and those who manage to reach the coast of Thailand may then be smuggled to Malaysia or held in jungle camps by smugglers and traffickers until a ransom is paid. In April and May 2015, mass graves of Rohingya were discovered in southern Thailand and northern Malaysia (Human Rights Watch 2015a), highlighting that it is not a recent crisis but Rohingya refugees have been subject to human rights violations in jungle camps for years. In May 2015, thousands of stateless Rohingya refugees, other migrants and human trafficking victims were stranded on boats at sea, unable to safely disembark, while governments in the region actively engaged in a process to push boats back out to sea. Public outpouring of support for the stranded people encouraged Indonesia and

Malaysia to revise their initial policy and engage in search and rescue operations, as well as allow disembarkation and provide temporary shelter. Nevertheless, Thailand continues to pursue its policy of not allowing boats to disembark within its territory.

Despite these rising numbers and the above outlined adverse measures, to date, there has been a tendency for debates to focus on refugee protection through the lens of national security and border control, instead of guaranteeing access to rights. For example, Australia's refugee policies have raised significant concern amongst human rights defenders. These changes include the re-introduction of off-shore processing of asylum seekers who attempted to reach Australia by boat, instead transferring them to detention centres on Manus Island, Papua New Guinea and the Republic of Nauru, bilateral agreements (for example the Australia–Cambodia refugee 'deal'), incidences of refoulement, indefinite detention, military control over asylum operations and other restrictive measures. All of these developments have set a dangerous precedent for refugee protection, and have resulted in further shrinking protection spaces affecting the entire region. The portrayal of refugees and asylum seekers in mainstream and social media also perpetuates negative stereotypes and perceptions, for example that refugees are a 'burden' on host communities. This has further added to the challenges facing refugees, as well as those advocating for refugee rights.

Legal context and protection gaps

International instruments

The key instruments of international refugee law are the 1951 Convention relating to the Status of Refugees ('Refugee Convention') and its 1967 Protocol (UNHCR 2015f). In South Asia, only Afghanistan and Iran have acceded to the 1951 Refugee Convention. In Southeast Asia, only the Philippines, Cambodia and Timor-Leste are signatories. International refugee law also intersects with international human rights law and international humanitarian law. Some countries in the region are parties to the Convention against Torture and Other Cruel, Inhuman or Degrading Treatment or Punishment (CAT), the International Covenant on Civil and Political Rights (ICCPR), the Convention on the Rights of the Child (CRC) and the Convention on the Elimination of All Forms of Discrimination Against Women (CEDAW). Many of these treaties include language which refers to refugee rights. The principle of non-refoulement is considered to be part of international customary law and, as such, is binding on any state; although in reality it is often not respected.[8] Throughout the Asia Pacific region, there have been a number of cases of refoulement—as recently observed in the crisis in the Andaman Sea. It is a matter of serious concern when countries like Australia, a signatory to the Refugee Convention, do not respect their international obligations, refoule refugees and push boats back on several instances.

As argued by academics such as Davies (2006) and Chowdhury (2001), international refugee law is rejected in Asia because it is considered to be 'Eurocentric' and was framed as a response to persons displaced in Europe after the Second World War and did not take the situation in Asia into account. Others argue that states are apprehensive to sign on to international instruments because of the related obligations (especially financial obligations). Research has highlighted that countries such as Malaysia and Thailand are reluctant because they believe it would act as a pull factor and that there are associated security risks (Mathew & Harley 2014: 1). Chowdhury (2001: 22) also argues that in South Asia, states have hosted refugees as a matter of hospitability and have already been 'generous', and therefore feel there is no need to sign onto the 1951 Convention because it would not necessarily improve conditions for refugees (Chowdhury 2001: 22).

Regional frameworks

Other regions, such as Europe and Africa, have developed comprehensive regional frameworks to deal with refugees. Yet there is no such framework in place for South Asia, Southeast Asia or the wider Asia-Pacific region. There have been regional agreements in the past such as the Comprehensive Plan of Action (CPA) for Indochinese refugees (adopted in 1989) that brought together countries of origin, countries of asylum and countries of resettlement to address the issue of 'boat people' out of Indochina. The plan ended in March 1996, when all refugee camps under the CPA in Indonesia, Philippines, Hong Kong, Thailand and Malaysia were deemed closed. The Bangkok Principles on the Status and Treatment of Refugees (Bangkok Principles) were adopted by the Asian-African Legal Consultative Organization (AALCO)[9] in 1966. The principles, however, only serve as a guide; they are not legally binding, and there is no enforcement in place.

In Southeast Asia, the Association of South East Asian Nations (ASEAN) does have the potential to lead the development of regional protection mechanisms. ASEAN is an intergovernmental organisation with ten member states (Brunei, Cambodia, Indonesia, Laos, Malaysia, Myanmar, the Philippines, Singapore, Thailand, Vietnam).[10] Despite the establishment of the ASEAN Intergovernmental Commission on Human Rights (AICHR) in October 2009 and the adoption of the ASEAN Human Rights Declaration (AHRD) in 2012, economic interests have very much taken precedence over discussions on human rights amongst ASEAN member states. With regards to the rights of refugees, there appears to be a lack of political will to discuss regional approaches, although there is some protection language provided in the AHRD, such as non-refoulement and the right to asylum (Kneebone 2015). Refugees are often considered to be a politically sensitive topic, with debates frequently compromised by ASEAN's principle of non-interference in internal affairs of member states. Regardless, refugee issues in ASEAN are not only an 'internal affair' but also a regional issue, affecting neighbouring countries. The South Asian Association for Regional Cooperation (SAARC), comprising Afghanistan, Bangladesh, Bhutan, India, Maldives, Nepal, Pakistan and Sri Lanka as members, has been similarly critiqued by human rights groups.

Recent discussions on 'regional cooperation' have very much focused on the securitisation of national borders, as well as combatting the trafficking and smuggling of people rather than the adoption of a rights-based perspective to refugee protection. The Bali Process on People Smuggling, Trafficking in Persons and Related Transnational Crime (Bali Process) was incepted in 2002 and is co-chaired by the governments of Australia and Indonesia. In March 2011, Bali Process ministers adopted the Regional Cooperation Framework (RCF) in consultation with UNHCR and the International Labour Organization (IOM). The framework was created with the purpose of:

> enabl[ing] interested Bali Process members to establish practical arrangements aimed at enhancing the region's response to irregular movement through consistent processing of asylum claims, durable solutions for refugees, the sustainable return of those not owed protection and targeting of people smuggling enterprises.
>
> *(Bali Process 2015)*

In September 2012, the Bali Process Regional Support Office (RSO) was then established to operationalise the RCF. While the establishment of the RCF and RSO was initially met with great enthusiasm, little progress has been made and a lack of engagement with civil society actors has been observed, highlighting the reluctance of states to look at protection elements and look at regional cooperation through a border control lens.

National legislation

In Southeast Asia and South Asia, the majority of countries do not have national legislation in place to protect refugees. Furthermore, in most countries, any foreigner who does not have recognised documentation is treated similarly under immigration law and usually considered to be an 'illegal alien/immigrant'. States generally do not have any protection mechanisms or processes to draw upon in order to provide differentiated protection to refugees or asylum seekers.

Since most countries are not signatories of the 1951 Refugee Convention, the mandate of recognising refugees falls on the UNHCR. Even Cambodia, which has signed the Refugee Convention, has not fully incorporated international instruments into its domestic laws. Nevertheless, there are some positive examples in the region, such as the Philippines, which now has functioning national laws that could serve as a model for other countries to follow. Civil society in the region has also been advocating for the development of national laws that would provide protection to refugees and are based on relevant international law and guiding principles while taking into account the regional context. Groups in Thailand and Nepal have drafted domestic refugee laws; however, the progress made is limited because of a lack of political will and obstacles such as political instability. In India, the status of refugees is governed through political and administrative decisions, and no progress has been made on the Indian Act on Refugee and Asylum Seeker Protection (Asia Pacific Refugee Rights Network 2013a: 7).

Filling the gaps

With governments in the region reluctant to take on their responsibilities and international agencies operating with limited resources and in constrained spaces, the role of civil society is becoming increasingly important. National NGOs as well as community-based organisations (CBOs) provide essential services such as health, education, shelter, cultural orientation, legal aid, counselling etc. In Malaysia for example, the government provides no access to education and refugees are reliant on NGO or CBO-led schools. NGOs also provide essential health services such as support with hospital costs, mobile clinics, community programmes, counselling and other psychosocial support. NGOs also provide crucial legal advice, which is important as refugees often struggle to understand complex international law and their rights, as well as how to claim asylum. National NGOs can also play an important role in advocacy with governments. In both South and Southeast Asia, governments are more reluctant to engage with international NGOs and UN agencies because they are perceived as having a 'Western perspective' and as trying to interfere with domestic politics. In this context, national civil society cannot be so easily dismissed as wanting to 'interfere' and the idea that refugee protection is a Western construct becomes more difficult to defend (Sukumaran 2011). South Korea passed a Refugee Act in July 2013 after several years of persistent and effective advocacy conducted by national actors. National NGOs in Thailand, Nepal, India and other countries are also on the forefront of advocacy on changing national laws. However, overall civil society advocating for refugee rights in this region continues to be weak and much more needs to be done to strengthen national civil society and create stronger movements at the national level.

Protection challenges

In an environment where governments disregard the rights of refugees and protection is inadequate, refugees are exposed to a number of protection challenges in their host countries. The following section provides an overview of these challenges.

Access to legal status, safety and security

Because refugees are mostly undocumented or have overstayed their visas and are thus considered as 'illegal aliens/immigrants', refugees in both South Asia and Southeast Asia are often subject to arbitrary detention, deportation, discrimination, harassment, different forms of violence and immigration detention. In most countries, refugee protection is temporary, ad hoc and also differentiated, resulting in different policies for some groups. Across the region, the lack of a legal status is a barrier for refugees to access even the most basic commodities such as health and education services, opening of bank accounts, rental of secure private accommodation, registration of SIM cards as well as travel documents. There are also significant challenges in registering and documenting refugees, for instance, in urban centres many refugees are in hiding and remain very difficult to access. In most countries, UNHCR only operate an office in the capital city, making it difficult to register those staying outside these urban areas. In Iran for example, access to the field sites requires going through different layers of government approval.

Adding further complexity, there is also a lack of accurate data for refugee populations. In Afghanistan the lack of accurate data assessment coupled with an overlap of information creates an information imbalance—either information is entirely missing or information is duplicated. The operational reality in Afghanistan is characterised by NGOs coming together with different data and figures that often do not match, creating obstacles to proper interventions and coordination. Lack of data and lack of access create a cyclical problem of: how do you capture data on refugees when you don't have access and how do you access refugees when you don't have data demonstrating the need?

Without any documentation or legal status, governments across the Asia-Pacific region also increasingly use immigration detention as a migration/border management tool and means to deal with refugees, asylum seekers, stateless persons and irregular migrants. Without national protective legislation, police and government officials often do not screen-out refugees or asylum seekers during immigration raids, putting such individuals at risk of arbitrary detention, often in conditions that fall well short of international standards. Research has shown that immigration detention is costly, ineffective and psychologically damaging (International Detention Coalition 2015: 1). International law also stipulates that the use of immigration detention should be proportional, necessary and a measure of last resort, which is often not the case in the detention of refugees (International Detention Coalition 2015: 71).

Detention is often applied in a blanket, arbitrary manner, and alternatives to detention (ATD) are still not commonplace. While immigration detention is less of an issue in South Asian countries, it is increasingly used in Southeast Asian states, such as Thailand, Malaysia and Indonesia. Detainees do not only include adults but also children and unaccompanied minors. For individuals, the effects can be particularly devastating: immigration detention violates children rights', risks their health and wellbeing and affects their normal development. In 2012 the Committee for the Rights of the Child asked governments to 'expeditiously and completely cease the detention of children on the basis of their immigration status' (Committee on the Rights of the Child 2012: 18). In Thailand, despite being a signatory to the CRC, immigration detention of children can be arbitrary and indefinite. Reports demonstrate that children lack access to education, social and intellectual development opportunities, adequate nutrition, medical services and physical exercise. This is exacerbated by bad sanitary conditions, overcrowded cells and exposure to violence/abuse (Human Rights Watch 2015b: 3).

In some countries, however, positive policies can be observed. In India, for example, UNHCR recognised that refugees can now apply for long-term residency visas and work permits (awarded for one year at a time) that are renewable for up to five years. Prior to 2012, residency and work permits were only available to specific refugee ethnicities and for very short periods of time. This decision is a step forward for refugee protection but much more needs to be done to ensure tangible benefits from this policy. Another example is the Proof of Registration card (POR card) in Pakistan, which is an identity document that provides temporary legal status and also allows refugees to obtain a drivers licence, open a bank account and purchase mobile SIM cards.

The Philippines is perhaps one of the most advanced countries in the region on this issue, having acceded to the 1951 Refugee Convention and its 1967 Protocol in 1981. The Philippines traces its refugee law as far back as 1937. In October 2012, the Department of Justice of the Philippines issued Department Circular No. 058, 'the rules on Establishing the Refugee and Stateless Status Determination Procedure' (Republic of the Philippines, Department of Justice 2012). As part of the Circular No. 058, the Philippines has become the only state in the ASEAN region to have a mechanism to identify and provide protection to stateless persons along with refugees.

Access to justice

In Southeast and South Asia, refugee status determination (RSD) is mostly conducted by UNHCR. Even though UNHCR has developed procedural guidelines, there are significant challenges in UNCHR's process. Firstly, RSD may take a number of years to be completed; in some cases first instance interviews are given four years from registration. Once recognised, it may take several additional months or years for recognised refugees to be resettled in a country capable and willing to provide a durable solution. During this time and while refugees are waiting to be resettled, UNHCR provides registration cards but these cards are not recognised by all governments and may not protect against arrest and immigration detention by authorities. During this time refugees receive UNHCR registration cards but, in particular in Southeast Asian countries, those cards do not protect refugees from arrest and detention by authorities. Second, it has also been found that RSD can be discriminatory against certain nationalities; in Thailand for example Pakistani refugees are given first instance interview dates three to four years from their initial registration. Somali or Syrian refugees on the other can be recognised within a two-year timeframe. Third, practices of the national UNHCR offices in the different countries also vary. In some countries refugees do not receive sufficient explanation in their rejection letters, preventing refugees from submitting targeted appeals in response to the specific reasons for rejection. Guidelines issued by UNHCR also spell out the right of asylum seekers to be informed of their right to legal counsel. Legal representation, however, continues to be a challenge and is currently not allowed by UNHCR in countries such as Thailand and Malaysia.

In this context legal aid is crucial. Generally speaking, refugee law is complicated, and refugees rarely have a good understanding of refugee law. In addition to navigating the complexities of refugee law, refugees also experience communication difficulties as they often have to speak with officers through interpreters. As is common when working through interpreters, miscommunication and misunderstandings prevent refugees from accurately and clearly conveying their stories in their own language. With all of these challenges, the consequences are significant; the rights that are at stake could not be more serious. A rejection on the wrong grounds could mean deportation back to a setting of persecution or much worse.

Refugees may often be subject to harassment, abuse or violence in host countries but are unable to access domestic legal remedies for fear of retribution by locals or detention by officials due to a lack of legal status. For example, if undocumented or out-of-status refugees experience harassment or discrimination at work, they often do not feel safe reporting such violations in case they are then reported by the perpetrator to immigration for deportation. But even in countries with some legal protections in place, there is often a lack of implementation combined with a lack of awareness among local police officers. Additionally, refugees are often also not aware of their own rights and opportunities for redress. Other barriers include language, financial constraints, community pressure and feelings of shame associated with different forms of violence including sexual and gender-based violence (SGBV). On the Thai–Myanmar border, 'fear, uncertainty, and a feeling of powerlessness contribute to a fatalistic attitude among camp refugees about whether justice is available to them' (Human Rights Watch 2012).

Access to health

Refugees across the region struggle to access health services, given the high costs involved. This is often perceived by refugees as one of the biggest challenges, especially in the urban context since refugees may not be able to access local government hospitals without documentation and often rely on NGOs and UNHCR for support. The real and perceived fear of being arrested may also make refugees reluctant to seek medical services from hospitals. In Malaysia, for example, a case was reported were a refugee mother and her new-born child were sent to immigration detention from the hospital after the mother gave birth (Health Equity Initiatives 2014). In refugee camps, the situation is slightly better since at least basic health services are provided by NGOs and are more easily accessible.

The health needs of refugees are complex and may require special considerations because of the often traumatic events to which they have been exposed. Specific groups such as unaccompanied minors, children, orphans, former child soldiers, women and girls as well as survivors of torture and sexual harassment are particularly prone to develop mental health problems. 'Clinical and research literature in mental health also indicate that refugees and asylum seekers experience a significant degree of psychological distress and physical and psychological dysfunction arising due to uprooting and adjustment difficulties and symptoms of somatization, depression and post traumatic stress disorder (PTSD), which may be evidenced even five years after resettlement' (Verghis & Pereira 2009: 1). This is compounded by the distress that refugees feel as foreigners in an unstable situation. In Southeast Asia, the constant fear of arrest and immigration detention, paired with a lengthy refugee status determination process, dire living conditions and an unknown future, puts severe distress on those who may already be traumatised. Furthermore, in many countries mental health needs are often not recognised and even if they are, service providers often lack the skills and experience to handle them adequately, as well as having limited options for referral to a specialist physician.

Among refugee communities there is also a lack of education on reproductive and sexual health (Asia Pacific Refugee Rights Network 2013b: 14). Stigma and shame contribute to the lack of education and services relating to sexual health, as well as gender inequality. Lack of knowledge makes it difficult to protect oneself and seek out appropriate services. Furthermore, there are significant gaps in post-natal care and delivery services. Maternal and infant mortality are significant consequences of a lack of reproductive healthcare. Early or underage pregnancy and the spread of disease can also be seen as the result of a lack of access to appropriate sexual and reproductive services. In Pakistan and Afghanistan, health services are sporadic—for example, gynaecological services are frequently inadequate and basic needs, such as adequate cloth and washing facilities for menstruating women, are overlooked. Serious problems, such as infections and cervical cancer, as well as harmful practices such as female circumcision, go all but undetected. The first set of UNHCR guidelines mentioning the importance of birth-spacing was drafted over 20 years ago; however, contraceptive services have failed to become an integral part of the primary healthcare services offered to many refugees, despite broad awareness of the high fertility levels and poor health status of many refugee women, such as in Pakistan, Afghanistan and Iran. There is also a lack of official support for family planning and sex education and legal abortion options are limited or completely prohibited, resulting in clandestine and risky abortions. In addition, there is also a lack of AIDS education and prevention, the diagnosis and treatment of other sexually transmitted diseases and gynaecologic conditions, rape prevention and counselling or programmes to assist the victims of sexual abuse.

Sexual and gender-based violence

UNHCR has documented that about 50% of refugee, internally displaced and stateless communities are composed of women and girls (UNHCR 2013: 9). This group suffers heightened vulnerability to different forms of violence including sexual and gender-based violence (SGBV), sexual exploitation, domestic violence and abuse. Additionally, the lack of appropriate official response to SGBV and the common social stigma attached to SGBV increases the risk of SGBV for men, young boys and individuals who identify, or are perceived to identify, as LGBTI.

Incidences of rape and other forms of sexual violence are common within refugee communities and can result in internal injuries, children of rape, complications from pregnancy and other health-related impacts. Rape survivors experience depression, anxiety and diminished self-esteem and confidence. Survivors of sexual violence are often unable or unwilling to seek formal justice for the crimes committed against them because of a number of hurdles. In communities where the likelihood of community shaming of victims is high, survivors are unable to seek proper redress against their attackers and often fear that there will be social consequences if the trauma they experienced is widely known. For example, women who have been raped may face fewer marriage opportunities, which can have a significant impact on their futures and their families' abilities to provide for them. Such complications increase their vulnerability to traffickers and other exploitation. In South and Southeast Asia, additional barriers to seeking help after sexual violence include a lack of support by police or other law agents and inadequate or absent health services that respond to sexual violence, including a lack of female doctors or proper rape documentation kits. In many South Asian countries SGBV is also not understood as human rights violations, but rather as cultural or private issues that are best left alone.

In situations of armed conflict, the risk of SGBV against women and girls is heightened but many governments in South Asia have yet to ratify the international commitments designed to protect the rights of women and girls during and after armed conflict. Furthermore, during armed conflict, forced displacement and SGBV are often deliberate strategies of war that destabilise families and communities. Physical and sexual violence, particularly towards women and children, occur with greater regularity during and after armed conflict. Women experience rape and forced pregnancy, forced sex work and sexual slavery often at the hands of peace keepers, police or occupying forces, as occurred in Afghanistan. In Eastern Myanmar it has also been documented that rape has been used as a systematic weapon of war to traumatise whole communities (Burma Campaign UK 2014: 1). However, these victims often do not and cannot get sufficient medical, mental, or physical support because of the chaos of conflict.

Access to education

Access to primary and secondary education is an obstacle in both South and Southeast Asia, particularly outside of refugee camps. In some countries in Southeast Asia, refugee children may in theory be allowed to enrol in local schools; however, there are a lot of practical challenges such as language, transportation, discrimination from the other students, fees for school materials and uniforms as well as school administrators that might refuse to enrol refugee children. In other countries such as Malaysia, refugee children do not have access to the national education system at all (Jesuit Refugee Services 2012: 61). As a result, refugee children in urban settings and also camps often rely on classes and schooling provided by NGOs and CBOs, which are limited and also not formally recognised. In cases were refugees can access the national schooling system, such as Pakistan, there is a need to sensitise stakeholders to ensure that the education provided also fulfils the needs of refugees and prepares them with useful skills.

Access to further education and skills development is another significant gap in the refugee protection framework. There are often very limited further education opportunities available, mostly because of the lack of legal documentation that prevents refugees from attending university. Finances, language, community pressure and invalid visas are other barriers. In Thailand for example, even if refugees have the financial resources to study at a university, they would not be able to do so because they would need a valid student visa (which is almost impossible for refugees to obtain).

Access to livelihoods

Research has shown that allowing refugees employment and self-employment is beneficial to hosting countries (Arnold-Fernández & Pollock 2013: 92). However in none of the Southeast Asian countries are refugees allowed to work without valid visas and work permits. Thailand has benefited from the employment of Burmese migrant workers; many of them in fact being refugees residing outside of refugee camps. However there is no political will to consider providing camp-based or urban refugees a formal right to work—the argument often provided by governments is that the right to work would act as a pull factor, attracting more refugees.

Many refugees are therefore forced to work illegally, which makes them more vulnerable to exploitation and abuse. This is particularly the case for women who may engage in prostitution to make ends meet or may become victims of trafficking. Working conditions are also often poor with little pay. In Malaysia, abuse of migrants and refugees has been well documented and researched (Jesuit Refugee Services 2012: 57). The constant fear of arrest also reduces mobility to travel and restricts job opportunities.

The most obvious impact of a lack of access to employment is the lack of sufficient income. This lack of income means basic needs cannot be met. For refugee women, a lack of income may also mean a lack of financial independence, which may lead to other issues such as women staying in unsafe domestic settings and increased vulnerability. Refugee children are also at increased risk of engaging in child labour, as well as sexual exploitation and trafficking. Forced into early adulthood by the need to work, these children are subsequently not accessing education.

In the refugee camps on the Thai–Myanmar border, many of the refugees have been in these camps for over 20 years and many more are born there. After all these years, refugees have not been allowed to work, making them dependent on humanitarian aid (Human Rights Watch 2012). Some risk sneaking out of refugee camps on a daily basis to earn money as day labourers, placing them at additional risk of exploitation and arrest.

Access to durable solutions

While refugees in the Philippines and Cambodia have some options for local integration, there is a lack of durable solutions available to refugees in Thailand, Malaysia and Indonesia.

With countries resistant to allow for local integration, resettlement often remains the only option but is only available for a small percentage of the refugee population. As a result many refugees remain stuck in limbo for years.

Voluntary repatriation is currently in discussion for Burmese refugees on the Thai–Myanmar border due to some positive political developments inside Myanmar. However, peace inside Myanmar is still fragile and certain preconditions need to be in place to ensure that refugees can return in safety and dignity. Specific concerns include the on-going presence of Burmese military troops, reports of human rights violations, thousands of uncleared landmines, oppressive laws, landownership issues, the lack of healthcare and education services, the lack of assistance for vulnerable people, livelihood issues, re-integration issues with local communities and limited or no citizenship/nationality rights. Refugee communities have also raised the concern that no consultation has taken place with them and only very limited information has been received which has resulted in anxiety and the spread of rumour.

For refugees in Pakistan, insecurity, disputes, intimidation and extortions, mines and unexploded ordinances are among the key factors that affect the physical safety and well-being of Afghan returnees. Recognition of their identity is also a challenge for returnees who are faced with obstacles to obtain proper legal documentation—in part due to the difficulty in going back to the area of origin to obtain identity cards. The lack of official identity documentation leads to severe challenges in accessing basic services for children, political representation and social inclusion. For Afghan refugees much more could be done to prepare them for return and more effective information sharing should be implemented to enable refugees to make an informed decision about their opportunities to return.

Conclusion

While refugee flows are increasing and becoming more complex, states are increasingly reluctant to provide asylum and protection for those in need. Protection on all levels (international, regional and national) is weak, inadequate and does not allow refugees to access their fundamental rights. Only a small number of states have acceded to international instruments and the majority do not have national laws in place nor is there any regional framework that provides protection to those in need of it. Even countries which have acceded to international refugee law instruments (such as Australia) do not fully respect their international obligations. This frequently leaves refugees in a 'legal limbo', desperately in search of protection, and forced to seek other migration channels with people smugglers and traffickers who thrive on the desperation of others. This legal limbo and the lack of legal status prevents refugees from accessing their rights, such as education, health and livelihoods.

Refugee protection starts at the national level, it starts with states developing national laws that are in line with international standards but it also starts with providing the access to rights outlined in such laws. In the context of mixed migration and irregular maritime movements, a rights-based regional response is desperately needed that addresses root causes and explores different models of responsibility sharing.

Notes

1 Edited by Anoop Sukumaran, Helen Brunt, Hina Tabassum and Michelle Ferns.

2 For this chapter, South Asia includes the following countries: Afghanistan, Bangladesh, Bhutan, India, Iran, Nepal, Pakistan and Sri Lanka.

3 For this chapter, Southeast Asia includes the following countries: Cambodia, Brunei, Indonesia, Laos, Malaysia, Myanmar, Philippines, Thailand, Timor-Leste and Vietnam.

4 When a refugee population is in exile for over five years, and exceeds a population of 25,000, it is considered as to be in a 'protracted' situation.
5 This figure is what UNHCR describes as people from Myanmar in refugee-like situations.
6 UNHCR's 'Framework for Durable Solutions for Refugees and Persons of Concern' identifies three durable solutions: resettlement to a third country, voluntary repatriation or local integration (UNHCR 2003: 5).
7 An asylum seeker is someone who is outside their country of origin and has a well-founded fear of persecution due to race, religion, nationality, membership of a particular social group, or political opinion and is unable or unwilling to return to that country, but whose status as a 'refugee' has not yet had their claim assessed by the relevant status determination body.
8 According to Article 33 of the 1951 Refugee Convention, 'no Contracting State shall expel or return ("refouler") a refugee in any manner whatsoever to the frontiers of territories where his life or freedom would be threatened on account of his race, religion, nationality, membership of a particular social group or political opinion'.
9 AALCO is an intergovernmental body with 47 members.
10 Since its independence in 2002, Timor-Leste has held 'observer' status in ASEAN, pending the country formally becoming a member.

References

Arnold-Fernández, E & Pollock, S 2013, 'Host economies benefit when refugees work: Nations seeking economic growth and political stability should allow refugees to access employment and to enjoy employment-related rights', *Forced Migration Review*, vol. 44, viewed 28 June 2015, www.fmreview.org/detention/arnoldfernandez-pollock.

Asia Pacific Refugee Rights Network 2013a, 'Urban refugees in Asia Pacific: Resiliency and coping strategies—Pilot study report', viewed 27 June 2015, www.aprrn.info/1/images/PDF/sasakawa-report-final-4.pdf.

Asia Pacific Refugee Rights Network 2013b, 'Women and girls at risk working group: Training of the trainers report', viewed 22 July 2015, www.aprrn.info/1/pdf/WAGAR%20Report%20Updated.pdf.

Bali Process 2015, 'About the Bali Process', viewed 27 June 2015, www.baliprocess.net/.

Burma Campaign UK 2014, 'Rape and sexual violence by the Burmese Army', viewed 23 July 2015, http://burmacampaign.org.uk/media/Rape-and-Sexual-Violence-by-the-Burmese-Army1.pdf.

Chowdhury, RA 2001, 'Legal protection of refugees in South Asia', *Forced Migration Review*, vol. 10, pp. 21–23.

Committee on the Rights of the Child 2012, 'Report of the 2012 day of general discussion: The rights of all children in the context of international migration', www2.ohchr.org/english/bodies/crc/docs/discussion2012/2012CRC_DGD-Childrens_Rights_InternationalMigration.pdf.

Davies, SE 2006, 'The Asian rejection?: International refugee law in Asia', *Australian Journal of Politics and History*, vol. 52, no. 4, pp. 562–575.

Health Equity Initiatives 2014, 'Stop the arrest and detention of asylum seeking women accessing maternal health care', viewed 28 June 2015, http://rightsinexile.tumblr.com/post/84534484837/stop-the-arrest-and-detention-of-asylum-seeking.

Human Rights Watch 2012, 'Refugees in camps on the Thai–Burma border', viewed 28 June 2015, www.hrw.org/zh-hans/node/109633/section/8.

Human Rights Watch 2015a, 'Thailand: Mass graves of Rohingya found in trafficking camp', viewed 27 June 2015, www.hrw.org/news/2015/05/01/thailand-mass-graves-rohingya-found-trafficking-camp.

Human Rights Watch 2015b, 'Two years with no moon: Immigration detention of children in Thailand', viewed 27 June 2015, www.hrw.org/sites/default/files/reports/thailand0914_ForUpload_0.pdf.

International Detention Coalition 2015, *There are alternatives: A handbook for preventing unnecessary immigration detention (revised version)*, viewed 13 January 2016, http://idcoalition.org/publications/there-are-alternatives-revised-edition/.

Jesuit Refugee Services 2012, 'The search: Protection space in Malaysia, Thailand, Indonesia, Cambodia and the Philippines', viewed 28 June 2015, www.jrs.net/Assets/Regions/APR/media/files/The_Search.pdf.

Kneebone, S 2015, 'The labeling problem in Southeast Asia's refugee crisis', viewed 11 January 2016, http://thediplomat.com/2015/08/the-labeling-problem-in-southeast-asias-refugee-crisis/.

Mathew, P & Harley, T 2014, 'Refugee protection and regional cooperation in Southeast Asia', *The Australian National University Research Publications*, viewed 27 June 2015, https://digitalcollections.anu.edu.au/bitstream/1885/11662/1/Mathew%20%26%20Harley%20Refugee%20protection%20 2014.pdf.

Republic of the Philippines, Department of Justice 2012, 'DOJ formalizes rules and mechanisms for the protection of refugees and stateless persons', October 22, viewed 28 June 2015, www.doj.gov.ph/news.html?title=DOJ+FORMALIZES+RULES+AND+MECHANISMS+FOR+THE+PROTEC TION+OF+REFUGEES+AND+STATELESS+PERSONS&newsid=138.

Sukumaran, A 2011, 'Shifting paradigms and building national civil society: Refugee protection in South and South East Asia', *FOCUS*, vol. 65 (September), viewed 23 June 2015, www.hurights.or.jp/archives/focus/section2/2011/09/shifting-paradigms-and-building-national-civil-society-refugee-protection-in-south-and-south-east-asia.html.

United Nations High Commissioner for Refugees 2003, 'Framework for durable solutions for refugees and persons of concern', viewed 16 July 2015, www.unhcr.org/3f1408764.html.

United Nations High Commissioner for Refugees 2013, 'UNHCR statistical handbook 2013', viewed 22 July 2014, www.unhcr.org/54cf99109.html.

United Nations High Commissioner for Refugees (Bureau for Asia and the Pacific) 2014a, 'UNHCR: Bureau for Asia and the Pacific, regional update', viewed 27 June 2015, www.unhcr.org/5000139a9.html.

United Nations High Commissioner for Refugees 2014b, 'UNHCR: Nepal fact sheet', www.unhcr.org/50001f3c9.html.

United Nations High Commissioner for Refugees 2014c, 'Southeast Asia: Irregular maritime movements', viewed 27 June 2015, www.unhcr.org/53f1c5fc9.html.

United Nations High Commissioner for Refugees 2015a, 'World faces major crisis as number of displaced hits record high', viewed 27 June 2015, www.unhcr.org/5582c2f46.html.

United Nations High Commissioner for Refugees 2015b, 'Bangladesh', viewed 27 June 2015, www.unhcr.org/pages/49e487546.html#.

United Nations High Commissioner for Refugees 2015c, 'UNHCR: Asia and the Pacific', viewed 27 June 2015, www.unhcr.org/pages/4a02d8ec6.html.

United Nations High Commissioner for Refugees 2015d, 'UNHCR: Urban refugees', viewed 27 June 2015, www.unhcr.org/pages/4b0e4cba6.html.

United Nations High Commissioner for Refugees 2015e, 'Southeast Asia: Irregular maritime movements', viewed 27 June 2015, www.unhcr.org/554c6a746.html.

United Nations High Commissioner for Refugees 2015f, 'Convention and Protocol Relating to the Status of Refugees', viewed 27 June 2015, www.unhcr.org/3b66c2aa10.html.

US Bureau of Democracy, Human Rights and Labor 2014, 'Country reports on human rights practices for 2013', viewed 21 June 2015, www.state.gov/j/drl/rls/hrrpt/humanrightsreport/#wrapper.

Verghis, S & Pereira, X 2009, 'Health concerns of refugees and asylum seekers in Malaysia', viewed 28 June 2015, www.healthequityinitiatives.com/wp-content/uploads/2012/06/HEALTH-CONCERNS-OF-REFUGEES-AND-ASYLUM-SEEKERS-IN-MALAYSIA.pdf.

17

Between protection and harm

Trafficked persons in Southeast Asia – where do the violations end?

Emma Bowers and Elaine Pearson

Introduction

A young teenage girl forced to submit to sex with cruel middle-aged clients to pay off an exorbitant debt. Gaunt faces of 'boat people' on rickety vessels floating in the clear azure waters of the Andaman Sea. These two starkly different but recognisable scenes are what most people picture when they hear of human trafficking in Southeast Asia. But, while these scenes do play out, misconceptions hide the reality that the vast majority of men, women and children are trafficked for forced labour (UNDOC 2014: 78). Some may cross borders illegally on boats, but trafficked people are just as likely to enter countries undetected on work or tourist visas, and then wind up sold to those who exploit them. In Southeast Asia, invisible victims of trafficking are everywhere: Burmese boys and men enslaved on a Thai fishing boat, forced to work long hours each day and beaten if they fail to catch their quota. Cambodian domestic workers on legal work permits in Malaysia, locked and abused in the homes of their employers, their travel documents confiscated. A disabled woman from the Thai countryside sewing labels day and night in a Bangkok sweatshop to pay back a large debt.

International law defines 'trafficking' as the buying, selling, receipt or movement of people, through deceptive and coercive means, into a situation of slavery, forced labour or severe exploitation (UNGA 2000: Art. 3). Southeast Asia remains a well-known 'hotspot' of human trafficking (Ford, Lyons & van Schendel 2012: 1). While the hidden nature of trafficking makes it difficult to assess its scale reliably, the International Labour Organization (ILO) (2012) estimates that 11.7 million people in the Asia-Pacific region are in conditions of forced labour. This figure is by far the highest of any region in the world (UN-ACT 2015: 4). Looking closer at Southeast Asia, there are extensive domestic and interregional trafficking networks in Myanmar, Cambodia, China, Indonesia, Laos, Malaysia, the Philippines, Thailand and Vietnam. With over 12,000 kilometres of land borders shared between the countries of the Greater Mekong Subregion (which includes Myanmar, Cambodia, Laos, Thailand, Vietnam and China's southern province of Yunnan), victims regularly cross into richer neighbouring countries in search of economic opportunities, or to escape poverty, inequality and persecution (UNODC 2015: 10).

Contrary to the traditional narrative that the trafficking trade is controlled by sophisticated transnational criminal networks, victims are often recruited by traffickers who have links to their family or friends (UNODC 2014: 28). Many victims initially consent to assistance from a trafficker posing as a recruiter, paying a large fee for the journey and are subsequently lured into exploitation with the false promise of employment at higher wages. The United Nations Office for Drug Control and Crime Prevention (2013: 14) estimates that in Thailand 4% of irregular labour migrants fall into the hands of traffickers.

Trafficking victims in Southeast Asia are recruited into a diverse range of industries, from fishing and agriculture to manufacturing, construction and domestic work (UN-ACT 2015). Women and girls are also trafficked into the sex industry or forced into marriage. Exploitative labour conditions are particularly prevalent in Thailand's fishing and seafood industry (Environmental Justice Foundation 2015). The ILO (2006: 83–85) has documented how trafficked persons are forced to work on fishing boats for more than 12 hours a day and are subjected to frequent violence, sleep deprivation and inadequate food and medical care. Take for instance two young boys from Myanmar, aged 14 and 15, who explained their fear working on Thai fishing boats: 'We work all day and all night on the boat. During working hours, we are not allowed to rest. If we do rest, we risk punishment . . . we are scared because we have seen some crew members thrown off the boat or beaten with hooks and anchors' (ILO 2006: xvi).

Other victims are deceived by traffickers into situations akin to debt bondage, where recruiters demand repayment of exorbitant fees for their journey. Human Rights Watch (2011) reported how Son Souen, aged 30, was recruited by a broker to migrate as a domestic worker from Cambodia to Malaysia. The broker promised Son Souen easy work and a salary of US$2,000 over two years. Like many other domestic workers who undertake the journey from Cambodia to Malaysia through recruitment brokers, she was offered money and sacks of rice as incentives to migrate. But these 'incentives' of food, cattle and sometimes cash are not gifts, but loans and advances. Women are often forced to forgo six to seven months of their salary once in Malaysia in order to repay their loans in addition to recruitment fees ranging between US$900 to US$1,300 (Human Rights Watch 2011: 26). Sadly, for many trafficked persons in Southeast Asia, the abuse and confinement they have suffered can persist in a different form even after they escape their traffickers. Poorly designed anti-trafficking policies often fail to respect the dignity, agency and human rights of those affected most by the crime.

This chapter will explore some of the instances where human rights have been left in the periphery of government responses to human trafficking in Southeast Asia. It begins by examining how the international and regional legal frameworks established to respond to human trafficking address and incorporate human rights concerns. Human rights violations as a consequence of inadequate anti-trafficking measures in Southeast Asia are also discussed using examples such as the practice of detaining trafficking victims in closed shelters and other restrictions on freedom of movement. We explore how anti-trafficking policies have undermined the rights of other groups, particularly sex workers and irregular migrants, when counter-trafficking is used as a pretext for 'crackdowns' on the sex industry or illegal migration. As a result of sustained international pressure and advocacy from civil society actors, governments in Southeast Asia are replacing anti-trafficking policies and practices which tended to violate human rights with approaches that respect them. The final section of this chapter explores how anti-trafficking measures in Southeast Asia can be further strengthened by drawing on successful policies and practices from around the globe.

The anti-trafficking legal framework

The origins of the sometimes precarious relationship between anti-trafficking measures and human rights can be traced to the international legal framework established to address trafficking. In 2000, the Protocol to Prevent, Suppress and Punish Trafficking in Persons, Especially Women and Children (the Protocol) was adopted by the United Nations General Assembly (A/RES/55/25 of 15 November 2000). The Protocol, which laid out the first comprehensive international legal definition of trafficking in persons, has become the foundational framework of the global response to human trafficking. The signing of the Protocol generated international momentum to address the problem and prompted a wave of global, regional and national anti-trafficking initiatives. In Southeast Asia, the Protocol's entry into force had considerable impact. Prior to December 2003, only four countries in the Asia-Pacific had legislated a specific 'trafficking in persons' offence that met international standards. By 2008 this figure had quadrupled, primarily due to gains in the Southeast Asian region (UNODC 2014: 80).

Despite these successes, the Protocol does not fully address the human rights of trafficking victims. Its approach to trafficking is heavily informed by its parent treaty, the UN Convention on Transnational Organised Crime (the Convention). Through the lens of transnational organised crime, the Protocol adopts a criminal justice response to trafficking (Gallagher 2015: 19). States parties are required to criminalise trafficking under their domestic law, prosecute and punish offenders, and cooperate with other governments to prevent the illicit movement of people across borders (UNGA 2000: Arts 5 and 11).

Human rights and women's rights groups lobbied hard during the protocol negotiations in Vienna in 1999 and 2000 to insist on the inclusion of human rights protections for victims in the treaty. During negotiations, activists pointed out that human rights violations are not only both a root cause of trafficking and a central part of the exploitation traffickers subject their victims to, but can emerge once a trafficked person is removed from a trafficking situation due to inadequate counter-trafficking policies. Initially, governments regularly failed to provide access to justice for victims, and too often victims were deported or detained, rather than protected and assisted. Consider the following case: Dinah, a Cambodian woman, was duped by an agent who promised her high wages and a legal job working in Thailand (Pearson 2001: 54). Soon after she arrived in Bangkok however, she found herself confined to a factory where she was forced to work 12 hours per day except Sunday, without any pay. During a police raid on the factory, Dinah was rescued from her dire situation. The police did not recognise Dinah as a victim of a serious crime requiring assistance and support, but instead arrested her for working illegally without a permit. She was not provided with a translator or lawyer, and during police investigations she was held in a detention centre where she slept on the floor and received only two meals a day. When she was unable to pay the US$100 fine issued for working without a permit, Thai authorities deported her after a month in immigration detention (Pearson 2001: 54). Activists used cases like Dinah's to drive home the point that countries have an obligation to protect the rights of victims of trafficking, and that these rights should be safeguarded in the UN Trafficking Protocol.

These efforts met with partial success. Although both the Protocol and Convention contain a number of provisions relevant to the protection of trafficked persons, these measures are optional. Article 6(3) of the Trafficking Protocol obliges states to 'consider' implementing measures to promote the recovery of trafficked persons, for instance through the provision of housing, counselling, medical assistance and employment opportunities. In some cases, victim assistance is implicitly tied to the trafficked person's involvement in criminal proceedings against their exploiters. In appropriate cases, states parties are required to ensure their legal or administrative systems provide victims with access to information about judicial proceedings and assistance to enable their views and concerns to be presented during criminal proceedings against offenders. Other articles broadly refer to the possibility of compensation and encourage states to 'consider' permitting trafficked persons to remain temporarily or permanently in their territory (UNGA 2000: Arts 6(6) and 7).

In 2002, a growing awareness of the inadequate human rights protections provided by the Protocol prompted the then UN High Commissioner for Human Rights, Mary Robinson, to formulate a set of recommended principles and guidelines on human rights and human trafficking (OHCHR 2002). The Principles, which emphasise the primacy of human rights, are a soft-law instrument and therefore non-binding on states. The principles expressly affirm that anti-trafficking measures shall not adversely affect the human rights and dignity of persons (UNGA 2000: Arts 1 and 3).

In Southeast Asia, the law enforcement focus underscoring the Trafficking Protocol has resurfaced in some regional initiatives to address trafficking. There is a secondary focus on rights, but this has sometimes not filtered down into national policies and practices. In 2004, members of the Association of Southeast Asian Nations (ASEAN) signed the Declaration against Trafficking in Persons, Especially Women and Children. The Declaration focuses heavily on trafficking of women and children in the sex industry. Reflecting the interregional nature of trafficking flows in Southeast Asia, the ASEAN Declaration encourages regional coordination of law enforcement and immigration policy to better detect and disrupt trafficking networks, and punish offenders (Khoo 2010: 69). Under Article 6 of the Declaration, member states are obliged to respect and safeguard the dignity and human rights of trafficking victims. Countries are also required to distinguish victims of trafficking from their perpetrators, and ensure that victims are treated humanely and provided with essential medical care and other forms of assistance (UNGA 2000: Art. 5).

The Coordinated Mekong Ministerial Initiative against Trafficking (COMMIT) is a memorandum of understanding between the governments of the Greater Mekong Subregion. Under the agreement, countries coordinate their anti-trafficking policy efforts through subregional plans of action and task forces. The COMMIT preamble reiterates the important contribution that survivors of trafficking can, on a strictly voluntary basis, make to developing, implementing and evaluating anti-trafficking interventions (COMMIT 2004: Art. 10). In doing so, COMMIT has been quite successful in shifting the focus away from an exclusively criminal justice response to human trafficking. While the ASEAN Declaration and the COMMIT process both afford some level of protection to trafficked persons, the degree to which governments have implemented these human rights measures varies considerably in practice. Governments in Southeast Asia have not always adopted policies that reflect a rights-respecting approach, as envisaged in regional agreements.

Fifteen years after the adoption of the Protocol, trafficking is squarely on the radar of most governments. Countries have adopted and harmonised laws that criminalise all forms of trafficking. Over $120 million is spent annually by OECD countries to fund anti-trafficking initiatives in countries across the globe (Walk Free Foundation 2013, cited in Dottridge 2014: 5). This concerted international effort to eradicate trafficking is in part due to the influence of the US State Department's Trafficking in Persons (TIP) Report. The Report, published annually, evaluates and ranks countries according to their anti-trafficking efforts. Countries placed on the lowest ranking, Tier 3, can face economic sanctions from the US government, including termination of non-humanitarian aid and withdrawal of US support for loans in multilateral financial institutions.

Although initially criticised for encouraging reactive policies that sometimes neglected the human rights of victims, over time the country assessments contained in the TIP Reports have become more rigorous and comprehensive, taking into account the needs and experiences of victims (Gallagher 2015: 25). For instance, the Report has called on countries in the region to provide support for trafficking victims, regardless of their cooperation with prosecutors.[1] The report has shone a spotlight on the negative impact of some anti-trafficking policies and practices, including victim detention and deportation without compensation. Gallagher (2015: 8) notes that these impacts have not been consistently addressed in the Report's country assessments, because 'collateral damage' does not fall neatly within the report's tripartite 'prevent, protect, prosecute' criteria.

In the wake of the Protocol, a number of Southeast Asian countries have adopted measures to protect trafficking victims. Government-funded shelters, hotlines and counselling services have been established to provide victim assistance and support. Some countries have created special visa categories to prevent the imminent deportation of trafficking victims and others have improved witness protection measures for victims and their families. With these measures has come a shift in perceptions among governments in the region. Today, there is greater recognition that a female domestic worker or a male construction worker can be just as vulnerable to trafficking as young women working in the sex industry.

While the quality of services to victims across Southeast Asia has generally improved, there remains a fundamental problem that paternalistic attitudes continue to pervade the anti-trafficking space. In some Southeast Asian countries, the desire to 'protect women and girls' still comes at a cost of violating basic rights, such as the freedom of movement. Protection does not always mean the protection of basic rights.

Shelters: blurring the line between protection and paternalism

A primary challenge across a number of Southeast Asian countries is the detention of victims in closed shelters. During a raid on a fish-processing factory in Thailand, Bu from Laos told officials that she was not trafficked in order to avoid being taken to a closed shelter:

> I said no, because I didn't want to go to the Home. I've heard stories that it's like a prison and I have heard you can get stuck there for many months. At least if I go to the IDC [Immigration Detention Centre] then they will send me back to the border after a few weeks. I need to earn money – that's why I left. I didn't like being locked up in the factory, why would I want to be locked up again?
>
> *(Pearson 2012)*

When victims like Bu choose to avoid the support measures designed to protect them, this calls into question the effectiveness of anti-trafficking initiatives. Many trafficking victims have experienced trauma and sometimes abuse. Locking them away in shelters, isolated from their family and support networks, can prevent them from beginning their healing process and regaining autonomy.

Not all shelters in the Southeast Asian region detain victims. Many shelters, particularly those run by non-government organisations, provide protection and assistance to victims without restricting their movement. However, in some cases, instead of providing trafficked persons with proper support to recover from their traumatic experience, victims are placed in closed environments that can closely resemble prisons (Gallagher & Pearson 2010: 77). Victims may even be detained for months or years, being closely monitored by shelter staff and denied the ability to freely come and go (Lisborg 2014: 23). As a result, many trafficked persons brought to shelters view themselves as 'captured', not rescued, by the authorities (Pearson 2002: 33).

In Southeast Asia, the practice of confining trafficked persons in closed shelters has been reported to occur in Cambodia, Malaysia, the Philippines and Thailand (US Department of State 2014: 260, 315, 375; Gallagher & Pearson 2010: 77). Women and girls tend to be the main target for shelter detention, highlighting paternalistic attitudes and gendered perceptions that underlie and legitimise the policy (Gallagher & Pearson 2010; Lisborg 2014: 24–25).

In Malaysia, foreign trafficking victims identified by the government are placed in approved shelters where they are detained 24 hours a day and are not permitted to work or leave the shelter, except for supervised hospital appointments or court appearances (US Department of State 2014: 262). During her visit to Malaysia in March 2015, UN Special Rapporteur on Trafficking in Persons Joy Ngozi Ezeilo, described how these shelters did not offer victims appropriate educational and vocational training to promote their economic empowerment (Giammarinaro 2015). Instead, women and girls were trained in traditionally feminine domestic skills, such as sewing, cooking and handicraft. As the Special Rapporteur observed, these skills 'may not correspond with their ambitions and talents, or the needs of the labour market' (Giammarinaro 2015: 59). By restricting vocational opportunities to the domestic sphere, these programmes can weaken rather than improve the autonomy and future economic prosperity of trafficked women and girls.

Limited external or judicial oversight means these shelters can become sites of abuse, reproducing the harms that trafficked persons suffered at the hands of traffickers. The 2014 TIP Report found that in Cambodia, despite the government issuing standards of care guidelines for facilities housing trafficking victims, there were reports of abuse and inadequate care in some NGO-run shelters (US Department of State 2014).

Even shelters that are held out as 'model responses' to trafficking have disregarded or undermined human rights. For instance, in Thailand, the Baan Kredtrakarn shelter effectively detains up to 500 trafficked women and girls in a remote island location (Gallagher & Pearson 2010: 82). Despite the shelter's prominence as the centrepiece of the Thai government's anti-trafficking response, the Empower Foundation (2012: 62) has documented how the shelter 'operates a system of punishments' for women who 'misbehave'.

A number of arguments have been mounted in support of shelter detention. In order to prosecute the crime of human trafficking, proponents argue that shelter detention is necessary to ensure that victims are available as witnesses in criminal proceedings in order to secure the conviction of traffickers. From a practical perspective, confining victims to shelters guarantees that they will be available when required to give evidence in court (Gallagher & Pearson 2010: 110). When the focus is on law enforcement, the imperative of a successful conviction can sometimes be privileged over human rights.

The detention of trafficked persons can also be linked to their status as irregular migrants. In Cambodia and Thailand for instance, women and children identified as trafficking victims and who do not have a visa or residence permit are generally sent to government-run shelters as opposed to immigration detention (Gallagher & Pearson 2010: 105). Governments justify shelter detention of foreign victims, reasoning that they would otherwise be arrested and charged with immigration offences. Yet closed detention would seem to be a disproportionate solution. Governments could just as easily grant temporary or permanent visas and work permits to allow foreign victims to remain in their territory during the recovery process.

To avoid a lengthy stay in a closed shelter, some trafficked persons like Bu do not identify as victims and so end up in immigration detention facilities in poor conditions. Research conducted by Human Rights Watch (2013b) found that many Thai immigration detention centres are severely overcrowded and lack basic medical services and other necessities. In 2013, eight people reportedly died while in immigration detention in Thailand from health conditions that appeared to have been exacerbated by extreme heat and limited access to health care. The circumstances of detention can also take a toll on the mental health and well-being of trafficked persons, as they are separated from their families, unable to work, and left uncertain about their future.

Shelter detention is also justified on the grounds of victim safety and protection from reprisals or re-trafficking. In some cases, there may be compelling safety and security concerns to justify detention, especially in the early post-trafficking stages where reprisals are a real risk. However, there are alternative ways of affording protection that do not deny trafficked persons their freedom of movement. Protection measures can include increased staffing, closed circuit cameras, alarm systems, police protection or even providing victims with mobile phones (Gallagher & Pearson 2010: 108–109). The evidence suggests that these alternatives are often more effective than detention. In practice, closed shelters can make victims easy targets for people smugglers and traffickers (Human Rights Watch 2013a). Desperate to escape confinement, trafficked persons are willing to take a chance and trust strangers to facilitate an escape. For instance, in June 2013, traffickers promised to reunite Narunisa, a 25-year-old Rohingya woman confined in a shelter in Phang Nga province, with her husband in Malaysia for a 50,000 Baht (US$1,660) fee, but instead raped her repeatedly (Human Rights Watch 2013a). Clearly, closed detention for extended periods of time should remain a last resort. In cases where a victim's safety is at risk, an individualised assessment of the likelihood and severity of risks should be conducted, instead of adopting a blanket policy of closed detention.

Some shelter staff express fears that victims would run away if they were not confined, or that victims have consented to restrictions on their freedom of movement (Gallagher & Pearson 2010). These arguments are often informed by paternalistic moral judgements of the women and girls housed in shelters, particularly those who have been trafficked into the sex industry. According to this narrative of vulnerability, foolishness and immorality, victims are viewed as incapable of making respectable and responsible choices, and instead it is assumed that staff know what is 'best' (Lisborg 2014: 23). Yet the effective imprisonment of victims in shelters with inadequate care and support can unintentionally exacerbate the harms suffered by victims during their trafficking experience. Confining trafficked persons in closed shelters violates their sense of autonomy and independence and, in the process, can undermine their recovery. The Trafficking Principles and Guidelines regard detention of victims as an inappropriate violation of trafficking victims' freedom of movement (Gallagher & Pearson 2010: 86).

Detention can discourage victims from self-identifying as victims, which has an impact on effective prosecutions of traffickers and cooperation with law enforcement. A recent report into trafficked persons in the Greater Mekong Subregion by the United Nations Action for Cooperation against Trafficking in Persons (UN-ACT) (Surtees 2013: 61) underscored the critical importance of trust for trafficked persons in deciding whether to decline or accept assistance from authorities. A policy approach which respects the human rights of trafficking persons is more likely to achieve better law enforcement outcomes than one that disregards them.

Anti-trafficking and border control

For victims who are irregular migrants, trafficked persons are often at risk of being charged with immigration offences and deported. Unidentified trafficking victims can be subject to harsh immigration laws. In Malaysia, irregular migration is illegal under the country's Immigration Act (1959) and subject to significant penalties including fines of up to MR10,000, five years imprisonment and deportation (Giammarinaro 2015: para. [23]). Deportation disrupts the recovery process and effectively denies trafficked persons their right to redress since many countries require the victim to present in their territory to file a claim for compensation (Pearson 2009: 2).

Trafficked persons are often treated as undocumented migrants partly due to poor victim identification processes. Authorities are sometimes not properly trained to identify trafficking victims, particularly those that do not neatly fit the archetypal young, female victim trafficked into sex work. The US TIP Report (US Department of State 2015: 333) has reported that screening interviews conducted among fishermen returning to Thailand

> were often brief and conducted in open environments where brokers sometimes were present in the same room. Interpretation services for potential victims remained limited, and poor understanding of trafficking indicators by front-line officers, as well as the lack of private spaces to screen potential victims, may have led to many trafficking victims not being identified.

Confusion over the distinction between trafficking and smuggling can also come into play (Winterdyk, Perrin & Reichel 2011: 199). In practice the distinction between smuggling, the illegal movement of people across national borders for a fee with their consent, and trafficking, the movement of people by deception or force for the purpose of exploitation, can be problematic. Like Dinah, many trafficking victims in Southeast Asia initially consent to their journey, relying on the false assurances of a trafficker. If law enforcement officers mistake a case of trafficking for smuggling, trafficked persons will be viewed as complicit in the crime and deported as a result. In reality, thousands of people cross borders illegally into Southeast Asian countries every year, making the task of distinguishing between trafficking victims and irregular migrants all the more challenging for authorities. Victim identification is also complicated by the reluctance of trafficked persons to seek assistance. Some trafficked persons deliberately evade detection by the authorities, often out of fear of the repercussions. Some trafficked persons prefer the quick process of deportation as an illegal migrant than the possibility of being caught up in lengthy criminal justice proceedings and locked away in a closed shelter (Surtees 2013: 57).

Even where trafficking persons *are* identified, the 'solution' is often to repatriate victims back to their country of origin, regardless of the risks of persecution or hardship they may face (Lisborg 2014: 30). In some countries, harsh immigration laws are a deliberate aspect of counter-trafficking policy. Although Article 7 of the Protocol encourages states parties to allow trafficked persons to stay in their territory either temporarily or permanently, this is rarely observed in practice. Some Southeast Asian countries do provide temporary residence for victims, but this is often not available to all victims. In 2014, the Thai government issued 57 foreign victims with six-month work permits and visas which allowed them to work temporarily in Thailand during the course of legal proceedings against their traffickers (US Department of State 2015: 333). However female victims that did not receive a work permit, representing the vast majority, were generally confined to government shelters until their repatriation (US Department of State 2015: 333).

In Cambodia, foreign trafficked persons are generally repatriated to their country of origin. No viable legal alternatives are provided to victims who may face retribution or hardship upon return to their home countries (US Department of State 2015: 111). This puts trafficked persons in danger and encourages re-trafficking, since many are likely to risk exploitation again to escape from the conditions they left to begin with.

Those that do not cooperate in criminal proceedings are more likely to face deportation. In Malaysia, despite some limited protections against prosecution for status-related offences in the Anti-Trafficking Act (2007) (Giammarinaro 2015: paras. [25], [55]), victims who do not provide testimony in a successful prosecution are generally not granted immunity from criminal offences. As a result, they are usually transferred to immigration detention centres and deported.

Inadvertent harms

Anti-trafficking measures can also have a knock-on effect that restricts the rights of migrants and sex workers (Global Alliance Against Traffic in Women 2007: 16–17). Under the guise of preventing trafficking, governments sometimes refuse entry or exit visas to individuals deemed 'at risk' of being trafficked. By restricting freedom of movement for broad categories of people, these 'protection' measures can increase the vulnerability of individuals to trafficking by denying a safe and legal pathway to migration. Vulnerable people may take even more risky migration journeys in order to avoid detection. Victims who have crossed borders illegally may be less likely to approach authorities for help when they are being exploited by traffickers due to fear of prosecution. With young single women the primary target, the policies can also amount to discrimination. The UN Special Rapporteur on violence against women has noted that 'Policies and practices that either overtly discriminate against women or that sanction or encourage discrimination against women tend to increase women's chances of being trafficked' (SRVAW 2000: 43).

In the Southeast Asian region, so-called preventative measures are employed in a number of countries. In Myanmar, there are reports that the government has denied passports to women aged under 26 seeking to travel outside the country without a chaperone (Farrelly 2012: 142). Similarly, the Philippine government uses 'screening' procedures at airports and seaports to prevent potential trafficking victims from travelling.[2] Known as the 'off-load' strategy, travellers can be subject to further questioning by immigration officials and prevented from leaving the country if deemed vulnerable to human trafficking (Philippines Bureau of Immigration 2015). In 2012, the vice president of the Philippines explicitly tied the government's 'off-load' policy to the US TIP Report: 'The offloading policy has contributed to our gains in the drive against trafficking, and as a result, our country was elevated to Tier 2 in the US State Department's Trafficking index. This year, we hope to be elevated to Tier 1' (ABS-CBN News 2012). These comments suggest that through the language of victim protection and border security, discriminatory policies which deny agency and autonomy to potential victims of trafficking are celebrated as successful counter-trafficking interventions.

The rights and needs of 'rescued' victims can again be sidelined in raids or crackdowns on facilities suspected of hiding trafficking practices. Amid the chaos of a police raid, trafficked persons are sometimes not informed of their rights, or, like Dinah, detained and arrested. The physicality and high visibility of raids make them a powerful advertisement for a government seeking to prove they have adopted a strong stance on human trafficking. As a result, the public relations value of an intervention is sometimes prioritised over the human rights of victims. The UN Special Rapporteur on Human Trafficking reported in 2012 that during anti-trafficking raids in the Philippines, victims were filmed by media in 'little or no clothes before being taken to police stations' (Ezelio 2012: para. [51]). The need to send a strong message to the international community that trafficking is being dealt with head on can result in breaches of privacy and dignity of trafficked persons.

'Crackdowns' on trafficking can also be used as a pretext for harsh immigration policies or discriminatory campaigns against the sex work industry. In 2010, in response to the Cambodian Prime Minister's appeal to end trafficking in women through a nationwide crackdown, the police widened their search beyond brothels and began raiding cafes and massage parlours.

Sandy (2012: 51) highlights that during the raids, the only individuals brought into custody were female sex workers. Similarly, Human Rights Watch (2010: 9) reported how in cases it investigated of police arrests of sex workers in Cambodia in 2008 and 2009, there was no attempt to distinguish between women voluntarily in sex work and those who were victims of trafficking.

The way forward: a rights-based approach

Over the past decade, there have been significant advances in how governments in the Southeast Asian region address trafficking. Anti-trafficking laws have been adopted and are being implemented, with varying degrees of success. The quality and breadth of victim services have improved and governments are making more of a concerted effort to train officials to detect victims, and to ensure counter-trafficking measures are victim sensitive. The advocacy efforts of numerous human rights and anti-trafficking organisations have fostered a growing awareness that policy responses to trafficking should place the rights of victims first. Looking ahead, anti-trafficking efforts in Southeast Asia may be further strengthened by reviewing numerous initiatives and measures being developed around the world. These policies, guided and informed by human rights, can offer a template for the region.

Governments increasingly recognise that providing safe, legal and inexpensive pathways for migration is crucial to eradicating trafficking. Many people in Southeast Asia depend on labour migration for their livelihoods and are willing to risk exploitation if legal avenues for migration are not available or too costly or bureaucratic. The exclusive focus on trafficking has sometimes obscured the other human rights violations labour migrants can face, for instance underpayment and poor working conditions. Creating fair and safe migration policies is one way to reduce both trafficking and a host of other abuses as well.

Removing barriers to legal migration, for instance by opening up work permits to various sectors of work in high-demand, can dramatically decrease the vulnerability of migrant workers to trafficking by offering a viable alternative. Legal avenues for migration are not risk free; however, victims who are in countries legally enjoy better legal protections and are able to access support services and law enforcement. Some progress has been achieved in this area through bilateral agreements. For instance, in 2014 1,351 Bangladeshis entered Malaysia legally to work under a January 2013 memorandum of understanding between the two countries (US Department of State 2014: 262). Similar agreements exist between Malaysia and Indonesia and the Philippines, as well as Thailand and Cambodia, Laos and Myanmar.

A number of organisations have pioneered alternative 'open' models for shelters that seek to empower victims of trafficking and restore their dignity. These shelters provide comprehensive support services for trafficked persons without restricting their freedom of movement. In Nepal, the grassroots organisation Shakti Samuha, meaning 'Women of Power', operates a shelter that is run and managed by survivors of trafficking. The shelter is the first of its kind in Nepal and provides a range of services designed to empower victims to regain control of their lives. The staff provide individualised legal and medical assistance, psychological counselling and vocational training to assist trafficked persons in their long-term reintegration into society. As former victims themselves, the staff at Shakti Samuha come from a place of empathy and understanding, rather than paternalism. Outside the shelter, Shakti Samuha runs victim-centric educational programmes and group activities targeting potential victims to build their self-confidence and ensure they are informed of their rights (The Protection Project: 55). These programmes adopt a proactive approach to prevention and respect the rights, needs and choices of the women and girls involved.

Another positive development has been the emergence of awareness campaigns which inform and educate potential victims of trafficking as workers and rights-holders, rather than simply as potential victims. Research conducted by UN-ACT (Surtees 2013: 52) found that many trafficked persons in the Greater Mekong Subregion remain unaware of the support systems available to them. To address this information gap, governments in Southeast Asia are engaging of civil society, the media and the private sector to empower vulnerable populations. In Hong Kong, the government publishes information pamphlets in six major languages to educate migrant workers of their employment rights and the risks of trafficking. In 2014, the Malaysian government launched over 5,000 public awareness campaigns across various platforms including radio, television and publications. Information was distributed in Bahasa Malaysia, Mandarin, Tamil and other languages (Giammarinaro 2015: para. [79]). These awareness campaigns should be combined with longer term educational and empowerment initiatives that give agency to trafficked persons and those vulnerable to trafficking.

An innovative feature of the European Union's response to trafficking has been the introduction of a 'reflection and recovery' period for victims. Under the Council of Europe Convention, if there are reasonable grounds to believe that an individual is a victim of human trafficking, countries must guarantee a minimum of 30 days 'reflection and recovery period' to allow the victim to make an informed decision about whether and to what extent they chose to cooperate in a prosecution (Council of Europe 2005: Art. 13). This approach, which is included in the UNDOC model anti-trafficking law, reduces the pressure on victims to participate and shifts the focus towards their mental and physical wellbeing. Measures have also been put in place to allow victims to legally resettle in their destination country, regardless of whether they have cooperated with law enforcement.

In some parts of the globe, trafficked persons have been reconceptualised from victims to rights-holders entitled to compensation. The recognition that trafficked persons should receive compensation for crimes committed against them both promotes the human rights of victims and enhances counter-trafficking prevention measures by acting as a financial deterrent to traffickers. Although compensation is contemplated by the Convention and Protocol, in practice it remains limited in the Southeast Asian region. Without legal protections against detention or deportation and limited access to adequate support services, including legal representation, there is little scope for victims to bring an action for compensation successfully in most Southeast Asian countries.

In Europe, a group of anti-trafficking organisations known as La Strada International launched the European Action Pact for Compensation for Trafficked Persons Project (COMPACT) in 2010. In conjunction with Anti-Slavery International, the project seeks to remove any practical, legal and procedural barriers to adequate compensation for trafficked victims. As part of the project, researchers have prepared national handbooks on trafficking compensation to assist lawyers and non-government organisations representing trafficked persons, and developed specific working plans to identify ways to improve compensation mechanisms at a national level (The Protection Project 2012: 36). In viewing trafficked persons as rights holders with a legal remedy, the COMPACT initiative and others like it have the power to place trafficked persons in a position of autonomy, empowerment and help contribute to their future recovery.

Conclusion

Anti-trafficking measures in Southeast Asia have at times ignored human rights. For some trafficking victims, their post-trafficking experience is of detention rather than support, or deportation rather than protection. Counter-trafficking measures have also interfered with the rights, dignity and agency of persons who are not trafficked, from young women seeking to travel, to sex workers who are stigmatised in the name of eradicating trafficking. With advocacy and international pressure, Southeast Asian governments have begun the slow process of refocusing their counter-trafficking policies to place human rights at their core. In this regard, global initiatives that have successfully adopted a rights-based approach to trafficking can serve as valuable templates for the region. If we are to combat human trafficking effectively, our response should be centred on a consideration of human rights, particularly of those most affected by the crime.

Notes

1 See for example, the 2014 recommendation to Malaysia:

> Amend the anti-trafficking law and government regulations to allow trafficking victims to travel, work, and reside outside government facilities, including while under protection orders; provide, and refer all victims to, protective services within Malaysia, regardless of the likelihood their cases will go to trial.
>
> (*US Department of State 2014: 261*)

2 Governed by the Bureau of Immigration 2012, *Guidelines on Departure Formalities for International-Bound Passengers in All Airports and Seaports in the Country*, www.philembassy.org.nz/images/2012/advisory/guidelinesindepartureformalities.pdf.

References

ABS-CBN News 2012, 'New offloading rule to boost anti-trafficking drive – Binay', viewed 2 August 2015, www.abs-cbnnews.com/global-filipino/01/18/12/new-offloading-rule-boost-anti-trafficking-drive-binay.

COMMIT 2004, *Memorandum of Understanding on Cooperation against Trafficking in Persons in the Greater Mekong Sub-Region (COMMIT)*, http://evaw-global-database.unwomen.org/-/media/files/un%20women/vaw/full%20text/asia/cambodia%20%20-%20commit%20mou%20(2004)/cambodia%20%20-%20commit%20mou%20(2004).pdf?vs=1929.

Council of Europe 2005, *Convention on Action against Trafficking in Human Beings*, 16 May, CETS 197.

Dottridge, M 2014, 'How is the money to combat human trafficking spent?', *Anti-Trafficking Review*, vol. 3, pp. 3–14.

Empower Foundation 2012, *Hit and Run: Sex Workers' Research on Anti-Trafficking in Thailand*, Nonthaburi: Empower Foundation, viewed 2 August 2015, www.empowerfoundation.org/sexy_file/Hit%20and%20Run%20%20RATSW%20Eng%20online.pdf.

Environmental Justice Foundation 2015, *Pirates and Slaves: How Overfishing in Thailand Fuels Human Trafficking and the Plundering of Our Oceans*, London: Environmental Justice Foundation, viewed 2 August 2015, http://ejfoundation.org/sites/default/files/public/EJF_Pirates_and_Slaves_2015.pdf.

Ezelio, J 2012, *Report of the Special Rapporteur on Trafficking in Persons, Especially Women and Children, Ms. Joy Ngozi Ezeilo: Addendum – Mission to the Philippines*, A/HRC/23/48/Add.3, Geneva: Human Rights Council.

Farrelly, N 2012, 'Exploitation and escape: Journeys across the Burma–Thailand frontier', in M Ford, L Lyons and W van Schendel (eds), *Labour Migration and Human Trafficking in Southeast Asia: Critical Perspectives*, Abingdon: Routledge.

Ford, M, Lyons, L & van Schendel, W (eds) 2012, *Labour Migration and Human Trafficking in Southeast Asia: Critical Perspectives*, Abingdon: Routledge.

GAATW 2007, *Collateral Damage: The Impact of Anti-Trafficking Measures on Human Rights around the World*, Bangkok: Global Alliance against Traffic in Women.

Gallagher, A 2015, 'Two cheers for the trafficking protocol', *Anti-Trafficking Review*, vol. 4, pp. 14–32.

Gallagher, A & Pearson E 2010, 'The high cost of freedom: A legal and policy analysis of shelter detention for victims of trafficking', *Human Rights Quarterly*, vol. 32, pp. 73–114.

Giammarinaro, M 2015, *Report of the Special Rapporteur on Trafficking in Persons, Especially Women and Children, Maria Grazia Giammarinaro: Addendum – Mission to Malaysia*, A/HRC/29/38/Add.1, Geneva: Human Rights Council.

Human Rights Watch 2010, *Off the Streets: Arbitrary Detention and Other Abuses against Sex Workers in Cambodia*, www.hrw.org/sites/default/files/reports/cambodia0710webwcover_2.pdf.

Human Rights Watch 2011, *They Deceived Us at Every Step: Abuse of Cambodian Domestic Workers Migrating to Malaysia*, New York: Human Rights Watch, viewed 2 August 2015, www.hrw.org/sites/default/files/reports/cambodia1111webwcover.pdf.

Human Rights Watch 2013a, *Thailand: Release and Protect Rohingya 'Boat People'*, Press Release, 20 August, viewed 2 August 2015, www.hrw.org/news/2013/08/20/thailand-release-and-protect-rohingya-boat-people.

Human Rights Watch 2013b, *Thailand: Traffickers Access Government-run 'Shelter'*, Press release, 27 June, viewed 2 August 2015, www.hrw.org/news/2013/06/27/thailand-traffickers-access-government-run-shelter.

International Labour Organization 2006, *The Mekong Challenge – Underpaid, Overworked and Overlooked: The Realities of Young Migrant Workers in Thailand*, Bangkok: ILO.

International Labour Organization 2012, *Global Estimate of Forced Labour: Results and Methodology*, Geneva: ILO.

Khoo, O 2010, 'Regional approaches to trafficking in women in South-East Asia: The role of national human rights institutions and the new ASEAN human rights body', *Australian Journal of Human Rights*, vol. 15, no. 2, pp. 59–82.

Lisborg, A 2014, 'The good, the bad and the ugly: In the name of victim protection', in S Yea (ed.), *Human Trafficking in Asia: Forcing Issues*, Abingdon: Routledge, pp. 19–34.

Office of the High Commissioner for Human Rights 2002, *Recommended Principles and Guidelines on Human Rights and Human Trafficking*, E/2002/68/Add.1, Geneva: United Nations High Commissioner for Human Rights.

Pearson, E 2001, *Human Rights and Trafficking in Persons: A Handbook*, Bangkok: Global Alliance Against Trafficking in Women.

Pearson, E 2002, *Human Trafficking, Human Rights: Redefining Victim Protection*, New York: Anti-Slavery International.

Pearson, E 2009, 'No sanctuary: Trafficking of Burmese people at the Thai–Malay Border', Human Rights Watch, 12 February, www.hrw.org/news/2009/02/12/no-sanctuary-trafficking-burmese-people-thaimalay-border.

Pearson, E 2012, 'Do not harm: "Post-Trafficking Abuses"', in M Worden (ed.), *The Unfinished Revolution: Voices from the Global Fight for Women's Rights*, New York: Seven Stories.

Philippines Bureau of Immigration 2015, 'FAQ – travel requirements', viewed 2 August 2015, http://immigration.gov.ph/faqs/travel-req.

The Protection Project 2012, *100 Best Practices in Combating Trafficking in Persons: The Role of Civil Society*, Washington, DC: The Protection Project at Johns Hopkins University, viewed 2 August 2015, www.ungift.org/doc/knowledgehub/resource-centre/CSOs/100-Best-Practices-in-Combating-TIP.pdf.

Sandy, L 2012, 'International politics, anti-trafficking measures and sex work in Cambodia', in M Ford, L Lyons and W van Schendel (eds), *Labour Migration and Human Trafficking in Southeast Asia: Critical Perspectives*, Abingdon: Routledge.

Special Rapporteur on the Violence Against Women, Its Causes and Consequences (SRVAW) 2000, *Rep. on Trafficking in Women, Women's Migration and Violence Against Women, Comm'n Hum. Rts*, E/CN.4/2000/68, 29 February 2000 (by Radhika Coomaraswamy).

Surtees, R 2013, *After Trafficking: Experiences and Challenges in the (Re)integration of Trafficked Persons in the Greater Mekong Sub-region*, Bangkok, UNIAP/NEXUS Institute.

UN-ACT 2015, *Reflections from the Greater Mekong Sub-region on the Occasion of the 10 Year Anniversary of COMMIT*, Bangkok: United Nations Action for Cooperation against Trafficking in Persons, viewed 2 August 2015, http://un-act.org/publication/view/commit-10-years-reflections-from-the-gms/.

United Nations, General Assembly (UNGA) 2000, Resolution 55/25, *Protocol to Prevent, Suppress and Punish Trafficking in Persons, Especially Women and Children, Supplementing the United Nations Convention against Transnational Organised Crime*, A/RES/55/25 (15 November 2000), available from undocs.org/A/RES/55/25.

United Nations Office for Drug Control and Crime Prevention 2013, *Transnational Organised Crime in East Asia and the Pacific: A Threat Assessment UNODC* Vienna: UNODC, viewed 2 August 2015, www.unodc.org/documents/data-and-analysis/Studies/TOCTA_EAP_web.pdf.

United Nations Office for Drug Control and Crime Prevention 2014, *Global Report on Trafficking in Persons*, Vienna: UNODC, viewed 2 August 2015, www.unodc.org/documents/data-and-analysis/glotip/GLOTIP_2014_full_report.pdf.

UNODC 2015, *Regional Programme for Southeast Asia 2014–2017: Promoting the Rule of Law and Health to Address Drugs and Crime in Southeast Asia*, Bangkok: UNODC, www.unodc.org/documents/southeastasiaandpacific/procurement/draft_SEA_RP_masterversion_10_10_13_tcSPU_option_1.pdf.

United States Department of State 2014, *Trafficking in Persons Report*, Washington, DC: US Department of State, viewed 2 August 2015, www.state.gov/j/tip/rls/tiprpt/2014/index.htm.

United States Department of State 2015, *Trafficking in Persons Report*, Washington, DC: US Department of State, viewed 2 August 2015, www.state.gov/documents/organization/245365.pdf.

Winterdyk, J, Perrin, B & Reichel, P (eds) 2011, *Human Trafficking: Exploring the International Nature, Concerns and Complexities*, Boca Raton, FL: CRC Press.

18

Southeast Asian regional cooperation and combating human trafficking

Huong Le Thu

Introduction

Trafficking in persons, next to other forms of transnational and organised crimes, is a serious problem across the world. In Asia, particularly Southeast Asia, human trafficking is a fast-growing phenomenon. In fact, it is estimated that human trafficking is the fastest growing organised crime, after trafficking in drugs and firearms (Crossette 2000: para. 1). It is expected that within the next decade, trafficking in human beings will surpass all other forms of trafficking in terms of numbers and profitability, notwithstanding the costs to human wellbeing (Schauer & Wheaton 2006: 146–169). The region's growing socio-economic disparity, political unrest and ethnic-religious tensions create vulnerabilities that are leveraged by the human traffickers.

Before analysing prevalent trends of the human trafficking industry, the impact of this in Southeast Asia and then evaluating the effectiveness of regional cooperation to mitigate trafficking, this chapter commences with a consideration of the ramifications of the problem.

The United Nations Protocol to Prevent, Suppress and Punish Trafficking in Persons Especially Women and Children, supplementing the United Nations Convention against Transnational Organized Crime (the Palermo Protocol) (UNGA Res 55/25 of 15 November 2000, Article 3(a)) defines trafficking in persons, also known as trafficking in human beings, as follows:

> 'Trafficking in persons' shall mean the recruitment, transportation, transfer, harbouring or receipt of persons, by means of the threat or use of force or other forms of coercion, of abduction, fraud, of deception, of the abuse of power or of a position of vulnerability or of the giving or receiving of payments or benefits to achieve the consent of a person having control over another person, for the purpose of exploitation. Exploitation shall include, at a minimum, the exploitation of the prostitution of others or other forms of sexual exploitation, forced labour or services, slavery or practices similar to slavery, servitude or the removal of organs.

In Southeast Asia, trafficking in persons, wildlife and drugs remains a prolific problem for the region. According to United Nations (UN) estimates, in the last decade the number of trafficked persons in Southeast Asia has soared up to three times the number of people that were 'trafficked into slavery over four centuries in Africa' (US Committee for Refugees and Immigrants 2000: 3; Crossette 2000: 2–3). With an estimated 11.7 million persons as at 2011, the world's highest concentration of forced labour victims are located in the Asia-Pacific region (ILO 2012a). Other estimates, including one given by the director of the United Nations Office for Drug Control and Crime Prevention (UNODC), state that from between 1990 and 2000, the number of victims of trafficking in Southeast Asia has reached an astounding 30 million (Richard 1999).

The Association of Southeast Asian Nations (ASEAN) is an intergovernmental organisation established in 1967 and includes the representation of Brunei, Indonesia, Malaysia, the Philippines, Singapore, Thailand, Cambodia, Laos, Myanmar and Vietnam. ASEAN is a multilateral framework established to advance political, economic, socio-cultural matters, among others, between member states in the Southeast Asian region. ASEAN has been based on an informal style of cooperation with rules and norms founded on non-intervention and consensus, even gaining its own name, 'the ASEAN-style' (Acharya 1998; Narine 2002). Given the complex conditions of the post-Cold War era, the development of regional structures remained challenged by the diverse political and economic preferences of the member states. Continuous territorial disputes in the region add to the integration process, whereas disparate economic progress has increased the cohesion gap within the Association. ASEAN has hence been an important, but limited, regional cooperation initiative.

Originally a collection of newly independent postcolonial states (with the exception of Thailand), over the past few decades the Association has transformed, gaining legal personality in 2008 with the adoption of the ASEAN Charter. In the same year, the ASEAN Intergovernmental Commission on Human Rights (AICHR) was established. Since the early 2000s, the Association had been committed to the creation of an 'ASEAN Community' occurring in 2015. The aims of the ASEAN Community are structured around the three pillars of political security, economy and socio-cultural interests. These pillars are intended to ensure a peaceful, stable and prosperous region (ASEAN 1997b). Among the long list of commitments outlined in the ASEAN Vision 2020 member states agreed to confront human security threats and transnational crimes, including trafficking in persons (ASEAN 2009).

This chapter has three objectives: First, to examine the phenomenon of trafficking in persons across Southeast Asia. Second, to explain the connection between the integration of ASEAN member states, the increased movement of people, and growing challenges of trafficking in persons across the region. Third, to evaluate the region's anti-trafficking measures. In the wake of the burgeoning ASEAN Community, this challenging issue exemplifies the achievements and limitations that the region faces. This chapter considers two vulnerable groups of trafficked persons: women and children. While women and children remain the majority victims of trafficking, the number of men and boys trafficked, particularly for labour exploitation, are growing fast. There is imbalanced attention in research and policy in addressing trafficking in men and boys.

Trafficking in persons in Southeast Asia

Prevalence of the problem

Of the different forms of trafficking in persons, most prevalent in Southeast Asia is trafficking for the purposes of sexual exploitation (whether sexual slavery or commercial sexual exploitation), labour exploitation, forced marriage, forced begging, surrogacy, organ harvesting and forced adoption. Particularly prone to exploitation through trafficking are persons escaping poverty and fleeing political, religious and ethnic prosecution.

Southeast Asia as a region has one of the highest occurrences globally of trafficking in persons. The US Department of State's annual Trafficking in Persons (TIP) Report on the problems and progress of human trafficking have been a benchmark monitoring and evaluation tool for over a decade. The TIP report adopts a tier standard for differentiating levels of compliance that a country has achieved with the Trafficking Victims Protection Act (the Act). According to the TIP Report: a 'Tier 1 reporting standard represents countries whose government fully complies with the Act's minimum standards'; 'Tier 2 represents those countries whose government does not fully comply with the Act's minimum standards, but are making significant efforts to bring themselves into compliance'; the 'Tier 2 Watch List represents countries whose government does not fully comply with the Act's minimum standards and the number of victims are significant or increasing, there is a failure to provide evidence of increasing efforts or the efforts toward compliance were based on a country's commitment to take additional future steps'; 'Tier 3 refers to those countries whose government does not fully comply with the minimum standards of the Act and are making no significant efforts to do so' (US Department of State 2015). ASEAN members have been repeatedly placed on either the Tier 2 or Tier 2 Watch Lists with some even being ranked as Tier 3 (see Table 18.1). Nine of ASEAN countries joined the list of notoriety where trafficking in persons is rampant.

Southeast Asia is a region in which trafficked persons originate, transit and settle. Trafficking in women and children is most prevalent in the region, however, the number of trafficked men and young adults for labour exploitation is also growing. In Southeast Asia, trafficking in women and children is mainly driven by the increased demand for women in the sex industries, the bride trade and for domestic work. Children are often trafficked for the purposes of forced begging, domestic work, adoption, marriage, or other forms of labour. The vulnerability of trafficked women and children is exacerbated by a combination of factors such as poverty, sexism and racism (Chuang 1998: 68–70), together with gender-based policies, cultural values or societal practices. In the Asia-Pacific region in general, and Southeast Asia in particular, economic and socio-cultural conditions often do not favour women and children. In some cases, political contexts relating to ethnic and religious division can contribute to unregulated migration, which further exposes vulnerable persons to a danger of being trafficked. For example, a large group of stateless Rohingya from Myanmar and Bangladesh were denied refugee status or citizenship by a number of neighbouring ASEAN countries, including Malaysia, Indonesia, the

Table 18.1 Trafficking in persons minimum reporting standard tier ranking system for Southeast Asian countries

Country	*2010*	*2011*	*2012*	*2013*	*2014*	*2015*
Brunei	2WL	2WL	2	2	2	2
Cambodia	2	2	2	2WL	2WL	2WL
Indonesia	2	2	2	2	2	2
Laos	2WL	2	2	2	2WL	2WL
Malaysia	2WL	2WL	2WL	2WL	3	2WL
Myanmar	3	3	2WL	2WL	2WL	2WL
Philippines	2WL	2	2	2	2	2

Source: Compiled by the author, based on US Department of State Trafficking in Persons Reports

Philippines and Thailand. Of this group, the United Nations High Commissioner for Refugees (UNHCR) has estimated that there were 25,000 victims of trafficking between January and March 2015 (Miles 2015). The crisis remains unresolved, with statistics of those who died on boats growing. None of the regional mechanisms proved to be helpful in the wake of individual ASEAN members being implicated in the crisis.

The prevalence of trafficking in women and children in Southeast Asia has been attributed to the 'feminisation' and 'illegalisation' of labour migration, as well as demands from the tourism industry, which often engages with the sex industry (Piper 2005). Growing demand for tourism-based sex is a difficult issue to address due to a common desire among Southeast Asian states to boost tourism development. In some continental Southeast Asian countries, this trend is reportedly deteriorating due to the growing demand from China—the fastest growing market for trafficking. China is a society built on imbalanced gender structures due to family planning policies, coupled with a cultural preference for a boy child, which has led to an increased need for the illegal 'import of people'. Women are trafficked into China for the purpose of forced marriage, prostitution or forced surrogacy. Children are trafficked for forced adoption or sexual or labour exploitation (Le Thu 2015). While these trends are known to be prevalent, the real scope of the problem is yet to be fully captured. The dynamics of the global economy are tightly linked to the push and pull for migration and also opportunities for organised crimes for the illicit movement of people (Rahman 2011).

In 2013, in order to assist the newly established ASEAN Intergovernmental Commission on Human Rights (AICHR) to identify the most pressing concerns, the ASEAN Human Rights Resource Centre (AHRRC) initiated a report portraying the situation of violence, exploitation and abuse affecting women and children in all member states. The report summarised the prevalence of the trafficking problem occurring across the region, with the sexual exploitation of women and children cited as a common and growing problem across Southeast Asia. Often this has been fuelled by the growing demand from abroad for sex-based tourism. Intra-ASEAN irregular movements are of serious concern, but also extra-regional trafficking, including to East Asia, Europe, America and Australia, are also prevalent. Economic, political, ethnic and religious refugee claimants are another vulnerable group being exploited by traffickers and smugglers.

The forms of exploitation that take place after the act of trafficking are summarised in Table 18.2:

Table 18.2 Forms of exploitation and the predominant Southeast Asian countries affected

Issue of concern	*Countries affected*
Trafficking in women	Cambodia, Indonesia, Malaysia, Myanmar, Philippines, Singapore, Thailand, Vietnam
Trafficking in children	Cambodia, Indonesia, Lao PDR, Myanmar, Philippines, Thailand, Vietnam
Sex tourism	Thailand, Cambodia
Sexual exploitation and prostitution	Cambodia, Indonesia, Myanmar, Philippines, Vietnam
Sexual exploitation of children	Cambodia, Indonesia, Lao PRD, Malaysia, Myanmar, Philippines, Vietnam
Exploitation of domestic workers (esp. female)	Indonesia, Malaysia, Singapore
Child labour	Cambodia, Lao DPR, the Philippines
Children involved in armed conflict	Myanmar, Philippines, Thailand

Source: Compiled by the author based on the Human Rights Resource Centre 2013 Report on Forms of Recruitment

In terms of recruitment, most trafficked persons are reported to be deceived into believing they would receive a gainful employment with a range of enticing opportunities being offered by destination countries. In other cases, some trafficked persons were aware that they would be engaging in sex-related activity, but were otherwise deceived about the conditions attached to those activities and were subjected to forced prostitution under the threat of serious harm. Migrant workers have faced confiscation of their passports, restrictions on their movement and illegal withholding of their pay, making them vulnerable to forced labour (UNODC 2015). The vulnerabilities of trafficked persons may be exacerbated by their lack of familiarity with the language, geography, law and other relevant information of the destination country. Thus, they often have no choice but to abide by the rules of traffickers.

There are also high incidences of voluntary migration that lead to involuntary servitude during the course of the migration process. This is true for women, but more apparent in cases of children migrants because of their vulnerability. For example, in Lao, studies show that there were no cases of the selling or kidnapping of children in the pre-departure stage; rather, movement is initiated independently. In the Burmese-Thai context, women and girls have been observed to move voluntarily, largely for economic and human rights reasons, with exploitation occurring during or after the movement. Officials in the Ranong and Sakaew provinces of Thailand, bordering Myanmar and Cambodia respectively, believe trafficking cases to be very rare; instead, they describe the current situation as a labour and migration issue (AHRRC 2013).

The ASEAN Human Rights Resource Centre's reports indicated that information technology is increasingly being used to facilitate exploitation. For instance, in Singapore, an increasing number of teenagers are said to use the internet or mobile phones to advertise or sell sex services. The Country Report on Thailand also noted that the internet has been used to facilitate the recent rise of child sex tourism with websites being used to provide potential child sex tourists with pornographic accounts and information on how to procure child prostitutes.

The root causes

Widespread poverty, high unemployment, low levels of literacy, few income-earning opportunities and persecution or denial of human rights by authorities (particularly by those commonly targeting ethnic and religious minorities) have been commonly cited as causes of exploitation. A widespread misperception that greater income opportunities are available in rapidly developing urban areas may provide an additional incentive to migrate. In the case of Myanmar, protracted armed conflicts along territorial border regions as well as political instability remain driving forces for trafficking to/from the country. Aside from the above-mentioned 'push factors', demand for cheap sex and labour fuels exploitation. The imbalanced gender ratio in China and strong demand for a male child contributes to the prevalence of trafficking in women and children from Vietnam to China.

Weak law enforcement, corruption, widespread inequality, vulnerabilities including difficulties in obtaining birth certificates, together with an inadequate understanding of trafficking contribute to the prevalence of exploitation. Culture and gender roles, the widespread use of the internet, consumerism, ease of travel and geographic proximity are also said to facilitate exploitation. Aside from these factors, other causes included a lack of awareness of the dangers involved, a lack of access to financial institutions, lack of safety nets and shattered or dysfunctional families (AHRRC 2013).

The shadow economy of trafficking

'Porous' governance is not the only feature facilitating trafficking. The so-called 'shadow economy', being the profit that this illicit business creates, remains a significant factor.

While understanding of the shadow economy remains based on assumptions, in Southeast Asia it is a significant contributor to the economy. In developing economies, like most ASEAN countries, the shadow economy is heavily affected by an incomplete tax system, limited enforcement of national legal systems and ineffective monitoring measures.

Trafficking in persons is a 'monopolistically competitive market supplying products in many forms' (Wheaton, Schauer & Galli 2010: 119). The profitability of trafficking was studied by establishing a formula that would determine the difference between the costs of trafficking and the price that the traffickers can get per victim. They have identified the actors involved in the process as: (1) vulnerable individuals, (2) traffickers, (3) employers and (4) users of slave-produced products or services. In such arrangements, the vulnerable individuals are prone to become victims who would be transported and traded by the traffickers, and then become exploited by the employers.

Trafficking is hence 'an opportunistic response to the tensions between the economic necessity to migrate, on the one hand, and the politically motivated restrictions on migration on the other' (Chuang 1998). The real challenge of trafficking in persons is that the business is extremely dynamic and adapting as populations become vulnerable and areas of demand shift. For example and as noted above, the former one-child policy in China has caused the explosion in demand for females, which has led to growing numbers of trafficked women, particularly from Southeast Asia, for the purposes of enforced marriages, sexual exploitation or forced surrogacy as well as children for forced adoptions. War, conflict and the mass movement of refugees are other examples of how the trafficking industry adapts to global changes. Vulnerable groups with limited or no protection or formal identification, like the Rohingya from Myanmar, become a target for the traffickers. Pervasive denial of basic human rights, including citizenship and rights related to it, such as education, housing registration or employment, are often related to discriminations that create the vulnerability of these groups. Individual ASEAN member state's policies towards certain ethnic and religious groups are also believed to be among the factors that cause large-scale unregulated movements. Such situations create opportunity for illicit exploitation, such as smuggling and trafficking of the people affected.

Regional collaboration against trafficking

This part of the chapter outlines a range of collective challenges facing the ASEAN region in respect of problematic anti-trafficking mechanisms. Most countries in Southeast Asia have even been identified as major sources, transit points and destination countries for trafficking in persons for the purpose of sexual and labour exploitation. Following the footsteps of other regions and governments, the countries in Southeast Asia have started to raise awareness to combat trafficking in women and children. Each Southeast Asian country has enacted laws criminalising trafficking in persons, especially in women and children, under domestic laws either by enacting specific laws and regulations or incorporating it into their respective penal code. Table 18.3 lists the anti-trafficking instruments enacted by each Southeast Asian country.

ASEAN multilateral efforts in counter-trafficking

ASEAN affirmed its commitment to women and children by establishing the ASEAN Intergovernmental Commission on Human Rights (AICHR) and the ASEAN Commission for the Promotion and Protection of Women and Children (ACWC). Further, all ASEAN member states are parties to the Convention on the Elimination of All Forms of Discrimination Against Women (CEDAW) and the Convention on the Rights of the Child (CRC).

Table 18.3 Anti-trafficking legislation enacted by ASEAN member states

Countries	*Domestic legislation on anti-trafficking*
Brunei Darussalam	The Trafficking and Smuggling of Persons Order of 2004
Cambodia	Law on the Suppression of Human Trafficking and Sexual Exploitation of 2007
Indonesia	Law No. 21 of 2007 concerning the Elimination of Trafficking in Persons
Laos	The Lao Penal Law of 2005 (Arts 24 and 27)
Malaysia	The Anti-Trafficking in Persons Act of 2007 (Act 670)—as Amended in 2010
Myanmar	The Anti-Trafficking in Persons Law of 2005
Philippines	The Anti-Trafficking Act of 2003
Singapore	Women's Charter of 1966 (as amended in 1996) and the Penal Code
Thailand	The Anti-Trafficking in Persons Act of 2008 (BE 2551/2008)
Vietnam	Viet Nam Penal Code of 1999 (Arts 119–120) Law on Prevention, Suppression against Human Trafficking 2011 (Le Thu 2013)

Source: Based on the ASEAN Human Rights Resource Center Report (AHRRC 2013)

ASEAN has placed a high priority on combating trafficking in women and children since the late 1980s. The Association has adopted various key instruments to overcome the growing number of trafficking victims in the region (see Table 18.4) such as the ASEAN Plan of Action for Children, ASEAN Declaration to Combat Transnational Crime, and ASEAN Plan of Action to Combat Transnational Crime. Moreover, all ten countries have enacted laws, adopted programmes, and have signed a number of bilateral and multilateral cooperation agreements addressing trafficking in persons. However, Singapore, Thailand and Brunei have not ratified the UN Palermo Protocol and hence are not bound by the Palermo definition of 'trafficking in persons' (David 2010). Such incoherence in terms of legal norms complicates and limits the regional cooperation.

In 1995, the ASEAN member states adopted the ASEAN Vision 2020 during the 2nd Informal ASEAN Summit (ASEAN 1997b). In this document, member states pledged to cooperate in formulating 'agreed rules of behaviour and cooperative measures' to address 'problems that can only be met on a regional scale', which include trafficking in women and children (ASEAN 1997b). The ASEAN Vision 2020 serves as a basis of further plans of action and declarations on counter-trafficking efforts in Southeast Asia. In the same year the Association adopted the ASEAN Declaration on Transnational Crime in Manila (ASEAN 1997a). In the 1997 Declaration ASEAN members agreed to take 'firm and stern measures' to combat transnational crime, including trafficking of women and children. Most importantly, the 1997 Declaration established the ASEAN Ministerial Meeting on Transnational Crime (AMMTC) to coordinate activities to fight transnational crimes (ASEAN 1997a). Furthermore, the 1997 Declaration also requires the involvement of the ASEAN Chiefs of National Police (ASEANAPOL) and considers the establishment of an ASEAN Centre on Transnational Crime (ACOT). The commitment to combat trafficking, especially in women and children, was once more reiterated in the 1998 Hanoi Plan of Action which emphasised the implementation of the 1993 ASEAN Plan of Action for Children (ASEAN 1998). In 2000 the ASEAN Plan of Action for Cooperation on Immigration Matters (Immigration Action Plan) was adopted, listing several objectives relating to anti-trafficking immigration measures such as developing a strong network among ASEAN immigration authorities.

In 2004, ASEAN made a tremendous leap in terms of enhancing its anti-trafficking policies and regional cooperation in criminal matters by adopting the ASEAN Declaration against Trafficking in Persons Particularly Women and Children (2004 Anti-Trafficking Declaration)

(ASEAN 2004a) and the Treaty on Mutual Legal Assistance (MLAT) in Kuala Lumpur (ASEAN 2004b). The 2004 Declaration is the first ASEAN Declaration adopted to specifically address the issue of trafficking in women and children in Southeast Asia. The Declaration reaffirmed ASEAN's commitment to the UNTOC and in respect of the Trafficking Protocol, declaring that the parties acknowledge that trafficking in women and children was an emerging regional problem and that rigorous efforts would be taken to effectively address the problem. The 2004 Declaration has ushered in some improvement in terms of victims' protection compared to the 2000 Immigration Action Plan (Yusran 2011). Some of the key commitments in the Declaration which reflect a victim-oriented approach include:

> To distinguish victims of trafficking in persons from the perpetrators, and identify the countries of origin and nationalities of such victims and thereafter ensure that such victims are treated humanely and provided with such essential medical and other forms of assistance deemed appropriate by the respective receiving/recipient country, including prompt repatriation to their respective countries of origin; and to undertake actions to respect and safeguard the dignity and human rights of genuine victims of trafficking in persons.
>
> *(ASEAN 2004a: paras. 5–6)*

The Mutual Legal Assistance Treaty (MLAT) was adopted on the same day. Originally, the MLAT was not categorised as an ASEAN instrument since it was adopted on the initiative of the Malaysian government and at the beginning, not all ASEAN member states signed and ratified the MLAT. However, all ten members, except Thailand, have now signed and ratified the MLAT. The MLAT provides a basis for international cooperation in criminal matters between ASEAN member states, which, among others, enables the collection of evidence in one state for use in another state. Article 5(2) of ASEAN MLAT makes it possible for the Central Authorities to expand their cooperation to INTERPOL or ASEANAPOL (ASEAN 2004b: Arts 1, 4).

The ASEAN Declaration on Transnational Crime was the first regional joint statement on cooperation in anti-trafficking. As a part of the ASEAN Plan of Action to Combat Transnational Crime in 1999, a Senior Officials Meeting on Transnational Crime was formed to assist the implementation process. The Work Programme was initiated to strengthen legal cooperation, harmonise national legislation and assist in bilateral and multilateral agreements. ASEAN Directors General of Immigration Departments and Heads of Consular Divisions of the Ministries of Foreign Affairs became the highest institutional bodies to deal with human trafficking (Emmers, Greener-Barcham & Thomas 2006: 490–511). Harmonisation of national legislation, in particular the legal definition of trafficking in persons, remains the goal to date. Although the Declaration on Transnational Crime defines trafficking in persons as:

Table 18.4 Some of ASEAN's major developments addressing trafficking

1997	ASEAN Declaration on Transnational Organized Crime
1998	Hanoi Action Plan
1999	ASEAN Plan of Action to Combat Transnational Crime
2000	Plan of Action for Cooperation in Immigration Matters
2004	ASEAN Declaration against TIP, particularly Women and Children
2007	ASEAN Declaration on the Protection and Promotion of the Rights of Migrant Workers
2008	ASEAN Human Rights Declaration
2015	ASEAN Convention on Trafficking in Persons (ACTIP)

Source: Author's compilation

> the recruitment, transportation, transfer, harbouring or receipt of persons, by means of the threat or use of force or other forms of coercion, of abduction, of fraud, of deception, of the abuse of power or of a position of vulnerability or of the giving or receiving the payments or benefits to achieve the consent of a person, having control over another person, for the purpose of exploitation (which includes at minimum, the exploitation, forced labour or services, slavery or practices similar to slavery, servitude or removal of organs).
>
> *(ASEAN 1997a)*

The ASEAN community and remaining limitations

While there are a number of ASEAN commitments toward combating the numerous challenges in the region, including trafficking (Linton 2008), one primary concern remains in sharp focus. That is, can a non-binding institution such as ASEAN be effective and consistent in fighting this particular form of transnational crime? Particularly as ASEAN member states do not hold unanimous views on human rights or offer consistent civil protections.

The founding principle of ASEAN was not legally binding in its nature and the Association has adhered to this during the nearly 50 years of its existence. This principle was critical for all member states to feel comfortable in joining ASEAN. Given the difference in political systems, outlooks on foreign and regional policies, different strategic interests, economic disparities and cultural settings, ASEAN had to be malleable from the beginning. Legally non-binding, on a principle of non-interference and with operations based on consensus and consultation was a mantra repeated before each gathering of the regional leaders. In fact, established in 1967, ASEAN did not have distinct legal personality until 2008, when the ASEAN Charter was adopted. With different phases of enlargement, ASEAN has become increasingly diverse on all levels, and therefore reaching a common position on many issues remains a significant challenge which threatens the Association's longevity. Of regular contention are issues related to human rights (Renshaw 2013).

With the Charter adopted, ASEAN was registered with the Secretariat of the United Nations. With legal personality, ASEAN entered a new phase of intensified political commitment. The 'ASEAN Community 2015' initiative included additional internal collaboration, more fluid movement of people and goods and more opportunities in each member's job markets. Visa waivers had been previously adopted for tourists from within the ASEAN region. All of these steps have worked toward bringing sovereign nations and people closer together within the borders of Southeast Asia. New blueprints to achieve an ASEAN Community have been complemented by strategies designed to enhance connectivity, including through institutional, people-to-people and physical connectivity platforms. However, the increased movement of people and trade, coupled with pre-existing inequality in income and opportunity, creates growing room for illicit crimes such as trafficking in persons or the smuggling of migrants.

The ASEAN Community encompasses three pillars: Political-Security, Economic and Socio-Cultural. Migration and trafficking are cross-cutting issues which affect all three pillars of the ASEAN Community. However, this three-pillar structure also complicates the anti-trafficking activities of ASEAN. For instance, transnational crime is a part of the ASEAN Political-Security Community (APSC), whereas labour migration affairs are in the domain of the ASEAN Socio-Cultural Community. Human trafficking, being regarded as a form of transnational crime falls under the APSC, but there is a danger in this as the issue may become separated from the regulations of labour migration, which is intensifying within as well as beyond ASEAN. Trafficking should not be conflated with migration; however, separating the two in a legal and regulatory sense fails to recognise the necessary relationship between them, causing each process to become less effective. In fact, human trafficking cuts across all sectors, as for example the trafficking industry is affected by economic inequality or agreement of exchange of services etc., which falls under the purview of the ASEAN Economic Community.

Human trafficking is a very complex issue that intersects at many levels, including: security, crime, jurisdiction and health. Beyond this, there are a variety of levels on which human trafficking operates, including: (a) transnational–national; (b) short term–long term; and (c) push and pull factors.

Singling out the responsibilities of one pillar to address trafficking can work against the community's purpose. A significant amount of coordination and information sharing is needed, not only between each ASEAN member state, but also among the various ASEAN institutions in order to improve the effectiveness of cooperation in the region. Two of ASEAN's milestones, directly related both to the issue of protection of human rights as well as to strengthening regional cooperation, were the establishment of the ASEAN Intergovernmental Commission on Human Rights (AICHR) and in reaching a consensus with the ASEAN Declaration on Human Rights. The issue of human rights has been a long-standing point of contention for many authoritarian regimes among the member states. As much as the AICHR was welcomed with enthusiasm (Le Thu 2010), it also caused some frustrations due to its numerous limitations. Similarly, with the ASEAN Human Rights Declarations, the anticipation of this achievement was hampered by the structural (and habitual) 'ASEAN Way' (Davies 2014).

Bilateral arrangements

Apart from the range of above-mentioned multilateral instruments, the ASEAN member states have also entered into various bilateral arrangements as a means to combat trafficking. These include the Mutual Legal Assistance Laws, a summary of which are provided in Tables 18.5 and 18.6.

Progress and challenges

One of the major challenges in the trafficking in persons discourse is a lack of reliable methodology available to provide accurate information and data relating to trafficking in persons globally

Table 18.5 Mutual legal assistance laws in ASEAN

ASEAN member states' national mutual legal assistance laws	
Brunei Darussalam	Mutual Assistance in Criminal Matters Order (2005)
Cambodia	No national mutual legal assistance law
Indonesia	Law Concerning Mutual Legal Assistance in Criminal Matters (Law No. 1 of 2006)
Lao DPR	Law on Criminal Procedure (2004), Part XI
Malaysia	Mutual Assistance in Criminal Matters Act 2002
Myanmar	Mutual Assistance in Criminal Matters Law (Law No. 4/2004)
Philippines	No national mutual legal assistance law; however, some mutual legal assistance provisions in the Anti-Money Laundering Act 2001
Singapore	Mutual Assistance in Criminal Matters Act (Chapter 190A) (Act 12 of 2000, as amended)
Thailand	Act on Mutual Assistance in Criminal Matters BE 2535 (1992)
Vietnam	Law on Mutual Legal Assistance (Law No. 08/2007/QH12)

Source: Compiled by the author

Table 18.6 Bilateral agreements of individual ASEAN member states

ASEAN member states' bilateral MLA arrangements	
Brunei Darussalam	–
Cambodia	–
Indonesia	Australia; PR China; Hong Kong
Lao DPR	Vietnam
Malaysia	Australia; Hong Kong; United States of America
Myanmar	–
Philippines	Australia; Hong Kong; PR China; Switzerland; United States of America
Singapore	Hong Kong; India
Thailand	Australia; Belgium; Canada; PR China; France; India; Korea; Norway; Peru; Poland; Sri Lanka; United Kingdom; United States of America
Vietnam	Korea; Lao PDR; Mongolia; PR China; United Kingdom

Source: Compiled by the author

and in any given region. With a growing and more robust ASEAN, and with the high mobility of people within the region, the problem of trafficking in women and children is an increasingly significant concern of member states. This is particularly so since trafficking in persons has become harder to distinguish from the broader human smuggling phenomenon occurring within Southeast Asia.

Research suggests that the absence of sufficient and reliable data on trafficking in persons in Southeast Asia is attributable to: (1) a lack of a systematic and holistic research (Piper 2005); (2) the lack of a common standard and unambiguous definition on trafficking in persons offences and also victims; and (3) institutional resistance by law enforcers to making trafficking-in-persons-related data accessible or available. The reliance on poor research and the absence of reliable data or estimates on the number of people falling victim to trafficking, trafficking investigations and prosecutions, for example, make it difficult for states to determine a precise and effective design for trafficking in persons counter-measures. A second problem relating to anti-trafficking measures is that most governments have a tendency to treat trafficking in persons as a migration problem (Lee 2011).

The third problem is the tendency to equate trafficking in women and children with prostitution or for other sexual purpose. This perception has influenced trafficking-in-persons-related research and counter-trafficking policies and regulations; consequently it can undermine or neglect the need to address other forms of exploitation. For example, a great extent of research has been conducted to scrutinise the issue of trafficking in women and children for sexual purposes in countries within the Greater Mekong Sub-region; however, research into the trafficking in women and children phenomenon occurring in other Southeast Asian countries such as Indonesia and East Timor hardly addresses this issue (Piper 2005).

The fourth challenge represents a long-standing problem that has shrouded the region: corruption in the criminal justice system. Traffickers are known to use corruption as a means to guarantee the safety of their operation and to escape prosecution. Many political leaders and government officials benefit from trafficking in persons and law enforcers receiving bribes from traffickers restrain themselves from conducting proper investigations and prosecution of the traffickers (Pretorius 2008). This problem has hampered counter-trafficking efforts in the region significantly, has secured impunity for the traffickers, and has obstructed the victims' right to access justice.

Last but not least, the approach towards victims also calls for adjustment. Victim identification and victim protection remain the most challenging of issues for ASEAN states to address.

According to the International Labour Organization, the practices of victim identification and victim protection are neglected, especially when it comes to undocumented migrant workers (ILO 2012b). There is incoherence across the region regarding provisions for immunity for trafficking victims. Only five out of the ten ASEAN members—Indonesia, Malaysia, Myanmar, the Philippines and Thailand—allow victims protection from prosecution. But even among those five, the issues of immediate protection and support, including providing shelters, physical and psychological treatment and vocational training etc. remain problematic (David 2010). In the context of regional cooperation, this calls for the establishment of a more integrated and coherent norm to be respected across the ASEAN region.

A number of factors contribute to ASEAN's dysfunctionality in anti-trafficking mechanisms. The limited power of existing ASEAN Human Rights bodies, a lack of monitoring and evaluation mechanisms and poor data and information-sharing practices are among the main barriers to effective protection against trafficking. To begin with, member states have conflicting interpretations of the legitimacy of ASEAN and its bodies (Poole 2015). Although the AICHR has the power to receive member states' data on domestic laws and policies that reinforce human rights, its terms of reference have not required AICHR to examine and assess these laws and policies (Kranrattanasuit 2014).

ASEAN relies heavily on external resources and capacity. Many of ASEAN's initiatives are financed by external partners and donors. The issue of trafficking in persons is of a transnational nature and hence cannot be separated from global processes. An example of monitoring to be consistently taken into consideration is the annual US Department of State TIP Report. No such equivalent is published in the Southeast Asian region by ASEAN. The two most prominent multilateral frameworks which include Southeast Asian countries are the Bali Process and COMMIT. In 2002 in Bali, Indonesia, the Regional Ministerial Conference on People Smuggling, Trafficking in Persons and Related Transnational Crime initiated an informal dialogue, inclusive of Asia-Pacific members, to regularly address issues of people smuggling, trafficking and refugees. Co-chaired by Australia and Indonesia, the Bali Process membership is over 45 countries, together with numerous United Nations agencies whose mandates focus on migration, refugees and transnational crime. With trafficking a significant problem in the Mekong region, the Coordinated Mekong Ministerial Initiative against Trafficking (COMMIT), an inter-governmental process between China, Thailand, Laos, Cambodia, Myanmar and Vietnam, was established in 2003. COMMIT Taskforces work on multilevel cooperation among different agencies of the Mekong countries (COMMIT 2007). The United Nations Action for Cooperation against Trafficking in Persons (UNACT), previously the UN Inter-Agency Project on Human Trafficking (UNIAP), serves as the Secretariat of COMMIT. UNACT is active in engaging with a wide range of multi-sectoral partners who contribute to the COMMIT Process, including UN agencies, NGOs, inter-governmental organisations, donor organisations and academia. UNACT's monitoring exercises and best practice reports can be a good point of reference for the ASEAN anti-trafficking process. The cooperation and coordination among these multilateral initiatives, as well as with civil society and NGOs working on trafficking, is essential and should be further enhanced. However, there is an even higher need for member states of ASEAN to take more responsibility and allocate more resources to commit to anti-trafficking efforts.

Conclusion

Southeast Asia is highly vulnerable to human trafficking, forced labour and the irregular movement of people. The scale of forced labour linked to global production chains in many cases exposes long-term practices that have a global reach and which indirectly affect consumers everywhere in the world. At the national level, anti-trafficking mechanisms are highly problematic in each of the ten Southeast Asian countries. This is because of inconsistencies in domestic definitions and international approaches to understanding human trafficking. Moreover, issues like the regulation of labour law, limited regulation of recruitment agencies, corruption, inadequate protection, insufficient resources to protect and rehabilitate victims of trafficking, a lack of awareness, poor coordination and information-sharing among different agencies are just a few of the problems. For ASEAN to successfully tackle trafficking is understandably challenging. ASEAN's collective commitment to combat trafficking remains marred by inconsistent and limited political will among individual member states.

Throughout the ASEAN region, prosecutors have reportedly noted that victims of trafficking cases frequently disappear prior to trial, or file affidavits of desistance to withdraw their complaints. The lack of cooperation may be attributed to the following factors: lengthy delays in the adjudication processes, a failure to adequately protect victims from intimidation or inducement by the accused or their lawyers, police corruption, and a failure to keep victims informed on the progress regarding their case. Authorities failed to provide child- and victim-friendly spaces for those waiting to give testimony—victims have had to share waiting rooms with their traffickers. Furthermore, within the ASEAN region, cooperation between investigators and prosecutors from the early stages of an investigation to ensure that investigative strategies are well conceived, arrests supported by sufficient evidence, and the collection of the right evidence are said to be very rare.

There is noticeable political will in Southeast Asian countries to address the issues facing the region regarding trafficking in persons. Nevertheless, research suggests that there is an absence of adequate legal protections for women and children, as well as for others who are vulnerable to exploitation, such as domestic workers. Key issues include weak law enforcement, poor implementation of laws, inadequate training, in some cases societal insensitivity, a lack of understanding of women's and children's rights, a failure to effectively investigate and prosecute, an inability of officials to identify trafficking cases, and a lack of coordination among the agencies tasked to address exploitation.

The remaining challenges facing anti-trafficking efforts in the Asia-Pacific are no different from the challenges apparent in other regions around the world. In the case of Southeast Asia in particular, despite the intensity of the global and regional anti-trafficking measures, there are still some gaps that need to be addressed. The absence of a reliable methodology to deliver accurate information and data relating to trafficking in persons has been a long-standing problem that needs to be resolved. Available information and data relating to the description and gravity of trafficking in persons in Southeast Asia is based on the application of various definitions and is often unreliable with conflicting estimates. In addition, this absence of reliable information across the Asia-Pacific region is due to a lack of systematic and holistic research, as well as resistance by enforcers to make trafficking-in-persons-related information accessible. Even though producing and quantifying comprehensive information related to trafficking in persons is not an easy task, relevant stakeholders can start addressing this issue by solving the already identified root causes in order to determine a methodology that would best cover these deficiencies for now.

Another main challenge restraining global counter-trafficking measures is the tendency for governments to treat trafficking in persons as a part of migration problems. This tendency is reflected in various international instruments, including various ASEAN instruments outlined in this chapter relating to anti-trafficking. This leads states to implement stricter border control measures that operate to criminalise victims of trafficking for violating immigration law due to having entered the country illegally, even as trafficked persons. Additionally, re-trafficked persons seeking repatriation to their countries of origin may face prosecution if they do not have proper identification; and for stateless groups, this is particularly alarming.

With regard to trafficking in women and children, the general prevailing trend has been to associate this form of trafficking with prostitution and other forms of sexual exploitation. This damaging approach influences research and anti-trafficking policies in Southeast Asia. Hence, many counter-trafficking efforts in Southeast Asia are focused on prostitution and sexual exploitation in the countries of origin, rather than in the countries of transit or destination. Furthermore, focusing on trafficking in women and children for the purposes of prostitution and other forms of sexual exploitation ultimately overshadows occurrences of trafficking for unrelated purposes, causing many victims to go under the radar. Men and boys are also under-researched as a consequence and are often victims of secondary forms of discrimination through not receiving adequate protection. Moreover, systemic corruption in the law enforcement and criminal justice system further frustrates anti-trafficking efforts in Southeast Asia.

This chapter has argued that trafficking in persons affects Southeast Asian societies in three ways: (1) as a human security threat; (2) as a threat to mobility and labour due to economic, political, climate-related, religious and ethnic reasons; and (3) by operating as a shadow economy. The outcome of this is that the efficacy of ASEAN's operations through the Security Community, Social Community and Economic Community are critically important but have been historically marred on the point of trafficking in persons. ASEAN cannot and should not neglect the issue, leaving it to non-state actors or international actors to take the lead in combating trafficking. The proliferation of trafficking poses costs to humans, but also reflects badly on the health of an economy as well as the reliance on strong law enforcement by ASEAN countries. To strengthen ASEAN's anti-trafficking capacity, it should prioritise trafficking in persons as part of its integration process.

References

Acharya, A 1998, 'Culture, Security, Multilateralism: The "ASEAN Way" and Regional Order', *Contemporary Security Policy*, vol. 19, no. 1, pp. 55–84.

AHRRC 2013, *Violence, Exploitation and Abuse in Migration Affecting Women and Children in ASEAN Countries: A Baseline Study*, 3 vols, Jakarta: ASEAN Human Rights Resource Center.

ASEAN 1997a, *ASEAN Declaration on Transnational Crime*, Jakarta: ASEAN Secretariat.

ASEAN 1997b, *ASEAN Vision 2020*, Jakarta: ASEAN Secretariat.

ASEAN 1998, *Hanoi Action Plan*, Jakarta: ASEAN Secretariat.

ASEAN 2000, *ASEAN Plan of Action for Cooperation on Immigration Matters*, Jakarta: ASEAN Secretariat.

ASEAN 2004a, *ASEAN Declaration against Trafficking in Persons Particularly Women and Children*, Jakarta: ASEAN Secretariat.

ASEAN 2004b, *Treaty on Mutual Legal Assistance in Criminal Matters*, Jakarta: ASEAN Secretariat.

ASEAN 2009, *Roadmap to the ASEAN Community 2009–2015*, Jakarta: ASEAN Secretariat, www.asean.org/storage/images/ASEAN_RTK_2014/2_Roadmap_for_ASEAN_Community_20092015.pdf.

Chuang, J 1998, 'Redirecting the Debate over Trafficking in Women: Definitions, Paradigms, and Contexts', *Harvard Human Rights Journal*, vol. 11, pp. 65–107.

COMMIT 2007, The Joint Declaration of the Coordinated Ministerial Initiative Against Human Trafficking, Beijing, http://un-act.org/wp-content/uploads/2015/07/COMMIT_2007_Joint_Declaration.pdf.

Crossette, B 2000, 'UN Warns That Trafficking in Human Beings Is Growing', *The New York Times*, 25 June, pp. 2–3, www.nytimes.com/2000/06/25/world/un-warns-that-trafficking-in-human-beings-is-growing.html.

David, F 2006, *ASEAN and Trafficking in Persons: Using Data as Tools to Combat Trafficking in Persons*, Geneva: International Organization for Migration.

David, F 2010, 'Law Enforcement Responses to Trafficking in Persons: Challenges and Emerging Good Practices', in L Territo & G Kirkham (eds), *International Sex Trafficking of Women and Children: Understanding the Global Epidemic*, Flushing, NY: Looseleaf Law Publications.

Davies, M 2014, 'An Agreement to Disagree: The ASEAN Human Rights Declaration in the Absence of Regional Identity in Southeast Asia', *Journal of Current Southeast Asian Affairs*, vol. 33, no. 3, pp. 107–129.

Emmers, R, Greener-Barcham, B & Thomas, N 2006, 'Institutional Arrangements to Counter Human Trafficking in the Asia Pacific', *Contemporary Southeast Asia*, vol. 28, no. 3, pp. 490–511.

ILO 2012a, *ILO 2012 Global Estimate of Forced Labour: Executive Summary*, www.ilo.org/wcmsp5/groups/public/---ed_norm/---declaration/documents/publication/wcms_181953.pdf.

ILO 2012b, *Ensuring the Right to Social Security for ASEAN Migrant Workers through Social Security Agreements*, ILO Research Series, Social Security Extension Initiatives in Asia.

Kranrattanasuit, N 2014, *ASEAN and Human Trafficking: Case Studies of Cambodia, Thailand and Vietnam*, Leiden & Boston, MA: Brill Nijhoff.

Le Thu, H 2010, 'Many Faces and One Identity? ASEAN in the Case of Human Rights Regime', *Asia-Pacific Journal of Social Sciences*, Special Issue No. 1, pp. 56–70.

Le Thu, H 2013, 'Vietnam Country Report', in *Violence, Exploitation and Abuse in Migration Affecting Women and Children in ASEAN Countries: A Baseline Study*, Jakarta: ASEAN Human Rights Resource Centre.

Le Thu, H 2015, 'Trafficking in Persons in Vietnam: The Root Causes and State Response to Human Security', in JY Song and ADB Cook (eds), *Irregular Migration and Human Security in East Asia*, Abingdon: Routledge.

Lee, M 2011, *Trafficking and Global Crime Control*, London: Sage.

Linton, S 2008, 'ASEAN States, Their Reservations to Human Rights Treaties and the Proposed ASEAN Commission on Women and Children', *Human Rights Quarterly*, vol. 30, no. 2, pp. 436–493.

Miles, T 2015, 'Bay of Bengal People Smuggling Doubles in 2015: UNHCR', *Reuters*, 8 March, www.reuters.com/article/us-thailand-rohingya-unhcr-idUSKBN0NT11D20150508.

Narine, S 2002, *Explaining ASEAN: A Regionalism in Southeast Asia*, Boulder, CO: Lynne Rienner.

Piper, N 2005, 'Problem by a Different Name: A Review of Research on Trafficking in Southeast Asia and Oceania', *International Migration*, vol. 43, no. 1–2, pp. 203–233.

Poole, A 2015, '"The World Is Outraged": Legitimacy in the Making of the ASEAN Rights Body', *Contemporary Southeast Asia*, vol. 37, no. 3, pp. 355–380.

Pretorius, W 2008, 'Law Enforcement Responses to Trafficking in Persons in Southeast Asia', in *Asia Regional Trafficking in Persons Project*, Cardno.

Rahman, M 2011, 'Human Trafficking in the Era of Globalization: The Case of Trafficking in Global Market Economy', *Transcience Journal*, vol. 2, no. 1, pp. 54–71.

Renshaw, C 2013, 'The ASEAN Human Rights Declaration 2012', *Human Rights Law Review*, vol. 13, no. 3, pp. 557–579.

Richard, A 1999, *International Trafficking in Women to the United States: A Contemporary Manifestation of Slavery and Organized Crime*, Washington, DC: Bureau of Intelligence and Research.

Schauer, EJ & Wheaton, EM 2006, 'Sex Trafficking into the United States: A Literature Review', *Criminal Justice Review*, vol. 31, no. 2, pp. 146–169.

United Nations (UNODC) 2015, *The Role of Recruitment Fees and Abusive Fraudulent Practices of Recruitment Agencies in Trafficking in Persons*, Vienna: United Nations.

United States Committee for Refugees and Immigrants 2000, *Trafficking in Women and Children: A Contemporary Manifestation of Slavery*, Refugee Reports, vol. 21, no. 5.

United States Department of State 2015, 'Tier Placements', www.state.gov/j/tip/rls/tiprpt/2015/243366.htm.

Wheaton, EM, Schauer, EJ & Galli, TV 2010, 'Economics of Human Trafficking', *International Migration*, vol. 48, no. 4, pp. 114–141.

Yusran, R 2011, 'Trafficking in Women and Children and an Observation on ASEAN Counter-Trafficking Efforts', 8th Asian Law Institute Conference: Law in a Sustainable Asia, Kyushu, Japan, 26–27 May, https://cil.nus.edu.sg/wp/wp-content/uploads/2011/06/ASLI-8th-Conference-ASEAN-and-Trafficking-in-Women-and-Children-RY-pdf.pdf.

Part VI

Age, identity and sexuality

19

Towards a regional framework for adherence to children's human rights in ASEAN?

Sharon Bessell

Introduction

This chapter focuses on the shift within ASEAN from a regional association that explicitly rejected the concept of universal human rights, to one that explicitly seeks to foster human rights through a range of regional mechanisms. The chapter argues that the human rights of children have been central to the shift that has taken place within ASEAN.

The chapter begins with an overview of ASEAN's journey towards accepting—and ultimately adopting—international human rights standards, noting ongoing areas of concern in the emerging regional human rights framework. It then examines the extent to which individual member states of ASEAN have accepted the concept of children's human rights, before analysing the progress towards realising children's rights, and the remaining gaps in key areas of health, education and protection. Finally, the chapter discusses the severe violations of the rights of minority children or those who have been denied statehood, focusing on the situation of the Rohingya in Myanmar. The chapter concludes by arguing that the credibility of ASEAN in fostering the human rights of children, and the progress made since the early 2000s, is under threat if the Association is unable to respond to the state-sponsored killing of children.

ASEAN's journey towards accepting the human rights of children

For the first three decades of its existence, ASEAN was criticised by human rights advocates for its neglect of human rights issues and failure to address violations within member states. ASEAN adopted a policy of strict separation between human rights and trade issues, strongly opposing pressure to address human rights from foreign states or international organisations (Thio 1999: 1). Prominent ASEAN member states, particularly Malaysia and Singapore, championed a cultural relativist approach, framed as 'Asian values', that prioritised an alternate set of values characterised as 'disciplined, group-oriented rather than atomized, and valuing duty to the community over the assertion of rights' (Thio 1999: 2). By the 2000s, however, ASEAN's position on human rights had shifted dramatically and in 2012 the ASEAN Declaration on Human Rights was adopted. While many issues shaped critiques of ASEAN's human rights record, and drove change, the human rights of children were central to the eventual development of human rights mechanisms with the Association.

ASEAN's position on human rights became a flashpoint for international attention in 1997, when Burma (now Myanmar) sought and gained entry to the Association. Burma, then a military dictatorship governed by the State Law and Order Restoration Council (SLORC), was subject to opprobrium in the West for the extent of human rights abuses. Throughout the 1990s, there was documentation of the recruitment of children into Burma's national armed forces, and by a range of opposition groups. Some reports suggested that children made up as much as 20% of government forces, with forced recruitment of children a common practice (Becker 2009: 111–112). Moreover, United Nations documentation suggested the systematic use of rape and other forms of sexual violence, including against children (IHRC 2009). Such violations of children's human rights were not central to discussions within ASEAN about Burma's membership, which were instead dominated by political and strategic considerations. They were, however, a focus for the human rights organisations, both within Southeast Asia and beyond, that campaigned against Burma's membership. The violation of children's human rights also underpinned the concerns raised by Western governments. The United States, in particular, sought to apply pressure to ASEAN members to reject Burma's entry to the Association on human rights grounds, with then US Secretary of State writing directly to ASEAN heads of government urging them to postpone Burma's admission (Cribb 1998: 54). Burma's entry to ASEAN in mid-1997 was widely seen as ASEAN's public rejection of human rights (and the human rights of children specifically), but—importantly—was a decision that also raised concerns *within* ASEAN countries (Cribb 1998).

Over the two decades since the international debate around Burma's entry to ASEAN, significant shifts have occurred both within member states and within the association itself in regard to human rights. Particularly significant was Indonesia's transition to democracy in 1999, and subsequent shifts in thinking on human rights within successive Indonesian governments. Indeed, Radtke (2014: 99) argues that by 2014, ASEAN officials emphasised the important role played by the Association in supporting Myanmar's transition towards democracy. Ideas of human rights were no longer rejected in favour of a relativist position of 'Asian values', even as the latter ideas remained influential. In 2015, the ASEAN Community was formally established, with ASEAN leaders endorsing ASEAN 2025, which included a set of commitments to further development of the region. The 2025 vision is for an ASEAN community where 'peoples enjoy human rights and fundamental freedoms, higher quality of life and the benefits of community building'.

A new era?

The adoption in 2004 of the Vientiane Action Programme (VAP) represented a watershed in ASEAN's approach towards human rights. The VAP identified the promotion of human rights as one of six programme areas under the strategic priority of political development. As a first step towards the creation of human rights machinery within ASEAN, the VAP called for a stock-take of existing mechanisms within the region, including sectoral bodies promoting the rights of women and children, and the establishment of a network of cooperation among them (Davies 2013: 387). Significantly, the Action Plan called for the 'establishment of an ASEAN commission on the promotion and protection of the rights of women and children' (Program Area 1.1.4.7).

In large part, the inclusion of human rights in the VAP was the result of the efforts, not only (or primarily) of international agencies, international non-government organisations or foreign governments, but of internal pressure in the form of the 'Regional Working Group for an ASEAN Human Rights Mechanism' (Working Group). The Working Group was established in 1995 by a high-profile group of human rights advocates from ASEAN member countries. The group was co-chaired by Marzuki Darusman, former attorney general of Indonesia and former chairperson of that country's National Human Rights Commission, and Vitit Muntarbhorn, professor of law at Chulalongkorn University, Thailand. What is of particular significance for this chapter is the centrality of the human rights of women and children to the Working Group's agenda from the outset (Phan 2008). Significantly, Professor Muntarbhorn is a long-time advocate of children's human rights and was UN Special Rapporteur on the sale of children, child prostitution and child pornography from 1990 to 1994. Protecting the human rights of children featured consistently in the efforts of the Working Group, and was on the agenda of its annual meetings, from 2001 to 2006 (Phan 2008).

In 2007, at the 13th ASEAN Summit, leaders from each member state signed the ASEAN Charter, setting in train the process for establishing a regional human rights body. Two years later, in 2009, the Roadmap for an ASEAN Community 2009–2015 established the terms of reference for the establishment of an ASEAN human rights body. The ASEAN Intergovernmental Human Rights Commission (AIHRC) was established in October of that year. In line with the Roadmap for an ASEAN Community, AIHRC proceeded to draft a regional human rights instrument. In November 2012, ASEAN heads of government adopted the ASEAN Human Rights Declaration. The establishment of AIHRC and subsequent adoption of the Declaration represents a significant shift towards ASEAN's engagement with the international human rights framework, and a move away from the strongly relativist position that had previously dominated within the Association. But it does not represent full acceptance of international human rights. The response from human rights advocates and scholars to the ASEAN Human Rights Declaration (AHRD) was far from euphoric—ranging from cautious optimism for the future of human rights in the ASEAN region to condemnation. Chief among the main criticisms of the AHRD is the limitations the document places on internationally recognised human rights, particularly civil and political rights. Article 6 of the AHRD states that 'human rights and fundamental freedoms must be balanced with the performance of corresponding duties as every person has responsibilities to all other individuals, the community and the society where one lives'. Article 7 states that human rights must be considered in the regional and national context, 'bearing in mind different political, economic, legal, social, cultural, historical and religious backgrounds', indicating that ideas of cultural relativism have not been replaced by acceptance of human rights as universal in nature. Article 8 states that limits may be placed on the exercise of human rights in the name of 'national security, public order, public health, public safety, public morality, as well as the general welfare of the peoples in a democratic society'. A joint statement from over 60 local, regional and international human rights organisations described it as 'highly regrettable that governments in ASEAN who are more democratic and open to human rights succumbed to the pressure of human rights-hostile governments into adopting a deeply flawed instrument'.

Towards a children's rights framework?

As discussed above, the Regional Working Group for an ASEAN Human Rights Mechanism from its establishment focused on the human rights of children. The advocacy of the working group was important in ensuring that children's human rights remained central as discussions about regional human rights mechanisms unfolded. In 2004, ASEAN leaders adopted the Vientiane Action Programme 2004–2010, which called for the establishment of an ASEAN commission on the promotion and protection of the rights of women and children. Five years later, the Roadmap for an ASEAN Community 2009–2015 again committed to the establishment of such a commission (ASEAN 2009: 9). In 2010, the ASEAN Commission on the Promotion and Protection of the Rights of Women and Children was finally established. The Commission's terms of reference identify the first of its purposes:

> To promote and protect the human rights and fundamental freedoms of women and children in ASEAN, taking into consideration the different historical, political, sociocultural, religious and economic context in the region and the balances between rights and responsibilities.
>
> *(ASEAN 2010: para. 2.1)*

This stated purpose raises questions about the commitment of ASEAN to fundamental principles of human rights, paralleling the criticisms made by human rights organisations about the ADHR. The inclusion of the phrase 'taking into consideration the different historical, political, sociocultural, religious and economic context in the region' seemingly sets limits on the extent to which internationally recognised human rights are accepted among ASEAN members. It suggests that children could be treated in ways that contravene the United Nations Convention on the Rights of the Child or other international human rights instruments, if that treatment can be justified on the grounds of local beliefs or behaviours. Given the extent to which issues around child-rearing and discipline are located within deeply held cultural and religious beliefs, a broad statement that subordinates human rights to context is of concern. The inclusion of the phrase that calls for a balance between rights and responsibilities reflects a long-held position among ASEAN states that presents responsibilities as essential to the communal values of many Southeast Asian societies.

The significance of the Commission should not be downplayed. It provides a clear regional mechanism for the promotion of children's human rights, but nor should the extent to which its mandate to promote internationally agreed human rights is constrained be underestimated. References to context and responsibilities provide caveats that potentially conflict with key principles of the United Nations Convention on the Rights of the Child. Moreover, ASEAN's approach of bundling women's and children's human rights together makes assumptions, in some situations problematic assumptions, about the necessary complementarity of those rights.

Children's participatory rights

An important focus of ASEAN's adherence to children's human rights has been in the area of children's participation. In October 2010, the first ASEAN Children's Forum was held in the Philippines. In 2011, terms of reference were established for the ASEAN Children's Forum, establishing it as a regular event. The objectives of the Forum are to serve as a venue through which children can participate in ASEAN community building; express their views and pursue their aspirations on issues affecting their lives; and work together to contribute to regional development. The terms of reference further develop the objectives of the Forum to promote mutual respect, promote awareness of ASEAN among children, advocate for children's rights, and enhance the capabilities of children as leaders and representatives of their generation.

The terms of reference for the Forum reveal some tension in the conceptualisation of children's participation, which are common to many adult-led efforts to create spaces for children to express their views. The recognition of children as leaders and representatives of their generation is important, particularly as it recognises the children's human rights and their role as children, rather than focusing on their future roles as adults. However, paragraph 18 of the terms of reference state that 'child delegates shall be informed of the issues affecting their lives prior to the Forum'. This sits awkwardly with Article 12 of the United Nations Convention on the Rights of the Child, which provides for children's right to express their views on matters affecting their lives and to have these views taken into account in any judicial or administrative proceedings affecting the child. Other articles of the UCRC are also relevant: under Article 13, children have the right to freedom of expression, while Article 17 recognises children's right to information, particularly information aimed at promoting 'social, spiritual and moral well-being and physical and mental health'. Together these articles contribute to what have become known as children's participation rights. While information is an essential foundation for the realisation of children's right to express their views, the wording of paragraph 18 of the terms of reference for the Forum create considerable ambiguity about the nature of information. It is unclear whether children receive information on which to base their own decisions, or are informed of the position they should take. Such ambiguity is particularly problematic given the tensions within the terms of reference of the Commission on the Promotion and Protection of the Rights of Women and Children, discussed above.

National adherence to children's human rights

The progress towards regional recognition and promotion of children's human rights within ASEAN has been supported by the ratification of the UN Convention on the Rights of the Children (CRC) by all ASEAN members. On the face of it, the ratification of the Convention by all ten countries within the ASEAN regions may be interpreted as a signal of commitment to children's human rights. Yet on closer examination, the ratifications placed on the Convention by key countries reflect the ongoing tension between adherence to the human rights of children and what may be described as cultural values. Brunei Darussalam, Malaysia, Singapore and Thailand have each placed reservations on their acceptance of the CRC. Thailand has limited the applicability of Article 22, on the rights of children seeking refugee status. While Brunei partially withdrew its reservations in August 2015, a sweeping reservation remains, whereby, 'provisions of the said Convention which may be contrary to the Constitution of Brunei Darussalam and to the beliefs and principles of Islam, the State, religion' are not accepted. The UNCRC, together with the Optional Protocol on the Sale of Children, Child Prostitution and Child Pornography, and the Convention for the Elimination of All Forms of Discrimination Against Women are the only international human rights treaties that Brunei has ratified. Thus, children's rights have been recognised, if in a circumscribed manner, within a broader context of disregard for international human rights.

Significantly, both Malaysia and Singapore—each of which has been influential within ASEAN over time, and particularly in its early decades—maintain broad reservations to the applicability of the CRC. At the time of ratification, Malaysia placed a reservation on Article 28(1a), which requires states to 'Make primary education compulsory and available free to all'. In 2010, the government of Malaysia declared that primary education had been made compulsory and the government provided financial and other forms of assistance to those who are eligible. While not fully complying with the principle of making primary education free to all, Malaysia has progressively moved toward the realisation of the right to education (see CRC 2007). However, Malaysia maintains reservations on Articles 2 (non-discrimination), 7 (birth registration), 14 (freedom of thought, conscience and religion) and 37 (protection from torture and degrading treatment or punishment; protection for children deprived of their liberty).

Malaysia's reservation on the principle of non-discrimination—a core human right principle, set out in the Universal Declaration of Human Rights—is of particular salience when analysing human rights adherence and negligence. It is also a principle of particular relevance to the realisation of children's human rights. While the implementation of the principle of non-discrimination can range from mere toleration through to highly valuing diversity, it is important in providing a degree of protection to individuals who are disadvantaged, excluded or despised (see Donnelly 2013: 46). Non-discrimination is especially important for children. Children belonging to groups who are systematically excluded or despised are in particular need of protection against discrimination; yet, analyses that highlight the subordinate place of children within age-based hierarchies indicate the importance of non-discrimination to the realisation of human rights for all children. Indeed, a driving factor behind the drafting of the UNCRC was the recognition of children's particular vulnerabilities to rights violations as a result of their developmental stage *and* social status.

Singapore has placed declarations on a number of articles of the CRC, which limit the applicability of those articles or shape their interpretation. Significantly, Singapore's declarations reflect the approach adopted by ASEAN towards human rights early in its life, discussed earlier in this chapter. Principles of respect (particularly children's respect for elders), public order, government authority, and protection of social hierarchies underpin Singapore's declarations. In particular, limits are placed on those articles within the CRC—Articles 12–17—that entitle children to civil rights. The relevant declaration states that these rights must be exercised in accordance with 'the authority of parents, schools and other persons who are entrusted with the care of the child and in the best interests of the child and in accordance with the customs, values and religions of Singapore'. While this declaration is adultist in subordinating children to those who are older, it also reflects the hierarchical nature of Singapore's social, and perhaps more particularly, political systems. Singapore also limits its adherence to the CRC to rights that are set down in the country's Constitution, with its declaration stating:

> The accession to the Convention by the Republic of Singapore does not imply the acceptance of obligations going beyond the limits prescribed by the Constitution of the Republic of Singapore nor the acceptance of any obligation to introduce any right beyond those prescribed under the Constitution.

Thus, while the CRC has been ratified by all countries within the ASEAN region, an examination of declarations reveal both the limitations placed on formal adherence to children's human rights and the long-standing debates within ASEAN about the relative value of universalist conceptualisations of human rights and positions grounded in cultural relativism.

Children's human rights within ASEAN member states

Levels of human and economic development vary markedly between member nations of ASEAN. Brunei Darussalam, Malaysia, Singapore and Thailand are each classified as high-income countries by the World Bank, based on gross national income per capita. Singapore is classified as having a very high level of human development, according to UNDP's Human Development Index, while Brunei and Malaysia are both classified as having a high level of human development. While Thailand is categorised as a high-income country, its level of human development is classified as medium. Indonesia, the Philippines and Vietnam are all classified by UNDP has having medium levels of human development and by the World Bank as upper middle-income countries. Cambodia, Lao and Myanmar are classified as having low levels of human development and each is a low middle-income country. Table 19.1 shows countries' human development ranking and category and level of economic development based on GDP per capita and GNI.

Low levels of human development indicate that social and economic rights, particularly human rights to education, health and an adequate standard of living, are not being realised. Low levels of human development have significant implications for the human rights of children in Cambodia, Lao PDR and Myanmar. In each of these countries, under-five mortality rates remain high (see Figure 19.1), reflecting a lack of access to essential health care services, prevalence of disease, and inadequate levels of nutrition.

Table 19.1 Levels of human and economic development across ASEAN member nations

	HDI ranking	*Human development category*	*GDP per capita*	*Income category (based on GNI)*
Singapore	9	Very High	56,286.80	High income
Brunei Darussalam	30	High	40,776.30	High income
Malaysia	62	High	10,829.90	High income
Thailand	89	Medium	5,560.70	High income
Indonesia	108	Medium	3,514.60	Upper middle income
Philippines	117	Medium	2,843.10	Upper middle income
Vietnam	121	Medium	2,052.30	Upper middle income
Cambodia	136	Low	1,084.40	Low middle income
Lao PDR	139	Low	1,707.50	Low middle income
Myanmar	150	Low	1,197.50	Low middle income

Source: Information in this table is derived from World Bank (2014), UNDP (2016), and World Bank Development Indicators (August 2016)

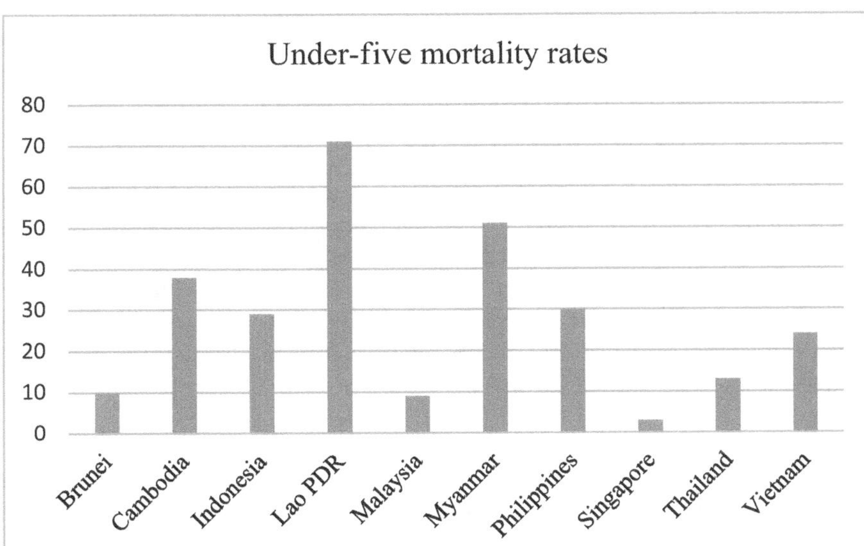

Figure 19.1 Under-five mortality rates in ASEAN countries

Source: UNICEF (2016)

In contexts of low human and economic development, such as Cambodia, Lao and Myanmar, the concept of progressive realisation of human rights is of special relevance. Progressive realisation recognises that social and economic rights, such as healthcare and education, are at least partially subject to resource allocation, which may be constrained in some contexts. Several human rights treaties recognised that some human rights must be attained progressively. For example, Article 28 of the United Nations Convention on the Rights of the Children calls on states parties to 'recognize the right of the child to education, and with a view to achieving this right progressively and on the basis of equal opportunity'. Progressive realisation is not, however, a justification for ongoing failure to secure social and economic rights, but places on governments the obligation to move progressively, through concerted effort, towards the realisation of these rights. Braveman and Gruskin (2003: 540) argue

> Poverty is not, in itself, a violation of human rights. However, government action or inaction leading to poverty, or government failure to respond adequately to the conditions that create, exacerbate, and perpetuate poverty and marginalization, often reflect—or are closely connected with—violations or denials of human rights.

The rights to health and health care

Within ASEAN member states, both government action and inaction has compounded the failure to realise fundamental human rights, including around child health and survival. Equality of access to and distribution of essential services remains highly problematic in most countries of ASEAN. For example, rates of immunisation against polio are significantly lower in Cambodia and Myanmar than in other ASEAN countries. Notably, inequalities in access to vaccines are marked within some countries. For example, in Lao PDR, children from the lowest socio-economic group are almost 50% less likely to receive vaccines against preventable diseases than children from the wealthiest socio-economic groups (OECD/World Health Organization 2014: 76). In Myanmar, approximately 40% of children from poor families suffering diarrhoea do not receive treatment. In Myanmar and Lao, there are large geographic disparities in access to essential childhood health services (OECD/World Health Organization 2014: 76), a major barrier to children's right to health care given that 66% and 62% of the population, respectively, live in rural areas. In situations of unequal access, human rights concerns come to the fore, as inequality and potentially discrimination, rather than poverty alone, present barriers to children's access to essential health services. These statistics indicate that the denial of the right to health care is not ultimately a matter of limited resources, but of distribution and equity. The failure of governments to address the barriers that prevent the most disadvantaged children from accessing health care, or other services is as much a factor in explaining poor health outcomes as is the low level of resources; it is also a human rights issue that contravenes Article 2 of the Convention on the Rights of the Child, that obliges states to ensure that children's human rights are respected without discrimination of any kind.

The right to education

In all ASEAN member countries, impressive gains have been made in basic education, with near universal completion of primary school in Brunei Darussalam, Malaysia, Singapore, Thailand and Vietnam (World Bank 2014). Progress towards universal primary school completion has also been significant in Indonesia, with challenges remaining in Cambodia, Lao PDR, Myanmar and the Philippines. While constraints on national resources provide a partial explanation for slower progress towards meeting the right to education, so too do structural inequalities that limit the opportunities for children from poor families to complete primary school.

All countries within ASEAN have legal provision for free and compulsory education, ranging from five years in Lao PDR, Myanmar and Vietnam to nine years in Brunei, Cambodia, Indonesia and Thailand (see Figure 19.2). In both Singapore and Vietnam, education is compulsory for nine years, but only primary education is free. Notably, Cambodia has free and compulsory education for nine years, but the lowest government spending on education in the region (at 2.6% of GDP), raising questions about the level of substantive commitment to the right to education despite legal provisions. Lao PDR and Singapore also have low levels of government spending on education, while Vietnam, Malaysia and Thailand have the highest levels of government spending on education in the region.

One of the most tangible outcomes of significant investment in education is student–teacher ratio. While Article 28 of the UN Convention on the Rights of the Child calls on states parties to make education compulsory and free to all, Article 29 focuses on the nature of education. Article 29 requires that education be directed to 'the development of the child's personality, talents and mental and physical abilities to their fullest potential'. If teaching is to be holistic and responsive to each child's needs and abilities, student–teacher ratio matters, particularly for children from disadvantaged backgrounds (Krueger 2002). The significant investment in education in Vietnam, Malaysia and Thailand is reflected in the teacher–student ratio. In Vietnam, the teacher–student ratio in primary school is 19; in Thailand, 16, and in Malaysia, 13 (World Bank 2014: 30). In contrast, in Cambodia, there are 46 students for every teacher. In the Philippines, the teacher–student ratio is 31, and in Myanmar, 28 (World Bank 2014: 30).

Low investment in education presents serious justice issues, resulting in the poor having less access to education. The World Bank (2014: 29) has explored the correlation between household wealth and primary school attendance in Thailand, Vietnam, Cambodia, Lao PDR and Myanmar.

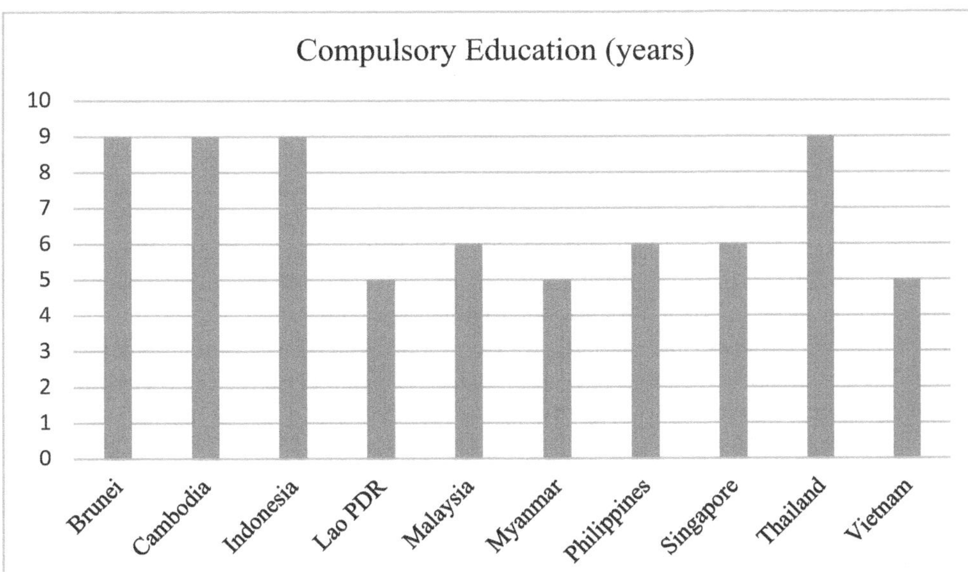

Figure 19.2 Compulsory education in ASEAN by years

Source: World Bank (2014)

In Thailand and Vietnam, where investment in education is relatively high, children from poorer households are almost as likely to attend school as children from wealthier households. In contrast, in Cambodia, Lao PDR and Myanmar, differences are substantial (World Bank 2014: 29). Brehm and Silova (2014: 160) describe Cambodia's education system as structurally disadvantaging the poor. By way of illustration the Cambodian curriculum is too long to be taught within the standard school day, resulting in a 'shadow curriculum' of private tutoring, often provided by class teachers, to teach elements of the curriculum that cannot be covered within the formal school system. Not surprisingly, the poor are less able to pay additional fees for private tutoring, resulting in poorer school achievement and greater likelihood of both repetition and drop-out. The 'shadow curriculum' that Brehm and Silova describe in Cambodia exists in other countries across ASEAN, and is, for example, very common in Indonesia. As Brehm and Silova (2014) argue, the practice can be understood not as individual teachers engaging in localised practices that are corrupt, but as reflecting systemic weaknesses of the education system that impact most deleteriously on the poor.

The right to protection

Rights to health care, education and living standards may be subject to progressive realisation but are also undermined by structural inequalities that leave children from poor families with fewer opportunities to claim their rights. Progressive realisation does not apply to what Green (2001: 1071) refers to as 'procedural rights that apply to all human rights without exception'. In particular, the right to non-discrimination, the right to legal remedies if one's human rights are violated, and the right to nationality are not subject to progressive realisation. Similarly, legislation and policy to protect children from abuse and violence are not subject to progressive realisation. This is not to suggest that all abuse and violence can be stopped through legislative and policy mechanisms—clearly it cannot. However, the establishment of a legislative and policy framework is an essential first step; such a framework should recognise resource constraints but not defer action until resources are available.

Progress towards domestic policy frameworks that incorporate either specific articles or the overarching intent of the UNCRC has been uneven across ASEAN member states. While ASEAN has taken up some issues around children's right to protection, such as sharing good practices on ending violence against children and addressing trafficking, the approach has been largely ad hoc. To date, there has been no move towards a coordinated regional approach towards child protection. UNICEF (2010) has advocated a systems approach to child protection, both within countries and regionally. Such an approach would move away from an issues-based approach towards building coordinated systems that respond to the interconnectedness of child protection issues and focus on prevention rather than response.

The Philippines arguably has the most well-developed child protection policy framework in the ASEAN region. While implementation has been extremely uneven, a strong commitment to children's human rights, and particularly to the right to protection, has developed within key government departments. With the accession of Rodrigo Duterte to presidency, children's right to protection came under direct challenge. In a number of media reports, President Duterte described the accidental killing of children by security forces as part of the 'war on drugs' as collateral damage (Holmes 2016). In 2016, the president proposed lowering the age of criminal responsibility from 15 years to nine years. In September 2016, the Department of Social Welfare and Development and the Juvenile Justice and Welfare Council issued a statement strongly opposing the lowering of the minimum age for criminal responsibility, drawing on the UNCRC to support their position. In the joint statement, the Department of Social Welfare and Development and the Juvenile Justice and Welfare Council stated:

> The UNCRC Committee, in its 2009 concluding observations to the Philippine report to UNCRC compliance commended the country's passage of the Juvenile Justice and Welfare Act of 2006 (or RA 9344), which raised the [minimum age for criminal responsibility] from 9 to 15 years old.
>
> *(Department of Social Welfare and Development 2014)*

At the time, the Secretary of the Department of Social Welfare and Development, Judy Taguiwalo, argued that the proposed change 'violates the fundamental principles of social protection of children as provided for by the law and by international treaties and internationally accepted standards and principles'. The strong policy commitment demonstrated to children's human rights within key government departments, such as the Department of Social Welfare and Development, is under direct challenge from an emerging political environment whereby 'respect for rule of law and human rights runs a distant second to the rule of violence and power' (Tidwell 2016: 3). Given the Philippines' important role in promoting children's right to protection within ASEAN, these developments are of grave concern not only at the national level, but also regionally.

The rather uneven uptake of the right to protection across other ASEAN member states is evident in the example of violent forms of punishment, often referred to as corporal punishment, particularly in schools. The UN Committee on the Rights of the Child, in General Comment number 8 has stated that 'eliminating violent and humiliating punishment of children, through law reform and other necessary measures, is an immediate and unqualified obligation of States parties'. Progress towards ending violent forms of punishment in ASEAN countries has been slow. No ASEAN member state prohibits the use of corporal punishment against children in all settings, although the Philippines and Thailand have each expressed a commitment to do so. Significantly, half of the ASEAN member states (Brunei Darussalam, Indonesia, Malaysia, Myanmar and Singapore) allow the use of corporal punishment in schools. The use of corporal punishment in schools breeches the principle of best interests (CRC: Art. 3), as well as undermining children's experience of school and sense of safety. Relatively few studies have been undertaken on the impacts of corporal punishment in ASEAN member states; however, small-scale studies conducted in various parts of Indonesia have suggested that being verbally or physically abused by teachers and by other pupils contributes to children leaving school before they complete primary education (Tampubolon et al. 2003; Ahimsa-Putra 1999; Daliyo et al. 1999). Thus, the use of violent forms of punishment violate not only Article 3 (best interests) and Article 19 (protection from all forms of physical and mental punishment) of the CRC, but also children's right to education (Arts. 28–29).

In 2014 the Malaysian Ministry of Women, Family and Community Development, with support from the ASEAN Commission on the Promotion and Protection of the Rights of Women and Children, produced a document of good practices in eliminating violence against women and children. Significantly, only the chapters documenting the approach of the Philippines and Thailand identified corporal punishment in schools as violence against children. Thailand was most progressive, framing corporal punishment, along with bullying, as a form of violence in schools that must be addressed. While the failure of other countries within the ASEAN region to identify corporal punishment as a form of violence is of concern, the efforts of the Philippines and Thailand to end all forms of violence in schools provide important models for other countries. Yet, as noted earlier in the discussion of the Philippines' move towards lowering the minimum age for criminal responsibility, its leadership role in relation to fostering children's human rights is greatly diminished in a political environment whereby human rights are violated with impunity.

A range of challenges continue to plague the ASEAN region, including severe violations such as the commercial sexual exploitation of children and human trafficking, including of children. The regional nature of the problem has long been recognised by ASEAN, with summit meetings throughout the 1990s raising the issues of commercial sexual exploitation and trafficking of children. Vision 2020, adopted in 1997, made a commitment to regional cooperation to end trafficking of women and children, although action was slow to follow. Over the past decade, ASEAN has increasingly played a role in supporting regional frameworks to address such violations. In 2015, the Association developed the ASEAN Convention and Plan of Action Against Trafficking in Persons Especially in Women and Children, representing an historic step towards addressing some of the most egregious violations of children's human rights within the region. While some human rights groups were critical of the slow response to the Convention and Plan of Action, it entered into force in February 2017, within two years of its adoption, when the Philippines became the sixth country to ratify it. The strong focus on a legal approach and lesser attention towards underlying causes does create concerns around its potential effectiveness. Nevertheless, as the region's first legally binding instrument addressing human trafficking, the significance of this instrument cannot be understated, and signals an ongoing movement towards efforts to address deeply entrenched human rights violations.

Statelessness and gross violations

Arguably, the greatest area of negligence towards human rights in the ASEAN region is the treatment of people whose citizenship status is uncertain or contested. While the resulting violations impact on people regardless of age, children's rights (to healthcare, education and protection in particular) are especially vulnerable. Gibney (2009: 50) has argued that the greatest injustice of statelessness is not that individuals 'cannot find a state to grant them citizenship but that the state which should grant them citizenship will, for various reasons, not do so'. This comment is especially pertinent to the situation of many children who are classified within the ASEAN region, and speaks to the failure to arrive at a regional solution despite the move towards greater adherence to human rights.

Within the ASEAN region, the situation of 'precarious residents' (Gibney 2009: 50) is a major human rights issue. These people, including large numbers of children, live in states where they have no right to stay. They have no claim to a range of human rights, including health care and education, and are vulnerable to deportation. In many cases, they were born in the country of their residence, but have no record of their birth and no recognition of their life from the country of their birth (Allerton 2013). The denial of these children's right to nationality occurs in a wider context of discrimination and leads to ongoing exclusion from a range of rights that are dependent of citizenship status or legal recognition of residency. Allerton (2013) has noted that among stateless children in Sabah (Malaysia) the denial of access to services and processes of justice results in precarious status, but more significantly creates a deeply damaging sense of 'exclusion from the nationality to which they feel they belong'.

The number of children without legal identity is high across ASEAN member states in part because of the historically porous nature of borders. For example, traditionally people have moved freely between what is now Malaysia, Indonesia and the Philippines; and also between Thailand and Myanmar. The establishment of national borders did not end the fluidity of people's movement but did lead to political claims of sovereignty that sought to control the entry and residency of 'foreigners'. The movement of peoples within the ASEAN region has been fuelled by both people's search for greater economic opportunity (for example, people of Indonesian origin in Malaysia) and by conflict that drives people away from their own country of birth (for example people from the southern Philippines in Malaysia) (Allerton 2013). Most fundamentally, children born into such situations of precariousness are often not registered at birth and have no subsequent claim to citizenship of any country. The denial of the right to identity from the time of birth locates them in a shadow world within which it is not possible to claim fundamental human rights because those rights are so bounded to citizenship. The politics of sovereignty within ASEAN, and the principle of non-interference in domestic issues, has prevented the development of a regional approach to addressing the rights of precarious residents.

Of the range of groups living in precarious situations within ASEAN, the Rohingya have been—and remain—particularly vulnerable. Despite the presence of Rohingya communities in Myanmar, mainly in the western Rakhine State, for centuries, their right to citizenship was denied by the 1982 Citizenship Act, with a litany of abuses perpetrated against them. The situation worsened from June 2012 with the outbreak of violence and the imposition of curfews and limitations placed on the movement of Rohingya (OHCHR 2017). The extent of human rights violations against the Rohingya has long been known within ASEAN and beyond. The United Nations High Commissioner for Refugees estimates that 25,000 Rohingya fled Myanmar in the period between January and March 2015 alone, when the situation in Rakhine State worsened. Many of those fleeing were subsequently stranded on boats at sea, as international debates emerged about how to respond to their plight. At the time, ASEAN foreign ministers met, but there was nothing in the way of coordinated response. The discovery of mass graves on the Thai–Malaysia border in 2015 resulted in cooperation between those two countries in bringing to trial in Malaysia those suspected of trafficking Rohingya out of Myanmar (Hunt 2015). At the time, the Malaysian government was openly critical of Myanmar's treatment of the Rohingya and denial of their citizenship rights, with former Prime Minister Mohammad Mahatir publicly stating that Myanmar should leave ASEAN if its treatment of the Rohingya continued (Hunt 2015). ASEAN, however, failed to take a leadership role in responding to the humanitarian crisis unfolding in the region, and originating within a member state.

In February 2017, the UN Office of the High Commissioner for Human Rights released a 'flash report' based on the testimony of 220 Rohingya who had fled Myanmar to Bangladesh following serious violence in October 2016. The report documented shocking violations against Rohingya communities by the Myanmar armed forces, the Border Guard Police Force of Myanmar and the Police forces of Myanmar (OHCHR 2017: 10–11).

The OHCHR Report included detailed appalling abuses against children. The human rights of children have long been violated in Rakhine State, of which poverty rates, literacy and health outcomes are among the lowest in Myanmar (OHCHR 2017). The testimonies gathered by the OHCHR team stated:

> Several testimonies gathered by the OHCHR team concern the killing of children—boys and girls of different age groups ranging from newborns to teenagers—by the security forces. Children were killed by live ammunition or stabbed while at home; while fleeing to safety; or while in the farms or fields. In several particularly disturbing cases, mothers witnessed the killings of their children by knife attacks.
>
> *(OHCHR 2017: 40)*

ASEAN, collectively, failed to respond adequately to the crisis in Myanmar. While individual member states, particularly Malaysia, spoke out, the Association's principle of non-interference in the domestic politics of states clearly conflicted with ASEAN's far newer commitment to regional human rights, particularly the rights of children. The state-supported killing of Rohingya children in Myanmar presents a serious challenge to the legitimacy of ASEAN's commitment to, and ability to protect, the human rights of children.

Conclusion

From the late 1990s, ASEAN moved from a position of rejecting international human rights standards, to the establishment of the Commission on the Promotion and Protection of the Rights of Women and Children in 2010 and the adoption of the ASEAN Declaration of Human Rights in 2012. The shift within ASEAN towards adherence to human rights was remarkable, with the human rights of children a consistent focus of the work of the Association. As the discussion in this chapter indicates, considerable progress has been made but areas of serious negligence remain. While the low levels of development in some member states mitigates against immediate realisation of some human rights, many of the failings to progress children's human rights to health care, education and protection are a result of structural discrimination and lack of political will, rather than resources.

While the progress of ASEAN towards adherence to the human rights of children during the twenty-first century is welcome, serious challenges remain. The most significant of these is ASEAN's ongoing commitment to the principle of non-interference, which prevents the possibilities of the Association genuinely leading human rights reform or dealing adequately with cross-border violations, such as trafficking, in a meaningful way.

The greatest ongoing test of ASEAN's ability to foster the human rights of children (and indeed of adults) across the region is, however, the ongoing persecution of minority groups in some member states. Most challenging of these is the treatment by Myanmar of Rohingya children. In 1997, when Myanmar sought entry to ASEAN, its record of using child soldiers and abusing the rights of children became an issue of international opprobrium. In 2017, Myanmar was again the subject of international condemnation as evidence emerged of the brutal murder of children by state forces. While ASEAN's increasing recognition of human rights is laudable, its inability to act when the most serious violations are committed by a member state undermines its credibility as a regional mechanism for promoting children's human rights.

Acknowledgement

Special thanks go to Jasmin Lim for her early contributions in conceptualising this chapter.

References

Ahimsa-Putra, HS 1999, 'A focused study on child abuse in six selected provinces in Indonesia', unpublished report, Jakarta, UNICEF.

Allerton, C 2013, 'Statelessness and the lives of the children of migrants in Sabah, East Malaysia', *Tilburg Law Review: Journal of International and European Law*, vol. 19, no. 1–2, pp. 26–34.

ASEAN 2009, *Roadmap for an ASEAN Community 2009–2015*, Jakarta, Association of Southeast Asian Nations.

ASEAN 2010, 'Terms of Reference: ASEAN Commission on the Promotion and Protection of the Rights of Women and Children', Jakarta, Association of Southeast Asian Nations.

Becker, J 2009, 'Child recruitment in Burma, Sri Lanka and Nepal', in S Gates and S Reich (eds), *Child Soldiers in the Age of Fractured States*, Pittsburgh, PA, University of Pittsburgh Press, pp. 108–120.

Braveman, P & Gruskin, S 2003, 'Poverty, equity, human rights and health', *Policy and Practice*, vol. 81, no. 7, pp. 539–545.

Brehm, W & Silova, I 2014, 'Ethical dilemmas in the education marketplace: Shadow education, political philosophy and social (in)justice in Cambodia', in I Macpherson, S Robertson and G Ward (eds), *Education, Privatisation and Social Justice: Case Studies from Africa, South Asia and Southeast Asia*, Oxford, Symposium Books, pp. 159–178.

Committee on the Rights of the Child (CRC) 2007, 'Consideration of reports submitted by states parties under Article 44 of the Convention: Concluding Observations: Malaysia', CRC/C/MYS/CO/1 2 February 2007, www2.ohchr.org/english/bodies/crc/docs/co/CRC_C_MYS_CO_1.pdf.

Cribb, R 1998, 'Burma's entry into ASEAN: Background and implications', *Asian Perspective*, vol. 22, no. 3, pp. 50–62.

Daliyo, Guest, P, May, M & Tirtosudarmo, R 1999, 'Child labour and education planning in Eastern and Western Nusa Tenggara Barat', Jakarta, AusAID.

Davies, M 2013, 'Explaining the Vientiane Action Programme: ASEAN and the institutionalisation of human rights', *The Pacific Review*, vol. 26, no. 4, pp. 385–406.

Department of Social Welfare and Development 2014, 'Lowering of the minimum age of criminal responsibility', 2 September, www.gov.ph/2014/09/02/statement-dswd-on-the-lowering-of-the-minimum-age-of-criminal-responsibility/.

Donnelly, J 2013, *Universal Human Rights in Theory and Practice*, Ithaca, NY, Cornell University Press.

Gibney, M 2009, 'Statelessness and the right to citizenship', *Statelessness*, Oxford, Refugees Studies Centre, University of Oxford.

Green, M 2001, 'What we talk about when we talk about indicators: Current approaches to human rights measurement', *Human Rights Quarterly*, vol. 23, pp. 1062–1097.

Holmes, O 2016, 'Duterte says children killed in Philippines drug war are "collateral damage"', *The Guardian*, 17 October.

Hunt, L 2015, 'ASEAN move on Rohingya, slow but forward', *The Diplomat*, 22 June.

IHRC (The International Human Rights Clinic at Harvard Law School) 2009, *Crimes in Burma*, Cambridge, MA, Harvard Law School, http://hrp.law.harvard.edu/wp-content/uploads/2009/05/Crimes-in-Burma.pdf.

Krueger, AB 2002, *Economic Considerations and Class Size*, National Bureau of Economic Research Working Paper no. 8875.

OECD/World Health Organization 2014, *Health at a Glance: Asia/Pacific 2014: Measuring Progress towards Universal Health Coverage*, OECD Publishing, http://dx.doi.org/10.1787/health_glance_ap-2014-en.

OHCHR 2017, 'Interviews with Rohingyas fleeing from Myanmar since 9 October 2016: Flash Report', *Report of the OHCHR Mission to Bangladesh*, 3 February.

Phan, HD 2008, 'The evolution towards an ASEAN human rights body', *Asia-Pacific Journal on Human Rights and the Law*, vol. 9, no. 1, pp. 1–12.

Radtke, K 2014, 'ASEAN enlargement and norm change: A window of opportunity for democracy and human rights entrepreneurs?', *Journal of Current Southeast Asian Affairs*, vol. 33, no. 3, pp. 79–105.

Tampubolon, LH, Adi, R, Nur Hayati, E & Haysim N 2003, 'Pengkajian Mengenai Kekerasan Terhadap Anak di Kabupaten SIKKA and ENDE, NTT', unpublished report, Jakarta, UNICEF.

Thio, L 1999, 'Implementing human rights in ASEAN countries: "Promises to keep and miles to go before I sleep"', *Yale Human Rights and Development Journal*, vol. 2, no. 1, pp. 1–86.

Tidwell, A 2016, 'Duterte, Mindanao, and political culture', *Asia Pacific Bulletin*, no. 362, pp. 1–2.

UNDP 2016, *Human Development for Everyone*, New York, UNDP.

UNICEF 2010, 'Child protection and child welfare in Asia and the Pacific', Discussion paper for High-Level Meeting on Cooperation for Child Rights in the Asia-Pacific Region, www.unicef.org/eapro/Child_Protection_and_Child_Welfare.pdf.

UNICEF 2016, *State of the World's Children: A Fair Chance for Every Child*, New York, UNICEF.

World Bank 2014, *Bridging the Development Gap: ASEAN Equitable Development Monitor*, Washington, DC, World Bank Group.

World Bank 2016, World Development Indicators. Washington, DC: The World Bank (producer and distributor). http://data.worldbank.org/data-catalog/world-development-indicators (accessed August 2016).

20

The human rights of older peoples in Asia

Christie M. Gardiner[1]

Introduction

The consequences of global population ageing are far reaching, affecting all societies, economies and governments and underscoring why the former United Nations Secretary-General Kofi Annan described ageing as 'one of the dominant themes of the century' (UN 2002: Foreword). The impact of ageing across Asia and the Pacific is so significant that it is widely viewed 'societies and economies need to be redesigned, with strategies to promote decent employment, lifelong learning and social participation for older persons and to make the voice of older persons heard' (UN ECOSOC 2017: 5). The purpose of this restructuring would be to 'ensur[e] older persons are provided with access to pensions, appropriate health care, technology, transport and built environment, including humanitarian and disaster response' (UN ECOSOC 2017: 5). This global phenomenon is most acute across Asia, which has the largest population of older peoples – a population which is itself rapidly ageing. As the world adjusts to this environment, major fault lines have emerged within the existing international human rights system, highlighting its inability to protect the rights and dignity of older peoples. Principally, older peoples are chiefly vulnerable to asymmetrical power relations in their public and private lives and are susceptible to social and structural prejudice and disadvantage, often compounding upon disadvantages from earlier in life. Widespread forms of ageism and elder abuse are significant causes of disadvantage and these have detrimental impacts on the safety and security, health and well-being and participation of older peoples. When left unaddressed, these issues can exacerbate the social and economic burden of population ageing and contribute to intergenerational disadvantage.

In the middle of the last century ageing was raised globally as a matter of pressing concern, though it was not until 1982 that the first international soft law instrument was endorsed by the UN General Assembly – the *Vienna International Plan of Action on Ageing*. Subsequently, recognition was given to how core human rights instruments should be construed with reference to older peoples given there are very few specific legal protections, producing both normative and implementation gaps within the human rights framework. In recent years United Nations-based discussions concerning the human rights of older peoples have focused heavily on the *substance* of these rights. While this issue is likely to remain open-ended for some time, given the pace at which discussions have thus far evolved, there has been a recent shift toward focusing more critically on the *form* through which newly construed rights should be enforced.

A growing number of states, UN bodies, UN special procedures and NGOs have advocated for the creation of a new binding instrument clarifying state responsibility, enhancing visibility of the range of human rights issues older peoples face and strengthening protection mechanisms. On the other hand, many other states urge for the stronger mainstreaming of the human rights of older persons through existing instruments in fulfilment of pre-existing soft law commitments, such as the landmark *Madrid International Plan of Action on Ageing* ('MIPAA') which is the leading instrument on the topic. While consensus is not needed to create a new instrument, the high level of abstentions recorded by the General Assembly on this issue has been a factor in the slow progress of this debate. Accordingly, states have focused their attention on addressing issues of populating ageing with reference to international soft law guidance, domestic policies and regional initiatives.

Without a clearer international legal framework guiding policies it is reasonable to foresee difficulties with this approach – including the inconsistent monitoring and evaluation of compliance, further impacting data collection and therefore policy making. Even if a treaty were to be forthcoming in the short to medium term, such decisions will likely impact communities for decades and any deficiencies in these domestic policies will ultimately translate into an imperfect legal protection framework for the remainder of this century. Accordingly, population ageing is indeed the dominant theme of this century.

There appears to be limited concrete interest in Asia for the formation of a new binding instrument, with its concomitant monitoring, reporting and other compliance burdens – at least until such time as the mainstreaming of existing instruments has been fully exhausted. If mainstreaming is genuinely preferred, this process may take years. Accordingly, a specific binding instrument may very well be the most effective way of dealing with this pressing issue while best enabling states to meet their concurrent commitments under the *Sustainable Development Goals* and other regional targets such as the ASEAN Community Vision 2025.

As population ageing demands immediate policy responses, many states within the Asia region have already engaged heavily with this issue on a domestic, regional and sub-regional basis, including in relation to social security, health, employment and accommodation. This has often occurred in disparate ways, reflecting pre-existing social and cultural norms and domestic economic challenges. Significantly, the public sector has emerged as a pivotal actor in relation to addressing issues facing ageing populations and whose conduct will heavily influence the quality of life of older persons, particularly in the rapidly expanding aged care, geriatric health care and technology sectors. The commodification of ageing requires close regulation to guard against the risks of exploitation of older peoples, to maximise opportunities, and to align development agendas with human rights frameworks.

The balance of this chapter explores each of these abovementioned themes in four parts: population ageing in Asia; issues of ageism and elder abuse; protecting the rights of older persons; and ageing and the private sector. Each of these sections draw on examples from within Asia to highlight the various ways in which older peoples are affected in this rapidly transforming landscape.

Population ageing in Asia

Population ageing – a phenomenon whereby older individuals become a proportionally larger share of the total population – is a normative global trend driven by development factors such as low birth rates and improved life expectancy (UN DESA 2017). There is significant variance in life expectancy across Asia and population ageing is occurring at different rates within the region. These changes are influenced by 'economic and social conditions as well as issues such as family planning, healthcare and religion' (Dlugosz & Razniak 2014: 44). In 2017, peoples aged 60 years and over ('older peoples') numbered 962 million (13% of the global total population), and this figure includes 137 million peoples aged 80 years and over ('oldest old') (UN DESA 2017: 1, 13; UN DESA 2001: 23).[2] Astoundingly, by 2030 there will be 1.4 billion older peoples in the world and by 2050 there will be 2.1 billion older peoples, including 425 million oldest old peoples – a group which is growing twice as fast as those aged 60–79 (UN DESA 2017: 1, 7, 13; UN DESA 2015: 1, 12). Europe currently has the largest percentage of older persons, but in overall numbers, the population of older peoples in Asia is unrivalled.

Sixty per cent of the world's population resides in Asia, with China and India comprising 1.41 billion and 1.34 billion peoples respectively (UN DESA 2017: 1, 5). Asia will shoulder a disproportionate 65% of the global increase in older peoples between 2017 and 2050 (UN DESA 2017: 13), growing even further in the following half-century. Developing regions will also carry a heavier burden associated with population ageing, with '54 per cent of the world's oldest old residing in less developed regions, increasing to 70 per cent by 2050' (UN DESA 2001: 24). The number of older peoples forecast to reside in Asia by 2030 is over 844.5 million and increasing to 1.3 billion by 2050 – representing the oldest population-based region globally by a significant margin (UN DESA 2017: 5; UN DESA 2015: 10). Japan's population includes 33% older peoples, which is the highest of any country globally (UN DESA 2017: 18, 19, 21); however, China has the largest population of older peoples in the region including over 12 million oldest old peoples, increasing to 99 million by 2050 (UN DESA 2001: 23). India's population is forecast to surpass China's by 2025 (UN DESA 2017: 5) and although its population is currently relatively young, by 2050 it too will have a significant aged population including 48 million oldest old peoples (UN DESA 2001: 24). Globally, Japan will lead a population of centenarians, increasing from '13,000 in 2000 to more than 1 million in 2050' (UN DESA 2001: 24). Evidently, the growing cohort of older peoples presents a unique and pressing challenge to current policy makers within countries of this region. The lessons learnt from population ageing in Asia will undoubtedly inform international laws and influence public policy making for all regions globally.

Ageing populations place considerable political and economic pressure on governments, largely due to a diminishing worker/retiree support ratio and an increase in old-age expenses (UN DESA 2015: 17). On average, by 2025 there will be 7.4 workers per retiree in Asia and for Japan this is drastically lower at just 2.1 workers per retiree, dropping to an estimated 1.3 workers per retiree by 2050 (UN DESA 2017: 11; UN DESA 2015: 17). This places a financial strain on 'public systems of health care, pensions and social protections for a growing older population' (UN DESA 2017: 11). Take for example the economic burden associated with retirement expenses in China. Hu (2017: 214) reports that 'by 2050 the total number of retired employees in China will surpass 100 million at a cost of RMB 18 trillion [US$2.8 trillion] – more than 20 times that in 1993'. In response, and as part of the 13th Five-Year Plan for Economic and Social Development of the People's Republic of China (2016–2020), the Central Committee has ushered in significant reforms permitting couples to have two children (Central Committee 2016: 184). However, early indicators suggest these measures have not triggered desired increases in birth rates (XinhuaNet.com 2018), largely due to the costs associated with raising a family in China, which is in addition to caring for the oldest old. Families have also now normalised a single child family structure. Additional reforms have been proposed relating to 'population strategies, employment systems, elderly care services, the social security system including a gradual increase in retirement age, health programs, training systems, environmental support, and social participation' (Central Committee 2016: 184). Improving administrative systems, access to services and delivery and aligning economic and social policies are also a priority for China (Central Committee 2016: 184).

It is easy to associate population ageing with economic burden, but as the UN General Assembly expressed in 1990, it is important that older persons are recognised as 'assets to society who can contribute significantly to the development process' (Res 46/106). Anticipating the pressures of population ageing enables countries to enact proactive policies to mitigate the burden, which UN DESA strongly encourages (2015: 1). Creating more opportunities for older peoples to continue to engage with the labour force is critical for economies and for improving the security, participation, health and well-being of older peoples generally. While many of the burdens associated with population ageing have broader public policy solutions, these may be overlooked due to pervasive social and structural prejudices against older peoples.

The problems of ageism and elder abuse

Ageism

Older peoples are vulnerable to systemic and social prejudices which perpetuate discrimination and negative stereotypes of the individual and of their place within society based on their age – a circumstance known as *ageism*.[3] Ageism has been linked to fear of ones' own mortality and to the generally greater social and political emphasis placed on the youth and working-age populations. In 1969 ageism was raised as a 'serious national problem' and in 1980 this issue was characterised as having three interrelated aspects:

> (1) prejudicial attitudes toward the aged, toward old age, and toward the ageing process, including attitudes held by older persons themselves; (2) discriminatory practices against older persons, particularly in employment, but in other social roles as well; and (3) institutional practices and policies which, often without malice, perpetuate stereotypic beliefs about older persons, reduce their opportunities for a satisfactory life and undermine their personal dignity.
>
> *(Butler 1980: 8)*

Ageism leads to the 'devaluation of older persons by depicting them as frail non-contributors and a burden to society' (UN DESA 2016). Devaluing attitudes can be disastrous for individuals, with research revealing that 'older people who hold negative attitudes about ageing do not recover as well from disability and live on average 7.5 years less than those with positive attitudes' (WHO 2016). Ageism can also deprive persons of opportunities to exercise personal autonomy and independence, particularly in relation to aged care, health care and end of life choices. It can impact the ability to make 'decisions about finances, work, property, who to vote for, where and with whom to live, access to health services, family life, and participation in community, voluntary or social activities' (HelpAge International 2018). It is not uncommon for older persons in Asia to be deprived of independence and autonomy, with decision making regarding health care, aged care and end of life issues often given to children in the absence of the individual parent's voluntary, informed consent. Issues of privacy and confidentiality are also exposed in this practice. While such incidents may be motivated by a sense of respect for the older person, perpetuated by social taboos regarding ill-health and death, the deprivation of autonomy has fundamental health consequences for older persons which must be closely considered. Having a system in place which enables older persons to legally delegate limited decision-making capacity to third parties can preserve the autonomy of the individual while simultaneously providing a legal remedy for breach of duties arising under that delegated authority. While these issues are not examined further in this chapter, they remain important regulatory mechanisms which should be utilised in ageing populations across Asia. However, caution should be exercised given these legal instruments also have the potential to promote instances of abuse if they are not supported by a strong regulatory, supervisory and educational framework.

Ageism manifests differently across various cultures and contexts. While it is often dismissed as a Western experience in contradistinction with Eastern cultural values of filial piety, researchers have identified pan-cultural characteristics of ageism which are widespread in both developed Western 'individualistic' countries and in Eastern 'collectivist' societies (Bodner & Lazar 2008; Cuddy, Norton & Fiske 2005). Greater negative denigration of seniors was found to arise in Eastern cultures, particularly in East Asia as compared to South and Southeast Asia. Individualism was also found to strongly correlate with positive attitudes of ageing, suggesting that 'collectivist traditions may backfire as an approach to generating elder respect in rapidly ageing societies' (North & Fiske 2015: 993). Accordingly, one can no longer apply traditional cultural typologies to issues of ageism alone, as the needs and interests of older peoples within countries and between individuals are influenced by diverse factors which increasingly challenge normative attitudes.

Common among ageist attitudes, practices and policies is an unfounded and invalid assumed degree of homogeneity among older peoples. Ageing itself is 'multidimensional and involves physical, psychological and social changes, impacting health, well-being and experiences in later life' (UNFPA 2012: 20). Individuals may identify as an older person by reference to social and health-related experiences, or by life events such as becoming a grandparent. There is no universal definition of an 'older person' and it is important to ensure that older peoples are not viewed as a homogenous group or something other than simply an adult person. However, it is often functionally necessary to define and delineate between population groups based on distinguishing characteristics which may be common to a class of persons on the basis that different social responses are often required based on age and physical circumstances. The United Nations commonly adopt 60 years as the age where someone is said to be an older person. An older age may be typical in some countries as this is often commensurate with eligibility for social security benefits, however these ages may vary between men and women. For many developing countries, or specific groups within countries, a younger age such as 50 years or even younger may be more appropriate relative to life expectancy. Accordingly, this chronological age varies across cultures and contexts (Gorman 2000; Thane 1978; Thane 1989; Glascock & Feinman 1980).

The words and phrases chosen to refer to older adults are challenging in the context of ageist attitudes and the tendency to normalise everyday discriminatory language (Gendron et al. 2016). The potentially discriminatory linguistic encoding for words such as 'old', 'elderly', 'older peoples', 'oldest old' should be the subject of further investigation, particularly when adopted by the international community.[4] As Fealy et al. (2012: 100) suggest, 'words and phrases to name and reference older people need to be chosen carefully to avoid imposing an implied homogeneity on older people with reference to their health, capabilities, dispositions, desires, socio-economic status and related social needs'. Recognising the heterogeneity of older peoples' capacities, needs and interests and how these are shaped by diverse social, cultural and environmental experiences earlier in life is essential for promoting the visibility of older peoples and safeguarding against risks of ageism. Further, advances in assistive technologies and personalised medicine, in combination with nascent philosophical concepts of life and death and concomitant rights frameworks, will inevitably change the way society views age.[5]

The *othering* of older persons is an expression of societal values. These values influence policy decisions in ways that promote or inhibit access, opportunity, health and security for older persons. For example, the design of modern urban environments often fails to facilitate the full participation of all persons at all ages and of all functional abilities – instead appealing to a present majority of people with a particular physiological identity who lead a particular kind of life. The World Health Organization's (WHO) Age-Friendly cities and communities initiative is an example of how international agencies are attempting to overcome these forms of implicit structural ageism in ways that deliver social and economic benefits to entire communities. Underpinned by the WHO's Active Ageing Policy Framework, eight domains are established as directly influencing quality of life and well-being: (1) outdoor spaces and buildings; (2) transportation; (3) housing; (4) social participation; (5) respect and social inclusion; (6) civic participation and employment; (7) communication and information; and (8) community support and health services (WHO 2002: 12; WHO 2007). These domains intersect with a range of MIPAA issues, including: active participation in society and development; work and the ageing labour force; intergenerational solidarity; health promotion and well-being throughout life; universal and equal access to health-care services; housing and the living environment. The 2030 Agenda for Sustainable Development, the UN Habitat Urban Agenda, the Global Strategy and Action Plan on Ageing and Health also objectively align with the principles of an age-friendly environment. According to the WHO, reconceptualising societies and environments by making them age friendly is one of the most effective economic and social policy responses to population ageing. The positive impacts this approach has on ageism should continue to be studied in line with MIPAA's priority direction for ensuring enabling and supportive environments.

Combating ageism appears to be a priority for most countries within Asia, whether for social, cultural or economic reasons. It is necessary to identify the boundaries of state responsibility and the extent to which their policies should also promote attitudinal shifts away from viewing older peoples as welfare dependents to rights holders with responsibilities. Adopted as part of the 2012 Asian Symposium on Building Sustainable Ageing Societies held in Changchun, China, it was held that:

> One of the main challenges of the ageing societies is the pressure that elderly care (including health and income support) will have on the country's fiscal sustainability and economic growth. One thing that is clear, however, is that older citizens are not idle beings, nor are they mere beneficiaries of social welfare benefits. They have been and will be contributors to the economy and the progress of societies at large with their multiple roles as producers, consumers, teachers of traditions, tenders of children in families, moral authorities in communities, and so on. The international agreed document, Madrid International Plan of Action on Ageing (MIPAA) proposes a social inclusion of older persons in all aspects of life in society.
>
> *(UN ESCAP 2012: 1)*

While evidence-based policy making in respect of ageing is increasingly advocated for across the region (see e.g. UN ESCAP 2012), there appears to be limited engagement with issues such as elder abuse relative to the severity of the issue.

Elder abuse

Elder abuse is a universal phenomenon. The WHO define elder abuse as 'a single, or repeated act, or lack of appropriate action, occurring within any relationship where there is an expectation of trust which causes harm or distress to an older person'.[6] Elder abuse encompasses a range of sub-categories including physical, psychological and sexual abuse, financial exploitation and intentional or unintentional neglect. It impacts the physical and psychological integrity of older peoples, their families and communities. It can lead to isolation, neglect, ill-health, forced care placement and is also known to generate higher mortality risks. Elder abuse can impact livelihoods, depriving older peoples of employment opportunities, and dispossessing them of physical and financial assets, resulting in financial and physical insecurity, further increasing the risks of abuse and exploitation. Data in relation to elder abuse is poor, with countries in Asia only beginning to confront this issue. Recent prevalence studies indicate that up to 16% of older peoples globally will experience some form of elder abuse (psychological abuse, 11.6%; financial abuse, 6.8%; neglect, 4.2%; physical abuse, 2.6%; or sexual abuse 0.9%) (Yon et al. 2017). It is also widely accepted that prevalence studies tend to underestimate the extent of abuse. This is because of underreporting or because of the misidentification or inconsistent characterisation of the nature of abuse perpetrated. Even if these figures are generally accepted, over half a million people in Asia will have experienced one or more forms of elder abuse. While the risk of abuse is known to increase with a victim's declining physical or cognitive abilities (Yan, Chan & Tiwari 2015: 201), research indicates that the oldest old are least likely to experience abuse compared with their younger counterparts (Dong & Simon 2010; Dong & Simon 2013; Dong, Simon, Gorbien, Percak & Golden 2007).

Mitigating elder abuse requires an intimate understanding of the conditions that surround and promote it. Elder abuse can be difficult to observe depending on the nature of the relationship between abuser and victim. The cultural contexts in which abuse occurs also influences the development of appropriate interventions (Yan, Chan & Tiwari 2015: 199). Research conducted in China, Taiwan, Hong Kong, India, Singapore, Japan and South Korea demonstrates that abusers are typically known to their victims and are often found to be adult children, predominantly sons and daughters-in-law (Yan, Chan & Tiwari 2015: 199, 215). Spouses, other family members and care givers are also common abusers. The UN appointed Independent Expert on the enjoyment of all human rights by older peoples, Rosa Kornfeld-Matte, has 'urged public action to halt the abuse of older persons by relatives' (UNGA 2017) and the United Nations has adopted the view that strengthening intergenerational interdependence is important to achieve this purpose. For developing countries, Gupta (2016) attributes abuse by family members to 'weakened filial piety' caused by 'changing socio-cultural contexts and weakening intergenerational bonds'. However, as noted above, arguments for increased collectivism over individualism may not hold true in all cases and greater research into the nature and causes of elder abuse across the region and between peoples is needed to better inform policy making.

Seeking help against perpetrators of elder abuse is also largely dependent on the willingness of the individual to speak out, often against their families. This is contingent on having an appropriate government authority to speak to and a clear basis for seeking help (i.e. seeking intervention services or accessing legal remedies). Research into elder abuse across Asia indicates a reluctance to report abuse due to privacy reasons (Dong, Simon & Gorbien 2007; Yan & Tang 2001), or concern for family honour. Other reasons for under-reporting have been linked to the personal difficulty that some parents experience in acknowledging the poor filial piety of their children (Cheng & Chan 2006), which can even be perceived as a parental failing, further attracting shame (Lee & Eaton 2009; Chan 2009).

Kornfeld-Matte has also noted that an inherent risk of speaking out against abuse is that victims may become more isolated – perpetuating a cycle of disempowerment. Accordingly, 'efforts should be made to build rapport with suspected victims on the basis that older Asian's are reluctant to report abusive practices outside of their families – stymying prevention and intervening efforts' (Yan, Chan & Tiwari 2015: 216). Strengthening interventions can also be stymied by a lack of political support and resourcing to investigate such behaviours in the community. For example, in response to a question posed in 2017 by the Open-ended Working Group in Ageing as to whether 'violence, abuse and neglect particularly affect specific groups of older persons', China stated: '[a]ccording to surveys, violence, abuse and neglect happens accidentally and it doesn't affect specific groups of older persons'. The surveys supporting this very general claim were not referenced in the submissions; however, this claim contradicts other findings that elder abuse is not accidental or nominal in mainland China. Take for example the widely reported incident of a 100-year-old Chinese woman kept in a pigsty for two years by her farmer son in Jiangsu province. This incident unambiguously aligns with the WHO conception of elder abuse.

In evidenced-based terms, studies regarding the prevalence of elder abuse in China range as high as 35% (16.9% caregiver neglect, 13.6% financial exploitation, 11.4% emotional abuse, 5.8% physical abuse, 1.2% sexual abuse and 0.7% abandonment) (Dong, Simon, Gorbien, Percak and Golden 2007; Yan, Chan & Tiwari 2015: 202) and 36.2% (27.3% psychological abuse, 15.8% caregiver neglect, 4.9% physical abuse and 2% financial exploitation) (Wu et al. 2012). These more reliable studies consistently report high rates of multiple forms of abuse. Older women are more likely to experience abuse overall than men, though men may experience greater neglect than women (Dong & Simon 2010; Dong & Simon 2013; Dong, Simon, Gorbien, Percak & Golden 2007). There have been inconsistent findings in relation to the correlation between abuse and a victim's relationship status in China (Dong & Simon 2008; Wu et al. 2012; Dong, Simon & Gorbien 2007; Dong & Simon 2013). There have, however, been consistent findings that lower education attainment levels are a significant risk factor for elder abuse victims in China (Dong, Simon & Gorbien 2007; Dong & Simon 2008; Dong & Simon 2013; Wu et al. 2012). Older peoples without an income are also more likely to be abused (Dong, Simon & Gorbien 2007), but are also more likely to report their abuse (Dong & Simon 2013). These studies demonstrate the complexities of elder abuse and highlight the importance of further research and creating access to reliable age and gender disaggregated data. These significant information gaps underscore key issues relating to ageism and development.

As expressed above, in addition to being aware of the avenues to report abuse, seeking help for elder abuse is dependent on public awareness of ones' rights in relation to elder abuse. These rights need to be clarified in domestic laws across the region. States should also provide appropriate outreach and education services, and reporting mechanisms, and improve investigative and prosecutorial capacities. Overcoming these barriers demands improved quality of laws which criminalise discrimination and elder abuse and provide better access to civil remedies. Such regulation is generally poor in the region, if not globally, as these concepts are often not clearly understood or defined in legislation. For example, while China has a range of laws protecting the equal interests of all citizens including from age-discrimination or abuse and neglect, these laws lack specificity and fail to provide legal definitions and elements to the offences which can be proven by the parties. Instead, they create ambiguity around the rights and obligations of parties regarding older persons which may promote barriers to access to justice on the one hand or vexatious litigation on the other. Without a strong legal and enforcement regime protecting older persons from ageism and abuse, the cycle of disadvantage and invisibility may be difficult to curb.

Protecting the rights of older peoples

An ageing agenda was first discussed by the international community in 1948 when Argentina proposed the *Draft Resolution on a Declaration of Old Age Rights*. The *Draft Resolution* declared:

> old age rights, having the same origin and purpose as other universal social safeguards, are essential for the improvement of the living conditions of the worker and for his welfare when his physical strength is at an end and he is exposed to poverty and neglect.
>
> *(UNGA 1948: A/C.3/213/Rev.1)*

The *Draft Resolution* creates rights to assistance, accommodation, food, clothing, care of physical health, care of moral health, recreation, work, stability and respect as necessary for safeguarding. However, it was not adopted. Instead, the inclusion of Article 25 in the *Universal Declaration of Human Rights* (1948) regarding broad reference to security in old age was seen as adequate at the time.

For several decades the issue of specific protections for older peoples has only received tangential recognition with no comprehensive commitments specific to the rights of older peoples. The first international document on ageing was the *Vienna International Plan of Action on Ageing* (VIPAA), adopted by the World Assembly on Ageing in 1982. This was followed by the 1991 *UN Principles for Older Persons*, which affirmed the fundamental and equal rights of all peoples, articulating key principles of independence, participation, care, self-fulfilment and dignity. The 1995 *General Comment No. 6 on the Economic, Social and Cultural Rights of Older Persons* was adopted by the Committee on Economic, Social and Cultural Rights, focusing on issues relating to the welfare of older peoples. Then in 2002 the landmark *Political Declaration and Madrid International Plan of Action on Ageing* (MIPAA) was adopted by the Second World Assembly on Ageing. Regional initiatives in Asia have included: the 1999 *Macao Plan of Action on Ageing for Asia and the Pacific*; the 2002 *Shanghai Regional Implementation Strategy on Ageing*; the 2010 *Brunei Darussalam Declaration on Strengthening Family Institution: Caring for the Elderly*; the 2015 *Kuala Lumpur Declaration on Ageing: Empowering Older Persons in ASEAN*; and the 2016 *ASEAN Plus Three Statement on Active Ageing*. Since 1982 the rights of older peoples in Asia have been cemented as a priority issue.

The MIPAA remains the leading soft law instrument on the topic. The *Plan of Action* was a culmination of collaborative initiatives directed toward better integrating ageing-related frameworks within social, economic and human rights-based norms. To achieve this, MIPAA sets three priority areas to guide policy making and programme actions: (1) older peoples and development; (2) advancing health and well-being into old age; and (3) ensuring enabling and supportive environments. In response, countries across the Asian region 'began the process of developing policies and legislation on ageing and integrating older people's concerns into broad policy-making' (Williamson 2015: i). This included the 2002 *Shanghai Regional Implementation Strategy on Ageing* which identified a pathway for issues of older peoples and development, advancing health and well-being, providing enabling and supportive environments, and implementation and follow-up to both the MIPAA and the Macao Plan of Action cited above. In 2017 the Asia-Pacific Intergovernmental Meeting on the Third Review and Appraisal of the *Madrid International Plan of Action in Ageing* was held in Bangkok.[7] Delegates affirmed that MIPAA and the 2030 *Agenda for Sustainable Development* (specifically goals 1, 3, 5, 10 and 11) are important instruments 'to overcome challenges and grasp the opportunities presented by population ageing' (UN ECOSOC 2017: 5).

Soft laws have attempted to enunciate how specific core human rights instruments are to be interpreted with reference to older peoples; however, these are non-exhaustive. Accordingly, a systematic and comprehensive approach to the circumstances of older peoples is urgently needed. The need for stronger legal protections for older peoples has been widely acknowledged, particularly as the core international human rights instruments contain very limited express reference to older persons. This results in few clear legal obligations on states to report on the situation of older peoples. Express reference is only contained in the *Universal Declaration of Human Rights* (Art. 25), the *International Convention on the Protection of the Rights of All Migrant Workers and Members of Their Families* (Arts 1.1 and 7), the *Convention on the Elimination of All Forms of Discrimination Against Women* (Art. 11.1e) and the *Convention on the Rights of Persons with Disabilities* (Arts 13.1, 16.2, 16.4, 23.1.b, 25b and 28.2.b). However, these obligations arise in very limited cases and fall short of providing an adequate standard of protection. The term 'other status' used throughout core instruments has not historically created an avenue of redress for older persons, as it creates no express obligation on states. Consequently, the voluntary reporting on the situation of the rights of older persons to the Human Rights Committee has been exceptionally poor. Implicit consideration of the rights of older persons by reference to 'all persons' or 'special measures' are similarly ambiguous and is thus inadequate for protecting the interests and needs of older persons (HelpAge International 2012).

The main avenues which have been proposed to close these protection gaps include: '(1) mainstreaming the rights of older persons in international human rights law; or (2) establishing a new legally binding mechanism specifically devoted to the rights of older persons' (UN DESA & UN ESCAP 2014: 7). This will likely involve creating a treaty specific to the rights of older peoples. The former option of enhanced mainstreaming is one which is favoured by many, including delegates of the Asia-Pacific Intergovernmental Meeting on the Third Review and Appraisal of the *Madrid International Plan of Action on Ageing*. The latter option could, however, help to provide a stronger, specific and common basis and frame of reference for the protection of the rights of the elderly. The Independent Expert on the enjoyment of all human rights by older persons' report to the Human Rights Council in September 2017 echoed her findings that 'the existing legal framework, regardless of its degree of implementation, is not enough to comprehensively and effectively ensure the enjoyment of all human rights by older persons' (UNGA 2017: A/HRC/36/48, 4. To this end, it has been established that there are normative, implementation, information and monitoring gaps in respect of the rights of older peoples. She also noted that it 'addresses the issues of ageing from a developmental rather than a human rights approach' (UNGA 2017: A/HRC/36/48, 4). However, as discussed below, this approach may be the most effective in the region.

To explore the issue of international protection for older peoples, on 21 December 2010 the UN General Assembly resolved to establish the Open-ended Working Group on Ageing (OEWGA):

> for the purposes of strengthening the protection of the human rights of older persons by considering the existing international framework of the human rights of older persons and identifying possible gaps and how best to address them, including by considering, as appropriate, the feasibility of further instruments and measures.
>
> *(see UNGA 2013: paras 1, 2, 4)*

The OEWGA has noted a distinct lack of universal mechanisms operating as a standard by which to benchmark the rights and interests of older peoples, as highlighted in this chapter above.

Between 2010 and 2018 the OEWGA held nine sessions focusing on thematic issues including the current situation of older peoples, international and regional frameworks and standard-setting processes; (multiple) discrimination; physical and mental health; violence and abuse; social protection and security; participation and exclusion; autonomy; independent living; aged care life and palliative care; dignity, social security and access to resources; abuse and violence; and access to justice, among others. However, some criticisms have been directed at the

OEWGA for not yet fulfilling its mandate to present a proposal of the main elements of an international legal instrument. Causes for delay are partially due to the protracted debate surrounding whether or not there should be a treaty at all and if so, the nature of its substantive content.[8] The burden of a new instrument on the pre-existing human rights system and the potential inefficiencies of this approach are further concerns expressed by states. Instead, a cautionary approach to resolving protection gaps has been urged by many, including China where, during the first session of the OEWGA, it stated 'in view of the major differences among the member states on the formulation of a new international legal instrument, a gradual process is required to ensure full consultations'.[9] This broad hesitation is echoed by the high level of abstentions for the pivotal General Assembly Resolution 67/139 on 20 December 2012, which refocused the OEWGA's efforts from investigating the feasibility of an international instrument to drafting its main elements. As the discussion toward developing stronger international law continues, domestic protection mechanisms for the rights of older persons must continue to be strengthened (UNGA 2011: A/RES/65/182, 3). Strengthening domestic protections additionally requires consideration of how, through regulation, the private sector can be leveraged to enhance the rights of older peoples.

Ageing populations and the private sector

By improving the private sector framework, individual rights can be better protected. As responses to population ageing in Asia necessarily involve market reform and investment, population ageing represents an important opportunity to help improve the quality of life for all persons in the region, including older persons. Known as the 'silver economy', ageing in Asia and the Pacific is a US$3.3 trillion market attracting mass international investment. The aged care and geriatric healthcare sectors specifically represent opportunities for the development of strategies which support economic growth while preserving rights. From education and vocational training, to establishing care robots and health monitoring, smart homes and driverless vehicles, the opportunities for improved health and participation are profound. China has been particularly engaged with this burgeoning market. As part of its 13th Five-Year Plan, China has committed to: opening up the entire elderly services market, and through means such as service procurement and equity cooperation, will support all types of market participants in providing more elderly care products and services' (Central Committee 2016: 186). During the fifth session of the OEWGA in 2014, China submitted that 'the role of the market should be given full play to improve the service system of older peoples and develop a service industry in this field', and claimed that it is necessary to 'tap the potential of civil society, the private sector and the family in meeting the needs of older persons' (PRC 2014).

The use of technology, including assistive and robotics technologies is an increasing phenomenon, improving the autonomy and dignity of older peoples, and improving equality of access and participation. In 2017 the Independent Expert on the full enjoyment of all human rights by older peoples examined this issue and has describes three main uses for assistive robotics technology: (1) monitoring the behaviour and health of older peoples; (2) providing assistance to older peoples or their caregivers with daily tasks; (3) providing social interactions (UNGA 2017: 5). The rapid deployment of such technologies can also address deficiencies in current aged care and health care systems in Asia.

The inadequacies of the current sector cannot be underestimated, but they also present massive opportunities. For example, the National Health and Family Planning Commission (NHFPC) of China has reported that just '50,000 aged care workers and 38,000 medical care workers are vocationally qualified, despite estimated demand for an aged care workforce of 10 million by 2020'.[10] As part of this workforce, China anticipates training half a million general practitioners. This includes raising the number of general practitioners, which is currently 1.5 per 10,000 peoples – a figure significantly behind the international standard of one general practitioner per 1,500–2,000 peoples (NHFPC 2018b). The qualifications of rural practitioners will also be supported under this scheme (NHFPC 2018b), and the introduction of artificial intelligence and big data are being explored as mechanisms to improve diagnostic and treatment deficiencies among professionals and to boost remote care services (NHFPC 2018a).

A fundamental risk of a rapidly expanding and developing aged care sector is poor regulation and fiscal pressure. For instance, pressures associated with increased medical expenditure in China have already reportedly resulted in the suspension of some medical consumables and the replacement of others with inferior products – placing all patients at increased risk (NHFPC 2018b). In partnering with the private sector, the 2012 Asian Symposium on Building Sustainable Ageing Societies concluded that 'the governance of [the] care industry must ensure that care is equitable, and that elderly care is not an opportunity for unreasonable profit making' (UN ESCAP 2012). For example, reports of the exploitative risks associated with the health-care industry are emerging, as healthy-ageing and anti-ageing products gain increased notoriety among older Chinese populations (*South China Morning Post* 2017), exacerbating the problems of elder abuse. While these products are often lawfully sold, the risks of financial over-exposure for older persons can be socially and financially devastating. When fraudulently sold, evidentiary issues often prevent successful investigation and prosecution (*South China Morning Post* 2017).

On the issue of engaging the private sector post-2015 to promote human rights and accountability:

> Corporate human rights violations occur when there is a lack of internal law regulating corporate activity and ensuring corporate responsibility, or when the state is either willing or unable to enforce existing regulatory law. This especially occurs when countries are reliant on foreign investment, and creates a crucial gap in governance: the host state is not willing or able to put laws in place and hold others to account, and home states fail to take the burden upon themselves, or offer justice for the victims.
>
> *(UN DESA 2015)*

Ford (2015: 9) describes how the attainment of a 'comprehensive and just human rights system' will, in the coming years, be greatly influenced by the 'role and regulation of business in society' as a means to prevent 'adverse impacts'. Ford (2015: 36) conceives of a business and human rights (BHR) paradigm where 'voluntary and mandatory measures capable of significant change at scale' coalesce into a form of 'regulatory ecosystem'. An opportunity to explore this regulatory ecosystem in the context of ageing in Asia is to be encouraged, particularly in the context of the work currently being undertaken by UNESCAP (2012) on building sustainable ageing societies. While a BHR perspective is yet to emerge in the context of ageing populations and the rights of older peoples, aspects of the agenda offer valuable insights into the utility of soft and hard regulatory approaches. The BHR agenda also highlights how the goals of the state and the private sector need not be mutually exclusive in relation to rights protection.

The economic benefits associated with ageing populations should and will continue to be exposed across the region. This represents a rare opportunity to align public–private sector interests with human rights frameworks, provided states remain cognisant of the multidimensional benefits of a stronger regulatory stance. As UN ESCAP reported, 'societies and economies need to be redesigned' (UN ECOSOC 2017: 5) in response to population ageing, and undoubtedly presents one of the most unique opportunities available to the region to develop a society for the benefit of all persons.

Conclusion

This chapter has explored many issues arising in relation to the complex topic of ageing and human rights in Asia. Although ageing impacts individuals and communities in different ways, universal consequences of population ageing include the reorganisation of societies, systems and resources. These mega-issues will remain priorities for Asia well into the second half of the twenty-first century. Notwithstanding the significance of the issue, the international human rights framework has proven inadequate and thus incapable of protecting the rights of older persons, leading to extensive normative, implementation, monitoring and data gaps. Reforms led by the work of the Open-ended Working Group on Ageing will likely see the endorsement of a treaty specific to the rights of older peoples in the coming decade. However, Asia's focus is directly aligned with the full implementation of the *Madrid International Plan of Action on Ageing* in conjunction with the *2030 Agenda for Sustainable Development* and ratification of a new treaty will likely be low across the region as a result. As this debate continues, the commodification of ageing presents opportunities to improve products and strengthen systems and services which positively impact older peoples and boost economies. However, poor regulation of the rapidly emerging aged care and geriatric healthcare sectors will adversely affect the rights and dignity of older peoples. To conclude with reference to a popular adage, 'Now that we have added years to life, we need to add life to years'.

Notes

1 ORCID ID 0000-0003-3990-6005..
2 In this chapter the population of those over 60 years is referred to as 'older peoples' and those over 80 years as 'oldest old peoples'. These concepts and their problematic terminology are discussed in some detail below. The term peoples and persons are used interchangeably throughout this chapter.
3 While ageism impacts people of any age, in this chapter it is used in reference to older peoples.
4 For a complete discussion on this issue, see Gendron et al. (2016).
5 Primus (2016) for example argues that a person is exclusively defined by their arbitrary desires (i.e. the aesthetic aspects of their human body and surrounding environment – the aspects they want but do not need), independently from infrastructure which serves their needs (e.g. the functional aspects of human biological bodies and their surrounding environment). This topic is beyond the scope of this chapter; however, it is important to note that the proliferation of such concepts into the future may help reduce attitudes of ageism and practices of elder abuse, through recognising the value of people at their conceptual core, irrespective of their physiological abilities.
6 See www.who.int/ageing/projects/elder_abuse/en/.
7 The Meeting was attended by representatives from Armenia, Australia, Azerbaijan, Bangladesh, Bhutan, Cambodia, Fiji, India, Indonesia, Iran (Islamic Republic of), Japan, Lao People's Democratic Republic, Macao (China), Malaysia, Maldives, Mongolia, Myanmar, Nepal, Palau, Philippines, Republic of Korea, Russian Federation, Sri Lanka, Thailand, Tonga, Uzbekistan and Viet Nam.
8 Specific rights are likely to address non-discrimination, freedoms of association and assembly, autonomy and independence, freedom of movement, equal recognition before the law, expression, self-fulfilment, access to justice, the right to life and the right to a dignified death, property, education, effective participation, ageing in place and housing, environment, accessibility and mobility, long-term support for independent living, information, health, social security and social protection, adequate standards of living, work, family life, freedom from torture, cruel, inhuman or degrading treatment

and violence and abuse. For more, see the Global Alliance for the Rights of Older People's report 'In our own words: What older people say about discrimination and human rights in older age', www.rightsofolderpeople.org/wp-content/uploads/2015/03/In-Our-Own-Words-2015-English.pdf.

9 Statement of the People's Republic of China to the 1st Meeting of the 7th Session of the Open-ended Working Group on Ageing, http://statements.unmeetings.org/media2/7664284/china-e-.pdf.

10 See www.austrade.gov.au/australian/export/export-markets/countries/china/industries/aged-care.

References

Bodner, E & Lazar, A 2008, 'Ageism among Israeli students: Structure and demographic influences', *International Psychogeriatrics*, vol. 20, no. 5, pp. 1046–1058.

Butler, RN 1980, 'Ageism: A foreword', *Journal of Social Issues*, vol. 36, no. 2, pp. 8–11.

Central Committee of the Communist Party of China 2016, 'The 13th Five-Year Plan for Economic and Social Development of the People's Republic of China: 2016–2020', Central Compilation & Translation Press, Beijing.

Chan, KL 2009, 'Protection of face and avoidance of responsibility: Chinese men's account of violence against women', *Journal of Social Work Practice*, vol. 23, pp. 93–108.

Cheng, ST & Chan, ACM 2006, 'Filial piety and psychological well-being in well older Chinese', *Journal of Gerontology. Series B: Psychological Sciences*, vol. 61, no. 5, pp. 262–269.

Cuddy, A, Norton, MI & Fiske, ST 2005, 'This old stereotype: The pervasiveness and persistence of the elderly stereotype', *Journal of Social Issues*, vol. 61, no. 2, pp. 267–285.

Dlugosz, Z & Razniak, P 2014, 'Risk of population aging in Asia', *Procedia – Social and Behavioural Sciences*, vol. 120, pp. 36–45.

Dong, X & Simon, MA 2008, 'Is greater social support a protective factor against elder mistreatment?', *Gerontology*, vol. 54, no. 6, pp. 381–388.

Dong, X & Simon, MA 2010, 'Is impairment in physical function associated with increased risk of elder mistreatment? Findings from a community-dwelling Chinese population', *Public Health Report*, vol. 125, no. 5, pp. 743–753.

Dong, X & Simon, MA 2013, 'Urban and rural variations in the characteristics associated with elder mistreatment in a community-dwelling Chinese population', *Journal of Elder Abuse & Neglect*, vol. 25, no. 2, pp. 97–125.

Dong, X, Simon, MA & Gorbien, M 2007, 'Elder abuse and neglect in an urban Chinese population', *Journal of Elder Abuse & Neglect*, vol. 19, no. 3–4, pp. 79–96.

Dong, X, Simon, M, Gorbien, N, Percak, BA & Golden, R 2007, 'Loneliness in older Chinese adults: A risk factor for elder mistreatment', *Journal of the American Geriatrics Society*, vol. 55, no. 11, pp. 1831–1835.

Fealy, G, McNamara, M, Treacy, MP & Lyons, I 2012, 'Constructing ageing and age identities: A case study of newspaper discourses', *Ageing & Society*, vol. 32, no, 1, pp. 85–102.

Ford, J 2015, *Business and human rights: Bridging the governance gap*, Royal Institute of International Affairs, Chatham House, London.

Gendron, T, Welleford, EA, Inker, J and White, JT 2016, 'The language of ageism: Why we need to use words carefully', *The Gerontologist*, vol. 56, no. 6, pp. 997–1006.

Glascock, AP & Feinman, SL 1980, 'A holocultural analysis of old age', *Comparative Social Research*, vol. 3, no. 3, pp. 311–332.

Gorman, M 2000, 'Development and the rights of older people', in Randel, J, German, T & Ewing, D (eds), *The ageing and development report: Poverty, independence and the world's older people*, Earthscan Publications, London.

Gupta, N 2016, 'Development, elder abuse and quality of life: Older women in urban India', *International Journal on Ageing in Developing Countries*, vol. 1, no. 2, pp. 158–173.

HelpAge International 2012, *International human rights law and older people: Gaps, fragments and loopholes*, https://social.un.org/ageing-working-group/documents/GapsinprotectionofolderpeoplesrightsAugust2012.pdf.

HelpAge International 2018, 'The freedom to decide: What older people say about their rights to autonomy and independence', www.helpage.org/blogs/bridget-sleap-24/the-freedom-to-decide-what-older-people-say-about-their-rights-to-autonomy-and-independence-1059/.

Hu, G 2017, *The cost of development in China*, Springer Nature Singapore & People's Publishing House, Singapore.

Lee, HY & Eaton, CK 2009, 'Financial abuse in elderly Korean immigrants: Mixed analysis of the role of culture on perception and help-seeking intention', *Journal of Gerontological Social Work*, vol. 52, no. 5, pp. 463–488.

National Health Commission of the People's Republic of China (NHFPC) 2018a, 'Greater use of tech urged in healthcare industry', 25 January, http://en.nhfpc.gov.cn/2018-01/25/c_72945.htm.

National Health Commission of the People's Republic of China (NHFPC) 2018b, 'China to train 500,000 GPs in 12 years', 26 January, http://en.nhfpc.gov.cn/2018-01/26/c_72939.htm.

North, M & Fiske, ST 2015, 'Modern attitudes toward older adults in the aging world: A cross-cultural meta-analysis', *Psychological Bulletin*, vol. 141, no. 5, pp. 993–1021.

People's Republic of China (PRC) 2014, 'Statement by Counsellor Yao Shaojun of the Chinese Mission to United Nations at the General Debate at the Fifth Session of the GA Open-Ended Working Group on Ageing', 30 July, New York, https://social.un.org/ageing-working-group/documents/fifth/China_En.pdf.

Primus 2016, *Purism (in English)*. Purist Press, Gold Coast.

South China Morning Post 2017, 'When old is gold for the unscrupulous: The hidden cost of buying a longer life in China', 22 July, www.scmp.com/news/china/society/article/2102753/when-old-gold-unscrupulous-how-chinas-lonely-elderly-are-being.

Thane, P 1978, 'The muddled history of retiring at 60 and 65', *New Society*, 3 August, pp. 234–236.

Thane, P 1989, 'History and the sociology of ageing', *Social History of Medicine*, vol. 2, no.1, pp. 93–96.

United Nations 2002, 'Madrid International Action Plan on Ageing', in United Nations, *Political Declaration and Madrid International Plan of Action on Aging: Report of the Second World Assembly on Ageing*, United Nations Publishing, New York.

United Nations Department of Economic and Social Affairs (UN DESA), Population Division 2001, *World population ageing: 1950–2050*, Department of Economic and Social Affairs, Population Division (ST/ESA/SER.A/207), United Nations Publications, New York.

United Nations Department of Economic and Social Affairs (UN DESA), Population Division 2015, *World population ageing 2015* (ST/ESA/SER.A/390), United Nations, New York.

United Nations Department of Economic and Social Affairs (UN DESA) 2016, 'Taking a stand against ageism', www.un.org/development/desa/en/news/social/taking-a-stand-against-ageism.html.

United Nations Department of Economic and Social Affairs (UN DESA), Population Division 2017, *World population prospects: Key findings and advance tables – 2017 Revision* (ESA/P/WP/248), United Nations, New York.

United Nations Department of Economic and Social Affairs (UN DESA) & United Nations Economic and Social Commission for Asia and the Pacific (UN ESCAP) 2014, *Workshop on the social integration and rights of older persons in the Asia-Pacific region*, 30 September–2 October, Bangkok.

United Nations Economic and Social Commission for Asia and the Pacific (UN ESCAP) 2012, *Conclusions and recommendations of the Asian Symposium on Building Sustainable Ageing Societies*, 6 July, www.unescap.org/sites/default/files/Ageing_Symposium_Outcome_document_1.pdf.

United Nations Economic and Social Council (UN ECOSOC), Economic and Social Commission for Asia and the Pacific 2017, *Report of the Asia-Pacific Intergovernmental Meeting on the Third Review and Appraisal of the Madrid International Plan of Action on Ageing* (E/ESCAP/MIPAA/IGM.2/3), United Nations Publications, New York.

United Nations General Assembly (UNGA) 1948, Third Session, *Draft Declaration of Old Age Rights* (A/C.3/213 and A/C.3/213/REV.1), United Nations, New York.

United Nations General Assembly (UNGA) 2011, *Follow-up to the Second World Assembly on Ageing* (A/RES/65/182), United Nations, New York.

United Nations General Assembly (UNGA) 2013, *Resolution adopted by the General Assembly on 20 December 2010 – Towards a comprehensive and integral international legal instrument to promote and protect the rights and dignity of older persons* (A/RES/67/139), United Nations, New York.

United Nations General Assembly (UNGA), 2017, *Report of the Independent Expert on the enjoyment of all human rights by older persons* (A/HRC/36/48), Human Rights Council, United Nations, New York.

United Nations, Population Fund (UNFPA) & HelpAge International 2012, *Ageing in the twenty-first century: A celebration and a challenge*, New York & London, www.unfpa.org/publications/ageing-twenty-first-century.

United Nations, World Health Organization (WHO) 2002, *Active ageing: A policy framework*, WHO, Geneva.

United Nations, World Health Organization (WHO) 2007, *Global age-friendly cities: A guide*, WHO, Geneva.

United Nations, World Health Organization (WHO) 2016, 'Discrimination and negative attitudes about ageing are bad for your health', www.who.int/en/news-room/detail/29-09-2016-discrimination-and-negative-attitudes-about-ageing-are-bad-for-your-health.

Williamson, C 2015, *Policy mapping on ageing in Asia and the Pacific analytical report*, HelpAge International, Thailand.

Wu, L, Chen, H, Hu, Y, Xiang, H, Yu, X, Zhang, T, Cao, Z & Wang Y 2012, 'Prevalence and associated factors of elder mistreatment in a rural community in People's Republic of China: A cross sectional study', *PLoS One*, vol. 7, no. 3, pp. 1–8.

XinhuaNet.com 2018, 'China's declining birth rate requires policy change', 25 January, www.xinhuanet.com/english/2018-01/25/c_136921905.htm.

Yan, E, Chan, K & Tiwari, A 2015, 'A systematic review of prevalence and risk factors for elder abuse in Asia', *Trauma, Violence & Abuse*, vol. 16, no. 2, pp. 199–219.

Yan, E & Tang, C 2001, 'Prevalence and psychological impact of Chinese elder abuse', *Journal of Interpersonal Violence*, vol. 16, no. 11, pp. 1158–1174.

Yon, Y, Mikton, CR, Gassoumis, ZD & Wilber, KH 2017, 'Elder abuse prevalence in community settings: A systematic review and meta-analysis', *Lancet Global Health*, vol. 5, no. 2, pp. 147–156.

21

Opportunities and challenges in implementing indigenous peoples' human rights in Asia

Raja Devasish Roy

Introduction

Asia is the home of nearly two-thirds of the estimated 300–370 million indigenous persons of the world (Roy, RCK 2009: 216, citing UN Habitat). It contains a large expanse of forests, most of which are related to indigenous peoples' livelihoods, culture and traditional knowledge systems (Minority Rights Group International 1999). Some of the most disempowered, vulnerable and impoverished indigenous communities live in Asia. Conversely, some of the highest forms of autonomous systems led by indigenous peoples also occur in Asia (Roy 2005: 15–16). Internal conflicts, including political movements countered by militarisation, are also among the highest in this region. Asia also has among the highest levels of corporate agribusinesses financing commercial plantations in territories inhabited by indigenous peoples, logging, hydroelectric dams and other enterprises, having a severe impact on the rights of indigenous peoples.

In *A Call to Action from Indigenous Peoples in Asia to the World Conference on Indigenous Peoples* (AIPP 2013), a unanimous declaration adopted in Bangkok in September 2012 (hereafter 'Asia Indigenous Peoples' Bangkok Declaration of 2012') by representatives of indigenous peoples from different parts of the region, Asian indigenous peoples drew attention to some of the most important features of Asia in the context of human rights. A part of the preambular section of the document includes the following:

> *Expresses concern* that indigenous peoples continue to be among the most impoverished sections of society, and that the specific needs and circumstances of indigenous peoples have not been adequately addressed and targeted by the Millennium Development Goals (MDGs) and in Poverty Reduction Strategies;
>
> . . .
>
> *Mindful* of the rich history of diverse civilizations, cultures and political and legal systems in existence in Asia;
>
> *Celebrates* Asia, as the global region, which is home to two-thirds of the world's indigenous population, with diverse peoples representing distinct identities, cultures and customary law regimes of indigenous peoples;

> *Recalls* that indigenous peoples in Asia have suffered colonization, marginalization, exclusion, discrimination, forced assimilation, and exploitation of their lands, territories and resources;
>
> *Concerned* that several treaties, agreements and other constructive arrangements between indigenous peoples and Asian states and their predecessor colonial or other states are not being recognized, observed and enforced in their true spirit;
>
> . . .
>
> *Alarmed* about the accelerating encroachment into indigenous peoples' territories and the exploitation of their natural resources by corporations as well as governmental, non-governmental and other entities, without the free, prior and informed consent of the peoples and communities concerned.[1]

Conceptual issues

Indigenous peoples' human rights

Different aspects of human rights are expressed and elaborated in different instruments, often responding to the differing needs and vulnerabilities of different sections of humanity, such as minorities, indigenous peoples, women, children, persons with disabilities, etc. Therefore, different social or other groups rely upon instruments that specifically address that group. In the case of indigenous (including 'tribal') peoples, the relevant instruments are the International Labour Organization (ILO) Convention No. 169 on Indigenous and Tribal Peoples of 1989, the ILO Convention No. 107 on Indigenous and Tribal Populations of 1957 and the UN Declaration on the Rights of Indigenous Peoples of 2007 (UNDRIP).[2]

Indigenous peoples, like many other sections of humanity, have multiple identities and contextually differing needs. Thus, in the case of the rights of indigenous women, in addition to invoking Convention 169 and UNDRIP, one would seek recourse through other instruments and regimes such as the Convention on the Elimination of All Forms of Discrimination Against Women (CEDAW) (gender-based discrimination); the Convention on the Elimination of All Forms of Racial Discrimination (CERD) (racial discrimination); and the ILO Convention 111 (discrimination concerning employment or occupation).

Indigenous peoples' rights are within the general fold of human rights, as Article 1 of UNDRIP clarifies, by reiterating that:

> indigenous peoples have the right to the full enjoyment, as a collective or as individuals, of all human rights and fundamental freedoms as recognized in the Charter of the United Nations, the Universal Declaration of Human Rights and international human rights law.

In order to help clarify the apparent dichotomy of indigenous and non-indigenous rights, this author has written elsewhere:

> Indigenous peoples' rights may need to be demystified from a human rights perspective. Indigenous peoples' rights are not a separate category of rights that recognize special privileges for indigenous peoples to the exclusion and detriment of others. Indigenous peoples' rights are the same as others', but the historical process of exclusion and discrimination necessitates a context-specific manner of enabling the exercise of equal rights. 'Special measures' may be called for, as repeated in so many articles of the UNDRIP, but these are not 'special rights' by any means.
> *(Roy 2016a: 387)*

Having said that, at the operational levels, there is one major distinction between the rights of indigenous peoples and that of other groups. Except for the right of peoples to self-determination, and perhaps a very few other collective rights, the rights that attach to members of groups other than indigenous peoples are, individual rights, rather than rights of groups. In the case of indigenous peoples, as elaborated in UNDRIP, in addition to the right of a people to self-determination, indigenous peoples possess collective rights, such as on the maintenance of their own institutions, freedom from genocide, forced assimilation and forcible removal from territories, rights to land, territories and resources and right to free, prior and informed consent.

A leading Canadian jurist explains the status of UNDRIP thus:

> The Declaration does not create any new rights. It responds to the 'urgent need to respect and promote the inherent rights of indigenous peoples'. It affirms a wide range of political, economic, social, cultural, spiritual and environmental rights. While individual rights are positively affirmed and protected in various ways, the rights in this new instrument are predominantly collective in nature.
>
> *(Joffe 2010: 124)*

The first debate over indigenousness: 'indigenous' versus 'tribal'

Except for Nepal and the Philippines, indigenous peoples in other countries of Asia are not recognised as 'indigenous' by national law, or at least not so in an unequivocal manner. The cases of Bangladesh, Bhutan and Japan are somewhat ambiguous. In other countries of Asia, indigenous peoples are recognised through various terms other than 'indigenous' (Roy 2016a).

A number of Asian governments have expressed their opposition to the application of the term 'indigenous' to citizens of their country, including Bangladesh, China, India, Indonesia and Myanmar (Gray 1995: 57; Kingsbury 2008: 106; Roy 2012a: 3). The rationale behind such assertions may be differently expressed, but they share the same motive and ethos.

The aforesaid states are primarily motivated by a concern to limit their duties and responsibilities. The reasoning usually involves a distinction between the situation in Asia with that of Australia, New Zealand and the Americas. In the case of Asia, the inhabitance by the groups claiming indigenous status in the territories concerned is of relatively recent origin, compared to the situation in America, etc. Moreover, the Asian groups concerned were not colonised by settlers from 'overseas', and subjugated, resulting in a state dominated by those trans-oceanic settlers, as was the case for the Americas, etc.

The basic fallacy in the Asian states' reasoning is the following. First, they have equated indigenousness with 'original inhabitants', rather than 'first settlers'. Second, they have artificially distinguished between trans-oceanic invaders and colonisers originating from the same landmass as the colonised peoples. Third, they have treated indigenousness as a primordial category, rather than as a social, political and human rights construct.

This writer has elsewhere critiqued the aforesaid approach, which he calls the 'Blue Water Colonization' theory, which distinguishes between 'indigenous' groups – largely, if not wholly, restricted to the Americas and the Pacific rim – and 'tribal' groups – to mean the non-mainstream populations groups in Asia and Africa. The approach implicitly denies the application of the international human rights regime concerning indigenous peoples to the 'tribal' groups and their members. He has argued that:

> [To] deny indigenous status to the indigenous peoples of Africa and Asia would . . . be immoral, and clearly discriminatory against them. To hold that the indigenous peoples of the Americas and the Pacific basin are indigenous while their Asian and African counterparts are not, merely on the basis that certain indigenous Asians and Africans were colonized not by European adventurers (the *blue water* or *salt* water colonizers) but by darker-skinned nations from within their own continent, sub-continent or region, is quite ironic, to say the least. Therefore, such *accidents* of history should not be used to discriminate against the indigenous peoples of Asia and Africa.
>
> *(Roy 2003: 8–9)*

Pragmatic and non-discriminatory approaches of such scholars as Gray (1995) and Kingsbury (2008) offer a good way out of this controversy, which one UN Special Rapporteur had called the 'Afro-Asian problematique' (Martínez 1999). Gray (1995: 38–39) simply equates 'tribal' with 'indigenous' within the context of international human rights law, and suggests that 'prior inhabitants' (such as in the Chittagong Hill Tracts, Bangladesh) can nevertheless qualify as indigenous, even if they cannot establish that they are the 'original inhabitants' (such as in the Americas). Similarly, Kingsbury (2008: 145) suggests that 'historical continuity' is an *indicator* rather than a *requirement* for the purpose of identifying indigenous peoples.

It is important to note that self-identification has been regarded as a 'fundamental criterion' to determine the groups to whom the provisions of ILO Convention 169 apply. This Convention, along with its earlier version, the ILO Convention 107 (which still applies in countries whose governments have not chosen to become a party to the later convention), gives a clear indication that the distinction between indigenous and tribal is, in the context of the primary purpose of applying the provisions of the convention, unimportant. This is unequivocally clarified in the two conventions' scope of application, which covers both 'indigenous' and 'tribal' groups, without distinction.[3]

The term 'indigenous' has not been defined in any legal instrument, and for good reason.[4] The same is the case for 'minorities'. The ILO Conventions No. 107 and 169, do, however, mention some subjective and objective criteria, to help identify indigenous and tribal groups, but these do not qualify as formal definitions. Nevertheless, these criteria are useful tools, to be used pragmatically and contextually, as are the criteria provided by UN Special Rapporteur Martinez Cobo (Cobo 1986). This author feels that some other additional criteria – as 'indicators' rather than as 'requirements' – are extremely relevant, and although they flow from the Cobo and ILO criteria, they may well be regarded in their own light.

However, whatever terminologies the national governments in Asia may choose to refer to their indigenous peoples, it is now clear that the United Nations has clearly come out in favour of the generic term, 'indigenous peoples', which is more than certain to sustain for a very long time. It is not practicable to expect that this global body can accommodate the subtle and not-so-subtle differences between 'tribal' and 'indigenous' groups, let alone cater to the different ethnic or socio-economic categories of citizens that national laws identify, in Asia, or elsewhere.

The second debate over indigenousness: 'indigenous', 'tribal' and 'minorities'

The terms 'tribe' and 'tribal' are used in a loose manner, and sometimes interchangeably with 'indigenous', even in countries where indigenous status is not a controversial issue, such as in the United States of America, Canada, New Zealand or the Philippines. However, the term 'tribe' is firmly ensconced in constitutional law in Asia, in Bangladesh, India and Pakistan, and perhaps Taiwan (as in several countries of Africa). In some countries, the term 'minorities' is used, such as in Laos and Vietnam. However, in all of the aforesaid countries, the groups referred to, or at least their representatives attending international forums, reject such terminology, and identify themselves as 'indigenous'.

All or most of the indigenous peoples in Asia do not form the majority of the national population of the countries that they live in, except perhaps in Bhutan, Laos, Papua New Guinea and Nepal. In that sense, they are a part of the 'minority'. They may be members of minorities groups on account of ethnicity, language, religion or spirituality, or even all of these.

With regard to the international legal regimes that apply to 'indigenous' and 'minorities', there are some areas of overlap, but there are several more areas for which the minorities rights regime is clearly inadequate to effectively protect the rights of those who self-identify as 'indigenous'.

The most important common area is with regard to discrimination, including that based on ethnicity, language, religion, etc., as is also obvious from the title of the only UN Declaration that deals expressly with the rights of minorities, the UN Declaration on the Rights of Persons Belonging to National or Ethnic, Religious and Linguistic Minorities. However, the rights pertaining to members of minority groups are individual rights (note the phrase 'persons'). In contrast, the ILO Convention 169 and UNDRIP not only expressly refer to 'peoples' in their titles, but contain provisions that deal substantively with collective rights (although they also deal with individuals' rights, and the UNDRIP clarifies this beyond any doubt).

As for the areas of human rights that are affirmed in UNDRIP and ILO Convention 169, but not in the Minorities Declaration, or at least adequately so, are the right to self-determination, the right of autonomy or self-government, rights over land and resources, the right to maintain indigenous institutions, the right to determine the membership of indigenous peoples, freedom from unjustified militarisation, and several other crucial rights and freedoms.

The inadequacy of the minorities regime in adequately safeguarding the rights of indigenous peoples is also evidenced by the overwhelming participation of indigenous peoples in UN Forums dealing with indigenous peoples' rights – the UN Permanent Forum on Indigenous Issues (UNPFII) and the Expert Mechanism on the Rights of Indigenous Peoples (EMRIP), contrasted with the absence or near absence of indigenous people in the UN Forum on Minority Issues.[5]

One of the most respected scholars on indigenous issues, Prof. Dr Erica-Irene A. Daes, also a long-time chairperson of the former UN Working Group on Indigenous Populations, states: 'where clarification or guidance is nevertheless needed on the difficult question of what makes a group indigenous as opposed to ethnic minority, United Nations practice typically applies . . . the . . . working definition contained in the landmark study . . . by Cobo' (Daes 2008: 18).

Daes goes further, and although she admits that in many cases, the difference between minorities and indigenous may be one of degree and context, she also clarifies the distinction under international law:

> Classification as an 'indigenous people' or 'minority' has very different implications in international law. Both kinds of groups possess the right to perpetuate their distinctive cultural characteristics and to be free from discrimination on the basis of those cultural characteristics. Both have the right to participate meaningfully in the social, economic and political life of the state as a whole – as groups if they choose, and in any case without adverse discrimination. *In my opinion, the principle legal distinction between the rights of indigenous peoples and those of minorities in contemporary international law concerns internal self-determination* [emphasis added]: the right of a group to govern itself within a recognized

> geographical area without state interference, albeit in some cooperative relationship with state authorities, as in any federal system of national government.[6]
>
> Some minorities today enjoy limited self-government, either *de facto* or pursuant to national legislation. But only indigenous peoples are currently recognized as possessing the *right* to a political identity and self-government as a matter of international law.
>
> *(Daes 2008: 27–28)*

Of course, in practical terms, an advocate of indigenous peoples' rights does not, and should not, confine herself or himself, to invoking only the indigenous-specific instruments – like UNDRIP and ILO Convention No. 169 – or the discrimination-related ones – CERD, CEDAW and ILO Convention No. 111 – but needs to make use of all relevant instruments. Thus, the ICCPR, which was framed in 1966, and well before 'indigenous peoples' became an important subject of international human rights law, has an important provision, namely, Article 27, that is crucial to safeguard indigenous peoples' rights, and particularly so as several states in Asia are party to this instrument. Article 27 deals with cultural, religious and language rights of ethnic, religious or linguistic minorities. This provision has been invoked to protect indigenous peoples' rights (MacKay 2015: 44).

Status and rights

The politics of exclusion

One of the criteria to help identify indigenous peoples that Cobo mentions is that they presently constitute 'non-dominant sectors of society' (Cobo 1986: para. 379). If one were to survey the extent of 'non-dominance' in higher level political – and consequently, economic – decision-making by Asian states over the last century or so, it would be difficult to find very many states in this region in which people who now identify as indigenous had much role in 'state-making', and its concomitant or associated development process (Roy 2016a).

The situation has changed somewhat for a number of countries in Latin American – e.g. Bolivia, followed by Ecuador, Nicaragua and a few others – over the past decade or so. Otherwise, one could safely equate indigenousness with 'non-dominance', in state decision-making, and consequent marginality, powerlessness, poverty, and even genocide and ethnocide. This was not necessarily the case prior to European colonisation and the development of the modern 'nation states'.[7] Thus, from an operational context, if one were to design a litmus test of who is, and who is not, a member of an indigenous people, one could probably get a fairly accurate picture by asking the following question: 'Did you or any other members of your indigenous people, or other indigenous peoples that you know of, have a role in framing the national constitution of your state? If so, to what extent?' It is fairly certain that, barring indigenous persons from the few Latin American states mentioned above, and perhaps sundry others in Asia (Myanmar or former Burma in the 1950s, and India, Nepal and the Philippines, for example), in most cases, whether in Asia or elsewhere, at least over the last century or so, the overwhelming answer would be: 'None, whatsoever'.

Marginality and vulnerability

Marginality and vulnerability generally go hand-in-hand with exclusion from state formation and 'nation building'. Unfortunately, development statistics, particularly data compiled by national offices or bureaux of statistics often do not disaggregate their data on ethnic, linguistic or other bases to enable policy-makers to obtain an accurate picture of the socio-economic status of their indigenous citizens, irrespective of the nomenclature used. Had the Millennium Development Goals and the process of achievement of those goals in particular, and the attainment of sustainable development in general, been indigenous-sensitive, such data could have been generated, and used, to combat the 'under-development' suffered by indigenous communities in Asia and elsewhere.[8]

Although the specific situation of different indigenous peoples varies from country to country within Asia, and even within different parts of each country, there is ample evidence to indicate that, indigenous peoples are among the 'most marginalised and disadvantaged of any population group, with high incidences of poverty, malnutrition, illiteracy and infant mortality, and low levels of education, employment and general well-being [including in studies] conducted by the World Bank and the Asian Development Bank' (Roy, RCK 2009: 219, 220).

Within the generic fold of indigenous peoples in Asia, there are of course several sub-groups. Women, in particular, are among the most vulnerable. In certain instances, they are said to face a 'triple burden', as indigenous, as women and as poor (Roy, RCK 2009: 225; Tugendhat & Dictaan-Bang-oa 2013). A section of a handbook on CEDAW on the rights of indigenous women highlights several areas in which Asian indigenous women's rights have been adversely affected, including sexual and other violence against women, land rights, militarisation, trafficking and prostitution (Tugendhat & Dictaan-Bang-oa 2013: 2–29).

However, despite the huge odds faced by indigenous women, they do not necessarily see themselves as 'victims', as noted in one study:

> Faced with discrimination and prejudice, indigenous women have been forced to develop skills and strategies for survival – for themselves, their peoples and their cultures. They have learnt to survive oppression and marginalization, discrimination and violence, without losing the wisdom and patience to build on and to share these experiences. Yet often their contribution to the struggle of indigenous peoples is not recognized or acknowledged.
>
> *(Roy, RCK 2009: 225)*

Major human rights themes and areas of concern for Asian indigenous peoples

Asia region indigenous peoples' statement on the World Conference on Indigenous Peoples

In the Asia Indigenous Peoples' Bangkok Declaration of 2012, attention was drawn to several areas of concern. Among these are: (a) the denial of appropriate constitutional safeguards; (b) the violation of treaties, agreements and other constructive arrangements between indigenous peoples and states; (c) the absence of regional and sub-regional human rights processes; (d) the legacies of colonial land and forest laws that violate indigenous customary law regimes and processes; (e) refusal of states to recognise indigenous juridical systems; (f) militarisation and use of special laws, including anti-terrorism laws against legitimate human rights defenders; (g) the mainstream paradigm of development and attendant violation of indigenous peoples' land rights and their right to free, prior and informed consent, including through commercial plantations and other agribusinesses, extractive industries and hydro-electric dams; and (h) the need for appropriately disaggregated data and indicators to guide context-specific development that is inclusive and non-discriminatory, among others.

The Asia regional preparatory meeting – along with other regional and thematic meetings (on women, youth, children and persons with disabilities) – was followed by a Global Indigenous Peoples Caucus meeting at Alta, Norway, on 10–12 June 2013, which resulted in the adoption of the Alta Outcome Document (UNGA 2014: para. 2). The Alta document, a consensus document negotiated by indigenous delegates from across the globe, attempted to synthesise major elements from the caucus declarations, including the Asia Indigenous Peoples' Bangkok Declaration of 2012, to feed into the preparatory process of the WCIP, and as a framework document, along with UNDRIP, to guide the proceedings of the WCIP.[9]

The World Conference on Indigenous Peoples and its Outcome Document

The World Conference on Indigenous Peoples (WCIP) was the first ever world conference on the subject of indigenous peoples. Coinciding with a high-level plenary meeting of the UN General Assembly, the meeting adopted a document known as the Outcome Document of the World Conference on Indigenous Peoples, in the drafting of which, indigenous peoples' representatives had a major role, facilitated by formal resolutions of the General Assembly (UNGA: 2011, 2012a, 2012b, 2014), although, of course, a resolution of the UN body can only be taken by its members. The process of involvement of indigenous peoples, who are non-state actors, within the world body's decision-making process on indigenous peoples, had thus been entrenched.[10]

The WCIP's main goal was 'to share perspectives and best practices on the realisation of the rights of indigenous peoples, including to pursue the objectives of the United Nations Declaration on the Rights of Indigenous Peoples' (UNGA 2011: para. 8). It was decided, among others, that the World Conference would result in 'a concise, action-oriented outcome document' (UNGA 2012b: para. 9). Although a number of priority issues of indigenous peoples, including the issue of militarisation, was not included, several crucial matters on indigenous peoples' rights now form part of the General Assembly resolution, facilitating political support by member states of the UN to implement the provisions of UNDRIP.[11]

Several of the provisions of the Outcome Document are a direct reflection of the issues highlighted in the Asia Indigenous Peoples' Bangkok Declaration of 2012 and the result of intense lobbying and negotiation by representatives of indigenous peoples, including from Asia, both at Alta and in New York. These include provisions on (a) ratification of or accession to the ILO Convention 169 (para. 6); (b) disaggregation of data and the utilisation of 'holistic indicators of indigenous peoples' well-being' to address specific situations and needs of indigenous peoples and their sub-groups (para. 10); (c) acknowledgement of the positive role of indigenous peoples' justice institutions (para. 16); (d) the contributions of traditional knowledge, innovations and practices of indigenous peoples in the conservation and sustainable use of biodiversity (para. 22); (e) support to indigenous peoples' occupations, traditional subsistence activities, economies, livelihoods, food security and nutrition (para. 25); (f) the contributions of indigenous peoples to ecosystem management and protection (referred to as 'Mother Earth') and in sustainable development based on their knowledge, sciences, technologies and cultures (paras 34, 35).

Of course, the mere adoption of the Outcome Document by itself is no guarantee that the UN member states will take their responsibilities seriously regarding the implementation of UNDRIP at country levels. The designation of a new Under Secretary-General, specifically on indigenous issues, as demanded in the Alta document, is a welcome development, particularly with regard to the mainstreaming of indigenous issues within the UN system. Ultimately, much will depend on how indigenous peoples engage at the international, regional, national and local levels. Some of the important challenges and opportunities in this regard are briefly discussed below.

Challenges and opportunities

There are, of course, innumerable challenges in the protection of indigenous peoples' rights in Asia, particularly where the groups concerned are socio-economically marginalised, and/or face acute discrimination from the government and mainstream society. Based on his experiences through his advocacy work at local, national and international levels, despite the overwhelming odds, this author believes that opportunities are also available, no doubt not in all cases, but at least in some cases. These opportunities have to be seized, to make strategic interventions, at least to improve the situation, and to mitigate the oppressive circumstances in which numerous indigenous communities survive.

Dealing with asymmetry: levelling and un-levelling the 'playing field'

The asymmetry in the status between indigenous peoples and others with whom they interface – e.g. governments, mainstream populations, private companies, etc. – is often stark. Therefore, in several contexts, such as those referred to below, such extreme asymmetry may be narrowed. These are, particularly, in the contexts of: (a) customary law; (b) customary or traditional institutions; and (c) strategic litigation or other engagements in judicial and human rights processes.

Invoking customary law

With regard to customary law, where the national legal system allows for such 'legal pluralism',[12] 'customary laws generally concern a body of laws, principles, norms and procedures that are regulated, and reformed, by the indigenous peoples themselves. This renders the playing field a little more even' (Roy 2011: 122–123; Roy 2016a). However, in such cases, the major challenge is not to have customary rights 'frozen' or 'fossilised' in a reductionist manner, in the attempt to have them provided with formal state recognition (Roy 2012b: 70–77).

Strengthening traditional institutions

In some countries of Asia, customary or traditional institutions have a legally mandated role in justice administration and in natural resource management, such as in Malaysia (Sabah and Sarawak), northeast India (Nagaland, Meghalaya) and Bangladesh (Chittagong Hill Tracts) (Roy 2005). The aforesaid roles often coincide with the application of customary law (Roy 2005). Such roles are crucial for indigenous peoples to safeguard their own interests, particularly where immigration of other population groups, leading to their demographic and political minoritisation, and the role of money from non-indigenous or 'elite-indigenous' business interests, prevent genuine representatives of indigenous peoples from holding elective offices. The major challenge here is to ensure that this does not perpetuate elite indigenous dominance to the detriment of the rest of indigenous society, and to ensure that women's rights, to equally participate in decision-making, and to hold property, among others, is not excluded in the name of 'tradition', which self-interested initiatives of patriarchal sections of indigenous society have often succeeded in 'fossilising' in the name of some imagined and so-called 'hallowed' tradition.[13]

Strategic and diversified engagement in international human rights mechanisms

Another challenge in the equation of asymmetry concerns the choice of field of engagement to secure the concerned rights. Obviously, political and economic clout is the best tool for change, in most cases, if not all. However, most indigenous peoples and their communities generally possess little or none of the two. While the value of engagement in the major political processes concerning electoral offices and political parties cannot be denied, where resources – human, financial and organisational – are finite, as is usually the case with indigenous peoples, engagement in arenas that are less asymmetrical than politics, such as in the human rights mechanisms, and as appropriate, in the courts of law, may well provide many more dividends. There are several examples of indigenous peoples obtaining remedies in national courts of law, such as in Nepal,[14] Bangladesh[15] and Indonesia.[16] Similarly, in international human rights mechanisms too, particularly through rulings of international treaty bodies and UN mechanisms dealing with human rights, customary law-related rights and rights of participation of indigenous peoples have been upheld, such as in Nepal (MacKay 2015: 43, 61; Roy 2016b: 10–13) and Indonesia (MacKay 2015: 28).

Of course, there are major hurdles to overcome in order to enable indigenous peoples to engage in the aforesaid human rights and judicial processes, again burdened by their socio-economically marginalised status, and these factors need to be accounted for. Nevertheless, access to these processes is often much easier than entering the realm of politics, especially in majoritarian polities that pose as democratic systems. But at the very least, once such access is ensured, the asymmetry between an indigenous people or its members vis-à-vis other groups – such as a government agency or private corporation – is visibly narrower.

However, here too, the remedy sought is often difficult to execute, even where a favourable ruling has been obtained. For, it is common knowledge in the human rights world that most international human rights processes – barring the European system – have few teeth with which to compel truant governments into complying with their treaty or other human rights obligations. But nevertheless, engagements in such processes are not valueless. Surely a case could be made, using statistics, to show, in many countries or parts of them, that the instances of human rights violations have at least remained static, if not decreased, after well-orchestrated engagements in international human rights mechanisms.

The basic strategic flaw that indigenous peoples' rights activists commit, along with their partners and allies, is to largely restrict their engagements to international human rights processes dealing specifically with indigenous peoples' issues (namely, UNPFII, EMRIP and the Special Rapporteur on the rights of indigenous peoples (SRIP)), and to a lesser extent, in processes dealing with the environment and climate change (Convention on Biological Diversity and the United Nations Framework Convention on Climate Change).[17] What about processes of mainstream human rights mechanisms barring the universal periodic review (UPR) under the Human Rights Council (in which indigenous peoples have been regularly participating)? Engagement of indigenous peoples with the treaty-monitoring bodies, other specialised mechanisms, including the Special Rapporteurs (except SRIP), and in processes dealing with trade and intellectual property, is still negligible, although the situation has changed for the better, at least marginally so. In the case of Bangladesh, India and Pakistan, engagement with the ILO system could help monitor the situation of customary land rights, rights to swidden cultivation, education and occupational rights, among others, in a far better manner, although the ILO monitoring system too has its shortcomings (Roy, RD 2009: 167–182).

Engagement with regional and national human rights institutions

Engagement with national human rights institutions (usually called 'human rights commissions') by or on behalf of indigenous peoples has grown in recent years, at least in several countries of South and Southeast Asia, and this trend needs to be sustained and deepened. In Southeast Asia, alliances between the major regional indigenous peoples' NGO, the Asia Indigenous Peoples Pact (AIPP) Foundation, with environment and human-rights-oriented international NGOs, including RECOFTC, Forest Peoples Programme and the Rights and Resource Initiative, has succeeded in sensitising leading members of the national human rights institutions (NHRIs) of the region and in facilitating the adoption of a number of declarations in partnership with civil society organisations, including of indigenous peoples, such as the Yangon Statement on Human Rights and Agribusiness, in November 2014. National human rights organisations of Malaysia (SUHAKAM) and Indonesia (Komnas HAM), for example, despite their shortcomings, have emerged stronger than before, in favour of indigenous peoples and other disadvantaged sections of citizens.

Although the ASEAN Human Rights Declaration of 2012 has practically been blind towards the region's indigenous peoples, at least formal and informal dialogues have started at the sub-regional and, to a lesser extent, the national levels. The formation of the South East Asian National Human Rights Institutions Forum (SEANF) is evidence of the goodwill of the NHRCs (Matibag 2014: 9). In contrast, SAARC, the regional organisation grouping the South Asian countries, is visibly lagging behind in this respect. There are neither visible dialogues here, nor a clear agenda for a South Asian Human Rights Declaration.

The biggest challenge concerning NHRIs is to make them financially and politically independent of national governments, although pressure of compliance with the Paris Principles has led to some positive reform in the structure and functions of Asian NHRIs (Matibag 2014: 1–5). Weak legal frameworks and other such impediments have compromised the work of several NHRIs, including in Bangladesh, India and Thailand, despite the commitments of those leading such institutions (Matibag 2014: 111, 112).

Litigation in constitutional and other superior courts

The situation of litigation by or on behalf of indigenous peoples varies across the region. Perhaps this avenue has been explored to a much greater extent by indigenous peoples in Malaysia than in other countries of Asia, although human rights activists in other countries, such as in India and Bangladesh, have also started to explore this avenue of redress. The important opportunity here is, if a positive ruling can be effected, the full force of the state is obliged to implement the judicial decision, which is not the case for rulings of human rights bodies, national or international (the European system excepted).

Advocacy networks and organisations at regional, national and local levels

A continuing challenge, and an opportunity, for indigenous peoples, in furthering their human rights, is to work through local, national and regional organisations and networks. At the international level, the work of several NGOs has proved to be a major catalyst in strengthening the work of indigenous peoples, including from Asia, which includes the International Work Group for Indigenous Affairs (IWGIA), the International Alliance of the Indigenous-Tribal Peoples of the Tropical Forests, and the Forest Peoples' Programme, among others. At the regional level, the Asia Indigenous Peoples Pact (AIPP) Foundation, which is composed of and managed by indigenous persons, has made tremendous strides in its advocacy, networking and capacity-raising work, including in facilitating annual conferences to prepare Asian indigenous representatives to participate effectively in international human rights processes.

At the national level, organisations of indigenous peoples, such as AMAN, in Indonesia, have proved to be a major force in influencing national-level decision-making through a combination of national and international advocacy campaigns and direct engagement with government policy-makers in formal and informal ways. Similarly, NEFIN, in Nepal, has successfully mobilised for indigenous peoples' rights both within Nepal, through civic campaigns, political engagement and litigation, and in international processes and mechanisms, among others, to enhance indigenous participation in legislative and other major decision-making bodies (Roy 2016b). However, in most of the other countries of Asia, indigenous peoples' national-level organisations and networks, although reasonably successful in rallying indigenous peoples in their work, have been impeded by organisational and logistical shortcomings, among others. Therefore, the support from, and alliances with, other human rights and related organisations and networks have much scope for improvement. In a study on Access to Justice for indigenous peoples of Bangladesh, the researchers, including this author, found that there was much scope for improvement in the way in which non-indigenous organisations support the human rights work of indigenous peoples. Some of the observations made in this case study are perhaps reflective of similar problems faced in several other countries of Asia. This study made several recommendations and observations, including the following:

> NGOs need to move away from a firefighting mode – of responding only to headlines of human rights violations – and instead engage in activities directly with [indigenous] communities, through their organizations on a regular basis.
>
> NGOs and CSOs also need to develop more effective linkages on the ground with [indigenous] communities to ensure more regular communications and follow-ups in cases that require their intervention and support.
>
> In developing the networks, special emphasis should be placed on giving priorities to the most marginalized and disadvantaged [indigenous] communities.
>
> A particular effort needs to be made to facilitate opportunities for women to raise their concerns within existing [indigenous] organizations, or, alternatively, to organize autonomously and articulate their concerns.
>
> *(Roy, Hossain & Guhathakurta 2007: 45–46)*

Conclusion

The aforesaid discussion shows that there are both opportunities and challenges in taking forward indigenous peoples' human rights in Asia, as elsewhere. Among the major opportunities, particularly in the field of economic, social and cultural rights, is the Outcome Document of the WCIP and the Sustainable Development Goals (SDGs) process.

The Outcome Document was adopted, without any dissent, at a high-level session of the UN General Assembly, which included heads of state and government, and hence embodies the political will of member states of the UN to achieve the full realisation of the provisions of UNDRIP. Apart from providing a strong political signal towards the national-level implementation of the provisions of UNDRIP, the Outcome Document includes measures on appropriate representation of indigenous peoples in UN processes dealing with their rights, the adoption of National Action Plans by national governments with the technical support of UN agencies, and the implementation of a System Wide Action Plan (SWAP) by the UN, to facilitate the promotion and protection of indigenous peoples' rights by UN agencies, funds and programmes at country levels.

The Sustainable Development Goals (SDGs) are decidedly an improvement on the Millennium Development Goals (MDGs) with regard to their contextualised application in the case of indigenous peoples. However, the extent to which the SDGs will actually address indigenous peoples' rights and concerns will depend, among others, upon how the process of operationalisation of the goals and targets is linked to disaggregated data on indigenous communities, whether it is truly inclusive of the peoples concerned, and whether it respects their right to free, prior and informed consent. Moreover, its success, generally, and in the case of indigenous peoples, will also depend upon whether a balance is maintained between the responsibilities of the government and that of the private sector, as the latter certainly needs to be held more responsible than it currently is, as the forces of profit are often seen to indiscriminately tread upon human rights, whether consciously or negligently.

In the field of civil and political rights too, the Outcome Document and SDGs may work as catalysts, such as to include different groups of indigenous peoples that need specific attention, including women, children, youth, elders and persons with disability. However, the Outcome Document and the SDGs will be insufficient *by themselves* to make marked improvements in the realm of civil and political rights, particularly concerning indigenous peoples' roles in governance and administration.

Apart from the few parts of Asia where indigenous peoples exercise a high level of self-government or autonomy – such as in east Malaysia and in some parts of northeast India (and perhaps Nepal in the near future?) – in most other parts of Asia, the small size of the indigenous peoples' populations and their socio-economic positions of marginality and disadvantage make it very difficult for them to be a substantive part of major decision-making processes. In such contexts, although the human rights regimes can invoke the peremptory norm of equality and non-discrimination to prevent or minimise discrimination and discriminatory exclusion perpetrated against them, substantive political empowerment cannot be achieved merely through human rights processes, but will require robust engagement in the political processes.

Moreover, even with regard to the implementation of the resolutions of international and national human rights bodies, except in the few cases where the national or regional regimes expressly so provide, the implementation of such rulings or advice needs to be facilitated through mass media campaigns, sustained advocacy or engagement in the political process.[18] Given the socio-economic disadvantage suffered by most indigenous peoples, this is the most difficult challenge to surmount: to ensure effective and substantive engagement in national political processes. And one of the few ways to make a bigger impact than may otherwise be possible is through forging alliances; alliances of indigenous peoples with progressive sections of the mainstream population of the country; the establishment of networks between and among indigenous peoples, and strategic engagement in human rights processes at national and international levels, combined with strategic litigations in national courts. At least in these spheres, the playing field is somewhat more level.

Notes

1 This document was the result of a preparatory meeting to provide inputs into the (then) forthcoming World Conference on Indigenous Peoples (WCIP), which subsequently took place at the United Nations headquarters in New York on 22–23 September 2014, and resulted in the adoption of the Outcome Document of the WCIP by the UN General Assembly, by consensus. See, AIPP (2013).

2 Among the most crucial documents on indigenous peoples' rights of global applicability since UNDRIP is the Outcome Document of the World Conference on Indigenous Peoples (UNGA 2014).

3 Within Asia, Convention No. 169 has been ratified by Nepal, while Convention No. 107 continues to apply in Bangladesh, India, Iraq and Pakistan.

4 In the debates and other discussions within the former UN Working Group on the Draft Declaration on the Rights of Indigenous Peoples, in which this author had participated at the last five or six sessions, indigenous participants unanimously rejected any attempts to provide a formal definition of the term, 'indigenous', as this would be difficult to agree upon, and is likely to exclude legitimate groups.

5 For a compilation of the recommendations of the first four sessions of the UN Forum on Minority Issues, viewed 18 July 2015, www.ohchr.org/Documents/HRBodies/HRCouncil/MinorityIssues/Forum_On_Minority_Pub_en_low.pdf.

6 Although, Daes has referred to 'internal self-determination', there are views that hold that self-determination cannot be distinguished into 'external' and 'internal' dimensions or contexts. Actual examples of the exercise of self-determination by indigenous peoples in 'external' contexts include: (a) the separate treatment of Greenland within the European Union, for trade purposes, and considering Greenland's separate and direct participation in some processes of the European Union and their representation in Brussels; (b) the direct participation of non-state indigenous peoples' organisations in the otherwise intergovernmental body called the Arctic Council; and (c) the use of indigenous national 'passports' or other travel documents by some nations of Canada and the US to travel to a few countries in Europe without using passports issued by the US or Canadian governments. In today's age of globalised free trade, transfer of humans, goods and capital, 'without frontiers', such examples will almost inevitably grow further.

7 In the pre-colonial period, indigenous peoples-led polities governed thriving rural and urban chiefdoms, tribal confederacies, kingdoms and empires, in Latin America, Africa, South and Southeast Asia. The descendants of many of these former ruling indigenous elite probably comprise current membership of peasant and workers' communities, or other marginalised groups.

8 The generation of disaggregated data and holistic indicators, including on indigenous peoples, is among the resolutions of the Outcome Document of the World Conference on Indigenous Peoples, 2014 (UNGA 2014).

9 Although the Alta document did not attain the status of a full-fledged UN document, its express acknowledgement in the Outcome Document (UNGA 2014: para. 2 and footnote 2) was a major achievement for the acknowledgment of indigenous peoples' views in an instrument adopted by the UN General Assembly. See also, AIPP (2013).

10 Based on recommendations of EMRIP, the UN Secretary-General submitted a report on the promotion of participation of indigenous peoples at the UN, in July 2012 (UN Doc: A/HRC/21/24). After the adoption of the Outcome Document, the president of the General Assembly started a process of consultations, facilitated by the IASG and four advisers appointed by her/him (including two indigenous experts) to produce specific recommendations. The consultations also took place during the 15th session of the PFII (May 2016) and at the 8th session of EMRIP (July 2016).

11 This information is based upon the author's participation in the final WCIP, and its preparatory stages, including the Bangkok meeting of September 2012, the Alta meeting of June 2013 (where he represented the PFII), and in the semi-formal open-ended consultations at UN headquarters in June–August 2014, facilitated by the president of the General Assembly, with the support of two co-facilitators appointed by him from among representatives of states and representatives of indigenous peoples. Among others, the author served as a member of the Drafting Committee, at the Bangkok meeting, the Alta meeting and in the preparatory engagements facilitated by the indigenous caucus-appointed Global Coordinating Group (GCG).

12 Such avenues are available in a large way in East Malaysia, India, Philippines, and to a lesser extent in Pakistan, Indonesia, Myanmar and Bangladesh (particularly the Chittagong Hill Tracts) (see Roy 2005). The situation in the Mekong region, East Asia and the Middle East are more problematic.

13 While recognising the important role of indigenous peoples' institutional structures, customs, traditions, juridical systems, etc., UNDRIP clarifies (at Art. 34), that this must be 'in accordance with international human rights standards'.

14 In 2009, soon after the adoption of the Interim Constitution of Nepal in 2007, the Supreme Court of Nepal instructed the government to include indigenous peoples' representatives in the constitution-making process. See, *LAHURNIP & Others v. Government of Nepal*, Supreme Court 2070, Nepal Kanoon Patrika, Additional Vol. DN8990, p. 491, as cited in www.lahurnip.org/userfiles/downloads_56.pdf.

15 *Aung Shwe Prue Chowdhury v. Kyaw Sain Prue Chowdhury and Others (Civil Appeal No. 8 of 1997)*, Supreme Court of Bangladesh (Appellate Division), 50 DLR (AD) 1998, pp. 73–80; *Rajkumari Unika Devi v. Bangladesh & Others*, 12 BLT, AD, 2004, 241. In the aforesaid two cases, the court held that the government was obliged to declare the succession to the chiefships of the Bohmong Circle and the Mong Circle (a circle is a traditional chiefs' territory in the Chittagong Hill Tracts), respectively, in accordance with the customs and practices of the circle concerned. In *Abrechai Magh v. District Judge Khagrachari & Others*, 19 BLC (2014), 358, a High Court bench declared that succession to the estate of a member of the Marma tribe must be done in accordance with the customary law of the tribe and

in consultation with the concerned Circle Chief and Mauza Headman (traditional authorities of the Chittagong Hill Tracts). This author was among the legal counsel in the two last-mentioned cases.

16 The Indonesian Constitutional Court, based on an application of the national indigenous peoples' body, AMAN, ruled on 21 May 2013, that customary forests were not 'state' forests; www.redd-monitor.org/2013/05/17/indonesias-constitutional-court-returns-customary-forests-to-indigenous-peoples/. See also MacKay (2015: 28).

17 The current Special Rapporteur on the right of indigenous peoples (SRIP) is Victoria Tauli Corpuz, a Kankanay-Igorot from the Philippines, who was also a former chairperson of the PFII. Corpuz's commitments and expertise are a huge asset for her work real and potential work for indigenous peoples' rights, but is impeded by the reluctance of Asian governments to formally invite the SRIP, without which a UN Special Rapporteur's work is rendered visibly weak, if not valueless.

18 The European system is the only system in the world where the decisions of the regional court, the European Court of Human Rights, are implemented through a Committee of Ministers. Such a process is absent in the Inter-American and the African systems (Asia does not have a regional human rights mechanism). At the national levels, the provisions of international treaties can be implemented through legal action in domestic courts only in a few countries of Europe and in Latin America and the US. These are known as *monistic* systems wherein international treaty law is regarded as part of domestic or national law. In most other countries of the world, which have *dualistic* systems, provisions of international treaties may not be directly implemented through legal action in national or domestic courts.

References

Asia Indigenous Peoples Pact Foundation (AIPP) 2013, *A Call to Action from Indigenous Peoples in Asia to the World Conference on Indigenous Peoples* (WCIP): A Declaration Emerging from the Asia Preparatory Meeting for the World Conference on Indigenous Peoples (WCIP), Bangkok, Thailand, 8–9 November, 2012, viewed 19 March 2016, http://iva.aippnet.org/wp-content/uploads/2013/09/Asian-IP-Statement-WCIP-final.pdf.

Cobo, JM 1986, *Study of the Problem of Discrimination against Indigenous Populations*, UN Document: E/CN.4/Sub.2/1986/7/Add.4.

Daes, EA 2008, *Indigenous Peoples: Keepers of Our Past – Custodians of Our Future*, International Work Group for Indigenous Affairs, Copenhagen.

Gray, A 1995, 'The Indigenous Movement in Asia', in RH Barnes, A Gray & B Kingsbury (eds), *Indigenous Peoples of Asia*, Association for Asian Studies, Ann Arbor, MI, pp. 35–58.

Joffe, P 2010, 'UN Declaration on the Rights of Indigenous Peoples: Canadian Government Positions Incompatible with Genuine Reconciliation', *National Journal of Constitutional Law*, vol. 26, no. 2, pp. 121–229, viewed 19 July 2015, www.afn.ca/uploads/files/education2/undripcanadiangovernments.pdf.

Kingsbury, B 2008, 'Indigenous Peoples in International Law: A Constructivist Approach to the Asian Controversy', in C Erni (ed.), *The Concept of Indigenous Peoples in Asia*, IWGIA Document No. 123, International Work Group for Indigenous Affairs (IWGIA), Asia Indigenous Peoples Pact (AIPP) Foundation, Copenhagen & Chiangmai, pp. 103–158.

MacKay, F (ed.) 2015, *A Compilation of UN Treaty Body Jurisprudence, Report of the Special Procedures of the Human Rights Council and the Advice of the Expert Mechanism on the Rights of Indigenous Peoples*, vol. 4, 2013–2014, Forest Peoples Programme, Moreton-in-Marsh [unpublished electronic copy].

Martínez, MA 1999, *Study on Treaties, Agreements and Other Constructive Arrangements between States and Indigenous Populations*, UN Document: E/CN.4/Sub.2/1999/20, 22 June.

Matibag, JG (ed.) 2014, *Indigenous Peoples and National Human Rights Institutions in Asia: Good Practices and Challenges*, Asia Indigenous Peoples Pact (AIPP) Foundation, Chiangmai.

Minority Rights Group International 1999, *Forests and Indigenous Peoples in Asia*, Report 98/4, London.

Roy, D 2003, 'The International Character of Treaties with Indigenous Peoples and Implementation Challenges for Intra-State Peace and Autonomy Agreements between Indigenous Peoples and States: The Case of the Chittagong Hill Tracts, Bangladesh', paper presented at the Expert Seminar on Treaties, Agreements and Other Constructive Arrangements between States and Indigenous Peoples, organised by the Office of the United Nations High Commissioner for Human Rights, Geneva, 15–17 December, viewed 19 March 2016, www.ohchr.org/EN/Issues/IPeoples/Pages/SeminarTreaties.aspx.

Roy, D 2011, 'Asserting Customary Land Rights in the Chittagong Hill Tracts, Bangladesh: Challenges for Legal and Juridical Pluralism', in M Colchester & S Chao (eds), *Divers Paths to Justice: Legal Pluralism and the Rights of Indigenous Peoples in Southeast Asia*, Forest Peoples Programme (FPP) and Asia Indigenous Peoples Pact (AIPP), Chiangmai, pp. 106–125.

Roy, RCK 2009, 'Indigenous Peoples in Asia: Rights and Development Challenges', in C Charters & R Stavenhagen (eds), *Making the Declaration Work: The United Nations Declaration on the Rights of Indigenous Peoples*, International Work Group for Indigenous Affairs, Copenhagen (Document No. 127), pp. 216–231.

Roy, RD 2005, *Traditional Customary Laws and Indigenous Peoples in Asia*, Minority Rights Group International, London.

Roy, RD 2009, *The ILO Convention on Indigenous and Tribal Populations, 1957 (No. 107) and the Laws of Bangladesh: A Comparative Review*, PRO 169, International Labour Standards Department, ILO Geneva and ILO Office in Dhaka.

Roy, RD 2012a, 'Promoting Partnerships in Implementing Intra-State Autonomy Agreements: Lessons from the Chittagong Hill Tracts, Bangladesh', unpublished paper presented at the Expert Group Seminar on Strengthening Partnership between States and Indigenous Peoples: Treaties, Agreements and Other Constructive Arrangements, organised by the Office of the High Commissioner for Human Rights, Geneva, 16–17 July, viewed 18 July 2015, www.ohchr.org/Documents/Issues/IPeoples/Seminars/Treaties/DevasishRoy.pdf.

Roy, RD 2012b, 'Indigenous Peoples and International Human Rights: Plural Approaches to Securing Customary Rights', in S Chao & M Colchester (eds), *Human Rights and Agribusiness: Plural Legal Approaches to Conflict Resolution, Institutional Strengthening and Legal Reform*, Forest Peoples Programme and Sawitwatch, Moreton-in-Marsh and Bogor, pp. 61–78.

Roy, RD 2016a, 'International Human Rights Standards and Indigenous Peoples' Land and Human Rights in Asia', in D Short & C Lennox (eds), *Routledge Handbook of Indigenous Peoples Rights*, Routledge, Abingdon & New York, pp. 371–393.

Roy, RD 2016b, *Inclusion of Indigenous Peoples in the New Constitution of Nepal – III: Prospects and Challenges of the 2015 Constitution* (unpublished); Technical Report on the Constitution of Nepal, 2015, commissioned by the International Labour Office, Geneva, January 2016.

Roy, RD, Hossain, S & Guhathakurta, M 2007, 'Access to Justice for Indigenous Peoples: A Case Study of Bangladesh', in UNDP, *Towards Inclusive Governance: Promoting the Participation of Disadvantaged Groups in Asia-Pacific*, UNDP Regional Centre, Bangkok, pp. 25–46.

Tugendhat, H & Dictaan-Bang-oa, E (eds) 2013, *Rationalizing Indigenous Women's Rights: A Handbook on the CEDAW*, Philippines Tebtebba Foundation: Baguio City, Philippines.

United Nations General Assembly (UNGA) 2011, *Resolution Adopted by the General Assembly: On the Report of the Third Committee* (A/65/453), 65/198, Indigenous Issues, UN Doc: A/RES/65/198, 3 March.

United Nations General Assembly (UNGA) 2012a, *Resolution Adopted by the General Assembly: On the Report of the Third Committee* (A/66/459), 66/142; Sixty-sixth Session, Agenda item 66(a), *Rights of Indigenous Peoples*, UN Doc: A/RES/66/142, 30 March 2012.

United Nations General Assembly (UNGA) 2012b, *Resolution Adopted by the General Assembly*; Sixty-sixth Session, Agenda item 66, *Organization of the High-level Plenary Meeting of the Sixty-ninth Session of the General Assembly, to Be Known as the World Conference on Indigenous Peoples*, UN Doc: A/RES/66/296, 15 October.

United Nations General Assembly (UNGA) 2014, *Resolution Adopted by the General Assembly on 22 September 2014*: Sixty-ninth Session, Agenda Item 65, *Outcome Document of the High-level Plenary Meeting of the General Assembly Known as the World Conference on Indigenous Peoples*, UN Doc: A/RES/69/2, 25 September.

22

No regional pattern

LGBTIQ rights and politics in Asia

Anthony J. Langlois

Introduction

One of the social media features of the 2015 Being LGBTI[1] in Asia conference held in Bangkok, was the sharing of brief statements on Twitter and Facebook that captured key aspects of what it is to be lesbian, gay, bisexual, transgender and intersex (LGBTI) in Asia (Being LGBTI in Asia 2015b). Here is one: 'The police investigation into my attack was both ineffective and homophobic. The police made it clear from the outset that, if I was indeed gay, I deserved the attack and that the reaction of my attackers was natural' (Being LGBTI in Asia 2015d). Another speaks of being sacked as a teacher for being a lesbian. Another of invasive and abusive medical practices. A tweet from the conference floor reads, 'We are listening to a very brave #SriLanka #Transgender delegate sharing awful physical, institutional and psychological abuse #BeingLGBTI' (Being LGBTI in Asia 2015c). From Pakistan, living a gay life 'is like putting yourself in a fire' (Being LGBTI in Asia 2015a). Suicide, broken family relationships, religious and social shunning, harassment, abuse by officers of the state – these are common experiences for LGBTIQ persons in Asia, as they are globally. Many of the shared statements from the conference also illustrated how lives vulnerable to such abuse can be protected and transformed through solidarity and social change – supported by civil society activism and politico-legal reform.

It is only recently that the global regime of human rights has pro-actively engaged the question of rights protection on the basis of sexual orientation and gender identity (SOGI) – and even then, it has been subject to severe resistance from certain regions. In Asia, there is both engagement and resistance; positive developments juxtaposed with sometimes severe resistance or mere cruel indifference. Below I will sketch the contemporary situation. First, I provide the broad context of human rights institutionalisation and observance in the region, and then indicate how it is that, once LGBTIQ rights are recognised as human rights, they may also be recognised within regional iterations of the global human rights regime. To illustrate this evolving process, I trace two threads of activity in the region: one concerns the engagement of National Human Rights Institutions (NHRIs) in Asia with LGBTIQ concerns; the other is the United Nations Development Programme's (UNDPs) regionally unique 'Being LGBTI in Asia' initiative.

Context: human rights in Asia

It is not possible to generalise about human rights in Asia. Conceptualising Asia as a region is itself a fraught exercise, and even within those parts of Asia that do form regional systems of one sort or another, engagement with human rights can vary enormously. It can also change over time: in the 1990s, 'Asian values' meant antipathy to human rights (Langlois 2001). Today, the Association of Southeast Asian Nations (ASEAN) has its own Bill of Rights (2012), developed under the auspices of the ASEAN Intergovernmental Commission on Human Rights (established in 2009). Much can be said about how to interpret this development, but it provides an important framework for regional human rights engagement (Langlois 2014; Tan 2011; Davies 2014).

In East and South Asia, there is no such organisational framework, and responses to the global human rights regime vary widely. Many states have signed key human rights conventions, such as the two central international covenants, in addition to the Universal Declaration. Many have gone further, signing covenants such as the Convention on the Elimination of all Forms of Discrimination Against Women (CEDAW) and those concerning the rights of the child, torture and racial discrimination. China, like the ASEAN states, has turned from scepticism and has formally endorsed human rights, signalling the respect and preservation of human rights through a national constitutional provision, as well as signing key United Nations (UN) treaties (Sanders 2015b). India was an original participant in the global human rights regime; like many more recently participating states however, it continues to struggle with the application of human rights standards in domestic policy.

While there is no broad human rights framework across Asia, it is important to observe that many Asian states have national human rights institutions (NHRIs) which are accredited according to the United Nations' Paris Principles. These include India, Indonesia, Malaysia, Mongolia, Nepal, the Philippines, Timor-Leste, South Korea and Thailand. Accreditation focuses on core human rights protection issues and is a key resource for mobilising human rights institutions for vulnerable populations.

This varied political, institutional and legal context for human rights in Asia is of great significance for how we approach the question of promoting LGBTI rights, as human rights, in Asia (cf. Mackie 2013). The trajectory of many states from scepticism to human rights institutionalisation has generated hope; in some states, it has issued in improvements for LGBTIQ persons. In other states, however, the very selective appropriation of human rights standards has meant continued exclusion.

More fundamentally, it has only been in the last decade or so that LGBTIQ rights have come to be regarded as rights within the broader UN human rights regime. Among member states themselves, it is not yet the case that respect for LGBTIQ rights can be considered an unambiguously 'settled' norm (D'Amico 2015). Contestation over LGBTIQ rights in the Asian region feeds into this broader global debate, and the developments taking place within individual states, across regional co-operative institutions, and in other norm-setting fora are therefore of great salience.

LGBT rights are human rights

The United Nations, the epicentre of the international human rights regime, has recently taken up the challenge of discrimination and abuse against LGBT persons. Ban Ki-moon, the UN Secretary-General, states that the struggle for the protection of LGBT rights is 'one of the great, neglected challenges of our time' (United Nations 2013). In 2011, the UN Human Rights

Council resolved (although not without opposition) 'that human rights should apply without distinction on the basis of sexual orientation or gender identity' (Altman & Beyrer 2014: 1). In a famous speech to the UN on Human Rights Day 2011, Hillary Clinton declared that 'gay rights are human rights' (Clinton 2011); the first ever UN report into LGBT rights – a chronicle of abuse, discrimination and neglect – was also released. In a subsequent statement from the UN, the case for respecting the human rights of LGBTI persons was put like this:

> In many parts of the world, lesbian, gay, bisexual, transgender and intersex (LGBTI) people face discrimination, stigmatization and acts of violence. Protecting and promoting the rights of LGBTI people to free expression, association, and peaceful assembly is crucial to end their discrimination and address the appalling human rights violations inflicted upon them. These are not only basic rights, but they are also essential in allowing individuals to claim other rights, in particular the rights to freedom from discrimination and equality before the law, and they can contribute to fostering public debate in society.
>
> We condemn acts of retaliation, intimidation, or harassment in any sphere (whether public or private) based on a person's manifestation or expression of their sexual orientation, gender identity or gender expression. . . . [W]e remind States of their obligation to protect, promote, and fulfil universal rights without discrimination. The existence of societal disapproval of diverse sexual orientations and gender identities does not justify discrimination or violence against LGBTI people.
>
> *(United Nations 2014)*

While there is no specific UN instrument for 'gay rights, a great many of the UN's already existing rights instruments apply to cases of abuse or discrimination based on sexual orientation or gender identity (SOGI). In 2006 in Yogyakarta, Indonesia, a meeting was convened at which a range of human rights experts drafted a document which sought 'to develop a set of international legal principles on the application of international law to human rights violations based on sexual orientation.' (Anon 2007: 7). While there has been some dispute about the extent to which these principles state the law as it is, versus the extent to which they push the envelope in an activist manner, there is no doubt that they have become a highly significant statement of the application of international law to SOGI matters. Brown (2009: 826) argues:

> They have become a fixture in the proceedings of the United Nations Human Rights Council; been incorporated into the foreign and domestic policies of a number of countries; been acclaimed and debated by regional human rights bodies in Europe and South America; and have worked their way into the writings of a number of United Nations agencies and human rights rapporteurs. They have even been cited by national courts in overturning their countries' discriminatory laws.

The Yogyakarta Principles were a clear and repeated inspiration to people of diverse sexual orientation and gender identity across Southeast Asia during the period in which ASEAN established its ASEAN Intergovernmental Commission on Human Rights and drafted its own Bill of Rights (for example, FORUM-ASIA 2011). Notwithstanding the fact that, predictably, SOGI matters were not accommodated as desired by civil society groups in ASEAN's bill, the existence of the Yogyakarta Principles acted as a powerful touchstone for deliberation and politicking around the question of how SOGI should be engaged by a newly emerging set of regional human rights principles and institutions (Langlois 2014). They have also become a clear reference point for a range of government and non-government organisations and agencies working in the region – the UNDP being a clear example. Taking the developments at the United Nations, and the development of the Yogyakarta Principles together, it becomes clear that the requirement to protect the human rights of SOGI persons is no longer 'the norm that dare not speak its name' (Thoreson 2009). We can now turn to the Asian region to consider how the treatment of LGBTQ people may be evaluated through a human rights lens.

Overview of regional rights protections for LGBTIQ people

In his opening comments at the 2015 UNDP Being LGBTI in Asia conference, Douglas Sanders painted a picture of global movements and allegiances with respect to LGBTIQ rights. These allegiances are centred on UN processes, but they also play out on the broader stages of global sexuality politics. Of critical note is a fault line between an alliance in opposition to LGBTIQ rights comprising a Russian led Eastern Europe, together with Sub-Saharan Africa and the Organisation of Islamic Cooperation states; and, in favour, a Western bloc and the Latin American states. Where does Asia fit in these global alliances? And does it follow a clear political trajectory either for or against support for SOGI rights? Sanders says,

> What of Asia? There really are no *regional* patterns in Asia. There are neither regional patterns of reform or of regression. . . . Nothing comparable either to the regression in Africa and Eastern Europe, or the reforms in the West and in Latin America.
>
> *(Sanders 2015a)*

This analysis is made clear by glancing at the state of play in the three conventionally articulated regions of Asia: East Asia, South Asia and Southeast Asia.

East Asia contains many manifestations of LGBTIQ life that are consonant with the familiar 'global' conceptions of gay social experience and identity. While homosexuality is basically de-criminalised, it is rarely protected by antidiscrimination laws. There are bars and other venues in most states; pride parades, film festivals, seminars and the like are possible in many of these jurisdictions. Sanders (2015b) reports that the largest gay event happens in Taipei in the autumn of each year, while Hong Kong has an annual 'Pink Season'. In addition, the UN is very active in the region on LGBT issues (Sanders 2015b). Despite these familiar global markers, sexual politics in the region is highly complex and contested. As Pendleton suggests, 'despite the apparent homogenization of global "gay" identities, understandings of sexual and gender identities in East Asia have coexisted with localized traditions and practices, resulting in processes of contested hybridisation' (Pendleton 2015: 25). Gaining social recognition and space is an ongoing political struggle, as is achieving incremental legal reforms concerned with alleviating discrimination.

While South Asia also has a rich tapestry of hybrid and non-normative sexualities and genders, and a similarly rich cultural landscape of communities and activities, the focus of attention is often on the battle for de-criminalisation. Developments in India have been closely watched in this regard. In 2009, after an arduous campaign, the High Court of Delhi handed down a judgment in the Naz Foundation case, which read down section 377 of the Indian Penal Code and de-criminalised homosexual relations between consenting adults. Legal developments in 2012 and 2013, however, led to a reversal of this decision, and the re-criminalisation of such relations. 'The country reacted in shock, terror, rage and solidarity' (Bose 2014: 499). The arduous campaign for sexual freedom was continued, however, with LGBTQ activists petitioning the Supreme Court in 2016. Their claim was that 'rights to sexuality, sexual autonomy, choice of sexual partner, life, privacy, dignity and equality, along with the other fundamental rights guaranteed under Part-III of Constitution, are violated by Section 377' (SCOI Report 2018).

The Supreme Court brought down a landmark decision in this case on 6 September 2018, repealing section 377 of the Penal Code, and affirming the full citizenship, dignity and equality of LGBTQ people in India. South Asia extends beyond India, however, and while the reversals and final triumph in India's case have garnered it much attention, it is not alone. Nepal, as Bose (2014) reminds us, overthrew its monarchy in 2007 and used the occasion to legalise homosexuality. Elsewhere still, in each of Afghanistan, Pakistan, Bangladesh, Sri Lanka, Bhutan and the Maldives, complex and distinctive histories are in play.

In Southeast Asia, here understood as the ASEAN nations, the regional development of human rights instrumentalities gives yet a different gloss on the matter of LGBT rights (cf. Offord 2013). In their pursuit of regional cooperation, inspired by the European Union model, ASEAN has pledged to become more 'people oriented'; its embrace of human rights commissions, declarations and other instrumentalities being a central part of this re-orientation. SOGI activists and communities in the region have argued that ASEAN cannot become more people oriented if it continues to fail on recognising and protecting their sexual orientations and gender identities. The legal, political and social sanctioning of sexual and gender diverse persons varies widely within ASEAN. The institutionalisation of human rights in the region through ASEAN and also through national human rights institutions, combined with the development of the Yogyakarta Principles, has provided an environment of unique traction for LGBTIQ advocates (cf. Croydon 2013). Change and reform across the region have been incremental, inconsistent and piecemeal, however; controversy and resistance in some states contrasts with a relatively benign accommodation in others (for example, Malaysia, as compared to Indonesia). The impact of the developing regional human rights architecture is apparent but still nascent (Langlois 2014).

The Asian region in general, then, offers a diverse patchwork of different levels of freedom, sanction, discrimination, reform, safety and political opportunity. As Sanders (2015a) suggested, there is no regional pattern or inclination. There are, however, threads of activity on SOGI matters which cut across the region and which provide an instructive window into possibilities for reform. In what follows I will trace two of these threads, using them to provide further detail on the state of play in the region, but also to illustrate the cautious optimism which may be identified. Both threads concern programmes conducted by the United Nations Development Programme, one in conjunction with the International Development Law Organization. The first is a project, reporting in 2013, titled Assessing the Capacity of National Human Rights Institutions to Address Human Rights in relation to Sexual Orientation, Gender Identity and HIV – 'the NHRIs Project', for short (UNDP, IDLO 2013). The second is a series of reports from the Being LGBTI in Asia programme, culminating in a Regional Dialogue on LGBTI conference in Bangkok in February 2015 (UNDP 2015). I will look at these in turn.

Advocating LGBTIQ rights in Asia: two recent programmes

National human rights institutions and LGBTIQ rights

The first thing to note about both of these programmes is that they illustrate a dynamic and complex network of activity in Asia around SOGI rights – a dynamism which might not at first appear if one simply looks to the relatively static and minimal institutional base for such protections. They build on regional activities that have been taking place within legal, institutional, governmental and civil society domains for a significant period. In the case of the NHRI Project, it emerged out of a series of prior meetings and reports, activities which themselves were following a pathway indicated by the Yogyakarta Principles. In 2009, a workshop facilitated by the Asia Pacific Forum in response to the Yogyakarta 'Additional Recommendations' was held which discussed how NHRIs could use their capacities to further SOGI concerns. This meeting in turn gave rise to a report from the Asia Pacific Forum's Advisory Council of Jurists (ACJ), which provided 'advice and recommendations on the question of the consistency or inconsistency with international human rights law, of laws in the Asia Pacific region concerning SOGI' (UNDP, IDLO 2013: 12). As well as the activities giving rise to the ACJ report (ACJ, AsiaPacificForum 2010), a number of organisations came together in 2011 for the South Asian Roundtable Dialogue – those organisations already mentioned plus the World Bank and UNAIDS. The NHRI Project emerged out of that Roundtable. The NHRI Project's Regional Report provides a great deal of detail about each of these steps, reinforcing the conclusion that despite significantly adverse political circumstances (in some states in particular), a wide coalition of interested actors are engaged at multiple levels within the structures of the region advocating for SOGI concerns.

The purpose of the NHRI Project was to examine 'the capacity and response of selected Asian National Human Rights Institutions (NHRIs) to the human rights issues faced by people of diverse sexual orientation and gender identity (SOGI)' (UNDP, IDLO 2013: 7) within a broader regional framework examining the evolving legal framework for responding to human immunodeficiency virus (HIV). The NHRIs included in the study were from the following states: Bangladesh, India, Indonesia, Nepal, Pakistan, the Philippines, Sri Lanka and Timor-Leste. The report found that while 'all NHRIs involved in the NHRI SOGI Project had some prior institutional exposure to SOGI, the issue remains highly sensitive in many jurisdictions' (UNDP, IDLO 2013: 7). In individual state reports provided for each participating NHRI, the nature and range of these sensitivities becomes clear. While, for example, in the Philippines it was possible for a political party formed to advocated for LGBT persons (the Ang Ladlad Party) to legally challenge its exclusion from the political process – and win (with the assistance of the Philippines NHRI, the Commission on Human Rights), in many other states such overt political activity would have severe consequences for both LGBTQ persons and NHRIs. As it is dryly put in the report on Bangladesh, 'These issues are not within the comfort zone of the [national] hegemonic ideology regarding sexuality' (National Human Rights Commission of Bangladesh 2013: 11).

The central analytical part of the NHRI Project report considers SOGI-related initiatives of the NHRIs in question. It does so by referring back to the earlier ACJ Report, which had made recommendations under four broad headings: '(A) capacity building and research; (B) education, promotion and dialogue; (C) monitoring; and (D) advocacy' (UNDP, IDLO 2013: 18). For each one of these headings, it considers the NHRIs of the South and Southeast Asian states included in the study (no East Asian NHRIs are considered). With respect to (A) capacity building and research, the report finds that the majority of NHRIs have taken some measures to inform themselves regarding SOGI rights issues. On (B), education, promotion and dialogue, educational activities in Southeast Asia among people of diverse SOGI are commended, but apart from in Nepal and Indonesia, NHRIs are not seen to engage in many educational or dialogue initiatives on SOGI with external stakeholders. With respect to (C) monitoring, NHRIs vary between those with an explicit mandate to monitor SOGI-related rights, and those who have found ways to construe their mandates to incorporate SOGI matters, particularly using discrimination mechanisms. While there are outstanding examples of (D) advocacy in the region by NHRIs, in general the cases of advocacy are few, and NHRIs seem reluctant to engage. This, it must be conceded strongly, is not surprising. As the report details, in South Asia, while Nepal may be making huge strides, evidenced by a serious commitment to the goal of same-sex marriage, in Bangladesh, the government view was characteristic of a number of antipathetic states in the region: 'Same-sex activity is not an acceptable norm to any community in the country' (UNDP, IDLO 2013: 26). Among the Southeast Asian NHRIs covered, the political environment has more scope for advocacy. In both Indonesia and the Philippines for example, NHRIs have been successfully involved in high-profile legal and social advocacy.

The NHRIs Project report observes certain critical factors which are present in NHRIs that have a 'well developed' capacity to address SOGI-related rights issues (UNDP, IDLO 2013: 35). One of these is the presence within an NHRI of a focal point for SOGI or HIV issues. This is particularly important given that the report concludes, from its surveys and interviews with almost 500 LGBT community members across the region, that 'in many countries, a lack of awareness of NHRI processes or lack of awareness of the willingness of an NHRI to address SOGI-related rights, may contribute to the reticence of LGBTI individuals to approach a Commission' (UNDP, IDLO 2013: 8). This then links with a second critical factor, which is 'the role of the community of people of diverse SOGI. . . . The impact and importance of the efforts of the LGBTI community: lobbying and advocating on not only rights, but stigma, social and cultural issues, cannot be understated' (UNDP, IDLO 2013: 35). Apart from the specific analysis and narratives which are communicated by the NHRIs Project report, what we learn is that the region is suffused by activity which seeks to ensure equality for people of diverse SOGI. That this is an ongoing struggle in which NHRIs can play a key part cannot be doubted.

Being LGBTI in Asia

The 'Being LGBTI in Asia' programme was launched on International Human Rights Day in 2012. A ground-breaking programme, its ambition was to undertake – in the words of its subtitle, 'A Participatory Review and Analysis of the Legal and Social Environment for LGBT Civil Society' (UNDP 2015). Between March 2013 and April 2014, community dialogues with LGBT civil society groups were held in eight countries in the region: Cambodia, China, Indonesia, Mongolia, Nepal, the Philippines, Thailand and Vietnam. A central part of this undertaking was to document the lived experiences of LGBT persons in these countries, in particular analysing them from human rights and development perspectives. Of its objectives, the programme's website says, '"Being LGBT in Asia" encourages networking between LGBT people across the Asia-Pacific region, building a knowledge and evidence baseline, developing an understanding of the capacity of LGBT organizations to engage in policy dialogue, and community mobilization' (UNDP 2015). The 'knowledge and evidence baseline' referred to here includes a series of country reports, which were developed out of the community dialogues held in each of the eight participating countries. These reports provide comprehensive assessments of the state of play for LGBTI populations in the states in question, and also provide detailed recommendations for policy change directed towards both governments and also the community sector.

The circumstances and experiences of LGBTI people among the eight states chosen to participate in this project are highly diverse. What is common among these states is that same-sex activities are not subject to criminal penalties under the law. The route that these states have travelled to this position is variable, and is part of the complex story of the differential treatment that LGBT people receive in the region. It is also, when baldly stated, significantly misleading. If we take China, for example, same-sex activity has never been directly criminalised, as the country report states. But, as it also details, in common with most other states discussed, other laws have been used to intimidate, harass and control LGBTI people. China's anti-hooliganism law, used for this purpose, was taken off the books in 1997. In Thailand same-sex activity was decriminalised in 1956. In the Philippines, a variety of laws are still used to harass; in Indonesia, while there are now no national laws which criminalise same-sex activity, there are some local ordinances that do. While states may have moved to decriminalise, this is still a long way from active protection of the rights of LGBTI persons. States have shown little or no interest to put in place anti-discrimination measures, or to ensure that sexual assault laws address LGBTI concerns, and in general civil rights are not protected. Mongolia is an exception, where efforts are being made to re-draft laws on domestic violence and labour, with SOGI concerns in mind.

In a number of the states in question, strong moves have been made to change relationship recognition laws. In Nepal, Thailand and Vietnam, significant steps have been taken, ranging from the efforts in Thailand by Civil Society Organisations (CSOs) and the Law Reform Commission to draft a gender neutral civil partnership bill, through to reforms in Vietnam which allow same-sex partners to wed publicly and live together, although these are not legally protected relationships. In Nepal, a 2007 Supreme Court ruling that anti-discrimination and same-sex marriage laws be investigated has not given rise to any further formal activity. In each of these states, possibilities for positive movement coexist with continued insecurity and vulnerability for LGBTI people.

As well as considering these and other legal aspects of LGBT life in the region, the country reports consider levels of social acceptance, and factors such as the influence of religion. Take, for example, this comment from the report produced by the dialogue in Mongolia:

> Mongolian culture is generally not open or welcoming to alternate or non-traditional sexual orientations and gender identity. Religion does not appear to play a significant role in contributing to negative attitudes but traditional norms place pressure on LGBT people to conform or hide their identities.
>
> *(UNDP, USAID 2014a: 7)*

A similar comment is made in the Thai report, notwithstanding Thailand's international reputation as an LGBT friendly locale (cf. Jackson 2011):

> LGBT behaviour and people who are seen as 'abnormal' or 'deviant' are not accepted by the norms of Thai society. There are those who choose not to conform to the accepted gender norms and societal constructs and there are also those who passively accept their situations out of the need to become a 'good' person as mandated by prevailing social norms.
>
> *(UNDP, USAID 2014b: 29)*

The Filipino report cites Pew Research which indicates high levels of approval for homosexuality; however, it goes on to argue that LGBTI Filipinos believe this only to be the case if certain stereotypes and occupational positions are maintained. The report details the complexities of the religion/sexuality nexus in the Philippines, with its majority Catholicism being a key, although not always stereotypical, factor.

Despite the diversity of the societies considered in this project, and notwithstanding the progress that is being made in many of them with respect to LGBTI persons, it remains the case that stigma, discrimination, prejudice and violence are experienced across the region. With that in mind, one of the evident benefits from this project has been the opportunity for LGBTI civil society members both within and across states to network with one another: the reports we have been sampling were developed out of national LGBT dialogue meetings in 2013–2014 which provided for national LGBTI actors to assemble together and talk.

As noted, in February 2015, a major conference was held in Bangkok, where LGBTI community members from across the region were able to come together to report to and learn from one another. The Being LGBT in Asia conference, held under the auspices of the UNDP, USAID and the Swedish Embassy in Thailand, brought 200 people from 30 states into dialogue with one another; it is a unique programme, there being no other regional meet of its kind. Much of its footprint and impact is archived on the internet, through its Facebook and Twitter accounts.

In his opening comments to the conference, Douglas Sanders (Sanders 2015a; cf. Sanders 2011) said:

> In June, 2011, almost four years ago, the UN Human Rights Council, for the first time, expressed concern over patterns of violence and discrimination against individuals on the basis of their sexual orientation or gender identity. After decades of marginalization at the UN we had finally been recognized by one of the UN's political bodies, a body established under the framework of the UN Charter.
>
> . . .
>
> The UN was not a friendly place. When I spoke as an 'out' gay man in 1992, there was 'open hostility' . . . But that has changed.
>
> . . .
>
> Few, if any, would have predicted that the UN Development Programme would become the lead international inter-governmental agency for LGBT rights in Asia. But that is what happened. And it began with its work on AIDS.

The conference canvassed a broad and detailed range of issues confronting the LGBTI communities from the region. Matters of law, social policy, education, political updates, economic impact, familial support and intervention and the future of LGBTI rights were all discussed by a wide range of speakers.

The Being LGBTI in Asia initiative has already met many of its goals – including researching and making available a wealth of information about LGBTI communities in the region. As well as being a sampler of that resource, the purpose of this discussion has been to demonstrate one set of threads of SOGI activity that extend across the region. Tracing these threads may not evince a formal regional pattern, but it clearly demonstrates a dynamic network of civil society human rights defenders at work together to see LGBTI rights recognised as human rights in the region.

Conclusion

My purpose in this chapter has been to outline the relationship between human rights and the experience of being LGBTIQ in Asia at the present time. In discussing the NHRI Project and the Being LGBTI initiative, I have sought to trace threads of activity across the region which show the utility of human rights as a tool for the protection and security of potentially vulnerable populations. In many of the states discussed, non-normative sexual and gender relations are still criminalised. Within many states that have formally de-criminalised, various other laws are routinely used to harass and persecute. And in states where there has been effective legal reform, it is commonplace for prejudice and discrimination to remain rife, with little in the way of legal redress. At the same time, there are local communities and civil society movements which provide a counter-point: a complex of interweaving narratives about sexual and gender relations which are building a different form of politics. The #BeingLGBTI hash tag on social media, associated with the Bangkok conference, is but one witness to these developments.

The use of human rights to articulate norms and enact protections for LGBTIQ persons is still relatively novel at the global level; within an Asia that is rapidly thickening its regional institutional infrastructure, including that pertaining to human rights, the rule of law and norms for governance, there are significant opportunities for reform to be had. As we have seen, however, there is no consistent regional pattern in Asia that can be discerned, no systemic political or social movement dedicated to bringing institutional, social and cultural norms into political engagement with SOGI rights. A watching brief must be retained.

Note

1 The exact length and inclusiveness of this acronym varies depending on who is using it, where and why. The default version adopted in this chapter will be LGBTIQ (lesbian, gay, bisexual, trans*, intersex, queer); however, when a source is being cited which uses a different version, that version will be used. Similarly, different versions are used in the names of texts, conferences and organisations.

References

ACJ AsiaPacificForum 2010, *ACJ Report: Human Rights, Sexual Orientation and Gender Identity*, viewed 6 June 2016, www.asiapacificforum.net/media/resource_file/ACJ_Report_Human_Rights_Sexual_Orientation_and_Gender_Identity.doc.pdf.

Altman, D & Beyrer, C 2014, 'The Global Battle for Sexual Rights', *Journal of the International AIDS Society*, vol. 17, no. 1, viewed 20 May 2014, www.jiasociety.org/index.php/jias/article/view/19243.

Anon 2007, 'The Yogyakarta Principles: Principles on the Application of International Human Rights Law in Relation to Sexual Orientation and Gender Identity', viewed 6 June 2016, http://yogyakartaprinciples.org/principles_en.pdf.

Being LGBTI in Asia 2015a, 'In a Muslim Country Living as a Gay Is Like Putting Yourself in a Fire', viewed 6 June 2016, https://pbs.twimg.com/media/B-cyn5UIAAAYYFZ.jpg:large.

Being LGBTI in Asia 2015b, 'Stories of #BeingLGBTI', viewed 6 June 2016, www.facebook.com/media/set/?set=a.423909121098846.1073741854.164639953692432&type=1.

Being LGBTI in Asia 2015c, 'We Are Listening to a Very Brave #SriLanka #Transgender Delegate Sharing Awful Physical, Institutional and Psychological Abuse #BeingLGBTI', *@beinglgbtinasia*, micro blog 8 April 2015, https://twitter.com/beinglgbtinasia/status/571165021654220800.

Being LGBTI in Asia 2015d, 'The Police Investigation into My Attack', viewed 6 June 2016, http://ow.ly/i/8MVvd.

Bose, B 2014, 'Notes on Queer Politics in South Asia and Its Diaspora', in McCallum, EL & Tuhkanen, M (eds), *The Cambridge History of Gay and Lesbian Literature*, Cambridge, Cambridge University Press, pp. 498–511, viewed 25 March 2015, http://universitypublishingonline.org/ref/id/histories/CHO9781139547376A038.

Brown, D 2009, 'Making Room for Sexual Orientation and Gender Identity in International Human Rights Law: An Introduction to the Yogyakarta Principles', *Michigan Journal of International Law*, vol. 31, no. 4, p. 821–879.

Clinton, H 2011, 'Hillary Clinton on Gay Rights Abroad: Secretary of State Delivers Historic LGBT Speech in Geneva (VIDEO, FULL TEXT)', *Huffington Post*, viewed 14 October 2014, www.huffingtonpost.com/2011/12/06/hillary-clinton-gay-rights-speech-geneva_n_1132392.html.

Croydon, S 2013, 'Two Rights Paths: East Asia's Emerging Regional Human Rights Framework', *Asia Pacific Perspectives*, vol. 11, no. 1, pp. 22–35.

D'Amico, F 2015, 'LGBT and (Dis)United Nations: Sexual Minorities, International Law, and UN Politics', in Picq, M and Thiel, M (eds), *Sexual Politics in International Relations*, New York, Routledge, pp. 54–74.

Davies, M 2014, *Realising Rights: How Regional Organisations Socialise Human Rights*, 1st edition, London & New York, Routledge.

FORUM-ASIA 2011, 'Gay, Lesbian, Bisexual and Queers Take Stage on ASEAN People's Forum' FORUM-ASIA, viewed 25 July 2012, www.forum-asia.org/?p=6934.

Jackson, PA 2011, *Queer Bangkok Twenty-first-Century Markets, Media, and Rights*, Hong Kong & Chiang Mai, Hong Kong University Press & Silkworm Books, viewed 4 March 2014, http://public.eblib.com/EBLPublic/PublicView.do?ptiID=863883.

Langlois, AJ 2001, *The Politics of Justice and Human Rights: Southeast Asia and Universalist Theory*, Cambridge, Cambridge University Press.

Langlois, AJ 2014, 'Human Rights, "Orientation", and ASEAN', *Journal of Human Rights*, vol. 13, no. 3, pp. 307–321.

Mackie, V 2013, 'Introduction: Ways of Knowing about Human Rights in Asia', *Asian Studies Review*, vol. 37, no. 3, pp. 293–301.

National Human Rights Commission of Bangladesh 2013, *Report to the Regional National Human Rights Institutions Project on Inclusion, the Right to Health and Sexual Orientation and Gender Identity*, Bangkok, UNDP IDLO.

Offord, B 2013, 'Queer Activist Intersections in Southeast Asia: Human Rights and Cultural Studies', *Asian Studies Review*, vol. 37, no. 3, pp. 335–349.

Pendleton, M. 2015, 'Transnational Sexual Politics in East Asia', in McLelland, M & Mackie, V (eds), *Routledge Handbook of Sexuality Studies in East Asia*, London, Routledge, pp. 21–34.

Sanders, D 2015a, 'How Did We Get Here?', viewed 11 March 2015, www.asiapacificforum.net/support/issues/sexual-orientation/downloads/role-of-nhris-in-promoting-and-protecting-the-rights-and-health-of-lgbti-in-asia-and-the-pacific-february-2015/presentation-professor-doug-sanders/view.

Sanders, D 2015b, 'What's Law Got to Do with It? Sex and Gender Diversity in East Asia', in McLelland, M & Mackie, V (eds), *Routledge Handbook of Sexuality Studies in East Asia*, London, Routledge, pp. 127–149.

Sanders, DE 2011, 'Out at the UN', in Weisbrodt, D & Rumsey, M (eds), *Vulnerable and Marginalised Groups and Human Rights*, Cheltenham, Edward Elgar, pp. 253–286.

SCOI Report 2018, 'Read the Wonderful New 377 Challenge by 5 Out-and-Proud Celebrities That'll Hit SC Today', viewed 12 September 2018, www.legallyindia.com/supreme-court/read-the-wonderful-new-377-challenge-by-5-out-and-proud-celebrities-that-ll-hit-sc-today-20160628-7762#liprefbox.

Tan, HL 2011, *The ASEAN Intergovernmental Commission on Human Rights: Institutionalising Human Rights in Southeast Asia*, Cambridge, Cambridge University Press.

Thoreson, RR 2009, 'Queering Human Rights: The Yogyakarta Principles and the Norm That Dare Not Speak Its Name', *Journal of Human Rights*, vol. 8, no. 4, pp. 323–339.

United Nations 2013, 'Ban Ki-moon: Struggle for LGBT Right One of the Great, Neglected Human Rights Challenges of Our Time', International Conference on Human Rights, Sexual Orientation and Gender Identity (Oslo, 15–16 April 2013), viewed 5 January 2015, www.youtube.com/watch?v=7uaHZWCgGss&feature=youtube_gdata_player.

United Nations 2014, 'Free Expression and Association Key to Eliminating Homophobia and Transphobia', viewed 23 March 2015, www.ohchr.org/EN/NewsEvents/Pages/DisplayNews.aspx?NewsID=14602&LangID=E.

United Nations Development Programme 2015, 'Regional Dialogue on LGBTI | UNDP in Asia and the Pacific', viewed 2 March 2015, www.asia-pacific.undp.org/content/rbap/en/home/presscenter/events/2015/february/Regional-Dialogue-on-LGBTI-Human-Rights-Health-in-AP.html.

United Nations Development Programme, IDLO 2013, *Regional Report: The Capacity of National Human Rights Institutions to Address Human Rights in Relation to Sexual Orientation, Gender Identity and HIV | UNDP in Asia and the Pacific*, Bangkok, UNDP, viewed 10 March 2015, www.asia-pacific.undp.org/content/rbap/en/home/library/hiv_aids/regional-report--the-capacity-of-national-human-rights-institutions.html.

United Nations Development Programme, USAID 2014a, *Being LGBT in Asia: Mongolia Country Report*, Bangkok, UNDP.

United Nations Development Programme, USAID 2014b, *Being LGBT in Asia: Thailand Country Report*, Bangkok, UNDP.

23

A rights-based approach to Indian speech laws

Raadhika Gupta

Introduction

The right to free speech and the right to equality can conflict with each other, particularly when speech is used to subordinate vulnerable groups in society. In India, these rights have stood in contrast with each another in sexual speech cases that involve some form of sexual representation of women. Divergent feminist positions have developed on the issue, each with a view to promote gender equality. For example, there are both pro- and anti-pornography feminists, with both groups using different conceptions of equality to examine the interaction of equality with the right to free speech. India's legal system is, however, divorced from this discourse, even though it has several laws restricting sexual speech. While these laws appear to have been enacted to 'protect' women, there appears to be an absence of jurisprudence in the interpretation of these laws through the lens of equality. Instead of promoting the right to equality, the discourse often pits the right to free speech against dominant morality, invading both liberty and equality.

This chapter uncovers the relative silence on the right to equality in Indian legal discourse relating to sexual speech, and examines how it is instead dominated by notions of morality. It is further argued that the reliance on dominant morality to examine the legality of sexual speech adversely affects both sexual liberty and freedom of expression. Accordingly, there remains a need to shift the narrative from 'dominant morality' to 'constitutional morality', to develop a human rights-based discourse on sexual expression.

The conflict between free speech and equality

The right to freedom of speech and expression and the right to equality are both well-recognised in human rights jurisprudence. Major international human rights instruments such as the Universal Declaration of Human Rights (UDHR) and the International Covenant on Civil and Political Rights (ICCPR), and most national constitutions, include both these rights as part of the guaranteed fundamental freedoms. While freedom of expression acts as a guarantee, the right to equality is increasingly understood in a substantive sense, allowing, and even requiring, the state to take positive steps to promote equality for historically and systemically discriminated groups. For example, while Article 1(4) of the International Convention on the Elimination of All Forms of Racial Discrimination (ICERD) permits affirmative action to ensure equal enjoyment of human rights by racial groups, Article 2(2) mentions that states 'shall, when the circumstances so warrant, take' such special measures. Further, the Human Rights Committee has recognised that the principle of equality requires states to take positive action to eliminate discrimination prohibited under the ICCPR (ICCPR General Comment 28 2000: para. 3; ICCRP General Comment 18 1989: para. 10). Similarly, the CEDAW Committee stated that states 'are obliged to adopt and implement' special measures 'if such measures can be shown to be necessary and appropriate in order to accelerate the achievement of the overall, or a specific goal of, women's de facto or substantive equality' (CEDAW General Recommendation 25: para. 24).

However, as mentioned earlier, the right to freedom of expression and the right to equality can conflict, particularly when speech is used to target or further subordinate marginalised groups. This is evidenced, for example, in hate speech cases in the US, such as those involving burning of the cross to express hatred and perceived inferiority of certain groups (*RAV v City of St. Paul* (1992); *Virginia v Black* (2003)), or putting on T-shirts with degrading messages about homosexuality in school (*Harper v Poway Unified School District* (2006)). If liberty allows using speech to keep marginalised groups in subordinated positions, then it directly injures the inclusive aspirations of the right to equality. When two rights of, in principle, equal value come in conflict, courts are often required to perform a balancing act.

It is challenging, and arguably even undesirable, to attempt to resolve the conflict by balancing or weighing fundamental rights against each other. Freedom of expression is considered essential to the autonomy, liberty and dignity of an individual; is necessary to search the truth in the 'marketplace of ideas'; and is fundamental to the precepts of a democratic society. At the same time, this freedom may be exploited to harm the autonomy, liberty and dignity of others who find themselves placed at the lower rungs on the social ladder, and to spread incorrect ideas, thus undermining democracy (Steenveld 2000: 26). While freedom of expression supports the right to equality by enabling all members of the society to participate in social and political decision-making, it is alleged that such an argument assumes that all members have equal access to this liberty. It is further argued that a substantive equality obliges the state to ensure that marginalised sections of society are not subordinated further by using dehumanising speech. Thus, equality should override liberty in anti-equality/identity speech (Gilreath 2009: 568–569, 571–572). In fact, based on a study of international principles, Professor Farrior (1996: 6) infers that 'if there is any right which enjoys primacy among rights, it is arguably the principle of equality and non-discrimination'. On the contrary, it may be argued that restricting speech may not be the best way to promote equality, and may instead run contrary to it. It is claimed that restrictions on speech are most often used to silence the most vulnerable groups (Strossen 1996: 465–470). Instead of increasing restrictions, the right to free speech should in fact be used as an ally in the cause of promoting equality (Branit 1986: 459–460).

International law recognises certain restrictions on the freedom of expression, some of which relate to concerns around equality. The ICCPR allows the right to freedom of expression to be restricted on the grounds of 'respect of the rights or reputation of others' and for protection of national security, public order, public health or morals (Art. 19(3)). International instruments also allow restrictions or prohibitions on hate speech. The ICCPR prohibits 'advocacy of national, racial or religious hatred that constitutes incitement to discrimination, hostility or violence' (Art. 20(2)). The UDHR prohibits incitement to discrimination (Art. 7). The ICERD requires states to outlaw 'all dissemination of ideas based on racial superiority or hatred' and 'incitement to racial discrimination' (Art. 4). The underlying principal behind these restrictions is to stop persons from engaging in activities aimed towards hampering the rights of others (Farrior 1996: 4).

Speech involving sexual content is another controversial issue within the speech-equality debate. India frequently witnesses expression of outrage and demands for restriction against various forms of sexual speech, such as sexually explicit scenes in movies, 'item songs' in Hindi cinema or paintings of nude or semi-clad women. While free speech proponents argue for maximum liberty and tolerance towards unpopular or uncomfortable expression, their opponents claim that such speech often objectifies and denigrates women, justifying violence against women and their sexual subordination.

The speech-equality controversy around sexual expression entered the courtroom perhaps most squarely in the US case of *American Booksellers v Hudnut* (1985), dealing with the constitutionality of an anti-pornography ordinance, which defined pornography as 'the graphic sexually explicit subordination of women', that includes representation of women as sexual objects who enjoy pain, humiliation or being raped, or as sexual objects for 'domination, conquest, violation, exploitation, possession, or use, or through postures or positions of servility or submission or display' (Indianapolis & Marion County Ordinance 1984, sect. 16-3(q)). Sex equality was clearly a primary motivator of the ordinance. The Court has also admitted that the ordinance did not concern violation of community standards of offensiveness, but was intended to challenge subordination of women. It also accepted the premise that '[d]epictions of subordination tend to perpetuate subordination' (*American Booksellers v Hudnut* (1985): 329). However, the fact that the ordinance attacked only those types of speech that involved the perspective of subordination of women led the Court to declare it unconstitutional. The ordinance led to discrimination, categorising speech with a specific kind of content as being unlawful, irrespective of its literary, artistic or political merits. This is against the tenets of the right to free speech, which does not discriminate between ideas.[1]

In contrast, feminist Catharine MacKinnon, one of the principal drafters of this ordinance, argues that the right to free speech need not protect pornography (MacKinnon 1993). She argues that pornography is not merely speech, but also conduct, since it involves physical abuse of the models (MacKinnon 1993). Prohibition of hate speech (e.g. 'No Blacks Served Here') and sexual harassment in the workplace are some examples of speech that is deemed unlawful not because of what is *says* but because of what it *does* (Gilreath 2009: 571). Further, MacKinnon argues that pornography promotes sexual violence against individual women and their subordination as a class (MacKinnon 1984). She also questions 'if a woman is subjected, why should it matter that the work has other value?' (MacKinnon 1985: 21).

Interestingly, even though international instruments recognise the right to sex equality, gender or sex is not explicitly mentioned in any of the hate speech provisions (Farrior 1996: 10). Unlike the ICERD, which contains a provision restricting hate speech on racial grounds, the CEDAW contains no corresponding provision restricting expression on the grounds of violation of sex equality.

While no doubt sex equality is a primary value that a state should aspire for, it is questionable if restricting expression would help. It may, on the other hand, be counterproductive. Moral conservatives may exploit the feminist anti-subordination agenda to target sexual speech they consider offensive. For example, after upholding a criminal ban on pornography in Canada in the interest of sex equality, books with homosexual content, and even books written by feminist scholars, became targets of seizure (Taub 1993: 606). It is also not certain if pornographic expression incites the sexual subordination of women.[2] Further, the link between pornography and sexual violence is questionable and has not been credibly established (Alternative Law Forum 2013: 6). Pornography may be taken up as an occupation by women out of choice, and may be sexually liberating for both female models and viewers.

It is also argued that if law starts restricting speech based on the perceived subordination of its content, much of the sexist speech one hears from the media and popular culture today may fall foul of such law, endangering the right to freedom of expression (Balmer 2010: 77). Indian popular culture involves a variety of such expressions, ranging from the portrayal of women as obedient wives and in-laws in television programmes and misogynistic rap songs. The latter includes songs by a popular rapper with lyrics clearly objectifying women, such as by seeking to choose among a 'buffet' of women or by calling a woman in a short dress a 'bomb'. These songs are widely popular, but have also generated debate over the freedom of such speech in the country. This includes a social media petition to stop a singer's concert performance as part of a wider demand to change social attitudes in the wake of a brutal gang-rape in Delhi (Kaushal 2014), as well as a female college student expressing an open letter against such lyrics by way or her own rap song (Nayar 2015).

What further problematises the speech-equality conflict in cases of sexual expression is the difficult question of whether it really damages equality, or instead promotes it. As mentioned earlier, sexual objectification may arguably equate to sexual empowerment provided the person being sexualised consents to the conduct and is depicted in the position of power (Ritchie 2015). Such expression gives space to create a feminist movement around sexual freedom and pleasure, and shifts the focus from violence and victimisation (Kapur 2012: 11). Discussions around sexual expression, especially pornography, have also complicated the understanding of sexual agency, with feminists presenting different viewpoints about the 'freeness' of a woman's choice in participating in and consuming such expression. This difficulty in categorising sexual speech as unequal makes it different from other anti-equality speeches such as hate speech where a particular group or community is clearly targeted and subordinated. This also calls for a need to consider a much wider equality discourse to inform the speech-equality conflict, including in the case of sexual expression.

Sexual speech law in India: dominance of morality over equality

Indian laws on the regulation of speech with sexual content are supported by the Indian Constitution. The Constitution guarantees both the right to equality (Art. 14) and the right to freedom of speech and expression (Art. 19(1)(a)), without indicating any hierarchical relationship between these rights. The right to free speech is subject to reasonable restrictions that may be imposed on the grounds stated in Article 19(2), which includes sovereignty and integrity of India, public order, decency and morality, incitement to an offence and defamation. These grounds do not mention equality, or any other fundamental right for that matter. The grounds of 'decency' and 'morality' have been points of contention in most cases involving restrictions to sexual speech. In addition to the fundamental rights, Article 51A(e) imposes a fundamental duty on all citizens of India to renounce practices that are derogatory to the dignity of women.

This section examines some of the laws governing sexual speech and their interpretation by the Indian judiciary. Several laws deal with the regulation of sexual speech in India, most notably laws governing obscenity, indecent representation of women and content in films and other media. Since the constitutional provision talks in terms of morality and decency, legislation and judicial jurisprudence reflect the same notions. This section argues that sexual speech discourse in India is based on a speech-morality conflict, with concerns around gender equality and sexual objectification rarely arising. The test to examine the validity of sexual speech has focused on its acceptance by and impact on 'public morality'. Considering the diversity of opinions in India, with people occupying a range of spaces on the spectrum from conservative to liberal morality, it will be incorrect to point to any one common 'public' morality. Therefore, I use the term 'popular', or rather, 'dominant' morality, to indicate that the moral standard applied is a populist view of morality.

Obscenity

Section 292 of the Indian Penal Code (hereinafter, IPC) prohibits the sale, distribution and circulation of obscene books, writings, objects and other materials. An object is considered obscene 'if it is lascivious or appeals to the prurient interest', or, when taken as a whole, it tends to deprave and corrupt persons in whose hands such object is likely to fall. This provision has certain exceptions, such as publications in the interest of science, literature or art, and materials kept or used bona fide for religious purposes.

In the landmark case of *Ranjit Udeshi v State of Maharashtra* (1965), the Indian Supreme Court declared the Hicklin's test as the appropriate test to determine obscenity. The Court declared the book *Lady Chatterley's Lover* written by DH Lawrence as obscene using the Hicklin's test, which it stated falls within the limitations of Article 19. As per this test, the judge should examine whether the impugned matter tends to 'deprave and corrupt those whose minds are open to such immoral influences, and into whose hands a publication of this sort may fall' (*Ranjit Udeshi v State of Maharashtra* (1965): paras 73–74). The judge should apply the test to the work as a whole, as well as to the obscene matter separately. Where art and obscenity coexist, art must preponderate to render the obscenity insignificant. The Court also noted that mere sex and nudity do not amount to obscenity; however, treating 'sex in a manner appealing [or tending to appeal] to the carnal side of human nature' is offensive to modesty and decency and is thus obscene (*Ranjit Udeshi v State of Maharashtra* (1965): para. 77). But the extent of such appeal needs to be examined in each case.

The Court in this case also briefly examined the legality of pornographic material. It stated that both pornography and obscenity fall within the public decency and morality exceptions under Article 19(2), with pornography being a more aggravated form of obscenity. This is quite different from the approach of the US Court in *American Booksellers v Hudnut* (1985), which suggested that a legislation that sought to ban pornography on the grounds of obscenity might be upheld. This seems to suggest that obscenity is considered narrower than pornography in the US, and only the pornographic content that passed the obscenity test[3] could be banned. On the other hand, the Indian Supreme Court's approach assumes all pornographic material as indecent, immoral and obscene, even though the Court itself states that mere sex and nudity should not be deemed obscene. Importantly, the question of the validity of obscene or pornographic material on the grounds of sex equality was not in question before the Court.

The Supreme Court rejected the Hicklin's test recently in the case of *Aveek Sarkar v State of West Bengal* (2014). A magazine reproduced a photograph of the famous tennis player Boris Becker posing nude with his dark-skinned fiancée Barbara Feltus, covering her breasts with his hand. The photograph was taken by her father. The accompanying article portrayed Becker as opposed to racial discrimination and signified love over hatred. The Court rejected the Hicklin's test because it allowed judging the material on the basis of isolated parts of the work taking into account the standard of sensitive persons, judged from the point of view of the average person. Instead, applying the 'community standard' test, the Court noted that only those nude/semi-nude pictures or sex-related materials could be called obscene that had a tendency to arouse lustful thoughts. Applying the test, the Court concluded that the impugned picture did not excite sexual passion, nor did it tend to deprave or corrupt the minds of people in whose hands it may fall. Further, the judges must examine the impugned material in its context, also looking at the message it sought to convey. In this case, the photograph and the article conveyed the message of racial equality and promoted inter-racial love and marriage. The Court also noted that the photograph was taken by none other than the father of Feltus.

In both obscenity tests adopted by the judiciary, the focus remained on the impact of the material on its audience.[4] There was relative silence from the litigants and judges alike on the issue of women's agency and the impact of such material on gender attitudes. This seems to confirm what MacKinnon stated about obscenity laws: 'It cares more about whether men blush than whether women bleed' (MacKinnon 2006: 113).

Indecent representation of women

The Indecent Representation of Women (Prohibition) Act, 1986 (hereinafter, IRWA) was enacted to prohibit indecent representations of women in advertisements, publications, paintings and other materials. The title of the Act makes it apparent that it was enacted specifically in the interests of women. Many cases filed under this Act (and under IPC: sect. 292) created an opportunity for the Indian judiciary to examine how concerns around objectification of women interact with the right to freedom of speech and expression. However, the Act is largely couched in the language of morality rather than equality. It defines 'indecent representation of women' as 'the depiction in any manner of the figure of a woman; her form or body or any part thereof in such way as to have the effect of being indecent, or derogatory to, or denigrating women, or is likely to deprave, corrupt or injure the public morality or morals' (IRWA: sect. 2). In accord with this text, the courts have focused on public morality, hardly even acknowledging equality-related concerns flowing from sexual speech.

An apt opportunity to address questions around objectification of women in advertisements and agency of models came before the Chhattisgarh High Court in *Babban Prasad Mishra v P.S. Diwan* (2006). The case dealt with a newspaper advertisement for oil and capsule titled *Kama Sutra* for strengthening the nerves. The advertisement contained a photograph of a woman in the lap of a man. Examining whether the IRWA was violated, the Court conflated the notions obscenity and decency, stating, '[t]he words "indecent" and "obscene" convey one idea, namely, offending against the recognized standards of propriety, indecent being at the lower end of the scale and obscene at the upper end' (*Babban Prasad Mishra v P.S. Diwan* (2006): para. 12). To decide if the photograph was indecent, the Court stated that the photograph contained the side pose of the woman, with 'no exposure of her breasts and genitalia' (*Babban Prasad Mishra v P.S. Diwan* (2006): para. 14). The Court also held that in the modern, sexually literate society, such depictions are not weighty enough to categorise them as indecent or derogatory to women or as likely to injure public morals. This is especially because the 'present depiction will fall in simple category among what has already been available to the society at large though the print and electronic media is much more higher than what has been depicted in the case in hand along with the overall surrounding circumstances' (*Babban Prasad Mishra v P.S. Diwan* (2006): para. 15). This judgment indicates that jurisprudence under the IRWA follows similar lines as the discourse involving issues of obscenity by focusing on public morality and community standards, without addressing equality-related concerns.

Looking at the broader context, the Court also stated that the impugned photograph appeared in the context of promoting sale of the oil and capsules as useful to strengthen nerves and to remove weakness. However, it failed to explain how the photograph was supporting the product. Notably, a committee on the prevention of undignified representation of women by media and television channels constituted by the Rajasthan High Court had noted the need for 'a direct co-relation between the nature/usage of product and its advertisement', suggesting that 'using scantily clad female models for products like car batteries, tobacco, electric inverters, shaving appliances for men, etc.' should be stopped (*Suo Moto v State of Rajasthan* (2005): para. 6).

In one case, instead of challenging objectification, the judiciary itself emphasised the bodily aspects of a woman's beauty in order to determine obscenity. In *PK Somanath v State of Kerala* (1990), the Kerala High Court entertained a petition against a magazine alleged to contain obscene and indecent photographs of women. The Court said that the judges must place themselves in 'the position of a reader of every age group in whose hands the book is likely to fall' (*PK Somanath v State of Kerala* (1990): para. 7). Like other cases, instead of any attempting to examine the perspective of the women models, the emphasis was on the viewpoint of the audience. The Court further went on to state that the literature often described the beauty of women. 'A pretty damsel is beautiful to behold. A thing of beauty is a joy for ever. Are the bodies of females obscene?' (*PK Somanath v State of Kerala* (1990): para. 9). To decide which nudity amounts to obscenity and indecency, the Court suggested some indicators, such as whether the nudity was properly covered, facial expression and pose. Examining the impugned photographs, the Court said that 'the models are seen with dress which can be described as an apology for a dress. The pose, facial expression and lay out are certainly objectionable and provocative' (*PK Somanath v State of Kerala* (1990): para. 11). This is a markedly non-empowering understanding of obscenity and indecency laws, reducing women to their bodily features and expressions, examining whether their photos provoke the (possibly male) audience, and discounting any notion of women's sexual agency, including in relation to the clothes they wear.

Cases calling for restrictions on sexual speech in the interests of minors have also focused on the moral development of children rather than on the sexist messages such expression may convey. For example, in *Akhila Publishers Pvt. Ltd. v State of Karnataka* (1987), the Karnataka High Court noted that exhibition of obscene magazines, advertisements and films with scenes involving sex and violence risk leading children and youth to undesirable habits and affect their moral strength, harming society as a whole. In another case, a petition was unsuccessfully filed requesting the Supreme Court to lay down regulations to prevent exposure of minors to sexually explicit content in newspapers, out of concerns around the moral health of children (*Ajay Goswami v Union of India* (2007)).

Petitions seeking restrictions on holding of beauty pageants in India present another set of interesting cases concerning the representation of women. The Andhra Pradesh High Court dealt with the legality of beauty contests in *Chandra Rajakumari v Commissioner of Police, Hyderabad* (1998).[5] Various women's organisations protested the holding of such contests, arguing that they lead to 'obscenity, exploitation of women and degradation of dignity and womanhood in all forms for commercialisation and lust' (*Chandra Rajakumari v Commissioner of Police, Hyderabad* (1998): para. 9). The Court recognised that the matter primarily dealt with concerns around gender equality. It also referred to women's rights recognised internationally against their media portrayal primarily as consumers, inappropriate targeting of girls and women and pornographic media expression, as recognised in the 4th World Conference on Women, Beijing, 1995 and the Convention on the Elimination of all Forms of Discrimination Against Women (CEDAW). However, the notion of decency hijacked the discussion. This is primarily because, as the judges admitted, the judiciary cannot interfere unless a law was violated, even if some sections of the society consider such shows 'indecent'.

The Court held that a beauty pageant, which is a form of speech and expression, would constitute indecent representation of women if it has the effect of being indecent or derogatory to women, which includes their modesty, or is likely to corrupt or injure public morality. The understanding of 'dignity' was thus linked to 'modesty', and the way modesty is defined by the

Court hardly takes account of the woman's perspective. Instead, it largely reeks of the dominant morality prevalent in the country. The Court holds that women possess the virtue of modesty, which refers to the 'womanly propriety of behaviour, scrupulous chastity of thought, speech and conduct (in men or women) reserve or sense of shame proceeding from instinctive aversion to impure or coarse suggestions' (*Chandra Rajakumari v Commissioner of Police, Hyderabad* (1998): para. 11). According to the Court, the indicators of a woman's modesty include her appearance or behaviour having or showing respect for conventional ideas of decency and purity, a modest dress, blouse, neckline etc., one that is not sexually provocative' (*Chandra Rajakumari v Commissioner of Police, Hyderabad* (1998): para. 11). The Court therefore perpetuates the view that beauty contests offend dress norms, exposing the body of women in a sexually provocative manner, thus violating the modesty of women. The Court reduced the question of women's rights to a notion of decency and modesty, by stating that such indecent representation of women violates Articles 14 (right to equality) and 51A (duty to renounce practices derogatory to the dignity of women). It also corrupts and injures public morals.

The judgment is a very disempowering one for women, even though it was initiated by women's rights groups. The Court adopts the viewpoint of the public instead of the women involved in the beauty pageants. It reduces equality to dignity; dignity to the popular or dominant understanding of what constitutes womanhood, woman's propriety and her modesty. Stepping against this popular understanding not only violates the dignity of women, but also causes injury to public morality. The Court does not stop here, but explicitly discounts the consideration of women's agency, by stating that where the consequence is outraging the modesty of a woman, '*the consent of the participants, the audience, or the viewers becomes redundant* . . . The converse of seduction of men in the same fashion must be equally true although nothing of the kind of modesty is attributed to the male society' (emphasis added) (*Chandra Rajakumari v Commissioner of Police, Hyderabad* (1998): para. 11). Thus, the Court totally accepts the socially dominant understanding of the kind of representation of women that should be limited, without examining whether the fundamentals of such understanding fulfil even the basic principles of equality.

Restrictions on films

Apart from the above-stated criminal laws, some other laws have been enacted to specifically place restrictions on public exhibition of films and cable television programmes. The Central Board of Film Certification (CBFC) is a censorship board that regulates the public exhibition of films in India. It was established under the Cinematograph Act, 1952 to pre-screen and certify films as, inter alia, suitable for unrestricted public viewing, suitable only for adults, or unsuitable for public viewing. The Act provides that a film shall not be certified for public exhibition if it is against decency or morality or is likely to incite the commission of any offence (Cinematograph Act, sect. 5B). The provision is largely based on the text of Article 19(2) of the Constitution. The Act empowers the central government to issue further directions in this regard (Cinematograph Act, sect. 5B(2)). As per the central government guidelines ('The Principles for Guidance in Certifying Films'), the Board must ensure that besides 'vulgarity, obscenity or depravity', 'scenes degrading or denigrating women' are not presented. Further, 'scenes involving sexual violence against women' and 'scenes showing sexual perversions' must be minimised.

The central government also added Guideline 2(iv-a) stating that 'visuals or words depicting women in ignoble servility to man or glorifying such servility as a praiseworthy quality in women' should not be presented. This is a content-based restriction, directly challenging portrayal of a particular kind of viewpoint about women.[6] In the case of *Union of India v Film*

Federation of India (1988), the Bombay High Court held that the guideline was within the scope of section 5-B(1) of the Cinematograph Act and Article 19(1)(a) of the Constitution. However, the reasoning had nothing to with the concept of viewpoint discrimination. Instead, the Court noted that both Article 19(2) and section 5B(1) include the words 'decency' and 'morality'. This guideline could not be justified under the latter category, which the Court understood as being limited to sexual morality. This was decided after considering some precedents that restricted the meaning of 'morality' under judicial examination to only the sexual aspect of morality. However, the Court concluded that the guideline was a valid restriction in the interests of 'decency'. Noting that immorality is a narrower aspect of indecency, it held that decency is not limited to sexual decency. To decide whether a film is indecent or obscene, the test is to examine whether if offends the 'contemporary standards of propriety' (*Union of India v Film Federation of India* (1988): para. 33). Since glorifying servility of women to men is not in conformity with contemporary standards of propriety, the guideline was declared valid.

This judgment has hinted at concerns over sexual subordination. But, such a provision also risks restricting a wide variety of speech and leaves a broad scope for arbitrary decision-making. The Court rejected the argument that the guideline was vague and permitted discriminatory treatment, holding that the words 'ignoble servility' were commonly understood by average persons, without giving a clear definition of what the phrase meant (*Union of India v Film Federation of India* (1988): para. 33). This case itself involved a challenge to the certification of a film *Pati Parmeshwar* on the ground the female protagonist was shown to be submissive. The film showed a female character who suffered harassment by her in-laws, but did not resist. She ultimately won her husband back. The Court noted that this film glorified 'not servility, but faith, compassion, courage and sacrifice' (*Union of India v Film Federation of India* (1988): para. 44). This petition exemplifies that such a provision opens doors for subjective interpretations of what constitutes servility, possibly risking censorship of content that depicts the reality of women in submissive and servile situations. Even the Court's interpretation in this case was influenced by what it considered as the ideal behaviour of an Indian woman. It stated: 'Unlike many in this modern world always turning westward for everything, the heroine Rekha is not colour blind to basis[sic] Hindu culture, heritage and tradition. She exemplifies the inner strength and character of Indian womanhood' (*Union of India v Film Federation of India* (1988): para. 33). This suggests that even a provision seeming to address sexual subordination of women can be interpreted from the lens of societal understanding of modesty and propriety.

These cases demonstrate how the Indian law has silenced women in freedom of sexual speech cases. While most cases presented apt opportunity for the judiciary to develop the jurisprudence around the conflict between speech and equality, the latter did not figure in the judicial deliberation, and often neither in the litigants' arguments. Instead of examining the agency of women, the law focuses on how sexual speech is taken by its audience. The dominant view of the confines of a woman's decency and modesty, and the impact of sexual speech on public morality, informed the Court's understanding of the limits of sexual speech. Even the snippets of equality-related concerns seen in a few cases were hijacked by notions of popular or dominant Indian morality.

The harm of morality-based discourse

The focus on dominant morality in sexual speech cases in India has furthered neither the right to speech nor the right to equality. Instead, it has had an adverse impact on both these rights. Contemporary India is witnessing greater restrictions on the freedom of expression, in a manner that is simultaneously diminishing sexual freedom of women and men. The focus on dominant morality reinforces conservative notions around ideal womanhood, adversely affecting the sexual liberty of women. Postcolonial scholar Ratna Kapur (2005: 53) argues that frequent protests and legal challenges against various forms of sexual speech suggest that sex is seen as a threat to Indian cultural values. According to Kapur, '[i]n India, motherhood, wifehood, domesticity, marriage, chastity, purity, and self-sacrifice constitute the primary features of normative sexuality' (Kapur 2005: 55).[7] This normative sexuality is also understood to be the location where the Indian, as opposed to Western, culture is situated (Kapur 2005: 53). Thus, where sexual expression and speech tries to challenge the notion of normative sexuality, it is also seen as a threat to Indian cultural values.

In many cases, restrictions on sexual speech are allowed in an attempt to preserve the Indian culture, located in Indian womanhood. For example, in a petition against the holding of Miss World 1996 contest in Bangalore, the Karnataka High Court brought in concerns surrounding the harm to Indian culture resulting from such contests. The Court noted the need to preserve and protect womanhood, including motherhood, wifehood and childhood, as well as our cultural heritage and social values. In the absence of materials on the nature of the contest in issue in the case, the Court did not, however, give a final decision on the pageant (*Mahila Jagran Manch, Bangalore v State of Karnataka* (1994)). In the case of *Union of India v Film Federation of India* (1988) discussed above, the Bombay High Court also lauded the sacrifice and tolerance of the Indian female protagonist in the movie *Pati Parmeshwar*, who chose not to follow the 'Western' methods of revolting against domestic mistreatment. In another case, complaints were filed against the TV channels of Star TV, Star Movies and V Channel for showing obscene and vulgar films, some of which included nude and topless dancers, scenes of love making and use of vulgar language. The Delhi High Court cautioned that cable operators owe an obligation to society to not display foreign programmes which are 'anti-national', obscene, indecent and vulgar (*R Basu v NCT of Delhi* (2007)). Interestingly, the same Court also noted the tendency of judges to restrict speech on the ground of preserving Indian culture, as was the case in *MF Husain v AS Naruka* (2008) where a painting was alleged to be obscene. The Court noted how graphical representation of sexual acts was a common feature of ancient Indian art. It further stated that in the name of 'cultural purity', a 'new puritanism' was being carried out. These cases suggest that the Indian judiciary largely views Indian women as repositories of an essentialist notion of Indian culture, threatened by a more sexually liberated West.

The reliance on dominant morality to judge sexual speech is creating greater space for moral policing, damaging both freedom of expression and sexual liberty of women and men. According to Kapur (2005: 59), the re-emergence of cultural nationalism in India is simultaneously making sexual speech more contentious. For example, introduction of sex education in schools is a tough battle in India, despite arguments for the need of such education to promote safe sex practices as well as for gender sensitisation. The issue raises anxiety over the impact of such education on the moral health of children, especially the risk of encouraging pre-marital sex. The topic has also instigated various remarks from law makers and enforcers, with the Union Health Minister making a personal comment to ban sex education in schools (Ghosh 2014) and a police commissioner calling for the need for 'moral education' instead of sex education (Marpakwar & Bhandary 2013).

The increasing restrictions on sexual speech are also causing self-censorship. Television channels are increasingly 'bleeping out' words such as sex, gay, lesbian, homosexual and underwear. This is a dangerous trend, and signifies a move towards sexual paranoia instead of sexual awareness and liberty, and further marginalises sexual non-conformers. The hiding of words like 'breast', even when it was used in the context of breast cancer, suggests a greater sexualising of women's bodies. Bleeping out words associated with homosexuality degrades homosexual persons, indicates non-tolerance towards homosexuality, and reduces homosexuality to sexual acts, something vulgar and obscene to be blocked from daily household TV. Currently, consumers can report any inappropriate television content to the Broadcasting Content Complaints Council (BCCC). If found genuine, the BCCC forwards it to the Ministry of Information and Broadcasting, who may impose heavy fines or suspensions on channels. Reportedly, even while BCCC receives requests to allow bold content, TV channels seem to be adopting a cautious approach to avoid any clash with the law (Sethuraman 2013). An approach that was grounded in the right to equality instead of morality would not have supported such restrictions, since a moral discourse has been used to promote sexual disempowerment instead of liberty.

From morality to rights

There is a need to redefine the understanding of morality in law using a rights-based approach. The above case law analysis shows that courts' reliance on the dominant view of what constitutes morality, whether understood as 'public morality', 'community standards', 'decency' or 'modesty', maps the notion of morality on to women's bodies and their expected social roles and behaviour, and has been a counter-productive approach to achieving the right to free speech and right to equality. While departure from the concepts of 'decency' and 'morality' is not feasible since Article 19(2) is couched in this language, it is possible to re-interpret these terms from a rights-based perspective.

A leading example of a judicial approach linking equality and morality is the Canadian Supreme Court case of *R v Butler* (1992). Upholding the validity of the impugned obscenity law, the Court held that the law prevented harm to the society, understood as the real harm of victimisation of women and change of behaviour and attitudes in a manner that hurt women, instead of merely harm to the moral sensibilities of people.[8] Section 168(3) of the Canadian Criminal Code provides that 'any publication a dominant characteristic of which is the undue exploitation of sex, or of sex and any one or more of . . . crime, horror, cruelty and violence, shall be deemed to be obscene'. According to the Court, the law passed the 'community standard of tolerance' test, which 'is concerned not with what Canadians would not tolerate being exposed to themselves, but with what they would not tolerate *other* Canadians being exposed to' (emphasis in original) (*R v Butler* (1992): para. 478), which needs to be determined on the basis of harm that may flow from such exposure. Exploitation of sex in a degrading or dehumanising manner violates community standards, 'not because it offends against morals but because it is perceived by public opinion to be harmful to society, particularly women' (*R v Butler* (1992): para. 479). In this case, harm would include the effect of the material in predisposing people to act anti-socially. Thus, the Court turned around the community standards test by making harm, and not public morality, as the basis of violation of community standards. If the material was found to offend community standards, as defined by the Court, it must be examined if such exploitation was 'undue' by applying the 'internal necessities test'. This test examines whether such portrayal of sex was essential to any wider artistic, literary or other purpose. Thus, the provision was understood as minimally limiting the freedom of expression, restricting only the expression that risked causing real harm to society. Under the *Butler* approach, mere explicit sexual expression will not be considered obscene, unless a substantial risk of harm to society is proved (*R v Hawkins* (1993)).

It must be pointed out that the *Butler* approach has also been criticised and concerns have been raised that it may work against gender equality if not implemented correctly. The Constitutional Court of South Africa noted that *Butler*'s harm-based approach may work as a cover for the morality approach, seen notably in the incidence of seizure of large quantities of feminist and homosexual material by Canadian police and customs officers (*Case v Minister of Safety and Security; Curtis v Minister of Safety and Security* (1996)). Even while the judicial intention may be to expand the rights-based approach, unless internalised by all authorities, it may actually allow implementation officers to repress expression they consider immoral on the pretext of preventing harm.

Another way to incorporate the rights-based approach within the meaning of 'morality' is to redefine 'morality' as 'constitutional morality'. The Delhi High Court recently used the notion of 'constitutional morality' to replace public morality while holding unconstitutional the criminal law provision penalising private and consensual homosexual acts between adults. To determine whether such provision violated the right to life and personal liberty, the Court noted that the only type of morality that may amount to compelling state interest may be 'constitutional morality'. It further noted that constitutional morality outweighed public morality. An individual's right to dignity and privacy cannot be denied merely on the grounds of moral outrage (*Naz Foundation v Government of NCT of Delhi* (2009): paras 64–66, 72).[9] This application of the concept of 'constitutional morality' offers space for further exploration on how it could be used in the context of sexual speech. The notion of constitutional morality will involve the application of basic principles guaranteed in our constitution to determine the boundaries of free speech, a fundamental principle being the guarantee of equality. Putting constitutional morality in opposition to 'public morality', as was done by the Delhi High Court, will further abstain litigants and judges from bringing in popular notions around morality and modesty. Such a discourse is therefore likely to shift focus from Indian womanhood to sexual subordination of women.

It must be cautioned that in the absence of a clear discourse around constitutional morality, there is need to understand and develop it further. Constitutional morality may itself have multiple meanings and elements (Mehta 2010). In fact, inevitably, both free speech and equality are likely to form part of constitutional morality, which brings us back to square one, leading courts to look at something beyond the notion of constitutional morality to resolve the debate. It also needs to be seen if shifting the understanding of morality will make any difference. If the judiciary brings in the right to equality in the debate through the adoption of constitutional morality standard, its application will still depend on the judicial understanding of the right to equality, which itself could be diverse.

The purpose of discussing the *Butler* and constitutional morality approaches here is to suggest some ways of introducing the notion of equality in sexual speech cases to initiate a change in the nature of the current discourse. The intention is not to pit two rights against each other and declare one winner. Instead, the attempt should be towards developing a discourse around sexual speech that ensures maximum liberty while taking into account valid concerns regarding sexual subordination. Further, the argument to include equality concerns is not to deny that there could be other concerns related to community standards that may also justify restrictions on speech. For example, it can be argued that an expression could be so perverse and repulsive that the community sees no value in protecting such speech. However, considering the experience of adopting the dominant morality standard in India, there is a need to ensure that popular notions of morality and decency do not usurp the discourse in a manner that harms both free speech and sexual liberty.

Conclusion

The need for gender sensitisation in India is indisputable. Women's rights groups, activists, politicians and others have called for the need to change the portrayal of women in popular culture and media as a means to alter gender attitudes and address discrimination and violence against women. Many laws in India govern sexual speech, some of which were overtly enacted in the interests of women. Several cases under these laws have given the Indian judiciary an opportunity to develop a rights-based jurisprudence around sexual speech. However, instead of engaging with challenging equality-related questions of objectification and agency, or examining their interaction with the right to free speech, the judiciary has largely allowed the notion of a 'dominant morality' to dictate the speech-equality debate. Such morality-based discourse has damaged both freedom of expression and personal sexual liberty.

To address valid concerns of sexual subordination flowing from speech, there is a need to theorise upon the freedom of expression from an equality perspective. Redefining 'morality' as 'constitutional morality' could be a first step towards a shift to a rights-based understanding of morality. Although the meaning of equality may itself be subjective, this discussion is vital to move towards a sexually empowering understanding of speech. The judicial acknowledgement of the speech-equality conflict in sexual expression cases can also generate an academic and political discourse on the issue. Through such debate and discussion, we may ultimately move towards a legal system that enhances both speech and sexual liberty in a sex positive and non-discriminatory manner.

Notes

1 See contra *R v Butler* (1992) 1 SCR 452 (Canada).

2 But see *Harper v Poway Unified School District* (2006), where a US Court upheld a high school ban on a student's T-shirt with a degrading message about homosexuality, acknowledging that such speech causes actual harm to homosexual students.

3 The test to determine obscenity in the US was laid down in the case of *Miller v California* (1973). As per the tripartite test, the Court must examine: (1) whether an average person, applying contemporary community standards would find the work, taken as a whole, as appealing to prurient interest; (2) whether the work depicts or describes sexual conduct specifically defined by the applicable state law in a patently offensive way; and (3) whether it lacks serious literary, artistic, political or scientific value.

4 See also *MF Husain v AS Naruka* (2008), where the Delhi High Court applied the test of obscenity under Section 292, IPC to nudity in paintings, examining whether the artistic material would arouse sexual interest in a perverted person or morally corrupt and debase the viewers.

5 See also *Amitabh Corporation Limited v Mahila Jagran Manch*, (1997) 7 SCC 91, where a petition was filed to restrain the holding of the Miss World contest in India. The Court held that merely because a section of the people were protesting against the holding of this world event, the event could not be put under severe restrictions. Different views may prevail on the issue of decency, and unless any law is violated the judiciary should not interfere.

6 See also Cable Television Networks Rules (1994), that provide that no advertisement in the cable television service shall be permitted which 'is against any provision of the Constitution of India' (Cable Television Networks Rules 1994: Rule 7(2)(ii)), or which,

> in its depiction of women violates the constitutional guarantees to all citizens. In particular, no advertisement shall be permitted which projects a derogatory image of women. Women must not be portrayed in a manner that emphasises passive, submissive qualities and encourages them to play a subordinate, secondary role in the family and society. The cable operator shall ensure that the portrayal of the female form, in the programmes carried in his cable service, is tasteful and aesthetic, and is within the well-established norms of good taste and decency.
>
> (Cable Television Networks Rules 1994: Rule 7(2)(vi)

7 For a historical analysis of how colonial encounters reconstituted the notions of culture and nationalism in India, such that women's bodies became the primary site for preservation of Indian culture, see Sarkar (1996), Chatterjee (1989) and Mani (1998).

8 The provision was considered justified under section 1 of the Canadian Charter of Rights and Freedoms, which provides that the rights and freedoms in the Charter are 'subject only to such reasonable limits prescribed by law as can be demonstrably justified in a free and democratic society'.

9 The judgment was reversed by the Supreme Court in *Suresh Kumar Koushal v Naz Foundation* (2014).

References

Ajay Goswami v Union of India (2007) 1 SCC 143.

Akhila Publishers Pvt. Ltd. v State of Karnataka (1987) (3) KarLJ 378.

Alternative Law Forum 2013, 'Response to the Petition on Cyber Pornography', viewed 5 July 2015, http://altlawforum.org/law-media-and-culture/response-to-the-rajya-sabha-on-petition-concerning-cyber-pornography/.

American Booksellers v Hudnut (1985) 771 F.2d 323 (7th Cir.).

Amitabh Corporation Limited v Mahila Jagran Manch, (1997) 7 SCC 91

Aveek Sarkar v State of West Bengal (2014) 4 SCC 257.

Babban Prasad Mishra v P.S. Diwan (2006) CriLJ 3263.

Balmer, S Jr. 2010, 'The Limits of Free Speech, Pornography and the Law', *Aberdeen Student Law Review*, vol. 1, pp. 66–82.

Branit, JR 1986, 'Reconciling Free Speech and Equality: What Justifies Censorship?', *Harvard Journal of Law & Public Policy*, vol. 9, pp. 429–460.

Case v Minister of Safety and Security; Curtis v Minister of Safety and Security (1996) 5 BCLR 609.

Chandra Rajakumari v Commissioner of Police, Hyderabad (1998) AIR AP 302.

Chatterjee, P 1989, 'The Nationalist Resolution of the Women's Question', in K Sangari and S Vaid (eds), *Recasting Women: Essays in Colonial History*, New Delhi: Kali for Women.

Committee on the Elimination of all Forms of Discrimination Against Women, General Recommendation No. 25, Article 4, paragraph 1 (Temporary special measures), UN Doc. HRI/GEN/1/Rev.7 at 282 (2004).

Farrior, S 1996, 'Molding the Matrix: The Historical and Theoretical Foundations of International Law Concerning Hate Speech', *Berkeley Journal of International Law*, vol. 14, no. 1, pp. 1–98.

Ghosh, D 2014, 'Harsh Vardhan Does It Again: "Ban Sex Education in Schools, Teach Yoga"' *NDTV*, 27 June, viewed 9 July 2015, www.ndtv.com/india-news/harsh-vardhan-does-it-again-ban-sex-education-in-schools-teach-yoga-581721.

Gilreath, S 2009, '"Tell Your Faggot Friend He Owes Me $500 for My Broken Hand": Thoughts on a Substantive Equality Theory of Free Speech', *Wake Forest Law Review*, vol. 44, pp. 557–615.

Harper v Poway Unified School District (2006) 445 F. 3d at 1170 (9th Cir.).

Human Rights Committee, General Comment No. 18, Non-discrimination, 37th session 1989, UN Doc. *HRI/GEN/1/Rev.*1.

Human Rights Committee, General Comment No. 28, Article 3 (The Equality of Rights between Men and Women), 68th session 2000, UN Doc. HRI/GEN/1/Rev.9 (vol. 1).

Indianapolis & Marion County, Indiana, Ordinance 35 (15 June 1984), § 16-3(q) (USA).

Kapur, R 2005, *Erotic Justice: Law and the New Politics of Postcolonialism*, London: Glass House Press.

Kapur, R 2012, 'Pink Chaddis and Slut Walk Couture: The Postcolonial Politics of Feminism Lite', *Feminist Legal Studies*, vol. 20, pp. 1–20.

Kaushal, S 2014, 'Honey Singh: Why He Shouldn't Face the Rap Alone', *Hindustan Times*, 12 November, viewed 6 July 2015, www.hindustantimes.com/music/honey-singh-why-he-shouldn-t-face-the-rap-alone/article1-983894.aspx.

MacKinnon, CA 1984, 'Not a Moral Issue', *Yale Law & Policy Review*, vol. 2, no. 2, pp. 321–345.

MacKinnon, CA 1985, 'Pornography, Civil Rights, and Speech', *Harvard Civil Rights-Civil Liberties Law Review*, vol. 20, pp. 1–70.

MacKinnon, CA 1993, *Only Words*, Cambridge, MA: Harvard University Press.

MacKinnon, CA 2006, *Are Women Human?: And Other International Dialogues*, Cambridge, MA: Harvard University Press.

Mahila Jagran Manch, Bangalore v State of Karnataka (1994) (4) KarLJ 295.

Mani, L 1998, *Contentious Traditions: The Debate on Sati in Colonial India*, Berkeley and Los Angeles, CA: California University Press.

Marpakwar, P & Bhandary, S 2013, 'Need Moral Education More Than Sex Education: Police Commissioner', *Times of India*, 16 January, viewed 9 July 2015, http://timesofindia.indiatimes.com/city/mumbai/Need-moral-education-more-than-sex-education-Police-commissioner/articleshow/18039373.cms.

Mehta, PB 2010, 'What Is Constitutional Morality?', *Seminar*, 615, viewed 5 July 2015, www.india-seminar.com/2010/615/615_pratap_bhanu_mehta.htm.

MF Husain v AS Naruka (2008), Criminal Revision Petition No. 114/2007 (New Delhi High Court).
Miller v California (1973) 413 US 15.
Nayar, A 2015, 'Watch This Gutsy Indian Girl Call Out Honey Singh for Misogynistic Lyrics with Her Own Rap', *Huff Post India*, 30 January, viewed 6 July 2015, www.huffingtonpost.in/2015/01/30/honey-singh-delhi-poetry-_n_6576564.html.
Naz Foundation v Government of NCT of Delhi (2009) 160 DLT 277.
PK Somanath v State of Kerala (1990) CriLJ 542.
R v Butler (1992) 1 SCR 452.
R v Hawkins (1993) 15 OR (3d) 549.
R Basu v NCT of Delhi (2007) (96) DRJ 722.
Ranjit Udeshi v State of Maharashtra 1965 SCR (1) 65.
RAV v City of St. Paul (1992) 505 US 377.
Ritchie, R 2015, 'How Can You Tell If You're Being Sexually Empowered or Objectified? Ask Yourself This Simple Question', *Everyday Feminism*, 14 April, http://everydayfeminism.com/2015/04/empowered-vs-objectified/.
Sarkar, T 1996, 'Colonial Lawmaking and Lives/Deaths of Indian Women', in R Kapur (ed.), *Feminist Terrains in Legal Domains: Interdisciplinary Essays on Women and Law in India*, New Delhi: Kali for Women.
Sethuraman, S 2013, 'The Big Bleep Theory', *Hindustan Times*, 5 October, viewed 9 July 2015, www.hindustantimes.com/brunch-stories/the-big-bleep-theory/article1-1130987.aspx.
Steenveld, L 2000, 'Equality and Expression', *Rhodes Journalism Review*, vol. 19, no. 26.
Strossen, N 1996, 'Hate Speech and Pornography: Do We Have to Choose between Freedom of Speech and Equality?', *Case Western Reserve Law Review*, vol. 46, no. 2, pp. 449–478.
Suo Moto v State of Rajasthan (2005) (1) WLC 116.
Suresh Kumar Koushal v Naz Foundation (2014) AIR SC 563.
Taub, N 1993, Book Review: 'A New View of Pornography, Speech, and Equality or Only Words?', *Rutgers Law Review*, vol. 46, pp. 495–607.
The Cable Television Networks Rules, 1994 GSR 729 (E).
The Cinematograph Act, No. 37 of 1952.
The Convention on the Elimination of All Forms of Discrimination Against Women, UNGA Res. 34/180, Sept. 3, 1981, 34 UN GAOR Supp. (No. 46), UN Doc. A/34/46.
The Indecent Representation of Women (Prohibition) Act, No. 60 of 1986.
The International Covenant on Civil and Political Rights, UNGA Res. 2200A (XXI), 16 December 1966, 21 UN GAOR Supp. (No. 16).
The International Convention on the Elimination of All Forms of Racial Discrimination, 660 UNTS 195, entered into force 4 January 1969.
'The Principles for Guidance in Certifying Films', viewed 8 July 2015, http://cbfcindia.gov.in/html/uniquepage.aspx?unique_page_id=1.
The Universal Declaration of Human Rights, 10 December 1948, GA Res. 217 A(II), UN Doc. *A*/8 10.
Union of India v Film Federation of India (1988) (90) BomLR 594.
Virginia v Black (2003) 538 US 343.

Index

Page numbers for figures are given in *italics*, for tables they are given in **bold** and notes are given as [page number] n [note number].

For Product Safety Concerns and Information please contact our EU representative GPSR@taylorandfrancis.com Taylor & Francis Verlag GmbH, Kaufingerstraße 24, 80331 München, Germany

Batch number: 10726294

Printed by Printforce, the Netherlands